PROPHECY WITHOUT CONTEMPT

PROPHECY
WITHOUT CONTEMPT

RELIGIOUS DISCOURSE IN THE PUBLIC SQUARE

CATHLEEN KAVENY

Harvard University Press

Cambridge, Massachusetts
London, England

First Harvard University Press paperback edition, 2018
First printing

Library of Congress Cataloging-in-Publication Data
Names: Kaveny, Cathleen, author.
Title: Prophecy without contempt : religious discourse in the public square /
Cathleen Kaveny.
Description: Cambridge, Massachusetts : Harvard University Press, [2016] |
Includes index.
Identifiers: LCCN 2015025416 | ISBN 9780674495036 (cloth : alk. paper) |
ISBN 9780674986879 (pbk.)
Subjects: LCSH: Prophecy—Political aspects—United States—History. | Jeremiads—
Political aspects—United States—History. | Rhetoric—Political aspects—United
States—History. | Christianity and politics—United States—History.
Classification: LCC BL633 .K38 2016 | DDC 322/.1014—dc23
LC record available at http://lccn.loc.gov/2015025416

To John T. Noonan, Jr.
a model of both prophetic witness
and practical deliberation

Contents

Preface . . . . *ix*

Introduction 1

I

THE STATE OF PUBLIC DISCOURSE: THREE INCOMPLETE EXPLANATIONS

1. Alasdair MacIntyre: Fractured Moral Traditions 15
2. John Rawls: Contests of Public Reason 46
3. Carter and Cuddihy: Constraints of Civility 85

II

THE JEREMIAD AND ITS EVOLUTION: A HISTORICAL EXPLORATION

4. The American Jeremiad: Covenant, Complaint, and Controversy 125
5. From Consensus to Division: The Jeremiad's Shifting Role in
   American Political Life 182

III

THE STATE OF PUBLIC DISCOURSE: A RHETORICAL ANALYSIS

6. Prophetic Indictment and Practical Deliberation: Identifying
   the Differences 239
7. Prophetic Indictment and Practical Deliberation: Describing
   the Relationship 286

IV

TOWARD AN ETHIC OF PROPHETIC RHETORIC: COMPASSIONATE AND HUMBLE TRUTH TELLING

8. Best Practices: Styles of Prophetic Indictment 319
9. Prophecy, Irony, and Humility: Lessons from Lincoln and Jonah 373

  Conclusion 419

  Acknowledgments 425
  Index 429

Preface

The title of this book, *Prophecy without Contempt: Religious Discourse in the Public Square,* encapsulates the basic thesis that is developed in the pages to follow. My focus is on the American jeremiad—the venerable tradition of religious and political speech modeled on the social indictments issued by Isaiah, Jeremiah, and other great and fiery Hebrew prophets. My project, however, is not mainly to conduct a historical study; rather, I want to draw insights from history in order to better understand and critique the current, almost hopelessly polarized state of political discourse in the United States.

Imitating their biblical models, American practitioners of prophetic rhetoric chastise their own people for fundamental violations of the basic social compact, which they frequently present as divinely sanctioned and supported. The rhetoric of the jeremiad, therefore, cannot but *condemn;* that is its core social function. At the same time, it is extremely important that its contemporary practitioners of the jeremiad resist the urge to *contemn* those whom they *condemn.*

The words *condemn* and *contemn* are exceedingly close; they are separated by one letter. At the same time, they have quite different meanings, which are supported by distinct etymological roots. According to the *Oxford English Dictionary, condemn* means "to pronounce an adverse judgment on; to express strong disapproval of, censure, blame." It made its way into English from Latin by way of Old French; *condemn* comes from the Latin word *condemnare,* which means "to sentence, condemn, convict." In both its current usage and its etymological roots, the word *condemn* conveys a context of law and justice;

the closely related Latin word *damnare* means "to occasion loss or damage to, to harm, damage," particularly as a punishment.

The verb *contemn* has a very different meaning. The *Oxford English Dictionary* defines *contempt* as "the action of contemning or despising; the holding or treating as of little account, or as vile and worthless; the mental attitude in which a thing is so considered." It comes from the Latin *contemnere,* which is defined in very similar fashion: "to consider a person or thing as unimportant or of small value, to value little, esteem lightly . . ." The closely related *temneere* comes from the Greek word τέμνειν, which means "to cut or to cut off," "to prune," or even "to wound or maim."

In the heated battles of the American public square, it is all too tempting for practitioners of prophetic rhetoric to let their condemnation mutate into contempt. They—we—must resist this temptation. In an increasingly pluralistic liberal democracy, prophetic condemnation of deep social evils can be justified on occasion, although such rhetoric never comes without ancillary costs. Citizens rightly call each other to account for violations of our most fundamental commitments as a people. Contempt, however, is a different matter entirely. To treat one's political interlocutors as vile or worthless is to risk undermining their equal status as participants in our political community. It is to treat them as unworthy of citizenship, as people who must be "pruned" from our common political endeavor.

Is it possible to condemn without contempt? I believe that it is. As I argue in the final chapter of this book, Abraham Lincoln, the sixteenth president of the United States, has shown us the way. He delivered his masterful Second Inaugural Address (1865) as the end of the Civil War appeared on the horizon, and he successfully laid the foundation of knitting a sorely divided country back together. I can think of no better way to open this book than with the final words of that address:

> With malice toward none, with charity for all, with firmness in the right as God gives us to see the right, let us strive on to finish the work we are in, to bind up the nation's wounds, to care for him who shall have borne the battle and for his widow and his orphan, to do all which may achieve and cherish a just and lasting peace among ourselves and with all nations.

PROPHECY WITHOUT CONTEMPT

Introduction

Religious beliefs have prompted human beings to perform acts of great courage and self-sacrifice. Such beliefs, sometimes even the same ones, have also persuaded them to engage in the most barbarous forms of cruelty. For those who are concerned about building a stable and sound political community, therefore, religion is always a double-edged sword.

What role should religious belief play in the political conversations of Western constitutional democracies such as the United States? This is by no means a new question. Over two centuries ago, James Madison worried about the role of religion as tinder for inflaming political factions. Many patriots valued the political participation of mainline Protestants who could be trusted to protect and promote the social order, but they worried about the subversive potential of so-called Papists and non-Christians. Nor has the question been an entirely theoretical matter in American history. In the nineteenth century, the growing political influence of Irish Catholics, many of them immigrants, provoked backlashes from native-born Protestant majorities in some American cities. In the twenty-first century, prompted by the terrorist attacks perpetrated by Islamic extremists in the United States and around the world, some politicians and pundits have expressed worries about the increasingly visible presence of Muslims in American life.

How should we think normatively about the role of religious discourse in the American public square in the contemporary era? This book makes the case that addressing this question fruitfully will require us to open up an entirely new front in our inquiries and analysis. Understanding the role that religious rhetoric has long played and continues to play in American political and social life will require us to attend not only to the content of the claims that religious persons (and others) make but also to the rhetorical form in which they are presented. More specifically, I argue that a full grasp of the nature, function, and limits of religious discourse in the American public square requires coming to terms with the rhetoric of prophetic indictment. In the contemporary era, of course, prophetic denunciations do not necessarily have religious content. What is decisive is the form of the denouncement. Those who employ prophetic indictments speak unequivocally and from on high: from a position of an unassailable authority, whether God, or Reason, or Common Sense. Consequently, attention to prophetic rhetoric will help us not only to understand passionate religious voices but also to grapple with a wide array of fractious discourse in the public square.

The rhetoric of prophetic indictment has been a staple of American public discourse from the time that John Winthrop led a small band of men and women out of England and founded the Massachusetts Bay Colony in 1630. These settlers saw themselves as establishing a New Israel in the New World—a religiously inspired polity that would be free of the corruptions of the established Anglican Church and immune to the compromises of the English government with heterodox or lax Christianity. These emigrant Puritans came to New England in order to construct godly congregations in a godly community, bound together in a network of covenantal relationships with God and with one another. The great Hebrew prophets decried the sins of their people in order to provoke repentance and avert God's wrath, and so did the great Puritan preachers, in sermons delivered at a variety of important public occasions in New England life. Sermons like these have come to be known as jeremiads because they echo the passionate condemnations of sinful behavior that pervades the biblical Book of Jeremiah.

Somewhat ironically, the rhetorical form of the jeremiad proved far more flexible, and therefore far more durable, than the Puritan culture that nurtured it. In the eighteenth century, both loyalist and patriot preachers availed themselves of it in the controversies surrounding the War of Independence. The nineteenth century witnessed fiery jeremiads delivered not only by abolitionists but also by those who saw Scripture as giving divine sanction to slavery. In the early twentieth century, a variety of social reformers emerged, most notably those advocating Prohibition, who decried the social evils they combatted in a language that would not be unfamiliar to the great Puritan preacher Cotton Mather. The flexibility of the jeremiad allowed it to traverse the lines of political commitment. In the 1960s, American political liberals prophetically denounced racism and the Vietnam War; in more recent years, political conservatives have chastised the country for practices such as abortion and sexual immorality.

Yet most influential accounts of political and moral disagreement in contemporary constitutional democracies deal uneasily with the rhetoric of prophetic indictment, if they deal with it at all. They proceed almost as if those disagreements are taking place in a seminar room rather than in the chaotic and overlapping social marketplace of cable television and the blogosphere. They focus their attention upon the substance of the arguments that participants in a public debate proffer for or against particular positions regarding law and public policy. They concentrate their analysis upon the intellectual pedigree of those positions. They examine whether arguments about controversial social matters depend, tacitly or explicitly, upon religious belief systems or other comprehensive worldviews that are not shared by everyone in a pluralistic society.

Also striking is the degree to which many accounts of the role of religious discourse in the public square pay scant attention to the rhetorical form that such discourse takes. Those accounts tacitly presume that the rhetoric of an argument—its form or its style—is simply the wrapper in which the substantive considerations are presented. To be sure, admonitions to be respectful or polite or civil are not uncommon; generally speaking, they presuppose that it is possible for participants in public discourse to rephrase their points without loss of substance.

This functional separation of the study of politics and political theory on the one hand from the study of rhetoric on the other is not surprising. Over the past century and a half, the field of rhetorical studies has largely belonged to the realm of language and literature studies. Harvard University's Boylston Professorship in Rhetoric and Oratory, the oldest and most distinguished such position in the country, was first occupied by John Quincy Adams. But his focus on public speech and democratic persuasion was an anomaly; the position quickly moved in another direction. In recent years, it has been filled by distinguished poets such as Robert Fitzgerald, Seamus Heaney, and Jorie Graham.

As Aristotle himself well understood, however, the study of rhetoric was not meant to be consigned solely to the realm of arts and letters; it is a key aspect of the study of politics. Rhetoric does not pertain solely to external matters, such as the "dressing" of an argument. The structure of what Aristotle called deliberative rhetoric is significantly different from what he called forensic rhetoric. The former is the pattern of discourse characteristic of city halls and policy analysts; it focuses on what courses of action are to be pursued in the future. The latter is the language of courtrooms and lawyers; it concentrates on how to assess and respond to actions committed in the past.

Form follows function in political discourse. The central argument of my book builds on this insight. To understand the role of religion in the American public square, it is essential to come to terms with the important and continuing role played by the jeremiad, which operates like a legal indictment. Precisely because it is structured as an indictment, a jeremiad is not best analyzed as a type of deliberative rhetoric; it belongs, rather, to the category of forensic rhetoric. As Aristotle's insights would suggest, an indictment forms part of the legal process for determining the violations of communal norms that have happened in the past. Its logical structure is not especially suited for settling on a plan for future action, other than by issuing a general call for repentance and reform. A jeremiad is an indictment, but it is not just any indictment. It has a particular communicative power that draws on its unique religious heritage. Echoing the fiery condemnations of the Hebrew prophets, it excoriates the people for violating their fundamental obligations before God, thereby opening the whole community to devastating punishment. It is a discourse that is at once both thoroughly religious and thoroughly political.

Prophecy without Contempt: Religious Discourse in the Public Square is divided into four major sections, each of which approaches the terrain to be explored from a different vantage point. The perspective offered by one part enriches and coordinates with that offered by the others. At the same time, however, I have tried to ensure that each of the four parts is also intelligible on its own. In Part I, "The State of Public Discourse: Three Incomplete Explanations," I make the case for taking a different path by considering some of the limitations and inadequacies of the more established approaches. Over the years, there have been many attempts to grapple with religiously influenced moral contentiousness in the public square, as well as to propose steps for amelioration of the situation. Three of the most important and distinct accounts have been proposed most fully by philosophers Alasdair MacIntyre and John Rawls and legal scholar Stephen Carter. In brief, MacIntyre maintains that the source of our dissension is that we have no common, full-blown framework for moral reasoning, so we are forced to offer competing analyses of moral and social problems by using bits and pieces of rival and incompatible moral theories. Rawls argues that the key to minimizing social dissension is encouraging citizens to shape their arguments according to the canons of public reason in discussing matters of fundamental political import in the public square. If citizens persist in casting their arguments in terms of particular comprehensive worldviews that are not shared by everyone in a society, they risk exacerbating division and causing unfair treatment to religious minorities. Carter takes another tack in explaining social bitterness and division: He suggests the problem is a fundamental lack of civility and mutual respect necessary to work together in a pluralistic society.

Despite their differences, MacIntyre, Rawls, and Carter share an important commonality. They all assume that most significant discourse in the American public square can be understood and analyzed as a form of practical deliberation. In my view, this assumption is false. Some of the most powerful—and polarizing—discourse takes the form of searing and bitter prophetic indictments, which operate in a very different way from deliberative discourse. While prophetic indictment can be bitter and harsh, its tone is not reducible to mere impoliteness or incivility, which can be eliminated at no cost to the substance. The tone and style is an essential component of its underlying moral message—an uncompromising condemnation of personal and social sin that triggers an urgent call to reform, often but not always issued in the name of God or divine law. Part I of my book therefore shows the necessity of grappling with prophetic rhetoric on its own terms so as to develop a more complete understanding of the role of heated religious and moral discourse in the public square.

In Part II, "The Jeremiad and Its Evolution: A Historical Exploration," I step back from present debates in order to uncover both the logic of prophetic rhetoric and its changing function over the course of American political life. More specifically, I delve deeply into historical sources, including numerous early colonial sermons, in order to investigate and illuminate the roots of contemporary prophetic rhetoric in the Puritan jeremiad.

I show that the jeremiad is moral discourse; it is not, however, *deliberative* moral discourse. It is modeled on a legal complaint and is therefore a type of forensic discourse. The use of the jeremiad in public discussion becomes particularly contentious, I argue, when speakers fail to recognize and comply with the constraints of form and content that are appropriate to its genre. The sermons of the great Puritan preachers of the seventeenth and early eighteenth centuries indicted their compatriots for violations of the national covenant, which commanded wide support in the community. Consequently, while their jeremiads might have stung on occasion, they did not generally fuel broad social controversy. As the decades moved on, however, the tight connection between covenant and jeremiad began to fray. As the New World expanded and the colonies moved toward nationhood, the terms of the covenant became less clear and commanded less agreement. Jeremiads began to be used by some members of the community to indict other members on the basis of a contested view of the national compact. Rather than serving to call the community together in repentance and reaffirmation of common commitments, they began to function as instruments of the culture wars of the time. The jeremiads on both sides of America's two major civil wars, the War of Independence and the Civil War, provide useful case studies of this phenomenon.

Having turned to historical sources to clarify the nature, origin, and evolving function of the American practice of prophetic indictment in Part II, I return to the present era in Part III, "The State of Public Discourse: A Rhetorical Analysis." My focus remains on primary sources, which are extensively quoted to illustrate my points. While I scrutinize sermons and political pamphlets in Part II, I attend to the arguments and accusations made by political leaders, church prelates, and public intellectuals in magazines and blog posts in Part III.

My central purpose in Part III is to examine how prophetic discourse operates in contemporary controversial situations and particularly to investigate how it functions in contrast and in competition with deliberative rhetoric. Needless to say, this is an extraordinarily broad topic. To sharpen the focus, I take the 2004 presidential election, arguably the high water mark of the culture wars, as the temporal frame for my investigation. For substantive material, I turn to the political discussions about abortion and torture among moderate and conservative Catholics and evangelical Protestants. By holding the time frame, the issues discussed, and the discussants constant, I hope to illuminate how the choice of a rhetorical path can both shape one's moral analysis and influence one's interventions in public debates.

Why focus on issues from 2004 rather than concentrate on issues dividing us now, such as same-sex marriage or even climate change? It seems to me that the perspective given by the passage of time allows us to analyze the rhetorical moves and countermoves with some degree of dispassion. It also assures some stability in the focus of the analysis; discussions of same-sex marriage and climate change are quickly evolving both rhetorically and substantively. In addition, I do not want to pretend that prophetic indictment and practical deliberation exhaust the range of rhetorical categories in the public square. I suspect, for example, that the fast-moving debate about same-sex marriage includes discourse about purity and taboo, and not only morality, while the discussion of climate change shades from prophetic into apocalyptic discourse. Treating these two topics adequately and in depth would require another book.

Why Catholics and evangelical Protestants? Broadly speaking, both groups are committed to reconciling participation in American civil life with the moral demands of their faith commitments. They generally see no barrier to drawing on the resources of their respective religious traditions in order to help them discern their public responsibilities. In addition, the political deliberations of Roman Catholics and evangelical Protestants are not irrelevant to American public life; taken together, members of these religious groups comprise nearly one-half of the population of the United States.

Why abortion and torture in particular? I have two reasons. First, in 2004, the two issues were marked by very different stages of social inflammation. Abortion at this point in time had long been an established flash point in the culture wars, while torture was an emerging issue only beginning to engage moral passions. Comparing the manner in which they were discussed allows us to compare how prophetic rhetoric functions at two different stages of social divisiveness.

Second, in the moral framework of the discussants, the two issues are arguably of comparable seriousness—matters of life or death. It is true, of course, that many Americans do not see them as comparable issues. On the one hand, someone who does not believe that the fetus is a human person may not be overly worried about abortion, but he or she may be repelled by our nation's practice of torture. On the other hand, someone who believes the fetus to be not only a person but an absolutely innocent person may be appalled by legalized abortion, but she or he may accept torture of our nation's enemies as a necessary practice to foil the plots of evildoers. For Catholics and evangelical Protestants, however, abortion and torture are arguably analogous in moral gravity. Both the unborn child and the terrorist bear the image and likeness of God. Intentionally defacing that image, through abortion or torture, is, at least prima facie, a serious moral wrong. For the civil government to be involved in promoting, protecting, or practicing such a violation is a deeply troubling social evil.

Consequently, an examination of how religious believers choose to talk about both issues in the public square at a particular moment in time is deeply revealing. What I discovered is that many of the same people who spoke about abortion in the adamant terms of prophetic denunciation used the more nuanced approach of deliberative assessment in discussing torture. The reverse was also true: Those who condemned torture as a fundamental violation of God's law were more open to nuance, circumstance, and qualification in discussing public policy on abortion.

In Part III, therefore, I show in some detail how prophetic rhetoric and deliberative rhetoric operate with very different presuppositions and create very different expectations in their respective audiences. I also examine how these differences can create significant tensions among those who think a particular issue should be discussed in terms of practical deliberation and those who judge it to be a fit topic for prophetic denunciation. It is a mistake, however, to think that prophetic discourse and deliberative discourse are hermetically sealed. Consequently, I also devote significant attention to exploring how they interact, including how deliberative rhetoric can be co-opted for prophetic purposes, and vice versa.

True prophets—those who understand themselves as called by God to deliver a message to the people—have no real option. They believe they must do as God commands and condemn the practices God tells them to condemn. Yet most of the people who use prophetic rhetoric in the public square do not understand themselves as actual messengers of God comparable to Isaiah or Jeremiah. They are *making a choice* to use prophetic rhetoric rather than deliberative rhetoric in order to advance their political views. What moral and practical considerations should guide their choice?

Part IV, "Toward an Ethic of Prophetic Rhetoric: Compassionate and

Humble Truth Telling," is dedicated to the development of a normative framework for assessing the use of prophetic indictment in the American public square. In my view, the most effective and suitable criteria for evaluating the use of this sort of rhetoric will be drawn from the genre itself rather than imposed externally. In developing these criteria, I draw on—and draw together—insights gleaned from the historical analysis in Part II and the contemporary rhetorical analysis in Part III. More specifically, I argue that Martin Luther King represents the gold standard in the modern American practice of the jeremiad precisely because he recognizes and incorporates key aspects of the biblical tradition of prophetic indictment. For example, King invokes rhetoric of lamentation and hope, not merely condemnation. Drawing largely on the "Oracles against Israel" in the prophetic books, King stands with the entire nation he condemns for its racism rather than calling for destruction of some part of that nation as evil and entirely other. In addition to drawing from King's example, I also reflect on prosecutorial ethics, the ethics of civil disobedience, and just war theory to illuminate the criteria for the fruitful and responsible use of prophetic rhetoric.

The book ends by considering what I think is the most pressing issue for the use of prophetic indictment in an increasingly pluralistic and postmodern society and an increasingly globalized and cosmopolitan world. Is it possible to incorporate a lively sense of humility into the practice of the jeremiad? Is it possible to condemn evil while still remaining suitably modest about one's knowledge of the divine will and one's own status in the eyes of God? I believe that these developments are both possible and necessary if prophetic speech is to continue to play a productive role in American public life in the years to come.

The greatest danger to moral character associated with the practice of prophetic indictment is arrogance. It is all too easy for its practitioners to assume not only that they stand in right relation with God but also that they are fully knowledgeable about God's purposes and endeavors. I examine Abraham Lincoln's Second Inaugural Address for insight about how to combine a strong commitment to combating social evil with a vivid sense of the inadequacy of one's own grasp of divine plans for dealing with that evil. I suggest that Lincoln's Second Inaugural Address offers a lesson in how modern-day jeremiahs might integrate self-criticism into their thought and speech. The issue remains, however, whether self-criticism and humility are values that are alien to prophetic rhetoric and must therefore be imported from an outside source. To grapple with this issue, I turn not to the Book of Jeremiah but to a much shorter and stranger prophetic text: the Book of Jonah. Rich with irony, the saga of Jonah, God's reluctant messenger to Nineveh, reminds all those who issue prophetic indictments how little they actually know about God's plans—and how much they stand in need of God's mercy. I show that the biblical tradition itself offers ample room for the cultivation of humility and self-criticism in prophetic speech.

Before turning to the substance of my argument, a few words about methodology are in order. The sources I draw upon and the arguments I consider come from a number of disciplines; I have tried to provide sufficient background and context, particularly in the notes, so that readers can find their own way into the material even when it does not come from their home fields of study. My own work is ultimately normative in character; I am an academic ethicist and law professor who works on questions at the intersection of religion, morality, and public policy. My study and teaching in ethics and law has convinced me that normative arguments are best proposed and understood in a rich narrative context that takes into account developments in both political and religious traditions. Consequently, I am deeply indebted to the work of Scripture scholars, literary critics, historians of early American religious history, and experts in the life of Abraham Lincoln and the Civil War. I do not pretend, however, to be making an original contribution to any of these academic fields, although I hope that what I say is of interest to those who work in them. Nor do I pretend that the work I rely on is totally uncontroversial in every respect; I fully recognize that ongoing, lively debates continue about the Book of Jonah, Puritanism, and the nature of Lincoln's religious beliefs.

At the same time, I do not think that the existence of disputed questions ought to deter scholars from using the most helpful insights they can find in related fields. Nor do I think the fact that certain texts have taken on a sacred character means that they are fit only for disinterested academic study. Their words and ideas are not pinned in amber under glass. To say that the prophetic books of Scripture, the Declaration of Independence, the Constitution, and the great speeches of Abraham Lincoln can no longer be absorbed, actively appropriated, and creatively applied is not the right way to protect their status as classics. Normative scholarly work in both ethics and law depends on active engagement with classical texts; theologians regularly marshal arguments using scriptural passages, while constitutional theorists do the same with the Bill of Rights or the Federalist Papers.

More important, however, is that the flourishing and development of a tradition depends crucially on the continual reappropriation of its classic texts, not only by scholars but by a wide range of people who live their lives within its overarching framework. Ordinary believers and pastors regularly interpret and apply biblical passages to address newly pressing social questions, while ordinary litigants and judges apply the provisions of the Bill of Rights to a wide range of emerging legal issues. So too do ordinary men and women read the words of the Gettysburg Address and the Second Inaugural Address engraved in marble on the walls of the Lincoln Memorial, and they ask themselves what being an American requires of them morally as they conduct their debates about the great issues facing our country.

Prophecy without Contempt: Religious Discourse in the Public Square seeks to chart a new direction in the normative discussion among political philosophers, lawyers, and ethicists on the one hand and religious studies scholars and theologians on the other about the role of religion in the public square. It is meant to serve as the catalyst for further conversation, not to offer the definitive word on the appropriate role for the rhetoric of prophetic indictment in pluralistic constitutional democracies such as the United States. At the same time, I hope that the book's cartography is sufficiently detailed to convince readers that this new region is worth exploring and that it highlights promising paths of further inquiry into the role that religious rhetoric should play in the public square.

I

THE STATE OF
PUBLIC DISCOURSE

THREE INCOMPLETE

EXPLANATIONS

Alasdair MacIntyre

Fractured Moral Traditions

In 1981, the philosopher Alasdair MacIntyre published his groundbreaking work, *After Virtue*,[1] which proffered a pessimistic account of the polarized state of contemporary moral and political discourse and of the possibility of overcoming that polarization.[2] Within the first few pages of that work, he observes that "[t]he most striking feature of contemporary moral utterance is that so much of it is used to express disagreements; and the most striking feature of the debates in which these disagreements are expressed is their interminable character."[3]

What has caused such disagreement? According to MacIntyre, it was the loss of a coherent tradition of moral reasoning once provided by Western Christianity. In MacIntyre's view, the Enlightenment project aimed to furnish the West with a rational, secular foundation for moral norms that was both universally applicable and universally acceptable, in the wake of the religious

1. Alasdair MacIntyre, *After Virtue: A Study in Moral Theory,* 3rd ed. (Notre Dame, IN: University of Notre Dame Press, 2007).

2. MacIntyre's work has generated keen interest, criticism, and debate in both philosophical and theological circles. For general anthologies, see, for example, Mark C. Murphy, ed., *Alasdair MacIntyre* (Cambridge: Cambridge University Press, 2003); John Horton and Susan Mendus, eds., *After MacIntyre: Critical Perspectives on the Work of Alasdair MacIntyre* (Notre Dame, IN: University of Notre Dame Press, 1994); Nancey Murphy, Brad. J. Kallenberg, and Mark Thiessen Nation, eds., *Virtues and Practices in the Christian Tradition: Christian Ethics after MacIntyre* (Notre Dame, IN: University of Notre Dame Press, 2003). Helpful monographs include Thomas D. D'Andrea, *Tradition, Rationality, and Virtue: The Thought of Alasdair MacIntyre* (Aldershot, UK: Ashgate, 2006); and Michael B. Fuller, *Making Sense of MacIntyre* (Aldershot, UK: Ashgate, 1998). See also Max L. Stackhouse, "Alasdair MacIntyre: An Overview and Evaluation," *Religious Studies Review* 18, no. 3 (July 1992): 203–8.

3. MacIntyre, *After Virtue*, 6.

wars of the early modern era. With the failure of that project, we are left with
bits and pieces of incompatible moral traditions, the flotsam and jetsam from
the shipwreck of innumerable attempts to formulate a coherent foundation for
moral norms and deliberation. Consequently, our moral discussion manifests a
chaotic and ad hoc quality, as various participants collectively put forward a
motley array of reasons supporting their moral judgments. Because the relationship of these reasons to each other is far from clear, the participants in our
key moral discussions frequently seem to be talking past each other rather than
coherently deliberating about the validity of a particular moral judgment.

MacIntyre's project in *After Virtue* is to provide an explanation of the origins of our pervasive and deep moral disagreement, which in turn can
make sense of the contentious and fruitless character of contemporary moral
debates. The goal of this chapter is to examine the degree to which his explanation adequately accounts for the nature and tone of moral and political
disagreement in the American context. In my view, his explanation is powerful; it is not, however, entirely satisfactory because it does not account for
the nature and source of the rancorous disagreements that occur *within* religious communities.

The Etiology of Moral Disagreement

MacIntyre illustrates his thesis by outlining the conflicting arguments that are
marshaled routinely in contemporary debates over justice in warfare, abortion, and the relative priority of social equality and individual liberty.[4] Here,
for example, is his presentation of the rival arguments on abortion:

> a. Everybody has certain rights over his or her own person,
> including his or her own body. It follows from the nature of these
> rights that at the stage when the embryo is essentially part of the
> mother's body, the mother has a right to make her own uncoerced
> decision on whether she will have an abortion or not. Therefore
> abortion is morally permissible and ought to be allowed by law.
>
> b. I cannot will that my mother should have had an abortion
> when she was pregnant with me, expect perhaps if it had been

4. Ibid., 6–7.

certain that the embryo was dead or gravely damaged. But if I cannot will this in my own case, how can I consistently deny to others the right to life that I claim for myself? I would break the so-called Golden Rule unless I denied that a mother has in general a right to an abortion. I am not of course thereby committed to the view that abortion ought to be legally prohibited.

c. Murder is wrong. Murder is the taking of innocent life. An embryo is an identifiable individual, differing from a newborn infant only in being at an earlier stage on the long road to adult capacities and, if any life is innocent, that of an embryo is. If infanticide is murder, as it is, abortion is murder. So abortion is not only morally wrong, but ought to be legally prohibited.[5]

MacIntyre concedes that each argument is logically valid; the conclusions follow from the premises. The premises of each argument, however, are mutually inconsistent. Option (a) places an emphasis on human rights; option (b) frames the question in terms of the Golden Rule, a test for impartiality and (often) universalizability; and option (c) discusses abortion in terms of exceptionless moral prohibitions. The problem is choosing *which* premises ought to guide our consideration of the question. According to MacIntyre, American society is at an impasse about abortion (and similarly controversial issues) because we have no way of coming to an agreement on the premises (or the moral goods presupposed in the invocation of those premises) that ought to inform our moral deliberation. Indeed, writes MacIntyre, "It is precisely because there is in our society no established way of deciding between these claims that moral argument appears to be necessarily interminable."[6]

MacIntyre goes on to explain the "slightly shrill tone" of most contemporary moral debates in terms of their unproductive, inconclusive, and seemingly interminable nature.[7] We might respond that this explanation is psychological, not philosophical. After all, there is an obvious and superficial connection to be drawn between fruitlessness and frustration in any

---

5. Ibid.

6. Ibid., 8.

7. "From our rival conclusions we can argue back to our rival premises; but when we do arrive at our premises argument ceases and the invocation of one premise against another becomes a matter of pure assertion and counter-assertion." Ibid.

and every human encounter. Anyone involved in a dead-end exchange with another person is likely to become frustrated. For MacIntyre, however, the discordance of our current moral discussions is not merely a matter of this sort of situational frustration. It has deeper roots, which are intertwined with the very way we conceive of moral argumentation in contemporary pluralistic societies.

Striking to MacIntyre is what he calls the "paradoxical air" of contemporary moral controversies. On the one hand, if we focus on "the way in which what at first appears to be argument relapses so quickly into unargued disagreement, we might conclude that there is nothing to such contemporary disagreements but a clash of antagonistic wills, each will determined by some set of arbitrary choices of its own."[8] On the other hand, the actual moral language we use functions "to embody what purports to be an appeal to objective standards."[9]

This paradox is central to MacIntyre's description of the ailments afflicting our current moral discourse and his diagnosis of the etiology of those ailments. More specifically, MacIntyre maintains that most people tacitly operate with an emotivist account of moral language, which holds that all statements of moral judgment are in fact nothing more than expressions of the speaker's emotional response, preference, taste, or attitude. Because we know we reason from rival premises on controversial issues such as abortion, war, and economic equality, it can begin to seem even to the rival parties themselves as if all moral positions, even their own, are ultimately nothing more than arbitrary commitments attributable to nonrational causes.[10]

Emotivism is not plausible as a theory of the *meaning* of moral language, as MacIntyre notes. To say "murder is unjust" is not the same thing at all as saying "murder! boo!"[11] At the same time, the fact that a theory is not fully plausible intellectually does not prevent it from exercising wide appeal or influence under certain conditions. MacIntyre's thesis is that emotivism is an

---

8. Ibid., 9.

9. Ibid.

10. "If I lack any good reasons to invoke against you, it must seem that I lack any good reasons. Hence it seems that underlying my own position there must be some non-rational decision to adopt that position. Corresponding to the interminability of public argument there is at least the appearance of a disquieting private arbitrariness. It is small wonder if we become defensive and therefore shrill." Ibid., 8.

11. This is my example. For MacIntyre's own examples, see ibid., 13.

appealing theory of how moral language operates in situations where moral argument seems to be at a standoff—as it does in our own culture. Because we do not make progress in reasoning with one another about moral questions, we reach the conclusion that the process of exchanging reasons must be about something else instead.

Emotivism, then, is a likely consequence of widespread despair about the possibility of moral reasoning.[12] A social world pervaded by emotivist sensibilities operates, according to MacIntyre, in certain baneful ways; its key feature is "the obliteration of any genuine distinction between manipulative and non-manipulative social relations."[13] One agent may *present* herself as giving objective, impersonal reasons to another for adopting or refraining from a particular course of action. Yet, if an emotivist account of moral language governs, that presentation must be illusory because there can be no such reasons.[14] Either the reason giver is deluded, or she is using the appearance of reason giving for other ends, which may not be so apparent to her conversation partner.

While MacIntyre does not explicitly attribute the volatility of contemporary moral debates to the emotivist tendencies of our contemporary culture, it is not difficult to draw a connection here as well. In an emotivist context, the use of seemingly objective moral language is simply one more tool with which some people try to move others to act or refrain from acting in a particular way. No wonder discourse gets testy from time to time. But we need not stop there. The expression of testiness itself can be one more form of manipulation. The characteristic understanding of the moral agent in an emotivist society is an individual stripped of all social connections and contingencies, an atomistic individual who is ultimately nothing more than an arbitrary chooser.[15] To such an individual, any attempt to limit her choices is

12. It "rests upon a claim that every attempt, whether past or present, to provide a rational justification for an objective morality has in fact failed." Ibid., 19.

13. Ibid., 23.

14. "I cannot genuinely appeal to impersonal criteria, for there are no impersonal criteria. I may think that I so appeal and others may think that I so appeal, but these thoughts will always be mistakes. The sole reality of distinctively moral discourse is the attempt of one will to align the attitudes, feelings, preference and choices of another with its own." Ibid., 24.

15. "The self thus conceived, utterly distinct on the one hand from its social embodiments and lacking on the other any rational history of its own, may seem to have a certain abstract and ghostly character." Ibid., 33.

bound to appear threatening and potentially unjustified. At the same time, she is constantly subjected to the efforts of other moral agents to conscript her into their own plans. In an emotivist society, human beings are generally manipulating one another, exercising resistance to those who are trying to manipulate them in an unwelcome manner, or both.

In fact, MacIntyre proposes that the three central figures or "characters" who anchor, embody, and enact the values of our cultural framework are all manipulators. *Rich Aesthetes* manipulate others in order to achieve their own ends, whether those ends are to achieve power, money, or fame—or even merely to stave off boredom.[16] *Therapists* help people manipulate themselves, turning badly adjusted patients into well-functioning members of society.[17] The complexities of modern social life, however, demand a broader and systemic manipulation. The task of the *Manager* is to muster resources, including human resources, to serve predetermined ends in an efficient manner.[18]

How did we get to this point? What caused popular conceptions of the role of moral discourse to turn toward emotivism? In *After Virtue,* MacIntyre argues that a coherent and productive moral argument can take place only within the context of a well-functioning moral tradition. The moral theory guiding the practical reasoning of such a tradition needs to include three elements: (1) an account of human-nature-as-it-is in all its messiness and disorderliness, (2) an account of human-nature-as-it-ought-to-be in its flourishing (the human *telos*), and (3) an account of ethical norms that can take us from the first stage to the second.[19]

Late medieval and early modern Western societies had forged a coherent moral tradition, incorporating all three elements, by fusing Aristotelian teleological ethics with a law-based ethics derived from a synthesis of Jewish and Christian moral commitments. Enlightenment thinkers, however, rejected

---

16. Ibid., 24–25, 27–30.

17. Ibid., 30.

18. Ibid., 25–27, 30.

19. Ibid., 52–53. See also Alasdair MacIntyre, "Intractable Moral Disagreements," in *Intractable Disputes about the Natural Law: Alasdair MacIntyre and Critics,* ed. Lawrence S. Cunningham (Notre Dame, IN: University of Notre Dame Press, 2009), 1–52. For interesting engagement of MacIntyre from a theological perspective, see two other essays in the same volume: Jean Porter, "Does the Natural Law Provide a Universally Valid Morality?," in Cunningham, *Intractable Disputes,* 53–95; and Gerald McKenny, "Moral Disagreement and the Limits of Reason: Reflections on MacIntyre and Ratzinger," in Cunningham, *Intractable Disputes,* 195–226.

both Protestantism and Catholicism along with Aristotelianism. Repudiating any normative notion of a *telos* for human life, they attempted to construct an ethics that combined the remaining two elements—a view of "untutored human nature," and a set of moral injunctions. MacIntyre maintains that this dyad, loosed from its moorings in a full-blown account of the nature and purpose of human life, was unstable from the beginning.[20] In fact, it was doomed to fail.[21]

MacIntyre buttresses his theoretical analysis with his analysis of the history of moral philosophy in the West. He maintains that the history of successive attempts by Enlightenment and post-Enlightenment thinkers to articulate a coherent set of moral norms based on an abstract, ahistorical notion of human nature, with each effort trying to remedy the deficiencies plaguing the previous effort, is practical evidence that the entire Enlightenment moral project was flawed from its inception. The negative arguments that Enlightenment philosophers mounted against one another succeeded— leaving no one standing.[22] In the end, argues MacIntyre, it proved to be impossible to justify moral precepts based on passions (Hume), on reason (Kant), or on will (Kierkegaard).[23]

The major strands of contemporary moral theory fare no better.[24] The

---

20. MacIntyre, *After Virtue*, 54–55.

21. He writes, "[s]ince the moral injunctions were originally at home in a scheme in which their purpose was to correct, improve and educate that human nature, they are clearly not going to be such as could be deduced from true statements about human nature or justified in some other way by appealing to its characteristics. The injunctions of morality, thus understood, are likely to be ones that human nature, thus understood, has strong tendencies to disobey." Ibid., 55.

22. Jeffrey B. Brenzel examines the role that explanatory power plays as a criterion of theory choice in his dissertation, "Nature, Origins and the Roots of Error: MacIntyre's Three Rival Conceptions of Moral Inquiry" (Ph.D. diss., University of Notre Dame, 2001). He argues in favor of the explanatory power of evolutionary naturalism, which is indebted to the Enlightenment "encyclopedic" tradition that MacIntyre rejects.

23. "Just as Hume seeks to found morality on the passions because his arguments have excluded the possibility of founding it on reason, so Kant founds it on reason because *his* arguments have excluded the possibility of founding it on the passions, and Kierkegaard on criterionless fundamental choice because of what he takes to be the compelling nature of the considerations which exclude both reason and the passions." MacIntyre, *After Virtue*, 49.

24. For interesting responses from philosophers sympathetic to various (and different) strands in liberal moral philosophy, see Philip L. Quinn, "Religious Ethics after *Ethics after Babel*: MacIntyre's Tradition versus Stout's *Bricolage*," in *Philosophy and Theological Discourse*, ed. Stephen T. Davis (London: Macmillan, and New York: St. Martin's, 1997), 151–68; Philip L. Quinn, Review of *Whose Justice? Which Rationality?*, *Faith & Philosophy* 8, no. 1 (1991): 109–15; Jeffrey Stout, "Homeward Bound: MacIntyre on Liberal Society and the History of Ethics," *Journal of Religion* 69, no. 2 (1989): 220–32;

dominant utility-based approaches and rights-based approaches to moral analysis also do not succeed in addressing the flaws exhibited by their Enlightenment
predecessors.[25] Famously (some would say notoriously), MacIntyre argues that
both the concept of utility and the concept of rights "are a matching pair of
incommensurable fictions."[26] Neither utilitarian thinkers nor neo-Kantians
have been able to address the criticisms that have been mounted against their
respective theories in a satisfactory manner.[27] At the same time, both theories
of morality animate our contemporary situation and frame our political and
social struggles. MacIntyre believes, for example, that our contemporary culture is characterized by political debates "between an individualism which
makes its claims in terms of rights and forms of bureaucratic organization
which make their claims in terms of utility."[28]

These struggles can never be won by either side, however, because the
weapons of the combatants are little more than conceptual ghosts. They are
the insubstantial remnants of the full-blown tripartite moral framework that

---

Richard J. Bernstein, "Nietzsche or Aristotle?: Reflections on Alasdair MacIntyre's *After Virtue*,"
Soundings 67, no. 1 (1984): 6–29; William K. Frankena, "MacIntyre and Modern Morality," *Ethics* 93, no.
3 (1983): 579–87; and Jeffrey Stout, "Virtue among the Ruins: An Essay on MacIntyre," *Neue Zeitschrift
für systematische Theologie und Religionsphilosophie* 26, no. 3 (1984): 256–73.

25. "The problems of modern moral theory emerge clearly as the product of the failure of the
Enlightenment project. On the one hand the individual moral agent, freed from hierarchy and teleology, conceives of himself and is conceived of by moral philosophers as sovereign in his moral
authority. On the other hand the inherited, if partially transformed rules of morality have to be found
some new status, deprived as they have been of their older teleological character and their even more
ancient categorical character as expressions of an ultimately divine law. If such rules cannot be found
a new status which will make appeal to them rational, appeal to them will indeed appear as a mere
instrument of individual desire and will. Hence there is a pressure to vindicate them either by devising
some new teleology or by finding some new categorical status for them. The first project is what lends
its importance to utilitarianism; the second to all those attempts to follow Kant in presenting the
authority of the appeal to moral rules as grounded in the nature of practical reason. Both attempts,
so I shall argue, failed and fail; but in the course of the attempt to make them succeed social as well as
intellectual transformations were accomplished." MacIntyre, *After Virtue*, 62.

26. Ibid., 71. About rights in particular he says: "The best reason for asserting so bluntly that there
are no such rights is indeed of precisely the same type as the best reason which we possess for asserting
that there are no witches and the best reason which we possess for asserting that there are no uni-
corns: every attempt to give good reasons for believing that there *are* such rights has failed." Ibid., 69.
See also Alasdair MacIntyre, "Are There Any Natural Rights?," Charles F. Adams Lecture, Bowdoin
College, Brunswick, Maine, February 28, 1983. He qualifies his rejection of rights in Alasdair
MacIntyre, "The Return to Virtue Ethics," in *The Twenty-Fifth Anniversary of Vatican II: A Look Back
and a Look Ahead*, ed. Russell E. Smith (Braintree, MA: Pope John XXIII Medical-Moral Research and
Education Center, 1990), 239–49.

27. MacIntyre, *After Virtue*, 69–70.

28. Ibid., 71.

disintegrated long ago. Emphasis on rights and their correlative duties recalls the middle part of the framework, the patterns and practices of activity meant to take human beings as they are and bring them to a condition of flourishing. In turn, the consequentialists who attempt to maximize utility or happiness or the satisfaction of people's preferences are working with the pale shadow of the idea of eudemonia or human flourishing as the end to which morally correct action is the means.[29] One reason that utilitarianism is so theoretically bereft is that it generally fails to treat virtuous activity as a constitutive part of the end of human flourishing rather than just a mere tool for achieving a desired consequence.[30]

MacIntyre maintains that this ultimately fruitless battle between the proponents of rights and the protagonists of utility also feeds into the stridency of contemporary moral discourse, giving rise, in MacIntyre's view, to a culture of protest and indignation. "The self-assertive shrillness of protest arises because the facts of incommensurability ensure that protestors can never win an *argument;* the indignant self-righteousness of protest arises because the facts of incommensurability ensure equally that the protesters can never lose an argument either."[31] Insightfully, MacIntyre goes on to observe that protestors generally address their remarks to those who already agree with them. "The effects of incommensurability ensure that protestors rarely have anyone else to talk to but themselves."[32]

The Proposed Remedy

What is the remedy for the incoherence of contemporary moral discourse and its consequent interminability and fractiousness? *After Virtue* closes with MacIntyre's famous appeal: "We are waiting not for a Godot, but for

29. Unlike utilitarians, classical teleological theorists did not view human actions as purely instrumental means to achieve the end of flourishing but rather as constitutive means. See MacIntyre's discussion of the differences between Aristotle's and Benjamin Franklin's account of the importance of virtuous activity at ibid., 185.

30. "If the deontological character of moral judgments is the ghost of conceptions of divine law which are quite alien to the metaphysics of modernity and if the teleological character is similarly the ghost of conceptions of human nature and activity which are equally not at home in the modern world, we should expect the problems of understanding and of assigning an intelligible status to moral judgments both continually to arise and as continually to prove inhospitable to philosophical solutions." Ibid., 111.

31. Ibid., 71.

32. Ibid.

another—doubtless very different—St. Benedict."[33] We need, in other words, to reconstitute thick communities that share a normative understanding of the nature and purpose of human life and the shape of human flourishing. Within such communities, and only within such communities, will productive moral reasoning again be possible. In *Whose Justice? Which Rationality?*, MacIntyre goes on to argue that conceptions not only of justice but also of practical rationality depend on and vary with the particular traditions in which they are embedded.[34]

Consequently, MacIntyre contends that it is only within the framework of particular communities, carrying forward particular normative traditions, that productive moral reasoning—and productive moral argument—will be possible.[35] Crucially important to MacIntyre's approach is his conviction that moral and political philosophy cannot rightly be viewed as abstract and disembodied pursuits. He maintains that judgments about moral action are made by—and made about—persons whose idea of good character and appropriate behavior is shaped by their social roles.[36] His commitment to an intelligible account of the development (or devolution) of moral theorizing situates it within the intellectual and political history of particular communities. For MacIntyre, productive moral reasoning must be understood and

33. Ibid., 263.

34. Alasdair MacIntyre, *Whose Justice? Which Rationality?* (Notre Dame, IN: University of Notre Dame Press, 1988).

35. MacIntyre's tradition theory has received particular attention. See, for example, Christopher Stephen Lutz, *Tradition in the Ethics of Alasdair MacIntyre: Relativism, Thomism, and Philosophy* (Lanham, MD: Lexington Books, 2004); Nancey Murphy, "MacIntyre, Tradition-Dependent Rationality and the End of Philosophy of Religion," in David Cheetham and Rolfe King, eds., *Contemporary Practice and Method in the Philosophy of Religion* (London: Continuum, 2008), 32–44; Micah Lott, "Reasonably Traditional: Self-Contradiction and Self-Reference in Alasdair MacIntyre's Account of Tradition-Based Rationality," *Journal of Religious Ethics* 30, no. 3 (2002): 315–39; Jean Porter, "Openness and Constraint: Moral Reflection as Tradition-Guided Inquiry in Alasdair MacIntyre's Recent Works," *Journal of Religion* 73, no. 4 (1993): 514–36; Jennifer A. Herdt, "Alasdair MacIntyre's 'Rationality of Traditions' and Tradition-Transcendental Standards of Justification," *Journal of Religion* 78, no. 4 (1998): 524–46; Ian Markham, "Faith and Reason: Reflections on MacIntyre's 'Tradition-Constituted Enquiry,'" *Religious Studies* 27, no. 2 (1991): 259–67; Peter J. Mehl, "In the Twilight of Modernity: MacIntyre and Mitchell on Moral Traditions and Their Assessment," *Journal of Religious Ethics* 19, no. 1 (1991): 21–54.

36. On MacIntyre and virtue theory, see, for example, Paul Blackledge and Kelvin Knight, eds., *Virtue and Politics: Alasdair MacIntyre's Revolutionary Aristotelianism* (Notre Dame, IN: University of Notre Dame Press, 2011); and Stephen D. Carden, *Virtue Ethics: Dewey and MacIntyre* (London: Continuum, 2006).

explained in a three-dimensional context, not reduced to the two-dimensional philosophical papers produced by academic theorists.

What are the elements of that three-dimensional context? First, human beings must not be viewed as isolated individuals but recognized as pursuing their own flourishing by inhabiting social roles made available to them by their communities. In well-functioning communities, persons are introduced into coherently defined social roles that allow them to develop expertise at the practices in which they hope to flourish and which interlock with other practices to contribute to the flourishing of the community as a whole.[37] They will develop the virtues by allowing their judgment to be shaped by others who are more advanced in the practices associated with their roles.[38] MacIntyre emphasizes that no worthwhile practice can be sustained unless its practitioners develop moral virtues such as truthfulness, justice, and courage.[39]

Second, key roles, and their associated practices, are administered, sustained, and modified throughout time by institutions, which muster external goods such as money and power to set up a physical and social framework in which those practices can flourish. The focus of institutions on external goods means that institutions can undermine the very roles and practices they mean to sustain by tempting people to lose sight of the far more important internal goods, such as meeting the internal standards of excellence of one's professional and personal vocation. A healthy community is one that finds ways to resist this sort of corruption.[40]

---

37. "In many pre-modern, traditional societies it is through his or her membership in a variety of social groups that the individual identifies himself or herself and is identified by others. I am brother, cousin and grandson, member of this household, that village, this tribe. These are not characteristics that belong to human beings accidentally, to be stripped away in order to discover 'the real me'. They are part of my substance, defining partially at least and sometimes wholly my obligations and my duties." MacIntyre, *After Virtue*, 33.

38. Ibid., 194.

39. Ibid.

40. "If my account of the complex relationship of virtues to practices and to institutions is correct, it follows that we shall be unable to write a true history of practices and institutions unless that history is also one of the virtues and vices. For the ability of a practice to retain its integrity will depend on the way in which the virtues can be and are exercised in sustaining the institutional forms which are the social bearers of the practice. The integrity of a practice causally requires the exercise of the virtues by at least some of the individuals who embody it in their activities; and conversely the corruption of institutions is always in part at least an effect of the vices." Ibid., 195.

Third, within such a framework, moral theorizing is second-order reflection that takes place within the context of such institutions and the communal life that is lived in and through them. That is, moral theorizing cannot be completely abstracted from the practices of daily life. It offers a view from somewhere, not a view from nowhere. MacIntyre argues that a coherent moral theory provides the following for its own moral community: (a) a description of the actual practices that are partially constitutive of human flourishing by making available to those who engage in them the goods internal to those practices;[41] (b) an account of the habits or virtues that allow people to experience the goods internal to the practices and not merely to rest content with external goods, such as money and power;[42] and (c) an account of the overarching *telos* or purpose of human life understood as a unity, which allows people to order and regulate various practices, as well as the goods they make accessible.[43]

Fourth, and finally, embedded within these components is a coherent description of the moral life, which includes a description of human beings as they are in their imperfection, a conception of human flourishing, and a set of moral precepts that help one move from the first state to the second. But these moral precepts are not abstracted from their normative context. They find their purpose and their meaning in relation to the view of the flourishing life they aim to foster and protect. Resisting the modern tendency to define virtue in terms of the willingness and ability to follow the law, MacIntyre stresses that the virtues are necessary in order to interpret and apply moral norms appropriately.[44]

41. MacIntyre defines a "practice" as "any coherent and complex form of socially established cooperative human activity through which goods internal to that form of activity are realized in the course of trying to achieve those standards of excellence which are appropriate to, and partially definitive of, that form of activity, with the result that human powers to achieve excellence, and human conceptions of the ends and goods involved, are systematically extended. Tic-tac-toe is not an example of a practice in this sense, nor is throwing a football with skill; but the game of football is, and so is chess. . . . So are the enquiries of physics, chemistry and biology, and so is the work of the historian, and so are painting and music." Ibid., 187.

42. "*A virtue is an acquired human quality the possession and exercise of which tends to enable us to achieve those goods which are internal to practices and the lack of which effectively prevents us from achieving any such goods.*" Ibid., 191 (original emphasis).

43. Ibid., 202–3.

44. "I remarked earlier upon the degree to which the concept of a rule acquired a new centrality in modern individualist morality. Virtues are indeed now conceived of not, as in the Aristotelian scheme, as possessing a role and function distinct from and to be contrasted with, that of rules or

MacIntyre's framework offers us a way of interpreting the current contentious state of political and moral dialogue in the public squares of liberal democracies. If he is correct, our basic problem is that we do not collectively subscribe to and participate in a rich and complex moral tradition that would enable us to reason together about the challenges facing our political community. Because we cannot reason together, we begin to despair of the powers of moral reasoning altogether, and we treat moral claims as nothing more than irrational preferences. The stridency of contemporary moral discourse in a pluralistic society is attributable to our frustration with this state of affairs. If we cannot convince one another intellectually, by using dialectical reason, we will co-opt one another emotionally, by manipulation or intimidation or strategic bargaining. For MacIntyre, the resort to nonrational means of persuasion is both a result and a symptom of the breakdown of a coherent moral tradition governing public life in a liberal democracy such as the United States.

Testing MacIntyre's Explanation for Moral Shrillness

If MacIntyre is right, we ought to see more coherence—and less fractiousness—within subcommunities that *do* have available to them full-blown moral traditions, such as those bound together by a particular tradition of faith.[45] Precisely because such traditions operate with an interlocking account of human beings as they are, human beings as they ought to be, and a set of moral norms and practices that promise to take an individual from the defective state to the second improved state, they ought not to fall prey to the same breakdowns of dialogue that characterize secular moral discussion. In addition, we might expect to find more progress within such subcommunities on morally contested social issues and less personal acrimony associated with

---

laws, but rather as being just those dispositions necessary to produce obedience to the rules of morality. The virtue of justice, as Hume characterizes it, *is* nothing but a disposition to obey the rules of justice." Ibid., 232. See also Alasdair MacIntyre, *Three Rival Versions of Moral Enquiry: Encyclopaedia, Genealogy, and Tradition* (Notre Dame, IN: University of Notre Dame Press, 1990), 174; in the modern framework, "[m]orality is thus primarily a matter of rules, and to be a good or just person, to be virtuous in character, is to be disposed to do what the rules require."

45. For an interesting account of tensions *between* different religious communities that is indebted to but not identical to MacIntyre, see John D. Barbour, "Religious *Ressentiment* and Public Virtues," *Journal of Religious Ethics* 11, no. 2 (1983): 264–79.

the inability to make such progress. We ought to observe subcommunities less pervaded by emotivism and more amenable to the dialectical exchange of reasons.

For all of those reasons, we ought to see less turbulence in the moral discussions of such subcommunities. But *do* we? As demonstrated by both sociological studies and emerging controversies, many religious bodies in the West are plagued by divisions every bit as difficult and fractious as those that bedevil the wider society.[46] Moreover, the tone of these discussions is not significantly better than that in the secular, pluralistic culture. In some respects, as we will see, it can be even more acerbic.

The evangelical Protestant community, for example, has been significantly divided on whether the use of torture is ever morally justified. In March 2007, the National Association of Evangelicals endorsed "An Evangelical Declaration against Torture: Protecting Human Rights in an Age of Terror,"[47] which was produced by the anti-torture activist group Evangelicals for Human Rights.[48] The declaration's blanket condemnation of torture drew sharp criticism from other prominent members of the evangelical community; for example, Daniel R. Heimbach, professor of Christian ethics at Southwestern Baptist Theological Seminary, argued that the declaration did not define torture with sufficient precision.[49] Keith Pavilschek from the Ethics and Public Policy Center, a politically conservative think tank in Washington, DC, echoed the criticism, stating, "I want to push up against the boundary of that [definition of what counts as impermissible treatment]. Why, because I am sadistic? No, because I want to protect innocent people."[50] According to a 2008 survey, more than three in five evangelicals believed torture can

46. See Robert D. Putnam and David E. Campbell, *American Grace: How Religion Divides and Unites Us* (New York: Simon & Schuster, 2012); and Kenneth D. Wald and Allison Calhoun-Brown, *Religion and Politics in the United States*, 7th ed. (Lanham, MD: Rowman & Littlefield, 2014).

47. An Evangelical Declaration Against Torture: Protecting Human Rights in an Age of Terror, http://nae.net/an-evangelical-declaration-against-torture/.

48. Evangelicals for Human Rights organized "A National Summit on Torture: Religious Faith, Torture, and Our National Soul." Most presentations appear in David P. Gushee, Jillian Hickman Zimmer, and J. Drew Zimmer, eds., *Religious Faith, Torture, and Our National Soul* (Macon, GA: Mercer University Press, 2010). See also the website of the National Religious Campaign Against Torture, www.nrcat.org,.

49. Peter Steinfels, "An Evangelical Call on Torture and the U.S.," *New York Times*, July 21, 2007, B5.

50. Christopher Quinn, "Evangelicals to Debate U.S. Use of Torture," *Atlanta Journal Constitution*, September 11, 2008, 8D.

"sometimes" or "often" be justifiable; moral acceptance of torture was highest among those that attended church services most frequently.[51]

Mainline Protestantism has also not been immune from serious moral disagreement. At the 2008 Lambeth Conference, a decennial assembly of Anglican bishops convened by the Archbishop of Canterbury, the world-wide Anglican community was riven with controversy over the moral status of homosexual relationships.[52] The more liberal branches of the communion, such as the Episcopal Church in the United States, viewed equal rights for homosexuals as a matter of social justice, while more traditionalist branches, such as the Anglican churches in Africa, consider homosexual activity an abomination condemned by God. Relationships between the two cohorts are strained not only in the United States but also around the world.[53] In June 2008, over a thousand traditionalist Anglicans, many from African nations, met in Jerusalem for the Global Anglican Future Conference (GAFCON), boycotting the Lambeth Conference and constituting a new network to defend traditionalist positions.[54] Some traditionally minded American Episcopalians attempted to secede from dioceses controlled by progressive bishops and submit themselves to the authority of traditionalist bishops in Africa.[55] At the end of the conference, Rowan Williams, the Archbishop of Canterbury, announced plans to draw up a "covenant" to which full members of the Anglican Communion would subscribe; among other things, it would

51. Eric Young, "Torture Survey Reveals Gap between NAE, U.S. Evangelicals," *The Christian Post*, May 4, 2009, www.christianpost.com/news/torture-survey-reveals-gap-between-nae-u-s-evangelicals-38453/.

52. Also controversial was the role of women's ordination. In 2008, the General Synod of the Church of England voted to ordain women bishops, rejecting measures that would have allowed traditionalists to set up separate structures of authority that would not entail recognizing the validity of the ordination of female bishops. "Church Vote Backs Women Bishops," *BBC News*, July 8, 2008, news.bbc.co.uk/2/hi/7494517.stm. In May 2012, the House of Bishops approved legislation that would admit women to the episcopacy, while conceding certain safeguards to traditionalists who cannot accept that step on theological grounds. See John Bingham, "Church of England to Allow Women Bishops," *Telegraph*, May 22, 2012, www.telegraph.co.uk/news/religion/9281336/Church-of-England-to-allow-women-bishops.html.

53. The Right Reverend Gene Robinson was consecrated as a bishop on November 2, 2003, and was invested as the ninth Episcopal Bishop of New Hampshire on March 7, 2004. He retired in 2013. See his biography on the website of the Episcopal Diocese of New Hampshire, http://web.archive.org/web/20090527084515/http://www.nhepiscopal.org/artman/publish/cat_index_66.shtml.

54. GAFCON has posted the conference proceedings at its website, http://gafcon.org/.

55. See, for example, Laurie Goodstein, "Episcopal Congregations in Virginia Vote to Secede in Dispute over Church's Direction," *New York Times*, December 18, 2006, A16.

place a moratorium on the ordination of bishops who were practicing homo-sexuals and suspend the practice of blessing gay unions.[56] A newly created pastoral commission would have the authority to issue binding interpreta-tions of the covenant.[57] It is not clear whether this strategy will suffice to keep the Anglican Communion together over the long term. Holding another major conference in April 2012, GAFCON reiterated its claim to be "not just a moment in time but a movement of the spirit," which suggests that Williams's strategy did not satisfy them.[58] After the 2015 conference in London, the group set up a charity for "the advancement of the Orthodox Anglican Christian Faith," which would likely be viewed by opponents as a schismatic and par-allel Anglican Church.[59]

How would MacIntyre respond to the foregoing examples? He has at hand a ready rejoinder. He could claim that it is not surprising that Protestant groups exhibit fissiparousness in their moral debates because they have jetti-soned the institutional structure that allows those debates to be settled pro-ductively. More specifically, MacIntyre emphasizes that productive moral discussions take place in communities guided by persons charged with the responsibility of arbitrating conflicts to prevent them from becoming too destructive. His line of argument suggests that a religious body with a clear line of teaching authority, along with a substantial body of authoritative interpretation, can prevent division and acrimony in its ranks. Such authority will permit contentious debates to be settled in an orderly manner, thereby allowing the community to move on in some sort of unison.[60]

With its highly developed account of the nature and function of magisterial

---

56. In 2011, the Church of England approved the ordination of openly gay bishops, provided they remained celibate. See Riazat Butt, "Church to Approve Celibate Gay Bishops," *Guardian*, June 20, 2011, home section, 4.

57. "Lambeth Diary: Anglicans in Turmoil," *BBC News*, August 4, 2008, http://news.bbc.co.uk/2/hi/uk_news/7509125.stm.

58. GAFCON, "The Movement Begins its Mission," April 27, 2012, http://gafcon.org/news/media-release-and-conference-commitment/.

59. Ruth Gledhill, "Conservative Anglicans Poised for 'Leap Forward,' Deny Schism," *Christianity Today*, April 17, 2015, www.christiantoday.com/article/conservatives.committed.to.anglican.communion.but.increase.funding.to.own.mission/52307.htm.

60. Reflecting on the successes of the Augustinian tradition, MacIntyre writes: "It was then the exercise of authority and the recognition accorded to authority which prevented the development of dialectical argument from fracturing the unity of enquiry into a multitude of disagreements, even though that enquiry drew upon heterogeneous philosophical sources." MacIntyre, *Three Rival Versions*, 91.

authority, the Roman Catholic Church appears to meet this requirement. Yet the Catholic Church is far from immune from the controversies plaguing other Christian groups. As of 2014, about one in five Americans identified as Roman Catholic.[61] According to the comprehensive *U.S. Religious Landscape Survey* conducted by the Pew Forum on Religion and Public Life in 2007, 19 percent of American Catholics believe "there is only one true way to interpret the teachings of my religion," while 77 percent believe "there is more than one true way to interpret the teachings of my religion."[62] Not surprisingly, given this view of authoritative interpretation, there is substantial variation on social and political issues: 48 percent of Catholics believe that abortion should be legal in all or most cases, while 45 percent believe it should be illegal in all or most cases;[63] 58 percent believe that homosexuality should be accepted by society, while 30 percent believe it should be discouraged by society;[64] 43 percent believe that "the government should do more to protect morality in society," while 49 percent believe that "the government is getting too involved in the issue of morality."[65] Moreover, many leaders in the church do not view these divisions with equanimity as legitimate prudential differences among people of goodwill. In an editorial published in June 2009, immediately before the first meeting of the U.S. Catholic bishops after Barack Obama's inauguration as president of the United States, the Jesuit magazine *America* addressed the

61. The percentage of the U.S. population who identify as Christian dropped from 78.4 percent to 70.6 percent between 2007 and 2014. The percentage who identify as Catholic dropped from 23.9 percent to 20.8 percent. Pew Forum on Religion and Public Life, *America's Changing Religious Landscape: Christians Decline Sharply as Share of Population; Unaffiliated and Other Faiths Continue to Grow* (May 12, 2015), www.pewforum.org/2015/05/12/americas-changing-religious-landscape/

62. Pew Forum on Religion and Public Life, *U.S. Religious Landscape Survey: Religious Affiliation: Diverse and Dynamic* (February 2008), 175, www.pewforum.org/files/2013/05/report-religious-landscape -study-full.pdf. The most recent survey did not make inquiries on such issues. Instead, it tracked the precipitous decline in religious believers in American society.

63. Ibid., 135.

64. Ibid., 128. Religious attitudes toward homosexuality have become even more supportive since that time. See Pew Forum on Religion and Public Life, "Changing Attitudes on Gay Marriage," July 29, 2015, www.pewforum.org/2015/07/29/graphics-slideshow-changing-attitudes-on-gay-marriage/. In June 2015, the U.S. Supreme Court announced its decision conferring constitutional protection upon the right to marry for same-sex couples. See *Obergefell v. Hodges*, 576 U.S. ___, 135 S. Ct. 2584, 192 L. Ed. 2d 609 (2015).

65. Pew Forum, *U.S. Religious Landscape Survey* (2008), 127. Sociologist John H. Evans recognized the increasing internal polarization on abortion among adherents of the same religious tradition in an article he published five years before the survey. John H. Evans, "Polarization in Abortion Attitudes in U.S. Religious Traditions, 1972–1998," *Sociological Forum* 17, no. 3 (2002): 397–422.

divisions, writing, "This polarization must stop; otherwise our identity as a faith community will be torn asunder and Catholicism will cease to be an elevating force for change."[66] In 2014, conservative *New York Times* columnist Ross Douthat expressed the hope that Pope Francis might be a unifier rather than a divider.[67] His hope was evidently short-lived; a few months later, he worried that the pope would ease Catholic teaching on marriage and divorce in such a fashion that would cause a schism.[68]

How could MacIntyre account for the divisions even within religious communities that have a strong institutional structure? Here too he has an obvious explanation ready at hand. He could simply maintain that the basic cause is the contamination of a formerly intact religious tradition by post-Enlightenment patterns of thought and practice. In *Whose Justice? Which Rationality?*, he suggests that many people in Western liberal democracies do not fully adhere to one tradition but live betwixt and between traditions. They move from one framework of norms to another as they move from one sphere of their lives to another: At work, they operate according to a version of utilitarianism, seeking to maximize profits; at home, they implement a domestic Kantianism, treating all their children with impartiality and fairness; on Sunday, they are Christians. They are deeply confused about their moral loyalties, and their attempts to integrate aspects of their secular lives into their coherent religious worldviews count as contamination, not enrichment. MacIntyre observes: "This type of self which has too many half-convictions and too few settled coherent convictions, too many partly formulated alternatives and too few opportunities to evaluate them systematically, brings to its encounters with the claims of rival traditions a fundamental incoherence which is too disturbing to be admitted to self-conscious awareness except on the rarest of occasions."[69]

This response, of course, would not require MacIntyre to modify his general account of moral disagreement and his related explanation of the grating tone of contemporary moral discussion. In fact, it would strengthen that account. Unfortunately, however, the response is not entirely sufficient,

66. "Community of Disciples," *America*, June 22, 2009, 5.

67. Ross Douthat, "Pope Francis as Unifier," *New York Times*, February 8, 2015, http://douthat.blogs.nytimes.com/2015/02/09/pope-francis-as-unifier/?_r=0.

68. Ross Douthat, "Will Pope Francis Break the Church?," *Atlantic*, May 2015, 118–35.

69. MacIntyre, *Whose Justice?*, 397.

even in MacIntyre's own terms. In *Whose Justice? Which Rationality?*, MacIntyre *also* makes it clear that well-functioning moral traditions are not hermetically sealed from one another. Adherents of one tradition regularly encounter adherents of different traditions and even draw from them in addressing their own "epistemological crises," situations in which a tradition, by its own standards, ceases to make progress on its own path of inquiry.[70]

MacIntyre describes, for example, how St. Thomas Aquinas integrated the insights of pagan and Muslim thinkers in order to address difficulties within the broader Christian Augustinian tradition to which he was committed.[71] In the same vein, one might argue that the Catholic Church's Second Vatican Council (1962–1965) integrated the insights of the Enlightenment by adopting the vocabulary of human rights in *Gaudium et spes*,[72] and explicitly recognizing a right to religious liberty in *Dignitatis humanae*.[73] By incorporating key elements of modernity into its own doctrine, the Roman Catholic Church overcame the so-called modernist crisis that made it very difficult for Catholics in Western liberal democracies to square their political commitments with their faith.[74]

MacIntyre might respond that those sterling examples of development within tradition are misleading when it comes to our current debates. He might argue that most of what is going on in contemporary American discussions of controversial issues such as abortion and homosexuality on the one hand or economic justice and conduct during war on the other is nothing more than a crude attempt to accommodate Christian views to the program of a particular political party. In his view, no major political party is untouched by the dominant culture.[75] Political liberals and political conservatives, MacIntyre

70. "It follows that the only rational way for the adherents of any tradition to approach intellectually, culturally, and linguistically alien rivals is one that allows for the possibility that in one or more areas the other may be rationally superior to it in respect precisely of that in the alien tradition which it cannot as yet comprehend." Ibid., 388.

71. Ibid., chap. 10.

72. Vatican II, *Gaudium et spes* [Pastoral Constitution on the Church in the Modern World], 1965.

73. Vatican II, *Dignitatis humanae* [Declaration on Religious Freedom], 1965.

74. For an account, see Marvin R. O'Connell, *Critics on Trial: An Introduction to the Catholic Modernist Crisis* (Washington, DC: Catholic University of America Press, 1994).

75. "Each of those [traditions] advances its claims, explicitly or implicitly, within an institutionalized framework largely informed by the assumptions of liberalism, so that the influence of liberalism extends beyond the effects of its explicit advocacy." MacIntyre, *Whose Justice?*, 392.

observes, are both engaged in maintaining the moral tradition of liberal individualism.[76]

Doubtless some of the key issues within religious communities, such as the role of women in positions of church leadership, reflect questions of central political concern in modern liberal democracies. At the same time, for several reasons, it is far too reductive to attribute religious controversies over such issues solely to the confused commitments of religious believers in liberal democracies. First, this explanation wrongly discounts the fact that many of our key liberal democratic values were originally advanced by religious believers on explicitly religious grounds. In both England and the United States, for example, Christian women rooted their claims for the right to vote in a scripturally based view of the world.[77] Martin Luther King's political activism on behalf of civil rights for African Americans was nurtured by his role-related obligations as a pastor in the black churches of the South.[78] The basic structures of American participatory democracy were forged by religious immigrants to the New World, who saw themselves as instituting a godly form of government as well as godly forms of worship.[79] The UN Universal Declaration on Human Rights, the linchpin of the modern human rights movement, was influenced not only by secular thinkers but also by European Christians. Abhorring both Nazi atrocities and the devastation of war, they

76. "But the outcome has been that modern conservatives are for the most part engaged in conserving only older rather than later versions of liberal individualism. Their own core doctrine is as liberal and as individualist as that of self-avowed liberals." MacIntyre, *After Virtue*, 222. See also MacIntyre's fall 2004 opinion piece, "The Only Vote Worth Casting in November," in which he says, "When offered a choice between two politically intolerable alternatives, it is important to choose neither." Originally published and now unavailable on the website of the University of Notre Dame's Center for Ethics and Culture, the piece is available at a number of other websites. See, for example, Philosophia Perennis, "Alasdair MacIntyre: 'The Only Vote Worth Casting in November,'" October 28, 2004, http://perennis.blogspot.com/2004/10/alasdair-macintyre-only-vote-worth.html.

77. One of the most influential advocates for women's suffrage was the Women's Christian Temperance Union, which advocated for the right to vote for women so that they could legally combat the baneful effects of alcohol on society and the family. See Alexander Keyssar, *The Right to Vote: The Contested History of Democracy in the United States* (New York: Basic Books, 2000), 186–7. See also Ian Tyrrell, *Woman's World/Woman's Empire: The Woman's Christian Temperance Union in International Perspective, 1880–1930* (Chapel Hill: University of North Carolina Press, 1991).

78. King's own autobiography makes clear the religious roots of his commitment. See Martin Luther King, Jr., *The Autobiography of Martin Luther King, Jr.*, ed. Clayborne Carson (New York: Warner Books, 1998).

79. See, for example, Michael P. Winship, *Godly Republicanism: Puritans, Pilgrims, and a City on a Hill* (Cambridge, MA: Harvard University Press, 2012).

pressed for the development of a dignitarian conception of human rights that reflects Christian anthropological and sociological commitments.[80] It is not so easy, then, to separate the values or the institutions of liberal democracy from the efforts of committed Christian believers.

Second, the "secular taint" theory of contentiousness within religious communities cannot account for a crucially important fact about that contentiousness: In some religious communities, the most divisive arguments are cast in distinctively religious terms. For example, noting that Jesus himself was tortured to death (*cruciare,* the Latin root of the word *crucifixion,* means "to inflict torture on, torture"), many progressive evangelicals press their arguments about torture's immorality by asking the rhetorical question "Who would Jesus torture?"[81] Their critics argue that this question is too "simple."[82] They do not, however, contest its basic legitimacy. For evangelical Protestants discussing torture, the touchstone is the Gospel, not the philosophy of John Rawls or John Locke.

Third, in other religious communities, such as the Roman Catholic community, the arguments for or against the morality of a particular practice are in principle accessible not only to members of that community but also to all people of goodwill as a matter of "natural law." To illustrate, Catholic teaching on matters of abortion, euthanasia, and contraception presents itself as based in reason, not merely in the tenets of the Catholic faith. So the religious tradition renders itself vulnerable, at least in principle, to challenges that are based on practical reason and put forward by any and all persons of goodwill. It does not see itself as a tradition that is free of the obligation to engage those outside its framework on moral and political issues.[83] Moreover, as John T. Noonan, Jr., has demonstrated, Catholic teaching on issues such as usury, marriage, slavery, and religious liberty have developed by dialogue with those who have different views in the broader world and by adopting

80. See also Mary Ann Glendon's *A World Made New: Eleanor Roosevelt and the Universal Declaration of Human Rights* (New York: Random House, 2001), which touches upon the religious faith of some of those involved in framing the UN declaration.

81. See, for example, David Batstone, "Who Would Jesus Torture?," *Sojourners,* November 9, 2005, http://sojo.net/sojomail/2005/11/09. This link is now defunct; the piece can be found on the website of the Progressive Action Alliance, www.progressiveactionalliance.org/node/771.

82. Greg Warner, "Evangelicals Seem Unfazed by Torture. Why?," *Religion News Service,* May 6, 2009, www.religionnews.com/2009/05/06/evangelicals-seem-unfazed-by-torture-why/ (subscription req.).

83. See International Theological Commission, "In Search of a Universal Ethic: A New Look at the Natural Law," 2009, www.vatican.va/roman_curia/congregations/cfaith/cti_documents/rc_con_cfaith_doc_20090520_legge-naturale_en.html.

their insights into its own analysis and judgments.[84] It is beyond dispute, for example, that *Dignitatis humanae,* Vatican II's Declaration on Religious Freedom, was inspired by the manner in which Roman Catholics had flourished in the United States, which constitutionally protects the free exercise of all religions while prohibiting the establishment of any of them.[85]

We cannot, then, dismiss the fact that even religious communities with fully articulated theories of human nature and human flourishing are not immune to of the argument and divisions that characterize moral and political debate in the broader society. Can we at least say that their arguments are more productive and their divisions less painful? After all, MacIntyre does not deny that conflict is an essential part of a moral tradition. He insists that well-functioning traditions are not mutual affirmation societies but support vigorous, rational, and fruitful arguments. In fact, he defines a moral tradition as "an historically extended, socially embodied argument, and an argument precisely in part about the goods which constitute that tradition."[86]

MacIntyre, then, might try to account for the divisions within religious traditions by claiming that they are, in essence, *fruitful* disagreements to be expected in well-functioning traditions. Will this strategy be successful? My sense is that it will not because the disagreements in question do not meet his criteria for productive arguments. While MacIntyre emphasizes that various traditions develop their own particular accounts of practical rationality (which are entwined with their accounts of justice), he also acknowledges that there are common patterns to sound moral argumentation in most well-functioning traditions.[87] What are some of these patterns?

---

84. See John T. Noonan, Jr., *A Church that Can and Cannot Change: The Development of Catholic Moral Teaching* (Notre Dame, IN: University of Notre Dame Press, 2005). For more extensive and specific studies of some of the topics he considers, see his *The Scholastic Analysis of Usury* (Cambridge, MA: Harvard University Press, 1957), *Contraception: A History of Its Treatment by the Catholic Theologians and Canonists,* rev. ed. (Cambridge, MA: Belknap Press of Harvard University Press, 1986), and *The Power to Dissolve: Lawyers and Marriages in the Courts of the Roman Curia* (Cambridge, MA: Belknap Press of Harvard University Press, 1972). I have written about the connections to be drawn between MacIntyre and Noonan in M. Cathleen Kaveny, "Listening for the Future in the Voices of the Past: John T. Noonan, Jr. on Love and Power in Human History," *Journal of Law and Religion* 11, no. 1 (1994–1995): 203–27.

85. See J. Leon Hooper, S.J., and Todd David Whitmore, eds., *John Courtney Murray & the Growth of Tradition* (New York: Sheed & Ward, 1996). More generally, see Charles E. Curran, ed., *Change in Official Catholic Moral Teaching: Readings in Moral Theology No. 13* (Mahwah, NJ: Paulist Press, 2003).

86. MacIntyre, *After Virtue,* 222.

87. MacIntyre, *Whose Justice?,* 359.

MacIntyre suggests that in a well-functioning tradition, arguments from the authority of established belief are the weakest form of argument but will prevail in the absence of stronger arguments. Incoherence in established belief will be identified and viewed as grounds for further enquiry. Rigorous dialectical testing of established positions will be encouraged, even demanded. Even first principles are not immune from critical scrutiny. "But such first principles themselves, and indeed the whole body of theory of which they are a part, themselves will be understood to require justification. The kind of rational justification which they receive is at once dialectical and historical. They are justified insofar as in the history of this tradition they have, by surviving the process of dialectical questioning, vindicated themselves as superior to their historical predecessors."[88] Furthermore, MacIntyre admits that a degree of humility about one's tradition's grasp of truth at any moment in time is a key characteristic of intellectuals in well-functioning traditions. "No one at any stage can ever rule out the future possibility of their present beliefs and judgments being shown to be inadequate in a variety of ways."[89]

From MacIntyre's description of argumentative habits encompassed by a well-functioning moral tradition, we can identify less helpful behavior that ought to be precluded or discouraged in conducting disputes. More specifically, his criteria would seem to exclude ad hominem attacks on one's interlocutors. At best, such attacks would be a serious distraction from the process of systematic dialectical challenge and response that he envisions. At worst, ad hominem attacks create an environment in which dialectical challenge is effectively precluded. If a serious question is regularly met by such an attack, it will inevitably appear that the very act of asking questions is taken as a sign that the questioner is about to betray the foundational principles of the tradition. No matter how coherent its worldview, a tradition whose discussions are marked by personal indictments is not engaging in productive moral discussion.

Moral Reasoning and Moral Indictments

Ad hominem attacks are not rare occurrences, however, in communities of faith struggling to address moral issues. They were not rare in the early

88. Ibid., 360.
89. Ibid., 361.

Christian church, as the Scriptures themselves attest.[90] And they are most certainly not rare in our era, as the earnest attempts to move beyond them make patently clear. At the beginning of the run up to the 2008 presidential election, a progressive group called Catholics in Alliance for the Common Good attempted to forestall the acrimonious rhetoric and mutual attacks among Catholics that had marked the 2004 presidential election season by issuing a statement calling for civility in politics. The statement exhorted Catholics to "disagree respectfully and without judgment to avoid rudeness in expressing our opinions to those whom we suspect will disagree with us, or in reacting to others' expressions of opinion." It implicitly equates lack of civility with lack of reasonableness. Catholics "should never lose faith in the power of reason" and should always "keep [themselves] open to a reasoned argument." The statement calls for Catholics to defend their views "with conviction and patience but without being obnoxious or bullying." It categorically rejects ad hominem attacks not only because they are inconsistent with rational deliberation but also because they threaten the "peace" of the church's community.[91]

Rather than generating goodwill, this call for civility fanned the flames of controversy. It was immediately opposed by Catholics who were more politically and socially conservative. They viewed the statement as a strategic move on the part of Catholic Democratic partisans to preempt strong criticism of politicians who do not support pro-life policies and the protection of traditional marriage. Moreover, they argued that justice, not civility, is the highest civic virtue. "If Catholic politicians advocated segregation or—even worse— slavery, would there be a call for civility toward them?"[92] To committed culture warriors, civility on certain matters is not an option; it is a betrayal of an overriding moral claim.

Consider, for example, the controversy that surrounded the invitation extended by the University of Notre Dame to newly elected President Barack Obama, who is pro-choice, to serve as its 2009 commencement speaker, which

90. See, for example, St. Paul's Letter to the Galatians, which describes his battle with St. Peter about the extent to which converts to Christianity needed to follow the Jewish law. Discord, selfish ambition, dissensions, and factions are described as sinful in Galatians 5:20.

91. Lay Catholics, "A Catholic Call to Civility in Public Life," *Origins* 37, no. 23 (November 15, 2007): 370–1.

92. 96 Catholics, "A Catholic Response to the 'Call for Civility,'" *Origins* 37, no. 34 (February 7, 2008): 550–51.

normally entailed the receipt of an honorary degree.[93] Cardinal Francis George, then the archbishop of Chicago, called the invitation "an extreme embarrassment."[94] John D'Arcy, then the bishop of Fort Wayne/South Bend and Notre Dame's local ordinary, boycotted the graduation ceremony.[95] The Cardinal Newman Society, dedicated to monitoring the activities on Catholic campuses to ensure conformity with magisterial teaching, organized a petition that called the invitation "an outrage and a scandal."[96] Ralph McInerny, a prominent professor at the University of Notre Dame and pro-life advocate, said, "By inviting Barack Obama to be the 2009 commencement speaker, Notre Dame has forfeited its right to call itself a Catholic university. It invites an official rebuke. May it come."[97]

Two features of this dispute are worth noting. First, those who vociferously criticized the decision of university officials to invite Barack Obama did so precisely because they believed abortion and stem-cell research ought *not* to be difficult issues for anyone within the Catholic community. Some, such as McInerny, thought it ought to be obvious to any Catholic that Notre Dame ought not to invite a pro-choice politician to speak at commencement.[98] Others framed the problematic issue more narrowly, focusing upon the honorary degree that Notre Dame confers as a matter of course upon its commencement speaker.[99] The vehemence of those who objected to the invitation

---

93. Dirk Johnson, "Invitation to Obama Stirs Up Notre Dame," *New York Times,* April 5, 2009, A12.

94. Liam Ford, "Cardinal Assails Notre Dame for Inviting Obama," *Chicago Tribune,* April 3, 2009, sec. 1, p. 11.

95. Joshua Rhett Miller, "Critics Blast Obama's Scheduled Notre Dame Commencement Address," *Fox News,* March 24, 2009, www.foxnews.com/politics/2009/03/24/critics-blast-obamas-scheduled -notre-dame-commencement-address/.

96. Cardinal Newman Society, Petition to Father Jenkins, April 29, 2009, www.notredamescandal .com/PetitiontoFrJenkins/tabid/454/Default.aspx. See also Mimi Hall, "Obama College Speeches Spark Controversy," *USA Today,* May 11, 2009, 10A.

97. Ralph McInerny, "Is Obama Worth a Mass?," *The Catholic Thing,* March 23, 2009, www .thecatholicthing.org/2009/03/23/is-obama-worth-a-mass/.

98. McInerny mentions the honorary degree but focuses his criticism on the attention received by the commencement speech.

99. See, for example, Cardinal Raymond Burke's address at the National Catholic Prayer Breakfast less than two weeks before Notre Dame's commencement: "The profound granting of an honorary doctorate at Notre Dame University [*sic*] to our President who is as aggressively advancing an anti-life and anti-family agenda is a source of the gravest scandal. Catholic institutions cannot offer any platform to, let alone honor, those who teach and act publicly against the moral law." Michael W. Chapman, "Notre Dame 'Betrayed' Catholic Identity with Obama Speech, Says Vatican Leader," cnsnews.com, June 16, 2009, cnsnews.com/news/article/notre-dame-betrayed-catholic-identity-obama-speech-says

was rooted in their conviction that Notre Dame was acting in flagrant disregard of key values in the Catholic moral tradition. Similarly, Anglicans opposed to the recognition of same-sex relationships believe it to be entirely clear that the Scripture and tradition oppose such relationships—no one can in good faith read the tradition differently. In 2006, the Anglican bishops in Nigeria urged the Archbishop of Canterbury to expel the American Episcopal Church for ordaining a bishop who was a practicing homosexual, arguing that "a cancerous lump in the body should be excised if it has defied every known cure."[100]

Second, close examination of the actual discourse used in these and similar cases shows that, while it definitely involves moral *discourse,* it does not involve moral *deliberation.* More specifically, many of the more neuralgic controversies within religious communities actually have not taken the form of conflicting chains of moral reasoning beginning with conflicting premises, in the manner suggested by MacIntyre's abortion example, which I discussed earlier in this chapter. Then what kind of moral discourse is being used in such controversies? In my view, the rhetoric is very similar in many cases to that found in a legal *indictment.* Catholics who opposed Notre Dame's invitation to Barack Obama, for example, were in effect charging the university with the offense of breaking the moral law. Consider the opening paragraphs of a letter written by a pro-life activist who not only attended Notre Dame but also sent his children to the university:

> Dear Father Jenkins,
>
> In your January 27 letter to my wife Phyllis and me, you thanked us for support "for our (Notre Dame's) most essential, and mission-bound, priorities." In the wake of the commencement announcement regarding Barack Obama, I am compelled to ask whether Notre Dame recognizes what those priorities are.
>
> Disillusionment, incredulity, betrayal—all describe my feelings. I am left questioning my own judgment in having encouraged our eight children to go to Notre Dame.

-vatican-leader. Needless to say, withholding an honorary degree from the first African American president would have raised the specter of racism, particularly since President Jimmy Carter, a prochoice Democrat, had received an honorary degree as the commencement speaker in 1977.

100. "Nigeria Bishops Scorn US 'Cancer,'" *BBC News,* July 4, 2006, http://news.bbc.co.uk/2/hi/africa/5144036.stm.

> Abortion is the unspeakable evil that causes my outrage—
> abortion and the fact that Barack Obama is the Abortion President.
> His first two months in office have constituted an all-out assault
> on the unborn child.[101]

The language of moral indictment and the tone of outrage that frequently accompanies it can be found across the political spectrum. It can also take the form of poetry as well as prose. For example, protesters against the Vietnam War directed stinging indictments against the U.S. government. One famous protester, Daniel Berrigan, S.J., was tried as part of the Catonsville Nine for burning draft cards outside a government facility in Catonsville, MD. He responded, in essence, by bringing an indictment against those who indicted him. In a play that he wrote about his trial in free verse, Berrigan reflected:

> Certainly
> "Some ten or twelve of us (the number is still uncertain)
> will if all goes well (ill?) take our religious bodies
> during this week
> to a draft center in or near Baltimore
> There we shall   of purpose and forethought
> remove the 1-A files   sprinkle them in the public street
> with home-made napalm   and set them afire
> For which act we shall beyond doubt
> be placed behind bars for some portion of our natural
>   lives
>
> in consequence of our inability
> to live and die content in the plagued city
> to say 'peace peace' when there is no peace
> to keep the poor poor
> the thirsty and hungry thirsty and hungry
> Our apologies   good friends
> for the fracture of good order   the burning of paper

---

101. Anthony J. Lauinger, letter to Rev. John Jenkins, C.S.C., reprinted in "National Right to Life Calls on Notre Dame to Rescind Obama Invitation," press release, March 23, 2009, www.nrlc.org /archive/press_releases_new/Release032309.html. Mr. Lauinger is the vice-president of National Right to Life.

> instead of children   the angering of the orderlies
> in the front parlor of the charnel house
> We could not   so help us God   do otherwise
> For we are sick at heart   our hearts
> give us no rest for thinking of the Land of Burning
>   Children.[102]

Moral indictments operate in ways significantly different than moral deliberation and argumentation does. Most important, an indictment is not an invitation to moral deliberation—it is an accusation of a moral violation. Generally speaking, it takes for granted the illicitness of the activity it charges against the defendant. It assumes, in other words, that the moral deliberation has already proceeded and that the moral argument has already been settled. Furthermore, unlike moral deliberation, moral indictments are necessarily ad hominem. They are *never* impersonal; by their nature, they accuse a particular agent or class of agents of breaking a fundamental moral bond of the community. Moreover, they frequently express a personal sense of outrage and betrayal against the accused's actions. For example, Berrigan's apology for the "fracture of good order" does not express regret but well-controlled anger against "the orderlies in the front parlor of the charnel house." The frustration prophetic indictments express proceeds not from a modern person's sense of the inconclusiveness of moral deliberation but from the clear moral certainty of a biblical prophet. Finally, Berrigan's verse expresses a combination of anger and deep sadness that also characterizes some biblical prophets, such as Jeremiah, who weeps over his people's sins even as he condemns them.

MacIntyre and Moral Indictments

MacIntyre's focus in *After Virtue* and his subsequent writings is the coherence of moral deliberation; his account of the cantankerousness in contemporary moral discourse in modern liberal democracies is based on the systemic

---

102. Daniel Berrigan, S.J., *The Trial of the Catonsville Nine* (New York: Fordham University Press, 2004), 93. Other examples of American prophetic indictment that are not embedded in straightforward prose include Michael Wigglesworth's "Day of Doom" (1662) and Julia Ward Howe's "Battle Hymn of the Republic" (1861–1862). The biblical prophets themselves often cast their indictments in the form of verse.

inconclusiveness of that deliberation. Yet in order to account for the harsh tone of the debate *within* religious communities, he needs to broaden his consideration to account for a different kind of moral discourse: the rhetoric of moral indictment. In my view, MacIntyre's analysis can be expanded to consider the role of moral indictments as a subset of moral discourse without too much difficulty.

After all, MacIntyre sees moral enquiry as an embodied endeavor, as taking place within a particular community that provides the necessary context for such enquiry.[103] He writes: "It is only because and when a certain range of moral commitments is shared, as it must be within a community structured by networks of giving and receiving, that not only shared deliberation, but shared critical enquiry concerning that deliberation and the way of life of which it is a part, becomes possible."[104] I would like to suggest that the role of the rhetoric of moral indictment is to defend the boundaries of the shared commitment that makes communal moral deliberation possible. To see why this is the case, it is necessary to highlight the often-overlooked role of law in MacIntyre's virtue theory. MacIntyre's virtue theory is not opposed to law; indeed, it depends on preserving a limited but essential place for it. As MacIntyre makes clear at various points, well-functioning traditions must integrate inculcation of the virtues with respect for the precepts of the moral law. For the Thomistic tradition (and the Christian tradition more broadly), respect for God's law, including the natural law, is a basic and constitutive aspect of human flourishing.

More specifically, MacIntyre recognizes that those involved in founding a common project, such as a religious cult or an expedition or a city, "need to develop two quite different types of evaluative practices." On the one hand, they need to identify praiseworthy and blameworthy "qualities of mind and character"—virtues and vices. On the other hand, they also need "to identify certain types of action as the doing or the production of harm of such an order that they destroy the bonds of community in such a way as to render

103. "In moral enquiry we are always concerned with the question: what *type* of enacted narrative would be the embodiment, in the actions and transactions of actual social life, of this particular theory?" MacIntyre, *Three Rival Versions,* 80. MacIntyre expands on this point by arguing that key negative moral precepts are rightly viewed as protecting the conditions necessary for moral enquiry and deliberation. See MacIntyre, "Intractable Moral Disagreements," 19–27.

104. Alasdair MacIntyre, *Dependent Rational Animals: Why Human Beings Need the Virtues* (Chicago, IL: Open Court, 1999), 161.

the doing or achieving of good impossible in some respect at least for some time."[105] These actions are prohibited by law. Although distinct, virtue and law are intimately related, on the levels of both moral theory and moral practice. Someone who does not accept and follow the basic requirements and prohibitions of the community is not likely to develop virtue; someone who does not possess a modicum of virtue is more likely to break the law. At the same time, the requirements of the law in difficult cases are only reliably interpreted by someone who has practical wisdom or *phronesis*—a virtue.

It is the task of law, particularly the criminal law, to identify and prohibit the most seriously problematic of those actions that "destroy the bonds of the community." Consequently, a legal indictment, particularly a criminal indictment, proclaims that the actions with which the defendant is charged are incompatible with the public good. Correlatively, the rhetoric of moral indictment, modeled on that of a legal indictment, functions much the same way with respect to moral deliberations. Some commitments must be taken as bedrock, as the touchstone for moral enquiry on particular points. They cannot be called into question without undermining the basis of the community. MacIntyre highlights Thomas's view of "the roots of intellectual blindness in moral error, with the misdirection of the intellect by the will and the corruption of the will by the sin of pride."[106]

More broadly, in describing the virtues of the Thomistic tradition, MacIntyre emphasizes the degree to which both philosophers and theologians on the one hand and ordinary persons on the other were held accountable for their moral beliefs. Indeed, he views such accountability as a condition of progress in moral inquiry.[107] "Within this tradition philosophical interrogations and accusations of heresy are both summonses to accountability; both refuse to separate the person from the thesis or argument or doctrine uttered by the person. . . . Yet, when accountability in enquiry is understood and practiced aright, how the person fares is a matter of how the thesis, argument, or doctrine fares and not vice versa. We flourish or fail to

---

105. MacIntyre, *After Virtue*, 151.

106. MacIntyre, *Three Rival Versions*, 147.

107. "To be accountable in and for enquiry is to be open to having to give an account of what one has either said or done, and then to having to amplify, explain, defend, and, if necessary, either modify or abandon that account, and in this latter case, to begin the work of supplying a new one." MacIntyre, *Three Rival Versions*, 201.

flourish, live or die, as our theses, arguments, and doctrines live or die."[108] Note the word *summons*. It too is a legal term. In medieval Christianity, the charge of heresy was an accusation that one's thinking was outside the realm of the community's fundamental moral and theological commitments. Not coincidentally, it was a legal charge, precipitating a trial and a judgment regarding guilt.

In my view, at least some of the "shrill" discourse in contemporary societies is best understood not as frustrated moral argument but as focused moral indictment. In MacIntyre's terms, we can say that those who engage in the practice of moral indictment see themselves as calling their fellow citizens (or believers) to account for adopting positions that undermine the basic moral commitments of the community. They see themselves as engaged in the distinct but related task of protecting the basic conditions under which such deliberation can be fruitful.

As powerful as it is, MacIntyre's analysis fails to take due account of the fact that moral reasoning—and moral argument—do not exhaust the category of moral discourse in Western societies, even Western liberal democracies. His theory does not explicitly account for the phenomenon of moral indictment within particular normative traditions. It is not that he is incapable of accounting for that phenomenon; the preceding paragraphs suggested a way for his theory to do so with relative ease. He has not focused sharply, however, upon the key differences between moral argument and moral indictment. The decision to deploy the rhetoric of moral indictment is a choice—and it can be subjected to moral and sociological analysis just like any other choice. When is it appropriate to engage in moral indictment? When is it inappropriate? As I hope to show in forthcoming chapters, coming to terms with the nature, scope, and appropriate limits of the rhetoric of moral indictment is a distinct and important task.[109]

---

108. Ibid.

109. I do not believe MacIntyre would disagree. See an earlier version of my argument in M. Cathleen Kaveny, "Prophetic Rhetoric and Moral Disagreement," in *Intractable Disputes*, ed. Cunningham, 131–65; see also MacIntyre's response in the same volume, "From Answers to Questions: A Response to the Responses," 325–28.

John Rawls

Contests of Public Reason

The late John Rawls devoted a great deal of effort, over an extended period of time, to specifying the conditions for peaceful and productive public conversations in liberal democracies such as the United States. As we will see, his diagnosis of the cause of socially divisive political discourse is very different from Alasdair MacIntyre's. Whereas MacIntyre attributes the shrillness of our public debates to liberalism's dangerously thin accounts of human flourishing, justice, and practical reason, Rawls worries that appeals to thick comprehensive religious or philosophical worldviews will result in far worse problems. In any modern pluralistic society, an attempt to settle a controversial issue by appeal to a single comprehensive worldview is bound to be ineffective at best and disastrous at worst. Such a settlement would not be widely accepted and could only be imposed by force. The very impetus for Western liberal democracies, after all, can be found in Europe's experience with bloody and fruitless wars of religion. Rawls applauds the wisdom of the American Constitution because it means that "various religions have been protected by the First Amendment from the state, and none has been able to dominate and suppress the other religions by the capture and use of state power."[1]

---

1. See John Rawls, *Political Liberalism,* exp. ed. (New York: Columbia University Press, 2005), "The Idea of Public Reason Revisited," 476. See also 476–77, note 75. For an older but still helpful attempt to bring public reason into conversation with a range of Christian political and moral thinking, see William Werpehowski, "Political Liberalism and Christian Ethics: A Review Discussion," *The Thomist* 48, no. 1 (1984): 81–115.

Unlike MacIntyre, Rawls finds hope for productive moral conversation in generating wide support for a broadly liberal account of justice and a corresponding account of "public reason" to guide our most important political conversations. He believes that his approach to public conversations on key political matters is the best way to preserve peaceful relations among citizens of diverse belief systems. I applaud his concern for the moral integrity of all citizens in our pluralistic society. In my view, however, neither his account of the causes of civil fractiousness nor his proposed remedies are ultimately fully adequate.

Public Reason

In Lecture Six of his book *Political Liberalism*, first published in 1993, Rawls sets forth criteria for appropriate public deliberation about important questions of politics and law in liberal democracies. He calls these criteria the requirements of "public reason." Rawls revised and fine-tuned his understanding of public reason over time, most notably in the introduction to the paperback edition of *Political Liberalism*, and then later in an article published in the *University of Chicago Law Review* in 1997.[2] His reflections regarding the nature, scope, and content of public reason have generated a vigorous academic debate[3] that is dwarfed only by comparison to the discussion prompted by his magnum opus, *A Theory of Justice*, in which he developed a comprehensive philosophical account of "justice as fairness."[4] Rawls does not pretend that

2. All of the relevant material is included in Rawls, *Political Liberalism*, exp. ed. This volume also includes the helpful "Reply to Habermas," first published in the *Journal of Philosophy* in 1995.

3. See, for example, Robert Audi and Nicholas Wolterstorff, *Religion in the Public Square: The Place of Religious Convictions in Political Debate* (Lanham, MD: Rowman & Littlefield, 1997); Nigel Biggar and Linda Hogan, eds., *Religious Voices in Public Places* (Oxford: Oxford University Press, 2009); Daniel A. Dombrowski, *Rawls and Religion: The Case for Political Liberalism* (Albany: State University of New York Press, 2001); Christopher J. Eberle, *Religious Conviction in Liberal Politics* (Cambridge: Cambridge University Press, 2002); Gerald F. Gaus, *The Order of Public Reason: A Theory of Freedom and Morality in a Diverse and Bounded World* (New York: Cambridge University Press, 2011); Kent Greenawalt, *Private Consciences and Public Reasons* (New York: Oxford University Press, 1995); Michael J. Perry, *Under God? Religious Faith and Liberal Democracy* (Cambridge: Cambridge University Press, 2003); Steven D. Smith, *The Disenchantment of Secular Discourse* (Cambridge, MA: Harvard University Press, 2010); Paul J. Weithman, *Why Political Liberalism? On John Rawls's Political Turn* (New York: Oxford University Press, 2010); and Paul J. Weithman, *Religion and the Obligations of Citizenship* (Cambridge: Cambridge University Press, 2002).

4. John Rawls, *A Theory of Justice* (Cambridge, MA: Belknap Press of Harvard University Press,

the requirements of public reason are legally enforceable; he knows that the First Amendment protects the freedom of Americans to violate the strictures of public reason with legal impunity. Nonetheless, he does hope that his criteria will function as a moral standard to which key participants in American public debates will hold themselves—and one another—accountable.

As Rawls notes, an essential feature of *A Theory of Justice* is his defense of "justice as fairness" as a "comprehensive philosophical doctrine" to be endorsed by all citizens.[5] Rawls came to recognize, however, that theory is one thing, and real life is another. He acknowledges that he cannot expect everyone in a pluralistic liberal democracy to adopt his own preferred comprehensive doctrine of "justice as fairness." Nor for that matter does he think it likely that everyone in such a society will adopt *any* single comprehensive doctrine. The task Rawls sets himself in *Political Liberalism,* therefore, is to articulate how citizens with irremediably different comprehensive worldviews might cooperate and converse in the political realm in a manner necessary to sustain a modern liberal democracy. Accordingly, he begins by drawing a key contrast between the "true" and the "reasonable"; for Rawls, "political liberalism, rather than referring to its political conception of justice as true, refers to it as reasonable instead."[6] Political liberalism, in a nutshell, is a theory that accounts for the ongoing commitment to the political life of a pluralistic society whose members believe that the comprehensive worldviews of many other people can be seen as reasonable, even if not ultimately true.

How, then, does Rawls define a reasonable comprehensive worldview? It is a comprehensive worldview, secular or religious, liberal or nonliberal, that endorses any one of a family of reasonable liberal conceptions of justice.[7] What is a reasonable liberal conception of justice? It is a conception of justice that makes fair social cooperation possible over generations among citizens who view each other as free and equal.[8] Rawls clearly recognizes that reasonable citizens may endorse a reasonable liberal conception of justice for nonliberal reasons; a religious comprehensive worldview might do so saying,

---

1971). See also the later version, in John Rawls, *A Theory of Justice,* rev. ed. (Cambridge, MA: Belknap Press of Harvard University Press, 1999). For an abridged version, see John Rawls, *Justice as Fairness: A Restatement,* ed. Erin Kelly (Cambridge, MA: Harvard University Press, 2001).

5. Rawls, *Political Liberalism,* exp. ed., "Introduction," xvi.

6. Ibid., xx.

7. Rawls, *Political Liberalism,* exp. ed., "Introduction to the Paperback Edition," xlvii.

8. Ibid., xlii.

as he notes, "such are the limits God sets to our liberty."[9] But reasonable citizens will not treat a reasonable conception of justice merely as a modus vivendi whose terms hold only until they can achieve sufficient political power to impose their comprehensive worldview on the state. Nor will reasonable citizens endorse a reasonable political conception of justice only on the condition that it does not result in their "religious or nonreligious doctrine losing ground in influence and numbers."[10] To endorse a reasonable liberal conception of justice requires real, open-ended commitment, not merely half-hearted acquiescence. Endorsement requires more than provisional or strategic acceptance.

It is important to see that Rawls's account of public reason works in tandem with his political conception of justice by asking how citizens loyal to different comprehensive worldviews should discuss the basic framework that determines their respective rights and responsibilities in a pluralistic liberal democracy. Public reason requires that discussions of these matters (and only of these matters) be carried out in accordance with the requirements of public reason, which are both substantive and procedural in nature. The substantive content of public reason is given by the content of "a family of political conceptions of justice, and not by a single one."[11] To qualify as a member of that family, a conception of justice must have three components:

> First, a list of certain basic rights, liberties, and opportunities (such as those familiar from constitutional regimes);
> Second, an assignment of special priority to those rights, liberties, and opportunities, especially with respect to the claims of the general good and perfectionist values; and
> Third, measures ensuring for all citizens adequate all-purpose means to make effective use of their freedoms.[12]

Moreover, in making arguments based on a reasonable conception of justice, citizens are also free to appeal to "presently accepted general beliefs and

9. Rawls, *Political Liberalism,* exp. ed., "The Idea of Public Reason Revisited," 484.
10. Ibid., 459.
11. Ibid., 450.
12. Ibid.

forms of reasoning found in common sense, and the methods and conclusions of science when these are not controversial."[13]

Public reason restricts not merely the content of deliberation, but also the process of deliberation, by emphasizing the criterion of reciprocity. Rawls states, quite strikingly, that the purpose of this criterion is to specify the nature of political relationship in a constitutional democratic regime as one of *civic friendship*. The crucial unstated premise of Rawls's argument is that friendship, even political friendship, requires an acknowledgment of basic equality. A condition of such friendship is that when we restrict the liberties of our fellow citizens, we do not merely give them reasons that they can understand, but we give them reasons that "they, as free and equal citizens, might reasonably also accept."[14] Consequently, as they deliberate about coercive laws, citizens ought to confirm that the principles derived from their conceptions of justice actually satisfy the criterion of reciprocity.[15] Rawls writes: "For what reasons can both satisfy the criterion of reciprocity and justify denying to some persons religious liberty, holding others as slaves, imposing a property qualification on the right to vote, or denying the right of suffrage to women?"[16]

Rawls insists that public reason, while important, is not hegemonic. He acknowledges, for example, that various corporate bodies within civil society, such as scientific societies, universities, churches, and other groups, may draw on nonpublic reasons in shaping their own respective cultures and terms of association.[17] Moreover, he insists that many questions of public life do not deal with the central subject matter of public reason, which encompasses constitutional essentials and questions of basic justice.[18] Normally, he says, we do not need to apply its strictures to "much tax legislation and many laws regulating property; statutes protecting the environment and controlling

---

13. Rawls, *Political Liberalism*, exp. ed., "The Idea of Public Reason," 224. While Rawls included this aspect of the content of public reason in his original articulation of the concept in "The Idea of Public Reason," it does not receive as much attention in his later essay, "The Idea of Public Reason Revisited."

14. Rawls, *Political Liberalism*, exp. ed., "The Idea of Public Reason Revisited," 447.

15. Ibid., 442.

16. Ibid., 447.

17. Rawls, *Political Liberalism*, exp. ed., "The Idea of Public Reason," 220.

18. See Rawls's summary of the scope in *Political Liberalism*, exp. ed., "The Idea of Public Reason Revisited," 442.

pollution; establishing national parks and preserving wilderness areas and animal and plant species; and laying aside funds for museums and the arts."[19] In addition, Rawls recognizes a sphere for nonpublic deliberation about public matters. The limits of public reason "do not apply to our personal deliberations and reflections about political questions, or to the reasoning about them by members of associations such as churches and universities, all of which is a vital part of the background culture."[20] It is only when arguments are made about the relevant political subject matter *in the public forum* that the strictures of public reason apply.[21]

Finally, and importantly, Rawls modified his position over the years to allow for an increasingly greater presence of nonpublic reason in the public square. In the later iterations of the theory, Rawls allowed that reasonable comprehensive "doctrines may be introduced in public reason at any time, provided that in due course public reasons, given by a reasonable political conception, are presented sufficient to support whatever the comprehensive doctrines are introduced to support." He refers to this condition as the "proviso."[22]

Rawls's account of public reason is a remarkable attempt to structure fruitful conversations about key political matters in pluralistic liberal democracies such as the United States. Rawls is no utopian; he fully recognizes that political discourse shaped according to the requirements of public reason will be accompanied by a substantial amount of debate and controversy. More specifically, he acknowledges the existence of "the burdens of judgment," which are common sources of reasonable disagreement, ranging from divergent ways of reading the empirical evidence (e.g., on climate change) to different approaches to social issues because of different past experiences (e.g., different attitudes toward police misconduct based on different experiences with the police).[23] Rawls believes, however, that these disagreements are not as threatening to social peace and civic friendship as those rooted in dueling comprehensive worldviews.

Despite its many strengths, I do not believe that Rawls's account can adequately account for or ameliorate the fractiousness in contemporary public

19. Rawls, *Political Liberalism,* exp. ed., "The Idea of Public Reason," 214.

20. Ibid., 215.

21. Ibid.

22. Rawls, *Political Liberalism,* exp. ed., "Introduction to the Paperback Edition," xlix–l.

23. Rawls, *Political Liberalism,* exp. ed., "The Power of Citizens and Their Representation," 54–58.

life that is related to clashing comprehensive worldviews. First, the requirements of public reason are not sufficient to achieve its interrelated objectives of civic peace and civic respect in a society such as our own. In fact, it is likely that implementation of those requirements will undermine these objectives, given the way in which discussions of controversial issues are likely to play out in American political life. Second, my pessimism about the usefulness of public reason is strengthened by an examination of two occasions when Rawls has commented on the implications of public reason for the discussion of specific controversial issues (abortion and same-sex marriage). Third, Rawls's account of public reason does not account for the fact that much American moral and political speech, especially religiously inspired moral and political speech, is rhetorically variegated. Most notably, some such speech involves the sort of reason giving contemplated by public reason, while other speech involves prophetic indictment or denunciation. The two types of speech do not pose the same dangers for public discourse. Nor, for that matter, do they have the potential to make the same contributions. Indeed, Rawls's failure to grasp the different types of religiously motivated political speech suggests that he is unable to account for the actual and specific contributions to public discourse of someone as important as Martin Luther King, Jr., who moved American society toward racial justice by both reason and prophetic utterances rooted in a Christian political vision.

I will expand on these three points below. Before doing so, however, it is worth signaling the common thread in my critique of MacIntyre and Rawls. Despite their differences, both thinkers fail to pay sufficient attention to the actual political-religious history of the United States. Their theories do not get to the "core" of the problem of civic discourse in American life because they have not devoted enough analysis to the development of that discourse, including its origins in a particular kind of prophetic indictment developed by the Puritans.

Civic Peace and Civic Respect

As revealed by both Rawls's own writings and the larger debate they generated, two general grounds justify restricting the role of claims rooted only in comprehensive worldviews in public discussion of important political matters. I will call them the ground of civic respect and the ground of civic peace.[24] As we will see, these grounds incorporate a diagnosis of the source of divisiveness in contemporary political discourse that is quite different from Alasdair MacIntyre's. While religious worldviews certainly do not exhaust the range of comprehensive worldviews that Rawls has in mind, they do provide central examples of tension and conflict with political liberalism, particularly in the American context. Accordingly, in the discussion below, I will focus on the way in which the strictures of public reason could affect citizens adhering to religious comprehensive worldviews.

The first major justification for restricting the role of distinctively religious (and other comprehensive) claims in the public square, the *civic respect* ground, pertains to the requirements of fundamental fairness in the deliberations of citizens of a liberal democratic republic. On the view advanced by Rawls and other theorists of public reason, religious believers are being unfair to their fellow citizens when they base their judgments about matters of key public concern on arguments whose force depends on the existence of a divine being or on the reliability of certain methods of discerning divine will. In Rawls's framework, it may be *wrong,* but it is not *unreasonable,* to deny the existence of God or to contest particular methods of discerning God's will for humanity. Consequently, it is unfair for believers to base their decisions about how to order a common political life on premises that they cannot expect every reasonable person to share because doing so imposes their worldview upon others without sufficient rational justification. Moreover, this unfairness is not merely one of the bumps and bruises that inevitably result from participation in contemporary political life. It is a manifestation of disrespect—a violation of what Rawls has called the principle of reciprocity, as I described earlier.

The second major justification for restrictions on the role of distinctively religious (and other comprehensive) claims in discernment and debate about public issues is more pragmatic in nature.[25] It is the *civic peace* justification.

24. Nicholas Wolterstorff offers an extremely helpful exposition and critique of these two strands in his essay, "Why We Should Reject What Liberalism Tells Us About Speaking and Acting in Public for Religious Reasons," in Paul J. Weithman, ed., *Religion and Contemporary Liberalism* (Notre Dame, IN: University of Notre Dame Press, 1997), 162–81. For my own take on the matter, see M. Cathleen Kaveny, "Religious Claims and the Dynamics of Argument," *Wake Forest Law Review* 36, no. 2 (2001): 423–48.

25. I read Kent Greenawalt as justifying the limitations he would place on the use of religious premises in arguments on political matters in the public square on these grounds. "Why should it

More specifically, we live in a highly pluralistic society in which many people have strong commitments to the truth of their religion that outrun the basis for rationally demonstrating its superiority to outsiders. Furthermore, many of the contending religious frameworks have vigorous and divergent views on how political life should be organized. In this context, the clash of religious beliefs can be a dangerous catalyst for social division, instability, and resentment.[26] The evident cause for concern in this context would be the use of such premises in the public debate. The invocation of a distinctly religious premise could be viewed as "fighting words," at least in a society in which there exists vigorous commitment to religious truth claims, substantial pluralism, and a number of religious belief systems whose rationally disputable truth claims extend to the structure of political society.

Both the civic respect and the civic peace justifications for establishing a robust conception of public reason can be subjected to further critical scrutiny. To foster civic respect and nurture civil peace, will it be sufficient to convince citizens to adhere to the requirements of public reason in their public discourse—that is, in their advocacy in town hall meetings, the op-ed pages of newspapers, and perhaps even on big political blogs? Or does achieving those goals actually require persons to restrict themselves far more radically, by constraining their thought processes and private deliberations about the political common good according to public reason's requirements? In other words, does fostering civic peace and civic respect mean that ideally all citizens should channel how they *think* about matters pertaining to public law and policy through the strictures of public reason? Rawls's answer to this question has evolved over time. In the final iteration of his theory, he presents public reason as an "ideal" for the deliberation of all citizens, although it is not a strict requirement.[27] In my view, however, whether it is construed as a

matter if religious premises are shared? . . . In a very religious but extremely tolerant society, public airing of particular religious views might work well, but in actuality such discourse promotes a sense of separation between the speaker and those who do not share his religious convictions and is likely to produce both religious and political divisiveness." Kent Greenawalt, *Religious Convictions and Political Choice* (New York: Oxford University Press, 1988), 219.

26. Conversely, however, on this view, there would be no reason to limit reliance or expression of religious speech in the political realm in a social context in which either religious belief or its fervor have nearly disappeared, or there is strong religious homogeneity, or the religions that do predominate take no stand on matters of political import.

27. Strictly speaking, the *idea* of public reason applies to government officials (from all three branches of government) and candidates for public office on fundamental political questions in the

requirement or as an ideal, public reason is not likely to lead to civic respect or civic peace, at least in the United States.

For example, suppose a group of religiously motivated citizens wants to enact a state law prohibiting homosexual couples from adopting children. On the one hand, their leaders might forthrightly but naively decide to cast their arguments in terms of the religious reasons that actually prompted their legislative program. On the other hand, if they are more politically astute, they might choose to draw upon "publicly accessible" reasons to make their case in the political realm by asserting that such parental arrangements might cause uncertain harm to children's psychosexual development, and so on. In so doing, they would conform to the *requirements* of public reason but not to its *ideal*. According to Rawls, the higher and unenforceable *ideal* of public reason requires participants in such discussions actually to be motivated by the publicly accessible reasons that they proffer.

Would those who object to the political activities of this religiously motivated group actually be satisfied by the group's shift in moral terminology in the public square? It seems to me that the answer is no. The objection would likely go far deeper than the language in which the religiously motivated citizens cast their political arguments; it would have to do with the substance of their position, not merely its rhetorical form. It would contest the reasoning that actually galvanized the religiously motivated citizens to political activity, not on the reasons adduced by their spokespersons on an ad hoc basis to make their case in the public square. Those who disagree with the religiously motivated citizens would likely judge it to be *substantively unjust*—a violation of civic respect—for one group of participants in a pluralist democracy to rely on a pattern of reasoning alien to another group in making public policy that affects everyone.

Moreover, encouraging citizens actually motivated by a religious comprehensive worldview to recast their arguments in terms acceptable to public reason might also impede civic peace, not merely civic respect. It is extremely

---

public forum. (See Rawls's elaboration of the five criteria in *Political Liberalism,* exp. ed., "The Idea of Public Reason Revisited," 442–43.) The *ideal* of public reason applies to the speech and conduct of government officials in broader contexts, and to citizens exercising their public duty. He writes, "[I]deally citizens are to think of themselves *as if they were legislators* and ask themselves what statutes, supported by what reasons satisfying the criterion of reciprocity, they would think it most reasonable to enact." They are also to hold their elected representatives accountable to the demands of public reason. Ibid., 444–45, original emphasis.

frustrating to carry on a conversation with individuals who do not offer their real reasons for holding the positions they hold. If we enter into an ostensibly frank discussion on a given controversial issue, such as abortion or gay adoption, we expect that if we refute the arguments put forward by our interlocutors, it is at least possible they will change their minds. But this may not be the case if our interlocutors are not offering us *the reasons they actually hold,* but rather are mustering an ad hoc argument drawn from the language of public reason to support their position. If we urge our interlocutors to put forward arguments in terms that are not really theirs, our interlocutors will not change their minds if we defeat them but instead will search for a more resilient replacement approach to make their case in the public square.[28]

Rawls and his defenders might reply that the foregoing scenario describes the abuse of public reason, not its proper use. Lawmakers and virtuous citizens are meant to deliberate in good faith, in terms set by the conception of justice they find to be the most reasonable; they are not meant opportunistically to raid such conceptions for arguments to justify conclusions reached on other grounds. Indeed, Rawls insists that valid public reasons must not be "puppets manipulated from behind the scenes by comprehensive doctrines."[29]

But this reply would raise the question whether Rawls had sufficiently relinquished the theoretical idealism presupposed in *A Theory of Justice.* The impetus for *Political Liberalism,* as I noted earlier, was Rawls's recognition that no actual liberal society will ever reach agreement on a comprehensive theory of justice; societies such as the United States, for example, are marked by an irreducible pluralism of comprehensive worldviews. As the political situation in the United States for the past two decades has made abundantly clear, it is also impossible to control the framework in which the citizens of liberal democracies actually conduct their practical deliberations about matters of public import. It is also impossible to prevent them from interjecting into public discourse arguments drawn directly from their own comprehensive worldviews (reasonable or not) or, alternatively, drawing upon the language of public reason in an ad hoc manner to cloak positions that they actually hold on entirely different grounds.

---

28. See Kaveny, "Religious Claims and the Dynamics of Argument," 429–30.
29. Rawls, *Political Liberalism,* exp. ed., "The Idea of Public Reason Revisited," 454.

Moreover, attempts to pressure religious believers to reframe the way they think or speak about important political issues may actually impede rather than advance the causes of civic respect and civic peace from the perspective of religious believers, not merely their secular interlocutors. As the political resurgence of the religious right under the administration of President George W. Bush demonstrated,[30] many believers did not take kindly to what they saw as an attempt to exclude distinctively religious voices from the public square.[31] Some believers think that the only way to be faithful to their religious commitments is to express the political convictions that flow from them in distinctively religious terms. Consequently, they experience the attempt to stifle their preferred language of civic participation as a deep form of disrespect for them, in an effort to favor more secular accounts of political life. Furthermore, requiring key matters of public concern to be cast in terms of public reason may discriminate against less educated religious believers, who may find it more difficult to express their views in the language of modern liberal democracies than their highly educated counterparts.

What about the proviso—the later Rawls's concession that key participants in public debates are permitted to make their interventions in the native terms of their comprehensive worldviews, provided that they eventually recast their argument in compliance with the demands of public reason? While the proviso manifests Rawls's deep commitment to revising his theory in light of the well-founded comments and concerns of others, I doubt that it will improve the chances that the norms governing the use of public reason will further the goals of civic respect and civic peace. The overall tone of any debate is set by the participants' ordinary contributions to it, not by one or two extraordinary interventions. If 80 percent of one's contributions to the public square are cast in the distinctive language of a comprehensive worldview, will the fears of those who feel excluded from that worldview really be assuaged by one or two prominent efforts to make one's point in the terms of public reason? Moreover, if religious believers comply with the proviso only sporadically, their interlocutors will understandably think that when they do

30. See, for example, Clyde Wilcox and Carin Robinson, *Onward Christian Soldiers? The Religious Right in American Politics,* 4th ed. (Boulder, CO: Westview Press, 2010).

31. See Richard John Neuhaus, *The Naked Public Square: Religion and Democracy in America,* 2nd ed. (Grand Rapids, MI: Eerdmans, 1988), for an early and influential manifesto against the exclusion of religious voices from public discussion.

cast their arguments in terms of public reason, they are doing nothing more than practicing a subterfuge. Finally, consider the matter from the perspective of religious believers. Will the proviso's concession be sufficient to address the objections that they have to the strictures of public reason, as I outlined them above? I think it is more likely that the proviso's requirement that they *eventually* reframe their public interventions in a way that is alien to them seems like an insulting test of their fitness to participate in public debate. If it is viewed in this manner, the proviso will further neither civic respect nor civic peace, despite Rawls's best intentions.

Abortion and Same-Sex Marriage

The inability of public reason to quell the fractiousness of political discourse in a pluralistic liberal democracy is suggested, although not demonstrated, by two concrete attempts Rawls made to frame controversial moral and legal issues in its terms. If Rawls's own application of public reason in addressing key political-moral questions facing our nation is highly problematic and contestable, it is highly unlikely that less philosophically astute citizens and activists will do any better with its requirements.

In a footnote appearing in "The Idea of Public Reason," and purporting to illustrate the application of the concept, Rawls articulates his judgment that *"any reasonable balance* of . . . [due respect for human life, ordered reproduction of political society over time, and the equality of women] will give a woman a duly qualified right to decide whether or not to end her pregnancy during the first trimester."[32] The offhand assertion about the limits of public reason is not only contestable; it should be deeply disturbing to anyone who has more than a passing acquaintance with the vigorous bioethical, legal, and political debate about abortion over the past forty years. Those opposed to abortion before the end of the first trimester make scientifically informed judgments about when an individual human life begins. Their judgments about this matter are not unanimous; some say a human life begins at fertilization, others say it begins at the end of the embryo's totipotent phase (which ends its capacity for twinning), and still others say it begins with the first brain wave or heartbeat. They conjoin their judgment about when

---

32. Rawls, *Political Liberalism*, exp. ed., "The Idea of Public Reason," 243n, emphasis mine.

human life begins with the conviction that all human life deserves equal legal protection to reach the conclusion that abortion should be legally restricted even before the end of the first trimester. The arguments of these various pro-life thinkers may be flawed—indeed, they cannot all be correct because they contradict each other as well as their pro-choice counterparts—but they are nonetheless arguments consonant with the requirements of public reason, which generally mandates the use of established scientific knowledge and the commitment to equal dignity of human beings in order to address controversial issues. In the end, then, it is impossible to treat Rawls's footnote as anything other than an expression of his own views on abortion rather than as an impartial deliverance of public reason.[33]

Indeed, in "The Idea of Public Reason Revisited," written some years later, Rawls minimizes the status of his remarks about abortion in that footnote.[34] Remarkably, however, in the very same essay, he goes on to make similarly abbreviated, suggestive, and controversial remarks about how public reason would assess the status of the traditional heterosexual family. Rawls writes that "the government would appear to have no interest in the particular form of family life, or of relations among the sexes, except insofar as that form or those relations in some way affect the orderly reproduction of society over time. Thus, appeals to monogamy as such, or against same-sex marriages, as within the government's legitimate interest in the family, would reflect religious or comprehensive moral doctrines."[35]

Here, as in the case of abortion, Rawls's judgment about the status of public reason with regard to same-sex marriage was disturbingly precipitous. While he goes on to acknowledge theoretically that there are arguments in favor of the traditional family that would pass muster (e.g., the argument that monogamy is necessary for the equality of women or same-sex marriages are harmful to children), he does not grapple with the actual arguments put forth by adherents of traditional family structure, which encompass but are not limited to those concerns. As demonstrated by the vigorous debates

33. For vigorous arguments that reasonableness does not require Rawls's position on abortion from different perspectives, see, for example, Michael J. Perry, *Love & Power: The Role of Religion and Morality in American Politics* (New York: Oxford University Press, 1991), 116–22; and John Finnis, "Public Reason and Moral Debate," in *The Collected Essays of John Finnis*, vol. 1, *Reason and Action* (Oxford: Oxford University Press, 2012), 256–76.

34. Rawls, *Political Liberalism*, exp. ed., "The Idea of Public Reason Revisited," 479, note 80.

35. Ibid., 457.

over same-sex marriage and homosexual rights between Michael Perry and
Paul Weithman on the one hand and John Finnis, Robert George, and Gerard
Bradley on the other, public reason is not likely to resolve these issues any
more than it is to resolve the abortion issue. Most significantly, an examination of the actual arguments used by these participants reveals no substantial
reliance on distinctively religious claims in mounting their arguments. Nor
can those arguments be framed as a battle between secularists on the one
hand and religious believers on the other. In fact, Perry and Weithman, who
supported same-sex marriage, and Finnis, George, and Bradley, who opposed
it, were all practicing Catholics at the time of their debate.[36] It is possible, of
course, that the U.S. Supreme Court's 2015 decision conferring constitutional
protection upon same-sex marriage may settle the issue. It is also possible that
it will inflame another battle in the culture wars, as *Roe v. Wade* did when it
conferred constitutional protection upon the right to abortion in 1973. It may
be too soon to say.[37]

36. Two of the journals sponsored by Notre Dame Law School have published symposia
addressing the rights of same-sex couples, including articles by these and other scholars. See *Notre
Dame Journal of Law, Ethics & Public Policy* 9, no. 1 (1995), *Notre Dame Journal of Law, Ethics & Public
Policy* 18, no. 1 (2004), and *American Journal of Jurisprudence* 42 (1997). For example, see John M. Finnis,
"Law, Morality, and 'Sexual Orientation,'" *Notre Dame Journal of Law, Ethics & Public Policy* 9, no. 1
(1995): 11–39; Michael J. Perry, "The Morality of Homosexual Conduct: A Response to John Finnis,"
Notre Dame Journal of Law, Ethics & Public Policy 9, no. 1 (1995): 41–74; Paul J. Weithman, "A Propos of
Professor Perry: A Plea for Philosophy in Sexual Ethics," *Notre Dame Journal of Law, Ethics & Public
Policy* 9, no. 1 (1995): 75–92; Gerard V. Bradley, "Law and the Culture of Marriage," *Notre Dame Journal
of Law, Ethics & Public Policy* 18, no. 1 (2004): 189–217; and "Same-Sex Marriage: Our Final Answer?,"
Notre Dame Journal of Law, Ethics & Public Policy 14, no. 2 (2000): 729–52. See also Robert P. George and
Christopher Wolfe, "Natural Law and Liberal Public Reason," *American Journal of Jurisprudence* 42
(1997): 31–49; and Robert P. George and Patrick Lee, "What Sex Can Be: Self-Alienation, Illusion, or
One-Flesh Union," *American Journal of Jurisprudence* 42 (1997): 135–57. More recently, as the national
debate over same-sex marriage intensified, Sherif Girgis, Ryan T. Anderson, and Robert P. George
published *What is Marriage? Man and Woman: A Defense* (New York: Encounter Books, 2012), which was
based on an article in the *Harvard Journal of Law and Public Policy*. While Girgis, Anderson, and George
are Roman Catholic, they do not see themselves as drawing upon specifically religious arguments in
making their case against same-sex marriage. After the Supreme Court gave constitutional protection
to same-sex marriage, the concern of social conservatives focused on protecting the rights of religious
people to resist the new definition. See, for example, Ryan T. Anderson, *Truth Overruled: The Future of
Marriage and Religious Freedom* (Washington, DC: Regnery Publishing, 2015). Yet one of the most influential defenders of same-sex marriage (as well as religious liberty) in the American context is a Roman
Catholic; see Andrew Sullivan, *Virtually Normal* (New York: Vintage Books, 1995).

37. The Supreme Court's decision in the same-sex marriage case was a 5-4 vote; see *Obergefell v.
Hodges*, 576 U.S. ___, 135 S. St. 2584 (2015). Polling immediately after the decision was handed down
suggested a slight decline in support for same-sex marriage. See Michael J. New, "In the Wake of

Rawls's offhand remarks about the clear verdict of public reason for abortion and same-sex marriage give plausibility to the fears of religious believers about the way public reason actually operates. They raise the suspicion that public reason is nothing more than a political tool designed to further legal policies that are consistent with a liberal comprehensive worldview rather than a set of sensible constraints on deliberation and argument appropriate for a truly pluralistic society encompassing religious believers as well as secular liberals.[38] They also seem to reflect Rawls's own inchoate suspicion that the arguments about the public good put forward by religious believers on the two controversial issues in question are not, in fact, arguments flowing from a reasonable conception of justice. In both cases, he seems inclined to dismiss arguments against early abortion or same-sex marriage as "puppets" manipulated by those advancing unreasonable aspects of comprehensive worldviews, religious worldviews in particular. In short, these two examples suggest not only that public reason is insufficient to resolve controversial issues such as abortion and same-sex marriage but also that the very invocation of its strictures can serve to exacerbate divisions. Secular thinkers like Rawls tacitly accuse religious believers of manipulating public reason for religious ends, while religious believers resent the accusation *and* suspect that it arises out of prejudice against religion. As I argued earlier, the multiplication of suspicions about the ulterior motives animating the interventions of our fellow citizens adduced in the public square is conducive neither to civic respect nor civic peace.

Is there an alternative to public reason? In my view, the best way to foster mutual respect in the public square is by undertaking, and asking others to undertake, the hard work of explaining our viewpoints on matters of public discourse in the terms that we *actually believe* to justify those viewpoints—whether or not those terms conform to the strictures of public reason.[39] We

---

Obergefell, Three New Polls Show Reduced Support for Same-Sex Marriage," *National Review*, The Corner, July 21, 2015, www.nationalreview.com/corner/421443/obergefell-same-sex-marriage-poll-reduced-support. By contrast, *Roe v. Wade*, 410 U.S. 113 (1973), which conferred constitutional protection on a woman's right to choose abortion, was decided by a 7-2 vote.

38. For example, Rawls's conception of the very thin interest in which government has in family life—limited to the "orderly reproduction of society over time"—seems oriented toward a particular, liberal, comprehensive philosophical understanding of the relationship between the state and the family.

39. See Kaveny, "Religious Claims and the Dynamics of Argument," 429–34.

are more likely to see our interlocutors as acting with moral integrity, and for the common good, if we can situate their judgments on controversial issues within a broader framework that allows us to see their moral values in oper-ation across a wide range of questions. It is harder, for example, to dismiss someone who opposes abortion as motivated by sheer disrespect for women if we see them expressing a consistent concern for vulnerable human beings, including the immigrant and the civilians caught in war.

In addition, we are more likely to make progress in convincing other people to accept our own conclusions about matters of law and public policy if we offer them reasons actually convincing to them rather than reasons that we think *ought* to convince them in a hypothetical, ideal political world. Suppose we want to persuade our interlocutors not merely to hold certain positions on political and moral matters but also to hold them for the very reasons that we hold such positions. This goal requires entering into a long and complex process of asking and replying to questions on both sides, in which we will likely need to convince them to change their minds about a number of interrelated matters in which their position in question is embedded. Ultimately, they will come to see a controversial question our way, for our reasons, only if they come to think that our way of approaching a range of related issues is more fruitful and compelling than theirs.[40]

Rawls's discussion of public policy does not pay sufficient attention to the fact that argument in the public square is activity that speakers conduct with a larger purpose in mind. On some occasions, we make our case in order to disclose ourselves and our deepest commitments to our fellow citizens. At other times, we make our case in order to convince others to join our political program. In still other contexts, we use our arguments as a bulwark, to push back a political agenda that we find objectionable.[41] To accomplish their ends, citizens make their case not just once but many times over, varying their words and their presentations to better connect with their audience. A savvy speaker does not make the same speech in a church basement that she does in a city bar frequented by Millennials or in a meeting of the ASPCA.

Unfortunately, in my view, much of the academic discussion of public reason proceeds as if participating in political discussion is rather like delivering

40. Ibid., 435–39.
41. Ibid., 442.

a single lecture to a group of homogenous college students, which may be recorded for later availability on smartphones and tablets to an unknown and amorphous audience. Rawls admonishes us to address "citizens as citizens," and furnish the same set of reasons backing our positions to all our political conversation partners.[42] But this is not possible in political discussions in the real world. Moreover, unless one has a Rawlsian political anthropology, which may well support an abstract understanding of a citizen as citizen, it does not seem necessary.

Our fellow citizens are particular persons, who have different backgrounds, different concerns, and different aspirations. They are moved by different reasons and rhetorical methods. To appeal to some, it is more effective to marshal facts and figures; to appeal to others, it is better to pull on their heartstrings. Some are moved by self-interest, others by altruistic concerns. Some are worried about communal safety, while others are more concerned about social fairness. Respecting our fellow citizens as the actual flesh-and-blood persons they are, in my view, requires us to address the worries they actually have, rather than the worries we think they should have if they are "reasonable" in Rawls's sense—or for that matter, in our own sense.

In *Democracy and Tradition*, philosopher of religion Jeffrey Stout makes a similar argument, contending that the rich process of mutual reason giving and reason requesting actually enhances mutual respect. He writes: "Real respect for others takes seriously the distinctive point of view *each* other occupies. It is respect for individuality, for difference."[43] Stout goes on to fault Rawls's view of a reasonable person for being too narrow in insisting that a reasonable person "play by the discursive rules" of public reason on all the essential political matters within its purview. He asks, "[W]hy not view the person who takes each competing perspective on its own terms, expressing his own views openly and practicing immanent criticism on the views of others, as a reasonable (i.e., socially cooperative, respectful, reason-giving) person?"[44]

I continue to think that both Stout's and my own earlier criticisms of Rawls's theory of public reason are sound. Nonetheless, I have also come to

---

42. Rawls, *Political Liberalism*, exp. ed., "The Idea of Public Reason Revisited," 441.

43. Jeffrey Stout, *Democracy and Tradition* (Princeton, NJ: Princeton University Press, 2004), 73 (original emphasis).

44. Ibid.

believe that they miss an important aspect of the actual role that religious discourse plays in the public square. The basic assumption of the entire discussion that has grown up around Rawls's account of public reason, among both supporters and critics, is that the central activity of citizens in the public square is giving *reasons* to one another in the course of engaging in moral and political argument. Rawls argues that civic peace and civic respect require the reason giving to be constrained in certain ways, while others, including Stout and myself, have questioned the necessity and usefulness of those constraints. Whatever the differences among us, we have all tacitly envisioned a certain ideal order to the moral and political conversation in the public square. Citizens should move from premises to conclusions, examining and reconsidering (and helping one another to examine and reconsider) premises and arguments in discussing and debating matters in the public square. As Stout says, the reasonable person in a pluralistic liberal democracy such as our own is a "socially cooperative, respectful, reason-giving" person.

Reason-giving people, people who are committed to the practice of immanent criticism and who are willing honestly to proffer and to reexamine their own premises, are not likely to threaten the stability of liberal democracies, no matter what worldview forms the basis of their arguments. That stability is not likely to be threatened when Catholic moralists make an elaborate argument for the full personhood of the zygote based on the latest embryology and a "natural rights" perspective on human dignity. Such an argument, as Rawls finally acknowledged, does conform to the requirements of public reason. But it is also not likely to be threatened when evangelical Protestant moralists make an elaborate argument for God's love and care for unborn children based on specific scriptural passages. Although such persons do not qualify as employing public reason, they are likely to be, as Stout argues, eminently reasonable.

But here's the rub. As I indicated in Chapter 1, reasonable argumentation is far from the only kind of speech, particularly religious speech, in the public square. And by its very nature, it is not the most incendiary. Citizens do not merely argue in the public square; they also proclaim the truth, exhort repentance, condemn, and call down the judgment of God—or the secular equivalent of the judgment of God, such as the judgment of nature. With utmost confidence, they condemn the actions of their fellow citizens, threatening divine wrath if their condemnations do not provoke reform and offering a better, and sometimes a beautiful, future if they do. They are, so to speak, social prophets. They have no need for public reason for their reason, so they think, is in direct conformity with God's own law. Like the Hebrew prophets, they are engaging in the discourse of prophetic indictment. If we are worried about civic respect and civic peace, we need to grapple not only with differences of reasons but also with differences of rhetorical style. The religious language of divine indictment, of clarion calls for moral and social reform, can have significant effect on the political sphere. I want to turn now to a discussion of a concrete case in which such rhetoric demonstrated the ability to shape political discourse and public policy.

The Limited Descriptive Reach of Public Reason

On March 31, 2005, forty-one-year-old Theresa Marie Schindler Schiavo died at a Florida hospice, thirteen days after her feeding tube was removed pursuant to court order.[45] Her death ended a protracted personal tragedy that had been transformed over the previous months into an emotional battle line in the culture wars. At the age of twenty-six, Schiavo had suffered serious brain damage due to respiratory and cardiac arrest, which resulted in a diagnosis of persistent vegetative state. After extensive efforts at rehabilitation failed, her husband and guardian Michael Schiavo decided to remove the feeding tube, arguing that his wife would decline such treatment if she were able to make the decision for herself. Terri Schiavo's parents disagreed with his decision, in large part on religious grounds (they were devout Catholics), and began a lengthy battle to preserve her life.

Long a cause célèbre among pro-life and disability rights activists, Terri's case became a national controversy in the spring of 2005. In the months before

45. The best account of the underlying dispute as it unfolded until late 2003 can be found in Jay Wolfson's guardian *ad litem* report (December 1, 2003), which is included in a FindLaw website collecting documents pertaining to the last couple of years of the saga, http://news.findlaw .com/legalnews/lit/schiavo/index.html. Another good resource for important documentation is Arthur L. Caplan, James J. McCartney, and Dominic A. Sisti, eds., *The Case of Terri Schiavo: Ethics at the End of Life* (Amherst, NY: Prometheus Books, 2006). The University of Miami Ethics Program also maintains a website with numerous resources, including a comprehensive time line: www6 .miami.edu/ethics/schiavo/schiavo.htm. Finally, the Wikipedia article, "Terri Schiavo Case," includes numerous hyperlinks to the relevant legal documents, http://en.wikipedia.org/wiki/Terri _Schiavo_case.

her death, pro-life activists stepped up protests outside Terri Schiavo's hospice, Michael Schiavo's home, and various Florida courthouse and capital buildings.[46] According to a *New York Times* reporter, "the signs included these sentiments: 'Hey Judge, Who Made You God?' 'Hospice or Auschwitz?' 'Murder is Legal in America.' 'Murderers!' 'You Wouldn't Let a Dog Die of Thirst.' 'Next They Come For You: America = Nazis.' 'Has Anyone Seen Jeb?' "[47] In 2003, the Schindlers asked Randall Terry, the leader of the extreme anti-abortion group Operation Rescue, to help save their daughter. His participation intensified the protests and the controversy.[48]

Not all the placards in favor of saving Teri's life were held by conservative Christians—the Reverend Jesse Jackson was a protester.[49] Not all the prophetic speech was specifically religious. Nat Hentoff wrote an article entitled, "Terri Schiavo: Judicial Murder," in which he stated: "For all the world to see, a 41-year-old woman, who has committed no crime, will die of dehydration and starvation in the longest public execution in American history."[50] Nonetheless, many conservative Christians did see the Schiavo case as a key battle in the culture wars.[51] Accordingly, many signs carried by protesters expressed strong religious judgments: "You are going to Hell, Murderers!," and "Jesus Lives, So Does Terri."

Most significantly for our purposes, the battle over Terri Schiavo's fate was not confined to warring placards outside her hospice. It extended into the halls of political power, at both the state and the federal level, in ways that seem astonishing after the passage of some time. After numerous attempts

46. Associated Press, "Schiavo Supporters Launch Protest Campaign," February 16, 2005, www.foxnews.com/story/2005/02/16/schiavo-supporters-launch-protest-campaign/.

47. Rick Lyman, "Protesters with Hearts on Sleeves and Anger on Signs," *New York Times,* March 28, 2005, A15. "Jeb," in the last of the signs described in the text, is a reference to Jeb Bush, who was governor of Florida at the time.

48. Abby Goodnough, "Victory in Florida Feeding Case Emboldens the Religious Right," *New York Times,* October 24, 2003, A1.

49. Abby Goodnough, "Jesse Jackson Takes up Cause of Schiavo's Parents," *New York Times,* March 30, 2005, A12.

50. Nat Hentoff, "Terri Schiavo: Judicial Murder," *Village Voice,* March 22, 2005, 36–38.

51. See Laurie Goodstein, "Schiavo Case Highlights Alliance between Catholics and Evangelicals," *New York Times,* March 24, 2005, A20. See also CNN Reliable Sources, "Battle over Terri Schiavo: Are Journalists Paying Enough Attention to Religion?" March 27, 2005, http://transcripts.cnn.com/TRANSCRIPTS/0503/27/rs.01.html. Needless to say, many groups saw the controversy as a fundraising opportunity. See David D. Kirkpatrick, "Conservatives Invoke Case in Fund-Raising Campaigns," *New York Times,* March 25, 2005, A15.

on the part of the Schindlers and their allies to wrest control over Terri's fate away from Michael Schiavo failed in the courts, they turned to the legislative branch for relief. The Florida legislature passed Terri's Law, in the fall of 2003; that law gave Governor Jeb Bush "authority to issue a one-time stay to prevent withholding of nutrition and hydration from a patient" who met the precise description of Terri Schiavo.[52] So, when Terri's feeding tube was removed on order of a Florida Court, Governor Bush ordered her feeding tube reinserted.[53] After another year of legal wrangling, in which Michael Schiavo was represented for some purposes by the American Civil Liberties Union, and the Schindlers were represented by the American Center for Law and Justice (founded by Pat Robertson), the Florida Supreme Court found Terri's Law unconstitutional in September 2004.[54]

With the battle to continue Terri's artificial nutrition and hydration losing ground in Florida, her parents joined forces with national religious and political leaders to take their daughter's cause to Washington.[55] The case was already of central importance to mainstream pro-life groups such as National Right to Life Committee and more extreme groups such as Operation Rescue. It also increasingly appeared on the radar of more broadly focused religious lobbying groups, such as the Traditional Values Coalition, which maintained that "Jesus Christ is the Son of God and the Lord has given us a rule book to live by: The Bible." The coalition also maintains that these values are politically relevant because "Bible-based traditional values are what created and what have preserved our nation. We will lose our freedom if we reject these values."[56]

52. Florida Legislature, Chapter 2003-418 (HB 35-E), approved by the governor on October 21, 2003.

53. Florida Governor's Office, Executive Order 03-201, October 21, 2003, http://news.findlaw.com/cnn/docs/schiavo/flagovexord03201.html.

54. *Bush v. Schiavo*, 885 So.2d 321 (Fla. 2004). The ground for unconstitutionality was separation of powers—the infringement by the legislative and executive branches upon matters within the purview of the courts.

55. See David D. Kirkpatrick and Sheryl Gay Stolberg, "How Family's Cause Reached the Halls of Congress," *New York Times*, March 22, 2005, A1. For a good account of the relationship between the religious leaders and political leaders, see Dan Gilgoff, *The Jesus Machine: How James Dobson, Focus on the Family and Evangelical America Are Winning the Culture War* (New York: St. Martin's Press, 2007), 124–32.

56. Traditional Values Coalition, "Traditional Values Defined," June 6, 2011. The phrase about the Bible as rulebook has been removed from the current definition of traditional values but has migrated to other groups. See, for example, Grace Chapel Christian Fellowship, "Traditional Values," www.gracechapeljax.com/TraditionalValues.html.

The Family Research Council, a powerful conservative Christian lobbying group associated with evangelical leader James Dobson's Focus on the Family, spearheaded the effort to have Congress intervene to save Terri's life. Key targets of their efforts were Senate Majority Leader Bill Frist and House Majority Leader Tom Delay, who were both courting the favor of "values voters." Congressman Delay assured the Family Research Council, "It is more than just Terri Schiavo. This is a critical issue for people in this position, and it is also a critical issue to fight that fight for life, whether it be euthanasia or abortion. I tell you, ladies and gentlemen, one thing God has brought to us is Terri Schiavo to elevate the visibility of what's going on in America."[57] Their efforts were joined by conservative Catholic senators Sam Brownback and Rick Santorum, both of whom had been for some time advocates of a more prominent, distinctively religious voice in the public square. Senator Santorum even flew to Florida to pray with the Schiavo's family by her bedside immediately before her death.[58]

The day that Schiavo's feeding tube was removed, March 18, 2005, Republicans in Congress summoned both Terri and Michael Schiavo to testify at hearings before House and Senate subcommittees later in the month. See Abby Goodnough and Carl Hulse, "Despite Congress, Woman's Feeding Tube Is Removed: Judge in Florida Rejects Effort by House," *New York Times,* March 19, 2005, A1. The idea was that the tube would need to remain in to keep her alive to make her appearance before Congress. When that move was rebuffed by Judge George Greer, the Florida state court judge in charge of the case, the Senate passed a bill on Palm Sunday, March 20, 2009, conferring jurisdiction over Schiavo's case upon the federal courts. The bill, sometimes called as the Palm Sunday Compromise, passed 3 to 0; ninety-seven senators were absent from the vote.[59] Congressman Delay then recalled the House of Representatives to consider the matter; the bill passed 203 to 58, with 174 representatives absent from the vote, which took place after midnight. President Bush, who had returned from Texas early for the purpose, signed the bill into law in the early morning on March 21.[60] Its title, An Act for the Relief of the Parents of

---

57. Karen Tumulty, "Tom DeLay: It Is More than Just Terri Schiavo," *Time,* March 23, 2005, www
.time.com/time/nation/article/0,8599,1040968,00.html.

58. Maeve Reston, "Santorum Prays with Schiavo's Family," *Pittsburgh Post-Gazette,* May 30, 2005,
www.post-gazette.com/stories/news/us/santorum-prays-with-schiavos-family-576119/.

59. The three senators present were Bill Frist, Rick Santorum, and Mel Martinez.

60. An Act for the Relief of the Parents of Theresa Marie Schiavo, P.L. 109-3, 1999 Stat. 15 (2005).

Theresa Marie Schiavo, indicated both its purpose and its highly particularized scope. In a statement Bush made on Schiavo's death a few days later, he invoked the language of the "culture of life" indebted to Pope John Paul II's 1995 encyclical *Evangelium vitae* and a prominent rallying cry among Catholic culture warriors.[61] Incorporating Schiavo's final days into the narrative of Holy Week, numerous pro-life commentators began framing her final ordeal as "the Passion of Terri Schiavo."[62]

In accordance with the act, the Schindlers made a motion to have the tube reinserted in federal district court. The motion was denied, largely on the grounds that the Schindlers were unlikely to prevail on the merits of their case alleging violation of their daughter's constitutional rights. A flurry of motions in federal court resulted in the U.S. Court of Appeals for the Eleventh Circuit declining the appeal. The Supreme Court of the United States declined to hear the case, thereby ending the matter at the federal level.[63] But further legal wrangling ensued on the state level, including an almost farcical stand-off between Judge Greer and the Florida Department of Children and Families, which at Governor Jeb Bush's request wanted to take custody of her and reinsert the feeding tube in order to investigate allegations of spousal abuse.[64] Finally, Judge Greer ordered "each and every singular sheriff of the state of Florida" to enforce his order denying the petition to take custody.[65] Rather than precipitating a conflict between the Florida National Guard and the state sheriffs, Governor Bush backed down. Fifteen years after her collapse and unsuccessful resuscitation, Terri Schiavo died in a hospice near St. Petersburg, Florida, on March 31, 2005.[66]

61. George W. Bush, "President's Statement on Terri Schiavo," March 17, 2005, http://georgewbush-whitehouse.archives.gov/news/releases/2005/03/20050317-7.html. See also Pope John Paul II, *Evangelium vitae* [The Gospel of Life], 1995.

62. See, for example, Bishop Thomas Wenski, "Holy Week and the Passion of Terri Schiavo," *Orlando Sentinel*, March 20, 2005, G3.

63. All these documents are available on the FindLaw website dedicated to the case, http://news.findlaw.com/legalnews/lit/schiavo/index.html.

64. CNN.com, "Florida Judge Rejects State Custody Bid in Schiavo Case," March 24, 2005, http://edition.cnn.com/2005/ALLPOLITICS/03/23/schiavo.jeb.bush/index.html.

65. Chris Hawke, "Report: State Tried Schiavo Grab," *Associated Press/CBS News*, March 26, 2005, www.cbsnews.com/8301-201_162-683300.html.

66. Michael Schiavo went on to marry the mother of his two children. The Schindler family began a non-profit organization called the Terri Schiavo Life & Hope Network, which provides assistance to the families of incapacitated persons. Deborah Hastings, "A Decade after Terri Schiavo's Feeding Tube Was Disconnected, Her Family's Pain Lives On," *New York Daily News*, March 17, 2015,

In my view, the Schiavo case demonstrates the inadequacy of examining the influence of religion in the public square solely in terms of the nature and source of the reasons that are brought to bear in the public discussion. In this case, rhetoric mattered as much as reasons. Religiously rooted, emotionally powerful rhetoric galvanized conservative religious leaders operating at the level of national politics to come to the rescue of an obscure middle-aged woman who had languished for years in a Florida long-term care facility. Religious commitment generated moral language that was passionate, unequivocal, and adamant about the need for legal intervention to save Terri Schiavo from "starvation" or "judicial murder." Moreover, it is not possible to treat the case as an anomaly; its course was deeply affected by the currents of contemporary America political life. Religiously based lobbying groups pressured key Republican lawmakers on behalf of the "values voters" who helped win the 2004 election for George W. Bush. Those lawmakers then took the extraordinary step of endorsing and promoting the passage of a federal law that applied to only one person: Theresa Marie Schindler Schiavo. Passionate religious commitment did not transform itself into public reason on the Capitol steps; in fact, religious motivation and emotion suffused the federal lawmaking process, a fact that was not lost on some observers and commentators.[67] For example, legal columnist Elaine Cassel observed "House Judiciary Committee Chairman James Sensenbrenner (R-Wisconsin) began and ended his speech during House debates Sunday with references to Holy Week."[68]

The most striking aspect of the controversy was precisely the fact that reason requesting and reason giving did not dominate the national discussion. Instead, emotionally laden appeals to religiously rooted moral truths

---

www.nydailynews.com/news/national/lessons-learned-bitter-divide-terri-schiavo-death-article
-1.2152267. Jeb Bush's actions in the Schiavo case may become relevant if he progresses as a Republican candidate in the 2016 presidential election. See Michael Kruse, " 'Jeb Put Me through Hell,' " *Politico*, January 29, 2015, www.politico.com/magazine/story/2015/01/jeb-bush-terri-schiavo-114730.html# .VdiHSflVhBd. A decade after the events, Jeb Bush has stated that he stands by his decisions. Zeke J. Miller, "Jeb Bush: No Regrets on Terri Schiavo," *Time*, April 17, 2015, http://time.com/3826605/jeb -bush-terri-schiavo/.

67. See Joshua E. Perry, "Biblical Biopolitics: Judicial Process, Religious Rhetoric, Terri Schiavo and Beyond," *Health Matrix* 16, no. 2 (2006): 553–630.

68. " 'As millions of Americans observe the beginning of Holy Week this Palm Sunday,' he noted, 'we are reminded that every life has purpose, and none is without meaning.' " Elaine Cassel, "The Terri Schiavo Case: Congress Rushes in Where Only Courts Should Tread," March 24, 2005, http:// writ.news.findlaw.com/cassel/20050324.html.

propelled the case from a local family tragedy to the battlefront in the national culture wars. The intensely heated controversy bore very little resemblance to the ordered discussions contemplated by Rawls's account of public reason. And the passions of those most heavily involved in the life-and-death debate were not conducive to the level-headed practice of what Stout calls "imminent criticism" in the public square. It is precisely because the case was reconfigured as a battlefront in the culture wars that some of the religious participants in the debate were not engaged in the process of mutual reason giving that Rawls and Stout join in recommending, despite their differences. Indeed, for several reasons, it would not go too far to say that some of those participants thought that this was a matter that required prophetic witness rather than public deliberation.

First, many of those who intervened in order to save Schiavo's life clearly did not see the matter as involving *hard* medical-moral questions. Reactions to her death on the part of several prominent religious and political figures made it clear that they did not see the case as a matter about which reasonable persons could disagree. While the bishop of their diocese in Florida refused to intervene in the case, high-ranking members of the Catholic clergy from elsewhere spoke out strongly on behalf of Terri Schiavo's parents. Archbishop Charles J. Chaput of Denver issued a statement saying that removal of the tube was "a form of murder"; actions doing so "attack the sanctity of human life. They reject any redemptive meaning to suffering."[69] Cardinal Renato Martino, prefect for the Pontifical Council for Justice and Peace, also called Schiavo's death "nothing else but murder, . . . a victory of the culture of death over life."[70] Pat Robertson said that Schiavo was "an innocent woman who was starved to death by the order of a judge who claimed to be a Christian."[71] Rhetorical form and meaning cannot be separated. Characterizing the act as murder, and especially judicial murder of an innocent person, conveys the speaker's judgment that there is no way the act could be justified.

---

69. Charles J. Chaput., O.F.M. Cap., "Statement by Archbishop Chaput on Terri Schiavo," *Catholic News Agency,* March 22, 2005, www.catholicnewsagency.com/document/statement-by-archbishop-chaput-on-terri-schiavo-252/.

70. CNN U.S., "Reaction to Terri Schiavo's Death," March 31, 2005, http://articles.cnn.com/2005-03-31/us/schiavo.reax_1_schiavo-s-schindlers-michael-schiavo?_s=PM:US.

71. Jody Brown, "Religious Leaders, Pro-Lifers Rip Judges for Terri's Death," *Crosswalk,* April 2, 2005, www.crosswalk.com/1321942/.

Second, precisely because they did not see the case as involving hard questions about which reasonable persons could disagree, many of those committed to saving Terri Schiavo's life cast aspersions on the character of those
who argued that it was morally legitimate to remove the feeding tube and
allow her to die. The hostility was strongest when it was directed against fellow
religious believers whom pro-life activists expected to support their cause. For
a Catholic moralist publicly to question whether in this case the removal of a
feeding tube was indeed morally the equivalent of "starvation" was likely to be
met by outraged cries of betrayal by Catholic pro-life activists.[72]

Third, for many pro-life activists, the overarching commitment to saving
Schiavo's life dwarfed any other considerations and trumped any other values,
including deeply embedded values of the American constitutional system. It
was not a question of securing a fair process; rather, it was a question of
achieving a correct result. In fact, many of them would probably say that a
process that did not result in a decision to continue artificial nutrition and
hydration was by definition unfair and unjust. In their view, any claim of individual rights asserted on behalf of Schiavo that resulted in the lethal withdrawal of nutrition and hydration had to be a false claim. As a consequence,
many pro-lifers were impatient with the idea that exhaustion of Terri Schiavo's
case in the Florida courts (and legislature) meant the end of the road. For
them, any constitutional balance of power that did not allow the federal government to step into the decision-making process to save the life of this vulnerable woman should not to be allowed to stand in the way of defending the
culture of life.

These three aspects of the Schiavo controversy reveal that the debate was
not conducted by free and equal citizens showing mutual respect in the recip-
rocal offering of reasons about a controversial public matter. Such mutually
respectful and reasonable discussions can take place only if both sides are
open to treating the claims of the other side as plausible, even if mistaken.

---

72. See, for example, Barbara Kralis, "Is Father Bouchard a Heterodox Dissident Vis à Vis Terri
Schiavo?," *Catholic Online*, March 24, 2005, www.catholic.org/featured/headline.php?ID=1958. See
also Terri Schiavo's brother's blistering critique of the local bishop, who refused to intervene in the
matter: "'Terri's legacy is one of life and love. Sadly, your legacy will be that of the shepherd that
stood silently by as one of his innocent disabled lambs was slowly and needlessly slaughtered by
removing her food and water—while you persistently ignored the cries of her family for help,' Terri's
brother added." Steven Ertelt, "Terri Schiavo's Brother Criticizes Florida Bishop over His Sister's
Death," *LifeNews.com*, March 28, 2007, www.lifenews.com/2007/03/28/bio-2046/.

Rawls might respond, so what? Advocates of public reason do not expect that each and every matter in the public square will be debated in terms of public reason; only fundamental matters pertaining to basic and constitutional essentials are subject to such restrictions. The Schiavo case, he might say, does not meet such lofty criteria because it affects only the fate of one person. In my view, however, that response is not persuasive for several reasons. An important category of basic rights are individual rights. At stake in this case was the nature and extent of an incompetent individual's constitutional right to refuse medical treatment through surrogate decision makers.[73] Also at stake was the meaning of freedom of religion as an individual right, and the degree to which that right could be asserted on one's behalf by a third party, such as a parent or guardian.[74] Third, the manner in which the federal government intervened in this one case touched on important constitutional principles such as federalism and separation of powers.[75]

Rawls's theory of political liberalism does not present itself as an abstract prescription for American politics. Instead, it aspires to engage and explain actual political debates, particularly those impinged upon by religious and other comprehensive worldviews. Yet any account of the place of religion in contemporary American political life needs to be able to grapple persuasively

---

73. *Cruzan v. Director, Missouri Department of Health*, 497 U.S. 261 (1990).

74. At the initial hearing, an expert witness testified that Catholic teaching would not require the continuation of artificial nutrition and hydration in Schiavo's case; while there was a presumption in favor of providing such treatment, that presumption could be overcome in specific situations. The trial court judge accepted that testimony. Moreover, he found that Schiavo was no longer actively practicing her faith. Throughout the course of the controversy, the Schiavos and their allies disputed both claims. In 2004, the Schindlers made a motion based on Pope John Paul II's March 20, 2004, allocution (www.vatican.va/holy_father/john_paul_ii/speeches/2004/march/documents/hf _jp-ii_spe_20040320_congress-fiamc_en.html), which limited the requirements under which artificial nutrition and hydration can be denied to patients in a persistent vegetative state. The motion was denied. See, for example, *In re Guardianship of Theresa Marie Schiavo*, Order, October 22, 2004 (Fla. Cir. Ct. Pinellas County, Greer, J), https://umshare.miami.edu/web/wda/ethics/documents/schivao /102204-denymotion.pdf.

75. Constitutional scholars who evaluated the case were divided about whether the act did indeed comport with constitutional requirements. Nonetheless, most agreed that it was an unwise exercise of congressional power in passing the bill, and presidential power in signing it into law. See, for example, Adam M. Samaha, "Undue Process: Congressional Referral and Judicial Resistance in the *Schiavo* Controversy," *Constitutional Commentary* 22, no. 3 (2005) 505–28, Steven G. Calabresi, "The Terri Schiavo Case: In Defense of the Special Law Enacted by Congress and President Bush," *Northwestern University Law Review* 100, no. 1 (2006) 151–70; Michael P. Allen, "Congress and Terri Schiavo: A Primer on the American Constitutional Order?," *West Virginia Law Review* 108, no. 2 (2005): 309–60.

with the Schiavo case, where the expression of religious commitments in the political context were pervasive, from Schiavo's parents briefs in Florida District Court to the statements of U.S. senators, who took it upon themselves to pass a highly unusual law on their behalf.

In my judgment, Rawls's theory of public reason cannot account for the Schiavo case for three reasons. First, it cannot account for the fact that the religious fervor driving this case was not the end result of a long process of deliberation and discernment; that fervor emanated instead from an absolute and confident determination to follow what many activists understood to be the clear will of God. Second, it cannot account for the distinctive manner of expressing that determination, which frequently involved the language of moral indictment, not the language of moral deliberation. Third, it cannot account for the fact that those most adamantly committed in religious terms to preserving Terri's life saw that commitment as fully consonant with their obligations as Americans; they saw themselves as fighting for the rights of a fellow citizen, not merely a fellow child of God. At least descriptively, therefore, the power of Rawls's approach to make sense of important debates in American public life is significantly limited.

The Limited Normative Grasp of Public Reason

In response to the foregoing argument about the inability of his account of public reason to account for the forms of religious intervention in the Schiavo case, Rawls might have replied, "so much the worse for those forms." He could claim, in other words, that the problem with most of the fevered interventions in the Schiavo controversy is precisely that they did not conform to the requirements of public reason. Rather than explaining what went on in that particular political crucible, he could simply reject the entire episode as an unacceptable confluence of political machinations. Granting the argument that the case did touch upon, at least in part, constitutional essentials, he could stand firm in the conviction that *no* intervention in the public square upon a matter of constitutional essentials is legitimate unless it is cast in the form of a rational argument tracking the requirements of public reason.

That claim, however, might throw out the baby with the bathwater, even in Rawls's own terms. It is easy to be nonplussed by the fiery indictments of the pro-life activists who wanted to preserve Terri's life, particularly if one leans toward the position that she was rightly allowed to die. Yet very similar rhetorical tools have been employed by activists agitating for a more broadly sympathetic cause. The most powerful—and obvious—rebuttal of a restrictive understanding of public reason are the examples of the nineteenth-century abolitionists and Martin Luther King, Jr., in the twentieth century. The speeches, pamphlets, and books of the abolitionists were instrumental in dismantling the institution of slavery, while King's work made it possible for millions of African Americans to enjoy the civil rights of free Americans. And even a cursory glance at the writings of abolitionists such as Charles Grandison Finney and Harriet Tubman reveals that they are suffused with religious concern, indeed animated by religious indignation. So were the writings of Martin Luther King. Many abolitionists relentlessly proclaimed that slavery is an abomination to God. A century later, many civil rights advocates insisted that racism is a betrayal of men, women, and children who are equal in God's sight and equally beloved by God.

In Rawls's terms, we can see that the political arguments of the abolitionists and King were consistently made in terms of their religious comprehensive worldviews. They did not, as Rawls would demand, strive to formulate a complete and distinct reasonable political conception of justice in which to make their claims about the rights and liberties that ought to be protected by the American Constitution. Their appeals to claims that could legitimately be incorporated into such a conception of justice were inextricably intertwined with passionate appeals to God's will and divine law, as revealed in Scripture and the natural law. And yet, in and through their religious convictions, they did more to establish basic civil rights and liberties than anyone operating purely within the constraints of public reason ever did or could have done in their time.

To his credit, Rawls does not deny the contributions to a just American political life made by religiously motivated abolitionists and Martin Luther King. In fact, he makes two serious attempts to incorporate their examples into his framework of public reason. His efforts are seriously flawed, however, because they fail to grasp the particular character of the political speech used in these cases, and the particular challenges that it poses to public reason. In fact, Rawls's second attempt to accommodate the abolitionists and King within the framework of public reason is less successful than his first attempt because it involves a more thoroughgoing distortion of the way they conceive their own projects in their own terms.

In "The Idea of Public Reason," Rawls's first attempt to address the issue, he maintains that the abolitionists and King were justified in invoking their religious worldviews in order to end slavery and racism because "the comprehensive reasons they appealed to were required to give sufficient strength to the political conception [of justice] to be subsequently realized."[76] In essence, he justifies their religiously based interventions in the public square on the grounds of political emergency. Both nineteenth-century abolitionists and twentieth-century civil rights activists were living in a time when "society [was] not well ordered and there [was] a profound division about constitutional essentials."[77]

Rawls does not claim, of course, that the abolitionists and King would themselves have thought of their own interventions on behalf of civil rights in terms of the requirements of public reason. Nonetheless, he constructs a hypothetical reasoning process by which their interventions could be justified in those terms. He verges quite close to attributing that reasoning process to the abolitionists and King; at the very least, he suggests that they could be brought to see the point of public reason and to justify their actions in its terms.[78] "The abolitionists could say, for example, that they supported political values of freedom and equality for all, but that given the comprehensive doctrines they held and the doctrines current in their day, it was necessary to invoke the comprehensive grounds on which those values were widely seen to rest."[79]

This tentative attempt to attribute to the abolitionists and King a tacit commitment to the ideal of public reason becomes more pronounced in Rawls's later work. More specifically, he adopts a "wide view of public reason," which allows greater latitude for the introduction of reasonable comprehensive worldviews into public discussions and therefore obviates the necessity for a "political emergency" exception to its requirements. As I noted at the beginning of this chapter, the later Rawls argued reasonable comprehensive doctrines "may be introduced in public reason at any time, provided

---

76. Rawls, *Political Liberalism*, exp. ed., "The Idea of Public Reason," 251.

77. Ibid., 249.

78. "To be sure, people do not normally distinguish between comprehensive and public reasons; nor do they normally affirm the ideal of public reason, as we have expressed it. Yet people can be brought to recognize these distinctions in particular cases." Ibid., 251.

79. Ibid.

that in due course public reasons, given by a reasonable political conception, are presented sufficient to support whatever the comprehensive doctrines are introduced to support."[80] This condition—the proviso—allows the abolitionists' and King's religious discourse to be admitted into public discourse. In a footnote, Rawls writes, "I do not know whether the Abolitionists and King ever fulfilled the proviso. But whether they did or not, they could have. And, had they known the idea of public reason and shared its ideal, they would have."[81]

Rawls understands and appreciates that both the abolitionists and King were motivated by religious belief. Yet he does not seem fully to appreciate the specifically Christian nature of those beliefs and the specific rhetorical form of biblically based rhetoric—prophetic rhetoric—corresponding to those beliefs. Instead, he focuses his attention on the parts of King's corpus that are most congenial to his own approach.

In "The Idea of Public Reason," for example, he writes: "Religious doctrines clearly underlie King's views and are important in his appeals. Yet they are expressed in general terms: and they fully support constitutional values and accord with public reason."[82] To buttress his claims, Rawls highlights selected passages from King's famous "Letter from a Birmingham City Jail" (1963), in which he discusses the nature of unjust laws in terms indebted to Thomistic natural law theory, terms that are consonant with the demands of public reason. Rawls quotes the following passage from King: "To put it in the terms of Saint Thomas Aquinas, an unjust law is a human law that is not rooted in eternal and natural law. Any law that uplifts human personality is just. Any law that degrades human personality is unjust. All segregation statutes are unjust because segregation distorts the soul and damages the personality."[83] After noting that King goes on to apply these general remarks to the case of racial discrimination in America, Rawls quotes this selection as well: "Unjust law is a code that the majority inflicts on a minority that is not binding on itself. This is difference made legal. . . . A just law is a code that a

---

80. Rawls, *Political Liberalism*, exp. ed., "Introduction to the Paperback Edition," xlix–l.

81. Ibid., page l, note 27.

82. Rawls, *Political Liberalism*, exp. ed., "The Idea of Public Reason," 250n.

83. Ibid., citing Martin Luther King, Jr., "Letter from Birmingham City Jail" (April 1963), paras. 14–16, in *A Testament of Hope: The Essential Writings of Martin Luther King*, ed. J. M. Washington (San Francisco, CA: Harper and Row, 1986), 293–94.

majority compels a minority to follow that it is willing to follow itself. This is sameness made legal."[84]

It is true, of course, that some of Dr. King's speeches were couched in general appeals to justice and injustice designed to appeal to as broad an audience as possible in addressing the problem of civil rights in the United States. That does not mean, however, that they transcend the specific moral and religious traditions in which they are rooted. Broadly speaking, the natural law tradition in ethics attempts to develop an approach to morality rooted primarily in the insights of practical reason, not in the specific commands of God to a particular religious community. Nonetheless, Christian thinkers from Aquinas to King himself did not *separate* reason from revelation; in their view, human minds, morally darkened as they are by sin, frequently need the additional light of revelation in order to perceive what is truly reasonable. Moreover, in interpreting the requirements of the natural law, Christian thinkers were not working in an abstract and ahistorical manner. They drew heavily on particular philosophical views of human flourishing with which they were acquainted. Aquinas, of course, was deeply indebted to Aristotle's *Ethics* for his understanding of the requirements of practical reason. King is no different in this regard. As Jeffrey Stout points out, King's immediate translation of the requirements of the natural law into the requirements of respect for human "personality" is indebted to the personalist philosophies he encountered while doing his doctoral work at Boston University School of Theology.[85]

Just as it is important not to stress King's appeal to the reasonableness of natural law at the expense of the broader, more specifically Christian intellectual tradition in which it is situated, so it is essential to refrain from highlighting his appeals to reason at the expense of his other rhetorical strategies. Particularly important in King's civil rights work is his use of prophetic rhetoric, which he perfected through years of preaching in African American churches. The use of prophetic rhetoric in the civil rights movement deeply resonates with the religious rhetoric deployed by nineteenth-century abolitionists such as William Lloyd Garrison. Unlike Rawls's articulation of public reason, it prioritized truth over reasonableness; it offered a fiery, uncompromising proclamation of God's law.

84. Ibid.
85. Stout, *Democracy and Tradition*, 241.

Consider, for example, a passage from Garrison's speech on the death of the violent radical abolitionist John Brown, who was executed after his unsuccessful attempt to start an armed revolt of the slaves by raiding a federal arsenal at Harper's Ferry, Virginia, in 1859.

> The slaveholder with his hands dripping in blood—will I make a compact with him? The man who plunders cradles—will I say to him, "Brother, let us walk together in unity?" The man who, to gratify his lust or his anger, scourges woman with the lash till the soil is red with her blood—will I say to him: "Give me your hand; let us form a glorious Union?" No, never—never! There can be no union between us: "What concord hath Christ with Belial?" What union has freedom with slavery?[86]

While suffused with moral concern, Garrison's language in the speech is not, strictly speaking, moral *reasoning*. He is not engaged in practical deliberation, carefully moving from premises to conclusions. He shows no inclination to engage in careful, dialectical exploration of the merits of his own premises and that of his opponents. Furthermore, he does not manifest civil respect toward those who disagree with him or any inclination to view their arguments within a hermeneutic of charity. No attempt is made to refrain from ad hominem remarks; in another passage, he calls his opponents "men-stealers and women-whippers." Nor is he interested in civil peace, as evinced by his question, "What concord hath Christ with Belial?"

William Lloyd Garrison's contributions to the abolitionist movement are inextricably intertwined with his mastery of the rhetoric of prophetic indictment. He is justly remembered not primarily for the subtlety or sophistication of his moral arguments but rather for the blazing certainty with which he expressed his moral convictions. Coming to terms with his towering influence in American public discourse means coming to terms with the particular rhetorical form he deployed in his relentless opposition to chattel slavery. A syllogism demonstrating the wrongfulness of that practice,

---

86. William Lloyd Garrison, "On the Death of John Brown," December 2, 1859, The History Place: Great Speeches Collection, www.historyplace.com/speeches/garrison.htm. For other speeches, see Mason I. Lowance, ed., *Against Slavery: An Abolitionist Reader* (New York: Penguin Books, 2000).

no matter how brilliant, would never have had the same effect on the public conversation.

How, then, are we to think of Garrsion's rhetoric and the relationship with the underlying moral belief about the abomination of slavery that it communicates? One tempting possibility for those who are committed to the role of reasoned argument in the public square is to treat the rhetoric as essentially ornamental, as not related in any substantive way to the underlying moral argument. It is simply the striking "dress" clothing the argument, designed to attract the masses to the underlying moral position by moving their emotions along with their minds. This approach emphasizes and hardens the classical distinction between dialectic, a process of reasoning designed to uncover the truth of the matter, and rhetoric, which is the skill of persuading an audience.[87]

But for a preacher like Garrison, or King a century later, the moral stance and the rhetoric are organically related to one another. The rhetoric, the language of divinely endorsed moral indictment, enacts the speaker's understanding of the enormity of the evil involved in chattel slavery. What is at stake, for the abolitionists, is not simply the success or failure of a moral argument, but the moral success or failure of an entire form of life—the life of the United States. Is the country going to betray its religious foundations, or is it going to be true to its basic Christian commitments? The rhetoric both embodies and communicates the gravity of the decision at stake.

Jeffrey Stout offers another, more promising and nuanced possibility for grappling with the rhetoric of the abolitionists and civil rights leaders like King. Stout criticizes Rawls for seeing this rhetoric as a series of IOUs requiring the speaker to provide arguments that comply with public reason. Instead, Stout frames them as a type of *expressivist* discourse appropriate in democratic societies such as our own. Drawing upon Hegel and Robert Brandom, Stout argues that what counts as "reasonable" is a function of the norms and conventions in place in a particular community at a particular time. He argues that some political discourse functions expressively, not merely

---

87. Aristotle defines *rhetoric* as an *"antistrophos"* of dialectic. Aristotle, *On Rhetoric: A Theory of Civil Discourse,* trans. George A. Kennedy (New York: Oxford University Press, 1991), bk. 1, chap. 1, paras. 1–2. Kennedy notes that *antistrophos* is commonly translated as "counterpart" but can also mean "correlative" and "coordinate," as well as "converse." George A. Kennedy, "Introduction," in *On Rhetoric: A Theory of Civil Discourse,* 28, note 2.

applying a static set of "reasonable" rules but instead changing what counts as "reasonable" by reshaping the terms of the conversation itself. A democratic expressivist, such as Stout himself, "sees democratic discourse as an unfolding dialectic in which the paradigmatic instances of 'reasonableness' involve either dramatically significant innovations in the application of an entrenched normative vocabulary or especially memorable exemplifications of discursive virtue. They are paradigmatic because they move 'reasonableness' forward, thus exercising some (defeasible) authority over future applications of the relevant concepts."[88]

Consequently, Stout defends the importance of "expressivist freedom." It is not merely negative freedom, freedom from existing laws or conventions that coercively restrain behavior and action. It is also and centrally positive freedom, "the freedom *to* transform both oneself and one's social practices through a dialectical progression of novel performances and their consequences."[89] By engaging in these novel forms of expression, speakers can change and develop a society's idea of what counts as "reasonable," which should never be understood in a fixed or static way.

Stout's commitment to expressivist freedom generates a critique not only of Rawls's program of argumentative restraint. He also critiques religious traditionalists (such as Alasdair MacIntyre and Stanley Hauerwas) who "have sometimes been willing to impose fairly severe restrictions on the expression of religious dissent in order to reap the rewards of expressive freedom and spiritual excellence they take to be possible only within a religiously unified community."[90] Instead, Stout defends a more freewheeling exchange as appropriate in our American society, whose political culture "was shaped in large part by immigrants in flight from restrictive religious orthodoxies."[91] Stout writes, "I do not propose to replace the contractarian program of restraint with its traditionalist counterpart—a different set of restrictions, typically designed to maintain a patriarchal orthodoxy, instead of a liberal professor's idea of discursive decorum."[92]

I think Stout's account of the expressivist function of the speech of the

---

88. Stout, *Democracy and Tradition*, 81.
89. Ibid., 80 (original emphasis).
90. Ibid., 83.
91. Ibid.
92. Ibid., 84.

abolitionists and King's sermons goes far in explaining an important aspect of their contributions to American public discourse. More specifically, their words, which were delivered orally as well as in written form, did indeed help redefine what counts as socially "reasonable" so that it excluded advocacy of chattel slavery. In my view, however, Stout's account does not adequately identify or describe *how* their rhetoric achieved these objectives, for two reasons. First, he does not specifically grapple with the fact that the innovative, transformative power of their rhetoric stemmed from its roots in very old sources—the prophetic books of the Hebrew Bible, the Christian Old Testament. Second, he does not directly address the problematic tone of abolitionist speech, which is permeated by expressions of derision for proslavery advocates.

As scholars of American history and historians of rhetoric have recognized, the language of prophetic indictment—the "jeremiad"—has been a crucially important form of social critique in the United States throughout its history. Formulated originally by pre-Revolutionary Puritan preachers in Massachusetts Bay Colony, it was successfully refurbished over the years to meet with changing political and social circumstances.[93] After the American Revolution, the jeremiad continued to grow and develop as itinerant preachers carried Christianity to the borders of the expanding nation.[94] As I have already noted, it was the form of discourse adopted by Christian abolitionists; later, it was revised and adopted by preachers in African American churches.[95] In the twentieth century, it came to be adopted, albeit in slightly different form, by both communists (e.g., Eugene Debs) and communist hunters (e.g., Joseph McCarthy), as James Darsey has persuasively demonstrated in his masterful work, *The Prophetic Tradition and Radical Rhetoric in America.*[96]

For present purposes, what is most important about the jeremiad in all its forms is that it does not present itself as innovative. Instead, it frames itself as

93. Perry Miller, *The New England Mind: From Colony to Province* (Cambridge, MA: Belknap Press of Harvard University Press, 1953); and Perry Miller, *The New England Mind: The Seventeenth Century* (Cambridge, MA: Belknap Press of Harvard University Press, 1954).

94. Sacvan Bercovitch, *The American Jeremiad* (Madison: University of Wisconsin Press, 1978).

95. David Howard-Pitney, *The African American Jeremiad: Appeals for Justice in America,* rev. ed. (Philadelphia, PA: Temple University Press, 2005). See also Willie J. Harrell, Jr., *Origins of the African American Jeremiad: The Rhetorical Strategies of Social Protest and Activism, 1760–1861* (Jefferson, NC: McFarland & Co., 2011).

96. James Darsey, *The Prophetic Tradition and Radical Rhetoric in America* (New York: New York University Press, 1997).

deeply conservative, or as Darsey would have it, *radical* in the proper sense of the word. It attempts to draw upon and renew dedication to the *root* commitments of a society whose members have gone frightfully wayward. In the religious forms of the jeremiad, such as those drawn upon by the abolitionists, Lincoln, and King, those root commitments are situated against the background of a fundamental national political covenant with God. Viewed within the conventions of the jeremiad, therefore, social progress is best understood as a return to the deepest and truest requirements of morality, which is understood by religious thinkers as fidelity to the demands of the divine law. In my judgment, then, one of the reasons that the abolitionists, Lincoln, and King were so successful in their political oratory was that they were able to graft their moral concerns into the form of the jeremiad, a form of speech to which many Americans were exposed on a regular basis in church. If this is the case, they succeeded in bringing to the American people not because, in their words, everything old was made new, but because everything new—the recognition of African Americans as fully equal human beings and citizens—was made *old*.

It is striking that neither Rawls nor Stout quote extensively from the speeches of the abolitionists, or the civil rights activists, for that matter. If they had done so, they would have had to grapple with certain aspects of their thought that concords not at all with either of their proposals for the shape of public discourse in American life. More specifically, political jeremiahs do not always respect interlocutors and opponents. For example, in the same sermon I quoted from earlier, William Lloyd Garrison makes quite clear what he thinks of slave owners. He thunders: "Let us tell the inexorable and remorseless tyrants of the South that their conditions hitherto imposed upon us, whereby we are morally responsible for the existence of slavery, are horribly inhuman and wicked, and we cannot carry them out for the sake of their evil company."[97] Stout does acknowledge that the language of the abolitionists is "dramatic." It is indeed. But it is also significantly more than that. It is deliberately deeply insulting to its targets, Garrison's political opponents.

Like Rawls, Stout is committed to a vision of public discourse as the respectful, albeit vigorous exchange and critique of reasons, although he is far more open than Rawls is to a plurality of sources for those reasons.

97. Garrison, "On the Death of John Brown."

Consequently, Stout recognizes the need for civility in public discourse, albeit balanced by the need for candor.[98] The trouble is that the language of the abolitionists was candid but obviously not civil, at least in the common meaning of the term. Nor, for that matter, was the language of many religious believers who saw themselves as saving Terri Schiavo from "judicial murder." In fact, if we abstract from the specific causes and the political programs supporting them, it is possible to find great similarities in the rhetoric of the nineteenth-century abolitionists and contemporary pro-life activists. Both sets of activists are morally adamant—but also rhetorically uncivil.

Why not say, then, that the threat to civic respect and civic peace does not stem from the specifically religious sources invoked by some contributors to political discourse or even from the "dramatic" and "expressive" turns religious language can take in the public square? Why not simply say the problem is more focused and therefore remediable: It is simply a failure to be civil to one's interlocutors and opponents. I will examine this approach critically in the next chapter.

98. "I would recommend the mixed rhetorical strategy of expressing one's own (perhaps idiosyncratic) reasons for a political policy while also directing fair-minded, nonmanipulative, sincere immanent criticism against one's opponent's reasons." Stout, *Democracy and Tradition*, 85.

Carter and Cuddihy

Constraints of Civility

On May 31, 2009, Dr. George Tiller, one of the few physicians in the United States who openly and regularly performed late-term abortions, was shot and killed while attending Sunday services at Reformation Lutheran Church in Wichita, Kansas.[1] To many members of the pro-life movement, Tiller was the most notorious of their opponents, the unapologetic living symbol of the "culture of death." For over twenty years, he had been subjected to harassment and even violence by more extreme members of the pro-life movement. In 1985, his Wichita clinic was bombed. In 1991, Operation Rescue, which employs theatrical tactics in its struggle against abortion, staged a six-week-long Summer of Mercy, a sit-in at his clinic which drew pro-life activists from all over the country and resulted in over 2,600 arrests of over 1,700 individuals.[2] In 1993, Tiller was shot in both arms by pro-life activist Rachelle Shannon, who later pleaded guilty to setting fires at other abortion clinics after being convicted of attempted murder in his case.[3]

About a decade later, Tiller's life and work received renewed attention in the national media. In 2005, a young woman with Down syndrome died after she underwent a late-term abortion at Tiller's facility. During the

1. Joe Stumpe and Monica Davey, "Abortion Doctor Shot to Death in Kansas Church," *New York Times*, June 1, 2009, A1.

2. See Mark Allen Steiner, *The Rhetoric of Operation Rescue: Projecting the Christian Pro-Life Message* (New York: T & T Clark, 2006), 9, citing Judy Lundstrom Thomas, "Tiller Rejects Compromise on Protests," *Wichita Eagle*, September 6, 1991, VUTEXT Database, document 250100, 2. See also Isabel Wilkerson, "Drive against Abortion Finds a Symbol: Wichita," *New York Times*, August 4, 1991, A20.

3. AP Wire, "Guilty Plea Expected in Fires at Clinics," *New York Times*, June 4, 1995, A24.

ensuing years, Tiller became a repeated target of the popular, conservative talk show host Bill O'Reilly, who often referred to him as Tiller the
Baby Killer. His donations to the political campaign of Kansas governor
Kathleen Sebelius were heavily publicized, particularly during the context of
the 2008 presidential election. Sebelius, a Roman Catholic who supported
Barack Obama's presidential candidacy, also came under heavy fire from pro-
life groups and conservative Catholics, who used her connection to Tiller to
highlight her pro-choice stance.[4] In March 2009, Tiller was tried and acquitted
on nineteen misdemeanor charges of failing to consult with a second, independent physician before performing an abortion on a viable fetus, as required
by Kansas law. Tiller's legal issues were not resolved by that acquittal, however; he faced an additional investigation by the state's Board of Healing Arts
on similar charges.[5]

That investigation, as well as Tiller's abortion practice, was abruptly ter-
minated when Scott Roeder killed Tiller with a single shot to the head.
Roeder, a fifty-one-year-old man with a history of mental illness, had connections with radical antigovernment movements as well as ties to more extreme
elements in the pro-life movement. More specifically, Roeder contributed to
Prayer and Action News, a magazine published by David Leach, which advocates killing abortion doctors as justifiable homicide.[6] He also posted on
Operation Rescue's "Tiller Watch," although the leadership of that group
denied that Roeder had any formal relationship to it.[7]

Shaken by the murder, many cultural commentators began to issue
anguished and broader calls for civility in public discussion, particularly over
morally explosive questions such as abortion.[8] In an essay in the *Nation,*
Eyal Press argued that those who vilified Tiller and other abortionists ought
to examine the connection between their violent rhetoric and Roeder's
violent actions:

4. After his election and inauguration, President Obama named Kathleen Sebelius secretary of
Health and Human Services, over the objection of pro-life groups.

5. Joe Stumpe, "Jurors Acquit Kansas Doctor in a Late-Term Abortion Case," *New York Times,*
March 28, 2009, A11.

6. Susan Saulny and Monica Davey, "Seeking Clues on Suspect in Shooting of Doctor," *New York
Times,* June 2, 2009, A1.

7. Laura Fitzpatrick, "Scott Roeder: The Tiller Murder Suspect," *Time,* June 2, 2009, www.time
.com/time/nation/article/0,8599,1902189,00.html.

8. See David Barstow, "An Abortion Battle, Fought to the Death," *New York Times,* July 26, 2009, A1.

Bullets kill. Inflammatory words merely incite. But those who deploy hateful language can hardly profess shock when their words are taken seriously, particularly over emotionally fraught issues that have sparked violence. Before he was murdered, George Tiller was a popular topic on Fox's *O'Reilly Factor*—the host referred to him as "Tiller the Baby Killer," a man guilty of "Nazi stuff." These are not innocent words, as doctors targeted by antiabortion protesters have pointed out in the past.[9]

At the *Huffington Post,* Frank Schaffer makes a similar point: "This 'lynch mob' mentality is the context in which Dr. Tiller was murdered. A lot of this emerging domestic terror has to do with a larger story. It has to do with what becomes thinkable under a barrage of hateful words."[10] Politically conservative commentators also expressed concern about some forms of pro-life rhetoric. Newspaper columnist and prominent blogger "Crunchy Con" Rod Dreher, who rejected the implication that pro-lifers should remain silent in the aftermath of Tiller's murder, nonetheless acknowledged that "[i]t is worth reflecting on, though, to what extent our words are seeds for violent deeds."[11] Randall Terry, the founder of Operation Rescue, did not denounce the murder but instead took the opportunity to reiterate his condemnation of abortion: "George Tiller was a mass-murderer. We grieve for him that he did not have time to properly prepare his soul to face God. I am more concerned that the Obama Administration will use Tiller's killing to intimidate pro-lifers into surrendering our most effective rhetoric and actions."[12] *National Review*'s Kathryn Jean Lopez criticized him for this statement, writing that "Terry is in no way responsible for Tiller's murder, and that he would be overwhelmingly

9. Eyal Press, "A Culture War Casualty," *Nation,* June 22, 2009, 6–7.

10. Frank Schaeffer, "Dr. Tiller, Murder, Domestic Terrorism and the Republican Right," *Huffington Post,* July 10, 2009, www.huffingtonpost.com/frank-schaeffer/dr-tiller-murder-domestic_b_212473.html.

11. Rod Dreher, "Tiller, Language and Violence," *Crunchy Con,* June 1, 2009, http://web.archive.org/web/20090605154300/http://blog.beliefnet.com/crunchycon/2009/06/tiller-language-and-violence.html. This link appears to be inactive; the relevant passage is quoted by Ken Ashford, *The Ashford Zone,* June, 2, 2009, http://www.ashford.zone/2009/06/reasonable-vs-unreasonable-voices.

12. "Randall Terry, Operation Rescue Founder, Says He's More Concerned about Obama's Reaction Than Tiller's Murder," *Huffington Post,* July 1, 2009, www.huffingtonpost.com/2009/05/31/randall-terry-operation-r_n_209531.html.

upset by what Tiller did is justified. But he needs to know that his statement is inevitably going to drown out the principled-but-merciful responses."[13]

What is the remedy for this unstable and dangerous situation? According to a wide number of commentators, both religious and secular, both liberal and conservative, it is a renewed commitment to *civility* in American public discourse. In a column for the *Washington Post,* conservative commentator Kathleen Parker argued that the "fire-breathers" on the margins of the Republican Party threatened to undermine its underlying message on life issues. "Rather than convincing people to think differently about abortion, the Terry-Keyes act [of theatrical protest] makes one want to write checks to Planned Parenthood."[14] Writing from a progressive perspective in an opinion piece in the *Los Angeles Times,* Tim Rutten contrasted Roeder's actions with the approach to moral disagreement on display at the University of Notre Dame's May 2009 commencement, at which newly inaugurated President Barack Obama, who is pro-choice, was the main speaker. Obama was joined on the stage by John T. Noonan, Jr., an eminent pro-life scholar and federal appeals court judge. Rutten argued: "In South Bend, both Obama and Noonan suggested that even irreconcilable views can coexist in a pluralist democracy— if they're civilly expressed, if each side concedes the other's goodwill and if both adjudge the other as mistaken rather than wicked."[15]

Calls for civility both preceded and followed the Tiller murder. Within the nation at large, discussions of civility were precipitated by the outburst of Representative Joe Wilson (R-SC), who shouted "You lie!" as President Obama addressed a joint session of Congress, on the topic of healthcare reform. He later apologized, saying, "While I disagree with the President's statement, my comments were inappropriate and regrettable. I extend sincere apologies to the president for this lack of civility."[16] The concerns about Wilson's agitated exclamation

---

13. Kathryn Jean Lopez, "Loving Life: Pro-life Is No Lie," *National Review Online,* June 15, 2009, www.nationalreview.com/article/227699/loving-life-kathryn-jean-lopez.

14. Kathleen Parker, "Carnival of the Fire-Breathers," *Real Clear Politics,* June 3, 2009, www.realclearpolitics.com/articles/2009/06/03/carnival_of_the_fire-breathers_96794.html.

15. Tim Rutten, "The Cost of Verbal Extremism," *Los Angeles Times,* June 3, 2009, A21.

16. Robbie Brown and Carl Hulse, "Heckler's District Mostly Supports the Outburst," *New York Times,* September 11, 2009, A15; Michael Scherer, "'You Lie!': Representative Wilson's Outburst," *Time* September 10, 2009, http://content.time.com/time/politics/article/0,8599,1921455,00.html. For commentary, see E. J. Dionne, Jr., "D.C. Mean Time: Joe Wilson's Character—And Ours," *Washington Post,* September 14, 2009, A15; Gail Collins, "So Much for Civility," *New York Times,* September 10, 2009, A43.

reinforced other worries about the tone and content of political talk radio and cable news commentators, such as MSNBC's Keith Olbermann and Fox's Glenn Beck (the latter appeared on the cover of *Time* sticking out his tongue).[17]

Not everyone, of course, responded to the passionate calls for civility with a chorus of amens. Some commentators offered responses that amounted to versions of *tu quoque*.[18] More significantly, other commentators viewed the call for civility around questions such as abortion and gay marriage as a political strategy meant to marginalize political opponents. As the debate about healthcare reform began in earnest in spring 2009, Tony Perkins of the Family Research Council wrote that "being cordial, while welcome in itself, fails to ameliorate the reality of entrenched and unflinching philosophical disagreement." He called on Americans to be "personally respectful," but also to remember that "we are in the midst of grim political combat over the direction of our country."[19]

But there were deeper objections as well. In response to the fracas over Representative Joe Wilson's outburst, Kevin Williamson of the *National Review* implicitly argued that the concern for civility is a distraction from truth telling. He asks us to "Set aside Joe Wilson's bad manners" and focus on "the substance of his accusation." Williamson maintains that Wilson was correct in saying that Obama's plan would force Americans to subsidize healthcare for illegal aliens. He concludes: "So, Representative Wilson could use a visit from Miss Manners. But he is telling the truth, and President Obama is not."[20] Truth, suggests Williamson, should be our primary concern. The marks of civility, such as good manners, are desirable, but not essential.

As the reader has doubtless noted, the examples of calls for civility that I have collected in the foregoing paragraphs have been taken from the popular press, not from academic essays. This locus is not accidental; it is meant to

---

For a different view, see Thomas Frank, "Liberals and Civility: Why Democrats Should Welcome a Rough Debate," *Wall Street Journal*, September 23, 2009, A23.

17. David Von Drehle and Michael Scherer, "The Agitator," *Time*, September 28, 2009, 30–36. It was reported that network executives at Fox and MSNBC put a damper on the on-air feud between Bill O'Reilly and Keith Olbermann. See Brian Stelter, "Voices from Above Silence a Cable TV Feud," *New York Times*, August 1, 2009, A1.

18. See, for example, Michael Gerson, "The Rhetoric of the Rant," *Washington Post*, May 15, 2009, A19; and Ross Douthat, "Palin and Her Enemies," *New York Times*, July 6, 2009, A19.

19. Tony Perkins, "Health Care: Civility Cannot Mask Bad Ideas," *FRCBLOG.com*, March 6, 2009, www.frcblog.com/2009/03/health-care-civility-cannot-mask-bad-ideas/.

20. Kevin D. Williamson, "Joe Wilson Is Rude but Right," *National Review Online*, September 10, 2009, www.nationalreview.com/article/228221/joe-wilson-rude-right-kevin-d-williamson.

emphasize that most ordinary discussion of the threats posed by competing religious and secular voices in the public square has been framed in terms of the effect of such discourse on civility. Not surprisingly, Alasdair MacIntyre's diagnosis of the underlying problem—the existence of rival and incompatible fragments of different moral traditions—has failed to gain much popular traction in a society not overly cognizant of the history of philosophy. No more surprisingly, John Rawls's elaborate attempt to trace morally permissible interventions in the public square back to their roots in a reasonable comprehensive worldview never attracted much public support. One reason, of course, was the suspicion expressed by some religious leaders that his framework would marginalize the voices of Americans operating out of a faith-based perspective. A second reason, however, also seems to be a likely factor. Rawls's account of the role of religiously based reasons in the public square is, so to speak, devilishly complicated. The implications of that account regularly confuse graduate students in a philosophy seminar; they are not likely to be easily grasped or deftly deployed by participants in the rough-and-tumble world of politics.

If we examine these popular calls for civility carefully, we see that they offer diagnoses of the problems afflicting contemporary discourse very different from the diagnoses offered by MacIntyre and Rawls. Unlike MacIntyre, they do not interpret the root problem as a *hidden* problem, understood only in the context of the history of philosophy and the breakdown of traditions in modernity. The problem is in important respects a *surface* matter—it lies in the way we actually talk to one another, no matter what our deepest moral beliefs and traditional commitments. Moreover, unlike Rawls, the advocates of civility do not locate the problem in the sectarian patrimony of certain arguments made in the public square—civility is a matter of the way an argument is cast here and now, not its past heritage or deep roots.

To its proponents, a key attraction of the call to civility is its apparent fairness. Civility, it seems, does not discriminate against any message or any messenger. It presupposes that all messages, no matter what their content, can be expressed in a nonoffensive way. As Barack Obama stated in defense of his decision to ask Rick Warren to speak at his inauguration, "[W]e can disagree without being disagreeable."[21] All participants in the discussion, no

21. Mimi Hall, "Obama Defends Inauguration Invitation to Warren," *ABC News*, December 18, 2008, http://abcnews.go.com/Politics/story?id=6492644.

matter what their viewpoint, are obliged to offer and are entitled to claim the benefits of civil interchange. Consequently, the call for civility seems to offer our nation the possibility that all issues, all positions, and all approaches to our common political life can be discussed in an even-handed manner. It also seems to imply that all those who want to enter into the discussion deserve a place at the table, where they can each take their turn contributing to the joint discussion—in a polite and respectful manner.

As we have seen, however, calls for civility have also garnered serious protests. These protests should prompt us to raise some critical questions about those calls. First, what exactly *is* civility? In the popular commentary just examined, most calls for civility were developed in negative rather than positive terms. They concentrated on avoiding the obvious tokens of *incivility* (such as yelling or insults) rather than advocating particular manifestations of civility. Can civility be defined in more affirmative ways? Second, what *sort* of requirements does civility impose? To what degree do those demands instantiate moral norms, even moral norms relatively independent of cultural context, and to what degree do they reflect changeable strictures of etiquette or manners? Is there a relationship between morals and manners, and if so, what is it? Third, are the norms of civility as fair-minded as they initially and attractively seem to be? Or do they favor a certain view of the world, either absolutely or in the American context?

These questions merit rigorous academic exploration. Surprisingly enough, however, the topic of civility has not received broad and deep attention from a wide range of normative theorists, although it has garnered slightly more scrutiny from sociologists, linguists, political scientists, and historians.[22] Perhaps the most influential contemporary normative account of civility is Stephen Carter's *Civility: Manners, Morals, and the Etiquette of Democracy*.[23] In the next

22. See, for example, the best-selling book by professor of linguistics Deborah Tannen, *The Argument Culture: Stopping America's War of Words* (New York: Ballantine Books, 1999). Needless to say, the topic of civility in politics has received a great deal of attention from all disciplines. See, for example, Marcus Daniel, *Scandal and Civility: Journalism and the Birth of American Democracy* (New York: Oxford University Press, 2009); Philip D. Smith, *The Virtue of Civility in the Practice of Politics* (Lanham, MD: University Press of America, 2002); and Burdett A. Loomis, ed., *Esteemed Colleagues: Civility and Deliberation in the U.S. Senate* (Washington, DC: Brookings Institution Press, 2000).

23. Stephen L. Carter, *Civility: Manners, Morals, and the Etiquette of Democracy* (New York: Basic Books, 1998). This is not to say that civility has been ignored throughout American history. The topic has been the subject of rule books, including a famous one by the first president of the United States;

section of this chapter, I will explore Carter's account, which has a distinct and important characteristic for this discussion: Its ultimate justification of the value of civility is religious, not purely philosophical. Carter argues that civility constitutes an important application of the biblical injunction to love one's neighbor as oneself. In short, Carter's account is not meant to foist secular norms on religious citizens; in fact, the very opposite is the case. Consequently, it provides us with a good way to test whether the fractiousness of the current political discussion is rightly attributable to incivility and whether an increase in civil discourse will ameliorate the problem. Precisely because he offers an explicitly religious account and defense of civility, he ought to be able to explain and address the objections of religious citizens who resort to more adamant forms of protest on issues of paramount concern to them. If he is unable to do so, we will have some reason to question whether the cause of fractiousness is rightly attributed to a lack of civility in the way in which we interact with each other.

Stephen Carter on Civility

Is civility a matter of manners or of morality? According to Carter, it is a matter of both. He does not merely situate civility at the intersection of manners and morality; he argues vigorously that the two are intertwined. "Rules of civility are thus also rules of morality: it is morally proper to treat our fellow citizens with respect, and morally improper not to."[24] Civility, then, is a manifestation of respect for other persons. Accordingly, a major goal of Carter's book is to reintegrate the norms of public morality and the norms of etiquette. Carter encapsulates the connection by drawing on the words of the nineteenth-century English evangelist and abolitionist William Wilberforce: "God Almighty has set before me two great objects, the suppression of the slave trade and the reformation of manners."[25] Echoing Wilberforce, Carter insists that "the connection between the great (fundamental human rights)

---

see George Washington, *Rules of Civility: The 110 Precepts That Guided Our First President in War and Peace,* ed. Richard Brookhiser (Charlottesville: University of Virginia Press, 2003).

24. Carter, *Civility,* 11.

25. Ibid., 100, citing Richard Lovelace, "The Bible in Public Discourse," in Rodney L. Peterson, ed., *Christianity and Civil Society* (Maryknoll, NY: Orbis, 1995), 62, 72.

and the small (basic manners) is at the heart of a proper understanding of civility."[26]

The connection between manners and morals is heightened in particular social contexts, particularly pluralistic and highly mobile societies such as our own. Carter reminds us that we do not travel through life alone, and our travel companions are not confined to a small group of relatives and intimate friends. The norms of civility are designed for relative strangers who cross each other's paths and who may even journey a short distance together. Carter repeatedly admonishes us that we are not to make friendship or even familiarity—common pasts, common interests, common purposes—a precondition to the duties of civility. The norms of civility are meant to facilitate social interaction and cooperation among *strangers,* not merely friends or relations; they are norms of obligation, not affection. As Carter stresses, "Our duty to follow those standards does not depend on whether or not we happen to agree with or even like each other."[27]

Inherent in Carter's articulation of the concept of civility is the demand for self-sacrifice, particularly in the form of self-restraint. Traveling on a crowded train, we cannot give in to every impulse to relieve ourselves, amuse ourselves, or make ourselves comfortable. We must consider the effects of our actions on those around us. "We should make sacrifices for others," says Carter, "not simply because doing so makes social life easier (although it does), but as a signal of respect for our fellow citizens, marking them as full equals, both before the law and before God."[28] Furthermore, we must sacrifice for the common good, the larger political community of which we are all a part. Building an orderly public life prohibits us from doing as we wish at all times.

So what are the basic requirements of civility? According to Carter, there are two: generosity and trust extended to others under less-than-ideal circumstances. "[S]acrificial civility has two components: generosity when there is cost, and trust when there is risk."[29] The cost of generosity and the risk of trust are part of the sacrifice required by civility. For Carter, generosity and trust are virtues required in matters both personal and political. We are tired,

26. Ibid., 28.
27. Ibid., 15.
28. Ibid., 11.
29. Ibid., 92.

but we ought to give up our seats on the bus to those who are infirm or elderly or carrying small children; we should not push to the head of the line but instead rely on the belief that everyone else will similarly refrain from asserting themselves. We do not always behave as we should in the personal realm. The political realm, however, is even more troubling. According to Carter, neither political liberals nor political conservatives regularly demonstrate the requisite combination of trust and generosity. "Conservatives refuse to call voters to be generous (for example, by supporting programs that might cost money), and liberals refuse to call voters to be trusting (for example, by looking to legislatures rather than courts in the effort to turn our desires into rights.)"[30]

An anecdote from his own life vividly exemplifies Carter's focus on the intersections between manners and morality, as well as between personal relationships and political transformation. Recounting how he moved with his family to Washington, DC, as a boy in the mid-1960s, Carter describes their feelings of isolation. They were the first African Americans to move into the predominantly white neighborhood of Cleveland Park.[31] Those feelings were overcome when a white woman named Sara Kestenbaum brought a huge plate of sandwiches over to welcome him and his siblings, who were sitting on the porch feeling alienated and unhappy in their new home.[32] Carter shows us that Kestenbaum's action was not only an instantiation of hospitality (etiquette) but was also an instantiation of political morality. She inscribed the moral imperative of racial integration in the personal habits of those dwelling in a particular neighborhood and, indeed, on a particular street. Carter points to the same integration of hospitality and political morality in the behavior of civil rights activists acting under the guidance of the Southern Christian Leadership Conference. When young workers for racial justice moved into a new community, they brought with them letters of introduction from respected elders along with their Bibles.[33]

It is no coincidence that Carter highlights the religious roots of this civil

---

30. Ibid., 92–93.

31. For other explorations of civility and race relations, see Elijah Anderson, *The Cosmopolitan Canopy: Race and Civility in Everyday Life* (New York: W.W. Norton & Co., 2011); and Danielle S. Allen, *Talking to Strangers: Anxieties of Citizenship since Brown v. Board of Education* (Chicago, IL: University of Chicago Press, 2004).

32. Carter, *Civility*, 60–63.

33. Ibid., 30.

manner of pursuing civil rights; he argues that commitment to civility is a natural fruit of a Christian worldview.[34] The two roots of civility, he claims, are awe and gratitude, which are both the result of seeing each human being as made in the image and likeness of God. This theological anthropology, in Carter's mind, enables compliance with the command to love one's neighbor, prominent not only in Christianity but also in other great religious traditions.[35] "Consequently," he writes, "we can see that the obligation of civility entails more than charitable acts; it entails a habit of the mind, perhaps an orientation of the soul, toward the other, the one who is outside of us and may seem very different from us, and yet is part of us through our equal share in God's creation."[36] Commitment to a transcendent God, who loves all human beings equally, inspires sacrifice on behalf of our fellow human beings. The story of the rich young man in the Gospels who refused to sell all he had to follow Jesus "is about the sacrifice that is at the heart of our relations with God. Once we accept our equality before God, our being made in the image of God, the story is also about the sacrifice that is at the heart of our relationship with others, and therefore is really about civility."[37] The rich young man failed to see that he needed to free himself from his desires for money, power, and comfort. Many people today also do not recognize the necessity of liberating ourselves from "anything about which we feel so strongly that we are unwilling to cast it aside in order to see the face of God in others." Such a failure is "a part of the structure of incivility that is so warping our world."[38]

What claim does civility have on us in the public square? For Carter, the claim is a strong one. He sees commitment to civility as nothing less than a "precondition of democratic dialogue."[39] He maintains that the incivilities we observe around us every day, such as general rudeness and unwillingness to contribute on behalf of the common good, corrodes the character of our people, ultimately threatening our democracy. At the same time, Carter does

---

34. For another perspective from a Reformed Christian point of view, see Richard J. Mouw, *Uncommon Decency: Christian Civility in an Uncivil World*, rev. ed. (Downers Grove, IL: InterVarsity Press, 2010).

35. Carter, *Civility,* 100–101.

36. Ibid., 102.

37. Ibid., 107.

38. Ibid., 108. At the end of the book, Carter offers a list of rules that crystallize his insights into civility; ibid., 277–86.

39. Ibid., 25.

devote substantial attention to the more focused question of *civil discourse;* he is concerned with how *words* can be the instruments of civility or incivility, particularly in the context of political activism or agitation. Carter observes, "Words are magic. We conjure with them. We send messages, we paint images. With words we report the news, profess undying love, and preserve our religious traditions. Words at their best are the tools of morality, of progress, of hope. But words at their worst can wound. And wounds fester. Consequently, the way we use words matters."[40]

How should we use words in political debate? How should we speak civilly to our interlocutors? Here Carter's advice corresponds to that of the more popular commentators whose writings were described above. It is negative in nature; he claims that we model civility by refusing to engage in or endorse the worst instances of incivility, no matter what the cost. Carter exhorts politicians to sacrifice some possibility of winning rather than resorting to attack ads against their opponents.[41] He also urges committed political activists working on moral issues such as abortion or school prayer to refrain from demonizing those on the opposite side of the issue—no matter how important they believe that issue may be. Carter articulates quite clearly the justification frequently offered for such demonization, saying, "[A]ll truly moral people agree on the issue; there is no reasonable alternative. Those on the other side then become monsters, and demonizing them is not incivility, it is simply description."[42] Nonetheless, he makes short shrift of this position, contending that those who hold it fail to regard their interlocutors with the awe that is due to them as creatures of God. Carter also maintains that demonization is a form of intellectual laziness. "Labeling as wicked those who do not agree with us is nothing but a transparent excuse for avoiding debate."[43] He hastens to add, however, that civility does not mean a reluctance to engage in criticism—even strong criticism. In his view, it simply places constraints on the way we engage in criticism.

Along with demonization, Carter rejects other ways of refusing to engage one's political and ideological opponents, which he groups together under

40. Ibid., 70.
41. Ibid., 120–22.
42. Ibid., 122–23.
43. Ibid., 123.

the chapter heading of "The Varieties of (Not) Listening."[44] We ought not to define the debate in a way that excludes some ideas from consideration from the beginning—Carter objects to this type of "bounded discourse."[45] We ought not to assume that our ideological opponents are evil; they may simply be misguided. If they are misguided, explaining the error of their ways requires being in conversation with them. Furthermore, Carter insists that we must acknowledge the possibility of being wrong ourselves—it is uncivil simply to enter into dialogue with the sole intent of refuting our interlocutors.[46] The process of attending to our conversation partners with an open mind and an open heart that are genuinely prepared to interpret what they say with a spirit of charity is what Carter calls "civil listening." The practice of civil listening requires his core virtues of generosity where there is potential personal sacrifice and trust where there is risk to self because those entering into a civil conversation are required to accept the possibility that their own views might be changed.

How might civility and respect operate in the context of deep social disagreement? Edward Langerak also tackles this question in his recent book.[47] Building on Rawls's notion of "the burdens of judgment," which outline sources of reasonable disagreement, Langerak argues that there are many contexts in which one might say, "I disagree with you but your position is one that I respect as reasonable."[48] Langerak develops six "variations on civil disagreement,"[49] which outline various ways in which interlocutors might ask themselves "whether [they] can respect the disagreeable position and whether [they] can tolerate or even cooperate with the associated actions or practices."[50] He contends that this sort of "open-mindedness is a matter of civility in a pluralistic society, and it enables people of strong conviction and integrity to live together with mutual respect along with their differences."[51]

44. Ibid., 132.

45. Ibid., 133–36.

46. Ibid., 137.

47. Edward Langerak, *Civil Disagreement: Personal Integrity in a Pluralistic Society* (Washington, DC: Georgetown University Press, 2014).

48. Ibid., 143. Langerak calls the ability to express this viewpoint "The essence of . . . reasonable pluralism." Ibid.

49. Ibid., 94–96.

50. Ibid., 94.

51. Ibid.

Langerak's approach is insightful. He shows, for example, how we might respect the position of parents who refused medically necessary blood transfusions for their children on religious grounds, even as we support laws overriding that position in order to save the children's lives.[52] At the same time, however, his account of civility does not ultimately move us significantly beyond that of Stephen Carter. Langerak's central model of political discourse is also conversation and discursive argumentation. In this context, civility means "treating others with appropriate courtesy and respect." It also involves "patience and *restraints*,"[53] such as refraining from questioning the motives of our interlocutors. But are these qualities always appropriate in the face of great social evil? Langerak recognizes that certain practices such as slavery became intolerable in American society,[54] but he does not grapple with the fact that some of the rhetorical interventions that helped make it socially intolerable were in no way courteous or respectful.

Is there a limit to civility's openness to dialogue? Are there some people whose views are so morally intolerable that they themselves ought not to be admitted into the conversation, such as those with hateful opinions of African Americans and Jews? Carter is extremely reluctant to admit this possibility, arguing that people are multifaceted, and those who are morally deficient, even seriously morally deficient in one area, may make valuable contributions in other areas. What about excluding them from conversations on the precise issues about which they are morally deficient? Even here, Carter has reservations:

> I do disagree, however, with the notion that people whose views are virulently hateful should be totally excluded from the possibility of the saving conversation, or that we can be sure that they say nothing worth listening to on any other subject. It is only through the process of *civil listening*—even to those whose views are hateful—that we can discover whether this is true. But even if we decide that the words of the hateful are as wrong as we thought, our duty to treat them with respect is in no way reduced.[55]

52. Ibid., 95–96.
53. Ibid., 20 (original emphasis).
54. Ibid., 77.
55. Carter, *Civility*, 145 (original emphasis).

Civility and Compartmentalization

How, then, does the virtue of civility operate in public conversations about political matters? At this point, drawing on Carter's normative account of civility, and with an eye on the more recent calls to civility in the public square, we are in a position to answer this question. One key to understanding how civility operates, in my view, is the legitimization of a certain type of compartmentalization or, to be precise, *two* particular types of compartmentalization.

One type of compartmentalization separates the form of the message from its content. Recall again Barack Obama's admonition, "[W]e can disagree without being disagreeable." This statement presupposes that the core of an argument, its "body," so to speak, can be separated from its presentation—the "clothing" in which it is "dressed." One can make the same point in either harsh or in mild language, without losing any of the point's integrity. One can rephrase one's objections to a particular practice (such as slavery, abortion, torture) in terms that minimize their appeal to emotions, and invite rational deliberation.

What might it mean "to dress" our moral arguments in the clothing of civility? It could mean, for example, avoiding colorfully tendentious descriptions of those actions that tended to arouse emotions in order to reinforce the speaker's moral viewpoint. The emotional valence framing a particular action or situation does not necessarily provide a reliable indication of its moral status. Even morally acceptable actions can be described in terms that appeal to the listener's emotions, particularly negative emotions. A wartime amputation to save a soldier's life can be made to sound even more gruesome than an incident of torture, a blow-by-blow description of an emergency C-section could easily sound far more repulsive than a step-by-step description of the operation of RU-486, which can function to terminate an early pregnancy.

It could also mean avoiding morally and legally conclusory labels. As political conservatives have pointed out, to call every form of intense enhanced interrogation "torture" begs the questions why and under what conditions are such forms of interrogation wrong—it does not argue the point. Conversely, as political liberals have emphasized, to call abortion "murder" takes for granted that it is a grievous and legally culpable form of intentional killing rather than, say, a form of justifiable homicide. Advocates of civility would doubtless ask participants in both debates to make each step in their argument explicit, nonconclusory, and therefore contestable at various points by reasonable persons. This approach can reduce acrimony by reducing and pinpointing the area of disagreement. For example, if I say, "I am opposed to torture, and I think waterboarding meets the definition," and you say, "I am opposed to torture, but I don't think waterboarding qualifies," it becomes clear that we share a common moral prohibition (against torture) and that our difference is a matter of how to categorize a particular practice.

Finally, it could mean accepting, if not openly acknowledging, the "joints" in our arguments—the places at which we are making factual or even normative judgments that might be made otherwise and that could be questioned, at least in principle. In some cases, it may mean acknowledging the competing values that are at stake in a particular decision. For example, in 2012, the United States Conference of Catholic Bishops organized a "fortnight for freedom" meant to highlight what they believed were violations of the religious freedom of Catholics on the part of the government. One example they cited was the Obama administration's mandate that employers cover contraceptive services for women as part of the basic benefits package; the bishops believed the regulation in question did not include a sufficiently broad exemption for Catholic colleges and healthcare institutions. Another example was the fact that in some states, Catholic Charities was refused licensure as an adoption agency because it refused to place children with same-sex parents. The bishops proclaimed these instances as clear violations of religious freedom. They did not note that for many of the decision makers involved, however, competing values were also involved in the decision, such as the right of women to obtain preventive healthcare, including contraception, and the state's repudiation of discrimination on the basis of sexual orientation. The bishops, of course, do not see the decision in this way because they do not recognize the competing values as legitimate. And civility does not require them to see those values as legitimate. It does require them to recognize that their interlocutors are positively motivated by those values and not by the negative desire to impede the free exercise of religion on the part of Catholic institutions.

In addition to separating the form of the message from its content, a second separation is equally necessary for civility: the separation of the messenger from the message. Bracketing our differences, we can deal civilly with those with whom we deeply disagree; we can treat them with respect and courtesy. This approach requires us to separate our evaluation of the moral character of other persons from the positions they hold or the arguments they make for those positions. In its stronger form, this approach would insist that a good person can make a morally bad argument or defend what their interlocutors believe is an objectively indefensible premise (such as the belief that African Americans or Jews or the unborn are less than fully human).

This second separation of civility insists that one area of moral failure does not besmirch an entire character. Furthermore, it highlights the fact that not every morally unacceptable position has its roots in moral corruption; in some cases, ignorance or mistake is to blame. Every instance of ignorance or mistake is in principle correctable. Moreover, not all instances of ignorance and mistake are morally culpable. Some are not even intellectually culpable. As Stephen Carter noted, the demands of civility remind us that we may even be making similar mistakes ourselves. We have no reason to think that our interlocutors, however mistaken, are not pressing their positions in good faith. In a weaker but still powerful form, civility's movement to separate a person from his or her positions can encourage us to refrain from evaluating our interlocutor's character at all.

By enabling this sort of thinking, civility's efforts to separate messenger and message are designed to minimize the occasions for ad hominem attacks. If we cannot licitly draw a conclusion about a person's character, or even her or his intelligence, from her or his bottom-line stance on a particular issue, ad hominem attacks become nothing more than a self-centered rhetorical indulgence that distracts from legitimate political debate.

In my view, therefore, at the root of the call to civility is the call for a dual separation in addressing political and moral arguments: (1) the separation of the content of a moral position from its presentation or form and (2) the separation of moral evaluation of a particular position from moral evaluation of the character of those who are advancing that position. This dual separation creates the possibility of civility defined theoretically by Stephen Carter and demanded more practically and intuitively by contemporary political advocates for civility. Yet we immediately run into a problem. Neither aspect of the separation is self-evidently justified, let alone self-evidently mandatory, in addressing our political interlocutors. Despite its initial appearance of fairness and viewpoint neutrality, the advocacy of this dual separation is arguably influenced strongly by a worldview that the critics of civility would consider anything but fair. In fact, they would treat it as an important aspect of the societal forces they believe themselves to be arrayed against, as some of the popular protests against the call to civility indicate.

John Murray Cuddihy on Civility

To understand why a call to civility would be viewed through such a skeptical lens, we must turn from law to sociology and in particular to the important, if idiosyncratic, writings of John Murray Cuddihy on religion and civility in twentieth-century America. In *No Offense: Civil Religion and Protestant Taste*, Cuddihy argues that civil religion in America is actually what he calls the "religion of civility."[56] Cuddihy argues that American civility, symbolized by the "national, protestant, and upper-middle-class smile," is actually anything but welcoming to traditional European religious and political groups immigrating to the United States.[57] Quietly but inexorably, the demands of civility reshape and reconfigure the way those groups approach the world. Cuddihy proposes an account of "the gossamer threads of civility in America as they bind down the giant Gullivers of religious and political fanaticism."[58] He argues that the American religion of civility has "tamed" all tendencies to fanaticism, teaching new immigrants how to "behave" appropriately in a pluralistic society.[59]

What is the underlying social factor that is responsible for this taming process? According to Cuddihy, it is Protestant denominationalism. Cuddihy argues that the early nation's acceptance of many different Protestant sects as

56. John Murray Cuddihy, *No Offense: Civil Religion and Protestant Taste* (New York: Seabury Press, 1978), 1.

57. Ibid., 4, 5–7. Both the ideal of "civility" and its content are, of course, socially conditioned. See, for example, Benet Davetian, *Civility: A Cultural History* (Toronto: University of Toronto Press, 2009); Jeffrey C. Goldfarb, *Civility and Subversion: The Intellectual in Democratic Society* (Cambridge: Cambridge University Press, 1998); Marvin B. Becker, *Civility and Society in Western Europe, 1300–1600* (Bloomington: Indiana University Press, 1988); Robert W. Hefner, ed., *Democratic Civility: The History and Cross-Cultural Possibility of a Modern Political Ideal* (New Brunswick, NJ: Transaction Publishers, 1998); and Edward C. Banfield, ed., *Civility and Citizenship in Liberal Democratic Societies* (New York: Paragon House Publishers, 1992). See also Leroy S. Rouner, ed., *Civility* (Notre Dame, IN: University of Notre Dame Press, 2000), as well as a more recent anthology: Austin Sarat, ed., *Civility, Legality, and Justice in America* (New York: Cambridge University Press, 2014).

58. Cuddihy, *No Offense*, 6.

59. Ibid.

having a place in the new country established theological pluralism as a foundational commitment of the new land. In turn, the key aspect of Protestant denominationalism is not merely grudging tolerance but rather active acceptance of the presence of other Protestant sects as one's citizens and neighbors. Within this framework, the central, civilizing commitment supports a change in belief "from 'you are there, and we are here' to 'it is good for all of us to be here.'"[60]

If, as Cuddihy argues, Protestant denominational pluralism is the de facto civil religion of the United States, the task for members of other religious bodies who find themselves landing on these shores from Europe is to find—or make—some way to come to terms with its demands. The most important of these demands, Cuddihy says, is differentiation, which, following Talcott Parsons, he maintains is the most striking and important feature of modern life. In contrast to premodern forms of society, we compartmentalize, distinguish, and separate various pieces of our social and personal worlds from each other. We arrange our lives by "crisscross," a complicated, compartmentalized, shifting array of alliances rather than one integrated seamless religious, political, and social world.[61] In America, all our coworkers are not co-religionists; in fact, all our family members may not be co-religionists. Similarly, all our co-religionists may not belong to the same social clubs or political parties. We Americans do not have a unified, integral worldview, in large part because we do not have a unified, integral life. To use Cuddihy's term, we live in the "crisscross" of competing frames of meaning and obligation.

According to Cuddihy, then, the key feature of American Protestant denominational pluralism is its drive to separate private life from public, civic life, and to locate religion squarely within the realm of the former. Just as the private realm should be separated from the public realm, so the church needs to be kept separate from the state. The political realm and the civil realm are the spheres where we all belong, equally, no matter what our religious commitments happen to be. Within this framework, religion becomes an individual question, a hidden affair, a matter of the heart. It is not a force that should permeate all aspects of one's life. Moreover, one's religious identity

60. Ibid., 164 (original emphasis).
61. Ibid., 183–89.

becomes reconfigured as an aspect of one's identity rather than its organizing core. We learn to separate our core identities—our "selves"—from various attributes of those selves, such as our religious identity or our ethnic background. These then become matters of choice or chance, as encapsulated in the phrase "I happen to be Catholic," or "I happen to be Jewish."

The American religion of civility, in Cuddihy's view, entails the acceptance of this sort of differentiation of roles and commitments. As he notes, it is anything but neutral in its effects on new immigrants coming to the nation's shores. It is far easier for Protestants, particularly those coming from the American Calvinist tradition, to make their peace with these separations than it is for Lutherans, Catholics, and Jews rooted in more holistic ways of viewing human life. In fact, Cuddihy contends that for those coming from integralist traditions to make their peace with modernizing compartmentalization is nothing short of an "ordeal," a painful test, a potentially mutilating form of torture. It is, in his view, "the ordeal" of civility.[62]

In three brilliant case studies, Cuddihy shows that the precise form the ordeal takes can depend on the particular form of integralism most important to the tradition being "civilized" for American life. His case study of Reinhold Niebuhr illustrates that, for German Lutherans, American civility required the sacrifice of their claims regarding the Gospel's universality, seen most sharply in the call to convert all nations, including the Jews, to belief in Jesus Christ. As Cuddihy notes, the singular contribution of Pauline · Christianity to world religions was the belief that the Christian God was the god of *all* human beings, including but not limited to the Jews. Whether or not they do believe in him, all human beings *ought* to believe in him and therefore worship him. Yet, according to Cuddihy, American civility requires that evangelical Christians relinquish their efforts at proselytization and return to a functional henotheism—a belief that different groups, different tribes, different peoples were each entitled to believe in and worship their own gods as they understood him.[63] Studying the tortured path of Reinhold

---

62. In his incisive and controversial book, *The Ordeal of Civility: Freud, Marx, Lévi-Strauss, and the Jewish Struggle with Modernity*, 2nd ed. (Boston, MA: Beacon Press, 1987), Cuddihy argued that the contributions of these three theorists could be illuminated by seeing them as efforts to universalize various aspects of the experience of European Jewry as they moved from the ghetto to full participation in European society.

63. Cuddihy, *No Offense*, chap. 3.

Niebuhr as he moved from a provincial German evangelical position that logically (if not practically) would require the evangelization of Jews to a stance that renounced evangelization out of "humility," Cuddihy asks, "[H]as Niebuhr removed, as Elmer Wentz charged, 'the offense of the cross' from Christianity?"[64] He strongly implies that the answer is yes. The lingering question, of course, is whether Christianity is still Christianity without the cross, offense or no offense.

If the main challenge for evangelical Christianity posed by the regime of civility was to its universalism, the main challenge civility posed to traditional Judaism was directed against its claim of being the chosen people.[65] The idea of a particular people, a particular ethnic group, being singled out by God for special attention directly conflicts with civility's command for universal equality. "The Christian, modernizing West could only experience Judaism's claim that 'more was expected of it because more had been given to it,' not as humble acknowledgment, but as theological arrogance in questionable taste."[66] Consequently, the harrowing sacrifice that American civility required of Jews was the reconfiguration of their tradition as a "religion" that was distinguishable from their family lives and ethnic roots. Cuddihy argues that conservative Judaism, with its emphasis on weekly temple worship, developed in the United States as a way of separating and highlighting the specifically religious components of Judaism's long-standing holistic traditions, which emphasized community, family, and shared heritage as much or more than religious belief. By so doing, it enabled Judaism to take its place as one of the "big three" free and equal *religions* in the United States, encapsulated in the title of Will Herberg's book *Protestant-Catholic-Jew.*[67]

If the challenge to Judaism posed by America's religion of civility was focused on its self-understanding as the chosen people, the challenge to Roman Catholicism also targeted its sense of uniqueness, its claim to be the

64. Ibid., 45, citing Elmer P. Wentz, letter, *Christian Century,* April 22, 1964, 525.

65. Ibid., chap. 5.

66. Ibid., 116.

67. Will Herberg, *Protestant-Catholic-Jew: An Essay in American Religious Sociology,* 2nd ed. (Chicago, IL: University of Chicago Press, 1983). According to Cuddihy, however, the ethnic identity of Jews did not disappear, but instead took another form. The emergence of the nation of Israel, a Jewish democracy, gave American Jews a way to assert simultaneously their commitment to America's universalist principles and to their own self-understanding as a distinct people.

one true church.[68] Whereas the integralism that Judaism promoted was between familial and ethnic identity and religion, the integralism particularly important to Catholicism was that between church and state. Before the Second Vatican Council, official Catholic teaching viewed the American model of religious pluralism as a distinctly inferior arrangement; ideally, the American state, like every sovereign nation, ought to promote and endorse the one true religion: Roman Catholicism. The fact that the Catholic Church developed its views on this matter to embrace religious liberty was in no small measure due to the work of the American Jesuit John Courtney Murray, who reframed both the American Constitution and Catholic church-state theory so that American Catholics could be both good Catholics and good Americans. More specifically, as Cuddihy observes, Murray's theory de-Romanized and de-Europeanized Catholic church-state theory by persuading it to drop its "ideal" demand for a confessional union of church and state. It did so by reinterpreting the background social and legal framework as theologically neutral rather than as geared toward Protestant Christianity. "If the 'Protestant' interpretation of 'America' and its Constitution is false— i.e., if America is not Protestant—there's no longer any need to insist it be Catholic."[69] The state could and should be *neutral* between the distinctive religious beliefs of Protestants and Catholics. Murray was confident that natural law, the Catholic term for the capacity for moral reasoning shared by all people of goodwill, could provide a substantive basis for civil interaction and a starting point for reasoned dialogue in the public square.

In Murray's view, the norms of civility provided a framework where Catholics could participate in civil society on equal terms with Protestants without sacrificing their fundamental identity or commitment to the truth. "Murray's dream was of a merger: to 'doctrinal exactness' there was to be joined 'a greatly *courteous* charity, which excludes any tendency to ally orthodoxy with undue suspicion, complacency, or rudeness.'"[70] Not every Catholic, however, was as convinced as this urbane Jesuit was that this sort of accommodation to American culture was a wise course for Catholics to pursue. In

---

68. Cuddihy, *No Offense*, chap. 4.

69. Ibid., 95.

70. Ibid., 67, quoting John Courtney Murray, S.J., "Christian Co-operation," *Theological Studies* 3, no. 3 (1942): 413–31, at 431 (italics are Cuddihy's).

fact, some American Catholics feared that Murray's type of "charity will end by devouring truth."[71]

Murray's fellow Jesuit, Leonard Feeney, was a case in point. A brilliant poet and a well-known Catholic intellectual, Feeney associated himself with the St. Benedict Center in Cambridge, Massachusetts, in the 1940s. Working in the shadows of Harvard, he labored to offer a "vision of an integrally Catholic culture" to combat the drift of American Catholics toward a Protestant sensibility. He offered a bold and unapologetic defense of traditional Catholic truths—including the truth "extra ecclesiam non salus est," which he interpreted quite literally as meaning that there was no salvation for anyone outside institutional Roman Catholicism. As the years progressed, however, Feeney also descended into an increasingly rabid anti-Semitism. Ironically, he himself was censured by the Holy Office for his overly restrictive interpretation of the doctrine "extra ecclesiam non salus est" and excommunicated in 1953 for "grave disobedience of Church authority." He was finally reconciled with Rome in 1974, four years before his death.[72]

As Cuddihy rightly points out, however, Feeney's main concern in preaching the idea of no salvation outside the Catholic Church was not converting Protestants and Jews. More specifically, his real targets were not non-Catholics; they were liberal Catholics (like Murray) who, he thought, watered down the truths of the faith because they cared too much for the good opinion of non-Catholics.[73] Feeney's primary goal was to stem the tide of Catholic indifferentism—the widespread failure on the part of American Catholics to guard their faith zealously and to transmit it to their children unadulterated and intact. And in Feeney's view, indifferentism was fostered by excessive social interaction with persons of other faiths, an interaction forced on Catholics by pluralistic American society.

To get along, many American Catholics were going along, and in going along, they drifted away from the faith of their fathers. Feeney refused to go along—to pull his theological punches in order to avoid offending Protestant

71. Ibid., 100.

72. See Avery Dulles, S.J., "Leonard Feeney: In Memoriam," *America*, February 25, 1978, 135–37. For another account, see James Carroll, *Practicing Catholic* (New York: Houghton Mifflin Harcourt, 2009), 69–77. Richard Cushing, the cardinal archbishop of Boston, had a Jewish brother-in-law, a man he grew to admire and love. Consequently, Feeney's anti-Semitic harangues were personally hurtful to him and his family. Ibid., 71–73.

73. Cuddihy, *No Offense*, 50, 54–56.

and Jewish sensibilities. He wanted to preach what he thought was Catholicism whole and entire, a Catholicism that, in its fullness, refused to be chopped up into the compartments demanded by American civility. Consequently, he both rejected and flouted those demands, much to the consternation of Boston's up-and-coming Catholic population. "To them," Cuddihy writes, "Father Feeney *had* to appear gauche and bigoted. What to him was *fides vere intrepida* was to them the claim to religious superiority, fanaticism, and vulgar group narcissism. To Feeney their urbane stance was a pusillanimous betrayal of the faith. Civil religion heard Feeney to be saying: 'Holier than thou.' Feeney heard back from them: 'Urbaner than thou.'"[74]

In my view, Cuddihy's work is important because it uncovers the normative presuppositions of American civility, which are *not* neutral but which largely presuppose and instantiate the values of Protestant denominational pluralism. The hallmark compartmentalization of modern civility—the separation of public from private, of church from state, of one's identity as a person from one's clan or religion—stand in great tension with the integralist approaches of religions whose worldviews had premodern roots. The price of acceptance and the precondition of success in American life was the willingness to lay one's belief system—and one's soul—down on the Procrustean bed of denominational pluralism, to give up the desire for a holistic universe in which one's personal, religious, and social worlds were completely integrated.

Civility's ornery critics accurately recognized the threat that it posed to integralist worldviews. As Cuddihy says,

> No, despite the word "civil" in its name, it is simply not true that civil religion knows its place and keeps its place, speaks only when spoken to, and runs politely "parallel" to the religions of the churches, coexisting platonically "alongside" their particular creeds. True, civil religion doesn't nail itself noisily to the portals of Protestant, Catholic, and Jewish houses of worship. Nevertheless, under cover of its prim title, civil religion, in its rites and practices, is activist, aggrandizing, subversive, intrusive, incivil.[75]

74. Cuddihy, *No Offense,* 63 (original emphasis).
75. Ibid., 1–2.

Civility and American Protestant *Agape*

Cuddihy's work allows us to put Carter's normative view of civility in some perspective. In no way is Carter's account of civility hostile toward religion; in fact, he emphasizes that religious communities committed to self-sacrificial neighbor love are essential in nurturing civility in the twenty-first century.[76] Moreover, Carter interprets civility as a manifestation of universal Christian love. It demands that we extend civic trust, in the form of respect, *to everyone*, not merely to everyone with whom we agree. Consequently, it is rooted in a Christian commitment to respect every human person as created in the image and likeness of God. He writes, "I suspect it will be possible to treat each other with love only if we are able to conceive doing so as a moral obligation that is absolute, something we owe others because of their personhood, bearing no relation to whether we like them or not."[77]

What would Cuddihy say about Carter's account of civility? First, he would doubtless agree with Carter's account of civility's religious roots. Civility, according to Cuddihy, is in fact the form that Protestant neighbor love—what Catholics tend to call charity—takes in a religiously pluralistic society. According to Cuddihy, Protestant denominationalism "institutionalizes *agape* as civility."[78] Furthermore, Cuddihy deeply values the benefits that this civilizing process has brought to American society, including social peace and the welcome absence of "movement" political fanaticism of the sort found in twentieth-century Europe. Unlike MacIntyre, Cuddihy is not nostalgic for a more integralist past. Yet he does not pretend that its loss has come without a cost—a great cost—to traditional Protestants, Catholics, and Jews whose commitments are rooted in more holistic and premodern worldviews. American civility's requisite split between public life and private belief demands a great deal of such persons because it demands that they forfeit a wholeness that they have come to expect and desire. What "America asks in the name of modernity and modernity's civil religion," according to Cuddihy, is this: "each sect is to remain the one true and revealed faith for itself and in

---

76. "Only religion possesses the majesty, the power, and the sacred language to teach all of us, the religious and the secular, the genuine appreciation for each other on which a successful civility must rest." Carter, *Civility*, 18.

77. Ibid., 101.

78. Cuddihy, *No Offense*, 23.

private, but each must *behave in the public arena as if* its truth were as tentative
as an esthetic opinion or a scientific theory."[79] Moreover, Cuddihy recognizes
that the public/private split is not as simple as donning and removing a mask.
The relationship between outward appearances and inner values is intimate
and complex.

> To accept and internalize such values is, in the end, to change
> one's outer appearance as much as one's inner disposition. The
> "look" of civic niceness takes over the human face, as it does the
> face each religion turns toward its public. Fanatical conviction is
> relativized and relegated like a private orgy to the home. What I
> call the "one-among-many-mien" is born and spreads itself across
> the democratic countenance. The American denomination, with
> its civil demeanor, is coming into being.[80]

As time goes on, the outward look transforms the inner self; one's religion
becomes one aspect of one's identity, not its defining feature. As I noted earlier in this chapter, the phrase that defines the transformation is, for Cuddihy,
the response of "I happen to be Catholic" (or "Jewish" or "Protestant") in
response to a question about one's religious affiliation.[81]

Carter's account of civility is based on mutual respect and a commitment
to participating in a shared community with others, despite our differences
from them. Nothing here would surprise Cuddihy. He would press Carter,
however, on the question what of sort of community civility makes possible. In Cuddihy's view, civility does not enable "the warm, dense closeness
of 'real' solidarity. It is 'formal' solidarity. In a regime of civility, everybody
doesn't love everybody. Everybody doesn't even respect everybody. Everybody 'shows respect for' everybody. . . . True, this is not 'solidarity forever'; it
is solidarity *ad interim,* for the time being."[82] In short, the Protestant ethic
of bourgeois civility defers full community indefinitely in order to forge a

---

79. Ibid., 108, quoting Arthur Hertzberg, "America Is Different," in Arthur Hertzberg, Martin E.
Marty, and Joseph N. Moody, *The Outbursts That Await Us: Three Essays on Religion and Culture in the
United States* (New York: Macmillan, 1963), 131 (italics are Cuddihy's).

80. Ibid., 125.

81. Ibid., 13.

82. Ibid., 210.

workable, limited formal community here and now. "Ultimate community and solidarity are for the 'end of days,' not for today."[83] It is a great merit of Cuddihy's analysis that it so sharply reveals that this limited view of community is not purely secular; it is, in fact, rooted in a particular strand of American Christianity, a Calvinist strand that prioritizes a certain type of self-denial and self-restraint.

Civility, Carter repeatedly asserts, does not preclude vigorous disagreement—provided that one disagrees "respectfully." In his view, respectful, and fruitful, political disagreements "must take place against the background of a shared understanding of what America most fundamentally means."[84] It presupposes that politics is only a small slice of American life. Furthermore, other arenas of social meaning must provide people with the moral weapons necessary to resist the political realm's tendency to expand beyond its proper sphere. Cuddihy's work forces us to question whether Carter's approach is feasible. Assuming Cuddihy is right, civility's "shared understanding" of what America means was not determined by consensus; instead, it was developed over centuries by the white Anglo-Saxon Protestant (WASP) elites of American social and political life. It is important to acknowledge that the norms of civility allowed for the categories of participants to be expanded; at the same time, however, those norms insisted that the basic structure of American life was to remain the same. Carter tacitly admits this is the case in his description of civil rights workers moving from city to city with their letters of introduction. Quite tellingly, he writes: "The goal of the movement, after all, was to ensure that black Americans could become full participants in the democracy, not to tear it apart."[85]

Here we find another problem. Carter's account of civility cannot fully and straightforwardly account for the fact that many of our most intense and bitter disputes are indeed battles over just what ideals America is supposed to embody. Nowhere is this clearer than in the way in which he deals with the abolitionists. Carter rightly notes that many of the abolitionists were motivated by Christian love. Furthermore, he clearly understands that religions must "preach not only love of neighbor but resistance to wrong,"[86] At the

83. Ibid.
84. Carter, *Civility*, 126.
85. Ibid., 30.
86. Ibid., 259.

same time, he remains too much at the level of generalities in grappling with abolitionist preaching. Yet it is the particularities of the discourse that matter for purposes of assessing its civility.

Carter simply does not address squarely the reality that many abolitionists did not merely call for the abolition of slavery out of love; they vividly condemned the institution, those who maintained it, and those who defended it in the strongest possible terms. They were not always, or even generally, "civil." They did not contribute to the orderly examination of moral arguments for and against slavery but rather deliberately provoked and played upon the emotions of their audience, and frequently attributed the worst of motives to their interlocutors. They saw themselves as fighting *to alter* the "shared understanding" of American identity in a way that, nonetheless, would bring that identity into greater conformity with the deepest and truest of American values. Neither the abolitionists nor the defenders of slavery believed the other was operating within the same view of the nation's nature and purpose. That nature and purpose were the ultimate grounds of their battle. Consequently, neither side would conform to Carter's qualifications for civility.

Carter also passes over in silence the fact that the language in which many of the most prominent abolitionists cast their calls to eradicate slavery was more indebted to the prophetic indictments of the Old Testament than to the beatitudes of the New Testament. William Lloyd Garrison and Wendell Phillips did not generally employ the rhetoric of "sweetness and light," to quote Matthew Arnold.[87] Instead, they deployed what Arnold referred to as the rhetoric of "fire and strength," of uncompromising moral witness about basic moral values.[88] Their blistering rhetoric denies what the rhetoric of civility presupposes—it denies that there is, in fact, a common commitment to core American values among the interlocutors. More generally, Carter does not address the potential of religious discourse to contribute to incivility,

87. Matthew Arnold, *Culture and Anarchy*, ed. Samuel Lipman (New Haven, CT: Yale University Press, 1994), chap. 5, "Porro Unum Est Necessarium," para. 171: "'Culture,' says an acute, though somewhat rigid critic, Mr. Sidgwick, 'diffuses sweetness and light. I do not undervalue these blessings, but religion gives fire and strength, and the world wants fire and strength even more than sweetness and light.'" Arnold, needless to say, places a higher value on "sweetness and light" because it avoids fanaticism.

88. Ibid. For an explanation of Arnold's use of these terms, see ibid., chap. 4, "Hebraism and Hellenism," paras. 142–66.

in our times as well as in the times of the Civil War. Writing in 1998, well after the civil rights movement and somewhat before the next eruptions of the culture wars, Carter played down that possibility. In fact, he maintained that religious voices have been too quiescent in recent years. He argued that the more pressing danger facing religion in American life is sloth; it manifests a collective failure to engage in civil protest against the wrongs of our society.[89] Carter writes: "I actually wish the critics were right. I wish the religiously faithful were more of a problem for America."[90]

Carter may have gotten his wish. The situation of religion in the public square in the first two decades of the twenty-first century, of course, looks somewhat different than it did when he was writing in the late 1990s. Whatever else it may be, religion is no longer quiescent; indeed, religious voices achieved significant prominence in the administration of George W. Bush and mounted a bitter critique of the Obama administration. Unfortunately, his account of civility does not help us in addressing the challenges of newly empowered and energized religious voices. Having glided over the rhetoric of prophetic denunciation in the abolitionists, having minimized the social challenge inherent in King's prophetic rhetoric, Carter's framework offers scant assistance in understanding the religiously motivated culture warriors of the second millennium. After all, contemporary culture warriors not only identify themselves as the contemporary heirs of the abolitionists and the civil rights workers; they also deliberately appropriate the prophetic rhetoric of the earlier causes.

Uncivil Protestants?

Can Cuddihy's work on civility fill in the lacuna left by Carter in addressing the twenty-first-century culture wars? In my view, no. Cuddihy can explain the mid-twentieth-century incivilities of Father Leonard Feeney and Rabbi Meir Kahane; he can help us see that they are attempting to defy the normative framework of Protestant civility in order to preserve or recapture the Old World wholeness of Catholic and Jewish life. He cannot account so easily, however, for important and distinctively Protestant forms of *incivility*. It is

89. Carter, *Civility*, 254–55, 257–61.
90. Ibid., 254.

true that Cuddihy can amalgamate Southern Baptists into the same paradigm with which he encompasses Catholics and Jews; he would argue that they too must give up their claims to religious exclusivity ("Jesus alone saves") as they move up the social ladder. Like Catholics and Jews, Southern Baptists must also absorb the demeanor of elite WASP society if they want to advance.[91] They must internalize its restraint and universal acceptance of the other. But Cuddihy's account is ultimately no more able than Carter's to explain a major moral and religious discourse of social controversy in America, which also has its roots in elite WASP society.

For example, while acknowledging the "trauma of Civil War" to the nation, Cuddihy does not grapple with the way in which barbed, distinctively Protestant rhetoric contributed to both sides of the controversy.[92] Instead, he focuses on the new terms of peace established by Lincoln's Second Inaugural Address, which he deems the second testament of American civil religion. Lincoln inscribed the theme of "sacrifice" onto the first testament, which Cuddihy understands to comprise key writings of the Founding Fathers. Moreover, Lincoln relocated the "major 'lines of cleavage'" to a point "*within* Americans rather than *between* them and non-Americans."[93] Cuddihy maintains that "the 'internalization' of conflict promoted by the pluralism and 'crisscross' of our *socio-economic* modernization coincided with the *cultural* symbolism bequeathed to us by Lincoln and the Civil War. The experience of cross-pressures at once modernizes us, middle-classifies us, and Americanizes us. The experience of crisscross is the social psychological coefficient of the modernization process. It makes us civil."[94] In short, Cuddihy is saying that civility now requires each person to conduct his or her own civil war entirely *within* the borders of his or her own psyche; interactions with others are to be peaceful, polite, and orderly.

Undeniably brilliant, Cuddihy's analysis cannot account nonetheless for the adamant demands of Protestant preachers in the various social reform movements in the century following the Civil War or, for that matter, for the passionate Protestant justifications for revolution against England in the

---

91. See Cuddihy's comments on Jimmy Carter, *No Offense*, 2–5.

92. Ibid., 188.

93. Ibid., 189 (original emphasis). Cuddihy borrows the phrase "lines of cleavage" from James Coleman, "Social Cleavage and Religious Conflict," *Journal of Social Issues* 12, no. 3 (1956): 46–47.

94. Ibid.

century preceding it. He might try to distinguish lower-class Protestants from the Brahmin class, claiming that the social agitators belonged to the former group, while members of the latter group fit into his pattern. That distinction, however, would be incorrect. Many of the most vehement and fiery American preachers before, during, and after the Civil War were by no means badly educated and socially marginalized rubes.

Consider, for example, the life of the abolitionist poet Julia Ward Howe, who wrote the "Battle Hymn of the Republic," one of the most popular songs of the Civil War era. After the war, she devoted her considerable efforts and energies to the causes of feminism and pacifism. Howe was born in New York to a wealthy banker whose grandfather was a governor of the colony of Rhode Island and a delegate to the Continental Congress. Highly educated, she learned to speak several languages in her youth. Her husband, Dr. Samuel Gridley Howe, founded the Perkins Institute for the Blind.[95] If anyone qualified as a Brahmin, Julia Ward Howe did. She rejected the dominant conventions of civility, writing an essay entitled "Is Polite Society Polite?," in which she argued:

> A doctrine which allows and encourages one set of men to exclude another set from claim to the protection and inspiration of God is in itself impolite. Christ did not reproach the Jews for holding their own tenets, but for applying these tenets in a superficial and narrow spirit, neglecting to practise [sic] true devotion and benevolence, and refusing to learn the providential lessons which the course of time should have taught them. At this day of the world, we should all be ready to admit that salvation lies not so much in the prescriptions of any religion as in the spirit in which these are followed.[96]

So far, so good. The foregoing passage could be endorsed by Stephen Carter. It also tracks the argument made by Cuddihy himself. Yet in advocating for abolition of slavery, Howe went in an entirely different direction in her

---

95. Her life was not without its difficulties. See, for example, Valarie H. Ziegler, *Diva Julia: The Public Romance and Private Agony of Julia Ward Howe* (Harrisburg, PA: Trinity Press International, 2003).

96. Julia Ward Howe, *Is Polite Society Polite? And Other Essays* (Boston, MA: Lamson, Wolffe & Company, 1895), 18.

critique of the dominant conventions of politeness. Her militant rhetoric in the "Battle Hymn of the Republic" was far from "polite"; it is recounting a harrowing vision of the second coming of Jesus Christ to judge the living and the dead. Consider the first two verses:

> Mine eyes have seen the glory of the coming of the Lord:
> He is trampling out the vintage where the grapes of wrath are stored;
> He hath loosed the fateful lightning of His terrible swift sword:
> > His truth is marching on.
>
> I have seen Him in the watch-fires of a hundred circling camps;
> They have builded Him an altar in the evening dews and damps;
> I can read His righteous sentence by the dim and flaring lamps:
> > His day is marching on.[97]

God's judgment over slavery and, by implication, over those who advocate or benefit from it, is swift, decisive, and terrible. Consequently, there is no room for discussion or argument with those who support the practice—only repentance. Nor was Howe anomalous in her use of prophetic, even apocalyptic rhetoric on behalf of the cause of freedom. The abolitionist Wendell Phillips

---

97. Julia Ward Howe, "Battle-Hymn of the Republic," *Atlantic Monthly* 9, no. 52 (February 1862): 10. The "Glory, Glory, Hallelujah" chorus was a hold-over from the original hymn, "Brothers, Will You Meet Us?," published in 1858 by G. S. Scofield, New York. See Julia Ward Howe, *Battle Hymn of the Republic: Adapted to the Favorite Melody of "Glory, Hallelujah"* (Boston, MA: Oliver Ditson, 1862). Many thanks to Notre Dame's research librarians Robert Simon and Lisa Welty for tracking this information down for me. The hymn continues:

> I have read a fiery gospel writ in burnished rows of steel:
> As ye deal with My contemners, so with you my grace shall deal;
> Let the Hero, born of woman, crush the serpent with his heel,
> > Since God is marching on.
>
> He has sounded forth the trumpet that shall never call retreat;
> He is sifting out the hearts of men before His judgment-seat:
> Oh, be swift, my soul, to answer Him! be jubilant, my feet!
> > Our God is marching on.
>
> In the beauty of the lilies Christ was born across the sea,
> With a glory in his bosom that transfigures you and me:
> As he died to make men holy, let us die to make men free,
> > While God is marching on.

was born to a prominent family in Boston, and attended Boston Latin School, Harvard University, and Harvard Law School. To say that not all of his rhetoric against slavery was polite or nice would be an understatement.

John Murray Cuddihy's account of civility can provide the etiology of Howe's concern with politeness. It cannot, however, furnish an explanation of how the same woman can pen "The Battle Hymn of the Republic." Nor can it explain how Wendell Phillips, from the same social class as Howe, would find it appropriate to deploy the invective he deployed against the pro-slavery forces.[98] What accounts for this substantial gap in Cuddihy's otherwise brilliant analysis? In my view, a clue can be found in the introduction to his book, where he briefly elaborates on the roots of the religion of civility. He writes that "[t]he norm of generalized 'niceness' that a 'civil religion' secularized from Christianity bids us practice in the presence of strangers has roots embedded in a unitarianized Calvinism."[99]

To explain the militant, prophetic side of Protestantism, we need to return to the beginnings of the history of American Christianity, to a time before the emergence of Unitarianism. We need to examine the rhetorical culture of the grandfathers and great-grandfathers of Unitarianism. In 1630, a band of Puritans set out for the New World in order to free themselves from the corruption of the English Church (which they saw as retaining too many "popish" inventions) and establish a "city on a hill," a "New Jerusalem," a polity whose total structure, through its coordinated political and religious governance, accorded with God's holy law. As Mark Noll details, the Puritans constructed a "canopy" over religious and political life, which was characterized by an interrelated set of covenants, or religiously infused contracts. These covenants structured the relationship of the regenerate Christian to God (the covenant of grace), the relationship of Christians to one another (the church covenant), and the relationship of God to the new Christian people

---

98. "The South is one great brothel, where half a million of women are flogged to prostitution, or worse still, are degraded to believe it honorable. The public squares of half our great cities echo to the wail of families torn asunder at the auction block; no one of our fair rivers that has not closed over the Negro seeking in death a refuge from a life too wretched to bear. . . ." Wendell Phillips, *Wendell Phillips on Civil Rights and Freedom,* ed. Louis Filler (New York: Hill and Wang, 1965), 37. See also Mason Lowance, ed., *Against Slavery: An Abolitionist Reader* (New York: Penguin, 2000). Other fiery abolitionists were from more modest backgrounds. See, for example, William Lloyd Garrison, *Selections from the Writings and Speeches of William Lloyd Garrison* (New York: Negro Universities Press, 1968).

99. Cuddihy, *No Offense,* 4.

(the political or national covenant).[100] The key prerequisite for American civility, as Cuddihy understands it, the separation of the private and the public realms, has no place in the Puritan worldview.

These adventurous reformers succeeded beyond their wildest dreams; in fact, they managed to maintain the purity of their Congregationalist vision in the New World for several decades after their counterparts in the Old World had been forced to modify that vision because of political expediency.[101] Human nature being what it is, however, the initial religious fervor of those making the trip to America waned at times. Moreover, the children and the grandchildren of the initial settlers sometimes appeared to be lukewarm in their faith. To reignite religious ardor, Puritan clergy availed themselves of a particular form of preaching that has come to be known as the jeremiad. As its name suggests, the jeremiad recalls the urgent call to moral repentance found most strikingly in the book of the prophet Jeremiah but is also prevalent in the other prophetic books of the Hebrew Bible, the Christian Old Testament.

In its initial forms, the rhetoric of the jeremiad presupposed and strengthened the interlocking set of Puritan covenants because it condemned gross violations of their terms and called attention to the ruin that would follow if those violations were not rectified. But the rhetoric of national chosenness— and with it, the jeremiad—survived the political and intellectual transformations that the colony would undergo from the time of its founding. The idea of America as the home to a people with a special relationship to God endured despite significant political upheaval. The sacralized idea of America took on anguished form in the era of the Civil War (which pitted Bible-believing Protestants against one another on the issue of slavery) and has reemerged in

100. Mark A. Noll, *America's God: From Jonathan Edwards to Abraham Lincoln* (New York: Oxford University Press, 2002), chap. 3.

101. Oliver Cromwell did not advance the interest of English Puritan Congregationalists in the Church of England as quickly as some American Puritans might have liked; he was forced to grapple with the conflicting interests and claims of Presbyterians and other dissenting parties. See, for example, Perry Miller, *The New England Mind: The Seventeenth Century* (Cambridge, MA: Belknap Press of Harvard University Press, 1954), 370; Harry S. Stout, *The New England Soul: Preaching and Religious Culture in Colonial New England* (New York: Oxford University Press, 1986), 50–53; Francis J. Bremer, *The Puritan Experiment: New England Society from Bradford to Edwards,* rev. ed. (Hanover, NH: University Press of New England, 1995), 127–28; and Blair Worden, "Oliver Cromwell and the Protectorate," *Transactions of the Royal Historical Society* 20 (2010): 57–83.

the twentieth century to ignite and structure social debates on matters from temperance to suffrage, to civil rights, to abortion.

Cuddihy is correct that the conventions of American civility owe a great deal to the New England Unitarians whose heritage was Puritan Calvinism. Yet those New England Unitarians carried forward only one strand of the Puritan tradition—its intellectualizing and disciplined side. There was another side of Puritanism—its affective power, rooted in an emotional connection with the divine, which was ignited by the preachers of the successive religious awakenings and which finds its contemporary expression in evangelical Protestantism. Moreover, this side of Puritanism fueled the passion of the jeremiad, encouraging successive generations to mount their moral and social critiques by drawing on its power.

Cuddihy is also correct in his observation that many upwardly mobile immigrants adapted to the broader culture by undergoing the "ordeal" of civility, construed in terms set by one strand of Calvinist thought that has its roots in our Puritan founders. But there is another strand of Calvinist thought that successive generations of more reform-minded immigrants made their own as well. Over the years, the conventions of the Puritan jeremiad were adopted and modified by American patriots, African American preachers, Catholic bishops, and secular social reformers.[102]

To come to terms with incivility in the United States, therefore, particularly the relationship of religion and incivility, it is not enough to call for neighbor love, as Carter does. It is not enough to identify incivility with the integralist presuppositions of new arrivals from the Old World, as does Cuddihy. We need to grapple with the integralist presuppositions of the Protestant founders of this nation and the form of political rhetoric that those presuppositions generated. The rhetoric of prophetic denunciation is every bit as American as the cool, detached, mutually respectful reason giving and orderly, emotionally detached consideration of arguments that is contemplated by MacIntyre, Rawls, and Carter.

The rhetoric of prophetic indictment is obviously not civil if we assume that the word *civil* means "polite and respectful." The fundamental problem

---

102. See James Darsey, *The Prophetic Tradition and Radical Rhetoric in America* (New York: New York University Press, 1997).

with Carter's analysis, and by extension with all those who lament the lack of civility in current political discourse, is that he does not take into account *why* it is not civil. Carter's account of civility presupposes that all participants in the discussion acknowledge each other's commitment to the foundational principles of the polity. It is on that basis that they call for mutual respect; however, the employment of prophetic rhetoric frequently denies that this is the case. Those deploying the rhetoric of prophetic indictment tend to see their opponents as threatening the basic foundations of the social order, which also serve as the foundations for calm and reasoned moral discourse. Accordingly, they view conversational niceties as at best a distraction and at worst as a betrayal of unswerving commitment to the truth.

Furthermore, those deploying prophetic rhetoric cannot accept the dual separation that I identified earlier as lying at the heart of Carter's justification of civility. They cannot separate their message from the form in which it is delivered. Their point is precisely that business as usual in moral argumentation is not an option because the foundations of the moral framework that ought to structure all subsequent moral argumentation are at stake in the debate. In addition, they cannot separate the moral merits of the person making an argument from the moral merits of the argument itself. Such a separation might be justifiable in a seminar room, but it makes no sense in real life. Those using prophetic rhetoric do not simply oppose their interlocutors' arguments, considered in some abstract, two-dimensional manner. Their opposition is concrete and three-dimensional; they deplore the fact that (in their view) their interlocutors are using the arguments in question to pursue a political course that they believe is ruinous for the entire society. Those deploying prophetic rhetoric oppose what their opponents are *doing* to the society by disseminating their arguments, not merely what they are *saying* by means of those arguments in a theoretical way. They would contend, along with the mainstream Christian tradition, that it is impossible to separate the evaluation of a person's actions from an evaluation of her or his character.

In short, the incivilities of prophetic discourse are not *mere* incivilities; they ought not to be dismissed as sheer rudeness or brutishness or attempts at political bullying, although at times they incorporate all three elements. In fact, they may not be incivilities at all, if *civil* means "committed to the foundational principles of the polity (*civitas*) in question." Consequently, to come to terms with the role of religion in the American public square and in particular its propensity to incivility as commonly understood, we need to come to terms with the nature and function of prophetic rhetoric in the public square. To do so, we need to recognize the place of prophetic indictment as a characteristically American form of religious and political discourse. This task in turn requires us to delve deeply into the historical and conceptual roots of prophetic rhetoric in the history and thought of the Puritans.

II

THE JEREMIAD
AND ITS EVOLUTION

A HISTORICAL EXPLORATION

The American Jeremiad

Covenant, Complaint, and Controversy

In previous chapters, I contended that three prevailing accounts of the role of religious discourse in the American public square are insufficient, both with respect to the problems they identify and with respect to the solutions they propose. Alasdair MacIntyre argues that the contentiousness of contemporary moral disagreement is attributable to the disintegration of a (once presupposed) normative account of human flourishing that supports a coherent pattern of moral reasoning and productive moral debate. John Rawls takes the opposite tack, suggesting that divisiveness in the public square can be attributed largely to the fact that citizens do not always present their moral arguments about fundamental political issues within the limits of public reason but rather draw on more idiosyncratic aspects of their comprehensive worldviews, which includes their religious beliefs. Stephen Carter maintains the problem is one of form, not substance—if religious believers (and others) made their points "civilly," public discourse would be enhanced and the "problem" of religious discourse in the public square would dissipate.

The specific problems of each account notwithstanding, I have argued that the failure of each author to articulate the origins of the problems of contemporary moral and political discourse is due to a set of assumptions shared by all three. First, each assumes that all significant moral claims in the public square are to be analyzed as moral argument, and second, each supposes that the substance of a moral claim can be separated from its form so that any moral claim can be repackaged and reframed in a civil or respectful manner. In my judgment, those two assumptions prevent the prevailing accounts from identifying and grappling with the crucial role played in American public life by the jeremiad, a particular form of discourse that is at once both thoroughly religious and thoroughly political. As Perry Miller so masterfully called to our attention, the jeremiad was notably employed by the Puritan preachers who settled Massachusetts Bay Colony.[1] Yet it long outlived their dreams for a godly polity run by Protestant Congregationalists. The jeremiad has proven itself to be both a durable and flexible form of political-moral speech in American life, as Sacvan Bercovitch and other scholars of rhetoric have demonstrated.[2] Some form of the jeremiad has been used in the battles over slavery, liquor, social justice, warfare, and civil rights.[3]

The jeremiad is without a doubt a type of moral *discourse;* it makes a moral claim on its audience. It is not a moral *argument,* however; it does not move by reason from stated premises to conclusions that certain actions ought to be performed or avoided. Nor is it a type of moral deliberation. Instead, it is best understood as a type of extended moral *indictment* or *complaint,* a law-like charge that certain actions, already performed, violate a socially binding agreement. Moreover, in the jeremiad, form and substance are intertwined. It is impossible to achieve the objectives of the jeremiad while recasting its point in less intransigent, more dialogical terms, just as

1. See Perry Miller, *The New England Mind: From Colony to Province* (Cambridge, MA: Belknap Press of Harvard University Press, 1953) and *The New England Mind: The Seventeenth Century* (Cambridge, MA: Belknap Press of Harvard University Press, 1954).

2. Sacvan Bercovitch, *The American Jeremiad* (Madison: University of Wisconsin Press, 1978). See also Sacvan Bercovitch, *The Puritan Origins of the American Self* (New Haven, CT: Yale University Press, 1975). For analysis of the tradition in broader context, see David Howard-Pitney, *The African American Jeremiad: Appeals for Justice in America,* rev. ed. (Philadelphia, PA: Temple University Press, 2005); Willie J. Harrell, Jr., *Origins of the African American Jeremiad: The Rhetorical Strategies of Social Protest and Activism, 1760–1861* (Jefferson, NC: McFarland & Co., 2011); James Darsey, *The Prophetic Tradition and Radical Rhetoric in America* (New York: New York University Press, 1997); and James A. Morone, *Hellfire Nation: The Politics of Sin in American History* (New Haven, CT: Yale University Press, 2003). Morone is particularly good about showing the continuing role of a fixation on sin—a violation of God's law—in American reform movements.

3. See, for example, Harrell, *Origins of the African American Jeremiad;* Timothy Patrick McCarthy and John Stauffer, eds., *Prophets of Protest: Reconsidering the History of American Abolitionism* (New York: New Press, 2006); Lyle W. Dorsett, *Billy Sunday and the Redemption of Urban America* (Grand Rapids, MI: Eerdmans, 1991); David L. Chappell, *A Stone of Hope: Prophetic Religion and the Death of Jim Crow* (Chapel Hill: University of North Carolina Press, 2004); Norman H. Clark, *Deliver Us from Evil: An Interpretation of American Prohibition* (New York: W.W. Norton & Company, 1976); James Dawes, *The Language of War: Literature and Culture in the U.S. from the Civil War through World War II* (Cambridge, MA: Harvard University Press, 2002); Adam M. Garfinkle, *Telltale Hearts: The Origins and Impact of the Vietnam Antiwar Movement* (New York: St. Martin's Press, 1995).

it is impossible to achieve the objectives of a criminal indictment in the same manner.

The aim of this chapter and the next is to show how our understanding of the role of religious language in contemporary political discourse can be greatly illuminated by examining the development of the jeremiad as a characteristically American form of religious and political speech. To do so, I analyze the origins of the jeremiad in the political and religious institutions of New England Puritanism, emphasizing its dependence on the covenant theology that animated the religious and social vision of those early American migrants. This analysis should help to explain an important and striking aspect of Puritan life and discourse in seventeenth- and eighteenth-century New England: Despite its trenchant criticism of the community's patterns of behavior, the jeremiad generally functioned as an instrument of social unity.

From the perspective of the contemporary era, the unifying function of the jeremiad in the Puritan era is nothing short of remarkable. We have become accustomed to the way in which fiery condemnations of social and moral evil tear our communities further asunder. What accounts for this dramatic shift in the social function of the jeremiad? When did it take place? In the following chapter, I argue that the jeremiad began to be a source of social contention when its practitioners no longer observed the constraints associated with its root genre, which is that of a legal indictment or complaint. In a nutshell, it is one thing to indict others for violating a law that is widely acknowledged in the community; it is another thing entirely to indict them for failing to obey a law that is not on the books and that they have no reason to accept. The first course of action may lead to reaffirmation of communal bonds, while the second is likely to produce only resentment and protest. By the onset of the American Revolution, political and religious commentators began to move from the first way of using prophetic indictment to the second, the reasons for which I will later explore.

Scholars of rhetoric have examined the social and political role of the jeremiad in Puritan times and beyond. My analysis differs from theirs by focusing on the close connection between the covenant and the jeremiad in the Puritan era, and by exploring the rhetorical presuppositions and constraints of that connection. More specifically, I examine what it means rhetorically for a jeremiad to be structured as a legal complaint or indictment for breach of covenant. This exploration requires as its basis an understanding of the covenantal framework that structured the Puritans' experience of themselves and their times. In other words, the rhetorical roots of the American jeremiad are intertwined with a particular history and understanding of the relationship between religious belief, politics, and law.

American Puritanism

Before turning to the task at hand, it may be helpful to provide a capsule summary of Puritan history.[4] Although American Puritanism has its own distinctive story to tell, many of its key elements cannot be understood without reference to the waxing and waning of Puritanism in England. In fact, as Stephen Foster has persuasively argued, the major lines of American Puritanism can be discerned in Elizabethan Puritanism, including the program for radical reform of the churches to extirpate the vestiges of Catholic "Papism," and the commitment to social and political facilitation of a godly life.[5]

As so often happens with social movements, the label "Puritan" was generated by detractors of the movement, who thought the "Puritans" were too rigid in their complaints that the English Reformation had not been

4. As its name suggests, a very brief summary of the Puritan movement can be found in Francis J. Bremer, *Puritanism: A Very Short Introduction* (New York: Oxford University Press, 2009). For a more extensive account, see Francis J. Bremer, *The Puritan Experiment: New England Society from Bradford to Edwards,* rev. ed. (Lebanon, NH: University Press of New England, 1995); Stephen Foster, *The Long Argument: English Puritanism and the Shaping of New England Culture, 1570–1700* (Chapel Hill: University of North Carolina Press, 1991); Edmund S. Morgan, *Visible Saints: The History of a Puritan Idea* (Ithaca, NY: Cornell University Press, 1965), and Alan Simpson, *Puritanism in Old and New England* (Chicago, IL: University of Chicago Press, 1955). Helpful anthologies of Puritan writing are Perry Miller and Thomas H. Johnson, eds., *The Puritans: A Sourcebook of Their Writings,* 2 vols., rev. ed. (New York: Harper Torchbooks, 1963); Alan Heimert and Andrew Delbanco, eds., *The Puritans in America: A Narrative Anthology* (Cambridge, MA: Harvard University Press, 1985); and David D. Hall, ed., *Puritans in the New World: A Critical Anthology* (Princeton, NJ: Princeton University Press, 2004). Helpful consideration of particular themes can be found in John Coffey and Paul C. H. Lim, eds., *The Cambridge Companion to Puritanism* (Cambridge: Cambridge University Press, 2008). A key reference work is Francis J. Bremer and Tom Webster, eds., *Puritans and Puritanism in Europe and America: A Comprehensive Encyclopedia,* 2 vols. (Santa Barbara, CA: ABC-CLIO, 2006).

5. "Some six decades separate the first assertion of militant Puritanism from the departure of the Winthrop fleet for America in 1630, but in broad outline the goals of the New England Way were still the agenda articulated by the Elizabethan radicals, and the reason for creating a New England at all was yet another setback in the continuing campaign to reshape English life on English soil." Foster, *The Long Argument,* 3.

sufficiently thorough in eradicating Roman Catholic beliefs, worship, devotions, and ecclesiastical structure from Christian practice in England.[6] In Elizabethan times, for example, the Puritans aimed to replace an episcopal church structure with a congregational model that they believed was more congruent with the early Christian communities depicted in the New Testament.

The Puritan cause was in favor in the latter years of the reign of Elizabeth I, as the tensions between England and Catholic Spain were at their height. Upon the ascension of James I to the throne, however, their fortunes shifted because the new king sided with the more moderate Anglican bishops against those who advocated for a more thoroughgoing reformation. Nonetheless, the Puritans were tolerated in Jacobean England, and many saw themselves as a Calvinistic reform movement within Anglicanism rather than as "separatists" who believed the English Church was beyond redemption.

The situation of the Puritans turned for the worse in 1625 when James's son ascended the throne. Charles I had taken a Catholic wife and (not surprisingly) had little tolerance for radical Protestant sensibilities. Moreover, William Laud, bishop of London and later the Archbishop of Canterbury, saw the Puritans as a threat to the unity and orthodoxy of the Anglican Communion. He cooperated closely with Charles I in attempting to curb what both viewed as the excessive rigidity of the movement. To implement his anti-Puritan measures, Charles I relied on the Star Chamber and the Court of High Commission (the highest ecclesiastical court in England). Both were under his direct control rather than under the control of Parliament. The perception of tyrannical abuses of the historical rights of Englishmen on the part of the king prompted the Puritans to ally themselves with the Parliamentarians against the Royalists in the English Civil Wars.

As their hopes of political and religious reform were dashed after Parliament was adjourned by Charles I in March 1629, and with no hope of it soon being called back into session, some of the more committed Puritans lost hope that England would soon reform and prompted the decision to band together to seek a fresh start in America.[7] John Winthrop, a wealthy

---

6. Morgan, *Visible Saints*, 5–6.

7. For an account of the intellectual underpinnings of American Puritanism, see Miller, *From Colony to Province* and *The Seventeenth Century*. No one can deny the towering contributions of Perry Miller to our understanding of American Puritanism. Miller focused largely on intellectual history,

lawyer from a merchant family, was the leader of one such band. He wrote to his wife about the English political situation: "The Lord hath admonished, threatened, corrected, and astonished us, yet we growe worse and worse, so as his spirit will not allwayes strive with us, he must needs give waye to his furye at last. . . . My deare wife I am veryly perswaded, God will bringe some heavye Affliction upon this lande, and that speedyle."[8]

The Puritans who built New England did not initially see themselves as forging such a destiny independent of their mother country. Their purpose was to engage in a strategic retreat from England's corruptions in order to provide a shining example of a purer way of organizing a Christian polity. In his farewell sermon to the Winthrop Fleet, John Cotton took as his text 2 Sam. 7.10, "Moreover I will appoint a place for my People Israel, and I will PLANT them, that they may dwell in a place of their OWN, and MOVE NO MORE."[9] After methodically outlining the justification for the migration, Cotton went on to outline salutary action guides for the new colony, including a plea that they *"Be not unmindful of our* Jerusalem *at home,* whither you leave us, or stay at home with us."[10]

A few hundred English émigrés had settled in New England during the . 1620s. Their population increased substantially from 1630 to 1640, the years of the Great Migration. During this period, approximately twenty thousand settlers, most of them Puritans, moved from England to the Massachusetts Bay Colony, which had the distinction of being the only English colony permitted to take its charter with it to the New World rather than being forced to leave it in London, where it could be more easily revoked. Under the leadership of John Winthrop, its first governor, Massachusetts set up its system of elected

---

however, not social and political history. One could read his work and mistakenly conclude that Puritan society can be exhaustively understood by examining the elaborate doctrines set forth by its most religiously committed intellectual leaders. Important correctives can be found in the works that vividly depict the various currents in early American religious life, such as David D. Hall's *Worlds of Wonder, Days of Judgment: Popular Religious Belief in Early New England* (Cambridge, MA: Harvard University Press, 1989) and Jon Butler's *Awash in a Sea of Faith: Christianizing the American People* (Cambridge, MA: Harvard University Press, 1990). For an account of the significant religious pluralism in that era, see Butler's *New World Faiths: Religion in Colonial America* (New York: Oxford University Press, 2000).

8. John Winthrop, *Winthrop Papers 1498–1649*, ed. Allyn B. Forbes et al. (Boston, MA, 1929–1947), 2:74–75, 91, 92, 96, cited in Foster, *The Long Argument*, 109. See also Edmund S. Morgan, *The Puritan Dilemma: The Story of John Winthrop*, 3rd ed. (New York: Pearson/Longman, 2007).

9. John Cotton, *God's Promise to His Plantations. . . .* (London, 1634), cover.

10. Ibid., 18.

representative government and congregational churches, with one eye fixed firmly upon those they had left behind in England. The New England Puritans were initially convinced that the purpose of their "errand into the wilderness" was to model a successful English Christian Protestant society that would prompt replication in their home country and Europe more generally. That understanding of their purpose became sharper and more acute during the early years of the Protectorate established by Oliver Cromwell after the execution of King Charles I,[11] when it appeared that Puritanism and Parliamentarianism were on the cusp of reforming and reorganizing society along the lines long advocated by Puritans.[12]

More specifically, the New England Puritans hoped that their model of congregationalism would be adopted in their native country because it fused "purity and power" by combining a congregationalist church structure with a civil government that maintained order and suppressed heterodox beliefs.[13] Tensions soon arose, however, as the Protectorate, in order to achieve and maintain political control, showed itself willing to extend religious toleration to religious groups that the New England Puritans believed to be of unsound doctrine or practice. The Americans were adamant that such toleration could not be permitted. It was nothing short of a danger to the salvation of souls and the proper ordering of the community. By contrast, their counterparts in England thought the rigidity of the Americans would be politically disastrous.[14] By this time the Anglican reform movement in England

11. After the overthrow of the English monarchy and the beheading of Charles I in 1649, England was declared to be a commonwealth by parliamentary declaration. In 1653, Oliver Cromwell disbanded Parliament and was declared Lord Protector of England. The protectorate lasted from 1653 to 1659. After Oliver Cromwell's death in 1658, he was succeeded for a short time as Lord Protector by his son, Richard Cromwell.

12. For a recent account that takes the religious dimension of the conflict very seriously, see Michael Braddick, God's Fury, England's Fire: A New History of the English Civil Wars (London: Allen Lane, 2008).

13. Harry S. Stout, The New England Soul: Preaching and Religious Culture in Colonial New England (New York: Oxford University Press, 1986), 52–53.

14. "The most humiliating element in the experience was the way the English brethren turned upon the colonials for precisely their greatest achievement. It must have seemed, for those who came with Winthrop in 1630 and who remembered the clarity and brilliance with which he set forth the conditions of their errand, that the world was turned upside down and inside out when, in June 1645, thirteen leading Independent divines—such men as Goodwin, Owen, Nye, Burroughs, formerly friends and allies of Hooker and Davenport, men who might easily have come to New England and helped extirpate heretics—wrote the General Court that the colony's law banishing Anabaptists was

had split into hopeless divisions between Presbyterians, Independents, and various other sects. The English reformers were incapable of appreciating and implementing the model that the New England Way had so vividly offered to them.

The failures of the Protectorate, however, were not the worst disappointment that New England had to endure. After the Restoration in 1660,[15] New England's hopes of attracting the attention and admiration of Protestant Christendom were thoroughly dashed. As Perry Miller observed, the Puritan errand into the wilderness of the New World could no longer be construed as a task given to fulfill the objectives of their English religious brethren. The project had to be understood and defended on its own terms. "Having failed to rivet the eyes of the world upon their city on the hill, they were left alone with America."[16] Left to their own devices by their mother country, the American Puritans turned to the task of working out their identity as the New Israel on their own.

The Puritans were not left alone quite as much as they would have liked to have been. The political challenges they faced after the Restoration were considerable. On the one hand, they needed to manifest their loyalty to the Crown, openness to mainstream Anglicanism, and tolerance of Independents. On the other hand, they were committed to preserving the political and religious power of the Puritan Congregationalists in their new land.[17]

In 1662, King Charles II wrote a letter to the colony, confirming their charter but demanding that all persons of honest lives be admitted to the Lord's Supper and that independent freeholders be admitted to citizenship, whether or not they were Puritans. A royal commission sent to New England

---

an embarrassment to the Independent cause in England." Perry Miller, *Errand into the Wilderness* (Cambridge, MA: Belknap Press of Harvard University Press, 1956), 13–14.

15. The Restoration of the English monarchy after the end of the Protectorate began when Charles II, the son of Charles I, assumed the throne in 1660.

16. Miller, *Errand into the Wilderness*, 15.

17. See, for example, John Norton's election sermon preached in 1661, the year following the beginning of the Restoration, "SION the Out-cast healed of her Wounds," in John Norton, *Three Choice and Profitable Sermons . . .* (Boston, MA, 1664), 1–15. "God make us more wise and religious then so to carry it, that they should no sooner see a Congregational-man, then to have cause to say, *They see an Enemy to the Crown.* Prov.24.21. . . . In matters of the State-Civil, and of the Church, let it be shewn that we are his Disciples who (*Matth.*22.21.) said, *Give unto Cesar the things that are Cesars, and unto God the things that are Gods:* and in matters of Religion, let it be known that we are for Reformation, and not for Separation." Ibid., 12. More generally, see Miller, *From Colony to Province*, chap. 9 ("Intolerance"), 119–29.

to investigate the situation found that the efforts made by the colony to comply with the king's command were superficial and deceptive. When confronted with their obvious deficiencies, the Massachusetts General Court said that they had complied with the command "'as farr as doth consist with conscience of our duty toward God, and the just liberties and priviledges' of the charter."[18] The incompetence of the Crown's government allowed the colony to evade and ignore the new policies on toleration for many years.

During the three decades following the time of the Restoration, the diverging perspectives and interests between England and the increasingly prosperous New England became apparent on a wide range of issues, including but not limited to religious matters. The second and third generation of colonists, in particular, did not shape their identity or interests with reference to the country of origin of their parents and grandparents. As a result of tensions over matters of trade and tariffs, the Chancery Court voided the charter of Massachusetts Bay Colony in October 1684, acting on the advice of the colonial agent of the Lords of Trade, Edward Randolph. At first the colony was not overly disturbed because New England native Joseph Dudley was appointed to rule. In 1686, however, Sir Edmund Andros arrived with a warrant making him governor of the Dominion of New England. While sorely trying for the New England Puritans, the dominion was mercifully short-lived. In 1668, William of Orange landed in England and recaptured the throne for Protestantism. When this news reached Massachusetts in April 1869, the colonists revolted. Andros, Dudley, and Randolph were arrested and eventually sent back to England by order of the new king.

This Glorious Revolution, which firmly returned England to Protestant rule, obviated tensions as the Puritans communicated their enthusiastic support for King William and Queen Mary, in part by aiding in the war effort against Catholic French Canada. Thanks in large part to Increase Mather, who crossed the Atlantic to engage in patient negotiations with representatives of the monarchy, a new charter was granted to the colony by William and Mary in 1691 under the name of the Province of Massachusetts Bay in New England.[19] While the autonomy conferred was generous, it was not unlimited. In particular, it required the colonists to extend religious toleration

18. Miller, *From Colony to Province,* 126–27. See also Bremer, *The Puritan Experiment,* 148–53.

19. Yale Law School, Lillian Goldman Law Library, The Avalon Project, The Charter of Massachusetts Bay–1691, http://avalon.law.yale.edu/17th_century/mass07.asp.

"to all Christians (Except Papists)." Unlike the original charter, which tied the right to vote to church membership, the new charter tied it to property ownership. In addition, under the new charter, the citizens did not elect their own governor, but he (along with his deputy) was appointed by the king. Technically speaking, the revocation of the first charter marked the decisive end of the Puritan theocracy, although the social and political influence of Congregationalist Puritans on New England politics and society would not diminish for decades.

Harry Stout has perceptively summarized the concerns of the American Puritans in terms of the motifs of purity, power, and liberty. They wanted to build and maintain churches that reflected the original pattern of the Gospels, untainted by impure, "Romish" additions or inventions. They intended to create a godly society embodying the principles of divine law undergirded by a political structure able and willing to exercise the coercive power of government toward that end. To achieve these goals, the Puritans needed liberty—not individual license, but *Christian* liberty—the freedom to build their individual, family, and social lives in accordance with Gospel truth.[20] All three motifs were worked out in a close but complicated relationship with their mother country.

The Covenantal Framework

The Puritan jeremiad is a form of rhetoric that is at once both thoroughly religious and thoroughly political. It is also historically and culturally embedded. Produced by the particular group of people whose beginnings were chronicled in the foregoing paragraphs, Puritan preachers used the jeremiad to reflect on their crises, opportunities, and challenges in the New World. They did so by embedding the key events of their times within the overarching framework that they used to make sense of themselves and the cosmos. That framework was thoroughly biblical.

The jeremiad is modeled largely on one strand of the prophetic literature in the Hebrew Bible, the Christian Old Testament——the strand of prophetic indictment. As many form-critical biblical scholars, such as Claus Westermann, have argued, many of the scathing denunciations of Jeremiah, Hosea, and

20. Stout, *The New England Soul*, 13–15.

Isaiah are frequently set forth in quasi-legal form; their content resembles a lawyer's complaint charging a party with breach of a legally binding agreement.[21] Yahweh entered into a covenant with the Jews; He promised to be their God and they promised to be His people. The prophets call attention to the ways in which the people of Israel and then Judah failed to abide by the terms of that covenant. The two most egregious breaches were their practice of idolatry—that is, failing to recognize that Yahweh alone is their God (the particular focus of the Book of Hosea) and utter disregard of the poor, the weak, and the marginalized (a prominent concern in the Book of Isaiah).

Puritan preachers adopted and adapted this form of rhetoric in order to decry the sins of their own community. Why did they do so? To answer this question, it is necessary to delve into the Puritan understanding of their relationship to God, their social and political relationship to one another, and their relationship with ancient Israel in the context of salvation history. The central concept for understanding the political, social, and religious goals of the Puritans is the concept of the covenant—a solemn, legally binding agreement—which is both deeply theological and deeply legal. It had strong underpinnings not only in biblical history but also in early modern English society, particularly the segment of society from which most Puritans were drawn. More specifically, the notion of covenant was of increasingly great importance in the developing tradition of English common law as it emerged from the medieval framework into the context of modern trade and mercantilism. It was unique in its capacity to accommodate a negotiated relationship between vastly unequal parties that could be relied on and enforced by each.

---

21. Claus Westermann, *Basic Forms of Prophetic Speech*, trans. Hugh Clayton White (Cambridge, UK: Lutterworth Press, and Louisville, KY: Westminster John Knox Press, 1991). Gene M. Tucker's foreword to the book helpfully reminds us that Westermann's work has not been entirely uncontroversial and should not be taken as an exhaustive account of all prophetic texts. Westermann was not the first to propose this idea of a covenant lawsuit. Other scholars, most notably Hugo Gressmann and Hermann Gunkel, worked on this topic before him. See Delbert R. Hillers, *Covenant: The History of a Biblical Idea* (Baltimore, MD: Johns Hopkins Press, 1969), 120–42. Furthermore, there is a dispute among biblical scholars about the degree to which this idea of covenant lawsuit can be found in biblical books written before the eighth century, especially in Deuteronomy. For a brief account, see Ernest C. Lucas, "Covenant, Treaty, and Prophecy," *Themelios* 8, no. 1 (1982): 19–23. For a helpful introduction to relevant critical scholarship, see Norman K. Gottwald, *The Hebrew Bible: A Socio-Literary Introduction* (Philadelphia, PA: Fortress Press, 1985). See also Joseph Blenkinsopp, *A History of Prophecy in Israel*, rev. ed. (Louisville, KY: Westminster John Knox Press, 1996); for a more sociological perspective, see Robert W. Wilson, *Prophecy and Society in Ancient Israel* (Philadelphia, PA: Fortress Press, 1980).

For Puritan theologians, this aspect of the covenantal structure was not only desirable, it was essential. The central relationship that the Puritans were concerned about negotiating was their relationship to God, a God who was infinite, omnipotent, and ultimately inscrutable.

To understand the Puritans' commitment to covenant theology and political theory, then, it is necessary to begin with their operative conception of God, which was deeply rooted in the Calvinist tradition. Christian theologians have long warned against identifying any of God's "attributes" too closely with God as He is in Himself, rather than as how human beings understand Him. Christians in the Calvinist tradition, however, were particularly concerned to protect God's absolute simplicity and unknowability. God is not to be manipulated by human beings for their own purposes; rather, human beings are obediently to play the role that they have been assigned in the divine plan, even if they are not fully cognizant of that role. As Perry Miller writes, in the minds and hearts of those with Calvinist sensibilities, "[t]he world is not governed by reason, or power, or love, but by 'I am,' who is a jealous God and wreaks vengeance upon those who idolize His titles instead of worshiping Himself."[22]

How, then, is one to describe or identify God? Puritan theologians steadfastly recognized that all theological descriptions of God were ultimately fragile and fallible human constructions. In addition, they placed much emphasis on absolute divine sovereignty and providence. For them, that emphasis meant affirming a thoroughgoing divine control over each and every event in the cosmos. In the natural realm, every event, down to every last microscopic detail, is positively willed by God to occur. In the spiritual realm, God has determined from all eternity not only who will be born, and when they will die, but also whether they will be saved or damned.

The terrifying doctrine of double predestination—of God's eternal decision to send each person to either salvation or damnation—was emphasized by John Calvin, who firmly resisted all attempts to understand, to control, or even to tame it.[23] After the fervor of the first generation of reform faded,

---

22. Miller, *The Seventeenth Century*, 13.

23. "When it is inquired, therefore, why the Lord did so, the answer must be, Because he would. But if you go further, and ask why he so determined, you are in search of something greater and higher than the will of God , which can never be found. Let human temerity, therefore, desist from seeking that which is not, lest it should fail of finding that which is." John Calvin, *Institutes of the*

however, believers in the Reformed tradition needed more predictability, and greater confidence in their ultimate fate, if they were to dedicate themselves to building Protestant communities. How to get that certainty? How to reconcile a divine, mysterious, transcendent, and sovereign God whose arbitrary ways were beyond human comprehension with the predictability in the natural and spiritual realms that human beings needed in order for their communities to grow and flourish? In the second generation, these questions were made particularly pressing by the need for orthodox Protestants to respond on the one hand to antinomians, who argued that, if God's gift of saving grace was arbitrary, living a moral life was either futile or redundant, or on the other hand to Arminians, who encroached upon God's sovereignty in order to make human free will and the choice to live an upright life count in the economy of salvation.

The idea of the covenant provided an ingenious way to provide for cosmic predictability, affirm the necessity of morality, and protect the overriding sovereignty of God. The so-called federal theologians modeled their notion of covenant roughly on the developing common law of contracts. Despite inequalities in all other realms, in the realm of bargained-for-exchange, the prince and the pauper could meet as equals. According to the developing common law, the will of a sovereign, which could not be legitimately limited by any external force, could be legitimately limited by itself. A king is able to enter into a valid, binding agreement with one of his subjects. By analogical extension, an unknowable, omnipotent, and essentially unpredictable deity may validly contract an agreement with one of his creatures. God's omnipotent will can be validly bound only by God's own free consent— but it can be so bound. The framework of the covenant, then, furnished a "scheme including both God and man within a single frame, a point at which, without doing violence to their respective natures, both could meet and converse."[24]

According to federal theologians—the Latin *foedus* means "pact"—God has consistently dealt with His human creatures within the framework of a covenant—or more precisely, a series of covenants. In the first covenant, the

Christian Religion, 2 vols., trans. John Allen (Philadelphia, PA: Presbyterian Board of Christian Education, 1936), 2:201 (bk. III, chap. 23, sec. 2).

24. Miller, *The Seventeenth Century,* 378. See also R. T. Kendall, *Calvin and English Calvinism to 1649* (Oxford: Oxford University Press, 1979).

covenant of works, God promised Adam and his descendants that He would grant them eternal life if they would obey the natural moral law whose terms were written on their heart. But Adam and Eve disobeyed, meriting the penalties described in the book of Genesis. God, however, did not give up on His creatures. Instead, beginning with Abraham, He instituted a new covenant, the Covenant of Grace, in which the obligation of human beings consists in faith. Ever merciful, God Himself supplied the irresistible grace that allowed the elect to believe in salvation.

While in some respects superseded, the covenant of works was not simply abrogated. That covenant was kept by God Himself on behalf of humanity in the person and work of Jesus Christ. This arrangement, some theologians said, was worked out within the Godhead as part of the covenant of redemption, when the second person of the Holy Trinity agreed to assume human form in order to save humanity from its sins. Moreover, the terms of the covenant of works emerged again as marking the shape of a regenerate life, situated within and supported by the covenant of grace. Having experienced God's gratuitous mercy, the elect were expected to live lives of moral righteousness, not in order to gain salvation but in grateful obedience for having already received eternal life as a free gift. From an external point of view, what mattered in the moral life was not the success but the striving for success. Belief and a good-faith effort to become progressively sanctified were reliable indications of one's status as a member of the elect.

So the idea of the covenant allowed the English Protestant theological heirs of John Calvin to be true to their theological heritage while responding to the contemporary needs of their congregations.[25] God's sovereignty was protected by the federal theologians' claim that He had voluntarily entered

---

25. See Miller, *The Seventeenth Century*, Book IV ("Sociology") for an explication of the interlocking covenants. Key figures in the development of English covenant theology include William Ames, William Perkins, and John Preston. See William Ames, *The Marrow of Sacred Divinity. . . . ,* bound with *Conscience with the Power and Cases Thereof. . . .* (London, 1639). For Perkins, see passages in his *The Workes of that Famous and Worthy Minister of Christ in the Universitie of Cambridge, M. William Perkins,* 2nd ed., 3 vols. (London, 1631). Preston's most important contribution is *The New Covenant, or the Saints Portion. . . .* (London, 1629). I do not mean to say that covenant theology was the exclusive providence of English-speaking theologians. That is most certainly not the case. David A. Weir's *The Origins of the Federal Theology in Sixteenth-Century Reformation Thought* (Oxford: Clarendon Press, 1990) provides detail about the technical developments in federal theology throughout Europe, and a valuable bibliography, although aspects of his account have been called into question by scholars such as Lyle Bierma and Richard Muller.

into this pact. God's essential unknowability was safeguarded by their insistence that the covenant did not describe God's internal life but only His freely chosen pattern of behavior toward humanity. The congregation's need for reliability and predictability was met by the clear and reliable terms of the divine–human relationship set forth in the covenant.

More specifically, the covenantal structure allowed Puritan preachers to minimize believers' fears of the whims of an arbitrary and inscrutable God while also inculcating the necessity of moral rectitude. Entirely free to do as He pleases, God nonetheless usually chooses to use secondary causes to bring about desired effects, in both the natural and supernatural realms. Normally, then, God chooses to save the elect by situating them within and giving them the benefit of established church structures, particularly preaching and the sacraments. Consequently, those who had the benefit of sound, persuasive preaching of the covenant and exhortation to a godly life could blame only themselves if they turned away from the bounty offered them. Conversely, those who profit from their preachers' efforts and who struggle to grow in piety and morality can rely confidently on the ironclad terms of the covenant.

While covenant theology was developed in theoretical form by English Puritans, it was enthusiastically and pervasively applied and subtly developed by their counterparts in America. Creating a new society from scratch, they had the opportunity to organize all facets of their ecclesiastical, social, and political life in accordance with the covenantal model. As David Weir shows, the early settlers of the New World saw the covenantal framework as a valuable tool for structuring the prosaic concerns of their mortal lives, not merely the terms of the salvation of their immortal souls.[26] Unlike their Old World counterparts, they were not faced, at least in their early years, with the pragmatic necessity of accommodating and compromising with Reformed Protestants, such as Presbyterians, who advocated competing models of church polity.

Consequently, American Puritans freely implemented their conviction that the ideal church structure is the congregational model exemplified in the New Testament itself.[27] According to this model, a group of the elect enter

---

26. David A. Weir, *Early New England: A Covenanted Society* (Grand Rapids, MI: Eerdmans, 2005).

27. The classic statement of American Puritan church polity can be found in *The Cambridge Platform* (1648). Sixty years later, Connecticut Puritans adopted a model that incorporated more elements of Presbyterianism and thereby gave less autonomy to individual congregations and more

into a church covenant that sets forth their rights and obligations to one another before God. Membership in a congregation was not automatic; it was to be limited to the "visible saints," those who, when subjected to reasonable and charitable assessment, satisfied one another that they were numbered among the elect. Membership in a church was not strictly required for salvation. Nonetheless, the Puritans maintained that, in the ordinary course of things, an individual's membership in the covenant of grace should lead him or her to welcome membership in a church congregation.[28] Membership had responsibilities as well as rights; one was not free to leave and join another congregation merely because it suited one's fancy. Because God ordinarily worked through secondary causes, membership in a church was a most fitting way to activate the stirring of grace in the hearts of one's own children, who needed to proffer their own experience of conversion in order to become full members of the church.

The covenant provided a model not only for ecclesiastical life but for political life as well. By the time the Puritans set sail for New England in 1630, they had available to them a well-articulated, contract-based model of government, articulated in the writings of the "judicious" Anglican divine Richard Hooker and others, that would later provide a source for John Locke's theory of government.[29] According to this model of the "social covenant," magistrates entered into a contract with the people that set forth their respective rights and duties; consequently, a magistrate could be justly deposed from office if he

---

power to "associations" of clergymen and "consociations" of area churches. Both approaches have been reproduced in paperback form. See *The Cambridge and Saybrook Platforms of Church Discipline . . .* (Boston, MA, 1829).

28. "All believers ought, as God giveth them opportunity thereunto, to endeavor to join themselves unto a particular church, and that in respect of the honor of Jesus Christ, in his example and institution, by the professed acknowledgment of, and subjection unto the order and ordinances of the gospel . . ." *The Cambridge Platform,* chap. IV, sec. 6. That passage is found on page 34 of *The Cambridge and Saybrook Platforms of Church Discipline.* Ibid., p. 34.

29. Richard Hooker, *Of the Laws of Ecclesiastical Polity,* ed. Arthur Stephen McGrade (Cambridge: Cambridge University Press, 1989). Scholars have debated the degree to which Hooker (d. 1600) can rightly be seen as a "mediating" figure between high-church Anglicanism and Puritanism. Some have argued that the *Of the Laws* must be interpreted in historical context and thus seen as a polemical tract justifying Tudor-style Anglicanism. See, for example, W. D. J. Cargill Thompson, *Studies in the Reformation: Luther to Hooker,* ed. C. W. Dugmore (London: Athlone Press, 1980). Moreover, others have questioned the degree to which Hooker's thought is rightly seen as an influential precursor to the contract theory of Locke and Hobbes. For a helpful attempt to situate Hooker's political thought in theological context, see. W. J. Torrance Kirby, *Richard Hooker's Doctrine of the Royal Supremacy* (Leiden: Brill, 1990).

failed to keep to the terms of the contract. Following this model in the first code of law of the Massachusetts Bay Colony, the Puritans took pains to specify the rights of Englishmen and to safeguard themselves from the abuses of tyrannical government. The contract metaphor allowed the Puritans not only to protect certain rights against tyrants but also to justify subordinating individuals to the collective will, provided that the state was properly designed, instituted, and managed to promote the common good.

According to the Puritans, government originated from God's will, corresponding to divinely created human nature, as well as engaging human consent. It functioned to restrain sin as well as to encourage Christians to live in a godly way. One entered into the compact freely, but one could no more negotiate its terms than one could the terms of the compact between husband and wife. The liberty guaranteed was the liberty to do right—to live in a regenerate way—not to do wrong. As Miller writes, "A Puritan state would give adequate liberty to its citizens if, after insuring the obvious rights of trial by jury and habeas corpus, it guaranteed them the ordinances of Christ, the means of conversion, faithful preaching and the sacraments. Civil law should be not so much a protection of subject' rights as an instrument by which the state defines their social duties and directs the exercise of their liberty."[30] Accordingly, Puritan preachers emphasized both the duty to obey lawful authority and the right to resist tyrants according to the terms of the political covenant.[31]

The Puritans saw a just government not only as the proper embodiment of the collective will of the citizens but also as something divinely willed. Consequently, they maintained that those who found themselves within the covenant of grace would also find themselves rightly drawn to submit themselves in obedience to a properly governed state. This positive attitude toward government was greatly intensified with respect to their own polity, however, because of the particular function that they saw it playing within the great cosmic drama of salvation history. Deeply identifying New England with ancient Israel, the Puritans saw their own nation as in a covenant with God that was modeled on the covenant God had compacted in ancient times with the Jewish people.

30. Miller, *The Seventeenth Century,* 425.
31. Ibid., 410–11.

The framework organizing the political and social life of Massachusetts Bay Colony was impressed upon the settlers even before they set foot on their new homeland in 1630. The first governor of the colony, John Winthrop, gave a speech to his little band aboard the *Arbella,* as it made its way across the Atlantic, titled "A Modell of Christian Charity." Styling himself a new Moses, he sketched their future life together in explicitly covenantal terms:

> Thus stands the cause betweene God and us. We are entered into Covenant with Him for this worke. Wee haue taken out a commission. The Lord hath given us leave to drawe our own articles. Wee haue professed to enterprise these and those accounts, upon these and those ends. Wee have hereupon besought Him of favour and blessing. Now if the Lord shall please to heare us, and bring us in peace to the place we desire, then hath hee ratified this covenant and sealed our Commission, and will expect a strict performance of the articles contained in it; but if wee shall neglect the observation of these articles which are the ends wee have propounded, and, dissembling with our God, shall fall to embrace this present world and prosecute our carnall intentions, seeking greate things for ourselves and our posterity, the Lord will surely breake out in wrathe against us; be revenged of such a [sinful] people and make us knowe the price of the breache of such a covenant.[32]

Rather than saying that their political covenant with God was modeled on that of the Jews, we should say that, in the Puritan view, the covenant between God and the Jewish people foreshadowed and anticipated the covenant between God and New England. Prophecy (understood here in the sense of prediction) and history were intimately related for the Puritans. As Nicholas Noyes said in his 1698 election sermon, *"Prophesie* is History *antedated;* and History is *Postdated Prophesie:* the same thing is told in both."[33] In the view of the American Puritan divines, all of human history led to Boston. As Miller writes, "The Puritan scholar studied all history, heathen or Christian, as an exhibition of divine wisdom, and found in the temporal unfolding of the

32. John Winthrop, "A Modell of Christian Charity" (1630), *Collections of the Massachusetts Historical Society,* 3rd ser., vol. 7 (Boston, MA, 1838), 31–48 at 46. See also Edmund S. Morgan, "John Winthrop's 'Modell of Christian Charity' in a Wider Context," *Huntington Library Quarterly* 50, no. 2 (1987): 145–51.

33. Nicholas Noyes, *New-Englands Duty and Interest . . .* (Boston, MA, 1698), 43.

divine plan that the entire past had been but a sort of prologue to the enact-ment of the New England commonwealths."[34]

For American federal theologians, the covenant of grace was exactly the same for Abraham as it was for them, with one difference. The ancient Jews were required to believe that Christ would come and redeem them, while Christians were charged with proclaiming the fact that he had come and redemption had been accomplished. At the same time, their elaborate "typo-logical" theory of biblical interpretation allowed them to scrutinize the his-tory for insight into their own obligations and destiny. Just as Moses was a "type" of Christ, so Israel and Judah were "types" of New England. In typo-logical readings, it is not simply that the Old Testament serves as a model for later imitation. It is rather that Old Testament "types" are models whose pur-pose and ultimate meaning are intelligible only in the light of their New Testament "antitypes."[35] For all their admiration of Israel and its prophets, the Puritans were clearly Christian supercessionists.

This typological reading of the relationship between Israel and New England shaped the Puritan religious and political consciousness for decades. So in *New-England Pleaded with*, a sermon given before the Massachusetts General Court in 1673, Urian Oakes explicitly invites his audience to consider the moral health of their polity by a series of close parallels between their situation and that of ancient Israel.[36] He writes, for example, "As the words of my Text respect the *Body of a Nation*, even *Israel*, that were sometimes the peculiar people of God: So give me leave to direct my *Exhortation* to the People of *New-England*, or the *Representative Body of the People of this Colony*, and to perswade the *New-England-Israel* to get and improve this Spiritual wisdome, *Understandingly and judiciously to consider what will be the latter End of your sinful wayes, and unworthy deportments before the Lord*."[37] Oakes tells his listeners, just as God gave Canaan to the Children of Israel, "[t]his *Wilderness* was the place which God decreed to make a *Canaan* to you."[38] He reminds them with respect to their civil government, "[y]ou have had Moses, Men, I

34. Miller, *The Seventeenth Century*, 463.

35. For a good example of a debate drawing upon this sort of typology, see, for example, the debate between Roger Williams and John Cotton: Roger Williams, *The Bloudy Tenent of Persecution* . . . (London, 1644); John Cotton, *The Bloudy Tenent, Washed* . . . (London, 1647); and Roger Williams, *The Bloudy Tenent Yet More Bloody* (London, 1652).

36. Urian Oakes, *New-England Pleaded with* . . . (Cambridge, MA, 1673).

37. Ibid., 17.

38. Ibid.

mean, of the same spirit, *to lead and go before you.*"[39] Oakes reminds his audience: "God hath instructed us, as he did *Israel* in the Wilderness."[40] He notes that "all that have attempted to devour you have offended, *and evil hath come upon them:* just as it was with the Adversaries of *Israel,* Jer. 2.3. God hath scattered his favors, and dealt out his blessings with a liberal hand to you."[41]

Thus when the Puritans landed on the shores of Massachusetts in 1630, they saw themselves as in the same position that Israel had been in before God. Like the Jews, they were also God's chosen national covenant partner. Yet the Puritans believed that thanks to Christ, they had greater spiritual resources (to fulfill the obligations of that position than ancient Israel had possessed. History tells us that both before and after the birth of Christ, most nations have experienced a waxing and waning of their power. Most cultures passed through periods of reform and flourishing followed by periods of moral decline and decay. The Puritans hoped, however, that God had chosen their religious and political endeavor to be an exception to this cyclical pattern of history. With the benefits given by the grace of Christ, assured through a covenantal relationship, they aspired to be a shining exception to the law of social growth and decline. Oakes nicely articulates the hope for the colony:

> And indeed, if we cast up the Accompt, and Summe up all our mercies, and lay all things together, this our Common-wealth seems to exhibit to us a *specimen,* or a *little model of the Kingdome of Christ upon Earth,* not in the wild sense of those that are called *Pift-monarchy men,* but in the sober sense of many of our Divines, wherein it is generally acknowledged and expected. This work of God set on foot and advanced to a good Degree here, being spread over the face of the Earth, and perfected as to greater Degrees of Light and Grace and Gospel glory will be (as I conceive) *the Kingdome of Iesus Christ so much spoken of.*[42]

---

39. Ibid.

40. Ibid., 20.

41. Ibid.

42. Ibid., 21. In the typescript of the time, "Pift" looks like "Pist" or "Pissed"; perhaps this was Oakes's derogatory commentary on the "wild" movement.

Why would God, in His infinite wisdom, pluck little New England from obscurity for such an unparalleled blessing? According to Puritan theologians, Christianity had been in decline since the time of Constantine, oppressed by corrupt popes and emperors. The Reformation had begun the process of restoring its theology and worship to its pristine form but, according to the Puritans, had failed to reestablish church polity in accordance with the model set forth in the New Testament. For various reasons, Switzerland, Holland, and England were incapable of reforming church structure in the congregationalist model that the Puritans believed to be divinely ordained. Without a shining model of that structure for all to follow and emulate, the Reformation would be fatally stalled in its progress through Christendom. As they settled their corner of the New World in the 1630s, the New Englanders were acutely conscious of their role in history. Echoing the words John Winthrop spoke to the pioneers aboard the *Arbella* years earlier, Peter Bulkeley admonished his fellow citizens:

> [L]abour to shine forth in holinesse above other people; . . . wee are as a City set upon a hill, in the open view of all the earth, the eyes of the world are upon us, because we professe our selves to be a people in Covenant with God, and therefore not onely the Lord our God, with whom we have made Covenant, but heaven and earth, Angels and men, that are witnesses of our profession, will cry shame upon us, if wee walke contrary to the Covenant which wee have professed and promised to walk in.[43]

According to the vision articulated by its founders, New England was destined to model the divine plan for both church and state by nurturing a flourishing set of congregational churches nested within a godly polity that took seriously its obligations to help its citizens experience grace and live according to divine law. As Winthrop said on the *Arbella*, "It is by a mutuall consent, through a speciall overvaluing providence and a more than an ordinary approbation of the Churches of Christ, to seeke out a place of cohabitation and Consorteshipp under a due forme of Government both ciuill and ecclesiasticall."[44] While the

43. Peter Bulkeley, *The Gospel-Covenant* . . . , 2nd ed. (London, 1651), 431. The first edition was published in 1646.
44. Winthrop, "A Modell of Christian Charity," 45.

Puritans recognized that the purposes of the church and the state were distinct, they also saw them as highly coordinated. A major purpose of the state was to protect and promote the congregational polity, while a key function of the church was to shape citizens of the requisite moral character, as well as to safeguard against the myriad ways in which their polity might fall short of its obligations to God under the covenant.

While the covenant of grace was an all-or-nothing relationship with God, the national covenant admitted of degrees of fulfillment. Individuals were predestined from all eternity to either salvation or damnation. The good or evil in their actions did not change this fate; at best it merely revealed it to others and to the individuals themselves. In contrast, the status of the political community's relationship with God in the national covenant was not so binary but instead was subjected to more nuanced assessment. That relationship could also be improved by pursuing virtue and avoiding vice. As good Calvinists, the Puritans insisted that no amount of good works could merit eternal life for an individual. The national covenant, however, dealt with well-being in this world, not the next. The Puritan preachers believed that God would precisely correlate the temporal prosperity of the new land to the degree to which its inhabitants kept His commandments.[45]

On the one hand, God held New England to a higher standard. "God is more offended with the miscarriages of such as He hath brought nearer to Himself than with others: It is in God's account an aggravation of sin."[46] On the other hand, God is patient and long-suffering with His covenant partner, choosing not to treat many serious transgressions as a total breach of the agreement. Instead, He treats them as an opportunity for improvement. Up to a certain point, God inflicts temporal suffering in almost a medicinal way so that the nation will be shocked into repudiation of its unhealthy way of life. At the same time, God's patience, while expansive, is not infinite. As the example of the Jewish people demonstrated, God would indeed terminate the covenant based on His covenant partner's egregious pattern of infidelity.

45. Harry Stout helpfully observes that the 1636 controversy in which Anne Hutchinson accused the New England preachers of advocating a covenant of works rather than a covenant of grace can be understood as exposing "latent tensions between the sermon as a proclamation of God's free grace and the sermon as an instrument of social direction." Stout, *The New England Soul*, 24. Peter Bulkeley attempted to reconcile the freedom of the covenant of grace with the need for coercion and good works in the national covenant in *The Gospel-Covenant*.

46. William Adams, *God's Eye on the Contrite* . . . (Boston, MA, 1685), 12.

In his 1668 Election Day sermon, William Stoughton summarizes the relationship between God and his Chosen People in the New World:

> When the Lord enters into Covenant with any people, this Covenant of his is a Covenant with Conditions. Foedus est prommisso sub certa conditione. Hence there are the Laws, as well as the Promises of the Covenant. As the Lord obligeth himself to us, so he requires something from us, and thus the Commandments & Statutes of God are frequently called his Covenant, Exod.34.28. Deut.4.13. The Lord doth not binde himself but upon terms to any people. In the purely spiritual Covenant, establish'd with Believers only, as there are the Laws of it, 1 Cor 9.21 so there is a sufficiency of grace provided, and absolutely engaged, that there may be a performance and obedience unto the end, and so that the Covenant can never be made void or disannulled to any that are ever brought into the bond thereof, Jer.31.31, 32, 33, 34 & 32.20. But as to that external political Covenant, which takes in A Body of People, here there is no such engagement of grace sufficient, infallibly to be bestowed for the keeping of the same; and therefore it may be and is most frequently broken and made void. God threatens to remove the Candlestick, Rev.2.5. and often hath he done it. Israel and Judah were in the issue cast off, for breaking the Lords Covenant.[47]

The Jeremiad and the Covenant

Just as the covenant of God with Israel and Judah provided the overarching framework for the interpretation of the fiery condemnations issued by the Hebrew prophets, the national covenant between New England and God provides the overarching framework within which Puritan jeremiads are intelligible.[48] The New England Puritan jeremiad, it must be stressed, was by no means an entirely novel creation. There were, of course, blistering

---

47. William Stoughton, New-Englands True Interest . . . (Cambridge, MA, 1670), 10–11.

48. As Michael Walzer writes: "Prophecy, in its critical mode, is hard to imagine without the covenant, for the prophets don't invent obligations for the people; they remind the people of the obligations they already have and know that they have." Michael Walzer, In God's Shadow: Politics in the Hebrew Bible (New Haven, CT: Yale University Press, 2012), 13.

indictments of sinful behavior in medieval Europe. Furthermore, such condemnations were not the exclusive province of Puritan preachers or even
Protestants; Roman Catholic preachers were also able to conjure the awful
specter of a vengeful God furious at human iniquity. More directly, however,
the New England jeremiad drew upon distinctive forms of sermonizing,
along with federal theology, firmly established by English Puritans. At the
same time, those features, combined with the dramatic perils and possibilities faced by the Puritans struggling to establish themselves in the New
World, allowed their jeremiad to gain new prominence as a characteristically
American form of religious and political speech.

As Harry Stout has so vividly described, the center of Puritan religious
life, week in, week out, was the sermon.[49] Generally, Puritan congregations
were treated to two sermons per week: one on Sundays and one on a weekday.
As Stout also emphasizes, during these ordinary sermons, the great doctrines
of Calvinist Christian thought were proclaimed, and the great drama of sin,
grace, and election were embedded in the hearts and minds of the congregation. The Puritan preachers were concerned first and foremost with the spiritual well-being of their congregations. Despite all the changes in society,
the basic structure of preaching in Congregationalist New England did not
change until the mid-eighteenth century.[50] Until that time, preachers preserved appeals to the head and to the heart in a fruitful tension, deftly avoiding
an Arminianism that would have granted too much rectitude to human
knowledge and will, and an antinomianism that would have decried any effort
to specify the shape of a regenerate life and a godly society.[51]

Stout reminds us, then, that the vast majority of preaching heard by
Puritan congregations did *not* take the form of the jeremiad. The jeremiad

49. Stout, *The New England Soul,* chap. 2. Puritan sermons took a highly structured form: First, a
verse from the Bible, quite frequently the Old Testament, was read by the preacher to the congregation. Second, the text was "opened" and its teaching or doctrine explained. Third, the "reasons" or the
rationale for the teaching were explained. Fourth, and frequently most elaborately, the "uses" or practical applications of the teaching were described and commended by the preacher.

50. Ibid., 152.

51. Ibid., 156. Around 1740, the ministers divided into rationalists, who would later become
Unitarians, and revivalists, who are the precursors of evangelical Protestantism. For a broader survey,
see Eugene E. White, *Puritan Rhetoric: The Issue of Emotion in Religion* (Carbondale: Southern Illinois
University Press, 1972); and Mason I. Lowance, Jr., *The Language of Canaan: Metaphor and Symbol in New
England from the Puritans to the Transcendentalists* (Cambridge, MA: Harvard University Press, 1980).

was not an ordinary form of address but rather an extraordinary form, which in part accounted for its initial power and popularity. It was a crucial part of the community's response to events of great blessing and trial, which were interpreted by the Puritans as a carefully calibrated comment by God upon His relationship with His chosen people. The Puritans relentlessly searched for the message of God in the events that blessed and troubled them. A vulnerable colony in a strange land, New England faced considerable troubles, including droughts, plagues (e.g., smallpox), blights, fire, and shipwreck. All potential calamities were to be feared not only because of the destruction they wrought by themselves but also because they revealed the anger of an omnipotent God with the state of their plantation and the state of their souls.

More specifically, the Puritans did not view material blessings or setbacks as matters of luck or chance but as events willed by God to reflect and to shape their covenantal relationship with Him. They did not find it the least improbable that an omnipotent God would work through secondary causes to reflect His reaction to the goings on in a little corner of North America. Precisely because they conceived of God as omnipotent and omniscient, the American Puritans easily believed that each and every event that takes place throughout the cosmos reflects divine will. Confident in their status as divinely chosen covenant partner, they took for granted that God was intensely interested in all their activities and particularly concerned with the quality of their responses to His manifest and particular interventions in their communal life.

Consider, for example, the response of the settlers to an earthquake that struck New England in late October 1727. Striking in the middle of the night, the tremors woke people out of a sound sleep and shook them out of their bed. What did they do? According to a pamphlet entitled *The Terror of the Lord,* they went to church,[52] where they heard the reflections of an aging Cotton Mather. Not surprisingly, he rejects the view that the earthquake was an impersonal matter of chance.[53] Instead, he offers a ringing and urgent call for New England to heed God's precepts:

52. Cotton Mather, *The Terror of the Lord.* . . . (Boston, MA, 1727).

53. "Shall we say, All this is but a *Chance that happens to us,* or the meer unguided *Motion* of *Matter?* Ah, profane *Philistine!*—'Tis a Language for none but a *Philistine. A Christian* cannot speak so." Ibid., 11.

> The VOICE of the glorious GOD *crying to the City* in His
> *Earthquake*, is This; Let the *Crimes* that Cry to the Holy GOD for
> all the Vengeance of an *Earthquake* upon you, be generally and
> thoroughly *Reformed* among you.
>
> The Cry is, REFORMATION, O *Degenerating Plants*, REFOR-
> MATION; *or more Evil to come upon you!*[54]

The Puritans were convinced that God works not only through natural
events but also through human actions to manifest His sentiments toward His
covenant partner. A striking example of this conviction can be found in a
book written by Cotton Mather's father, Increase Mather, with the title *A
Brief History of the Warr with the Indians in New England*.[55] The book gives a
detailed account of the Puritans' military clash with the Native American
population, which began in the summer of 1675 and concluded a little over a
year later.[56] Increase Mather interprets the finely detailed ebb and flow of the
conflict in terms of God's ultimate purposes with respect to New England,
seen through the lens of God's purposes with respect to Israel. He notes, for
example, that the English missed an early opportunity to end the war by pursuing Metacomt into a swamp and killing him there. "[I]f the *English* had
continued at the Swamp all night, nay, if they had but followed them but one
half hour longer, *Philip* had come and yielded up himself. But God saw that
we were not yet fit for Deliverance, nor could Health be restored unto us
except a great deal more Blood be first taken from us: and other places as well
as *Plimouth* stood in need of such a course to be taken with them."[57]

Fast Day Sermons

Generally speaking, the responses of the colony to supervening events took
two forms, days of thanksgiving, in which the community praised God for

---

54. Ibid., 17.

55. Increase Mather, *A Brief History of the Warr with the Indians in New-England* . . . (Boston, MA, 1676).

56. It is often called King Philip's War, after the English name for Metacomet, who was the
sachem of the Pokenoket Tribe and the leader of the native population hostile to the English settlers.
Eight hundred English colonists (approximately 1.5 percent of their population) and three thousand
Native Americans (approximately 15 percent of their population) were killed in the war. Eric B.
Schultz and Michael J. Tougias, *King Philip's War: The History and Legacy of America's Forgotten Conflict*
(Woodstock, VT: The Countryman Press, 1999), 5.

57. Mather, *A Brief History of the Warr*, 5.

blessings conferred or disasters averted, and days of humiliation, in which the community responded to threats and troubles by setting aside their quotidian activities in order to engage in acts of fasting and penance.[58] The structure of the call for a day of humiliation issued by the legislature followed a fairly standard form. The proclamation recited the material adversities experienced by the colonies. The matter was then committed to the churches to organize an appointed day of humiliation in order to repent of the sins that provoked divine wrath. On these days, ordinary work would cease because the community attended their houses of worship in order to beg divine indulgence. The sermon was the center of the occasion just as it was the focal point of ordinary Sunday worship.

Most fast day jeremiads also took a standard form, closely related to the ordinary four-part form of the ordinary Puritan sermon.[59] First, a verse from the Old Testament, often from the Book of Isaiah or Jeremiah, would supply the text for the occasion. Second, the "doctrine" would be articulated in order to show that the people were being rightfully chastised by God for their sinful behavior. Third, the "reasons" backing the doctrine would be elaborated, drawing on the national covenant with God and articulating the colonists' duties, their breach of duties, and the condign penalty imposed by God for the breach. Finally, the preacher would turn to the practical "applications" or "uses" of his assessment, outlining a proposed scheme of reformation and vividly depicting the increasing torments likely to be inflicted upon the colony and its denizens if reform were rejected, postponed, or evaded. Miller

58. See William DeLoss Love, Jr., *The Fast and Thanksgiving Days of New England* (Boston, MA: Houghton, Mifflin & Co., 1895). The identification of days of humiliation was a coordinated effort of church and state. In the early years of Massachusetts Bay Colony, the magistrates gave a general indication to the clergy that such a day would be welcome and helpful, leaving it to the latter group to call the congregation to prayer., The Massachusetts General Court acted solely on its own authority in calling for a general fast on January 19, 1637, to overcome "the dissensions in our churches" precipitated by the Antinomian Controversy. See Love, *The Fast and Thanksgiving Days*, chap. 9; see also David D. Hall, *The Antinomian Controversy, 1636–1638, A Documentary History* (Durham, NC: Duke University Press, 1990), chap. 6. Over the years, other precipitating events included frequent threat from Native Americans, smallpox, fire, hail, drought, earthquake, plague and pestilence, and witchcraft.

59. Key election sermons of the second generation, which generally bewail a loss of the religious zeal and moral rectitude of their parents' generation, include Thomas Shepard, *Eye-Salve* . . . (Cambridge, MA, 1673); William Hubbard, *The Happiness of a People* . . . (Boston, MA, 1676); Samuel Torrey, *A Plea for the Life of Dying Religion* . . . (Boston, MA, 1683); Samuel Willard, "The Only Sure Way to Prevent Threatened Calamity," in *The Child's Portion* . . . (Boston, MA, 1684), 163–97; and Adams, *God's Eye on the Contrite*.

observes: "A minister's reputation for eloquence came to be based upon the skill with which he could devise prognostications of a mounting disaster, by contrast with which the present suffering dwindled into mere annoyance."[60]

An outstanding model of a jeremiad written in a time of fasting is Michael Wigglesworth's *God's Controversy with New-England: Written in the time of the great drought Anno 1662.*[61] It is quite idiosyncratic in form; its idiosyncrasies, however, reveal more clearly and compactly its rhetorical structure to the modern-day reader. Not actually a sermon, it was written in verse (446 lines) and was doubtless, therefore, far more interesting to read than most jeremiads published by prominent Puritan preachers in sermon form.[62] The first stanza of the poem offers a reliable advertisement for its content:

> Good christian Read[r] judge me not
> > As too censorious,
> For pointing at those faults of thine
> > Which are notorious.
> For if those faults be none of thine
> > I do not thee accuse:
> But if they be, to hear thy faults
> > Why shouldest thou refuse.[63]

Closely intertwining the history of Israel with the history of New England, Wigglesworth begins by describing the initial phase of God's relationship with the Puritan colony in almost idyllic terms:

> The Lord had made (such was his grace)
> > For us a Covenant
> Both with the men, and with the beasts,
> > That in this desert haunt:
> So that through places wilde and waste
> > A single man, disarm'd,

60. Miller, *From Colony to Province*, 29–30.

61. Michael Wigglesworth, *God's Controversy with New-England* (1662, 1871), ed. Reiner Smolinski, *Electronic Texts in American Studies*, Paper 36, http://digitalcommons.unl.edu/etas/36.

62. Reiner Smolinski, introduction to Wigglesworth, *God's Controversy with New-England.* Wigglesworth's writings were quite popular; *The Day of Doom* (1662), his account of the Last Judgment, was also a best seller.

63. Wigglesworth, *God's Controversy with New-England*, lines 1–8.

> Might journey many hundred miles,
>   And not at all be harm'd.[64]

The early, halcyon days did not last forever; with the passing of the first generation, the tone and commitment of the colony changed, causing Jehovah to wonder whether he was dealing with the same nation. Not one to suffer from excessive humility, Wigglesworth adopts the voice of God to make his point more vividly to his countrymen:

> Are these the men, that now mine eyes behold,
>   Concerning whom I thought, and whilome spake,
> First Heaven shall away together scrold,
>   Ere they my lawes and righteous wayes forsake,
> Or that they slack to runn their heavenly race?
>   Are these the same? or are some others come in place?
>
> If these be they, how is it that I find
>   In stead of holyness Carnality,
> In stead of heavenly frames an Earthly mind,
>   For burning zeal luke-warm Indifferency,
> For flaming Love, key-cold Dead-heartedness,
>   For temperance (in meat, and drinke, and cloaths) excess?[65]

Jehovah warns His covenant-partner that He is sorely aggravated by their sins and that He is in no mood to bear much more disobedience and disregard of the covenant without considering retaliation:

> For thinke not, O Backsliders, in your heart,
>   That I shall still your evill manners beare:
> Your sinns me press as sheaves do load a cart;
>   And therefore I will plague you for this geare.
> Except you seriously, and soon, repent,
>   Ile not delay your pain and heavy punishment.[66]

---

64. Ibid., lines 101–8.
65. Ibid., lines 211–22.
66. Ibid., lines 259–64.

Reminding New Englanders of how He treated the Israelites when they were unfaithful, God elaborates on their sins, and informs them that the window for repentance and reform is quickly closing:

> Now therefore hearken and encline your ear,
>   In judgement I will henceforth with you plead;
> And if by that you will not learn to fear,
>   But still go on a sensuall life to lead:
> I'le strike at once an All-consuming stroke;
>   Nor cries nor tears shall then my fierce intent revoke.[67]

Resuming his own voice, Wigglesworth goes on to outline the temporal sufferings endured by the colony as a consequence of their deviation from the strictures of the covenant. He laments the pervasiveness of illness that saps the strength of the settlers:

> One wave another followeth,
>   And one disease begins
> Before another cease, becaus
>   We turn not from our sins.
> We stopp our ear against reproof,
>   And hearken not to God:
> God stops his ear against our prayer,
>   And takes not off his rod.[68]

The occasion of the jeremiad was a severe drought—a fundamental matter of life and death to the settlers. Wigglesworth unhesitatingly attributes the threat to the divine will.

> The clouds are often gathered,
>   As if we should have rain:
> But for our great unworthiness
>   Are scattered again.
> We pray & fast, & make fair shewes,
>   As if we meant to turn:

---

67. Ibid., lines 337–42.
68. Ibid., lines 375–82.

> But whilest we turn not, God goes on
> Our fields & fruits to burn.[69]

Wigglesworth brings the poem to a close with a carefully calibrated balance of fear and hope that is typical of the great jeremiads. On the one hand, as bad as the situation is now, it could be worse—and it will be surely be incomparably worse if New England does not repent of its sins. On the other hand, all is not lost—at least not yet. Sincere repentance can indeed renew God's favor, and reinvigorate the blessings of the land upon God's covenant people. Wigglesworth presents the sharp choice—and sharply contrasting fates—to his audience in two successive stanzas:

> Beware, O sinful Land, beware;
>   And do not think it strange
> That sorer judgements are at hand,
>   Unless thou quickly change.
> Or God, or thou, must quickly change;
>   Or else thou art undon:
> Wrath cannot cease, if sin remain,
>   Where judgment is begun.[70]

> Ah dear New-England! dearest land to me;
>   Which unto God hast hitherto been dear,
> And mayst be still more dear than formerlie,
>   If to his voice thou wilt incline thine ear.[71]

Wigglesworth ends the poem reassuring his audience of his abiding love—and implicitly, of God's abiding love—for the little colony in the wilderness. To the modern ear, the poem reads like a theological horror story:

> Cheer on, sweet souls, my heart is with you all,
>   And shall be with you, maugre Sathan's might:
> And whereso'ere this body be a Thrall,
>   Still in New-England shall be my delight.[72]

69. Ibid., lines 391–98.
70. Ibid., lines 423–30.
71. Ibid., lines 431–34.
72. Ibid., lines 443–46.

The protagonists are threatened with grave harm. They may even lose some of their friends, family, and property. Nonetheless, they manage to survive, with a deeper appreciation of the blessings that life can bring.

ELECTION DAY SERMONS

The subject and style of sermons given on fast days declared by the legislature migrated to another, more regular and predictable occasion, which highlights the close partnership between church and state in New England: the annual election day sermon. Before beginning its business on the first day of the new term each spring, the lawmakers of the colony listened to a sermon preached by a prominent clergyman who would give an account of the troubles facing the colony and the root of those troubles in faithlessness and deviation from godly behavior.[73] In addition to the magistrates and the deputies, other members of the clergy were also in the audience. This practice likely began in Massachusetts in 1634 and continued, with some exceptions, until 1884. The earliest sermon known to have been printed was delivered in 1661, although it did not go to press until 1664.[74] In the second generation, these sermons took on added importance, growing in length and complexity in anticipation of publication.[75]

The general purpose of the election day sermon was to remind the legislators and the governors of their responsibilities under the covenant, including their special obligation to promote sound religion and to foster its transmission to the next generation. Like fast day sermons, the premise of the election day sermons was that the material well-being of the colony was directly tied to its fulfillment of its covenantal obligations.

73. R. W. G. Vail, "A Check List of New England Election Sermons," *Proceedings of American Antiquarian Association* 45 (1935): 233–66. See also A. W. Plumstead, ed., *The Wall and the Garden: Selected Massachusetts Election Sermons, 1670–1775* (Minneapolis: University of Minnesota Press, 1968). Facsimiles of important sermons are collected in Ronald A. Bosco, ed., *Connecticut and Massachusetts Election Sermons*, 3 vols. (Delmar, NY: Scholars Facsimiles & Reprints, 1978).

74. Vail, "A Check List," 243. It is possible that Richard Mather's 1660 election sermon was printed, although Vail says there is no copy known to exist.

75. For an elaborate—and surprisingly witty—account of Massachusetts election sermons from the time of their institution until they were discontinued in the mid 1880s, see Lindsay Swift, "The Massachusetts Election Sermons," Publications of the Colonial Society of Massachusetts, *Transactions* 1 (1892-94): 388–451 (published in Boston, MA, 1895). Not surprisingly, the father-and-son team of Increase and Cotton Mather dominated the genre; each delivered four election sermons. Cotton's paternal grandfather, Richard Mather, gave three election sermons, and his maternal grandfather, John Cotton, gave the first election sermon in 1634.

The most well-known specimen of this genre, Samuel Danforth's *A Brief Recognition of New-England's Errand into the Wilderness*,[76] was given before the Massachusetts General Assembly on election day in Boston in 1670. It warned that New England had lost its zeal for God and was consequently likely to lose its prosperity. *"The Lord calls upon them seriously and thoroughly to examine themselves, what it was that drew them into the Wilderness, and to consider that it was not the expectation of ludicrous levity, nor of Courtly pomp and delicacy, but of the free and clear dispensation of the Gospel and Kingdome of God."*[77] Danforth asks the colony's leaders to consider "[w]hether we have not in a great measure forgotten our Errand into the Wilderness," whose holy and overriding purpose was *"your Liberty to walk in the Faith of the Gospel with all good Conscience according to the Order of the Gospel."*[78]

Other election sermons focused more directly on the responsibilities of the distinguished members of the audience, who were the leaders of government and civil society. In these cases, the intimate relationship between New England and Israel as people of the covenant is even more apparent. The full title of William Hubbard's 1676 election sermon, for example, is *"The Happiness of a People* in the Wisdome of their Rulers DIRECTING and in the Obedience of their Brethren ATTENDING Unto what Israel ought to do."[79] Echoing Winthrop, Hubbard calls for a tightly ordered hierarchical society whose members are knit together by Christian charity. In elaborating the qualifications and duties of electors, those elected to office, and the subjects of the government, Hubbard used ancient Israel as his touchstone.

One might expect Hubbard to highlight biblical analogies and religious obligations when considering the ecclesiastical duties of the ministers of New England. Nonetheless, it is striking how frequently he emphasizes the religious dimension of the political and military duties by constant analogies to ancient Israel. For God's divinely chosen covenant partner, there is no sharp separation

---

76. Samuel Danforth, *A Brief Recognition of New-Englands Errand into the Wilderness* . . . (Cambridge, MA, 1671).

77. Ibid., 5.

78. Ibid., 9, 10.

79. "It mût needs be a flourishing state, where may be seen due order in the constitusion of a Government, and administration thereof, True Wisdom in the Rulers, Entire Unity in the people, joyned with meet Courage for the execution of the prudent commands of their Leaders: of such a place it may be said, that it is *beautifull as Tirzah, comely as Jerusalem, terrible & c. Cant.6.4* . . ." William Hubbard, *The Happiness of a People* . . . (Boston, MA, 1676), 8.

between the spheres because every sphere of the colony's existence provides the stage for God to work out the relationship. Despite the fact that Hubbard began his election sermon with a discourse on political theory, he is ineluctably drawn to the language of biblical theology to work out his ultimate advice to the audience. That is, he is drawn to the conceptual framework of the jeremiad. After surveying the political and military setbacks of the region, he reframes his analysis to fit the jeremiad's inevitable conclusion:

> I fear, that as before it hath been said by some, God hath a contro-
> versie with New-England, so now that the rod of affliction, hath
> not only budded and blossomed, but brought forth its fruit, may
> we not all conclude, that there are some matters of offence, that
> God hath against us, that notwithstanding all threatenings, and
> solemn warnings both by the word as well as by the works of
> God, could not be reformed. Therefore God was not willing to lay
> aside his quarrel against us. And for this and that transgression
> would no tturn [sic] away the punishment of New-England.[80]

Generally speaking, election sermons were not immune to the political controversies of the day. A few years before Hubbard's election sermon, Thomas Shepherd's *Eye-Salve* resoundingly rejected "indefinite and boundless [religious] toleration" as "Satan's policy."[81] Other election sermons waded into matters that were more thoroughly secular. The first election sermon, delivered by John Cotton in 1634, urged the re-election of John Winthrop as governor.[82] Later sermons reflected the tension between the elites and the common members of the community, symbolized by the tension between the magistrates and the deputies.[83] Some election preachers remonstrated against the precarious state of the financial situation of the colony.[84] As a rule, however, election preachers did not go out of their way to court controversy in politically dangerous times but focused on the perennial problems of sin

---

80. Ibid., 54.

81. Thomas Shepard, *Eye-Salve* . . . , 14.

82. Swift, "The Massachusetts Election Sermons," 389. John Cotton pleading failed to convince his audience; they elected Thomas Dudley instead.

83. Ibid., 394. Eventually, an agreement was reached that the magistrates and deputies would each choose the election preacher every other year.

84. Ibid., 415, 417.

and repentance. Election sermons were likely not given in 1687 and 1688, the years in which Massachusetts was part of the Dominion of New England under the governorship of Sir Edmund Andros.[85] Moreover, the somewhat spotty evidence that exists suggests that the sermons given around the time that England revoked the colony's original charter in 1684 were not incendiary.[86] Nonetheless, several rather pointed election sermons did appear in print around the time of the Revolutionary War and the War of 1812.[87]

REVIVAL AND COVENANT RENEWAL SERMONS

The theme of decline from the religious fervor and moral probity of the founding generation was heavily represented in election day sermons in the 1660s and 1670s. The Puritans took the problem of religious declension far too seriously, however, to confine its treatment to an annual political event, no matter how solemn and important. That problem also took center stage in religious revivals held by New England congregations, the purpose of which was to motivate church members to renew their commitment to the covenant. The phenomenon of covenant renewal became an important feature of Massachusetts congregations in the 1770s and especially the 1780s. A typical renewal event would consist of a day of fasting and praying, the central focus of which was a sermon that outlined the peoples' sins and the need for repentance, followed by the solemn ceremony of renewal. While distinct, covenant renewal sermons preached to a particular congregation were also motivated by the same concerns that prompted election sermons and fast day sermons for the entire community. For example, seizing on an example given by the church of Norwich during the darkest moments of King Philip's War, Increase Mather contended that "Renewal of Covenant" is "the great Duty incumbent upon decaying or distressed CHURCHES."[88]

---

85. Ibid., 407.

86. Ibid., 405–7. More specifically, William Adams's *God's Eye on the Contrite* (1685) was a fairly typical, if especially vigorous, condemnation of the besetting sins of New England. No copy of Michael Wigglesworth's 1686 election sermon appears to have been made. Nonetheless, it does not appear that the topic was particularly controversial.

87. Ibid., 421–26, 430–31.

88. Increase Mather, *Renewal of Covenant* . . . (Boston, MA, 1677), title page. This sermon was actually given to a church in Dorchester. Mather preached at his own church's covenant renewal a couple of years later. See Increase Mather, *Returning unto God the Great Concernment of a Covenant People* (Boston, MA, 1680).

The Provoking Sins

Fast day sermons, Election Day sermons, and sermons preached at covenant renewal events all decried the sins of New England. What, precisely, were those sins? We do not have to comb through the sermons to collect and collate them ourselves; not surprisingly, the Puritans did the organizational work for us. In 1679, the Massachusetts General Court called the churches to convene a reforming synod that would examine two questions: *"What are the Evils that have provoked the Lord to bring his Judgements on New England?"* and *"What is to be done that so those Evils may be reformed?"*[89] By that point in time, the ordinary run of fast days had not proven to be particularly effective against the increasing number of calamities such as fire, shipwreck, and the ongoing threat from the Native American population. The Result of the 1679 Reforming Synod offered a full account of the besetting sins of New England, which in fact functioned as a digest and recapitulation of many themes of earlier jeremiads, as well as a twelve-point proposal to address the sins that impeded the spiritual well-being of the colony.

No one could say that the Puritans were not thorough in their analysis of the state of their souls. The Result systematically examined New England's provoking evils, organizing them into thirteen categories that consumed a little over thirteen printed pages of a cramped eighteenth-century reprint.[90] What exactly constituted the "visible manifest Evils, which without doubt the Lord is provoked by"?[91] According to the Puritan divines, the community was guilty of the following offenses:

---

89. *The Results of Three Synods . . .* (Boston, MA, 1725), v. The Result of the Reforming Synod of 1679 is the third result included in this volume, and begins on page 94, under the title "The Necessity of REFORMATION with the Expedients subservient thereunto, asserted, in TWO QUESTIONS." The General Court called the Reforming Synod at the behest of Increase Mather and eighteen fellow ministers. J. William T. Youngs, *The Congregationalists* (Westport, CT: Greenwood Press, 1990), 64. The synod convened in two sessions. The first, held in September 1679, drew up a list of New England's "provoking sins" and proposed remedies, while the second, held in May 1680, adopted the Savoy Declaration (a modification of the Westminster Confession), which was already in use in many congregations in New England, as a statement of faith. Youngs, *The Congregationalists*, 64, 66. See also James F. Cooper, Jr., *Tenacious of Their Liberties: The Congregationalists in Colonial Massachusetts* (New York: Oxford University Press, 1999), 141–44. Cooper suggests that scholars have paid too little attention to the focus of the Reforming Synod on covenant renewal, seen in their decision to reaffirm the 1648 Cambridge Platform, which was published as the first part of *The Results of Three Synods*.

90. *The Results of Three Synods*, 94–107.

91. Ibid., 96.

1. "There is a great and visible decay of the power of Godliness amongst many Professors in these Churches." Mentioned as offenders under this category are those who worship in public while committing "spiritual and heart Apostacy."[92]

2. "The Pride that doth abound in *New-England* testifies against us." Key offenses here include "refusing to subject to Order, according to Divine Appointment," pervasive "Contention," and "Pride in respect of Apparel," especially among the "Servants, and the poorer sort of People."[93]

3. "[W]e may fear that breaches of that [the Second] Commandment are some part of the Lords Controversy with *New-England*." The neglect of "Church-Fellowship," especially by the young, was a key concern to the pastors, as was the lack of church discipline in general. Also troublesome was the presence in the community of "false Worshippers" such as Quakers and Anabaptists, who accepted "into their Society those that have been for Scandal delivered unto Satan."[94]

4. "The Holy and Glorious Name of GOD hath been polluted and profaned amongst us," by too casual an approach to oath-taking, and too much "irreverent behaviour in the solemn Worship of God." Like the preachers, God disapproved when "[m]en (though not necessitated thereunto by any Infirmity) . . . give way to their own Sloth and Sleepiness, when they should be serving God with attention and intention."[95]

5. "There is much Sabbath-breaking." Not only do people fail to attend Sunday services, they dedicate the Lord's time to other purposes. Some people even "attend their particular servile Callings and Employments after the Sabbath is begun, or before it is ended."[96]

92. Ibid.
93. Ibid., 96–97.
94. Ibid., 97–98.
95. Ibid., 98–99.
96. Ibid., 99–100.

6. "As what concerns Families and the Government thereof, there is much amiss." Many families do not engage in morning and evening prayer. There is a lack of discipline, as evidenced by "Children and Servants that are not kept in due Subjection, their Masters and Parents especially, being sinfully indulgent towards them."[97]

7. "Inordinate Passions. Sinful Hearts and Hatreds, and that amongst Church-Members themselves, who abound with evil Surmisings, uncharitable and unrighteous Censures, Back-bitings, hearing and telling Tales . . ."[98]

8. "There is much Intemperance." Not only do the Puritans drink too much themselves, "but Indians have been debauched, by those that call themselves Christians, who have put their Bottles to them, and made them Drunk also." In addition, there have been "other hainous breaches of the seventh Commandment," including "[l]aying out of Hair, Borders, naked Necks and Arms, or, which is more abominable, naked Breasts, and mixed Dancings . . ."[99]

9. "There is much want of Truth amongst Men." Offenses here include promise-breaking, false reports, slanders, and reproaches.[100]

10. "Inordinate affection to the World," especially the tendency of some "to forsake Churches and Ordinances, and to live like Heathen, only that so they might have Elbow-room enough in the World." According to the Result of the 1679 Synod, "Religion is made subservient unto worldly Interests." Merchants charge excessive prices for their goods and engage in other forms of economic oppression. In general, "Men are under the prevailing power of a worldly Spirit, by their strait-handedness, as to public Concernments." Too many

97. Ibid., 100–101.
98. Ibid., 101.
99. Ibid., 101–3.
100. Ibid., 103.

people put their own private economic interest ahead of the common welfare.[101]

11. "There hath been opposition unto the work of Reformation." The Result complained that the people have not been responsive to God's message in His "awful Judgements, that we should return unto him, who hath been smiting us." What is worse, "[t]hey that have been zealous in bearing witness against the Sins of the Times, have been reproached, and other ways discouraged; which argueth an Heart unwilling to Reform."[102]

12. "A publick Spirit is wanting in the most of Men," in that "Matters appertaining to the Kingdom of God, are either not at all regarded, or not in the first place." School and other public ventures "are in a languishing state," and there are "unreasonable Complaints and Murmurings because of publick Charges."[103]

13. Finally, "[t]here are Sins against the Gospel, whereby the Lord hath been provoked." According to the Result, "[n]o Sins provoke the Lord more then Impenitency and Unbelief."[104]

How, then, are the people's evil ways to be reformed in order to divert divine judgment? The second part of the Result offered a twelve-point answer to this question, which drove home the necessity of renewed commitment to the political, social, and religious order instituted by the founding generation of Puritans.[105] The eighth point of the answer constitutes the heart of the proposed reform program; it calls for a "[s]olemn and explicit renewal of Covenant."[106] Here again, the model of Israel is decisive for the Puritans. "And as the Judgements which befel the Lords People of old are recorded for our

101. Ibid., 103–5.
102. Ibid., 105–6.
103. Ibid., 106.
104. Ibid.
105. Ibid., 107–17.
106. Ibid., 112–15.

Admonition, 1 Cor. 10. 11. so the Course which they did (according to God) observe in order to Reformation & averting those Judgements, is recorded for our imitation. And this was an explicit renovation of Covenant."[107]

Renewing the covenant was not merely a matter for the church but also for the state; Part II of the Result also recommended a program of legal reform. "In special it is necessary, that those Laws for Reformation of provoking Evils, enacted and emitted by the General Court in the Day of our Calamity, should be duly considered, lest we become guilty of dissembling and dallying with the Almighty, and thereby Sin and Wrath be augmented upon us." Of particular concern was the "Regulation of Houses for publick Entertainment."[108] At the same time, the magistrates were to ensure that the work of the ministers was supported financially and respected within the political community, if necessary by making the people "do their Duty in this matter."[109]

Having called for the Reforming Synod of 1679, the Massachusetts General Court could scarcely ignore its Result. On May 19, 1680, the General Court approved the Confession of Faith produced by the clergymen attending the synod and ordered it published together with the long-standing blueprint of congregational polity—the Cambridge Platform of church discipline.[110] The General Court quickly moved from expressing appreciation for the work of the synod to evaluating strategies for implementing its recommendations. Immediately following the first session, the General Court formed a committee to review the colony's laws "to see 'whether they were sufficiently warranted by the word of God, and other lawes not so well worded as may be effectuall to the end intended, or honorable to this Court.'"[111] Furthermore, it strengthened the legal powers of the "tithingmen" who were appointed by the towns to watch over Sabbath observance and discourage people from visiting taverns instead of attending services. In 1681, the Massachusetts General Court passed a comprehensive tavern reform law. Legal pressure was

107. Ibid., 112.

108. Ibid., 111–12.

109. Ibid., 110–11.

110. The account of this Action of the General Court has no page number; it can be found two manuscript pages after the account of the Result of the 1679 Synod, which ends on page 118 of *The Results of Three Synods*.

111. Richard P. Gildrie, *The Profane, the Civil, & the Godly: The Reformation of Manners in Orthodox New England, 1679–1749* (University Park: Pennsylvania State University Press, 1994), 37.

applied to ensure that the towns contributed to Harvard for the education of ministry and built grammar and writing schools for the education of the young.[112] Fifty years after John Winthrop had proposed his *Modell* for Puritan society, the colony he helped found reaffirmed the covenantal structure that made its political and religious life intelligible.[113]

Covenant, Breach, and Complaint

As the foregoing pages make abundantly clear, the Puritan jeremiad emerged out of and reinforced a colonial religious and political life structured by an elaborate series of covenants. Perry Miller has focused scholarly attention upon the integral relationship between covenant and jeremiad.[114] In my view, however, to understand the role prophetic rhetoric plays in contemporary public discourse, we need to delve more deeply into certain aspects of that relationship that Miller recognizes but does not emphasize. More specifically, we must bring to the foreground the distinctively legal framework that shapes both the structure and content of the covenant and jeremiad. Only by taking full account of this legal framework will we be able to understand how the jeremiad functioned to build up, rather than tear down, the moral consensus of the colonial Puritan community.

Let us begin with a more focused look at the definition of the term *covenant*. As I noted earlier, the Puritans' theological use of the term was deeply influenced by the way it operated in secular courts of law. Miller writes that "[b]y the word 'covenant' federal theologians understood just such a contract as was used among men of business, a bond or a mortgage, an agreement between two parties, signed and sworn to, and binding upon both. It was usually defined as 'A mutual agreement between parties upon Articles or

---

112. Ibid., 30, 37.

113. For further accounts of the Reforming Synod, see Miller, *From Colony to Province*, 33–39; Stout, *The New England Soul*, 96–99; Bremer, *The Puritan Experiment*, 166–67; and Gildrie, *The Profane, the Civil, & the Godly*, 19–40. See also Albert E. Dunning (with Joseph E. Roy), *Congregationalists in America: A Popular History of Their Origin, Belief, Polity, Growth and Work* (New York: J. A. Hill, 1894), 191–96. The Reforming Synod was in part an effort to shore up the authority of both the magistrates and the ministers; a recurring complaint of the latter group was that they (like the Hebrew prophets) did not receive enough respect or remuneration from their congregations.

114. Miller, *From Colony to Province*, 27–39.

Propositions on both sides, so that each party is tied and bound to performe his own conditions.'"[115]

In an economic era transitioning from feudalism to early capitalism, such legally enforceable agreements provided a way to allow persons to commit themselves beyond the role-related expectations of their respective social stations. Miller goes on to crystallize the implications: "An absolute monarch can change his laws every day, forswear his oaths, make promises and break them by the score, rewrite his testament as often as he pleases, but once he enters a covenant, though with but the humblest of his peasants, he is held as with hoops of steel."[116] These hoops are strong enough not only to fasten mortal rulers of earthly realms but also to bind the ruler of the universe Himself. In fact, as Miller notes, federal theologians used covenantal bonds to constrain the movements of an arbitrary, Calvinist God: "We must not make Gods Covenant with man, so far to differ from Covenants between man and man, as to make it no Covenant at all."[117]

To what degree is the discourse of covenant theology actually consistent with the legal use of the term? In fifteenth-century England, the action of "covenant" provided a legal remedy for breach of promise provided that the plaintiff could comply with certain legal requirements. To avail oneself of that remedy, a plaintiff had to produce a "speciality"—a written promise marked with a seal. This requirement was formal, not substantive—any kind of promise could be the subject of the action of covenant provided that it was marked by the specialty. Closely related actions were "debt" and "detinue." Debt was an action for a certain amount of money, based on an underlying transaction, sometimes called a contract. Detinue was an action similar to debt, although what was owed was chattel property rather than a liquidated amount of money.[118]

Like the action of covenant, debt and detinue also imposed specific requirements on plaintiffs seeking to recover under their auspices. At times, these requirements could be cumbersome, onerous, or subject to manipulation by

---

115. Miller, *The Seventeenth Century,* 375.

116. Ibid., 375–76.

117. Ibid., 376.

118. The evolution of the enforcement of promises from the medieval to the modern framework is exhaustively treated in A. W. B. Simpson, *A History of the Common Law of Contract: The Rise of the Action of Assumpsit* (Oxford: Clarendon Press, 1987). This summary is taken from pages 5–6 of Simpson's book. See also Kevin M. Teeven, *A History of the Anglo-American Common Law of Contract* (New York: Greenwood Press, 1990).

the defendant. Ultimately, these logistical flaws proved fatal to the older forms of actions. In his comprehensive account of the common law of contracts, A. W. B. Simpson recounts how the late fifteenth and early sixteenth century witnessed the development of the action of "assumpsit." This action is the ancestor of our contemporary understanding of contracts, which are generally defined as agreements in which each promise is supported by consideration. Initially, assumpsit was used by plaintiffs who could not meet the procedural requirements of covenant, debt, or detinue. Eventually, even plaintiffs who could meet those requirements turned to assumpsit for redress, effectively sidelining the actions of covenant, debt, and detinue.

The colloquial use of legal terms, in that time as in our own, overlaps but does not completely coincide with the strict legal use. As Simpson himself notes, *covenant,* not *contract,* was the general term for *agreement.* The meaning of the term *covenant,* then, was not narrowly restricted to promises that complied with the forms of the legal action by that name.[119] Moreover, then as now, the colloquial use of a legal term was situated in a family of related terms, used in the same nontechnical manner. As the action of assumpsit increasingly subsumed actions under covenant, debt, and detinue, the boundaries between these terms became increasingly porous in colloquial speech as well.

The colloquial language of agreements, of buying and selling, of promises and debts, would have been readily accessible to much of the English-speaking audience for covenant theology. Literacy increased in late sixteenth- and early seventeenth-century England among the Puritan middle class. It was driven not only by the desire to read the scriptural terms that would govern believers' relations with God but also by the need to read the legal terms that structured their relations with one another. One man offered this pithy summary: "[T]his is all we go to school for: to read common prayers at church; and set down common prices at markets; write a letter and make a bond; set down the day of our births, our marriage day; and make our wills when we are sick . . . these are the chief matters that we meddle with."[120]

As Max Weber and Matthew Arnold observed long ago, the Puritans in England belonged to the emerging merchant class, and their relationships

---

119. Simpson, *A History of the Common Law of Contract,* 5.

120. David Zaret, *The Heavenly Contract: Ideology and Organization in Pre-Revolutionary Puritanism* (Chicago, IL: The University of Chicago Press, 1985), 36, citing Mildred Campbell, *The English Yeoman under Elizabeth and the Early Stuarts* (London: Merlin Press, 1967), 265.

were increasingly governed by contract rather than status, as had been the case in the late medieval world.[121] Puritanism was by no means a movement confined to clerics; it also included a large number of lay men and women who spanned the ranks of gentry, yeomanry, and artisans. As England's transition to a market economy proceeded, the use of written contracts became more widespread, encompassing not merely sales transactions but also extensions of credit, bills of debt, and other commercial arrangements.

Lay Puritans were not only assiduous about their religious and work lives; they also treated them as integrally related because a pattern or practice of good works and prosperity could be interpreted as a sign of divine favor. This interrelationship also favored the intermixture of theological and legal terms in the development of covenant theology. As David Zaret argues in his study of the relationship between the economic status and theological commitments of pre-Revolutionary English Puritans, preachers regularly drew on transactional images likely to be familiar to their congregants in order to limn their relationship with God. Zaret observes that often "[t]hese principles and practices concern a very specific type of contract: the type used in acquisitive activities governed by a market rationality."[122] Consider this example from a sermon series on the new covenant:

> Like a household servant that is in covenant with his master, comes in from his work and calls for his dinner . . . so may we, as many as are in covenant with God, go to him in the like manner: Lord I want faith, give me it . . . As if he had said you are in covenant with me, and therefore perform your bargain; as you have allotted me work, so you must find me tools wherewithal to work . . . It is a flat bargain between us, therefore stand to it.[123]

121. Max Weber, *The Protestant Ethic and the "Spirit" of Capitalism and Other Writings*, ed. and trans. Peter R. Baehr and Gordon C. Wells (New York: Penguin, 2002); Matthew Arnold, *Culture and Anarchy*, ed. Samuel Lipman (New Haven, CT: Yale University Press, 1994). For helpful examinations of the relationship of American Puritans to capitalism, see Mark Valeri, *Heavenly Merchandise: How Religion Shaped Commerce in Puritan America* (Princeton, NJ: Princeton University Press, 2010); Joshua J. Yates and James Davidson Hunter, eds., *Thrift and Thriving in America: Capitalism and Moral Order from the Puritans to the Present* (New York: Oxford University Press, 2011).

122. Zaret, *The Heavenly Contract*, 164.

123. Robert Harris, *Treatise of the New Covenant* (London, 1632), I. 42–43, quoted in Zaret, *The Heavenly Contract*, 160–61.

Zaret also notes that preachers "glossed over" technical legal distinctions in order to make general points accessible to businessmen, such as the importance of mutual consent in forging a binding agreement. Not surprisingly, they tended to use the terms *contract* and *covenant* interchangeably.[124] George Walker, a Puritan preacher from London, wrote: "The word covenant in our English tongue signifies, as we all know, a mutual promise, bargain, and obligation between two parties." He went on to assert that the term "signifies all covenants in general, both God's covenant with men, and also the covenants which men make among themselves."[125] In addition, Puritan preachers deployed related concepts and contexts, such as earnests, seals, bonds of debt, leases, and (even) premarital contracts to fill out their theological framework.[126]

As Walker rightly noted, a contract involves "a mutual promise, bargain, and obligation between two parties." To put the point another way, a valid contract is an agreement with consideration. In most cases, the consideration consists of an exchange of promises. One party makes a promise to do or refrain from doing certain specified things in exchange for the other party's promise to do or refrain from doing certain things. A complaint for breach of covenant is a complaint that the other party failed to live up to his or her end of the bargain.

So the touchstone for a complaint for breach of covenant must be the contents of the covenant itself. In identifying a breach, then, Puritans would understand that the key is to look to the covenant to identify the duties that each party agreed to assume. Ideally speaking, discerning whether or not particular actions or omissions count as a breach should not be difficult or controversial. A breach is nothing more than a failure to fulfill an obligation that the party has freely assumed by agreeing to the contract. The crucial question, then, is what promises each party has actually made in a voluntary and knowing manner—not what promises she or he ought to have made, or what would have been fair or just for her or him to have made. The point of reference in determining whether a breach occurred is the set of obligations that the contract itself actually brings into existence, not some hypothetical set of

124. Zaret, *The Heavenly Contract,* 168. Their imprecise use of the terms *covenant* and *contract* is not idiosyncratic; it tracks Simpson's observation about the nontechnical use of the terms in a secular context, which I noted earlier.

125. George Walker, *The Manifold Wisdome of God . . .* (London, 1641), 39, 48, quoted in Zaret, *The Heavenly Contract,* 169.

126. Zaret, *The Heavenly Contract,* 174–83.

obligations that the parties would have imposed if they had been blessed with more foresight or better negotiating skill.

As the examples I invoked earlier in this chapter testify, the jeremiad is best construed as a stylized complaint for breach of covenant. Consequently, it looks to the covenant in order to identify the behavior it condemns. By structuring their jeremiads in this legalistic fashion, the Puritans were not acting idiosyncratically; they were not even acting creatively. They were simply following the tracks laid down in Scripture itself. As theologians and biblical scholars have argued, key passages in the prophetic books of the Bible are implicitly organized as if they are presenting a lawsuit brought by Yahweh against his people for violation of the covenant.[127] Prophetic literature prominently features the legal language of complaint and judgment, the invocation of heaven and earth as witnesses in a manner used in ancient treaties, and the deployment of curses common to breaches of treaty.[128] For example, the Book of Micah alludes to a civil complaint of Yahweh against His people:

> Hear what the LORD says:
>   Rise, plead your case before the mountains,
>   and let the hills hear your voice.

127. For examples of the covenant "lawsuit," see Micah 6:1–8; Jeremiah 2:4–13; Hosea 4:1–6; Deuteronomy 32; and Isaiah 1:2–3, 18–20; Isaiah 3:13–18; Isaiah. 49. See George E. Mendenhall, *Law and Covenant in Israel and the Ancient Near East* (Pittsburgh, PA: Biblical Colloquium, 1955); Herbert B. Huffmon, "The Covenant Lawsuit in the Prophets," *Journal of Biblical Literature* 78, no. 4 (1959): 285–95; R. E. Clements, *Prophecy and Covenant* (London: S.C.M. Press, 1965); R. E. Clements, *Prophecy and Tradition* (Oxford: Basil Blackwell, 1975); G. Ernest Wright, "The Lawsuit of God: A Form-Critical Study of Deuteronomy 32," in *Israel's Prophetic Heritage: Essays in Honor of James Muilenburg*, ed. Bernhard W. Anderson and Walter Harrelson (New York: Harper & Brothers, 1962), 26–67; and Kristen Nielsen, *Yahweh as Prosecutor and Judge: An Investigation of the Prophetic Lawsuit*, JSOT supp. series, no. 9 (Sheffield, UK: University of Sheffield, 1978). For overviews, see Dennis J. McCarthy, S.J., *Old Testament Covenant: A Survey of Current Opinions* (Oxford: Basil Blackwell, 1972); and Anthony Phillips, *Essays on Biblical Law* (London: T & T Clark, 2004), chap. 10, 164–78. For more recent work, see Shalom E. Holtz, "The Prophet as Summoner," in *A Common Cultural Heritage: Studies on Mesopotamia and the Biblical World in Honor of Barry L. Eichler*, ed. Grant Frame, Erle Leichty, Karen Sonik, Jeffrey H. Tigay, and Steve Tinney (Bethesda, MD: CDL Press, 2011), 19–34; Shalom E. Holtz, "Praying as a Plaintiff," *Vetus Testamentum* 61, no. 2 (2011): 258–279; Shalom E. Holtz, "A Comparative Note on the Demand for Witnesses in Isa 43:9," *Journal of Biblical Literature* 129, no. 3 (2010): 457–461. See also Ari Mermelstein and Shalom E. Holtz, eds., *The Divine Courtroom in Comparative Perspective* (Leiden: Brill, 2015). Thanks to Yonder Gillihan for his bibliographical suggestions.

128. Hillers, *Covenant: The History of a Biblical Idea*, chap. 6, 120–42.

> Hear, you mountains, the controversy of the LORD,
>> and you enduring foundations of the earth;
> for the Lord has a controversy with his people,
>> and he will contend with Israel.[129]

Yahweh goes on to argue that He has fulfilled His side of the agreement, thereby implying that Israel's failure to perform is unjustified.

> O my people, what have I done to you?
>> In what have I wearied you? Answer me!
> For I brought you up from the land of Egypt,
>> and redeemed you from the house of slavery;
> and I sent before you Moses,
>> Aaron, and Miriam."[130]

To take another example, Hosea pushes the theme in the direction of a criminal case, explicitly articulating the charge against Israel:

> Hear the word of the LORD, O people of Israel;
>> for the LORD has an indictment against the inhabitants of the land.
> There is no faithfulness or loyalty,
>> and no knowledge of God in the land.
> Swearing, lying, and murder,
>> and stealing and adultery break out;
>> bloodshed follows bloodshed.[131]

Yahweh is both prosecutor and judge; after conducting the trial, He pronounces the sentence:

> Israel's pride testifies against him;
>> Ephraim stumbles in his guilt;
>> Judah also stumbles with them.
> With their flocks and herds they shall go
>> to seek the LORD,

---

129. Micah 6:1–2. (All biblical quotations in this book are taken from the New Revised Standard Version of the Bible released in 1989 by the National Council of Churches; they were accessed through the website Bible Gateway.)

130. Micah 6:3–4.

131. Hosea 4:1–2.

but they will not find him;

   he has withdrawn from them.

They have dealt faithlessly with the LORD;

   for they have borne illegitimate children.

Now the new moon shall devour them along with their fields.[132]

Civil and criminal complaints normally occupy very different realms in the contemporary legal context. But in the Puritan worldview, as in the biblical worldview, they are connected, at least with respect to matters touching upon the divine–human relationship. Breaching the covenant with God is not only a breach of contract but also a criminal offense against the divine sovereign. Consequently, it is not surprising that the preachers' complaints invoke the language of criminal indictments in detailing the sins of the people. Consider, for example, Thomas Shepard's 1672 election sermon, *Eye-Salve,* which focuses on a passage from the book of Jeremiah (2:31) in a way that explicitly invokes a criminal charge. According to Shepard, the passage treats:

   1. The Lords Vindication and Acquittance of himself from all blame . . .

   2. The Lord's Crimination of *Israel, or* his Expostulatory Indictment and Charge drawn up against this People by the Lord himself . . .[133]

In many respects, the logical structure of a criminal indictment is similar to that of a civil complaint, especially for our purposes here. An indictment alleges that a particular action or omission took place, that the action or omission in question violated the duly enacted code of conduct binding upon the community, and that the offender should be punished in accordance with law.[134] In a popular eighteenth-century legal dictionary used by the

132. Hosea 5:5–7.

133. Thomas Shepard, *Eye-Salve* . . . , 2.

134. For a picture of the legal system in Puritan Massachusetts, see Edgar J. McManus, *Law and Liberty in Early New England: Criminal Justice and Due Process, 1620–1692* (Amherst: University of Massachusetts Press, 1993); and David Thomas Konig, *Law and Society in Puritan Massachusetts: Essex County, 1629–1692* (Chapel Hill: University of North Carolina Press, 1979). Particularly fascinating is Joseph H. Smith, ed., *Colonial Justice in Western Massachusetts (1639–1702): The Pynchon Court Record: An Original Judges' Diary of the Administration of Justice in the Springfield Courts in the Massachusetts Bay*

colonists,[135] an indictment is defined as "a Bill or Declaration of Complaint drawn up in Form of Law, exhibited for some Offence criminal or penal, and preferred to a Grand Jury; upon whose Oaths it is found to be true, before a Judge or others, having Power to punish or certify the Offence."[136] Citing Lord Chief Justice Hale, the 1750 edition of the dictionary goes on to say that an indictment "is nothing else but a plain, brief, and certain Narrative of an Offence committed by any Person, and of those necessary Circumstances, that concur to ascertain the Fact and its Nature."[137]

The indictment was read aloud to the accused in court; it too embedded the criminal law within a larger, religious framework. Until the mid-nineteenth century, for example, English criminal indictments generally alleged the defendant committed the crime "not having the fear of God before his eyes, but being moved and seduced at the instigation of the devil."[138] Those words

---

Colony (Cambridge, MA: Harvard University Press, 1961). See also Juliet Haines Mofford, *The Devil Made Me Do It! Crime and Punishment in Early New England* (Guilford, CT: Globe Pequot Press, 2012); and Michael P. Winship, *The Times & Trials of Anne Hutchinson: Puritans Divided* (Lawrence: University of Kansas Press, 2005). See also William E. Nelson, *The Common Law in Colonial America*, vol. 1, *The Chesapeake and New England, 1607–1660* (New York: Oxford University Press, 2008). For deeper background, see John Dykstra Eusden, *Puritans, Lawyers, and Politics in Early Seventeenth Century England* (New Haven, CT: Yale University Press, 1958).

135. The colonists used law dictionaries such as John Cowell's *A Law Dictionary* (1708) and Giles Jacob's *A New Law Dictionary* (1736). See Peter Charles Hoffer, "History of American Law: Colonial Period," in *The Oxford Companion to American Law*, ed. Kermit L. Hall (New York: Oxford University Press, 2002), 365.

136. "Indictment," in Giles Jacob, *A New Law Dictionary* . . . (London, 1729). For an account of the development of law dictionaries, see Gary L. McDowell, "The Politics of Meaning: Law Dictionaries and the Liberal Tradition of Interpretation," *American Journal of Legal History* 44, no. 3 (2000): 257–83.

137. "Indictment," in Giles Jacob, *A New Law Dictionary* . . . , 6th ed. (London, 1750).

138. See, for example, the main source on English criminal procedure, John Frederick Archbold, *A Summary of the Law Relative to Pleading and Evidence in Criminal Cases*, 5th ed. (New York, 1835), 314, which follows this rule. See Markus Eder, *"At the Instigation of the Devil": Capital Punishment and the Assize in the Early Modern England, 1670–1730*, 2nd ed. (CreateSpace Independent Publishing Platform, 2014); and the examples in Owen Davies, "Talk of the Devil: Crime and Satanic Inspiration in Eighteenth-Century England" (2007), www.academia.edu/224811/Talk_of_the_Devil_Crime_and _Satanic_Inspiration_in_Eighteenth-Century England. English indictments gradually began to take simpler form in the mid-nineteenth century as a result of new legislation: An Act for further Improving the Administration of Criminal Justice 1851, 14 & 15 Vict. c. 100, enacted on August 7, 1851, and effective from September 1, 1851 (sometimes, like several other Acts, called Lord Campbell's Act), provided by various provisions and especially s. 24 that formal defects could no longer be made the ground for demurrer during the trial and could in any case be cured by the Court. As a result, indictments became reduced to their essentials. See R. R. Pearce, *The New Law of Indictments* . . ., supplement to Archbold's Criminal Law (London, 1851); and John Frederick Archbold, *The New System of Criminal Procedure, Pleading and Evidence* . . . (London, 1852). See also Harry B. Poland, "Changes in

or similar ones commonly appeared in indictments in New England;[139] it was not until 1853 that they were declared unnecessary averments for indictments for murder in the Commonwealth of Massachusetts.[140]

The premise of the indictment is that the law in question is functionally *beyond* question—in both the sense that it is valid and in the sense that it is or ought to be known to be valid law. The very first article of the very first set of laws passed by the Puritans, the Massachusetts Body of Liberties (1641), expressly stated that no one was to be deprived of life, liberty, or property except pursuant to a valid and sufficiently publicized law:

> It is therfore ordered by this Court, & Authority therof, That no mans life shall be taken away; no mans honour or good name shall be stayned; no mans person shal be arrested, restrained, bannished, dismembered nor any wayes punished; no man shall be deprived of his wife or children; no mans goods or estate shal be taken away from him; nor any wayes indamaged under colour of Law or countenance of Authoritie unles it be by the vertue or equity of some expresse law of the Country warranting the same established by a General Court & sufficiently published; or in case of the defect of a law in any particular case by the word of God. And in capital cases, or in cases concerning dismēbring or banishmēt according to that word to be judged by the General Court. [1641][141]

Criminal Law and Procedure since 1800," in *A Century of Law Reform: Twelve Lectures on the Changes in the Law of England during the Nineteenth Century* (London: Macmillan and Co., 1901), 62–63. Thanks to John Finnis for help with this note.

139. See, for example, the forms of criminal indictment in Francis Wharton, *Precedents of Indictments and Pleas, Adapted to the Use Both of the Courts of the United States and Those of all the Several States* (Philadelphia, PA, 1849), book 3, chap. 1.

140. *Commonwealth v. Murphy,* 11 Cush. 472 (1853). The shift is duly incorporated in the legal practice books; see, for example, Joel Prentiss Bishop, *Criminal Procedure; or, Commentaries on the Law of Pleading and Evidence and the Practice in Criminal Cases,* vol. 2, 3rd ed. (Boston, MA: Little, Brown 1880), sec. 503. For a broader perspective, see Steven Wilf, *Law's Imagined Republic: Popular Politics and Criminal Justice in Revolutionary America* (Cambridge: Cambridge University Press, 2010).

141. *The Book of the General Lawes and Libertyes Concerning the Inhabitants of the Massachusets . . .* (Cambridge, MA, 1648), A3, in *The Laws and Liberties of Massachusetts 1648: Reprinted from the Unique Copy of the 1648 Edition in the Huntington Library,* introduction by Richard S. Dunn (San Marino, CA: Huntington Library, 1998).

We saw that a complaint for breach of contract assumes that the contract is valid and that the parties themselves agreed to its terms. Analogously, a criminal complaint assumes that the law is valid and that the defendant is bound to observe it because it was duly enacted by the legislative body. An indictment, therefore, rhetorically assumes that there is no need to argue that the class of behavior it is condemning is objectionable. It focuses its efforts on (1) showing that the defendant engaged in this type of activity on a particular occasion and (2) arguing that the appropriate penalty should be imposed.

Furthermore, within the framework of the indictment, there is virtually no room to consider systematically whether the actions or omissions with which the defendant is charged are indeed wrong or should be illegal. It is not true, of course, that such discussions cannot take place in other contexts and in other places or times. Citizens and lawmakers do debate about statutory prohibitions, just as contracting parties do dicker about terms to be included in the prospective agreement. But by the time a complaint or indictment is filed, those sorts of deliberations are closed—at least with respect to this case. Any attempt on the part of the defendant to reopen them would be met with a firm rejoinder: "This is the contract you signed," or "Take it up with your representative. This is the law that governs your actions here and now." Complaints and indictments are not meant to facilitate consideration of whether particular activity should be considered wrongful—they are meant to facilitate consideration of whether activity already deemed to be wrongful actually took place.

As I argued above, the complaint or indictment provides the model for the religious-political speech of the Puritan jeremiad, which outlines, with a limited amount of variation, "God's controversy with New England." While the heat of the rhetoric varies with the preacher, the basic framework remains the same: (1) the citizens of New England have engaged in certain types of behavior, (2) that behavior violates the national covenant with God, and (3) God has exacted or will exact damages or a penalty for that violation.

Significantly for our purposes, the Puritan jeremiad excoriated activities and attitudes that the clergy believed were far too prevalent among the people. They did not, however, believe it necessary to defend their judgment that the condemned behavior was morally wrong. It would have astonished the divines who participated in the 1679 Reforming Synod, for example, if any intelligent and respectable person defended any of the twelve categories of rebuked behavior as actually permissible according to the terms of the covenant. The point of the jeremiad—the purpose of the fiery condemnations and threats—was to urge the colonists to turn away from behavior that they themselves well knew was prohibited by God's covenant with New England. The phenomenon it sees itself as addressing is that of human sinfulness even among believers, as so vividly described by St. Paul: "For I know that nothing good dwells within me, that is, in my flesh. I can will what is right, but I cannot do it. For I do not do the good I want, but the evil I do not want is what I do."[142]

So the jeremiad, like a complaint, is meant in the first instance to call defendants to account for acting in ways that the contracting parties—in this case, the community—have already agreed is impermissible. Like an indictment, it is also meant to call for the punishment of such behavior and to exhort other potential wrongdoers to change their ways. It is not meant to be a vehicle to encourage deliberation about whether a certain set of actions is in fact morally wrong. In fact, it provides almost no opening for the kind of dialectical questioning that would constitute such deliberation. The firm condemnation of various types of wrongful activity does not encourage systematic consideration of what actions, under what circumstances, deserve such a fierce rebuke. In essence, the structure of the jeremiad assumes that there is no reasonable disagreement about what sort of behavior is wrongful. It assumes that the only pertinent questions are whether persons are engaging in such behavior and what the unpleasant consequences of such activities should be. Moreover, these assumptions are reinforced by the passionate terms in which social deviation from the covenant is deprecated.

A Cosmic Carrot and Stick

At first glance, it may seem as if the scolding tone and ominous threats of the jeremiad would render it a highly unpopular form of address. That initial impression, however, would be quite mistaken. In fact, the jeremiad was a very well-regarded type of rhetoric with the first generation of settlers. Moreover, and more surprisingly, it grew even more popular with their chil-

142. Romans 7:18–19.

dren and grandchildren. In the middle decades of the seventeenth century, jeremiads were almost the only form of printed materials for which there was sustained public demand.[143] Why were they so popular?

First, despite appearances, the jeremiad was actually a cosmically reassuring form of political and religious rhetoric precisely because it was firmly situated within the context of the national covenant. Other nations may pray to God for blessings or deliverance; their prayers may or may not be granted. God deals with them as He will, for His own inscrutable purposes. But God has made His intentions toward New England clear by entering into covenant with the Puritans who built the colony. And those intentions are beneficent; God desires New England to be both virtuous and prosperous. While God certainly holds His covenant partner to a higher standard than other nations, He does so only because of His great love for them. Moreover, God has promised to incline His ear to New England's prayers of repentance and petition; the Puritans were therefore able to rely confidently upon His favorable response, although that response might be delayed for a time for their own good. The New Englanders could count on the fact that, in their case, any temporal chastisements were meant to be medicinal rather than destructive. God wanted nothing more than to convert them from their wicked ways and to reward their renewed piety with renewed material blessings. As Sacvan Bercovitch writes,

> Why was it that "no place under heaven . . . will so highly provoke and incense the displeasure of God as . . . New-England"? Why were there *"no persons in all the world unto whom God speaketh as he doth unto us* [by His] . . . most awful Providences"? The reason was obvious. Because New England was God's country, its inhabitants must expect His lash. *"God is terrible out of his holy places."*[144]

---

143. Miller, *From Colony to Province*, 30.

144. Bercovitch, *The American Jeremiad*, 57. He is citing John Bale, *The Image of Both Churches* (1548), in *Select Works*, ed. Henry Christmas (Cambridge, MA, 1849), 295; Increase Mather, *The Times of Man* (Boston, MA, 1675), 16, 19–20; and John Sherman and Thomas Shepard, Jr., preface to Urian Oakes, *New-England Pleaded with* . . . (Cambridge, MA, 1673), sig. A2.

God's chastisements, in the case of other nations, were meant to destroy on account of sin and disobedience. In the case of the Puritans, and New England, and later the United States, they were meant to be a form of "corrective affliction."[145]

Second, the jeremiad nurtured an optimism that was not only a hope for a blessed existence in eternity on the one hand or a prosperous existence here and now on the other. The American jeremiads fused the two, by endowing New England's fate, and later the fate of America as a whole, with eternal significance. "Of all communities on earth, only the new Protestant Israel had 'the Blessings both of the *upper and nether Springs,* the Blessings of Time and of Eternity.'"[146] According to Bercovitch, the Calvinist virtues of diligence and self-restraint operated in an increasingly capitalistic culture to produce a "middle class" mind-set striving toward achievement in both the material and spiritual realms. The unique divine concern for this new land meant that prosperity and success were available both now on earth and hereafter in heaven.

Third, the jeremiad not only gestured toward a blessed future, it also manipulated the emotions of its audience so that they would work harder to bring that future into existence. "The very concept of errand, after all, implied a state of *unfulfillment.* The future, though divinely assured, was never quite there, and New England's Jeremiahs set out to provide the sense of insecurity that would ensure the outcome."[147] The jeremiad was a stimulant; it provoked both anxiety and renewed determination. Its energy prodded the early settlers to tame the wilderness, and (borrowing from Perry Miller) to evolve from colony to province and to develop from province to nation. Miller observed that it was success that flummoxed New England's jeremiahs, not the prospect of failure: "the jeremiad could make sense out of existence as long as adversity was to be overcome, but in the moment of victory it was confused. It had always to say that now the day of trouble may be ended, that God has thus far 'answered us by terrible things in righteousness'—if only our sins do not again undo us."[148]

145. Ibid., 58.

146. Ibid., 47. He is citing John Davenport, *A Sermon Preached at the Election* (Cambridge, MA, 1669), 16; and Richard Mather and William Tompson, *An Heart-Melting Exhortation* (London, 1650), 7.

147. Ibid., 23.

148. Miller, *From Colony to Province,* 33.

Fourth, the jeremiad helps to expiate communal guilt about what is necessary to do in order to create that prosperous future. Miller proposes that one reason the jeremiad became so popular in the second and third generations is that it assisted them in reconciling their increasing focus on commerce and trade with their commitment to the religious faith of their fathers and mothers. New England was settled by people whose mind-set was at least as much medieval as modern; Puritans operated with a fixed social hierarchy and a theory of the "just price." By adapting to early modern capitalist society and admitting the flexibility in social status that accompanied success in the increasingly competitive world of business, second- and third-generation Puritans created a world that was very different from that expected by their ancestors. The jeremiad's ritual of confessing and berating their sins—the ordinary sins of a busy, industrious and acquisitive people—assuaged their anxiety and allowed them to get back to work.[149]

In my view, however, these four reasons for the jeremiad's popularity, advanced by Miller, Bercovitch, and others, do not fully grasp the nettle of the problem. They provide a helpful, even an essential, account of the jeremiad's role within broader social and economic currents of the colony. But they do not attend sufficiently to the relationship between the rhetoric of the jeremiads and their reception in the community. We still need to ask: How could such sustained diatribes against bad behavior be so well-received? Why would they not immediately provoke social fissure and bitter resentments?

In my view, the answer lies in the fact that the behavior condemned in the jeremiads was widely acknowledged to be illicit. While some people, even many people, might engage in it from time to time, almost no one would *defend* doing so. Who could defend decay in godliness, sinful pride, or Sabbath-breaking, to invoke three items from the Result to the 1679 synod identifying the provoking evils of New England? The only real question was whether the people had in fact engaged in such activity and, if so, what was required of them in order to repent and repair the ensuing breach with God.

The fact that the acts and practices condemned in the seventeenth-century jeremiad were *unquestionably* wrong is strongly related, in my view, to the tight connection the preachers assumed between the jeremiad, the positive law of the colony, and a clear understanding of the national covenant. In

---

149. See ibid., 40–52.

seventeenth-century New England, the jeremiad was a stylized form of legal complaint or indictment, calling attention to deviations from the strictures of the covenant and warning of the dire consequences of such faithlessness. In that context, and in that society, the requirements of the covenant were not controversial; they were pervasively inculcated by both church and state. Even those who engaged in the behavior condemned in the jeremiad would not defend it; they would strive to repent and reform, or at least strive to pretend they would do so.

Modeled as a complaint for breach of contract, the jeremiad could only castigate actions or omissions that violated the clear agreement of the parties. Modeled as an indictment for wrongful behavior, it could call to account only actions whose criminality had been determined and promulgated by lawful authority. The jeremiad created no more room for discussion and debate about the underlying judgment that the condemned behavior is wrongful than a criminal indictment does about the impermissibility of the actions with which it charges the defendant. In both cases, it is assumed that the discussion is closed, and the relevant normative judgments about actions or omissions are both settled and known to be settled.

Over time, however, the conception of the covenant became more attenuated in New England society, as it was stretched to encompass the changing circumstances of the colony.[150] Moreover, the tight link between the jeremiad and the covenant began to dissolve, as did as the constraints that the link placed on the use of the jeremiad as a spur to social reform. By the time of the American Revolution, the fire of the jeremiad proved irresistible to those who wished to use it to forge a new social consensus about a controversial issue rather than simply to enforce an existing social consensus by discouraging behavior widely agreed to be sinful. At this point, the jeremiad began to shift its rhetorical function from a mechanism reinforcing social consensus to a vehicle propelling social change. The jeremiad began to be used to condemn behavior that the speaker believed *ought to be* against communal mores.

---

150. Another topic, beyond the scope of this book, is the shading of prophetic discourse into apocalyptic modes of speaking and thinking, which was not uncommon in the Puritan era or in subsequent eras. See, for example, Daniel Wojcik, *The End of the World as We Know It: Faith, Fatalism, and Apocalypse in America* (New York: New York University Press, 1997). Yet an apocalyptic imagination works against agitators for social reform and also against the use of a jeremiad to secure such reform. If repentance and reformation will not avert the coming destruction, prophetic indictment logically shades into lamentation.

At the same time, however, its use began to stoke controversy and create divisiveness rather than to unite the community by prompting renewed commitment to widely acknowledged values. What once functioned to unite a covenanted community through collective self-denunciation came to function as a means by which one might denounce persons perceived to be "outsiders" for reasons that were not always related to a clearly articulated set of covenantal values.

From Consensus to Division

The Jeremiad's Shifting Role in American Political Life

As Sacvan Bercovitch has persuasively argued, the jeremiad is a quintessentially American form of political discourse.[1] Its status as an American classic does not mean, however, that the jeremiad has remained the same over the centuries. After all, it is also quintessentially American to incorporate significant change within the framework provided by enduring forms. As Bercovitch rightly notes, the changes in the jeremiad were set in motion by the Puritans themselves as they were pressed to expand their notion of political community in response to their evolving circumstances. He writes: "they were being forced by history to enlarge their ideal of New Israel into a vision that was so broad in its implications, and so specifically American in its application, that it could survive the failure of theocracy."[2]

Bercovitch has also maintained, to my mind much less persuasively, that despite the changes, the jeremiad has continued to function as a ritual of consensus in American life by broadening its conception of America to encompass more and more heterogeneous populations. Through the successive

---

1. Sacvan Bercovitch, *The American Jeremiad* (Madison: University of Wisconsin Press, 1978). Bercovitch's classic account has been subjected to numerous critiques. See, for example, Andrew R. Murphy, *Prodigal Nation: Moral Decline and Divine Punishment from New England to 9/11* (New York: Oxford University Press, 2009), 166–67. Murphy argues that Bercovitch's interpretation of the jeremiad as an optimistic form of rhetoric is too strong; he thinks that the New England jeremiahs truly feared the withdrawal of God's favor. While Murphy is correct about later forms of the jeremiad, I think Bercovitch is closer to the truth about the Puritans. As I read them, the Puritans believed that the grace of Christ made their covenant with God stronger than that of the Hebrew people.

2. Bercovitch, *The American Jeremiad*, 92.

revolutionary upheavals of the Puritan Great Migration to New England (1620–1640), the American Revolution, and the Civil War, the country was advancing toward the New Jerusalem, an increasingly hazy religious and political ideal marked with urgency by the millenarian tendencies that were increasingly prevalent in American society throughout the eighteenth and nineteenth centuries. Harnessed to the notion of progress, the jeremiad maintained and legitimated mainstream capitalist, middle-class American culture. By insisting that revolution or improvement be justified in terms of our common *American* identity, our particular and glorious destiny, the jeremiad, according to Bercovitch, set limits on social criticism and forged social coherence.

Bercovitch's analysis fails, however, to take into account a key element of the classical Puritan jeremiad: the strong condemnation of a people's sins and failings. He recognizes that the "ritual of the jeremiad" shaped political discussions around the Revolutionary War, the Civil War, and even early feminist debates. What he does not grapple with is the fractious nature of both the tone and the substance of these later jeremiads at the time they were delivered. For example, it may be possible to look back at an abolitionist's speech and see in it the confirmation of the true nature of America, an articulation of our common consensus. At the time the speech was delivered, however, nothing could have been further from the truth. The abolitionists' fiery rhetoric condemning slavery was met with an equally blistering rebuttal from those who defended the institution on both religious and political grounds. It is important to remember that it was not rhetoric that settled the controversy over slavery in the United States but rather bullets and blood. The question Bercovitch fails to ask, and the question I hope to address in this chapter, is this: How did the jeremiad evolve from a mechanism of social consensus to an engine of division in American culture?

As I argued in the previous chapter, the castigations of the Puritan preachers were both widely popular and a source of communal unity in mid-seventeenth-century New England. They were effectively designed to call the community to recommit itself to its foundational values, as expressed in the national covenant, along with the positive laws passed in order to give that covenant concrete shape in the new world. In our own era, by contrast, most jeremiads are anything but unifying; in fact, they are usually strongly divisive. A jeremiad on a controversial topic such as abortion, torture, healthcare reform, same-sex marriage, or war in the Middle East tends to reinforce and entrench already existing social and political divisions. Those who agree with a particular "jeremiah" happily find their position confirmed, while those who disagree generally respond with anger and frustration.

What accounts for the socially fissiparous nature of many contemporary jeremiads? The immediate and obvious response is that they grapple with controversial topics. This response raises a deeper question: Why would a political controversialist think it appropriate to use this particular rhetorical form to discuss divisive matters? No community is totally homogenous—even Puritan Massachusetts.[3] The Puritans generally deployed the jeremiad to condemn behavior that was widely agreed to be wrong and refrained from using it as a vehicle for addressing contested matters. This was a wise decision because the jeremiad is not a rhetorical form that is conducive to systematic consideration of controversial issues. Consequently, employing a jeremiad in order to convince others of highly contested moral or political questions is very likely to lead to a fractious and frustrating discussion. In fact, it is very much like using an indictment to condemn behavior that has not yet been outlawed, or drafting a complaint to seek redress for breach of a term that one *wishes* had been part of the contract but that had not been incorporated into it.

How can we explain the shifting role that the jeremiad plays in American political and religious life?[4] The task of this chapter is to propose an account of the evolution of its role, which was in substantial part complete by the time of the Revolutionary War. In brief, I argue that over the span of a century or so, the Puritan colony lost a tight hermeneutical connection between the covenant and jeremiad. As that connection faded, the jeremiad did not lose its importance; it did, however, lose the sociopolitical context in which it originally played a constructive and formative role. It no longer functioned as an instrument that contributed to social unity by reinforcing widely

3. For a picture of the lively heterogeneity in Puritan America, see David D. Hall, *Worlds of Wonder, Days of Judgment: Popular Religious Belief in Early New England* (Cambridge, MA: Harvard University Press, 1989).

4. I do not mean to suggest that the evolution of American religious sensibilities from colonial times onward is anything but complicated and variegated. See, for example, E. Brooks Holifield, *Theology in America: Christian Thought from the Age of the Puritans to the Civil War* (New Haven, CT: Yale University Press, 2003); Mark A. Noll, *America's God: From Jonathan Edwards to Abraham Lincoln* (New York: Oxford University Press, 2002); Jon Butler, *Awash in a Sea of Faith: Christianizing the American People* (Cambridge, MA: Harvard University Press, 1990); Nathan O. Hatch, *The Democratization of American Christianity* (New Haven, CT: Yale University Press, 1989); and Sydney E. Ahlstrom, *A Religious History of the American People* (New Haven, CT: Yale University Press, 1972).

agreed upon social norms; instead, it became a rhetorical tool deployed on behalf of moral progress, in service of the adoption of *new* political and/or moral norms. As a consequence of this shift, the jeremiad evolved into an instrument of social division rather than remaining a vehicle that promoted social harmony.

In this chapter, I argue that three developments in the context, language, and structure of the jeremiad can explain how the jeremiad evolved to become a source of contentiousness in American life. First, the close-knit relationship between the jeremiad and a rich conception of a national covenant disintegrated, thereby unmooring the jeremiad from a more or less defined moral and social consensus. Second, the more focused framework of the national covenant was displaced by the more vague and contestable language of natural rights and common sense. Third, the biblical template for the jeremiad shifted from the "oracles against Israel," which prompts reform and renewal on the part of God's people, to the "oracles against the nations," which portends the destruction of the enemies of God's people. After detailing three developments in the colonial era, I turn to Thomas Paine's *Common Sense* as a case study. In my view, this immensely popular pamphlet defending the cause of the Patriots against the Loyalists nicely illustrates how the components of the jeremiad were reassembled to serve controversialist and polemical ends. Given these historical considerations, I then advance a thesis about how the jeremiad has come to function in contemporary society. For the Puritans, the *breach* of the covenant was their prevailing sins, which were more or less uncontroversial; the *penalty* was the loss of material prosperity. In our era, however, it seems that this structure is completely reversed. The uncontroversial covenantal obligation is to secure the nation's economic and military well-being. Political parties that do so are rewarded with the opportunity to implement their own, contested vision of what counts as virtue and vice.

Loosening the Bond between Covenant and Jeremiad

In the preceding chapter, I described the elaborate, interlocking set of covenants with which American Puritans organized their relationship to God and to one another. Echoing the Hebrew prophets in their heavy reliance on the legal language of complaint and indictment, Puritan preachers developed their jeremiads within the closed frame of that covenantal structure, particularly the structure of the national covenant. The covenant between God and the nation, whose content the Puritans believed they could determine with some certainty, set the terms of social and political behavior. The people breached the covenant and, as a consequence, God withdrew favor and exercised wrath on the colonists by directing natural and human events to work to their great disadvantage. Repentance and reformation would heal the breach, and God in His mercy would remove the penalty.

It is true that the center of gravity of many jeremiads is on the sins that provoke God's wrath, sins that the preachers viewed as lamentable in themselves, not merely because they triggered God's ire. Their perspective is not surprising; what was at stake for the Puritans was their self-understanding as God's chosen people, as a city on a hill. The loss of this self-conception, and not merely of the temporal blessings that accompanied it, would have been an unbearably heavy burden for devout Puritans to bear. The jeremiads of the second generation of Puritan preachers betray an overwhelming sense of their own inadequacy when compared to the religious fervor and moral fiber of their parents. A strong emphasis on the provoking evils of New England, with correspondingly lighter consideration of God's retribution for those evils, does not necessarily mark an erosion of the strong covenantal framework as both enabling and constraining the jeremiad. After all, the preachers could have assumed that their audience knew very well the material dangers to their personal, familial, and communal well-being. They did not need to be reminded of famine, war, illness, or the threats from the native population—those threats awaited them at the door of the meeting house.

What *would* mark an erosion of the covenantal framework, however, would be growing doubts about whether the material trials endured by the colonists were actually inflicted by God as a penalty for the breach of covenant. The Puritan covenantal structure depended, as we saw in the previous chapter, on the belief that God was finely calibrating His control of the cosmos to manifest His evolving attitude toward the colony. What if this was not the case? The Puritan self-understanding can survive, indeed thrive, in the face of the recognition that God has a "controversy" with New England. The Puritans recognized, after all, that special chastisement could be an expression of special concern and love. What cannot be a form of love, however, is indifference.

The Waning of God's Interest

What if the terrible trials, and considerable blessings, experienced by the Puritans in settling the New World were not sent by God as finely gauged assessments of the state of their covenantal relationship with Him? What if they were not rightly interpreted as divine messages at all? Moreover, what if the impact of natural events, as well as the success or failure of human endeavors, were not to be attributed to God's particular providence but instead to some form of chance? This line of questioning, of course, had the potential to undermine not merely the intelligibility of the jeremiad but the entire structure of Puritan thought.

Doubts about the correspondence between the trials and triumphs experienced by their community and qualms about God's attitude toward New England's standing as a covenant partner can be seen in seventeenth-century Puritan writings. Increase Mather manifested such doubts in his account of "King Philip's War," although he made every attempt to minimize them. How, he wondered, could the colonists' fervent attempts at repentance and self-abnegation before God be met with devastating defeats at the hands of the native population? These continuing losses threatened the intelligibility of the national covenant itself. Miller pithily summarized the problem: "How could men continue to believe that New England enjoyed a peculiar and sanctified relation to Jehovah, or that He would come to their aid against King Charles merely because the people repented and reformed? And if Jehovah would not help them, why should they repent at all?"[5]

The significant political failure experienced by the Puritans in England and in America was another cause of the erosion of the belief that natural and human events could be straightforwardly interpreted as manifestations of the divine will. New England was meant to be a beacon of light to European reformers, inspiring them to redouble their efforts to remake both church and society in accordance with the guidance of the Bible. The collapse of Cromwell's protectorate and the restoration of the monarchy in 1660 called into question not only the self-conception of American Puritans but also their view of divine providence. In addition, the increasing tensions that the colonists experienced

5. Perry Miller, *The New England Mind: From Colony to Province* (Cambridge, MA: Belknap Press of Harvard University Press, 1953), 143.

with their mother country could not but raise doubts about whether God indeed viewed New England as His covenant partner. Particularly painful for the colonists was England's revocation of their charter in 1684, followed by the years of their subjection to the Dominion of New England under the control of Sir Edmund Andros (1686–1689). Many of these doubts were alleviated in time after the Glorious Revolution, the ascension of Protestant rulers William and Mary to the English throne in 1689, the immediate expulsion of Andros by the colonists, and the Crown's issuance of a second charter to Massachusetts in 1691 after a series of negotiations conducted in part by Increase Mather. The Mathers, in fact, interpreted the years of the Dominion as a terrible divine affliction from which a merciful God delivered New England after its sincere repentance and prostration. Nevertheless, the doubts about God's intimate involvement with the fate of New England never entirely abated, in part because the new charter did not replicate the theocracy of the first charter but extended voting rights beyond the Puritan settlers.

The colonists' experiential doubts about whether God was indeed relating to New England through the terms and conditions of the covenant were strengthened by quickly spreading religious ideas indebted to the Enlightenment. The late seventeenth century and early eighteenth century were marked by the waxing influence of deism in English thought and in European thought more generally. Deists tended to perceive God in more remote and mechanistic terms; according to them, the divine being created the world and set it on its path but maintained very little involvement in day-to-day events. In their view, the "Supreme Architect" of the universe did not involve himself in petty human affairs; the course of events was determined by the laws of nature and of motion, not by the imprecations of human beings. Neither miracles nor petitionary prayer had any place in this world-view. Consequently, the idea that a day of fasting could turn the course of a decisive battle by calming divine anger would make little sense to those sympathetic to deist sensibilities.[6]

---

6. For a recent, revisionist history of deism's major and minor English proponents, see Jeffrey R. Wigelsworth, *Deism in Enlightenment England: Theology, Politics, and Newtonian Public Science* (Manchester, UK: Manchester University Press, 2009). The role of deism in American colonial history has received renewed scholarly attention. See, for example, Eric R. Schlereth, *An Age of Infidels: The Politics of Religious Controversy in the Early United States* (Philadelphia: University of Pennsylvania Press, 2013).

The Puritans attempted to shore up their notion of providence, in some cases by refocusing their lens upon individual cases rather than an overall national pattern. Increase Mather's most popular book was entitled *An Essay for the Recording of Illustrious Providences,* which painstakingly recorded particular instances of God's wonderful or terrible intervention in the natural world.[7] It addressed its readership as individuals, not as members of a national community. By and large, Mather argued, God continues to reward the virtuous and punish the wicked; it is therefore in a prudent individual's interest to live virtuously. In later years, however, the Mathers undermined this claim by arguing that the response to the smallpox epidemic that affected Massachusetts in 1721 should be a proactive medical program of vaccination against disease, not a reactive religious regimen of prayer and fasting.[8]

For many years, a commitment to the particular attention of divine providence coexisted uneasily with a growing propensity to explain events in terms of natural causality or human agency. A good example can be found in Jonathan Mayhew's two sermons delivered on October 9, 1760, a day of public thanksgiving for the British conquest of Canada.[9] The full title of the first sermon is "Considerations on divine Providence in the Success and Consequences of national Wars; with some short, general Reflections on the Success of His Majesty's Arms in the present War."[10] While Mayhew begins by affirming the importance of divine providence and covenantal commitment, his remarks in this area seem almost perfunctory. His real interest is the worldlier and more tangible causes of military victory.

> But, from these general reflections on the overruling providence of God in the success and issue of wars, we will, if you please, proceed now to take a nearer and more particular view of these important events. We will consider, what are the usual, the visible, and more immediate causes of military successes and victories: In doing which, we shall trace the vestiges of divine providence.[11]

7. Increase Mather, *An Essay for the Recording of Illustrious Providences* . . . (Boston, MA, 1684).
8. See Miller, *From Colony to Province,* 345–66.
9. Jonathan Mayhew, *Two Discourses Delivered October 9, 1760* . . . (Boston, MA, 1760).
10. Mayhew, "Considerations on Divine Providence . . . ," in *Two Discourses,* A3.
11. Ibid., 14.

The vestiges of divine providence, according to Mayhew, appear in superiority of wisdom and military skill, the number and dedication of the troops,
the advantage in natural resources, the fickleness of disease, and other forms
of luck or chance. Mayhew's God is not yet the disinterested creator of the
deists, but neither is He actively involved in managing the gritty details of
worldly events. Instead, God is more like a judge on the sidelines. "God really
sits as Umpire on his eternal throne, between contending nations in all their
contests, whether for right and justice only, or for proud dominion; giving
success and triumph to which soever he pleaseth?"[12] Mayhew attributes the
turnaround in English fortunes in only three years to divine providence and
urges his audience to thank God for the victory. While He might have
arranged for the British conquest of the French, it appears that God's reasons
were as much political as they were religious.

In his second discourse, Mayhew goes on to consider the causes of the
English victory in Canada, revealing that he is more interested in military
strategy than spiritual reflection. He speaks of the benefits of victory largely
in this-worldly terms, noting that they "seem to promise an honorable peace,
future security to us here in America, and many advantages both to Great-
Britain and her colonies."[13] Yet he again anticipates the criticism that it is "a
kind of affront to a christian [sic] assembly" if a preacher on this occasion
"wholly confined his views and discourse to things of a secular nature."[14] Even
in the section of the sermon dedicated to religious concerns, however, Mayhew
cannot resist framing his points in strategic terms. The Catholic Church, the
"great whore, or mystical Babylon," has been defeated in this battle.[15] The
"successes which God has given to the British arms in the present war" are a
step toward "the destruction of the papal power, and the establishing of christianity thro'out the world."[16] The Native American population will soon be
disabused of "[t]he prejudices which many of them have imbibed against us
and our religion."[17] Mayhew's focus throughout the sermon is not so much on
transforming hearts and minds, but rather on extending the political power

12. Ibid., 27.
13. Jonathan Mayhew, "Concerning the Late Successes of His Majesty's Arms . . . ," in *Two
Discourses*, 52.
14. Ibid.
15. Ibid., 56.
16. Ibid., 54. By "Christianity," of course, Mayhew meant "Protestant Christianity."
17. Ibid., 57.

of Protestant Christendom, in which religious and civil rights are intertwined. "For both our civil and religious privileges are secured to us by these successes; and there is a fair prospect, that both we and our posterity may possess this good land in great peace and prosperity."[18] Mayhew gestures at the historical format of the jeremiad, urging his audience to "have a proper sense of God's undeserved goodness to us, by forsaking all our evil practices."[19] But he does not enumerate those practices, much less dwell upon them. His focus is upon adopting the right cause, and taking all human measures to achieve success, in the hope that God will award victory from His throne.

A more serious undermining of the intelligibility of a covenantal framework came from the tragic event with which New England Puritanism became best associated: the Salem witchcraft trials. The Puritans believed that one of the afflictions a covenanted people had to bear was the presence of witches in their midst.[20] In 1689, Cotton Mather chronicled "direful effects of a (no less *palpable* than) stupendous WITCHCRAFT" on the children of Boston mason John Goodwin.[21] His account of the tortures was vivid and detailed; in his florid introduction, he urges his *"little Book, as a Lackey"* to "Go *tell* Mankind, that there are *Devils & Witches;* & that tho those *night-birds* least appear where the *Day-light* of the Gospel comes, yet *New-Engl.* has had Exemples of their *Existence & Operation."*[22]

The colonial hysteria about witchcraft reached its deadly apex in Salem, Massachusetts, in 1692–1693.[23] Over the course of that period, more than two hundred people were accused of witchcraft, nineteen men and women were hanged on Gallows Hill, one man was executed by being pressed to death,

18. Ibid., 62.

19. Ibid.

20. The Puritans were not idiosyncratic in their belief in witchcraft; early modern historians remind us that the belief in witchcraft was also common in Europe. For a helpful resource, see Brian P. Levack, ed., *The Oxford Handbook of Witchcraft in Early Modern Europe and Colonial America* (Oxford: Oxford University Press, 2013).

21. Cotton Mather, *Memorable Providences, Relating to Witchcrafts and Possessions* . . . (Boston, MA, 1689), i.

22. Ibid., introduction, unpaginated.

23. For an account of the proceedings, see, for example, Richard Godbeer, *The Salem Witch Hunt: A Brief History with Documents* (Boston, MA: Bedford/St Martin's, 2011); and Marilynne K. Roach, *The Salem Witch Trials: A Day-by-Day Chronicle of a Community under Siege* (Lanham, MD: Taylor Trade Publishing, 2002). For a comprehensive documentary account, see Bernard Rosenthal, ed., *Records of the Salem Witch-Hunt* (New York: Cambridge University Press, 2009).

and several other persons died in prison.[24] The matter of Mather's responsibility for the witchcraft hysteria is complicated and contested.[25] On the one hand, Mather's contemporary Robert Calef places much of the blame on him for the madness.[26] This verdict is echoed by the nineteenth-century historian Charles Upham, who writes that "it can admit of no doubt, that Increase Mather and his son, Cotton Mather, did more than any other persons to aggravate the tendency of that age to the result reached in the Witchcraft Delusion of 1692."[27] On the other hand, twentieth-century scholars have been significantly kinder to both Mathers,[28] emphasizing the way they urged caution in the use of so-called "spectral evidence" to convict alleged practitioners of witchcraft.[29]

24. Jess Blumberg, "A Brief History of the Salem Witch Trials: One Town's Strange Journey from Paranoia to Pardon," Smithsonian.com, October 23, 2007, www.smithsonianmag.com/history /a-brief-history-of-the-salem-witch-trials-175162489/. The height of the Salem hysteria was in the summer and early fall of 1692; all executions took place from June to September. See the description of the memorial to the victims erected in 1992 in Danvers, Massachusetts: Salem Witch Trials, Documentary Archive and Transcription Project, "Salem Village Witchcraft Victims' Memorial at Danvers," http://salem.lib.virginia.edu/Commemoration.html.

25. For a compact, nuanced account, see Rebecca T. Smith, "Cotton Mather's Involvement in the Salem Crisis," *The Spectrum: A Scholar's Day Journal* 2, no. 1, art. 11 (2013), http://digitalcommons .brockport.edu/spectrum/vol2/iss1/11. On the animosity between Mather and Calef, see Robin DeRosa, *The Making of Salem: The Witch Trials in History, Fiction, and Tourism* (Jefferson, NC: McFarland & Co., 2009), chap. 2.

26. See Robert Calef, *More Wonders of the Invisible World . . .* (London, 1700). The title echoes the title of Mather's own book in defense of his role in the Salem witchcraft trials: *The Wonders of the Invisible World: Observations as well Historical as Theological, upon the Nature, the Number and the Operations of the Devils . . .* (Boston, MA, 1693).

27. Charles W. Upham, *Salem Witchcraft and Cotton Mather: A Reply* (Morrisania, NY, 1869), 1. See also Upham, *Salem Witchcraft* (New York, 1859).

28. See, for example, Chadwick Hansen, *Witchcraft at Salem* (New York: George Braziller, 1985); and Bernard Rosenthal, *Salem Story: Reading the Witch Trials of 1692* (Cambridge: Cambridge University Press, 1993). Perry Miller has a nuanced view; he argues that Mather "is not responsible for killing Rebecca Nurse or George Burroughs. But he tried to make those killings legitimate when he knew they were murders by dressing them in the paraphernalia of federal doctrine. . . . He tried it even though he knew that the covenant remedy of confession had become a farce. By gathering the folds of that prophetic mantel around the gaping hypotheses of Stoughton's court, he fatally soiled it." Miller, *From Colony to Province*, 204.

29. "Spectral evidence" was testimony that the specter of a defendant appeared to a witness. See "The Return of Several Ministers Consulted by his Excellency, and the Honourable Council, upon the present Witchcrafts in Salem-Village" (Boston, June 15, 1692), widely understood to be written primarily by Cotton Mather. While it does not rule out spectral evidence, it urges caution in its use "*inasmuch as 'tis an undoubted and a Notorious Thing, That a* Demon *may, by God's Permission, appear even to Ill purposes, in the Shape of an Innocent, yea, and a vertuous man*" (point VI). Although he signed on to the "Return," Cotton's father Increase Mather later became an opponent of the use of spectral

For our purposes, however, it is important to see how the incident itself undermined the logic of the covenant. According to the Puritans, the practice of witchcraft not only threatened the compact between God and New England, it also perverted and mocked that holy agreement. Living publicly in the midst of the people covenanted to God, a witch executed a private covenant with Satan, thereby participating in the Devil's great assault on the New Jerusalem.[30] Not surprisingly, then, in his writings on witchcraft, Cotton Mather folded the outbreak of witchcraft into the great drama of God's intense engagement with New England, ringing the changes of impending doom and merciful rescue after sincere repentance.

Yet in the end, it was the Puritans' own response to allegations of witchcraft that itself undermined the intelligibility of covenant in at least two ways. First, as Perry Miller acutely recognized,[31] in federal theology, confession and repentance is meant to invite forgiveness and redemption. Accordingly, in the Salem witch trials, in most cases, the lives of those who confessed to witchcraft were spared by the community. Most of those who refused to confess, however, were hanged. When it became clear that the whole system created a perverse incentive for false confessions and resulted in the death of people who protested their innocence in good faith, the logic of the whole covenantal framework cracked irreparably, although it took several decades for those cracks to become fully apparent. The intricate logic of the covenantal system, based on repentance and forgiveness, could be twisted to diabolical ends in the name of resisting the Devil himself—and God did not step in to prevent it.[32]

Second, rather than illuminating the actual, death-dealing sins that were committed at Salem, the dominant conceptual framework wrapped them in the obfuscating boilerplate language of covenantal theology. In the reflection he produced soon after the hysteria abated, for example, Cotton Mather

---

evidence. See Increase Mather, *Cases of Conscience Concerning Evil Spirits* . . . (Boston, MA, 1693). The "Return" is reprinted in the unpaginated postscript of *Cases of Conscience*.

30. See, for example, Elizabeth Reis, "Witches, Sinners, and the Underside of Covenant Theology," in *New Perspectives on Witchcraft, Magic, and Demonology*, vol. 1, *Demonology, Religion, and Witchcraft*, ed. Brian P. Levak (New York: Routledge, 2001), 271–86.

31. See, generally, Miller, *From Colony to Providence*, chap. 13, "The Judgment of the Witches," 191–208.

32. Modern scholarship has investigated some of the socioeconomic triggers for the witchcraft hysteria. See, for example, Paul Boyer and Stephen Nissenbaum, *Salem Possessed: The Social Origins of Witchcraft* (Cambridge, MA: Harvard University Press, 1974).

strives to fold the events at Salem into covenantal-business-as-usual. He urges that "With a *Great Zeal*, we should lay hold on the *Covenant* of God, that we may Secure *Us* and *Ours*, from the *Great Wrath*, with which the Devil Rages."[33] Witchcraft, he tells his audience, is ultimately the result of the faithlessness and bad morals of New England. He writes: "*A Reformation of our Provoking Evils*, as the only way to avoid that *Wrath* of His. . . . 'Tis because we have been deaf to those *Calls*, that we are now by a provoked God, laid open to the *Wrath* of the Devil himself."[34] Moreover, Mather's enumeration of the "provoking evils" includes nothing that would not have appeared in dozens of prior Puritan jeremiads. In time, it seemed that Mather and other divines were obdurately blind to the real threats that the events at Salem posed to the covenant. Those threats did not come from the alleged witches or even the garden-variety peccadilloes of the community.

Ultimately, the crisis Salem precipitated for the covenant is epistemological. The execution of innocent men and women by the "godly" community raises the possibility that the leaders of that community do not, in fact, have reliable access into the truth about spiritual matters. Mather studiously avoids this problem; instead, he presents the challenges facing the Salem judges as a particularly difficult matter of prudence.[35] It was necessary, of course, to be careful in the application of proven methods for discerning the divine mind and cautious in differentiating godly persons from those in compact with the devil.[36] But there was no need to rethink the entire framework.

In response to the Salem witch crisis, Cotton Mather calls members of the community to humble themselves before God.[37] Yet there is something

33. Mather, *The Wonders of the Invisible World* . . . , 72.

34. Ibid., 62.

35. "What a Difficult, what an Arduous Task, have those Worthy Personages now upon their Hands? To carry the *Knife* so exactly, that one the one side, there may be no Innocent Blood Shed, by too unseeing a *Zeal for the Children of Israel;* and that on the other side, there may be no Shelter given to those Diabolical *Works of Darkness* . . ." Ibid., 71.

36. "If a Drop of *Innocent Blood* should be shed, in the Prosecution of the *Witchcrafts* among us, how unhappy are we! For which cause, I cannot express my self in better terms, than those of a most Worthy Person, who lives near the present Center of these things. *The Mind of God in these matters, is to be carefully look'd into, with due Circumspection, that Satan deceive us not with his Devices; who transforms himself into an Angel of Light, and may pretend Justice, and yet intend Mischief.* But on the other side, if the Storm of Justice do now fall only on the Heads of those Guilty *Witches* and *Wretches* which have defiled our Land, *How Happy!*" Ibid., 144. Perry Miller suggests that in his later days, Mather was haunted by his failure to stop the executions.

37. "How much more now ought we to *Humble ourselves*, under that *Mighty Hand* of that God who indeed has the Devil in a *Chain*, but has horribly lengthened out the *Chain!*" Ibid., 55.

oddly smug about this call for humility because it does not encourage the Puritans to cultivate modesty about their ability to read the mind of God about the state of the covenant. As we will see, the development of this new and necessary type of covenantal humility does not come to fruition for well over a century, in the anguished and brilliant soul of Abraham Lincoln confronting the horrors of the Civil War.

The Identity of the Covenant Partners

As the seventeenth century came to a close and the eighteenth century began, the nature and identity of both covenant partners began to become broader and less sharply focused. Obviously, the God of the deists was not the vivid, passionate, and intensely engaged Jehovah, God of the Old Testament, and personification of the covenant partner of the Puritans. To those influenced by deism, the idea that God revealed Himself in human scriptures, much less became incarnate in Jesus of Nazareth, was unnecessary superstition; the basic facts of divine creation of the universe and the reasonableness of the moral law could be established by human reason alone. While deism did not become a major intellectual force in the United States until the mid to late eighteenth century, we can see evidence that the sharp contours of the biblical Jehovah were already being smoothed out in the beginning of that century.

Moreover, the identity of the human partner to the covenant evolved to accommodate not only the Puritan Congregationalist but also Anglicans, Baptists, and other Protestants. Consequently, the Puritans were forced to grapple with the effects of increasing religious pluralism on their political life. After the Restoration and before the revocation of the first charter in 1684, Puritan preachers began to emphasize the national covenant as encompassing all denizens of New England, saints and sinners alike. This emphasis became more pronounced after 1691, when the colony received a second charter after enduring the terrible years of the Dominion. That charter substantially limited their political autonomy, however, especially when it came to matters of religious toleration. By law, Massachusetts was now required to welcome members of all religious traditions tolerated at that time in England. While New Englanders attempted tactfully to evade that requirement, it inevitably reshaped the colony and its public conception of itself. As a consequence, political sermons (e.g., election sermons) began to stress the common elements of Protestant Christianity rather than the distinctive elements of a strongly Calvinist view of God viewed through the lens of federalist theology.

Further, the notion that the "new land" itself had a special relationship with God began to develop as the Puritans relinquished the idea that their purpose was to provide England, and later the rest of Protestant Europe, with a viable model of a godly polity. The human partner began to be seen more as the land and people of New England, defined in terms of their broader religious and political commitments, and less as the specifically Congregationalist towns whose people were bound together by the elaborate set of interlocking covenants. Without the support of federal theology, the idea of a national covenant—the idea of an agreement with specific obligations on the part of both contracting parties—began to fade and to be replaced by the vaguer idea of national chosenness.

A good model of the covenantal framework that is reworked and smoothed out to meet the exigencies of the new century is Cotton Mather's *Magnalia Christi Americana,* a massive exercise in church history culminating in and centered upon Puritan New England. First published in England in 1702, the tome includes seven books. It is a veritable hodgepodge of observations and reflections, incorporating a wandering account of the trials and tribulations of New England, hagiographies of the political and religious leaders of its settlements in Plymouth, Boston, and Connecticut.[38] The purpose, as Mather states in the General Introduction, is to "WRITE the *Wonders* of the CHRISTIAN RELIGION, flying from the Depravations of *Europe,* to the *American Strand.*"[39] The God whom Mather describes in the *Magnalia* is unmistakably the Jehovah of the Old Testament. Yet Mather discusses God's working in general terms that can be appreciated by a broad array of Protestant Christians increasingly concerned about the reasonableness of their religion. He is the divine being whose "Divine Providence hath *Irradiated* an *Indian Wilderness.*"[40]

We see here the veneration of ancestors both political and clerical, as well as the great emphasis on loyalty to England and to Protestantism in general. The language of covenant is muted and there are many allusions to classical Roman and Greek literature. Nonetheless, the story of New England is told as if it is the story of the ancient Jews, intertwining spiritual and temporal blessings. If New England is Israel, Boston is Jerusalem; Mather devotes an

38. Cotton Mather, *Magnalia Christi Americana* . . . (London, 1702).
39. Ibid., "A General Introduction," § 1.
40. Ibid.

entire section to commemorating its history as if on an "ebenezer" or stone memorializing God's assistance.[41] Preserving the form of the jeremiad, although not the explicit language of covenant, he relates New England's sufferings to its moral failures, including drunkenness, reveling, and idleness. While tales of "wonders"—isolated workings of God in the lives of individuals and communities—are prominent, a strong note of uncertainty about the overarching purpose and outcome of the endeavor also marks the work:

> 'Tis possible, That our Lord Jesus Christ carried some Thousands of *Reformers* into the Retirements of an *American Desart,* on purpose, that, with an opportunity granted unto many of his Faithful Servants, to enjoy the precious *Liberty* of their *Ministry,* tho' in the midst of many *Temptations* all their days, He might there, *To* them first, and then *By* them, give a *Specimen* of many Good Things, which He would have His Churches elsewhere aspire and arise unto: And *This* being done, He knows whether there be not be *All done,* that *New-England* was planted for; and whether the Plantation may not, soon after this, *Come to Nothing.* . . . But we must therewithal ask your Prayers, that these *Golden Candlesticks* may not *quickly* be *Removed out of their place!*
>
> But whether *New England* may *Live* any where else or no, it must *Live* in our *History!*[42]

THE COVENANTAL OBLIGATIONS

The *content* of the jeremiads—and by implication, the contents of the national covenant—also began to evolve as the nervous New Englanders strived to prove their loyalty to the English sovereign. The beginnings of this development can be seen after the Restoration. Election day sermons began to place as much emphasis on the rights and duties of Englishmen as they did on specifically religious obligations. They also emphasized the material blessings of the covenant, doubtless to convince more commercially minded members of the community

41. Mather, *Magnalia Christi Americana,* 30–38. See 1 Sam 7:12. The prophet Samuel sets up a stone between Mizpah and Jeshanah, commemorating the assistance Yahweh gives to the Israelites in their victorious battle against the Philistines. Samuel names the stone "Ebenezer," which means "stone of help."

42. Mather, *Magnalia Christi Americana . . . ,* "A General Introduction," §§ 3–4.

of its importance.[43] It is important not to overstate the significance of these early shifts. The roots of the Puritan movement in England were deeply committed to political reform as essential to and intertwined with religious reform. Furthermore, the pressure on the covenantal worldview was significantly alleviated by the victory of William of Orange and his subsequent decision to issue the colony a new charter. Nonetheless, in the decades after the issuance of the second charter, Puritan clergymen began to use the jeremiad to stress the commitment of the colonists to their identity as British subjects, which included practicing the British virtue of tolerance. Trying to integrate their ecclesiastical commitments within a broader political vision, they emphasized their loyalty to Protestant Christianity, rooting their sacrifices in the sporadic conflicts with Native Americans and the French not only in their love of their mother country but also in their determination to battle against Papist France.[44]

Moreover, as part of the continuing adjustment on the domestic front, the jeremiads in the first few decades of the eighteenth century began to stress piety and moral rectitude as part of the adjustment to the situation of Protestant pluralism. An emphasis on "practical piety" minimized doctrinal divisions in favor of broad religious and moral agreement. Published in 1710, Cotton Mather's *Bonifacius* attempted to focus the lives of the colonists on the moral improvement of one another and society.[45] In the same year, Boston preacher Benjamin Wadsworth sounded similar themes, in *An Essay to Do Good: By a Disswasive from Tavern-Haunting, and Excessive Drinking.*[46] As the

43. See William Hubbard's *The Benefit of a Well-Ordered Conversation* . . . (Boston, MA, 1684), which was preached on June 24, 1682, a day of public humiliation, in more or less traditional Puritan style. Interestingly, the publication also includes "A Funeral Meditation . . ." (pp. 111–75), preached at the interment of Major Daniel Denison, a political and military leader in Massachusetts Bay Colony. The sermon emphasizes the virtues of wisdom and prudence in ways that allow for correlations between Hebrew and pagan virtues. Finally, the book also included *Irenicon, or a Salve for New England's Sore* (pages 176–218), penned by Denison himself and exploring the sources of social division in human nature.

44. Miller, *From Colony to Province*, 160-69.

45. Cotton Mather, *Bonifacius: An Essay upon the Good that is to be Devised and Designed by Those Who Desire to Answer the Great End of Life, and to Do Good While They Live* . . . (Boston, MA, 1710). See, generally, Miller, *From Colony to Province*, chap. 24, "Do-Good," 395–416; and Richard P. Gildrie, *The Profane, the Civil, & the Godly: The Reformation of Manners in Orthodox New England, 1679–1749* (University Park: Pennsylvania State University Press, 1994). Chapter 3 of Gildrie's book discusses tavern laws.

46. Benjamin Wadsworth, *An Essay to do Good: By a Disswasive from Tavern-Haunting, and Excessive Drinking* (Boston, MA, 1710). See also Samuel Danforth, *The Woful Effects of Drunkenness* . . . (Boston, MA, 1710).

title of Wadsworth's sermon suggests, being transformed by grace entailed doing good, which in turn involved combating vice, including swearing, drinking and blasphemy. In 1714, Samuel Whitman preached an election sermon in Hartford, Connecticut that emphasized "practical godliness" and the avoidance of the familiar litany of sins within the context of a generalized Christian belief.[47] As Richard Gildrie notes, referring to the continuing custom of fast day sermons: "Right into the American Revolution, the themes of social order, moral reform, and piety remained tightly linked in an important public ritual."[48]

Godliness also meant aiding the poor; while the Puritan preachers argued that social and economic inequalities were part of God's design, the rich had an obligation to use their money for the benefit of the community, including those who lacked resources.[49] It meant supporting one's preachers and avoiding luxury. As Mark A. Noll has shown, important roots of American evangelical Protestantism can be found in this early emphasis on moral and social improvement, which was given new focus and energy in the 1740s by itinerant preachers such as George Whitfield, who was a central figure in the Great Awakening.[50] This evangelical emphasis on doing good reflected a more fragmented and emotional conception of God's relationship to each believer, with less of an emphasis on the covenant as creating a cosmic framework for evaluating human action.

At the time Cotton Mather was modifying his theological apparatus, New England as a whole was also moving away from the complex biblical hermeneutic, elaborate logical framework, and mannered style of his father and grandfather. In England, the work of John Locke was swaying people toward the reasonableness of Christianity, the self-evident grasp of the basic elements of the natural law and the moral order. As a good Puritan, Cotton could not

---

47. Samuel Whitman, *Practical Godliness: The Way to Prosperity* . . . (New London, CT, 1714). As the title suggests, Whitman's election sermon avoids speculative theology and focuses on the beneficial moral consequences of belief in God: *"that 'tis matter of Lamentation when Religion Declineth, and Iniquity Aboundeth among a People."* Whitman, *Practical Godliness*, 25.

48. Gildrie, *The Profane, the Civil, & the Godly*, 114.

49. At the same time, the poor had obligations of their own. See, for example, Cotton Mather, *Some Seasonable Advice unto the Poor* . . . (Boston, MA, 1726).

50. As Noll reminds us, the Great Awakening "was not a tightly organized affair, but rather a series of memorable preaching occasions that sparked a major turn toward a more personal, emotional, inward, and experiential religion." Mark A. Noll, *The Work We Have to Do: A History of Protestants in America* (New York: Oxford University Press, 2002), 44. See also Mark A. Noll, *The Rise of Evangelicalism: The Age of Edwards, Whitefield, and the Wesleys* (Downers Grove, IL: InterVarsity Press, 2003).

endorse any view of humanity that did not pay due respect to the doctrine of the fall of humanity in the sin of Adam and Eve. Nonetheless, in practice, Cotton Mather and others of his generation manifested greater optimism than preachers of prior generations had about the general human capacity for recognizing moral truths, and the congruence of those truths with the revealed truths of Scripture. What he and others failed to reckon with, however, was the fact that, once the elaborate intellectual scaffolding for interpreting Scripture was taken down, disagreements would inevitably arise about what natural reason and common sense required. So too would disagreement about what constituted "doing good."

The Rhetoric of the Jeremiad

The evolution of the Puritan jeremiad was not limited to the covenant partners it presupposed and the substantive covenantal obligations that it proclaimed. In addition, the jeremiad's *rhetoric* began to shift, moving in two different ways and directions. On the one hand, a certain strand of preaching became more fiery and threatening. By the 1680s, the citizenry had grown used to the dire warnings of the preachers; those preachers needed to add something new and dramatic to the mix in order to capture the attention of the people and thus provoke them to reform. A strong millenarian streak began to appear in Puritan writings, emphasizing the second coming of Christ and his thousand-year reign on earth. The conclusion of that reign, of course, would be the Last Judgment; some Puritans began incorporating gruesome accounts of the torments of hell in their account of the penalties for breach of covenant. This tendency continued into the 1720s, as certain preachers attempted to reinforce the covenantal structure by pronouncing the terrors of hellfire in order to excite the population to repentance and church membership. Solomon Stoddard of Northampton, Massachusetts, pioneered this approach in his "revivals"; it was perfected by his successor and grandson, the great Jonathan Edwards.[51]

On the other hand, a younger breed of Harvard-trained preachers advocated measured, reasonable arguments to defend the created order. While not denying the notion of a covenant, their arguments suggested that the covenantal structure, at least in its elaborate, interlocking form, was not

51. See Miller, *From Colony to Province*, 276–87.

necessary to understand the nature of America.[52] They conveyed the impression that God's basic nature and requirements were readily accessible to the honest reflections of calm, collected minds. It was part of the genius of Jonathan Edwards that he was able to integrate an appreciation for reasonableness, through the epistemology of John Locke, into an unwavering commitment to Calvinist theology.[53]

The first two decades of the eighteenth century saw the emergence of disputes regarding the well-being of the community that were not conducted in the framework of the jeremiad, most notably the question of whether there should be a national bank that issued currency in exchange for security in land. The Puritan preachers were not experts in matters of finance; they dedicated themselves to condemning luxury, greed, and associated vices.[54] The financial difficulties at this time put pressure on those struggling to make a living; congregations balked at paying their ministers. The jeremiads responded by highlighting the importance of living simply and frugally. These sermons in turn raised the suspicion that the ministers were motivated by their own financial self-interest rather than the common good.[55] Whereas fifty years earlier, the jeremiad had been a means of promoting communal well-being and social unity, it was now seen as an instrument of a faction. For the first time, the jeremiad's socially divisive potential was exhibited on a broad and sustained basis.[56] It would not, however, be the last time.[57]

52. See ibid., 269–73.

53. See, for example, George M. Marsden, *Jonathan Edwards: A Life* (New Haven, CT: Yale University Press, 2003). It is wrong to think that Edwards focused only on the terrors of hell; he also preached movingly on the delights of heaven. See, for example, Jonathan Edwards, "Heaven is a World of Love," in *The Works of Jonathan Edwards*, vol. 8, *Ethical Writings*, ed. Paul Ramsey (New Haven, CT: Yale University Press, 1989), 366–97. See also Mark A. Noll, who observes that, while New England churches split between those drawn to more emotional articulations of religious belief and those drawn to more intellectual approaches, "outside New England, the revival fires associated with the Great Awakening did more to build churches than to fragment them." Noll, *The Work We Have to Do*, 45.

54. Miller, *From Colony to Province*, chap. 19, "A Medium of Trade," 305–23.

55. Ibid., 328.

56. "From this situation arose a suspicion, gradually becoming a settled conviction, that preachers of the jeremiad, when calling upon citizens to observe simplicity and sobriety in expenditures, were not so much expounding Scripture as supporting the restrictive policy of Wigglesworth and the 'Court party,' that they were trying to browbeat the people into going without the few available comforts in order to pocket the money themselves." Ibid.

57. Quite significantly, around this time there emerged in New England prominent instances of the only form of rhetoric that is effective against the jeremiad: satire and mockery. Some of John Wise's

Moving beyond the Covenant

While pressing its boundaries, many of the foregoing developments took place largely within the framework of federal theology. It was a matter of emphasis. Consequently, the corresponding revisions in the jeremiad also remained within the strictures of the covenant and were therefore rhetorically constrained by the idea of an indictment. In the beginning of the eighteenth century, however, the intelligibility of federal theology was threatened in New England from two different directions. In Western Massachusetts, Solomon Stoddard's sermons and writings tended to retrieve a starker, purer form of Calvinism, which refused to admit that the majestic and terrible divine will could be tamed and understood by the petty agreements of the English common law. At Harvard University, the logic of Petrus Ramus began to fade from prominence. Ramus's logic had long enabled both English and American Puritans to treat their covenantal frameworks as clearly implied and endorsed by Holy Scripture.[58] This shift from Ramus to other approaches to logic in turn cleared the way for younger theologians to downgrade federal theology by arguing that it was simply one more debatable interpretation of the Bible, not the hermeneutical key. As Miller writes, "Thus in the first years of the eighteenth century multiplicity continued to grow out of simplicity; the covenant theology, having conceived and cradled the principle of voluntary consent, set the New England mind at work destroying that theology. The whelps were eating up the dam."[59]

Destroying covenant theology is one thing, but finding a substantive alternative to put in its place is quite another. Influenced by the philosophical currents in Europe, the moderate preachers began to consider the possibility that rights, including the right of freedom of conscience, were justified by reference to human nature rather than explicitly conferred by a divinely ordained covenant. The jeremiads thus became more democratic

---

writings took this form; the most prominent example, however, was the short-lived *New England Courant* (1721–1726), whose editor was James Franklin and whose most well-known satiric contributor was James's younger brother Benjamin, who wrote under the pseudonym "Silence Dogood."

58. Peter Ramus (1515–1572) developed elaborate and comprehensive anti-Aristotelian theories of logic, rhetoric, and pedagogy, which allowed his adherents to synthesize all branches of theoretical knowledge, as well as to integrate theoretical and practical knowledge. See, for example, Walter J. Ong, S.J., *Ramus, Method, and the Decay of Dialogue: From the Art of Discourse to the Art of Reason* (Chicago, IL: University of Chicago Press, 2004).

59. Miller, *From Colony to Province*, 267.

and less hierarchical. The clergy emphasized the rights and duties of the citizens and downplayed the power of the governor and his deputy, who were appointed by and directly responsible to the Crown. Religion and private property were defended together as intertwined rights of Englishmen. By the early 1720s, political controversies between the governor (Samuel Shute) and the General Court (led by Elisha Cooke) were framed in secular terms, assuming that the purpose of government was to promote the material happiness and well-being of the people. The preachers found themselves making the argument that religious piety and moral rectitude were conducive to these secular goals. When tensions between the colony and its mother country arose at that time, Jeremiah Dummer wrote *A Defence of the New-England Charters* (1721), which scarcely mentioned the colony's religious roots in favor of articulating its identity in terms of its commercial prosperity and prospects.[60]

As noted earlier in this chapter, Jonathan Mayhew's sermons exemplify this ongoing trend of secularization, serving as a vivid harbinger of the religious and political sensibilities that would later animate the Revolution. In 1749, on the centennial of the execution of King Charles I of England. he preached a sermon entitled *A Discourse Concerning Unlimited Submission and Non-Resistance to Higher Powers. . . .*[61] It is an astonishingly bold sermon. In essence, his argument was that the late king should not be commemorated by English Protestants as a saint and martyr but reviled as a tyrant. Mayhew excoriates the political flattery and maneuvering that led to the anniversary of his execution being treated as a day of fasting and humiliation in England. On the contrary, he believes it ought to be treated as a day of thanksgiving.

The force of his argument is taken from a Lockean understanding of the nature of political authority rather than some form of covenant theology. In fact, so far is Mayhew from the conceptual world of his forebears that he describes the ancient Jews who believed they were divinely entitled to a unique political status as laboring under the influence of a "strange conceit."[62] He emphasizes the New Testament, not the Old; he labors mightily to demonstrate that the Pauline instruction that "every soul be subject unto the

---

60. Jeremiah Dummer, *A Defence of the New-England Charters* (London and Boston, 1721). See Miller, *From Colony to Province*, 388–92.

61. Jonathan Mayhew, *A Discourse Concerning Unlimited Submission . . .* (Boston, MA, 1750).

62. Ibid., 3.

higher powers" (Rom. 13:1) applies only to legitimate political authority, not to tyrants.[63] Mayhew knows that his intimate intertwining of religion and politics will raise eyebrows and he attempts to fend off criticism in the preface: "Besides, if it be said, that it is out of character for a christian minister to meddle with such a subject [civil government], this censure will at last fall upon the holy apostles. They write upon it in their epistles to christian churches: And surely it cannot be deemed either criminal or impertinent, to attempt an explanation of their doctrine."[64] He goes on to contend that this insight applies equally to monarchical forms of government. "What unprejudiced man can think, that God made ALL to be thus subservient to the lawless pleasure and phrenzy of ONE, so that it shall always be a sin to resist him!"[65]

After establishing that the Scripture enjoins submission only to legitimate higher powers, Mayhew goes on to raise the possibility that resistance to illegitimate powers is morally acceptable. He contends that, according to the true sense of the Pauline doctrine, when a ruler "turns tyrant, and makes his subjects his prey to devour and to destroy, instead of his charge to defend and cherish, we are bound to throw off our allegiance to him, and to resist."[66]

Ostensibly looking back a century to the Glorious Revolution against King Charles I, Mayhew's sermon was eerily prescient of the arguments to be made by the Patriots a quarter of a century later. "For a nation thus abused to arise unanimously, and to resist their prince, even to the dethroning him, is not criminal; but a reasonable way of vindicating their liberties and just rights; it is making use of the means, and the only means, which God has put into their power, for mutual and self-defence."[67]

As his account of the iniquities of King Charles I demonstrates, Mayhew sees religious and political tyranny as more or less intertwined in both cause

---

63. Ibid., 25. Mayhew writes on the previous page (24): "So that whenever that argument for submission, fails, which is grounded upon the usefulness of the magistracy to civil society, (as it always does when magistrates do hurt to society instead of good) the other argument, which is taken from their being the ordinance of God, must necessarily fail also; no person of a civil character being *God's minister*, in the sense of the apostle, any farther than he performs God's will, by exercising a just and reasonable authority; and ruling for the good of the subject."

64. Ibid., preface.

65. Ibid., 35.

66. Ibid., 30.

67. Ibid., 40.

and effect. Tyrants and prelates cooperate with one another in order to preserve the domination of each in their respective spheres:

> Civil tyranny is usually small in its beginning, like "the drop of a bucket," till at length, like a mighty torrent, or the raging waves of the sea, it bears down all before it, and deluges whole countries and empires. Thus it is as to ecclesiastical tyranny also,—the most cruel, intolerable and impious, of any. From small beginnings, "it exalts itself above all that is called GOD "and that is worshiped" People have no security against being unmercifully priest-ridden, but by keeping all imperious BISHOPS, and other CLERGYMEN who love to "lord it over God's heritage," from getting their foot into the stirrup at all. Let them be once fairly mounted, and their "beasts, the laiety," may prance and flounce about to no purpose: And they will, at length, be so jaded and hack'd by these reverend jockies, that they will not even have spirits enough to complain, that their backs are galled; or, like Balaam's ass, to "rebuke the madness "of the prophet."[68]

Mayhew's approach, in a nutshell, was to integrate political and religious rights by situating each in the political framework of Lockean liberalism as well as a larger and relatively vague framework of congregationalist Christianity. His 1754 election day sermon offers faint echoes of the religious themes of his ancestors, while shifting his focus to the political and pragmatic questions facing the colony.

> Consider then, Gentlemen, in the name of God, consider, what you owe Him, and to your holy religion; what, to the protestant interest in general; what, to your King and to Great-Britain, in particular; what, to your native country; what, to the honour of your Ancestors; what, to the present generation; what, to future ones; what, to yourselves; and what, to those whom the God of nature has made dearer to you than yourselves, your children. It is even uncertain, Gentlemen, how long you will have an *House* to sit in, unless a speedy and vigorous opposition is made to the present

68. Ibid., preface (citations omitted).

encroachments, and to the farther designs, of our enemies! This, surely, is not a time to be saving, unless in our private expences.[69]

While Mayhew attempted to cast a protective religious aura over his justification of civil rights, another New England public intellectual approached the issues from the reverse direction. John Wise, an enigmatic preacher and farmer from Ipswich, Massachusetts, attempted to encompass New England's distinctive religious life under the umbrella of the civil rights of Englishmen.[70] His enemy here was not the Crown but the old theocrats, typified by Cotton Mather, Samuel Willard, Benjamin Colman, and Benjamin Wadsworth. To shore up their authority in the early eighteenth century, they advocated moving toward a presbyterian model of polity, which would impose a significant amount of conciliar control upon hitherto independent congregations. In the fall of 1705, delegates from the five ministerial associations in the colony issued *Proposals* written so that "Associations of the Ministers in the several Parts of the Country may be strengthened."[71] Wise doubtless saw the threat to congregational autonomy, but he did not put pen to paper until Connecticut's ministers adopted a similar approach in the Saybrook Platform in 1708.

Wise wrote two short books defending congregational polity. The first, *The Churches Quarrel Espoused . . .* , was a satire attacking the presbyterian polity by gleefully poking hole after hole in the proposals of the ministerial associations. Not surprisingly, given that he was taking on the powerful Cotton Mather, Wise published under a pseudonym, which satirized its own necessity: Abjiciendus Pudor, Quoties urget Necessitas.[72] Several years later, he went on to produce a more systematic defense of the church structure set forth in the Cambridge Platform in his *A Vindication of the Government of New-England Churches.*[73] Like Mayhew, Wise wrote in a style that was fresh,

69. Jonathan Mayhew, *A Sermon Preach'd in the Audience of His Excellency William Shirley, Esq . . . ,"* (Boston, MA, 1754), 47. Mayhew goes on to make his usual apology for saying too much about politics and not enough about religion (p. 49).

70. For an introduction to Wise's work, see Clinton L. Rossiter, "John Wise: Colonial Democrat," *New England Quarterly* 22, no. 1 (1949): 3–32.

71. Miller, *From Colony to Province,* 261; see, generally, his chap. 16, "The Failure of Centralization," 248–68. See also Francis J. Bremer, *The Puritan Experiment: New England Society from Bradford to Edwards* (Lebanon, NH: University Press of New England, 1995), 216–17.

72. John Wise, *The Churches Quarrel Espoused . . .* (New York, 1713). The pseudonym roughly means "Propriety must be cast aside whenever necessity encroaches."

73. John Wise, *A Vindication of the Government of New-England Churches . . .* (Boston, MA, 1717).

blunt, and clear—he did not engage in the wordy circumlocutions of the previous generation of Puritans. His arguments were relentless, logical, systematic, and exhaustive. In structure and tone, they read more like a legal brief than a sermon.[74]

Like Mayhew as well, Wise's sensibilities and interests were largely secular. Obviously familiar with the writings of John Locke and Samuel Pufendorf, he based his argument for the rights of Englishmen on natural reason and common sense, not upon an authoritative interpretation of the Bible promulgated by the founders of the colony. In his view, the primary commitment was to the land, liberties, and traditions of New England and its people. He defended the church covenant not because of its place in a cosmic structure of agreements but because it was an essential part of New England's democratic way of life. He maintains, for example, that "The End of all good Government is to Cultivate Humanity, and Promote the happiness of all, and the good of every Man in all his Rights, his Life, Liberty, Estate, Honour, &c. without injury or abuse done to any."[75]

After arguing that democracy was the preferable form of civil government, Wise goes on to maintain that it is a preferable form of church structure as well—particularly as embodied in the New England Way. The problem with the papacy was that its monarchical structure was a distorted form of both political and religious government.[76] In all important respects, he argues, the congregational church structure echoes the structure of the primitive church, whose democratic structure is revealed by natural reason to be the best form of government for church and state alike. "The Divine Establishment in Providence of the fore-named Churches in their Order is apparently the Royal assent of the supream Monarch of the Churches, to the grave Decisions of Reason in favour of Mans Natural state of Being, and Original Freedom."[77]

74. A striking similarity in tone is apparent between Wise's writings on church polity and his argument for a bank of credit, *A Word of Comfort to a Melancholy Country* . . . (Boston, MA, 1721), which he also published pseudonymously as "Amicus Patriae."

75. Wise, *A Vindication*, 61.

76. Of the papacy, Wise asks the rhetorical question, "But the sad Enquiry is, Whether this sort of Government has not plainly subverted the Design of the Gospel, and the end for which Christ's Government was Ordained, *viz.* the Moral, Spiritual, and Eternal Happiness of Men?" Ibid., 55.

77. Ibid., 30.

Wise, of course, defends the Congregationalist church structure on biblical grounds. Strikingly, although not surprisingly, he reads Scripture as if God were the force behind a cosmic constitutional democracy:

> Now to conclude, Let the Reader lay all these Scriptures together, which contain Rules of Judicatory for the Churches; and then let him answer me with good reason if he can, and tell me why these Scriptures may not be esteemed the Churches *Magna Charta,* in matters of Censure and Judicature; as well as that be held such a Golden Rule in the Judicial Proceedings of *English* Government, mentioned in the great Charter of *English Liberties,* Chap. 29. *No Freeman shall be Taken, or Imrpisoned, or be Dis-seised of his Freehold, Liberty or free Customs, or be Out-Law'd or Exiled, or any other ways destroyed, nor will we press upon him, nor condemn him, but by lawful Judgment of his Peers.* Now Gentlemen! Don't you think that the Lord Jesus Christ, the King of Heaven, is as careful and tender of his Subjects, as the King of *England* is of his?[78]

For purposes of rhetorical analysis, the emergence of a natural rights–based approach to articulating the political and religious duties and claims of New England is highly significant. Its practitioners doubtless thought that they were simplifying moral and political judgments and placing them on firm, indisputable ground. They understood themselves as appealing to common sense, as capturing and articulating the judgments of every sound and sober God-fearing man or woman. By avoiding the elaborate, mannered, and increasingly debatable arguments and rhetoric of the Puritans, they doubtless perceived themselves as leading their communities toward a firmer, less arcane, and less contentious basis for political decision making.

In actuality, however, they were creating numerous openings for dispute and controversy. Why? First, as I argued in the previous chapter, situating the jeremiad in the context of the covenant, and treating it more or less as an indictment for breach of covenant, placed significant constraints on its contents. The basis for the condemnation was *the audience's agreement* (express or implied) to perform or not to perform certain particular actions or classes of

78. Ibid., 85.

action. The covenantal basis of the jeremiad constrained its content; as I illustrated earlier, the provoking sins tended to be activities disapproved of by the entire community.

In contrast, a jeremiad based on a conception of the natural rights of men, or the natural rights of citizens, is untethered to any agreement. It is based instead on the speaker's own perception of reality, of nature, of the very structure of humanity. Consequently, a jeremiad based on natural rights does not have the same constraints binding a jeremiad based on a covenant. A preacher delivering a jeremiad based on a political covenant could only indict his audience for violations of the terms of that covenant, which, in principle, were binding upon and therefore in principle accessible to everyone. But a preacher delivering a jeremiad based on natural rights was not similarly constrained. He could indict his audience for violating his own particular conception of natural rights and self-evident truths—even if they were self-evident only to him.

Second, the shift from covenant to natural rights as a basis for the jeremiad greatly increases the potential for ad hominem arguments and consequently for social discord. The covenant-based jeremiad did not characteristically attack the persons of the audience; it challenged their actions. It presumes that audience members agree with the speaker about the nature and requirements of the covenant, but they sin out of lust or weakness of will. Such a stance does not necessarily place the preachers above the audience because, as sons of Adam, they themselves are not immune to the same temptations. In short, the jeremiad, particularly in the second generation, presupposes the goodwill of the audience, who were haunted by the achievements of their ancestors.

Within the framework of natural rights, however, the fundamental question is whether one has the eyes to see human nature and the will to respect the concrete requirements of natural rights. If the preacher of a jeremiad based on natural rights believes that the requirements he sets forth are self-evident, and should be apparent to all persons of goodwill, he is not going to view the members of the audience who are skeptical of his position in a favorable light. In fact, the preacher will likely conclude that they must be uncommonly dim of mind or distorted in soul. Consequently, the natural rights–based jeremiad creates a strong temptation for the preacher to frame those who refuse to go along with him as morally blind, perhaps even perversely so. The rights in question may be written in the hearts of men, but in many cases the script is rather murky. To the preacher, however, that is no excuse, merely evidence of defective moral vision.

Before and during the Revolutionary War, American Patriots drew on the conventions of the jeremiad to make their case for the independence of the colonies from their mother country, as well as for the justice of the war that had to be fought in order to achieve that independence. Interpreting the plight of the colonies in light of the sacred history of Israel, they argued that the revolution was legitimate resistance against tyranny, divinely sanctioned in order to protect the civil and religious liberties that would allow America to fulfill its divine destiny.

For our purposes the most striking aspect of many Patriot jeremiads delivered during this time is that they were controversial in character. First, they took a clear position on a disputed question of political morality. Not all colonists supported the War of Independence and many took a strong Loyalist position for both pragmatic and principled reasons. Second, these jeremiads were framed in a disputatious way: the language of the Revolutionary jeremiads was caustic and derisive toward the English and, by extension, toward American Loyalists. In these two respects, some of the Revolutionary jeremiads should sound familiar to contemporary Americans because the same sort of contentiousness is visible in the jeremiads of the contemporary culture wars.

Moreover, these two features of the Revolutionary jeremiad are not by and large characteristic of the jeremiad as practiced by the New England Puritans in the late seventeenth and early eighteenth century. As we saw, the seventeenth-century jeremiad generally reinforced already existing communal commitments. It was a striking exercise in unity, not an expression of division. Nonetheless, developments that took place in the genre over the course of a century can help us understand how the jeremiad became a more fractious type of religious-political discourse. What are those developments?

While continuing to exert some influence in the background, the idea of the national covenant was increasingly outside the explicit and dominant framework of the jeremiad. The idea that America was a chosen nation remained a prominent theme, but the nature of chosenness was not as frequently articulated in terms of covenantal rights and responsibilities. Instead, it was worked out by analogy to the history of Israel, which provided the blueprint for all divinely chosen nations, including New England and, by extension, America as a whole. The fact that the covenant receded into the background meant that the function of the jeremiad as an indictment or complaint for a communal breach of covenant also began to drift into the background. Consequently, speakers were less constrained by the rhetorical and logical limits of those legal forms in shaping their jeremiads. In turn, the loss of these constraints allowed the scope of the jeremiad to expand in two key ways that contributed to its potential for social fissiparousness.

First, loosening the connection between the jeremiad and an indictment meant that speakers were not restricted to treating their audience—and themselves—as wrongdoers standing together before a divine judge. In the first instance, an indictment or complaint is addressed by the wronged party to the wrongdoer. Accordingly, in the Puritan jeremiad, God is the wronged party, and the community as a whole has done the wrong. The preacher articulates God's complaint to the community. At the time of the Revolutionary War, however, that relationship of speaker and audience was no longer adequate because the speakers wanted to portray the audience—and themselves— as the wronged party, who was entitled to seek redress and claim justice against its wrongdoing oppressor.

Second, traditional jeremiads modeled on indictments condemned *past* stances of wrongful behavior, which clearly violated an agreement or a statute legally binding on the community. The future actions they called for generally had to do with repentance and reformation. Needless to say, this backward-looking orientation was not adequate for the rhetorical needs of the American Revolution because Patriot preachers needed to be able to construct the future, not merely to condemn the past. More specifically, the jeremiad began to be used to justify a prospective and highly debatable course of action: waging war against England to gain political independence.

Placing less emphasis on the covenant framework did create a new problem for the New England Puritans. How could they maintain their self-identity as God's new chosen people, the New Jerusalem, even while escaping the constraints of covenant-based preaching? Increasing attention to typological biblical interpretation helped to resolve this challenge. As I described in the previous chapter, typological interpretation treats New Testament events and figures as the ultimate meaning and fulfillment of figures in the Old Testament. Puritan theologians placed great emphasis on this mode of biblical interpretation, extending the typological patterns beyond the text of the New Testament times into the subsequent life of the church. This extension, of course, enabled the American Puritans to see their "city on a hill" as an "antitype" both revealing and fulfilling the sacred meaning of the "type" provided by ancient Israel.

From a rhetorical perspective, increased attention to typological interpretation offered preachers not only continuity with sacred history but also strategically necessary flexibility to deal with their changing political and religious situation. When the Puritans were concerned with defending their loyalty to King William and Queen Mary in order to regain their charter after the Restoration, the stories of how Israel flourished under King David and King Solomon provided fertile material. Later, however, when American Patriots protested the injustice of the English monarchy toward the colonies, the stories of the catastrophes that befell the Jewish people under corrupt and incompetent kings offered more enticing points of comparison. Finally, as the idea of independence from monarchical rule became more attractive, the flourishing of the Jews before the time of the kings became an increasingly visible theme. Focusing on the Book of Judges, Puritan preachers increasingly began to see themselves as the heirs of Jewish constitutionalism rather than Jewish monarchy. The story of the Jews was elaborate and varied enough to ensure that different aspects of it could be used to illustrate or highlight certain features of the contemporary situation.

In certain respects, then, typological interpretation was culturally conservative. It was practiced by the undisputed leaders of American Puritanism. Cotton Mather's *Magnalia Christi Americana* (1692) was an elaborate typological enterprise painstakingly relating each major figure in the saga of American Puritanism to corresponding figures in the saga of ancient Israel and Judah. At the same time, however, highlighting typological relationships rather than the covenant encouraged political and theological innovation, enabling the jeremiad to develop in significant ways beyond the form prescribed by an indictment model. For example, by inviting the audience to identify with the Jews in their struggles, triumphs, and defeats, a typological approach enabled the speaker to position himself and his audience as divinely assisted protagonists in an episode of sacred history, not as defendants in a lawsuit brought by God Himself. This shift was a matter of rhetorical emphasis, not theological commitment. In fact, the premise of the jeremiad is that God is specially angered by the sins of New England because His love for them is great and unique. Nonetheless, by emphasizing the audience's affinity with the trials and tribulations of ancient Israel, the typological approach reinforced the commitment of the audience to the endeavor as a righteous one and minimized the impetus for critical self-reflection.

The difficulty with a purely typological interpretation, of course, was that the flexibility it offered was available to one's adversaries as well. In London in 1776, the leading Methodist theologian John Fletcher penned a sermon entitled "The Bible and the Sword," which defended the Royalist cause. A British subject residing in London, Fletcher issued a heartfelt call to national repentance, manifested by public fast and humiliation. This call would not have been out of place in the pulpit of a New England Patriot. He too employed analogies with the history of Israel to shed light on the current controversy between England and its American colonies, but the lessons were very different from those drawn by the Patriots. He compared the perpetrators of the Boston Tea Party to the sons of Belial, who horribly violated the concubine of a Levite in the Book of Judges, and the Massachusetts government to the corrupt children of Benjamin, who went to war against Israel rather than turn over the wrongdoers for their just retribution. To Fletcher, the lesson to be learned from Scripture was clear:

> And "accordingly the Lord smote Benjamin before Israel." Judges xx. 26, &c. And the few Benjamites that escaped the edge of the vindictive sword lamented the obstinacy with which their infatuated tribe had taken up arms for the sons of Belial who had beset the house in the inhospitable city of Gibeah. And so will the revolted colonies one day bemoan the perverseness with which their infatuated leaders have made them fight for the sons of Belial who beset the ship in the inhospitable harbour of Boston.[79]

79. John Fletcher, "The Bible and the Sword . . ." (December 6, 1776), in *The Works of the Rev. John Fletcher, Late Vicar of Madeley,* vol. 8 (London, 1859), 186–204, at 197.

From the Oracles against Israel to the Oracles against the Nations

When the Revolutionary War jeremiads situated the Patriots in the position of a fragile and noble Israel struggling to instantiate God's will for itself, what position could Loyalists hold?[80] They could obviously be cast in the role of the enemies of Israel, including the Egyptians, the Philistines, the Ammonites, and especially the Assyrians and Babylonians. In the biblical narrative, God regularly uses these neighboring kingdoms as instruments to chastise his chosen people, but inevitably they go too far in their brutalities, thereby precipitating divine anger against them and reigniting God's sympathies for the Jews. This phenomenon, often repeated by different nations in the ancient Near East, is treated by the prophets in some of the most strikingly violent passages of the prophetic books, the so-called oracles against the nations.

Unlike the oracles against Israel, on which the older Puritan jeremiads are based, the oracles against the nations do not generally predict corrective or medicinal corrections for the offending enemies of Israel. Rather, these passages vividly portend total destruction as condign punishment for the excessive suffering they inflicted on Israel. An oracle against Babylon from the Book of Jeremiah gives a flavor of the genre:

> For thus says the LORD of hosts, the God of Israel:
> Daughter Babylon is like a threshing floor
>   at the time when it is trodden;
> yet a little while
>   and the time of her harvest will come.
> "King Nebuchadrezzar of Babylon has devoured me,
>   he has crushed me;
> he has made me an empty vessel,
>   he has swallowed me like a monster;

---

80. For a broader investigation of the sources of the war, see, for example, Bernard Bailyn, *The Ideological Origins of the American Revolution*, enl. ed. (Cambridge, MA: Belknap Press of Harvard University Press, 1992). For sermons from this period see, for example, John Wingate Thornton, ed., *The Pulpit of the American Revolution: Or, the Political Sermons of the Period of 1776* (Boston, MA, 1860); Ellis Sandoz, ed., *Political Sermons of the American Founding Era, 1730–1805*, 2nd ed., 2 vols. (Indianapolis, IN: Liberty Fund, 1998). For a good survey, see Michael Warner, ed., *American Sermons: The Pilgrims to Martin Luther King Jr.* (New York: Penguin Putnam, 1999).

he has filled his belly with my delicacies,
>   he has spewed me out.
May my torn flesh be avenged on Babylon,"
>   the inhabitants of Zion shall say.
"May my blood be avenged on the inhabitants of Chaldea,"
>   Jerusalem shall say.
Therefore thus says the LORD:
I am going to defend your cause
>   and take vengeance for you.
I will dry up her sea
>   and make her fountain dry;
and Babylon shall become a heap of ruins,
>   a den of jackals,
an object of horror and of hissing,
>   without inhabitant.[81]

Themes and language inspired by the prophetic oracles against the nations began to seep into the speeches of ministers supporting the Patriot cause, offering a structure to denounce England and the Loyalists who supported her.

The integration of the American Revolution into the broader Puritan framework can be seen in two New England sermons preached in commemoration of the battle of Lexington, Massachusetts, which took place on April 19, 1775.[82] Jacob Cushing (d. 1809), the minister of a church in Waltham, Massachusetts, preached a sermon entitled "Divine Judgments Upon Tyrants" on the third anniversary of the Lexington massacre. Like earlier preachers, he draws on the type of Israel as God's chosen people; however, he does not limit the analogy so narrowly to New England's congregationalist polity. In fact, the antitype is left rather vague: "The prophecy then before us, is not limited to the *Israelites;* but may be understood as extending to all GOD's chosen, though oppressed and injured people, in all generations,—that he will recompense their wrongs—plead their cause—and do justice upon their

---

81. Jeremiah 51:33–37.

82. I do not mean to imply that only New England clergy advocated revolution. For an account of a Southern Anglican clergyman's perspective, distinctly more moderate in tone, see Charles Wilbanks, ed., *The American Revolution and Righteous Community: Selected Sermons of Bishop Robert Smith* (Columbia: University of South Carolina Press, 2007).

enemies."[83] He notes that "it pleased GOD to single out a nation from the rest of mankind, and to erect them into a sacred polity" but leaves the argument implicit that this elected nation, in his time, is not New England but rather the new American nation.[84]

The bulk of Cushing's attention is given to God's vengeance on behalf of His chosen people. America is clearly in the position of Israel, while England is configured as Edom or Babylon. "The enemies of GOD's church and people, are GOD's adversaries. 'The Lord's portion is his people,—he keeps them as the apple of his eye' . . . Whoever grieves or afflicts them, provokes GOD, for they are 'his peculiar treasure.'"[85] While God uses other nations as instruments to chastise His chosen people, He also holds them accountable for their atrocities. "Thus utter destruction is denounced upon *Edom*, for their unnatural enmity against the *Jews,* and cruelty towards their brethren . . ."[86] And there can be no doubt that for Cushing, the British went too far in Lexington:

> In pursuance of their oppressive measures (if not intentionally to begin the barbarous and bloody scene) the enemy came upon us like a flood, stealing a march from *Boston,* through by-ways. under the darkness and silence of the night; and, like *cowards* and *robbers,* attacked us altogether defenceless; and cruelly murdered the *innocent,* the aged and helpless. Accordingly they are described by the prophet, as persons whose *hands are defiled with blood;*—adding, "their works are works of iniquity, and the act of violence is in their hands. Their feet run to evil, and they make haste to shed innocent blood; their thoughts are thoughts of iniquity, wasting and destruction are in their paths."[87]

83. Jacob Cushing, *Divine Judgments upon Tyrants: And Compassion to the Oppressed* . . . (Boston, MA, 1778), 8.

84. Ibid., 13. See also page 7: Of God's words and actions toward Israel, he writes: "though, in their primary meaning, they respect that nation only, yet they may be accommodated and fairly applied to GOD's faithful and obedient people, at all times, and in all ages; inasmuch as the latter part of the prophecy reaches unto the latter days, and is not yet wholly fulfilled."

85. Ibid., 12 (citation omitted).

86. Ibid.

87. Ibid., 21. Cushing goes on, however, to quote a passage from Isaiah 59, which is an oracle against Israel, not an oracle against the nations. See also Jonas Clark *The Fate of Blood-Thirsty Oppressors* . . . (Boston, MA, 1776). Clark's sermon takes Joel 3:19–21 as its scriptural basis; see page 5:

Distinguished preacher and patriot Henry Cumings (d. 1823) sounds many of the same themes in his anniversary sermon. Repentance is necessary because God will use the wrath of foreign nations to punish the iniquities of His chosen people. Nonetheless, while He uses the wrath of the nations to His purposes, He does not let it run unchecked: "But as the Assyrian acted freely, being under no constraint, it was no excuse for him, that GOD made his pride and ambition, instrumental in bringing his righteous judgments on the Jewish nation; but his conduct was highly affrontive to Heaven, and exposed him to the righteous resentments of the Supreme Governor."[88]

This rhetorical turn was more than slightly ironic. About two decades earlier, the same group of ministers had drawn inspiration from the oracles against the nations to defend the English cause in the French and Indian War. The jeremiads against the French focused on the necessity of defending the integrity of New England's political system against foreign invaders who would subvert both political liberty and freedom to worship according to the dictates of the Gospel, as those ministers understood the Gospel. A thanksgiving sermon preached after the English won the war pithily encapsulates the sentiment: "The *American* DUNKIRK and the Western BABYLON are fallen!"[89] France, as a Catholic country, was easily configured as a nemesis of true Christianity, which in the preachers' view was Protestant Christianity. Not only was France depicted as Babylon, the mortal enemy of the Jewish people, it was also configured as the whore of Babylon, the enemy of true Christianity because of its Roman Catholicism.

The whore of Babylon, of course, makes her appearance not in ancient Israel but at the end of sacred history in the events described in the Book of

---

"EGYPT *shall be a desolation, and* EDOM *shall be a desolate wilderness, for the violence against the children of Judah, because they have shed INNOCENT BLOOD in their land. But Judah shall dwell for ever, and Jerusalem from generation to generation. For I will cleanse their blood that I have not cleansed; for the LORD dwelleth in Zion."*

88. Henry Cumings, *A Sermon Preached at Lexington on the 19th of April, 1781* . . . (Boston, MA, 1781), 13–14.

89. John Mellen, *A Sermon Preached at the West Parish in Lancaster, October 9, 1760* . . . (Boston, MA, 1760), 16. An important military site in World War II, the European Dunkirk is in northern France, about six miles from the Belgian border. Long disputed territory, it came under French rule when the Catholic king Charles II of England sold it to France in October 1662. Mellen is preaching the sermon on the general occasion of the fall of Montreal and what he deems the "Total Conquest of CANADA" (title page).

Revelation.[90] The strong millenarian sensibilities in Puritan preaching (and among Christians of that era more generally) added to the urgency to defeat the enemy of Christ—to defeat the Antichrist, whom many Puritans identified with the pope. The fact that the "papists" were attempting to subvert the New Jerusalem was not surprising to the New England Puritans; it only made them more determined to win the cosmic battle between good and evil.

In certain respects, it was a natural move to extend the language of the prophetic oracles against Israel's enemies from the war against France to the war against England. The Patriots had in that language a ready-made rhetorical framework for self-justification and self-motivation. Nonetheless, it is important to emphasize that the colonists' use of this aspect of the prophetic literature in the war against England was also significantly incongruous. Unlike France, England was a firmly Protestant nation by this point in time. England had in fact been the birthplace of Puritanism; it was the seedbed of the very conception of political and religious rights that the colonists wished to claim for themselves. In the late 1750s and early 1760s, Americans were fighting side by side with the British to defend these values. Fifteen years later, the colonists were casting their mother country in the role of those nations who sought to destroy God's chosen people in ancient times and those who would act as the mortal enemies of Christ at the end of times. The swift reversal in treating England as a valuable Protestant ally to the whore of Babylon was nothing short of rhetorically dizzying.

What made the rhetoric even more striking, however, was the context in which these addresses were delivered. In the French and Indian Wars, the language echoing the oracles against the nations and the final confrontation between good and evil treated the French bitterly;[91] it is likely, however, that most Frenchmen never encountered that rhetoric. Nor, for that matter, did most Native Americans. But they were not the intended audience of these

---

90. "So he carried me away in the spirit into a wilderness, and I saw a woman sitting on a scarlet beast that was full of blasphemous names, and it had seven heads and ten horns. The woman was clothed in purple and scarlet, and adorned with gold and jewels and pearls, holding in her hand a golden cup full of abominations and the impurities of her fornication; and on her forehead was written a name, a mystery: 'Babylon the great, mother of whores and of earth's abominations.' And I saw that the woman was drunk with the blood of the saints and the blood of the witnesses to Jesus. When I saw her, I was greatly amazed." Revelation 17:3–6.

91. See, for example, John Mellen, *Sermon Preached at the West Parish*; Samuel Haven, *Joy and Salvation by Christ; His Arm Displayed in the Protestant Cause* . . . (Portsmouth, NH, 1763).

sermons, which were meant to galvanize the English colonists to victory. In fact, the sermons in the French and Indian Wars represented a well-established genre of English preaching. More specifically, in addition to election, feast, and fast day sermons, the Puritans also developed a distinct genre of preaching, commonly known as artillery sermons or muster sermons. They focused on motivating colonial military forces to struggle wholeheartedly against New England's enemies, who were also God's enemies. After all, the colonists in the wilderness could not afford to forget that "[t]he Little Flock of Christ, is hem'd round with devouring Wolves, who are always spiteing of it, gnashing their teeth upon it, and ofttimes actually making a prey thereof."[92] These artillery and muster sermons were often fierce in tone, frequently drawing on or alluding to biblical imagery modeled on the battles of ancient Israel and Judah.[93] These sermons were sharper when the hostilities with the Native American population were raging than in times of relative quiescence.[94]

In contrast to the French and Indian Wars, the Revolutionary War was a battle *among* people who shared the same culture, language, and history. The question whether America should obtain its independence, by the sword if necessary, was disputed not only between the Old World and the New, but *within* the New World itself. Scholars estimate that as many as 20 percent of the colonists were opposed to the revolution. To a considerable extent, therefore, the American Patriots were targeting their fellow colonists with invective that they modeled on the biblical oracles against the nations.[95] In a

92. Henry Gibbs, *The Right Method of Safety* . . . (Boston, MA, 1704), 7.

93. As Harry S. Stout notes, "Too often, historians have mistaken the restraint in these [fast and thanksgiving] sermons for the whole of New England preaching, and they have therefore missed more radical sentiments that appeared on other, more local occasions and that reveal the full range of pulpit ideology. Of these, the most striking were the artillery election sermons and the local militia muster sermons." Harry S. Stout, *The New England Soul: Preaching and Religious Culture in Colonial New England* (New York: Oxford University Press, 1986), 287.

94. See, for example Samuel Nowell, *Abraham in Arms* . . . (Boston, MA, 1678); John Richardson, *The Necessity of a Well Experienced Souldiery* . . . (Cambridge, MA, 1679); Grindal Rawson, *Miles Christianus* . . . (Boston, MA, 1703); Thomas Bridge, *The Knowledge of God* . . . (Boston, MA, 1705); and Ebenezer Pemberton, *A Sermon Preached to the Ancient and Honourable Artillery-Company* . . . (Boston, MA, 1756).

95. Kenneth S. Lynn, *A Divided People* (Westport, CT: Greenwood Press, 1977). Lynn examines the backgrounds of prominent Loyalists and Patriots. See also William Allen Benton, *Whig-Loyalism: An Aspect of Political Ideology in the American Revolutionary Era* (Rutherford, NJ: Fairleigh Dickinson University Press, 1969); G. N. D. Evans, ed., *Allegiance in America: The Case of the Loyalists* (Reading, MA: Addison-Wesley, 1969); Robert McCluer Calhoon, *The Loyalists in Revolutionary America, 1760–1781* (New York: Harcourt Brace Jovanovich, 1973); and Christopher Hibbert, *Redcoats and Rebels:*

sermon preached in Salem at the commencement of the war and dedicated to George Washington, Nathaniel Whitaker makes it clear that there is no room for good-faith disagreement about the wisdom of revolution. His fifth doctrinal observation is: "That God requires a people, struggling for their Liberties, to treat such of the community who will not join them, as open enemies, and to reject them as unworthy the priviledges which others enjoy."[96] Those who do not join them "are accursed of God, and we are commanded to curse them, we ought, at least, to shun their company."[97]

In the rhetorical history of the jeremiad, this turn was extremely significant. There were certainly disagreements within New England Puritanism prior to the Revolutionary War. The disagreement over the halfway covenant in the mid-seventeenth century was extremely heated,[98] as was the tensions that arose over the Great Awakening and the itinerant preachers in the mid-eighteenth century. Yet in these cases the disputants did not tend to configure each other as enemies of the chosen people, as whores of Babylon who were to be utterly destroyed for their sins rather than medicinally corrected because of them. The Revolutionary War rhetoric condemning fellow members of the community in a manner resonant of the oracles against the nations is an important root of the acerbity characterizing the present-day culture wars. As I show in the next section, however, the culture wars are by no means an exclusively contemporary phenomenon.

Was Thomas Paine the First American Culture Warrior?

Widely acknowledged to be the most influential piece of pro–Revolutionary War rhetoric, Thomas Paine's *Common Sense: Address to the Inhabitants of America* was first published anonymously in Philadelphia in January 1776.[99] By

---

The American Revolution Through British Eyes (New York: Norton, 1990). For more information, see Robert S. Allen, *Loyalist Literature: An Annotated Bibliographic Guide to the Writings on the Loyalists of the American Revolution* (Toronto: Dundurn Press, 1982).

96. Nathaniel Whitaker, *An Antidote Against Toryism* . . . (Newbury-Port, MA, 1777), 10.

97. Ibid., 32. For a good flavor of the life and times of Patriot preachers, see Joel Tyler Headley, *The Chaplains and Clergy of the Revolution* (Springfield, MA: G. & F. Bill, 1861); and Frank Moore, *The Patriot Preachers of the American Revolution: With Biographical Sketches* (New York: C. T. Evans, 1862).

98. The "halfway covenant" was a way in which the children and grandchildren of the original Puritans could participate to some degree in the life of their congregations, despite the fact that they did not undergo a personal conversion experience that was the condition for full covenantal church membership. Most important, they could baptize their own children in the church.

99. Thomas Paine, *Common Sense*, February 14, 1776, in *Collected Writings*, ed. Eric Foner (New

the end of the year, at least twenty-five editions of the pamphlet had been printed.[100] According to Eric Foner, "What made Paine unique was that he forged a new political language. He did not simply change the meanings of words, he created a literary style designed to bring his message to the widest possible audience."[101] In my view, Foner's observation is entirely correct: Paine did forge a new political language. Yet Foner's observation is also incomplete: Paine forged that new language not out of virgin rhetorical metal but by combining and building on recognizable components of existing forms of public discourse. In addition to his breathtakingly sharp turns of phrase, what made Paine's *Common Sense* uniquely influential was his ability to draw on, recombine, and extend familiar themes and rhetorical tropes in a way that supported his case for revolution. Paine did not simply make a new case for independence; he made that case in a way that exhibited significant rhetorical continuities with long-standing American themes, including religious themes. Ultimately, his rhetorical power derived from his combination of innovation and tradition. Edward Larkin argues that Paine invented the American public to which he spoke by casting his arguments in plain forms that could be understood by the common person and not merely by members of the intellectual and cultural elite.[102] Larkin's analysis, I think, supports my own view that Thomas Paine was the first major American "public intellectual," presenting sophisticated arguments in a simplified form that is accessible to a broad readership.

A close examination of *Common Sense* reveals a brilliant rhetorical consonance with many of the themes we have traced in the evolution of the Puritan jeremiad. The first part, "Of the Origin and Design of Government in General. With Concise Remarks on the English Constitution," makes the

---

York: Library of America, 1995), 5–59. In view of the large number of colonial reprints, I use Foner's edition in my analysis below.

100. Eric Foner, *Tom Paine and Revolutionary America* (New York: Oxford University Press 1976), xi, 79. Paine was far from the only pamphleteer. See Bailyn, *The Ideological Origins,* for a fuller account of the role of pamphlets in the Revolutionary War. Bailyn notes, "The American writers were profoundly reasonable people. Their pamphlets convey scorn, anger, and indignation; but rarely blind hate, rarely panic fear. They sought to convince their opponents, not, like the English pamphleteers of the eighteenth century, to annihilate them" (pp. 18–19). See also Bernard Bailyn, ed., *Pamphlets of the American Revolution 1750–1776,* vol. 1, *1750–1765* (Cambridge, MA: Belknap Press of Harvard University Press, 1965).

101. Foner, *Tom Paine,* xvi.

102. Edward Larkin, *Thomas Paine and the Literature of Revolution* (Cambridge: Cambridge University Press, 2005).

case against monarchy largely in the Lockean framework of natural rights and the social contract made in the state of nature rather than in the terms of the biblical covenant. The second part, "Of Monarchy and Hereditary Succession," duplicates and extends the points made in the first chapter by means of an elaborate appeal to Scripture rather than to the deliverance of natural reason.[103] It is striking that the appeal is made in terms of analogy to ancient Jewish history rather than to the legal terms of the covenant. Praising the fate of Israel under the Judges, Paine paints the move to monarchy as an idolatrous delusion. "As the exalting one man so greatly above the rest cannot be justified on the equal rights of nature, so neither can it be defended on the authority of scripture; for the will of the Almighty, as declared by Gideon and the prophet Samuel, expressly disapproves of government by kings."[104]

Both these argumentative strategies allow the rhetoric of the pamphlet to become far more heated than the Puritan jeremiad. Precisely because Paine sees himself as appealing to the evident truths of natural reason—to common sense—the opponents of his plan must be intellectually or morally benighted. In the "Introduction" to the pamphlet, Paine affirms that his arguments will not take the form of personal insults: "the author hath studiously avoided every thing which is personal among ourselves. Compliments as well as censure to individuals make no part thereof."[105] Nonetheless, this disavowal of personal insult is disingenuous. Paine cannot see how anyone could, with intellectual competence and good faith, argue against him. This inability to interpret his interlocutors with charity is apparent in the third part, "Thoughts on the Present State of American Affairs."

> Though I would carefully avoid giving unnecessary offence, yet I am inclined to believe, that all those who espouse the doctrine of reconciliation [with England], may be included within the following descriptions. Interested men, who are not to be trusted; weak men, who *cannot* see; prejudiced men, who *will not* see; and a certain set of moderate men, who think better of the European

103. Not that Paine accepted his own arguments in this regard. His later work, *The Age of Reason,* was a militant defense of deism. See Paine, *Collected Writings,* 663–830.

104. Paine, *Common Sense,* in *Collected Writings,* 13.

105. Ibid., 5.

world than it deserves; and this last class, by an ill-judged deliberation, will be the cause of more calamities to this continent, than all the other three.[106]

Paine soon moves on to question even the basic human grasp of morality and fellow feeling of those who are passively disinclined to war. No contemporary culture warrior could best this rhetoric of insult:

> Have you lost a parent or child by their [English] hands, and yourself the ruined and wretched survivor? If you have not, then you are not a judge of those who have. But if you have, and still can shake hands with the murderers, then are you unworthy the name of husband, father, friend, or lover, and whatever may be your rank or title in life, you have the heart of a coward, and the spirit of a sycophant.[107]

Paine is not above appealing to long-standing anti-Catholic sentiment to make his arguments against England. In Paine's view, "monarchy in every instance is the Popery of government."[108] He calls Sir John Dalrymple, the English author of an anti-independence pamphlet, "the putative father of a whining jesuitical piece," and tars him with the sin of idolatry.[109] And he is no kinder to Americans who seem to support the Crown, brutally castigating the Quakers who counsel against revolution for inconsistency in not staying completely out of politics.[110] So much for Paine's "no personal insults" policy.

While Paine freely draws on venerable American religious tropes and images, he feels equally free to broaden and even recast them to serve his current purposes.[111] The sufferings of Boston under British domination are made to serve as a symbol of a broader threat: "that seat of wretchedness will teach us wisdom, and instruct us for ever to renounce a power in whom

106. Ibid., 25–26.
107. Ibid., 26–27.
108. Ibid., 15.
109. Ibid., 47.
110. Ibid., 54–59.
111. A helpful compilation of religious sources used to justify the revolution is Page Smith, ed., *Religious Origins of the American Revolution* (Missoula, MT: Scholars Press, 1976).

we can have no trust."[112] At the same time, Boston is only a symbol; its distinctive religious commitments are not merely swept away but reversed entirely. In the course of arguing that the authority of England over America "was never the design of Heaven," Paine recasts the purpose of the founding of the colony. "The reformation was preceded by the discovery of America, as if the Almighty graciously meant to open a sanctuary to the persecuted in future years, when home should afford neither friendship nor safety."[113] The Puritans, of course, did not see themselves as especially godly *because* they were unjustly persecuted; they saw the persecution as unjust *because* they were especially godly.

Like our contemporary culture warriors, Paine's strategy and tactics were not entirely well regarded by his sometime allies, who envied his fame and influence even as they deplored his ideas. John Adams, who viewed Paine's radical democratic ideals as dangerous and his deism foolhardy, made his opinion clear in this comment on Paine's *The Age of Reason*. Not incidentally, it competes with Paine's fiery rhetoric even as it denounces its effects on civil life.

> I am willing you should call this the Age of Frivolity as you do, and would not object if you had named it the Age of Folly, Vice, Frenzy, Brutality, Daemons, Buonaparte, Tom Paine, or the Age of the Burning Brand from the Bottomless Pit, or anything but the Age of Reason. I know not whether any man in the world has had more influence on its inhabitants or affairs for the last thirty years than Tom Paine. There can no severer satyr on the age. For such a mongrel between pig and puppy, begotten by a wild boar on a bitch wolf, never before in any age of the world was suffered by the poltroonery of mankind, to run through such a career of mischief. Call it then the Age of Paine.[114]

112. Paine, *Common Sense,* in *Collected Writings,* 26.
113. Ibid., 25.
114. Larkin, *Thomas Paine,* 8, citing David Freeman Hawke, *Paine* (New York: Norton, 1974), 7.

The Jeremiad after the Revolution

Thomas Paine may have been one of the first culture warriors, but he certainly was not the last. As Sacvan Bercovitch, James Darsey, David Howard-Pitney, Andrew Murphy, and others have detailed, the jeremiad went on to become a staple of major American social and political controversies throughout the nineteenth and twentieth centuries.[115] No longer the instrument of social cohesion that it was in Puritan times, it became a tool of social division, for reasons I detailed earlier in this chapter. The jeremiad became a rhetorical vehicle to demand innovative social change rather than a call for the community to repent of well-worn and familiar sins. The tight connection between jeremiad and national covenant was loosened, but it was not entirely eliminated. In fact, the reconstructed jeremiad presented its call for social change as clearly demanded by faithfulness to the nation's deepest values. Needless to say, those opposed to the proposed change did not understand the values of the national covenant in the same way. The nation's periodic culture wars have reflected and reinforced each side's configuration of its opponents as inimical to the nation's basic commitments.

It is beyond the scope of this book to examine in detail the shifting relationship between the jeremiad and the covenant as it was revealed in our nation's controversies over matters such as slavery, women's suffrage, Prohibition and its repeal, worker's rights, and civil rights.[116] My goal here is to draw on historical

115. Bercovitch, *The American Jeremiad;* David Howard-Pitney, *The African American Jeremiad,* rev. ed. (Philadelphia, PA: Temple University Press, 2005); James Darsey, *The Prophetic Tradition and Radical Rhetoric in America* (New York: New York University Press, 1997); Murphy, *Prodigal Nation.* See, in particular, Murphy, *Prodigal Nation,* chap. 3: "Decline, Slavery, and War: The Jeremiad in Antebellum and Civil War America," 44–76.

116. I discuss slavery and the jeremiad later in this chapter, and preaching about civil rights in Chapter 8. On women and voting, see, for example, Ellen Carol DuBois, *Women's Suffrage & Women's Rights* (New York: New York University Press, 1998); and Jean H. Baker, *Sisters: The Lives of America's Suffragists* (New York: Hill and Wang, 2005). On Prohibition, see, for example, Andrew Sinclair, *Prohibition: The Era of Excess* (Boston, MA: Little, Brown and Company, 1962); and David E. Kyvig, *Repealing National Prohibition,* 2nd ed. (Kent, OH: Kent State University Press, 2000). On the social gospel, see, for example, Gary Dorrien, *Social Ethics in the Making: Interpreting an American Tradition* (Malden, MA: Wiley-Blackwell, 2009). Given the recent dominance of more conservative, evangelical Protestants in American political life, it is important to recognize the enormous contributions of Protestant liberals. See, for example, David A. Hollinger, *After Cloven Tongues of Fire: Protestant Liberalism in Modern American History* (Princeton, NJ: Princeton University Press, 2013).

sources in order to illuminate the contemporary context rather than to provide an exhaustive account of political and religious rhetoric in the American public square. At the same time, it is worth examining some influential sermons in the nation's battle over slavery, if only because they so clearly illustrate the evolution of the jeremiad's social function.[117]

The great antislavery preachers knew they were being divisive in calling for social change. Moreover, they acknowledged that their tools were not the precise instruments of practical deliberation. For example, in his essay, "Philosophy of the Abolition Movement," Wendell Phillips writes: "The charges [against the abolitionists] to which I refer are these: that, in dealing with slaveholders and their apologists, we indulge in fierce denunciations, instead of appealing to their reason and common sense by plain statements and fair argument."[118] Putting himself in the shoes of the prophets, he goes on to ask:

> What is the denunciation with which we are charged? It is endeavoring, in our faltering human speech, to declare the enormity of the sin of making merchandise of men—of separating husband and wife, taking the infant from its mother, and selling the daughter to prostitution—of a professedly Christian nation denying, by statute, the Bible to every sixth man and woman of its

---

117. The literature on antislavery preaching and writing is voluminous. See, for example, Timothy Patrick McCarthy and John Stauffer, eds., *Prophets of Protest: Reconsidering the History of American Abolitionism* (New York: New Press, 2006); Albert J. Raboteau, *Slave Religion: The "Invisible Institution" in the Antebellum South*, updated ed. (New York: Oxford University Press, 2004); Eddie S. Glaude, Jr., *Exodus! Religion, Race, and Nation in Early Nineteenth-Century Black America* (Chicago, IL: University of Chicago Press, 2000); Wolfgang Mieder, *"No Struggle, No Progress": Frederick Douglass and His Proverbial Rhetoric for Civil Rights* (New York: Peter Lang, 2001); Stanley Harrold, *American Abolitionists* (Essex, UK: Pearson Education Ltd., 2001); Stanley Harrold, *The Abolitionists and the South, 1831–1861* (Lexington: University Press of Kentucky, 1995); John Auping Birch, *Religion and Social Justice: The Case of Christianity and the Abolition of Slavery in America* (Colonia Lomas de Santa Fe, Mexico: Universidad Iberoamericana, 1994); Victor B. Howard, *Conscience and Slavery: The Evangelistic Calvinist Domestic Missions, 1837–1861* (Kent, OH: Kent State University Press, 1990); C. Eric Lincoln and Lawrence H. Mamiya, *The Black Church in the African American Experience* (Durham, NC: Duke University Press, 1990); Paul Finkelman, ed., *Articles on American Slavery*, vol. 16, *Religion and Slavery* (New York: Garland Publishing, 1989); John R. McKivigan, *The War against Proslavery Religion: Abolitionism and the Northern Churches, 1830–1865* (Ithaca, NY: Cornell University Press, 1984); and Eugene D. Genovese, *Roll, Jordan, Roll: The World the Slaves Made* (New York: Random House, 1974).

118. Wendell Phillips, *Wendell Phillips on Civil Rights and Freedom,* ed. Louis Filler (New York: Hill and Wang, 1965), 30. See also Andrew Delbanco, *The Abolitionist Imagination* (Cambridge, MA: Harvard University Press, 2012).

population, and making it illegal for "two or three" to meet together, except a white man be present![119]

We do not often think of the abolitionist preachers as advancing a contested and contestable account of the nation's fundamental moral and religious commitments, but they assuredly were. Proslavery forces defended the institution on the basis of the very same Bible that abolitionists used to attack it.[120] Arguing against racial equality, Alexander Stephens maintained that "[o]ur new government is founded upon exactly the opposite idea: its foundations are laid, its corner-stone rests upon the great truth, that the negro is not equal to the white man; that slavery—subordination to the superior race—is his natural and normal condition."[121] Thornton Stringfellow averred: "I affirm then, first (and no man denies,) that Jesus Christ has not abolished slavery by a prohibitory command: and second, I affirm, he has introduced no new moral principle which can work its destruction, under the gospel dispensation. . . ."[122] An essay examining the scriptural basis of slavery concluded that if the Bible "is of divine origin, the holding of slaves is right: as that which God permitted, recognized and commanded, cannot be inconsistent with his will."[123]

119. Phillips, *Wendell Phillips on Civil Rights and Freedom*, 36. For other primary abolitionist texts, see, for example, Mason Lowance, ed., *Against Slavery: An Abolitionist Reader* (New York: Penguin Books, 2000); Owen Lovejoy, *His Brother's Blood: Speeches and Writings 1838–64*, ed. William F. Moore and Jane Ann Moore (Urbana: University of Illinois Press, 2004); Frederick Douglass, *Frederick Douglass: Selected Speeches and Writings*, ed. Philip S. Foner, abr. Yuval Taylor (Chicago, IL: Lawrence Hill Books, 1999); Horace Mann, *Slavery: Letters and Speeches* (Boston, MA, 1851); and William Lloyd Garrison, *Selections from the Writings and Speeches of William Lloyd Garrison with an Appendix* (Boston, MA, 1852).

120. See, for example, Jeffrey Robert Young, ed., *Proslavery and Sectional Thought in the Early South, 1740–1829: An Anthology* (Columbia: University of South Carolina Press, 2006); Paul Finkelman, *Defending Slavery: Proslavery Thought in the Old South—A Brief History with Documents* (Boston, MA: Bedford/St. Martin's, 2003); John R. McKivigan and Mitchell Snay, eds., *Religion and the Antebellum Debate over Slavery* (Athens: University of Georgia Press, 1998); Paul Finkelman, ed., *Articles on American Slavery*, vol. 12, *Proslavery Thought, Ideology, and Politics* (New York: Garland Publishing, 1989); William Sumner Jenkins, *Pro-Slavery Thought in the Old South* (Chapel Hill: University of North Carolina Press, 1935); and E. N. Elliott, ed., *Cotton Is King, and Pro-Slavery Arguments: Comprising the Writings of Hammond, Harper, Christy, Stringfellow, Hodge, Bledsoe, and Cartwright on this Important Subject* (Augusta, GA, 1860).

121. Alexander Stephens, "The Cornerstone Speech" (1861), in Finkelman, ed., *Defending Slavery*, 91.

122. Thornton Stringfellow, "The Bible Argument: Or, Slavery in the Light of Divine Revelation" (1860), in Finkelman, ed., *Defending Slavery*, 126.

123. De Bow's Review, "Slavery and the Bible" (1850), in Finkelman, ed., *Defending Slavery*, 114.

In his important book, *The Civil War as a Theological Crisis,* Mark A. Noll details the way in which the struggle over slavery also functioned as a battle over how America, which configured itself at that time as a Christian nation, ought to read the Bible.[124] As Noll recounts, European Christian observers of the battle clearly saw the elements of what we today would call a culture war. An editorial in the *London Times* observed: "The Northern fanatic, who declared slavery to be humanly wrong, produced the Southern fanatic, who declared it to be divinely right."[125] Because the culture war over slavery was decisively settled long ago by actual military engagement, we now tend to focus on the fiery preaching of the abolitionists and lose sight of their equally committed religious and political opponents. More specifically, it is all too easy to see the abolitionists as drawing upon an indisputable understanding of this nation's moral foundations, including its scriptural foundations, in order to press their argument against slavery. Noll's book demonstrates that this is not the case. In fact, the dueling declamations of the North and the South were *contesting* the correct way to read Scripture and the scripturally infused national compact. As Noll writes, the religious battle over slavery "was never only a matter of interpreting individual biblical texts, but always a question of putting actively to use the authoritative Book on which the national culture of the United States had been built."[126]

If we are going to understand the evolving role of prophetic discourse in the American public square, it is important to look at the full range of jeremiads preached in the social battle over slavery and not merely to focus on the abolitionist literature. A narrow concentration on the abolitionist literature would suggest that the social function of the jeremiad had not ranged too far from that of the Puritans—or at least that it had ranged no further than its function at the time of the Revolutionary War. More specifically, such a concentration could easily lead one to conclude that the abolitionists, like the Patriots, were deploying a more or less widely agreed upon conception of

124. Mark A. Noll, *The Civil War as a Theological Crisis* (Chapel Hill: University of North Carolina Press, 2006). See also Harry S. Stout's magisterial volume, *Upon the Altar of the Nation: A Moral History of the Civil War* (New York: Penguin Books, 2006).

125. "The Civil War in America," *London Times,* March 23, 1863, p. 9, col. e, cited in Noll, *The Civil War,* 107.

126. Noll, *The Civil War,* 29.

Scripture, together with a more contestable account of natural rights and common sense, to press their emancipatory cause.

Such a conclusion would be sorely mistaken, which becomes clear when the abolitionist jeremiads are set next to their anti-abolitionist counterparts. Functionally, the debate was not merely about the practice of slavery. Instead, it was centrally concerned with how to interpret the basic commitments of the country and most particularly with how to understand the scriptural basis of those commitments. Did the fundamental terms of our social compact include a commitment to the legitimacy of slavery? As Noll emphasizes, those questions were definitively settled for nineteenth-century Americans not by pamphlets and broadsides but by bullets and bayonets.

For our purposes, it is important to note the stress that the shape of the nineteenth-century debate over slavery placed on the form of the jeremiad. As I noted in the previous chapter, the jeremiad is centrally designed to lodge an indictment against those who engage in behavior prohibited by the national covenant. Its form *presupposes* general agreement on the requirements of that covenant; it is not designed to litigate their nature and acceptability. The rhetorical battle over slavery, however, *did* involve a contestation about the basic requirements of the covenant. On each side, the battling jeremiahs elaborated and presupposed their understanding of America's basic commitments in order to press their respective views about the legitimacy of slavery. Yet by its very rhetorical nature, the jeremiad did not and could not facilitate critical reflection about the antagonists' different views on Scripture and constitutional values. A legal indictment is not designed, after all, to facilitate critical reflection about the normative worth of the law whose violation is charged; it presupposes that worth as a given.

One might object that from time to time criminal lawyers do indeed challenge the moral worth of a law; they ask for the jury to refuse to convict the defendant for moral reasons despite the fact that he or she is clearly guilty of breaking the law. It could be argued that the abolitionists, in particular, were asking the jury to refuse to enforce extant laws recognizing and protecting slavery. Although this objection is intriguing, in my view, it ultimately fails. First, calls for "jury nullification" are highly problematic in the legal system precisely because they threaten to undermine the rule of law. Second, to the extent that they succeed, they tend to invoke a "higher law," which trumps the particular legal provision that the defendant is accused of violating. What is at stake in the jeremiads over slavery, of course, is precisely the nature of that higher law.

Perusing only the abolitionist side of the verbal battles over slavery may lead readers to think that the jeremiad was a vigorous and well-functioning form of political-religious speech. Fiery abolitionist prophets indicted slave owners for their treacherous betrayal of constitutional and biblical values. As jeremiads typically do, the only option they left to their rhetorical defendants was confession and repentance. From the contemporary vantage point, it is easy to read the abolitionist rhetoric and think that the slave owners and supporters of slavery could respond only by repudiating their objectionable practices and positions. But that was not the case. Their own preachers defended slavery and attacked the North on the basis of a very different understanding of constitutional and biblical values. For all their fierceness, the dueling jeremiahs could not convict their target defendants, who refused to acknowledge each other's framing of the foundational commitments of the country. A jeremiad may be full of sound and fury, but its rhetorical power is thwarted if it does not and cannot appeal to a broadly accepted account of the national covenant or basic law of the country.

Reversal of Breach and Penalty

As the covenant became an increasingly tenuous anchor for the jeremiad, the identity of the partners to this special relationship between God and the chosen people became more diffuse, and the human obligations of this relationship and the consequences of breaching it became less definite. In my view, one development first observed in the Puritan era has particularly striking effects for the long-term evolution of the jeremiad. Perry Miller details how even the second-generation Puritans began confusing the breach—the offending conduct—with the punishment. In other words, the jeremiad was originally structured so that the common sins of the people were the breach, while the temporal misfortunes suffered by the little colony were divine penalty for the breach. But that structure soon began to be turned around. The jeremiads began to treat the sins and dissensions of the community as punishments rather than as the precipitating causes of the punishments. If so, what were the breaches? In some cases, it was not entirely clear.

On October 19, 1652, the Massachusetts General Court mandated a fast day in the usual manner, pointing to the customary list of temporal troubles as the justification. In addition, however, the court identified the provoking sins— worldliness, oppression, and hard-heartedness—among the afflictions suffered by the colonies. Perry Miller writes: "Corruption itself now appeared not as a cause but a visitation of wrath."[127] Miller argues that this transformation, which began as a slight shift in emphasis, began to dominate the genre within a decade; "proclamations concentrated more and more upon the sins themselves, reducing the resulting distresses to footnotes."[128]

In a homogenous community, where there is near-universal agreement on what constitutes just moral and political action, this confusion between breach and penalty would not have been particularly problematic. Everyone knew the requirements of the covenant. Everyone acknowledged what constituted betrayal of God's law and what constituted fidelity. But coupled with the other changes—the expansion of the human covenant partners, the more diffuse identity given to the divine covenant partner, and the increasing vagueness of the terms of the covenant itself—the propensity to confuse breach and penalty is significantly greater. I think this is one of the problems characterizing the appropriation of the images and languages from colonial Puritanism in the contemporary context.

The belief that America is a chosen nation has been challenged, of course, on principled theological, political, and historical grounds.[129] My concern here is more pragmatic; I am concerned about the practical consequences of this belief. The Puritans balanced their belief that the American people were specially chosen for great privilege with the conviction that they were also called to great duties. Moreover, they were convinced that both privilege and duties were not a matter of entitlement or good luck but were conferred by God for His own purposes. In contrast, in our era, we have retained the idea of chosenness without any firm conception of a chooser. We have maintained the ideal of national privilege but have not always sustained a clear sense of

127. Miller, *From Colony to Province*, 28.

128. Ibid. For a preliminary exploration of themes discussed in this section, see M. Cathleen Kaveny, "The Remnants of Theocracy: The Puritans, the Jeremiad and the Contemporary Culture Wars," *Law, Culture and the Humanities* 9, no. 1 (2013): 59-70.

129. See, for example, Andrew Kohut and Bruce Stokes, *America against the World: How We Are Different and Why We Are Disliked* (New York: Henry Holt, 2006).

national duties. Our destiny is far from manifest. We think of ourselves as a shining city on a hill, but our view of the path from that august vantage is decidedly cloudy. Contemporary Americans may still see themselves as "chosen" for special blessings. We have largely lost sight, however, of the cosmic religious and moral framework, including the traditional covenantal structure, which makes sense of our chosenness.

In our highly divided society, it has become more difficult for culture warriors to treat widespread American support for (or opposition to) abortion, same-sex marriage, stem-cell research, or euthanasia as *breaches* of the terms of the national covenant. It is far easier to treat the existence of divided public opinion on these matters as in some sense a *penalty* imposed on our nation. What kind of penalty? In my view, it is twofold: It is a penalty harming our moral integrity and a penalty undermining our national unity. To a conservative culture warrior, for example, the fact that same-sex marriages are being performed in the United States mars the moral integrity of the nation. To a progressive culture warrior, the fact that same-sex marriage is resisted in some quarters of the country constitutes the moral black mark. Moreover, the divided nature of American public opinion on these matters reveals the fragile bonds of our union. Our unity in diversity has long been a key part of our national self-understanding. In fact, Congress authorized the phrase "e pluribus unum" (which means "out of many, one") to be placed on the Great Seal of the United States in 1782. Our deep and persistent social division can easily be seen to mock the aspiration that this phrase articulates.

What actions count as *breaching* our national covenant, in the contemporary situation, in which culture warriors treat the partial social acceptance of (or opposition to) abortion, same-sex marriage, and other controversial practices as the *penalty* for such breaches? I think that a breach is generally perceived to be any failure to do what is required to protect and advance the material interests of the nation, particularly its military security and its economic advancement. More specifically, one way of interpreting the dynamics of the contemporary culture wars is in terms of an *inversion* of the covenantal structure adopted in colonial Massachusetts. For the earliest Puritans, the national covenant demanded social conformity to divinely imposed moral and social norms. If the nation conformed to those covenantal duties, God would grant His covenant partner material security and prosperity as a reward for good behavior. Conversely, in Puritan times, widespread failure to comply with moral and social norms constituted a *breach* of the covenant, which would trigger a penalty characterized by severe threats to the political and economic well-being of the colony. In earlier times, the logic of American exceptionalism focused primarily on the nation's covenant-based moral obligations, seeing the blessings of material prosperity as *a reward and result* of fulfilling those obligations.

In our era, by contrast, the blessings and the obligations seem to be inverted or reversed. The overriding obligation of the contemporary national covenant generally seems to involve securing America's military and economic interests.[130] Such security triggers a duty in itself; it is *not* a divinely given national reward for having successfully performed other duties defined by a clear (and divinely mandated) set of moral norms. Recent presidential campaigns strongly suggest that the essential task of America's political leaders is to protect and promote America's global power and influence. Candidates for national office compete by showing that their party is best able to fulfill that crucial term of our national pact.

If securing American material prosperity is now a political leader's main covenantal duty, what is the blessing associated with success in that endeavor? The reward for political parties and party leaders who successfully promote the country's economic and military well-being is the opportunity to advance their own understanding of the nation's binding moral and social norms. In our increasingly pluralistic and fractious society, the nature of one party's controversial moral vision as a true "blessing" is demonstrated in part by its association and correlation with a clear and effective program of national material prosperity.

To put it another way, in this reconfigured and reversed understanding of the covenant, many people see the failure of a political party to secure the military and financial security of the country as a *breach* of a fundamental term of the national covenant, and they treat the lost opportunity to implement the correct policies on contested moral and social issues as a *penalty* for the breach. The penalty is inflicted most immediately upon the political party that failed to bring about prosperity by securing America's interests in economic prosperity and military dominance; it loses political

---

130. See Vincent D. Rougeau, *Christians in the American Empire: Faith and Citizenship in the New World Order* (New York: Oxford University Press, 2008).

power. But those committed to the moral vision advanced by the losing party will also say that the nation as a whole has suffered a penalty. In their view, the nation has been set further adrift in moral error because it is now subject to the baleful moral influence of the winning party. So, for example, after Barack Obama won the 2008 presidential election, many social conservatives blamed George W. Bush for mishandling the economy. They did so not only because his failed economic policies threatened the country's material prosperity but also because those policies cost the Republicans the White House, which in turn seriously hampered their pro-life and pro–traditional marriage social agenda.

In the modern context, then, honoring American exceptionalism increasingly seems to consist, first, in promoting the material prosperity that ideally characterizes the nation and, second, in reaping the blessings associated with the implementation of what one's party believes to be the true, even the divinely sanctioned, moral vision in a contentious society. Why is this reversal of breach and penalty occurring? The preceding exploration of the structure of the jeremiad helps us to formulate an answer to this question. The substance of the national covenant must be the subject of widespread consensus. In the Puritan era, the moral norms of society were indeed widely accepted. The fact that those norms were not always widely followed was attributable to the snares of the devil, the attractiveness of sin, and weakness of will—not to fundamental dissent. In our era, of course, we are faced with widespread and principled disagreement about which actions qualify as sinful and, even more fundamentally, disputes about whether the category of "sin" is useful in the first place. In contrast, contemporary Americans do not generally disagree about the importance of promoting material prosperity and national security. Consequently, those values have increasingly come to dominate the duties specified in the national covenant, in practice if not always in theory. Our disagreements in these realms generally tend not to be about the value of a robust economy and a powerful and secure nation-state but rather about the best means to achieve those ends.

At the same time, contemporary American political discussion remains marked by prophetic discourse that treats our moral duties as central terms of our national covenant, either tacitly or explicitly. Yet this use of prophetic indictment is problematic precisely because it depends on a nonexistent moral consensus as the basis for its complaint. My goal in Chapters 4 and 5 was to show how and why the indictments of the jeremiad depend on a shared, solid understanding of the national covenant for their political intelligibility and fruitfulness. In Chapters 6 and 7, I will return to the contemporary era and explore how the language of prophetic indictment is used—and abused—in situations where the background terms of the covenant cannot be taken for granted.

III

THE STATE OF PUBLIC DISCOURSE

A RHETORICAL ANALYSIS

Prophetic Indictment
and Practical Deliberation

Identifying the Differences

In this chapter, I attempt to show that, with all due respect to MacIntyre, the intractability of contemporary moral disagreement does not arise solely from the inevitable tensions among clashing fragments of moral argumentation plucked from incompatible moral theories. Our difficulties do not stem solely from the challenge of brokering the rival moral claims of Kantians and utilitarians or negotiating the tension between hedonists and stoics. In the contemporary United States, we also confront serious moral disputes among persons who see themselves as belonging to the same moral tradition and as holding themselves accountable to the same values and same account of the virtues. Furthermore, with all due respect to Rawls, there is no evidence that these tensions could be ameliorated by a commitment to use public reason on the part of all sides of the disputes in question. In fact, Rawls's recommended restrictions are somewhat beside the point, since these disputants share the same comprehensive worldviews. Finally, even Carter's powerful and eloquent call for civility will not be effective because some of the discussants believe that the issues at stake are too fundamental for ordinary rules of civil discourse to govern.

My touchstone for analysis will be the debates generated by the 2004 American presidential election, which in my view was a high point of the culture wars. It was widely perceived to be an election that turned to a significant degree on "moral values."[1] Yet it generated bitter controversy even between and among members of the same religious communities, who presumably view the nature and purpose of human life in much the same way.[2] By limiting my primary sources to one election season, I hope to make up for in depth what I lose in breadth, as well as to avoid the need to account for the changing variables that affect the shape of political debates over the years. It is difficult to say, for example, how much of the conservative opposition to the presidential candidacy of Barack Obama in 2008 and in 2012 was based on key social issues and how much of it was based on race, and how much the reasons for the opposition shifted over time.

I recognize, of course, that political coalitions cut across religious communities. I also understand that the range of religious beliefs in the United States is broad and ever-expanding. My goal here, however, is not to offer a full account of the role of religious belief and disbelief in the 2004 election; I am not a political scientist. Rather, my aim is to use that election as the frame for a case study that investigates the sharp moral disagreements among religious believers who would claim to share the same normative worldviews. Broadly speaking, the subset of believers I will be discussing consider themselves to be "orthodox" Christians, of a conservative to moderate political bent. Yet they split sharply over American politics in 2004. My goal is to explore the moral language of their divisions.

Many of my examples will be taken from interventions from Roman Catholics and evangelical Protestants. By and large, the aim of these interventions

---

1. CNN Election Results, 2004, www.cnn.com/ELECTION/2004/pages/results/states/US/P/00/epolls.o.html. A question in a CNN poll asked which issue was the most important. Twenty-two percent of those polled said "moral values" was the most important issue, although the category was not defined by the pollster. The other options and their results were: taxes (5 percent), education (4 percent), Iraq (15 percent), terrorism (19 percent), economy/jobs (20 percent), and healthcare (8 percent). All of these categories implicate "moral values." For example, the question of Iraq raises issues of when and under what conditions it is just to wage war, and both the economy and healthcare raise issues of social justice. All these issues have been the subject of extensive reflection by moralists working within the Christian tradition, as well as other moral traditions. For an article putting the poll questions in a broader context, see Dick Meyer, "Moral Values Malarkey," CBS News, www.cbsnews.com/2100-500159_162-653931.html. For more extensive analysis, see Pew Research Center, "Moral Values: How Important? Voters Liked Campaign 2004, but Too Much 'Mud-Slinging,'" (November 11, 2004), www.people-press.org/files/legacy-pdf/233.pdf.

2. See John C. Green, Corwin E. Smidt, James L. Guth, and Lyman A. Kellstedt, *The American Religious Landscape and the 2004 Presidential Vote: Increased Polarization* (February 1, 2005), www.issuelab.org/resource/american_religious_landscape_and_the_2004_presidential_vote_increased_polarization.

was not to convert the secular world of their arguments but to convince (or sometimes compel) other Roman Catholics and evangelical Protestants to view political-moral matters in the same way. While focusing on their discussions is specific, it is not narrowly sectarian. Taken together, Roman Catholics and evangelical Protestants constitute about one-half of the American electorate.[3] Moreover, beginning in the Clinton era, significant attempts were made to coordinate their moral and political sensibilities and harness their votes, particularly by Republican strategists.[4] While some of their theological commitments may differ, there is significant overlap in the moral views of the two religious groups. In fact, evangelical Protestants have increasingly borrowed language and concepts from the Roman Catholic moral tradition to make their points in the public square, because that tradition has been developed more fully and systematically over the centuries.

In attempting to probe the nature of the disputes among co-religionists surrounding that election, we must tread cautiously. Some disagreements no doubt turned on factual questions. For example, did President Bush have a reasonable basis for thinking there were weapons of mass destruction in Iraq? Other disagreements turned on narrowly prudential judgments regarding the intermediate and long-term consequences of various courses of action: For example, what was the likely effect of the American presence in Iraq for the stability of the Middle East?

Nonetheless, setting those cases to one side does not eliminate the problem. We continue to see deep clashes of moral judgment among well-educated, committed adherents of the same religious tradition.[5] They do not

3. For data over several election cycles, see Pew Research Center, Religion & Public Life Project, "How the Faithful Voted: 2012 Preliminary Analysis" (November 7, 2012), www.pewforum.org /2012/11/07/how-the-faithful-voted-2012-preliminary-exit-poll-analysis/.

4. See, for example, Charles W. Colson and Richard J. Neuhaus, eds., *Evangelicals and Catholics Together: Toward a Common Mission* (Dallas, TX: Word Publications, 1995). For a unique perspective, see Damon Linker, *The Theocons: Secular America under Siege* (New York: Anchor Books, 2007). Linker worked for Neuhaus before developing increasing reservations about the project.

5. According to a CNN exit poll, Protestants comprised 54 percent of the voting population in the 2004 presidential election; 59 percent of them voted for Bush, while 40 percent voted for Kerry. Catholics, who constituted 27 percent of voters, gave 52 percent of their votes to Bush, and 47 percent to Kerry. Twenty-five percent of Jews, who comprised 3 percent of the voting population, voted for Bush, while 74 percent voted for Kerry. Among those who acquiesced to the description "white evangelical/born-again" (23 percent of the voting population), 78 percent voted for Bush, while 21 percent voted for Kerry. Fifty-eight percent of those who attended church weekly voted for Bush, while 41 percent voted for Kerry; the numbers for Bush were even higher among those who attended more than

give rise to fruitful discussion about differences but instead signal the break-down of conversation, and frequently even the breakdown of community. My hypothesis is that some of these clashes, and some of these ensuing breakdowns, are not precipitated by factual disputes or by the application of mutually inconsistent moral premises. Instead, they are driven by clashes in moral sensibility, which in turn shapes and reflects clashes in choice of moral discourse. More specifically, I believe that they are driven by tensions between a prophetic and a deliberative style of discourse—between prophetic indict-ment and moral deliberation.

In this chapter, I begin by explaining what I mean by the prophetic style of discourse and the deliberative style of discourse. I then proceed to illus-trate how the decision to use one or the other genre of moral discourse con-strains the shape of the ensuing moral conversation, even among people who share much the same moral and religious worldview. My analysis throughout will focus on two issues that provoked a tremendous amount of discussion among many committed Christians before and in the aftermath of the 2004 presidential election: abortion and torture.

I need to emphasize a crucial point here: My primary objective is *not* to engage the *substantive* arguments about torture or abortion themselves. Instead, I want to explore the *form*—prophetic or deliberative—in which those arguments were cast around the time of the 2004 election. I also want to examine the consequences of that choice of rhetorical form for the ensuing moral conversation among persons who claim to share the same basic world-view. In a nutshell, my goal is to try to understand the significant and bitter political and moral disagreements *between and among* American Christians who share the belief that abortion likely involves the taking of a human life and who are troubled by the fact that torture inflicts unbearable pain upon a fellow human being.

In the Christian tradition, all human beings are viewed as having an inherent and inalienable dignity because all have been created in the image and likeness of God. That view would suggest that the subset of Christians who accept the full humanity of the unborn would respond to abortion and

once a week. Breaking down this statistic by religion gives an interesting picture: 70 percent of Protestants who attend church weekly voted for Bush (29 percent voted for Kerry), while only 56 per-cent of Catholics who attend church weekly voted for Bush (43 percent voted for Kerry). CNN 2004 Election Results, www.cnn.com/ELECTION/2004/pages/results/states/US/P/00/epolls.o.html.

torture with similar repulsion. As we will see, however, that is not the case. Many people who are horrified by the violation of human dignity in the case of abortion are more qualified in their assessment of the violations involved in torture. The reverse is also true; some people who are utterly opposed to torture call for nuance and pragmatism in the political response to abortion— even if they do accept the humanity of the unborn. In my judgment, the differences among these groups of people have as much to do with rhetorical style as substantive moral belief.

The rhetorical clash on the question of abortion is well-established—the language of both prophets and deliberators is practiced, the rhetorical moves they make well-rehearsed. By contrast, in 2004 and early 2005, the rhetorical lines around the question of torture were only beginning to form. Both prophets and deliberators were only starting to find ways of framing the discussion in their preferred mode of address. Taken together, therefore, an analysis of the rhetorical styles used in the discussions of both abortion and torture will give a more complete picture of the tensions between the respective practitioners of prophetic and deliberative discourse.

Describing the Two Forms of Discourse

Both prophetic indictment and moral deliberation are discursive practices with long histories in Western moral discourse. Naturally, the meaning of either term cannot be fully understood apart from those histories. It will suffice here, however, to provide brief, working definitions that will facilitate my own analytical purposes. I hope that a fuller picture of these two types of moral discourse will emerge from the ensuing discussion.[6]

---

6. Others have attempted to capture the key differences between various forms of speech. The nineteenth-century English poet and critic Mathew Arnold distinguished between "Hellenism" and "Hebraism," which he correlated to the language of the philosophers and artists on the one hand and the language of adamant moral reformers on the other. See Matthew Arnold, *Culture and Anarchy*, ed. Samuel Lipman (New Haven, CT: Yale University Press, 1994). More recently, John O'Malley has identified four "cultures" that have shaped Western civilization: (1) "Prophecy and Reform"; (2) "The Academy and the Professions"; (3) "Poetry, Rhetoric, and the Common Good"; and (4) "Art and Performance." A key strength of O'Malley's book is that he recognizes that written and oral conversations take place within a broader, three-dimensional pattern of intelligibility—what he calls a "culture." See John O'Malley, *Four Cultures of the West* (Cambridge, MA: Belknap Press of Harvard University Press, 2004).

PROPHETIC DISCOURSE

The term *prophet* is bandied about quite frequently in contemporary discourse. Some people would call Nostradamus a prophet and treat his predictions as prophecy. Others would say that Bob Dylan was a prophet and proclaim that his life and songs channeled something of a divine spirit. In my view, the use of the terms *prophet, prophecy,* and *prophetic* in both these contexts should be viewed as analogical extensions of their core biblical meanings. As I am using them here, the paradigmatic meaning of the terms *prophet* and *prophecy* centers around the prophetic writings in the Old Testament or Hebrew Bible. The term *prophetic discourse* refers in the first instance to the rhetorical forms and substantive concerns that are characteristic of the biblical prophets.

Who were the biblical prophets? The Hebrew language suggests they were a diverse group of people—or at least people who performed a diverse group of functions. Four words are commonly used to describe prophets in the Hebrew Bible: "*hōzeh* ('seer'), *rō'eh* ('diviner'), *'îš hā'ĕlōhîm* ('man of God'), and *nābî'* ('prophet')."[7] In general, the first term connotes a person who is the recipient of a vision from or ordained by a divinity, while the second refers to someone who can grasp useful information through contact with the supernatural world, such as the prophet Samuel.[8] Broadly speaking, these two terms accord with the fact that even today, we sometimes use the term *prophet* to refer to someone with the power to predict future events, such as Nostradamus, or to access arcane truths. The third term, which frequently appears in the biblical stories of Elijah and Elisha, refers to men who "possess the power of the holy and hence are dangerous, powerful, and due appropriate respect."[9] Fans who sense that Bob Dylan has an unsettling connection with the divine realm may be calling him a prophet in this sense.[10]

---

7. David L. Petersen, *The Prophetic Literature: An Introduction* (Louisville, KY: Westminster John Knox Press, 2002), 5. Specialists in the field emphasize the impossibility of pinning mutually exclusive univocal meanings on these terms; see Petersen, *The Prophetic Literature,* 6–8. See also Joseph Blenkinsopp, *A History of Prophecy in Israel,* rev. ed. (Louisville, KY: Westminster John Knox Press, 1996), 26–30, for a more specialized historical discussion.

8. Petersen, *The Prophetic Literature,* 6.

9. Ibid.

10. Prophetic language has been a pervasive phenomenon in Western cultures. To grapple with this phenomenon, in my view, it is important to begin by asking how the prophetic language at issue

Nābî' is the most common term for prophet in the Hebrew Scriptures. It is a general term; over time it acquired a very broad range of meanings that overlapped with the meaning of the three other terms.[11] Nonetheless, the root meaning of this term, *nabū,* which means "to call," appears to be significant.[12] Many biblical prophets are called and commissioned by God to deliver a message to God's people.[13] Very often that message details the ways in which the Israelites or Judeans were ignoring or betraying their obligations under their covenant with God. The message conveys, in vivid terms, God's perspective on the state of the rocky and passionate relationship.

This is the facet of prophetic discourse that is most relevant to our discussion because it is the aspect that drives social critique and advocates for societal reform. As the great Jewish thinker Abraham Joshua Heschel stated, "[t]he prophet was an individual who said No to his society, condemning its habits and assumptions, its complacency, waywardness, and syncretism. . . . His fundamental objective was to reconcile man and God. Why do the two

---

functions. To answer that question, it is helpful to be aware of the various ways that prophetic language operates in Scripture. In his *Oracles of God: Perceptions of Ancient Prophecy in Israel after the Exile* (New York: Oxford University Press, 1986), John Barton distinguishes between four modes of prophetic discourse, which draw upon different aspects of the Hebrew terms: (1) "Prophecy as Ethical Instruction"; (2) "Prophetic Foreknowledge of the Present Day"; (3) "Prophecy and the Divine Plan for History"; and (4) "The Prophet as Theologian and Mystic." Prophetic indictment falls centrally under the first category, although the punishments for failing to comply with divinely given ethical norms can fit under the second and third categories as well. In the Middle Ages, a new "theology of the spirit" was proposed by Joachim of Fiore (d. 1202) and his followers, in part to break through the rigidities in thought and practice that Christianity had developed by that time in its history. See Marjorie Reeves, *The Influence of Prophecy in the Later Middle Ages: A Study in Joachimism* (Oxford: Oxford University Press, 1969). I think the phenomenon that Reeves discusses falls largely under Barton's categories 3 and 4.

11. Michael Walzer's important discussion of the prophet as social critic would have been enriched if he had, first, kept the functional distinctions rooted in the different terms in mind in his analysis and, second, focused more clearly on the way in which the social criticism of biblical prophets was framed as an *indictment* on the basis of the covenant between the Hebrew people and God. See Michael Walzer, *Interpretation and Social Criticism* (The Tanner Lectures on Human Values) (Cambridge, MA: Harvard University Press, 1987), 69–71. He is right, in one sense, that the prophets adopted a "social and workaday ethic" (p. 80). At the same time, that ethic was embedded in a legal relationship with a divine being closely involved with His people and attentive to their fulfillment of covenantal obligations. For the Hebrew prophets, breach of workaday norms had cosmic significance.

12. See, for example, Blenkinsopp, *A History of Prophecy,* 28–29; Petersen, *The Prophetic Literature,* 6; and Bruce Vawter, C.M., "Introduction to Prophetic Literature," in Raymond E. Brown, S.S., Joseph A. Fitzmayer, S.J., and Roland E. Murphy, O.Carm., eds., *The New Jerome Biblical Commentary* (Englewood Cliffs, NJ: Prentice Hall, 1990), 188–89.

13. Blenkinsopp, *A History of Prophecy,* 29–30.

need reconciliation? Perhaps it is due to man's false sense of sovereignty, to his abuse of freedom, to his aggressive, sprawling pride, resenting God's involvement in history."[14] I will refer to this aspect of the writings of the Hebrew prophets as *prophetic indictment.* Unless I indicate otherwise, when I refer to prophetic discourse, I will be speaking of prophetic indictment, and when I refer to speakers and writers in the contemporary context as *prophets,* I will be alluding to those who are employing the rhetoric of prophetic indictment within the context of a particular social struggle or political debate.

One can speak "prophetically" in the sense described by Heschel without actually appropriating for oneself the mantle of a prophet. Social critics can and do draw on the forms and the themes of prophetic discourse found in the Hebrew Bible/Old Testament without claiming that they themselves are actually delivering specific messages from God. They simply make use of the rhetorical framework of prophetic indictment in order to focus attention upon the moral and political failings of their own societies. Such critics do not actually think that they have been called or chosen to be a conduit for God's own words of reproach to the contemporary world. They may, however, understand themselves as following in the footsteps of the biblical prophets, using blistering words and images from ancient times in order to expose the moral dangers of the current situation.

What are the basic characteristics of prophetic indictment more generally, particularly as invoked in contemporary discussion of moral issues? In the Stob Lectures at Calvin College, the distinguished Protestant ethicist James Gustafson maintained that prophetic discourse characteristically "takes the form of moral or religious indictments. It is the word of the Lord proclaimed *against* the moral evil and apostasy of the world and societies. It shows in dramatically vivid language just how far the human community has fallen from what it ought to be."[15] Gustafson believes these indictments have two characteristics. "First, they usually, though not always, address what the prophet perceives to be the *root* of religious, moral, or social waywardness, not specific instances in which certain policies are judged to be inadequate or wrong."[16] Second, prophetic discourse "use[s] language, metaphors, and symbols that

14. Abraham J. Heschel, *The Prophets* (New York: HarperCollins, 2001), xxix.

15. James M. Gustafson, *Varieties of Moral Discourse: Prophetic, Narrative, Ethical, and Policy,* The Stob Lectures, 1987–88 (Grand Rapids, MI: Calvin College and Seminary, 1988), 7–8.

16. Ibid., 8.

are directed to the 'heart' as well as to the 'head.' The prophet usually does not make an argument; rather he demonstrates, he shows, he tells."[17]

Gustafson also points to an additional characteristic of prophetic discourse, which is its *utopian* nature. Gustafson does not use this term technically but merely to indicate that "prophets sometimes proclaim and depict an ideal state of affairs which is radically in contrast with the actual state of affairs in which we live together in society." As Gustafson also notes, the path from the real to the ideal is not necessarily clear: "Of itself, the utopian vision does not precisely show how we are to get . . . to the fulfilment of the alluring ideal future."[18]

As we have seen, the use of prophetic rhetoric has a long tradition in American political and social controversies. As James Darsey has noted, American social reformers who used the rhetoric of prophetic indictment can rightly be understood as a certain kind of "radical."[19] "Radicalism . . . is defined by its concern with the political roots of a society, its fundamental laws, its foundational principles, its most sacred covenants. It is common for radicals to claim to be the true keepers of the faith; they oppose their society using its own most noble expressions and aspirations."[20] Both so-called liberals and so-called conservatives can be radicals in this sense. Darsey's case studies in the use of prophetic rhetoric include the abolitionist Wendell Phillips;[21] the socialist Eugene V. Debs;[22] the Communist hunter Joseph McCarthy;[23] and the founder of the John Birch Society, Robert Welch.[24] The political scientist Andrew Murphy offers some further insights. He notes that both "traditionalist" and "progressive" jeremiads lament over the deplorable state of the present and turn to the past for inspiration. Whereas the traditionalists decry the moral decline of contemporary social practices from those of an earlier era, progressive jeremiahs look to the past for "emancipatory ideals and fundamental principles."[25] In my own terms, the fundamental

17. Ibid., 11

18. Ibid., 13.

19. James Darsey, *The Prophetic Tradition and Radical Rhetoric in America* (New York: New York University Press, 1997).

20. Ibid., 9.

21. Ibid., 61–84.

22. Ibid., 85–108.

23. Ibid., 128–50.

24. Ibid., 151–74.

25. Andrew R. Murphy, *Prodigal Nation: Moral Decline and Divine Punishment from New England to 9/11* (New York: Oxford University Press, 2009), chap. 5, "Competing Jeremiads," 109–24, at 114.

difference lies in the way the diferent parties understand the terms of the basic social covenant.

The rhetoric of prophetic indictment is not "polite" or "civil." In fact, it is frequently perceived by its audience as corrosive of communal bonds. Nonetheless, its presuppositions and purpose are not ultimately negative. Those who engage in prophetic discourse (or prophetically symbolic activity) are attempting to break through a community's entrenched habits of apathy and injustice in order to prevent them from smothering the fundamental values and commitments upon which that community is founded and its flourishing depends. But it cannot be denied that these constructive intentions frequently remain unrealized and that attempts to invoke prophetic language only exacerbate moral balkanization and even breed moral cynicism. The use of prophetic discourse is risky business, both for the prophet and for the community.

DELIBERATIVE DISCOURSE

Moral deliberation, of course, is an extremely broad category. Its general focus is how an agent should go about making a decision to act rightly in a particular case. There are many theories about how moral deliberation should be conducted and many examples of it being carried out well or badly. A basic question is how to describe human acts in a way that will facilitate moral analysis. Of all the possible true things we can say about an agent's action, ask: what counts from a moral perspective and what is irrelevant? Some modern theories attempt to provide a simple answer to this question, although that answer invariably provokes many and complicated follow-up questions. For utilitarians, the decisive feature of an action is its likely consequences. For those indebted to Kant, the maxim that the agent expresses in and through the action is decisive.

In my view, however, moral deliberation is best accounted for by a broadly Aristotelian approach to ethics, which maintains the interlocking relevance

---

Murphy argues that a "more expansive jeremiad" is necessary; the traditionalist jeremiad "is unable to do justice to the full citizenship of the broad and diverse American populace of the twenty-first century. Its use of the past is too limiting, its view of the present too despairing, its vision for the future too divisive" (p. 168). For further insight into what Murphy would call the "traditionalist" mindset, see Charles Mathewes and Christopher McNight Nichols, eds., *Prophesies of Godlessness: Predictions of America's Imminent Secularization from the Puritans to the Present Day* (New York: Oxford University Press, 2008).

of (1) a view of human flourishing, both individually and in community; (2) a description of virtues or habits that allow one to actualize such flourishing; and (3) a group of rules and principles that highlight actions or patterns of behavior that are commanded, commended, discouraged, or prohibited in light of that normative conception of human flourishing and the virtues that instantiate it. Such an approach strikes me as not only theoretically sound but also accords fairly well with common experience, even in the contemporary era. When people deliberate about what to do in a morally fraught situation, all of these factors frequently come into play as bearing upon the decision.[26]

Moral deliberation is centrally about particular actions or courses of action. How, then, do we describe and frame prospective and past actions in a way that facilitates our moral consideration of them? Perhaps because it is more comprehensive, a broadly Aristotelian framework is more useful than other approaches that focus on only one aspect of an action as decisive for moral evaluation. The Aristotelian schema analyzes actions in terms of three basic factors: (1) the immediate object or purpose of the acting agent, which describes what he or she is actually "doing;" (2) the larger purposes or motives for which the agent is performing the action; and (3) the broader circumstances under which the action is being performed.

In his *Summa Theologica,* Thomas Aquinas (d. 1274) adopted (and adapted) both Aristotle's virtue theory and his schema for analyzing human action.[27] That schema in turn directly influenced Western Christian thought before the Reformation, and Roman Catholic moral thought long after it. In addition, however, the Aristotelian-Thomistic schema had a tremendous, albeit indirect, influence on the Anglo-American common law tradition, in part because of its influence on the Anglican divine Richard Hooker.[28]

One continues to find, for example, the contemporary criminal law system using this basic approach to identify, classify, and evaluate criminal acts. Murder is centrally defined by acting with the object, or immediate purpose, of killing

26. In this regard, I am indebted to Alasdair MacIntyre's *After Virtue: A Study in Moral Theory,* 3rd ed. (Notre Dame, IN: University of Notre Dame Press, 2007); and *Whose Justice? Which Rationality?* (Notre Dame, IN: University of Notre Dame Press, 1988).

27. Thomas Aquinas, *Summa Theologica,* 3 vols., trans. Fathers of the English Dominican Province (New York: Benzinger Bros., 1948).

28. For an examination of Hooker's role in English political theory, see Alexander S. Rosenthal, *Crown under Law: Richard Hooker, John Locke, and the Ascent of Modern Constitutionalism* (Lanham, MD: Lexington Books, 2008).

another human being. Larger motives can exacerbate or attenuate the gravity of the act; so, for, example, murder for monetary gain is judged more harshly than mercy killing. Other circumstances can also affect the judgment about the act. An agent who kills another human being in self-defense, with no options to escape, is often relieved of criminal responsibility. An agent who kills another human being in the course of committing another serious crime is judged more harshly.[29] The detailed categories of analysis of contemporary American criminal law would not be at all foreign to many medieval and early modern moralists.

Principles and rules generally highlight some features of actions as more relevant to ethical or legal analysis than others. Which features ought to be highlighted? The answer to that question is itself a normative decision, which both informs and is informed by the background view of human flourishing for the society in question. For example, consider the statement: "Adam shot and stabbed four people who were ahead of him in the Starbucks line." If the circumstance "Adam is the king's son" is relevant to the moral analysis of Adam's action in a given society, we learn a great deal about the way that such a society is organized and what its values are. Or, to strike closer to home, consider the claim "An American hospital has an obligation to provide life-saving care and treatment to Belle, who appears broken, bloodied, and bruised at the bay of its emergency room." If the circumstance "Belle is an illegal alien" creates a valid exception to the claim, we learn a great deal about our own society's organization and values.[30]

How should we think about cases in which a normally applicable rule does not seem to apply? How are exceptions generated? In some cases, it appears that we are deepening, extending, and qualifying the meaning of a rule as it confronts circumstances not included in the central cases of its application. For example, the rule against private killing admits of an exception for self-defense, in part because the point of the rule is to protect the innocent,

---

29. A good place to see how motives and circumstances can operate to qualify the gravity of the offense is to take a look at the Federal Sentencing Guidelines, www.ussc.gov/guidelines-manual/2014/2014-ussc-guidelines-manual.

30. In 2004, the House of Representatives rejected a bill requiring hospitals to obtain information on the immigration status and employment of a person presenting for emergency medical treatment, and mandating the Homeland Security Department to initiate deportation proceedings against those found to be illegal aliens. Undocumented Alien Emergency Medical Assistance Amendments of 2004, H.R. 3722, 108th Cong. (2004).

not to allow the guilty to commit wrongful acts without danger to themselves. In other cases, the exception is made because the rule's application would conflict with another value or goal more important in that particular context. While Aquinas acknowledged that one had a general duty to return deposits to their owners, he also saw that it was appropriate to make an exception in the case of enemies of the state.[31]

The process of moral deliberation is complicated. It is not completely captured either by the linear process of applying rules to facts or by the analogical process of drawing comparisons between factual circumstances. The rules matter, but the facts of a case can shape the way a rule is understood, not merely by justifying an exception at the margins but more integrally by affecting the breadth, depth, reach, and strength of a rule. Facts make a rule multidimensional. For this reason, moral deliberation, in my view, is also multidimensional. One cannot realistically expect to formulate a completely exhaustive series of moral rules with well-defined exceptions. Different aspects of a superficially similar situation—including character, place, and circumstance—can combine with one another in different ways to yield different judgments about what is to be done. Sometimes, the most important question is not how to apply the rule but which rule to apply. But this depends on how one frames the moral question, which in turn depends on how one perceives the total constellation of the facts in light of the total constellation of relevant moral norms. Ultimately, the successful resolution of hard cases requires the virtue of prudence or practical wisdom, as both Aristotle and Aquinas emphasized.[32]

Obviously, not every moralist is a Thomist or even an Aristotelian virtue theorist. Many contemporary ethicists and political theorists adopt some form of consequentialism, or a deontological framework indebted to Immanuel Kant. Some of the most powerful contemporary moral theories have been focused on articulating and defending rights claims. In my view, however, most discussions of political morality and public policy in the public square

---

31. Aquinas, *Summa Theologica*, II-II, q. 57, art. 2, rep. ob. 1.

32. See Daniel Mark Nelson, *The Priority of Prudence: Virtue and Natural Law in Thomas Aquinas and the Implications for Modern Ethics* (University Park: Pennsylvania State University Press, 1992). I have applied this description of moral deliberation to deliberation in the common law. See M. Cathleen Kaveny, "Between Example and Doctrine: Contract Law and Common Morality," *Journal of Religious Ethics* 33, no. 4 (2005): 669–95.

fall into the category of what I call *messy* virtue theory—in some fashion, they try to take into account consequences, and duties, rights, and rules, but also pay attention to questions of personal and national character. In deliberating about key social questions such as abortion, torture, same-sex marriage, and euthanasia, many citizens ask themselves, "What sort of nation, what sort of people, do we want to be?"

TERMINOLOGY AND ITS LIMITS

As mentioned above, I use the term *prophet* in this chapter to refer to a person engaging in the rhetoric of prophetic indictment, unless it is clear from the context that I mean to refer to the biblical prophets themselves. Likewise, I will use the term *deliberator* to refer to a person engaging in the complicated, multifaceted discourse of moral deliberation, using some or all of the Aristotelian elements. It is important to emphasize, however, that the terms do not describe fixed personal attributes. More specifically, those who are prophets with respect to one moral issue, or even with respect to one context in which that issue is discussed, can be deliberators with respect to another moral issue, or with respect to the same issue in a different context. Furthermore, the two types of discourse are not entirely parallel. Deliberative discourse is our normal mode of moral reasoning. Prophetic discourse, in contrast, is anything but normal. It is a clarion call to respond appropriately to what the prophet believes to be a moral crisis. While it is possible that a person could approach each and every moral issue he or she faced with the tools provided by deliberative discourse, it is almost inconceivable that someone might be similarly devoted to prophetic discourse. No one can treat every moral decision as a moral crisis because the attempt to do so would destroy the very concept of a crisis. Consequently, the fact that a person engages in the rhetoric of prophetic indictment in some circumstances but not in others does not, in itself, count as a sign of moral incoherence or hypocrisy. Prophetic indictment, by its nature, is an episodic form of discourse.

Before proceeding further, I want to emphasize that the descriptions offered above are meant to function in a typological rather than a purely empirical manner. They are frames meant to bring into focus important rhetorical aspects of our contemporary debate over important political and moral issues; they are not intended as rigid definitions. I am not claiming that all moral deliberation in the public square takes a broadly Aristotelian form of analysis. I am suggesting that the moral sensibilities captured by its nuanced, multifaceted framework are also at work, sometimes in less philosophically rigorous ways, in those who engage in the rhetoric of moral deliberation in the public square. Similarly, I do not mean to imply that everyone who uses the rhetoric of prophetic indictment about an issue of passionate importance is taking to heart the rhetorical conventions of the Hebrew prophets. Those conventions, however, provide a powerful way of understanding both the impetus for their speech and its effect on the broader conversation, particularly within the American context and its unique history of the jeremiad.

In my view, attention to political rhetoric can also shed light on the scriptural world, and indirectly, upon the Western political cultures shaped by Scripture. Writing as the distinguished political theorist he is, Michael Walzer analyzes the political and legal framework of ancient Jewish society in his fascinating book, *In God's Shadow: Politics in the Hebrew Bible*.[33] He acutely observes that what gave Israel's political culture its distinctive character was it legal focus; "from fairly early on, a significant number of people, virtually the whole of the nation's intelligentsia, such as it was, were engaged in arguing about the law."[34] He highlights the fact that the disputants occupied a wide variety of social roles, and included "priests, judges, elders, prophets, and scribes."[35] But he does not go on to correlate these social roles with distinct forms of rhetorical engagement.

Walzer understands that the clashes between prophets and kings stem in large part from their very different roles with respect to the ongoing political life of the community. Kings and their advisers deal with day-to-day matters and challenges, while something urgent and unusual prompts the intervention of prophets. As Walzer writes, "monarchy is a form of normal politics,

---

33. Michael Walzer, *In God's Shadow: Politics in the Hebrew Bible* (New Haven, CT: Yale University Press, 2012).

34. Ibid., 32. Walzer attributes the argumentative culture to several features, including the fact that Israel's law was "justified law"—which opened room for disputes about the law's purpose and scope, as well as the fact that the law was "pluralized." He maintains that "[t]he existence of three codes [Sinai, Exodus, Deuteronomy] means that Israel's legal tradition was pluralist in character, encompassing (with what degree of strain we don't know) argument and disagreement" (p. 31).

35. Ibid., 32.

whereas the prophets defend an abnormal politics that is sometimes admirable and sometimes not. The opposition is reenacted again and again."[36] Yet Walzer does not connect the opposition to different ways of relating to the law that are channeled through different rhetorical paths. Rhetorical analysis plays at best an unsystematic and peripheral role in his book. He notes, for example, that "[m]uch of what the prophets say, though not deliberative, is certainly argumentative,"[37] but he does not grapple with the precise sort of argumentativeness they exhibit—the argumentativeness characteristic of an indictment, not a policy argument. He also acknowledges the persistent tensions between prophets and royal policy advisers, observing that the former frequently denounced the latter "because of the pragmatic advice they give and because they give it in their own name and not in God's name."[38]

Walzer does not uncritically endorse the prophets' dim view of those who deal in prudential judgments; he remarks that "[t]he worldliness of the wise should not be taken to mean that they were impious or immoral; in their own fashion they were teachers of righteousness."[39] He also does not help us understand precisely how the "fashion" of righteousness exhibited by the wise counselor differs from that of the prophet. Walzer asserts that the prophet represents God's interests, while the king and his advisers represent "the full and often contradictory set of human interests—personal, dynastic, and national."[40] It is tempting to respond to Walzer by pointing out that for a people in a covenant relationship with an all-powerful God, human interests are intimately entwined with divine interests. Yet the modern category of "interests" may not be the most helpful in understanding the relationship between Yahweh and His people. It is not merely Israel's interests but her very identity that is constituted in the covenant with Yahweh. Fulfilling that covenant is a matter of life and death for the Jewish people; a total breach can amount to total annihilation at the divine hand. Ultimately, therefore, the question facing the Hebrew people must be how the covenant is to be interpreted—which provisions are central and which are more peripheral. The

36. Ibid., 68.
37. Ibid., 74.
38. Ibid., 150.
39. Ibid., 151.
40. Ibid., 67.

prophets and the purveyors of practical deliberation to the Hebrew kings not only see this question differently, they speak and hear it differently.

Consequently, fully understanding the clash between the prophets and the royal advisers in ancient Israel and Judah requires attention to rhetoric. Disputes about the obligations of the covenant between these groups are both embedded in and exacerbated by the rhetorical forms characteristically used by each group. The forensic rhetoric of the prophets operates differently, and with a different focus, than deliberative rhetoric of the king's sage counselors. An Aristotelian reintegration of rhetorical and political analysis would have allowed Walzer to account for the tensions between Hebrew prophets and kings in a broader and perhaps more comprehensive fashion. In the ancient Middle East, as in our own times, political analysis needs to be supplemented by rhetorical analysis.

Analyzing Mixed Forms of Discourse

What about *mixed* forms of discourse? Many examples of interventions in the public square incorporate both prophetic indictment and moral deliberation. In my view, however, these mixed forms of intervention are not as prevalent or as important as one might initially surmise.[41] First, as I will attempt to show more fully in Chapter 7, practitioners of each form of moral discourse can and do appropriate the other for their own purposes. In my view, these cases are not rightly viewed as the good-faith use of two forms of moral discourse. Instead, they are better analyzed as cases of conscription: the subordination of one form of discourse—and the criteria for its appropriate use—to the constraints of the other.

Second, the two forms of discourse do not have the same effect on the quality of the conversation. Unsurprisingly, prophetic discourse—the language of fire and strength—has far more power to shape the overall tenor of a conversation than deliberative discourse. Its emphatic and unequivocal condemnations, conjoined with its vivid language, have a disproportionate effect on the way the communication in which it is embedded is received. One might analogize it to a powerful spice, which can overpower bulkier and blander foods with its flavor. The deliberative message of a careful argument against abortion, slavery, or torture can be overwhelmed with even one vivid and

---

41. Many thanks to Jeffrey Stout for pressing me to expand on this point.

emotional prophetic indictment. Rhetorically speaking, therefore, a mixed form of discourse tends to operate more like prophetic indictment. It is generally interpreted as, and frequently combined with, an ad hominem attack on the target of the indictment.

Suppose, for example, someone named George thinks that all mammals are equal as moral persons. Suppose also that he is outraged that someone named Ann owns a pharmaceutical company in his town and it tests new cancer drugs on thousands of animals as part of a process to ensure that these drugs are safe and effective for human beings. He may write a blistering manifesto, which begins by making the case for the moral personhood of animals (arguing, say, that they have the same intelligence as toddlers, as well as the same capacity to experience fear and pain); goes on to argue that the company is engaged in unjust killing; and moves to a crescendo by accusing Ann, in searing prophetic language, of being a torturer and mass murderer akin to Hitler or Pol Pot. As a bonus, the manifesto labels all those who benefit from animal testing as vampires feeding on the blood of the innocent or as scavengers picking through the belongings of those gassed as Auschwitz.

Ann's attention is not likely to be drawn to the deliberative moral argument in the first part of George's manifesto; it is more likely to be entirely captured by what she will doubtless view as a character assassination in the indictment at the end. Moreover, the very existence of that indictment is likely to block Ann's willingness to engage in deliberation with George on the issue of the moral status of animals and animal testing for at least four reasons. First, and most obviously, Ann's attention will be drawn to the indictment—to the accusation that she is a moral outlaw—rather than to the justifications George offers for that claim.

Second, and crucially, the nature of an indictment does not invite moral deliberation between free and equal citizens of a democracy. From a rhetorical perspective, the one issuing an indictment assumes a position of power and authority over the one being indicted. An actual legal indictment is a call to respond to a charge issued in the name of the government. It is issued in the name of those who claim authority over the defendant. It is coercive. It is also threatening; a looming consequence of a criminal indictment can be the loss of freedom. Even a civil complaint can threaten financial loss. By wrapping one's moral analysis in the rhetorical form of an indictment, George is no longer approaching his conversation with Ann as if they are moral and political equals. He is signaling his claim that he is a moral authority with the power to stand in judgment over Ann. Moreover, he is expressing his view that she is morally compromised or even morally corrupt. Consequently, Ann would not be unreasonable to think that the prospects of fair-minded and respectful deliberation under these circumstances would be rather dim. From a rhetorical perspective, George has already reached the conclusion that her practices are morally inconsistent with the foundational moral commitments of a just community—for him, that debate is closed. The only open question in his mind is whether Ann will repent and reform.

Third, indictments do not generally foster nuanced argumentation or the acknowledgment of uncertainty. If George mounts an argument for the full moral personhood of animals in the context of indicting Ann's pharmaceutical company, he will likely not consider in a full or fair way the case to be made against treating animals as persons. He will be unlikely to consider how a person could mistakenly, although justifiably, think that animals are not equal in dignity to human beings. He will be unlikely to explore the possibility that Ann is reasonable, although wrong, in her belief that animal testing can be justified to ensure the safety of drugs that will save the lives of men, women, and children with cancer. If he presented her views in this more sympathetic manner, he would not be able to group her with Hitler and Pol Pot. Yet it is only by attempting to enter imaginatively into her differing positions at key points in his argument that he will be able actually to engage in fruitful deliberation with Ann and (by extension) with those who think like she does.

In short, I do not deny that examples of mixed rhetoric exist; obviously, they are not uncommon. Yet for all the reasons adduced in the foregoing paragraphs, I think that examples of mixed rhetoric function much more like prophetic indictments than they do deliberative encounters among free and equal citizens.

POTENTIAL TENSIONS

Where might prophecy and moral deliberation clash in their respective approaches to reflection on particular cases? Such a clash seems possible on five levels. First, prophetic and deliberative approaches can clash with respect to the priority they assign to certain issues. For example, prophets and deliberators can agree that abortion or torture is morally unacceptable; prophets are more inclined, however, to see the issue as dwarfing every other issue on the horizon, while deliberators generally tend to see it as situated within a broader range of issues deserving moral attention in the course of making political judgments.

Second, prophets and deliberators can clash with respect to first-order moral analysis of given action. Generally speaking, prophets tend to be impatient with the analytically nuanced descriptions of human actions proposed by deliberators as well as with the efforts of deliberators to identify and justify exceptional situations that warrant a departure from the general moral rule. No doubt some of their impatience is due to the constraints of prophetic discourse. For example, the rhetorical power of a prophetic denunciation of idolatry or abortion would be significantly diluted if the prophet devoted significant attention to the precise features that an action must exhibit in order to fall under the moral prohibition of abortion or idolatry.

In addition, prophets are not likely to be sympathetic with the attempts of deliberators to justify exceptions to a general moral rule by probing its rationale and tacit assumptions. A prophet is likely to view such attempts as a morally bankrupt effort to get around the rule for one's own venal purposes. Furthermore, to the extent that the prophet views the moral rule as directly or indirectly given by God, she is less likely to believe that its rationale and scope can or should be probed by human reason. Deliberators, for their part, believe that prophets are intellectually crude and even self-indulgent in issuing broad condemnations without taking care to specify precisely the range of activity to which those condemnations apply.

Third, prophets and deliberators can clash with respect to the manner in which they assess the character of those who engage in the morally troublesome practices in question. Prophets generally take an agent's engagement in the acts in question (and sometimes even her toleration of such acts) as conclusive evidence of bad character. They tend tacitly to apply a strong belief in the "unity of the virtues."[42] More specifically, prophets tend to perceive other people who engage in or defend actions they believe to warrant prophetic

---

42. This controversial position has been advocated by a number of the philosophical luminaries of the West, including Plato, Aristotle, and Aquinas. See, for example, Plato, "Protagoras," 329b5–334c3, in *Plato: The Collected Dialogues,* ed. Edith Hamilton and Huntington Cairns (Princeton, NJ: Princeton University Press, 1961), 324–29; Aristotle, *Nicomachean Ethics,* trans. Terence Irwin (Indianapolis, IN: Hackett Publishing Company, 1999), bk. 6 sec. 13; and Aquinas, *Summa Theologica,* I–II, q. 65.

indictment as so lacking in the virtue of justice that it is impossible for them to possess more than cheap imitations of the other virtues. Deliberators are more likely to assess character in light of a broader scale of virtues and vices. They are more likely to be sympathetic to the claim that a generally good person engaged in or authorized morally unacceptable acts for mistaken but nonetheless understandable reasons.

Fourth, prophetic and deliberative discourse can clash with respect to the proper response of the society to the practices in question, particularly if those practices are already entrenched. Prophets are more likely to think that the immorality of a practice such as abortion or torture calls for its immediate and total abolition, while deliberators are more likely to regard the question of societal response as deserving of separate moral analysis.

Fifth, and finally, prophets experience the temporal horizon of their moral decision making in a very different way than deliberators. Prophets experience themselves and their society as held within a moment of crisis (*kairos*), as facing a decisive turning point about whether to pursue a path toward salvation or toward damnation. Deliberators, in contrast, tend to see even very important moral decisions as occurring in a long, drawn-out span of history (*chronos*) in which analogous decisions have arisen before and will arise again. The idea that any one moral issue can, by itself, constitute a turning point in history is not one to which deliberators are naturally attracted.[43]

The Rhetoric of Religious Debates over Abortion and Torture

The foregoing reflections suggest that prophetic discourse and deliberative discourse do not make tranquil companions. In fact, the choice to use one or the other mode of moral reflection to frame a particular topic sets one down a path that is almost guaranteed to make it difficult to have a fruitful conversation with someone who has chosen to use the other mode *even if* the prophet and the deliberator share the same basic moral and religious values. This claim, it seems to me, is empirically supported by public discussion

---

43. An older but still respected study of Greek notions of time is James Barr's *Biblical Words for Time*, 2nd ed. (London: SCM Press, 1969). Barr argues that the distinction in the use of the two words (*kairos, chronos*) has largely disappeared in the Greek of the New Testament.

of abortion and torture in the context of the 2004 American election and its aftermath.

Why did these two issues become flash points at that particular time? Abortion, while an important moral question in its own right, became a heightened political issue in 2004 because the Republican candidate for president, the incumbent George W. Bush, intimated that he would appoint judges to the U.S. Supreme Court who would overturn *Roe v. Wade*,[44] the 1973 decision conferring constitutional protection on a woman's right to choose an abortion.[45] His Democratic opponent, Senator John Kerry, was an unequivocal supporter of the rights conferred by *Roe* and pledged to appoint only judges who would uphold the decision. Torture rose to public attention because the revelation of the atrocities at Abu Ghraib prison in Iraq in the spring of 2004 coincided with the leaking of legal memos from the Attorney General's office and its Office of Legal Counsel that seemed to facilitate, if not entirely to endorse, these practices and to spurn international law in the course of doing so.[46] The attacks of September 11, 2001, had created a crisis—a turning point in time for the United States. The revelations of torture and abuse revealed how far we would be willing to sacrifice moral principles in order to preserve our way of life.

Abortion and torture are problematic practices within many Christian circles, particularly among evangelical Protestants and Roman Catholics. Both practices are condemned as "infamies" by the Second Vatican Council, the most recent ecumenical council of the Roman Catholic Church.[47] More broadly, whether or not they are believers, few people indebted to Western

44. *Roe v. Wade*, 410 U.S. 113 (1973).

45. To my knowledge, President Bush never actually made the appointment of anti-*Roe* judges an explicit campaign promise, although he did promise to appoint judges similar in philosophy to Justice Antonin Scalia and Justice Clarence Thomas.

46. Shocking photographs of the abuse of Iraqi prisoners by American soldiers were first published by Seymour M. Hersh, "Torture at Abu Ghraib," *New Yorker*, May 10, 2004, 42. (The May 10 issue first appeared online on April 30.) More photographs were broadcast on May 4, 2004, by CBS on the news show *60 Minutes*. *Newsweek* broke the story of the torture memos in a special report; see John Barry, Michael Hirsh, and Michael Isikoff, "The Roots of Torture," *Newsweek*, May 24, 2004, 26–34. The article argues that the torture memos, which explicitly concerned only al-Qaeda operatives and members of the Taliban, constituted the first step on "the road to Abu Ghraib." The first article in the *New York Times* about the memos appeared on May 21, 2004. Neil A. Lewis, "Justice Memos Explain How to Skip Prisoner Rights," *New York Times*, May 21, 2004, A10.

47. Vatican II, *Gaudium et spes* [Pastoral Constitution on the Church in the Modern World], 1965, para. 27.

culture for their moral framework consider abortion and torture as unambig-uously good.[48]

Nonetheless, both practices are often engaged in under the color of necessity. In a perfect world, women would not need to seek abortions; how-ever, we do not live in a perfect world. Women sometimes find themselves pregnant when they are not physically, emotionally, financially, or socially equipped to raise a child. Under such circumstances, many seek abortions. In a perfect world, no government would be faced with a choice between com-plying with the laws of war and safeguarding its people. Yet nations some-times find themselves faced with ruthless adversaries who will stop at nothing in order to achieve their political objectives. Under such circumstances, many of their agents will engage in torture and similar practices in order to pre-serve their way of life.

Neither prophets nor deliberators, in my judgment, would dispute the foregoing statements as empirical descriptions. They would differ funda-mentally, however, in their basic strategy regarding how to respond to the complex reality those statements describe. Prophets tend to emphasize the need for radical and unambiguous compliance with the patterns of action appropriate for denizens of the kingdom of God, no matter the circum-stances. Deliberators, on the other hand, tend to focus on the fact that God's kingdom is not yet perfectly instantiated in our midst and that our responsi-bilities to those made in God's image and likeness require that we take due account of this fact. What is "due account"? In some cases, taking due account may mean attempting to define the prohibition in question as precisely as possible in order to take into account the other values at stake. In other cases, it may mean demanding that other values, including the persistence of sin, be accounted for in the formulation of legal efforts to impose prohibi-tions on such practices, even if they do not affect one's judgment of their moral status.

---

48. Gallup polling on abortion is instructive on this point. For over a decade, Gallup has asked the following question: "Regardless of whether you think it should be legal, for each [issue] please tell me whether you personally believe that in general it is morally acceptable or morally wrong. How about abortion?" In May 2015, 45 percent of those surveyed said it was morally acceptable, 45 percent said it was morally wrong, and 8 percent said that it depends on the situation. One percent said that it was not a moral issue and 1 percent had no opinion. These responses were not substantially different from those given in May 2001 in response to the same polling question. Gallup, "Abortion," www.gallup.com/poll/1576/abortion.aspx.

Abortion and torture are prime examples of two areas in which there has been increasing tension between traditional Christianity and modern Western society. The increasingly strained relationship between Roman Catholicism and American values provides a vivid case study because it is possible to point to specific authoritative documents that mark the points of increasing tension and distance. During the early years of the Second Vatican Council, which began during the presidency of John F. Kennedy, American Catholics were buoyed by the hope that American values and Catholic values would reflect and reinforce one another. This optimism was generated in part because an American theologian, John Courtney Murray, S.J., had helped convince the church that the American experiment with religious liberty was a positive development with universal implications.[49] Yet the optimistic mood had begun to dissipate by the end of the 1960s. Murray's confidence that the insights of the natural law—available in principle to all human beings, not merely to Catholics—would ensure that Catholic moral teaching remained in the cultural mainstream, alas, was not entirely justified.

Consider first the tensions in the realm of sexuality and procreation. In 1965, the U.S. Supreme Court declared that married couples had a constitutionally protected right to use contraception.[50] In 1968, Pope Paul VI reaffirmed the church's traditional prohibition of artificial contraception, as well as all sexual activity outside marriage.[51] In 1972, the Supreme Court extended constitutional protection to the use of contraception by unmarried couples,[52] and in 1973 found that the Constitution protects a pregnant woman's right to obtain abortion prior to fetal viability,[53] a right that it steadily protected and expanded over the next fifteen years.[54] While most other Western democracies were also liberalizing their laws related to contraceptives and abortion, the Vatican not only stood firm in its rejection of both practices but also

49. See Vatican II, *Dignitatis humanae* [Declaration on Religious Freedom], 1965.

50. *Griswold v. Connecticut*, 381 U.S. 479 (1965).

51. Pope Paul VI, *Humanae vitae* [On Human Life], 1968.

52. *Eisenstadt v. Baird*, 405 U.S. 438 (1972).

53. *Roe v. Wade*, 410 U.S. 113 (1973); *Doe v. Bolton*, 410 U.S. 179 (1973).

54. The line of cases expanding abortion rights came to an end in *Webster v. Reproductive Health Services*, 492 U.S. 490 (1989). The current framework for the Supreme Court abortion jurisprudence was set in *Planned Parenthood v. Casey*, 505 U.S. 833 (1992), which affirmed *Roe*'s core holding while abandoning its trimester framework and adopting a new "undue burden" test, which appears less hostile to restrictions on abortion than *Roe*'s "strict scrutiny" test.

increased the forcefulness of its opposition under the papacy of John Paul II, which lasted from 1978 to 2005.[55] The recent expansion in the rights accorded to same-sex persons in the United States, as well as the increasing openness to transgendered persons, has deepened the gap between American sexual mores and official Catholic teaching.[56] A second area in which there has been significant tension between the evolving teaching of the Roman Catholic Church and American culture is the arena of war and peace.[57] Before the end of the Cold War, nuclear deterrence symbolized the potential conflict between American values and Christian values in the realm of statecraft. Deterrence policies based on mutual assured destruction and other counter-population targeting strategies ultimately depended on the conditional willingness to engage in an action utterly inconsistent with respect for human beings as made in the image and likeness of God. Christian moralists working within the just war tradition were in general agreement that the actual infliction of indiscriminate destruction would be radically immoral. Some made powerful arguments that the deterrence policy itself was radically immoral on the grounds that it is illicit to threaten to do that which is illicit to do.[58] Others, cognizant of the likely consequences of immediate unilateral disarmament, argued that the system of nuclear deterrence was (barely) tolerable while efforts to develop a morally superior alternative could be implemented.[59] In short, in the Cold War era, the dilemma of nuclear deterrence

55. Pope John Paul II writes: "Among all the crimes which can be committed against life, procured abortion has characteristics making it particularly serious and deplorable. The Second Vatican Council defines abortion, together with infanticide, as an 'unspeakable crime.'" Pope John Paul II, *Evangelium vitae* [The Gospel of Life], 1995, para. 58, citing Vatican II, *Gaudium et spes* [Pastoral Constitution on the Church in the Modern World], 1965, para. 51.

56. See, for example, Obergefell *v.* Hodges, 576 U.S. ___, 135 S.C.t 2584 (2015), in which the U.S. Supreme Court conferred constitutional protection on same-sex marriage. While Pope Francis has softened the Catholic Church's tone about same-sex relationships, he has not changed official teaching. See Rachel Donadio, "On Gay Priests, Pope Asks, 'Who Am I to Judge?,'" *New York Times*, July 30, 2013, A1.

57. While most Christian teaching has never advocated pacifism, it also has not treated the waging of war as free from significant moral constraints. See Roland H. Bainton, *Christian Attitudes Toward War and Peace: A Historical Survey and Critical Re-evaluation* (Nashville, TN: Abingdon Press, 1979); and Lisa Sowle Cahill, *Love Your Enemies: Discipleship, Pacifism, and Just War Theory* (Minneapolis, MN: Augsburg Fortress, 1994).

58. John Finnis, Joseph M. Boyle, Jr., and Germain Grisez, *Nuclear Deterrence, Morality and Realism* (New York: Oxford University Press, 1987).

59. The most notable articulation of this position was the pastoral letter on war and peace written by the U.S. Catholic bishops; see National Conference of Catholic Bishops, *The Challenge of*

constituted an acute reminder that there is no easy way to harmonize one's commitment to the values embedded within a Christian moral framework with the exigencies of preserving the American way of life.

In my judgment, the use of torture to obtain information concerning potential terrorist activity will come to symbolize the tension between American values and Christian values in the political sphere in the era of global terrorism. In the first decade of the twenty-first century, the war on terror became America's paradigmatic battle to defend its way of life.[60] Like nuclear deterrence, torture was perceived by some governmental officials as necessary to protect American society from an implacable enemy's devastating terrorist attacks. At the same time, like nuclear deterrence (particularly counterpopulation forms), it is a practice that is inconsistent with respect for the dignity of a human being as an integrated unity of body and soul. Whereas nuclear deterrence involves the (conditional) willingness to destroy the physical integrity of other human beings, torture involves the unconditional willingness to destroy their psychic integrity by (almost) destroying their physical integrity. The willing of either type of destruction, even for a supremely important end, is not consistent with what most Christians consider due respect for human dignity.

Abortion and torture, then, are moral issues of the highest importance, raising fundamental questions about the nature and the scope of our obligation to respect human dignity. At the same time, significant and urgent practical pressures can lead to the decision to engage in both these practices, which means that they will not be easy to ban or to eradicate. Consequently, both abortion and torture are issues that are ripe for the confrontation between prophecy and moral deliberation.

Clashing Rhetorical Styles in a Well-Established Controversy

In analyzing the clash between prophetic indictment and moral deliberation in the context of abortion, I will concentrate on the rhetoric among Roman

---

Peace: God's Promise and Our Response (Washington, DC: United States Catholic Conference, 1983), paras. 162–99.

60. President George W. Bush, "Address before a Joint Session of the Congress on the United States Response to the Terrorists Attacks of September 11," *Public Papers of the Presidents,* 2001, book II, 1140–44 (September 20, 2001).

Catholics, which brings that clash into sharpest relief. In addition to a long, adamant, and passionate history of opposition to abortion, the Roman Catholic tradition also has a highly developed framework for moral deliberation, sometimes known as casuistry.[61] Manuals of moral theology, developed over centuries as guides to assist confessors in assessing the nature and gravity of the sins confessed to them by penitents, are models of distinction and nuance. While certain acts are always prohibited (such as abortion), great care is taken to define precisely what constitutes the prohibited act. For example, the removal of the cancerous uterus of a pregnant woman would not count as a prohibited abortion because the doctor's object, or immediate aim in acting, would not be to kill the fetus but to eliminate the cancer that would otherwise kill both mother and fetus. Furthermore, the moral manuals were very sensitive to the way one's responsibilities and role-related obligations could affect one's obligations with respect to prohibited acts. While a doctor could never be obliged to perform an abortion, a custodian would not necessarily be required to quit his job at a hospital that performs abortions—particularly if he has children to feed. In short, thanks to its roots in the writings of Aquinas, the Catholic casuistical tradition has engaged in a nuanced practice of deliberative discourse, and a rather Aristotelian one at that.

Prophetic Voices

In my view, prophetic discourse on the issue of abortion in the context of the 2004 presidential election is characterized by several features, all of which are reflected in Gustafson's definition of prophecy.[62] First, we find a broad use of the language of moral indictment. Legalized abortion was portrayed as the gravest of all moral issues facing that generation.[63] Vivid words are deployed

61. For a history, see John Mahoney, *The Making of Moral Theology: A Study of the Roman Catholic Tradition* (New York: Oxford University Press, 1989). See also Albert R. Jonsen and Stephen Toulmin, *The Abuse of Casuistry: A History of Moral Reasoning* (Berkeley: University of California Press, 1988).

62. A helpful list of the writings mainly from what I have termed the prophetic perspective on abortion and the election can be found at "Senator John Kerry, Abortion and the Relation between Church & State," The Church & the Liberal Tradition: Contributions to the Debate, www.ratzingerfanclub.com/liberalism/john_kerry_catholic_election.html.

63. "Therefore, I want to say, clearly and distinctly, as your brother and your Bishop, that abortion is the greatest moral evil of our age. As the deliberate killing of an innocent human being, there is 'no circumstance, no purpose, no law whatsoever' that can justify or excuse abortion. 'It is contrary to the Law of God which is written in every human heart, knowable by reason itself, and proclaimed by the Church' (*Evangelium Vitae*, para. 62)." Bernard W. Schmitt (Bishop of Wheeling-Charleston),

to evoke revulsion and horror at how the practice of abortion has destroyed millions of unborn lives. Legalized abortion is analogized to Nazi genocide,[64] the enslavement of African Americans,[65] or the perpetuation of racist practices such as segregation.[66] Those who supported legalized abortion, like John Kerry, were compared to Nazi leaders[67] or anti-abolitionists.[68] Roman Catholics adopting this stance depicted legalized abortion as the most indisputable mark of the United States' pervasive complicity in what the late Pope John Paul II called the "culture of death."

Advocates of this position believed that it was not only legitimate, but necessary, for Catholic voters to cast their ballots in the presidential election with primary reference to the issue of legalized abortion. By "primary reference" I do not mean to imply that such advocates thought that abortion was the only issue that was morally relevant to the choice of president. Rather, I am suggesting that prophets employed a lexical ordering: A candidate who

---

pastoral letter on abortion, October 20, 2004, www.priestsforlife.org/magisterium/bishops/04-10 -20schmitt.htm.

64. Archbishop Raymond Burke of St. Louis began a pastoral letter about the election by invoking Nazi Germany. "On Our Civic Responsibility for the Common Good," October 1, 2004, www.ewtn .com/library/bishops/burkecom.htm. In an interview he gave to a reporter from *Inside the Vatican*, he articulates his views more completely: "I don't think it's a question of if we're heading down that way [down the path taken by the Nazis]. I mean, it's a fact that 40 million unborn children have been aborted since 1973. In some way, and I make the point at the end of the letter, too, even as Catholics we have to ask ourselves, 'What have we done?' If all Catholics would join those Catholics and other people of good will who were working to promote the respect for human life, this situation wouldn't be what it is." Thomas A. Szyszkiewicz, "I, A Catholic Bishop," *Inside the Vatican* (special dossier), October 2004, 3, johnmallon.net/Site/Inside_the_Vatican_files/ITV%20Dossier%20Catholic%20Vote %202004.pdf. Burke was named a cardinal by Pope Benedict XVI in November 2010.

65. "But with abortion (and for example slavery, racism, euthanasia and trafficking in human persons) there can be no legitimate diversity of opinion. The direct killing of the innocent is always a grave injustice." John J. Myers (Archbishop of Newark), "A Time for Honesty," May 5, 2004, http:// rcan.org/may-2004.

66. Michael J. Gaynor, "Illicit Reception," Catholic Media Coalition, www.catholicmediacoalition .org/illicit%20reception.htm.

67. Valerie Mierzwa, "Could Kerry be the 'Hitler of the Unborn'?," October 31, 2004, Catholic Online, www.catholic.org/featured/headline.php?ID=1483. Barbara Kralis, "John Kerry Was an Altar Boy—So Was Adolf Hitler," October 25, 2004, www.renewamerica.us/columns/kralis/041025.

68. "To vote for John Kerry in 2004 would be far worse, however, than to have voted against Lincoln and for his Democratic opponent in 1860. Stephen Douglas at least supported allowing states that opposed slavery to ban it. And he did not favor federal funding or subsidies for slavery. John Kerry takes the opposite view on both points when it comes to abortion. On the great evil of his own day, Senator Douglas was merely John Kerry-lite." Robert P. George and Gerard V. Bradley, "Not in Good Conscience," National Review Online, October 12, 2004, www.nationalreview.com/article/212506 /not-good-conscience-robert-p-george-gerard-v-bradley.

supports abortion rights (particularly with the dedication that Kerry devoted to the cause) had, in essence, morally disqualified himself from the race. From their perspective, he had shown himself to be fundamentally mistaken about a morally prismatic issue,[69] and his fitness to lead the nation could not be rehabilitated by his stands on a number of other issues, no matter how morally superior they might have been to George W. Bush's policy positions. Accordingly, several Catholic bishops suggested that a Catholic would commit a serious sin if he or she voted for John Kerry for president.[70]

Moreover, we can see a type of utopianism at work in the arguments of the prophetic opponents of abortion. To be sure, it was a particular kind of negative utopianism defined by an absense of a perceived evil; these prophetic voices frequently proceeded as if overturning *Roe v. Wade* would make a dramatic, almost total difference in the way unborn life is treated in America. Moreover, as Gustafson suggests, we find relatively little concentrated analysis of the steps likely to lead to this negative utopia. George W. Bush was a good candidate because he was opposed to *Roe;* John Kerry was a bad candidate because he supported *Roe.* Very few prophetic opponents of abortion spent a great deal time soberly considering whether either candidate was likely to make much difference in the legal status of abortion if elected president. Indeed, arguments that Kerry's social and economic policies would in fact reduce the number of abortions by giving more options to women facing crisis pregnancies were frequently met with hostility because prophets viewed his pro-choice position as morally disqualifying in itself. Utopias, even negative utopias, are not built on the soft sands of differential policy analysis but on the stony ground of radical commitment to moral principle.

The palpable urgency of the prophetic approach to abortion and the 2004 election is also impossible to ignore and not difficult to understand. The pro-life movement had been struggling for decades to reverse *Roe v. Wade* and the

69. Some American Catholic bishops declared that they would not give Holy Communion to Catholic politicians who were pro-choice. The majority of bishops did not follow this course of action. Kevin Eckstrom, "Cardinal Says 'Majority' of Bishops Wouldn't Deny Communion," July 11, 2004, Beliefnet, www.beliefnet.com/story/170/story_17061_1.html.

70. See, for example, Michael Sheridan (Bishop of Colorado Springs), "A Pastoral Letter to the Catholic Faithful of the Diocese of Colorado Springs on the Duties of Catholic Politicians and Voters," May 1, 2004, www.priestsforlife.org/magisterium/bishops/sheridanmay2004.pdf. See also John J. Myers (Archbishop of Newark), "A Voter's Guide: Pro-Choice Candidates and Church Teaching," *Wall Street Journal,* September 17, 2004, W13.

widespread practice of legalized abortion that the decision had enabled. At the time of the 2004 election, the elements at last seemed aligned in their favor; they hoped to take advantage of Republican control of both houses of Congress, as well as a national mood that saw many Americans recoiling from too much emphasis on autonomy and individuality, and expressing renewed concern for the fragile connections among family, friends, and community. The pro-life movement thought there was a high likelihood that at least one vacancy would occur on the Supreme Court during the upcoming presidential term and with the right appointments, which President Bush implied that he would supply, *Roe* could be reversed. By contrast, if Kerry were elected, the next round of Supreme Court appointments would almost surely support a broad constitutional right to abortion, thereby settling matters for the next generation, if not indefinitely. The notion of this particular moment in time as *kairos,* as a unique opportunity to make an important and decisive change in the course of events, sharpened the tension between pro-life prophets and co-religionists who approached the election in more deliberative terms.

DELIBERATIVE VOICES

What about the deliberators in the debate over abortion and the presidential election? Let me begin by being clear: The deliberators *agreed* with the prophets that abortion is a grave moral wrong. They did not, however, begin their reflections from that stance. They began with the particular question to be decided. And that question was who should receive one's vote for the next president of the United States. In approaching this question, they considered a number of different moral and pragmatic factors.

Unlike the prophets, therefore, the deliberators stressed the distinctions and differences between having or performing an abortion on the one hand and voting for a pro-choice presidential candidate on the other. The task was to do decide how to vote—and to make that decision in full cognizance of all the issues that would be affected by the decision—not simply the issue of abortion. How did pro-life deliberators grapple with the fact that their vote would inevitably affect the issue of abortion, whether or not they intended it to do so?

Whether they knew it or not, the Catholic deliberators were able to draw on their own moral heritage in addressing the question whether and under what circumstances to vote for a pro-choice candidate. More specifically, the Catholic tradition of moral deliberation has long supported the drawing of such distinctions and differences in its framework for analyzing problems of "cooperation with evil." This framework, given its first definitive formulation by St. Alphonsus Liguori (1696–1787) in the eighteenth century,[71] considers how far, if at all, agents should alter their own plans of action in order to avoid facilitating the wrongful actions of others. Anthony Fisher, O.P., a lawyer and moral theologian who was named the Archbishop of Sydney, Australia in 2014, summarizes the fundamental issue at stake in cooperation:

> [T]hough co-operating in the [wrongful] project, the agent in question is not the one most directly involved, conceiving, instigating, directing, coordinating and actually engineering the operation. Rather she is in a secondary or subordinate role to the principal agent(s) and contributes something which facilitates the wrongdoing of the principal agent(s). What she wants to know is how close she can properly get to taking part, without becoming, as it were, an accessory, a conspirator. How involved can she be without becoming tainted by it?"[72]

Whether explicitly or implicitly, many Catholic deliberators framed the question of voting for a pro-choice politician as a cooperation with evil problem: Could a Catholic vote for John Kerry in the 2004 presidential election despite the fact that he or she could predict that the vote would help maintain a pro-choice legal regime? While the analytical framework of cooperation is elaborate and complicated, its application to this case was fairly straightforward. Catholics could vote for pro-choice candidates in good conscience provided that (1) they did not intend to promote abortion in so doing, and (2) their vote was justified on the basis of "proportionate reasons." The meaning of that phrase is notoriously nebulous, but it indisputably points not to a bright line rule, but rather to what lawyers call a facts-and-circumstances

71. See Roger Roy, C.Ss.R., "La coopération selon Saint Alphonse de Liguori," *Studia Moralia* 6 (1968): 377–435.

72. Anthony Fisher, O.P., "Co-Operation in Evil," *Catholic Medical Quarterly* 44, no. 3 (February 1994), 15–22, at 15.

test.[73] Cardinal Joseph Ratzinger, the head of the Sacred Congregation of the Doctrine of the Faith who later became Pope Benedict XVI, articulated that standard in a memo initially written to the U.S. bishops, later leaked, and finally made public.[74]

What should shape a voter's assessment of "proportionate reasons" regarding a pro-choice candidate for the American presidency? Essentially, voters need to keep in mind the full range of tasks involved in serving as the political leader of the only remaining superpower on earth. First and foremost, voters need to remember that they are electing a person, not a platform. They need to consider the character, skills, and temperament of the candidates for office; they also must assess the character, skills, and temperament of the men and women the candidates are likely to choose as their closest advisers. What degree of the virtue of prudence do the candidates and their respective teams possess? For many Catholic deliberators, George W. Bush's record during his first term disqualified him on these grounds. For example, before the election, it became impossible to deny the fact that Bush's two major reasons for going to war against Iraq (to combat al-Qaeda and to neutralize Saddam Hussein's alleged supply of weapons of mass destruction) were seriously flawed, if not entirely specious. Revelations of the torture and abuse of prisoners in American custody, as well as the memos that justified such torture and abuse, called into question Bush's commitment to the laws

73. It was observed in one well-respected pre–Vatican II manual: "In estimating the sufficiency of the excuse for material co-operation, we must consider the spiritual character and needs of another, our relations to him, and how great is his offense against God, the harm that may accrue to a third person, the public harm likely to ensue, how close the co-operation, how indispensable it may be. So many factors enter into all questions of material co-operation, that only the most general principles can be laid down. Great varieties of opinion, therefore, on any given case except the most obvious, are inevitable, and there is no more difficult question than this in the whole range of Moral Theology." Henry Davis, S.J., *Moral and Pastoral Theology*, vol. 1, *Human Acts, Law, Sin, Virtue*, 6th rev. and enl. ed. (London: Sheed & Ward, 1949), 342.

74. "[N.B. A Catholic would be guilty of formal cooperation in evil, and so unworthy to present himself for holy communion, if he were to deliberately vote for a candidate precisely because of the candidate's permissive stand on abortion and/or euthanasia. When a Catholic does not share a candidate's stand in favor of abortion and/or euthanasia, but votes for that candidate for other reasons, it is considered remote material cooperation, which can be permitted in the presence of proportionate reasons.]" Cardinal Joseph Ratzinger, "Worthiness to Receive Holy Communion: General Principles," in Cardinals Joseph Ratzinger and Theodore McCarrick, "Vatican, U.S. Bishops: On Catholics in Political Life," *Origins* 34, no. 9 (July 29, 2004): 133–34. The statement was controversial, prompting efforts by prominent pro-life activists to reinterpret it. See, for example, Frank Pavone, "The Ratzinger Fiasco," Priests for Life, www.priestsforlife.org/columns/columns2004/04-09-13theratzingerfiasco.htm.

of war and the commitment to human dignity they are meant to promote and protect. On that basis, some Catholic deliberators concluded that he had conclusively demonstrated that he lacked the practical wisdom and moral judgment to serve as commander-in-chief, because his actions in that capacity had inflicted serious harms on the nation and the world.[75]

For example, consider these reflections of the Catholic ethicist Sidney Callahan, which were written in the summer before the 2004 elections: "I voted for George W. Bush and I'm heartily sorry now. My support was motivated by prolife convictions, but so is my present dismay. I opted for Bush in 2000 because I thought he'd try to protect embryonic life in and out of the womb, and also support faith-based social initiatives. As for foreign policy, Bush's promises of 'humility' were reassuring." Contrasting her views of Bush in 2000 with her assessment four years later, Callahan writes: "Our present policies, now dubbed the Bush Doctrine, are morally suspect and prudentially disastrous. . . . Has this kind of 'war on terrorism' really made us safer?"[76]

Second, one needs to consider the evil that is prompting the invocation of the matrix of cooperation. How, in other words, does one assess the causes of and remedies for the evil with which one is cooperating? Catholic deliberators recognized that the abortion issue must be given due weight; they did not dispute Ratzinger's judgment that the over 1.5 million abortions performed each year under the national regime of legalized abortion inaugurated by *Roe v. Wade* was a pressing moral issue.[77] Yet they did not believe that this issue, considered by itself, pointed toward a vote for George Bush. They questioned whether Bush actually intended to ensure that *Roe* would be overruled. They pointed out that Republicans had been running on an anti-*Roe* platform for nearly thirty years and that the justices Republican presidents had appointed to the Supreme Court had supported *Roe*, at least in its core.[78] Furthermore, they

75. I develop this point more extensively in M. Cathleen Kaveny, *Law's Virtues: Fostering Autonomy and Solidarity in American Society* (Washington, DC: Georgetown University Press, 2012), chap. 8.

76. Sidney Callahan, "A Prolife Case against Bush," *Commonweal*, June 4, 2004, 15.

77. "The number of induced abortions performed annually in the United States increased dramatically in the decade following its legalization. After reaching a peak of 1.61 million in 1990 . . ., the number declined to about 1.22 million in 2004, even as the population of the country continued to grow." Stanley K. Henshaw and Kathryn Kost, *Trends in the Characteristics of Women Obtaining Abortions, 1974 to 2004* (New York: Guttmacher Institute, 2008), 7.

78. See editorial, "Politics, Piety, and the Catholic Vote," *National Catholic Reporter*, April 30, 2004, 24.

noted that, in the event that *Roe* were to be overturned, abortion would be returned to the states, many of which would not ban the procedure.[79] Catholic deliberators judged that in a situation in which abortion was likely to remain legal for the foreseeable future, John Kerry's social policies were likely to make it possible for more women to choose childbirth rather than abortion. These factors, for example, were decisive for Fordham professor of sociology James R. Kelley, who wrote an essay in the Jesuit weekly *America* defending his vote for Kerry. He claimed: "I am voting for Kerry because I am pro-life. I will make my case as a social scientist who believes that voting involves a prudential judgment that must look at the facts and not just what candidates say. I believe that President Bush, if re-elected, will not deliver on his promises and that a Kerry administration would support economic programs that would in fact reduce the number of abortions."[80]

Third, in choosing a candidate, Catholic deliberators considered a wide range of issues pertaining to human dignity and the common good.[81] These included the war in Iraq, the war on terror; and other issues of military policy. They also encompassed questions of social justice and solidarity, such as the status of Social Security and other social welfare programs, the impact of the tax structure on the most vulnerable, and the status of undocumented immigrants and other vulnerable populations under American law. In addition to abortion, other life issues were relevant, such as euthanasia, stem-cell research, capital punishment, and the protection and promotion of marriage

79. In 2004, the Center for Reproductive Rights estimated that twenty-one states were at high risk of banning abortion, nine states at some risk, and that in twenty states abortion rights were secure. It is in the interest of pro-choice groups, in my view, to overestimate the number of states that will restrict abortion as well as the severity of the restrictions that will be adopted. Center for Reproductive Rights, "What if Roe Fell?: The State –by-State Consequences of Overturning *Roe v. Wade*," September 2004, http://reproductiverights.org/sites/default/files/documents/bo_whatifroefell.pdf.

80. James R. Kelly, "A Catholic Votes for John Kerry," *America*, September 27, 2004, 13. According to a study done in the year 2000–2001, women with incomes below 200 percent of poverty made up 30 percent of all women of reproductive age but accounted for 57 percent of the abortions in 2000. Adjusting for different pregnancy rates, it is still the case that high-income women were the least likely to abort their pregnancies (15 percent) and poor and low-income women were the most likely to do so (33 percent). Rachel K. Jones, Jacqueline E. Darroch, and Stanley K. Henshaw, "Patterns in the Socioeconomic Characteristics of Women Obtaining Abortions in 2000–2001," *Perspectives on Sexual and Reproductive Health* 34, no. 5 (2002): 226–235, at 231.

81. For other representative examples of the Catholic deliberator position supporting a vote for John Kerry, see Margaret O'Brien Steinfels, "Time to Choose," *Commonweal*, October 22, 2004, 10–13; and John Langan, S.J., "Observations on Abortion and Politics," *America*, October 25, 2004, 9–12.

and family life. On each of these issues, deliberators were inclined not merely to focus on passing laws prohibiting morally objectionable actions, but also on insuring that social structures were in place to help dissuade people from seeking to engage in prohibited behavior. For example, Catholic deliberators would be inclinded to ask not only whether there was a law on the books prohibiting euthanasia, but also whether there were sufficient public services to care for the impoverished elderly. Deliberators emphasized that to ensure the well-being of vulnerable populations, it is not sufficient to see that they are not unjustly harmed by third persons; by definition, a vulnerable person is in need of the aid and comfort of others.[82]

The framework of cooperation with evil, of course, did not *compel* a vote in favor of John Kerry—it merely *permitted* one. Some deliberators reviewed the relevant factors and decided that they pointed toward reelecting George W. Bush. The key difference between these deliberators and the pro-life prophets who voted for Bush is that the former recognized the existence of a multi-factor test and acknowledged that persons could come to disagreement in good faith about how to assess each of those factors.

THE TENSION BETWEEN PROPHETS AND DELIBERATORS

How do the practitioners of these two modes of moral discourse view each other? As the rhetoric surrounding abortion in the context of the 2004 presidential election demonstrates, they take a very dim view of each other. Let us begin with how the prophets view the deliberators. First, the prophets' radicalism means that they tend to adopt an "if you are not for us, you are against us" approach. The prophets view anything short of full agreement, both with respect to ultimate values and with respect to strategy, as a betrayal of the duty to offer uncompromising witness to the truth. More specifically, the prophets tend to view more pragmatic approaches as demonstrating an inadequate understanding of the enormity of the moral problem of abortion, both with regard to the number of unborn lives taken and with regard to the particular horror involved in the taking of completely innocent, vulnerable life.

---

82. I make this point more elaborately in Kaveny, *Law's Virtues*. See also M. Cathleen Kaveny, "How Views of Law Influence the Pro-Life Movement," *Origins* 34, no. 35 (February 17, 2005): 560–65.

Second, many prophets seem to have more respect for the radical prophets of the opposition than they do for the deliberators on their own side, whom they dismiss as at best morally blind and at worst as morally disingenuous. Radical pro-choice prophets mirror and reinforce the pro-life prophets' belief in the centrality of the abortion issue to the fundamental moral character of our community.

Third, prophets are impatient with, and often disdainful of, the intricacies of argument in which the deliberators engage. Prophets see deliberators as "rearranging the deck chairs on the Titanic when the ship is sinking,"[83] when what is required is an immediate and radical turn in course.

How do the deliberators view the prophets? Not much more favorably than the prophets view the deliberators! First, the deliberators find the prophets' radicalism deeply troubling. The prophets' concern with one issue, which they identified with the moral health of the country, is judged by deliberators to be a drastic oversimplification of the moral issues at stake in the election. In addition, the deliberators think that the prophets' commitment to an all-or-nothing attitude on that issue forecloses the possibility of incremental improvement.

Second, on the surface, deliberators may seem to have more respect for prophets, than vice versa; they see prophets as performing an important hortatory function, reminding us all about the transcendent importance of certain values. But scratch the surface, and more than a little condescension and wariness is revealed: Deliberators tend to view the single-minded commitment of prophets as the immature passion of youth; it is harmless when tightly cabined on a college campus but dangerous when allowed to threaten the basic structures of society.

Third, if prophets see deliberators as rearranging the deck chairs on the *Titanic,* deliberators see prophets as expecting God Himself to turn the ship to avoid the iceberg. Deliberators accuse prophets of engaging in a form of self-indulgent behavior: Mesmerized by the power of their own rhetoric of condemnation, they excuse themselves from the hard work of designing and implementing a workable plan for ameliorating the evil that they condemn.

83. Gustafson, *Varieties of Moral Discourse,* 9.

Choosing a Rhetorical Voice on an Emerging Question

Our discussion thus far raises a question: How do people of goodwill decide whether to adopt a prophetic or a deliberative approach to a particular issue? The obvious rejoinder to this question is to cast doubt on its presuppositions. Perhaps the use of prophetic style or deliberative style is not a matter of "decision" at all. Perhaps it is a matter of personality; some people are more drawn to one style by their temperament and training.

Yet to gain even a minimal hearing, would-be prophets need to choose an issue that is worthy of their rhetoric. It is, of course, not logically impossible to address every question of the slightest moral significance within a prophetic framework. One could attempt to cast each decision, no matter how small, as an essential battle in the war between good and evil. At the same time, however, some concentration of effort on issues of particular importance seems pragmatically wise. How do moralists who are open to engagement in prophetic rhetoric decide which issues merit their concentrated fire?

Obviously, the issue must be seen as highly significant by the would-be prophet. Yet significance is not enough. No one denies, for example, that the deeds of serial killers such as Ted Bundy are horrendous. They are seen (rightly or wrongly) as social and cultural aberrations, which our society firmly rejects and punishes. In addition to being significant, therefore, an issue deemed worthy of prophetic attention must seem to crystallize a fundamental moral or spiritual flaw in our society. By demanding that the society look upon that issue in all its stark horror, the prophet attempts to force the society to see itself for what it really is and therefore to move toward repentance and reform of life.

Abortion and torture, of course, are both issues that can easily qualify as worthy of prophetic attention from American Christians. A review of the public discussion during the time immediately surrounding the election strikingly reveals that many American Christians did not apply the same style of discourse with respect to both issues. Many of those who took a prophetic stand with respect to voting and abortion sympathized with a more deliberative approach with respect to President Bush's policies on the applicability of the Geneva Conventions and the definition of torture or at least remained

silent about the atrocities. Conversely, those who were more vocal in advocating a deliberative approach to voting and abortion were more prophetic
about the administration's willingness to rethink the definition and the
restraints on torture in order to win the war on terror.

Needless to say, the debate over the appropriate American stance toward
torture has not been developed as extensively or as deeply as the debate over
our nation's appropriate stance toward abortion. Although academics have
long discussed the definition of torture, the harm it causes, and the circumstances (if any) under which it might be justified, it was not a topic that captured the attention of the American public until the spring of 2004. That
season in time saw three distinct though not unrelated events: the exposure
of atrocities committed by American soldiers at Abu Ghraib prison in Iraq;
the emerging worries about the treatment of prisoners at the American
detention center at Guantanamo Bay, Cuba; and the declassification of memos,
written by high officials in the legal arm of the Bush administration, arguing
that prisoners held on terrorism-related charges were entitled to diminished
legal protections against torture and other forms of mistreatment.[84] The
debate over torture came to a head in December 2004 and January 2005 during
the congressional hearings to confirm Alberto R. Gonzales as attorney general of the United States.[85] This flashpoint occurred because the so-called torture memos revealed that Gonzalez, while serving as White House counsel
under George W. Bush, endorsed and defended the administration's purported justification of torture, acting on the advice given him by the attorney
general's office, in particular the Office of Legal Counsel.

As actually conducted in the fall of 2004, the debate over the role of torture in the war against terrorism was not precisely parallel to the debate over

84. See Karen J. Greenberg and Joshua L. Dratel, eds. *The Torture Papers: The Road to Abu Ghraib*
(New York: Cambridge University Press, 2005). The volume contains a wealth of documentation,
including the main memos providing a legal justification for the Bush administration policy toward
the treatment of incarcerated Taliban and al-Qaeda forces. Two memos in particular are worth particular scrutiny; both were written by assistant attorney general and head of the Office of Legal
Counsel Jay S. Bybee to White House Counsel Alberto R. Gonzales. The first of these is dated January
22, 2002, and is entitled "Application of Treaties and Laws to al-Qaeda and Taliban Detainees." The
second, dated August 1, 2002, is entitled "Standards of Conduct for Interrogation under 18 U.S.C.
§§2340–2340A." These memos were originally drafted by John Yoo while he was serving as deputy
assistant attorney general under Bybee.

85. Gonzales was confirmed by the Senate on February 3, 2005; see Eric Lichtblau, "Gonzales Is
Confirmed in a Closer Vote Than Expected," *New York Times*, February 4, 2005, A13.

abortion and the election that I described above. The tension between prophets and deliberators over abortion centered around the question whether and when one ought to vote for a candidate who favored a permissive legal stance toward the practice. In contrast, the tensions over torture were centered on far more basic questions, including what counts as morally prohibited "torture." Not surprisingly, prophets were uninterested in parsing the definition of the term and comparing it carefully with the evidence of pain and suffering inflicted on prisoners, whereas deliberators thought such parsing was essential to proper evaluation. The rhetorical clashes over torture are illuminating precisely because they reveal how the tensions shape up with respect to an emerging issue of controversy.

PROPHETIC CHALLENGES

So how did the prophetic voices react to revelations of abuses at Abu Ghraib and to the torture memos? By and large they did not engage the intricate arguments mounted by the Office of Legal Counsel. More specifically, they did not respond by calling into question the validity of the analysis itself; that is, they did not point to particular flawed arguments or highlight particular assumptions they believed to be questionable. With some modifications, their response can be understood in terms of the two main features that James Gustafson has associated with prophetic discourse: visually oriented moral indictment and utopianism. They swept away arguments and focused on the underlying reality.

Because torture was not a broadly prominent issue in American public life before this point, its emergence allows us to appreciate the roots of prophetic indictment in an immediate experience of moral shock and horror. The primary form of the indictment against American torture and abuse was not verbal but visual—the horrifying spectacle of the abuses of prisoners that took place at Abu Ghraib prison. The public saw the photographs of a smiling American soldier pulling a desperate, naked prisoner by a leash, and of a detainee's bloodied and bruised corpse being carried out of the prison on a stretcher.[86] The revulsion evoked by those photographs constitutes the core

---

86. David Griffith makes the insightful point that the cropping of the photographs affects whether one views the problem as one of a few bad apples in the military or a systemic problem of abuse: He notes that "[c]ropped, yes, the pictures suggest the work of only a handful of reservists. But uncropped they show more soldiers, some identified as military intelligence officers, standing around,

of immediate prophetic opposition, and it is this experience that prophets tried to re-create in their audience.

What about the fact that the torture memos were never intended to apply to prisoners at Abu Ghraib? Prophetic voices did not make a detailed argument regarding the relevance of the torture memos to the abusive conditions in Iraq. Instead, they relied on the fact that the photographs raised a host of questions in the minds of those who saw them. If this was the sort of treatment that merits a visual record, what was happening in situations where there was no photographer present? What sort of ethos pervades a military operation that can engender this sort of behavior on the part of American soldiers charged with guarding prisoners of war? If the ultimate justification of torture was that it is necessary to win the war on terror, was the mere fact that the Bush administration recognized that Iraqi prisoners, unlike members of the Taliban or al-Qaeda, were clearly protected by the Geneva Conventions likely to make any real difference? President Bush, after all, had initially justified the war against Iraq at least in part on the grounds that Saddam Hussein's administration was giving aid and comfort to terrorists.[87]

From the perspective of the prophets, what was the basis of the indictment against the decision makers in the Bush administration? What was the root cause of their disastrous policy? Fundamentally, the prophets thought that the root cause was the failure of American political leaders to obey divine law. In an open letter to Alberto R. Gonzales (who is an evangelical Christian) signed by more than two hundred religious leaders,[88] we can see the development of a

---

a few watching, others preoccupied with the most mundane activities. One picture reveals a man cleaning his fingernails." David Griffith, "A Good War is Hard to Find: Flannery O'Connor, Abu Ghraib, and the Problem of American Innocence," in *A Good War is Hard to Find: The Art of Violence in America* (New York: Soft Skull Press, 2006), 27–40, at 30. He goes on to observe that the photos are "icons, Rorschachs used by commentators to justify, criticize or deconstruct the war and the United States." Griffith writes that one of the perpetrators had a stone in his flower bed inscribed with a verse from the prophet Hosea: " 'Sow for yourselves righteousness, reap the fruit of unfailing love and break up your unplowed ground; for it is time to seek the Lord, until he comes and showers righteousness on you, [Hosea 10:12 NIV]." He also notes that the "stone is mentioned in most of the early news coverage of the scandal" a fact that suggests to me the continuing power of prophetic voices the American imagination (p. 32).

87. George W. Bush, "Address before a Joint Session of Congress on the State of the Union," January 28, 2003, *Public Papers of the Presidents*, 2003, book I, 82–90, at 89. "Evidence from intelligence sources, secret communications, and statements by people now in custody reveal that Sadaam Hussein aids and protects terrorists, including members of Al Qaida."

88. Church Folks for a Better America, "An Open Letter to Alberto Gonzales," January 4, 2005,

prophetic indictment along these lines. The open letter illustrates the difference between a moral indictment, which centrally attempts to pin down responsibility for a past action, and moral deliberation, which centrally aims to decide on a future course of action.

First, the open letter articulates the requirements of God's law, which constitute the basis against which all human conduct is to be judged: "We invite you to affirm with us that we are all made in the image of God—every human being. We invite you to acknowledge that no legal category created by mere mortals can revoke that status. You understand that torture—the deliberate effort to undermine human dignity—is a grave sin and affront to God."[89] Second, the open letter issues its moral indictment, detailing the manner in which Gonzales's actions failed to conform to the requirements of the divine law: "How could you have written a series of legal memos that disrespected international law and invited these abuses? How could you have justified the use of torture and disavowed protections for prisoners of war? How could you have referred to the Geneva Conventions as 'quaint' and 'obsolete.' We fear that your legal judgments have paved the way to torture and abuse."[90]

Can we also find utopianism in prophetic responses to the Bush administration's policy on torture, as Gustafson would predict? My sense is that we come upon a type of reversal here because the utopia in question for those denouncing torture is a dystopia. More specifically, the prophetic voices did not gesture toward a blissful world that will come into being if their prohibition against torture is accepted by the American government (after all, according to common accounts, that has been our world to date) but rather toward the hellish existence that we will all be forced to endure if we no longer comply with divine prohibitions.[91] Most important, the prophetic voices on torture repeatedly suggested that we would lose our national moral

http://www.apfn.net/messageboard/01-22-05/discussion.cgi.15.html. The liberal Catholic magazine *Commonweal* also published an editorial on the Gonzales nomination, "The President's Lawyer," *Commonweal*, December 3, 2004, 5–6.

89. Church Folks for a Better America, "An Open Letter."

90. Ibid.

91. One of the most powerful responses to the revelations at Abu Ghraib was written by Dianna Ortiz, O.S.U., a religious sister who was a victim of torture while teaching Mayan children in Guatemala. Sister Diana Ortiz, O.S.U., "Mr. President, Stop the Torture!," *U.S. Catholic*, July 2004, 50.

identity if we proceeded along this path. An editorial in *National Catholic Reporter* began by asking: "Who are we in America? What is being done in our name?"[92] Bishop John Ricard, chair of the International Policy Committee of the National Conference of Catholic Bishops, wrote, "The abuse and torture of Iraqi prisoners have brought shame upon our nation, are an affront to our most basic ideals, and will undermine legitimate efforts to confront the very real threats faced by our nation and the world."[93]

This threatened loss of identity, through loss of one's fundamental commitments, is a recurrent theme in the Old Testament prophets. Consider this passage from the book of Isaiah:

> For Jerusalem has stumbled
>   and Judah has fallen,
> because their speech and their deeds are against the LORD,
>   defying his glorious presence.
>
> The look on their faces bears witness against them;
> They proclaim their sin like Sodom,
>   they do not hide it.
> Woe to them!
>   For they have brought evil on themselves.[94]

The prophetic response to the torture memos and the abuses at Abu Ghraib assumed that both events revealed something deeply troubling about the American character.[95] The fact that we have stooped to both torturing

---

92. Editorial, "Difficult Questions Won't Go Away," *National Catholic Reporter,* November 5, 2004, 24. For another argument about American identity, see James Ross, "Bush, Torture and Lincoln's Legacy," *America,* August 15, 2005, 10–13. For another critique highlighting the inconsistency of torture with American values, see editorial, "Torture's Apologists," *Commonweal,* February 11, 2005, 5.

93. John H. Ricard, S.S.J. (Chairman, Committee on International Policy, United States Conference of Catholic Bishops), "Statement on Abuse of Iraqi Prisoners," May 14, 2004, www.usccb .org/issues-and-action/human-life-and-dignity/global-issues/middle-east/iraq/statement-by-bishop -ricard-on-abuse-of-iraqi-prisoners-2004-05-14.cfm. See also John H. Ricard, S.S.J., "Letter to House and Senate Conferees on Human Rights and Torture," July 12, 2004, www.usccb.org/issues-and-action /human-life-and-dignity/global-issues/middle-east/iraq/letter-to-house-and-senate-conferees-from -bishop-ricard-on-human-rights-and-torture-2004-07-12.cfm.

94. Isaiah 3:8–9.

95. The Vatican newspaper responded in prophetic terms by focusing on the symbolic function of the photos at Abu Ghraib. "In its May 10 edition, *L'Osservatore Romano* commented on the widely published photo showing a U.S. soldier holding a naked Iraqi detainee on a leash. Of all the images

our prisoners and justifying torture was a sign of our radical departure from the bedrock values upon which our nation was founded. To the prophetic critics of torture, the idea that the United States could effectively defend itself by engaging in acts so thoroughly inconsistent with our fundamental moral commitments was both foolhardy and dangerous.[96]

Deliberative Responses

Needless to say, it was impossible for Christians of any stripe to defend what happened at Abu Ghraib. What, then, was the response of Christian deliberators with respect to the question of the American policy on torture? As several commentators have pointed out, the predominant response around the time of the 2004 election and the immediate aftermath was silence.[97] Notwithstanding the silence, it is possible to reflect more generally upon the shape of a deliberative response to torture and the abuse of prisoners exemplified by Abu Ghraib as well as to find key elements of this response in some commentary, particularly from politically and religiously conservative quarters.

As we have seen, many religious thinkers who took a prophetic stance on torture saw the abuses at Abu Ghraib as revealing something both important and disturbing about the American character. In contrast, for those who adopted a deliberative stance, the abuses at Abu Ghraib were essentially unfortunate *anomalies*. While deeply wrong and repulsive, they did not uncover

---

that have been released, this one is the most 'tragically symbolic' because it shows a desire to treat the enemy almost as an animal, it said." John Thavis, "Vatican Newspaper Condemns 'Inhuman Acts of Torture' by U.S. Soldiers," Catholic News Service, May 10, 2004, www.catholicnews.com/data/stories/cns/20040510a.htm (subscription req.).

96. According to a survey conducted by the Pew Research Center and released November 17, 2005, "The American public is far more open than opinion leaders to the use of torture against suspected terrorists in order to gain important information. Nearly half of the public (46 %) say this can be either often (15 %) or sometimes (31 %) be [*sic*] justified." The Pew Research Center for the People and the Press in association with the Council on Foreign Relations, "America's Place in the World 2005," 24, www.people-press.org/files/legacy-pdf/263.pdf. For an illuminating examination of the conflicted American stance on torture, see Joseph Lelyveld, "Interrogating Ourselves," *New York Times Magazine*, June 12, 2005, 36 (L).

97. In October 2004, Richard John Neuhaus unequivocally condemned torture and flatly rejected the theory that Abu Ghraib is attributable to "a few bad apples." See his "Drawing the Line against Torture," in "The Public Square," *First Things*, October 2004, 82. In the next issue, however, Neuhaus defended the decision of his magazine to "shy away" from the question of torture on the grounds that it is a subject that is "amply, and more or less adequately, addressed in other publications." See "Internationalisms," in "The Public Square," *First Things*, December 2004, 64.

anything of significance about the American moral character. An early example of this approach can be found in a column by the politically conservative Catholic writer George Weigel titled "Abu Ghraib and Just War in Iraq." For Weigel, what was important was the "revulsion" that most Americans expressed at the revelations of the abuses of Iraqi prisoners; he writes: "If anything proves that America is not a Realpolitik country in which it's simply assumed that might makes right, it's the reaction to Abu Ghraib."[98] Weigel maintains that "no one knows the stain on military honor that Abu Ghraib represents better than the officers and enlisted personnel who believe they came to Iraq to liberate its people from a vicious dictatorship in which murder, rape, and torture were normal instruments of state policy, not aberrations."[99]

Moreover, the deliberators would not be as quick as the prophets to connect the torture memos, which were designed to justify a range of coercive interrogation techniques with respect to members of al-Qaeda and the Taliban, with the abuses that occurred at Abu Ghraib. What prophets saw as meaningful connections, deliberators viewed as coincidences. In this case, as in the case of abortion, deliberators emphasized the need to draw distinctions. Deliberators resisted the prophetic tendency to offer a holistic interpretation of reality in terms of the nation's verging on fundamental disobedience to divine law. They viewed the situation as more nuanced and complicated.

A good example of the deliberative approach can be found in Heather Mac Donald's essays in *The City Journal* in early 2005. In essence, Mac Donald, a politically conservative journalist, suggested that the key memo on the topic of torture, Jay S. Bybee's August 1 Memo to Alberto R. Gonzales, was at least two steps removed from the atrocities at Abu Ghraib. First, she argues that the memo was directed toward interrogations conducted by the Central Intelligence Agency; they "had nothing to do with the interrogation debates and experiments unfolding among *Pentagon* interrogators in Afghanistan and Cuba" (emphasis added). Second, she contends that the Pentagon's interrogation practices in Afghanistan and Cuba were also irrelevant to the misdeeds at Abu Ghraib, which were attributable instead to other failures, including the failure to keep military discipline from collapsing at Abu Ghraib.[100]

98. George Weigel, "Abu Ghraib and Just War in Iraq," Ethics and Public Policy Center, July 13, 2004, http://eppc.org/publications/abu-ghraib-and-just-war-in-iraq/.

99. Ibid.

100. Heather Mac Donald, "How to Interrogate Terrorists," *City Journal*, Winter 2005, 24–35, at 32.

In a second article, written in response to Marty Lederman's vigorous critique of her first article,[101] Mac Donald argues that "[t]he abuse in Iraq resulted from a violation of the rules, not from compliance with them. Had interrogators and military guards followed the guidelines governing their behavior, none of the sadistic treatment of detainees would have occurred."[102] Whereas the prophets interpreted Abu Ghraib as revealing a fundamental flaw in the national character of the United States, the deliberators attributed it to the grubby failures of uncontrolled and undisciplined individuals, whom Mac Donald refers to as the "grunts on the ground."[103]

From Mac Donald's deliberative perspective, the problem was not with American law or commitment to fundamental law. She emphasizes that the applicable "Interrogation Rules of Engagement" were "provided to all military interrogators and soldiers in Iraq" and that these manuals clearly prohibited the morally atrocious behavior engaged in by American soldiers at Abu Ghraib.[104] The problem was with a small number of individuals whose characteristically human failings were undisciplined and uncontrolled in a way that facilitated those atrocities. Taken as a whole, Mac Donald's essays suggest that Abu Ghraib did not require Americans to examine their own moral values and commitments; it simply prompted us to demand that the relevant norms are enforced with sufficient discipline among the young soldiers acting in our name.

What could religiously committed deliberators make of the torture memos? It is important to emphasize that a deliberator did not need to defend them in their entirety; indeed, it would be impossible for anyone within the moral framework of the Catholic Christian tradition to do so. While she does not draw explicitly on religious sources in making her arguments, Heather Mac Donald's essays are also instructive regarding how a deliberator's nuanced argument might proceed. She explicitly distances herself from Jay Bybee's August 1 memo, which focuses on the nature and scope of international and national laws against

101. Marty Lederman, "Heather Mac Donald's Dubious Counter-'Narrative' on Torture," Balkinization, January 11, 2005, http://balkin.blogspot.com/2005/01/heather-macdonalds-dubious-counter.html.

102. Heather Mac Donald, "Heather Mac Donald Responds to Marty Lederman on Abu Ghraib and U.S. Interrogation Policies," City Journal, January 13, 2005, www.city-journal.org/html/eon_01_13_05hm2.html.

103. Ibid.

104. Ibid.

torture.[105] At the same time, her analysis implicitly legitimates the two fundamental questions Bybee grappled with in that memo as well as in his earlier
January 22 memo.[106] Both of these questions open the way for the facts-and-
circumstances analysis characteristic of the rhetoric of moral deliberation.

More specifically, Mac Donald focuses attention on hard questions. First,
what precisely are the positive moral and legal obligations owed to members
of groups such as al-Qaeda and the Taliban, which do not comply with the
laws of war? With respect to this question, Mac Donald's argument accords
with the argument of the January 22 memo, which maintained that the
Geneva Conventions do not apply to al-Qaeda and Taliban detainees. She
writes, "Were the United States to announce that terrorists would be protected under the Geneva conventions, it would destroy any incentive our
ruthless enemies have to comply with the laws of war."[107]

Second, what are the moral limits on what we can do to such detainees in
the course of interrogations designed to obtain potentially life-saving information from them? Subsidiary questions include what constitutes "torture" that
is prohibited always and everywhere, what constitutes "inhumane treatment"
that is generally prohibited, and what counts as a sufficiently pressing reason or
set of reasons to engage in progressively more aggressive forms of interrogation? Mac Donald does not raise these questions in any systematic manner,
let alone address them with any kind of precision. Yet her essays are clearly
designed to precipitate their discussion. She argues, "[T]here is a huge gray area
between the gold standard of POW treatment reserved for honorable opponents and torture, which consists of the intentional infliction of severe physical
and mental pain. . . . To declare non-torturous stress off-limits for an enemy
who plays by no rules and accords no respect to Western prisoners is folly."[108]

As it first took place in 2004 and the early months of 2005, the emerging
debate over torture reveals how characteristic elements of both prophetic and

---

105. Of the August 1 memo, Mac Donald writes, "In response to the CIA's request, Assistant
Attorney General Jay S. Bybee produced a hair-raising memo that understandably caused widespread
alarm." Mac Donald, "How to Interrogate Terrorists," 32. While Mac Donald does not clearly articulate her objections to the memo, they appear to be, first, that Bybee's definition of torture is too
stringent and, second, that Bybee argues that the president is not bound by either international treaties or American law in wartime.

106. Bybee, January 22 memo.

107. Heather Mac Donald, "How to Interrogate Terrorists," 35.

108. Ibid., 28.

deliberative discourse can begin to coalesce around a particular issue. Moreover, the fault line dividing those inclined to frame the question in one way from those inclined to frame it in the other also became clearly visible. The prophets, shaken to the core by the pictures of torture and abuse, cannot drive those images out of their minds and hearts. The horror of those images became the focal point and driving force of their moral proclamation. Prophets strive to translate the intensity of their reaction to that riveting horror into words that will communicate it to others. Many prophets see their task not only as convincing their audience of the truth of their position on an issue but also as impelling them to prioritize that issue in the same way that the prophets do themselves. In contrast, deliberators literally do not *see* the issue in the same way. It is not the mesmerizing center of their attention and it does not exert an existential pull on their concern. They immediately grasp the complexities of the issue; they are impressed with both the theoretical and practical difficulties in defining the wrong at stake and in formulating a response. Whereas prophets are almost myopic in their concentration on the object of their concern, deliberators attempt to define and frame the question with the necessary subtlety to grasp not only their worries about torture but other moral and pragmatic concerns as well.

In this chapter, I have attempted to illustrate in some detail how the basic rhetorical clash between prophets and deliberators operates by examining the public discussion of abortion and torture around the time of the 2004 presidential elections, focusing largely, but not exclusively, on Catholic and evangelical Protestant voices. Taken together, the rhetoric surrounding these two issues at the time of the 2004 elections provides us with a rich basis for exploring and illustrating the clashes in moral perspective generating and generated by the clashes in rhetoric. Matters, however, are not so simple. The rhetoric of prophetic indictment and the rhetoric of moral deliberation do not only clash, they also conscript one another for their own purposes. I will attempt to untangle this and other more complicated aspects of the relationship between the two forms of moral rhetoric in the following chapter.

Prophetic Indictment
and Practical Deliberation

Describing the Relationship

Chapter 6 drew on the discussions of abortion and torture in the 2004 American presidential election to illustrate the contrasting manner in which prophetic and deliberative discourse approach controverted moral issues. We saw how the markedly different rhetorical characteristics of the two forms of discourse can create tension between their respective practitioners even when they share the same underlying worldview. Having described the distinctive characteristics of each form of discourse, I now take up the task of analyzing their sometimes complicated and tumultuous relationship. Like its predecessor, this chapter will not remain at the level of general observations. To understand how moral discourse operates in the context of particular disputes, I will descend to the level of detail, examining specific moral arguments in their wider rhetorical context. Let me remind the reader, therefore, that the purpose of this chapter is not to enter into the substantive moral and political debates over abortion or torture but rather to understand their character, their argumentative strengths and weaknesses, and their rhetorical vulnerabilities.

One might begin by asking whether there is any relationship to be analyzed. While it is tempting to conceive of these discourses as completely unrelated, the truth is that they are all too interrelated. After all, it is not as if each form of discourse exists in a vacuum, hermetically sealed from the influence of the other. A major source of the tension between prophets and deliberators is the tendency of each group to conscript the other's discourse for their own purposes. In most cases, that process of conscription distorts the competing form of discourse almost beyond recognition. First, and most obviously, the conscription of one form of discourse by its competitor raises the ire of those who purport to use it in good faith. Second, the disingenuous use of each form of the conscripted discourse itself easily becomes a straw man to be attacked.

Before attempting to develop criteria that would outline a healthier and more fruitful relationship between these two forms of discourse, it is necessary to examine and set aside the unproductive ways in which they often interact. The first two sections of this chapter, therefore, analyze several problematic ways in which the two forms of discourse surreptitiously draw on the other's rhetorical conventions to further their own purposes. The third section takes a closer look at one of the controversial torture memos drafted by produced by the Office of Legal Counsel for the Bush administration. I suggest that a major reason that this memo generated such disquiet was its rhetorical deceptiveness. Purporting to be a good-faith exercise in moral and legal deliberation of our obligations to enemy combatants, the document is better seen as a conscription of deliberative rhetoric in service of a larger prophetic indictment of the enemy.

Building on the insights into the two forms of moral discourse gleaned in this and the previous chapter, the fourth section attempts to begin formulating a normative account of the relationship between prophetic and deliberative discourse. My goal here is not only to account for their antagonistic moments but also to incorporate that antagonism into a fuller account of moral discourse in the public square. More specifically, I argue that the rhetoric of prophetic indictment is best understood as a sort of *moral chemotherapy*, a reaction to a potentially life-threatening distortion in ordinary, day-to-day moral discussion. Deliberative discourse is, in fact, that ordinary form of moral discussion. We reason from premises to conclusions, we analyze actions in terms of immediate goals, motives, and circumstances. In some cases, however, our ordinary form of discussion can be gravely corrupted, perhaps by the incorporation of a false major premise, perhaps because of the dependence on a mistaken minor premise. Such mistakes are made all the time in matters small and large. In some few cases, however, the mistake is about such a fundamental matter that it threatens to undermine the very possibility of moral and political reasoning within the community. It is in these desperate situations that the stark, harsh focus of prophetic indictment becomes necessary. Prophetic indictment relentlessly—and sometimes ruthlessly—targets the corruption that, left unchecked, would undermine the possibility of sound moral deliberation more generally.

Deliberative Misuse of Prophetic Discourse

Those inclined to a deliberative manner of framing their interventions in the public square can misuse prophetic discourse by putting it on a pedestal. By relegating prophecy entirely to the realm of an ideal world, deliberators can dismiss its normative claims upon the world we live in here and now. The prophetic calls to do justice to the widow, the orphan, and the stranger can be honored by the deliberator as the unalloyed norms that govern the kingdom of God, even as they are set to one side as too pure, too demanding, for gritty life in the world as it actually is.

In a closely related move, deliberative discourse can reduce prophecy to a mere moral admonition. The urgent demand of prophecy is politely paraphrased, its power reduced; it is moral nostrum and defanged. An example of this approach can be found in *Economic Justice for All,* a pastoral letter on the economy issued by the U.S. Catholic Bishops in 1986. It observes that:

> [t]he substance of prophetic faith is proclaimed by Micah: "to do justice, and to love kindness, and to walk humbly with your God" (Mi 6:8, RSV). Biblical faith in general, and prophetic faith especially, insist that fidelity to the covenant joins obedience to God with reverence and concern for the neighbor."[1]

While this summary is no doubt true, it is rhetorically incomplete; something important is lost in the translation of the prophetic faith found in the Hebrew Bible. Consider this passage from the book of Isaiah:

---

1. United States Conference of Catholic Bishops, *Economic Justice for All,* 10th ann. ed. (Washington, DC: United States Conference of Catholic Bishops, 1997), para. 37.

The LORD rises to argue his case,
    he stands to judge the peoples.
The LORD enters into judgment
    with the elders and princes of his people:
It is you who have devoured the vineyard;
    the spoil of the poor is in your houses.
What do you mean by crushing my people,
    by grinding the face of the poor? Says the LORD, the God of hosts.

The LORD said:
Because the daughters of Zion are haughty,
    and walk with outstretched necks,
    glancing wantonly with their eyes,
mincing along as they go,
    tinkling with their feet;
The LORD will afflict with scabs
    the heads of the daughters of Zion,
    and the LORD will lay bare their secret parts.[2]

The moral indictment of prophetic discourse cannot be separated from its fiery rhetoric of excoriation. The purpose of this form of discourse is meant to move the listener or reader in a holistic way by communicating a vivid picture of the travesty indicted by the prophet, a picture that is first meant to move the audience to see—and feel—in the same way as the prophet—and then, subsequently, to act appropriately.

The temptation to invoke prophetic discourse is often raised when deliberators are unable to supply arguments whose conclusions are as settled or impressive as they might wish. In other words, the temptation is strongest when the dictates of practical reason are less firmly grounded in the relevant principles, facts, and circumstances than the deliberator would like them to be. If one is tentative about one's assessment of key facts or circumstances, one ought to be correspondingly tentative about a course of action chosen on the basis of that assessment. Yet deliberators can fear, sometimes reasonably, that any tentativeness in judgment on controversial political or moral issues

2. Isaiah 3:13–17.

will be exploited by their opponents. As St. Paul once asked, "And if the bugle gives an indistinct sound, who will get ready for battle?"[3] Consequently, strategically minded deliberators might decide to play down the inescapably tentative character of their conclusions by drawing on a prophetic interpretation of the situation.

In my judgment, some pro-life opponents to human embryonic stem-cell research avail themselves of prophetic discourse to buttress the inherently debatable conclusions of a deliberative argument. More specifically, they invoke prophetic language to buttress their claim that such research is morally unacceptable because it involves the intentional destruction of human embryos, which is tantamount to the intentional killing of human persons, albeit very young ones. Cardinal Raymond Burke, former archbishop of St. Louis, denounced human embryonic stem-cell research, arguing that to sign a petition in support of an initiative favoring such research "is to promote the culture of death which tragically besets our nation."[4]

Outlined in syllogistic form, the basic pro-life argument runs as follows:

> *Major premise:* Each and every living, individual, human being merits equal respect as a human person made in the image and likeness of God.
>
> *Minor premise:* This entity is a living, individual human being.
>
> *Conclusion:* This entity merits equal respect as a human person made in the image and likeness of God.

The moral insight of the pro-life argument is carried by its major premise. Pro-life Catholics believe it is morally unacceptable, for example, to say that the dignity of human beings varies according to their capacity to reason or to will, or their relative state of physical dependence. So they would reject, for example, arguments that human infants do not qualify as persons until their brains reaches a certain level of maturity[5] or that adults who have lost the

---

3. 1 Corinthians 14:8.

4. Raymond Burke, "Safeguarding Human Life: The Very Beginning," *St. Louis Review,* November 23, 2005, http://stlouisreview.com/article/2005-11-23/safeguarding-human-life-very-beginning. (subscription req.). See also Tim Townsend, "Bishops Target Stem Cell Petition," *St. Louis Post-Dispatch,* November 25, 2005, A1.

5. Peter Singer adopts this position; see, for example, *Practical Ethics,* 3rd ed. (New York: Cambridge University Press, 2011), chap. 6.

capacity to reason no longer count as persons, although they are still living human beings.[6]

The minor premise, however, entails a factual judgment. In most circumstances, common sense suffices to identify individual, living members of the species *Homo sapiens*. But to determine the very beginning and the very end of an individuated human life, we need to draw heavily upon the best insights of biology and medicine. The determination that the biological life of an individual human being has begun or come to an end depends in significant part on an evaluation of scientific data, which is not reducible to an abstract debate about the norms of justice.[7]

As Burke himself recognizes, the pro-life argument against embryonic stem-cell research depends on the scientific judgment that an individuated human being comes into existence at fertilization.[8] Yet the available scientific evidence does not unequivocally support that judgment. Until it reaches the age of approximately fourteen days, the embryo can divide, creating two embryos (twinning). It is also possible, but rarer, for two embryos to join together to constitute one embryo, through a process of combination.[9]

6. See, for example, the debate between John Finnis and John Harris on the criteria for human personhood in *Euthanasia Examined: Ethical, Clinical, and Legal Perspectives*, ed. John Keown (Cambridge: Cambridge University Press, 1995), chaps. 1–6.

7. See Paul Ramsey, *The Patient as Person: Explorations in Medical Ethics*, 2nd ed. (New Haven, CT: Yale University Press, 2002), 63–64. Ramsey writes: "No doubt there are various levels of death (clinical death, physiological death, organ death, cellular death). No doubt also life and death fall within the continuum of all life's processes. . . . These facts are not crucial when, in a medical-ethical context, we ask the meaning of life and death. This is to ask when in the continuum of the beginning of life there is a human life among us, and when in the continuum of the dying process there is a life still among us who lays claim to the immunities, respect, and protection which in ethics and/or by law are accorded by men to a fellow man. Even if the 'moment' of death is actually a span of time, pronouncement of death has this significance: that we need some procedure for determining when a life is still with us, making its moral claims upon us, and when we stand instead in the presence of an unburied corpse." Ramsey goes on to state: "No more should the definition of what death is be confused with the methods by which it shall be determined that death has occurred. One of these may undergo change without changing the other; or both may be revised in the light of contemporary knowledge."

8. "The truth that the human embryo is a human being is not a matter of religious faith. It is a matter of biological science. Biology, and, more specifically, embryology, teaches us that once fertilization (or a procedure which replaces fertilization like human cloning) takes place, a new human being comes into existence." Burke, "Safeguarding Human Life."

9. A brief, helpful description of embryonic development can be found in the President's Council on Bioethics, *Monitoring Stem Cell Research* (2004), 157–81, http://bioethics.georgetown.edu/pcbe /reports/stemcell/pcbe_final_version_monitoring_stem_cell_research.pdf.

These biological phenomena weaken the basis for saying that an individuated human being comes into being at the time of fertilization because individuated human beings, who are mammals, do not reproduce by dividing days after coming into existence and because individuated human beings do not combine to form one human being. There is no question, of course, that the embryo is biologically human, in the sense that its component cells are not those of a plant or another animal. Yet more is required to constitute an entire individuated human being than the possession of living cells bearing a human genotype. Also required is a holistic, integrating organization with the prospect of maintaining a stable, individual identity through time. The possibilities of twinning and combination raise doubts about whether the very early embryo has developed the stability and coherence of biological identity that justify calling it an individual human being.[10]

Those opposed to embryonic stem-cell research have often been reluctant to admit that the case for the status of the early embryo as an individuated human being is susceptible to questions that gave pause to powerful figures in the pro-life movement such as Paul Ramsey.[11] At times, in fact, the rhetoric condemning embryonic stem-cell research as the slaughter of innocent human beings has been heightened, rather than qualified, despite the factual

---

10. Those who hold that the life of an individuated human being begins at fertilization have articulated responses to these objections; see, for example, Robert P. George and Christopher Tollefsen, *Embryo: A Defense of Human Life* (New York: Doubleday, 2008). For a concise presentation of the arguments on both sides, as well as a consideration of special cases, see President's Council on Bioethics, *Monitoring Stem Cell Research*, 74–93. See also President's Council on Bioethics, *Human Cloning and Human Dignity: An Ethical Inquiry* (2002), 133–40, 152–59.

11. "So in order to retain belief that life begins at conception, [Germain] Grisez . . . adopts the view that 'a certain number of human individuals . . . cease to be shortly after conception,' and at that point two others begin by asexual reproduction (p. 26). In the case of mosaics, Grisez relies on the fact that implantation cannot occur without definition of function, so long as the two morulae are distinct from each other they are distinct individuals, and 'once combined the two cease to be as such and form one new individual'—like a 'grafted plant.' With considerable astonishment we may ask whether any such 'individuality' is the life we should respect and protect from conception. In trying to prove too much, Grisez has proved too little of ethical import." Paul Ramsey, *Three on Abortion* (Oak Park, IL: Child and Family Reprints, 1978), 29–30, citing Germain Grisez, *Abortion: The Myths, the Realities, and the Arguments* (New York: Corpus Books, 1970), 26. A "mosaic" is an embryo that contains cells with different genotypes, which results from the combination of two morulae, which in turn are embryos at an early stage of development. Grisez says that, from the point of fertilization until combination, the two morulae are two individual human persons; say, A and B. When they combine, they form the mosaic, C, who is a third individual human person.

uncertainties.[12] Why? In my judgment, the heightened rhetoric was an attempt to overcome the wariness on the part of policy makers to take a stand on the issue. Once opposition to human embryonic stem-cell research becomes less about the concrete violation of the rights of particular human beings (i.e., human embryos) and more about the relatively abstract harms associated with exploiting the seeds of the next generation, the deliberative argument becomes harder to make in the public square. To counter the concrete appeals of the late Christopher Reeve or Michael J. Fox regarding the benefits of stem-cell research, some pro-life advocates believed they needed the concrete appeals of other helpless, vulnerable human beings—which is why President George W. Bush staged a photo opportunity with children born from frozen embryos.[13]

Nonetheless, it was a mistake for those who read the biological data as supporting the position that an individuated human life begins at fertilization to resort to prophetic rhetoric in their response to those who read that data in a different way. It is one thing to put forward factual, deliberative arguments in favor of life beginning at fertilization; it is another thing entirely to say that anyone who is not persuaded by those arguments is an advocate of the culture of death. This rhetoric of prophetic denunciation wrongfully obscures the fact that the dispute between at least some of the parties has not been at the level of fundamental moral commitments to the dignity of each individual human being. Instead, it has revolved around the difficult question of precisely when an individual human being comes into existence.[14]

---

12. See, for example, Matt Sande, "Back Again to Stem Cells: Bill Allowing the Destruction of Embryos Simply Advances the Culture of Death," *Milwaukee Journal Sentinel*, May 29, 2005, Jl. "Last week, the U.S. House of Representatives shamefully disregarded the right to life of innocent human beings by passing a deadly measure that would fully rescind President Bush's federal funding restrictions on human embryonic stem cell research."

13. Hilary White, "President Bush Meets with Families of Adopted Frozen Embryo-Children," May 25, 2005, https://www.lifesitenews.com/news/president-bush-meets-with-families-of-adopted -frozen-embryo-children.

14. Doubtless the refusal of many pro-lifers to acknowledge difficult questions around the status of the early embryo is rooted in political exigencies, not merely a concern for intellectual purity. After all, a significant number of those who advocate stem-cell research also do not think that unborn life possesses equal human dignity even after it passes the stage where twinning and combination are no longer possible. Some thinkers assess the value of fetal life in utilitarian or quasi-utilitarian terms until much later points in gestational development. These assessments can justify not only abortion but also nontherapeutic experimentation on fetuses destined for abortion. In this political context,

Prophetic Misuse of Deliberative Discourse

It is not only moral deliberation that misuses prophetic discourse; we can also find mirror-image situations in which prophets misuse deliberative discourse. First, prophets can deny that the fine distinctions of deliberative discourse make any legitimate contribution to moral reflection on controverted issues. They can portray moral deliberation as a type of malignant rationalization, as a thin excuse for realpolitik in the domestic, national, and international spheres of human existence. Very crude divine command theories of morality sometimes take this line in an explicit way. Obedience to God's command is set over and against attempting to find moral wisdom in the processes of discursive reason.[15]

Second, prophecy can at times attempt to subvert the analytical tools of deliberative discourse, employing its categories, grids, analogies, and decision-making procedures, in a way that leads to the practical uselessness of the categories themselves—thereby pointing the listener or reader toward a prophetic vista as the only possible alternative. For example, consider the debate between pacifists and advocates of just war. Although early Christians were pacifists, since the time of Constantine and the adoption of Christianity by the Roman Empire, a number of Christian thinkers have advocated the position that it may sometimes be just to wage war. Over the centuries, Christian political theorists developed just war theory, which in its present form identifies seven criteria that should govern a just decision to go to war (*ius ad bellum*) and two criteria that should govern just conduct in the waging of war (*ius in bello*).[16]

---

pro-lifers may well think that drawing a hard and clear line at fertilization is necessary in order to avoid stepping on a slippery slope.

15. Not all divine command theories are crude, of course; many divine command theorists attempt to reconcile human reason with the divine will in some way or another. See, for example, Paul Helm, ed., *Divine Commands and Morality* (New York: Oxford University Press, 1981); Richard J. Mouw, *The God Who Commands: A Study in Divine Command Ethics* (South Bend, IN: University of Notre Dame Press, 1991); and John E. Hare, *God's Call: Moral Realism, God's Commands, and Human Autonomy* (Grand Rapids, MI: Eerdmans, 2001).

16. The *ius ad bellum* criteria are generally held to include: (1) just cause; (2) competent authority; (3) comparative justice, (4) right intention; (5) last resort; (6) probability of success; and (7) proportionality. The *ius in bello* criteria include: (1) discrimination between combatants and noncombatants in targeting weaponry, and (2) proportionality. Sometimes added to the list of *ius in bello* criteria include: compliance with international law on prohibited weapons, benevolent quarantine for prisoners, and no means *mala in se*. See the *Stanford Encyclopedia of Philosophy*, "War." See also National

Some pacifists, however, have taken the just war criteria and turned them against the theory itself, interpreting the evidence so that no war could ever meet the criteria. An example of this approach can be found in the late Mennonite theologian John Howard Yoder's book, *When War Is Unjust: Being Honest in Just-War Thinking.*[17] A pacifist himself, Yoder sees this book as calling just war theorists to be true to the requirements of their own theory and insisting that they resist the temptation to concoct rationalizations for decisions made by nation-states and governments to augment their own power and influence.[18] And surely, just war theorists might profitably read his work for such purposes.

At the same time, Yoder does not consistently treat just war theory as the channel for practical reason that he explicitly recognizes it to be.[19] He recognizes in principle that it offers a structure in which Christians might legitimately grapple with the question whether a particular war is being waged justly. Practically, however, he treats it as if it were (at best) a toothless construct of Christian moralists relegated to the ivory tower of academia[20] or (at worst) a propaganda tool of politicians who proclaim their Christian commitments while actually practicing realpolitik in statecraft.[21]

In short, Yoder turns to finely grained deliberative discourse to advance prophetic ends. He attempts to use just war theory against itself, functionally leaving a form of pacifism as the only available option, at least for self-professed Christians.[22] Ultimately, however, Yoder's critique in *When War Is Unjust* is

Conference of Catholic Bishops, *The Challenge of Peace: God's Promise and Our Response* (Washington, DC: United States Catholic Conference, 1983), paras. 85–100 (*ius ad bellum*) and paras. 101–110 (*ius in bello*), from which this list is taken. For a general discussion, see James Turner Johnson, *Ethics and the Use of Force: Just War in Historical Perspective* (Surrey, UK: Ashgate, 2011).

17. John Howard Yoder, *When War Is Unjust: Being Honest in Just War Thinking,* 2nd ed. (Maryknoll, NY: Orbis Books, 1996).

18. "The just war position is . . . the one most Christians say they take. But is that claim accurate? We shall observe that there is reason to doubt that it is. My task is to ask what it would really mean to take a just-war position. As an ecumenical contribution to the integrity and the self-esteem of my just-war interlocutors, I shall proceed to examine the credibility of the dominant tradition." Ibid., 3.

19. "But before leaping to the basic question of credibility, we need a broader acquaintance with what the just-war tradition is about. The tradition is not merely a set of criteria to apply to a political situation. It is as well a culture, shaped by a long history of thought and application, which evolved along the way with more twists and turns than the popularizers or even the theologians tend to acknowledge." Ibid., 7.

20. Ibid., chap. 3.

21. Ibid., chap. 4.

22. He develops his own theologically grounded pacifism in John Howard Yoder, *The Politics of Jesus,* 2nd ed. (Grand Rapids, MI: Eerdmans, 1994).

deceptive. His own case for pacifism is rooted not in the failure of just war theory but in his own commitment to the "war of the lamb," that is, to the path of self-sacrifice and suffering freely accepted by Jesus Christ.[23]

Finally, prophecy sometimes uses deliberative discourse as a mere instrument to achieve its ends, just as deliberators sometimes use prophecy in the same manner. In some contexts, an explicitly prophetic voice is not likely to be either welcome or effective. For example, one such context is the legal realm, which is dominated by a deliberative approach, at least in the Anglo-American tradition. In the United States, the legal realm constructs an elaborate series of checks and balances in relation to political power and places significant constraints on the choice of means that any agent (i.e., an individual, a corporation, or a governmental body or functionary) may select in order to achieve chosen ends. In such contexts, prophetic voices must apply deliberative tools instrumentally in order to clear the way for them to give full allegiance to the prophetic vision.

Assuming that George W. Bush and his advisers were indeed operating from the conviction that the West is engaged in a "clash of civilizations" with militant Islamic forces,[24] it becomes plausible to view the torture memos as essentially a case of prophecy using deliberative discourse as an instrument to remove the legal and moral barriers that impeded full compliance with their prophetic vision.[25]

---

23. "The choice that he [Jesus] made in rejecting the crown and accepting the cross was the commitment to such a degree of faithfulness to the character of divine love that he was willing for its sake to sacrifice 'effectiveness.' Usually it can be argued that from some other perspective or in some long view this renunciation of effectiveness was in fact a very effective thing to do. 'If a man will lose his . . . life he shall find it.' But this paradoxical possibility does not change the initially solid fact that Jesus thereby excluded any normative concern for any capacity to make sure that things would turn out right." Ibid., 234.

24. "This is not, however, just America's fight, and what is at stake is not just America's freedom. This is the world's fight. This is civilization's fight. This is the fight of all who believe in progress and pluralism, tolerance and freedom." George W. Bush, "Address before a Joint Session of the Congress on the United States Response to the Terrorist Attacks of September 11," *Public Papers of the Presidents,* 2001, book II, 1140–44, at 1142–43 (September 20, 2001). See also George W. Bush, "Transform America's National Security Institutions to Meet the Challenges and Opportunities of the Twenty-First Century," (address to a joint session of Congress on September 20, 2001), chap. 9 of *The National Security Strategy of the United States of America: September 2002,* 29–31 at 31, www.state.gov/documents/organization /63562.pdf: "The war on terrorism is not a clash of civilizations. It does, however, reveal the clash inside a civilization, a battle for the future of the Muslim world. This is a struggle of ideas and this is an area where America must excel."

25. What of the fact that the Obama administration has not sharply distinguished itself from the

The Torture Memos

As I noted in the previous chapter, the ongoing American debate about torture was precipitated in part by the revelation of a number of confidential
memos from the administration of George W. Bush. Numerous commentators have strongly criticized the arguments in these memos on substantive
moral and legal grounds. My primary focus here is not on the substance per
se. Instead, I propose to examine how the arguments reveal the broader rhetorical purposes of the memos, purposes that in turn serve larger moral and
political ends. I hasten to add, however, that substance and rhetoric are intertwined. It is precisely because the memos fall so far short as exercises of deliberative reasoning that readers are driven to look for another explanation of
their underlying aim and function.

Two memos in particular merit close analysis. They were submitted by
Jay S. Bybee, then assistant attorney general for the Office of Legal Counsel,
to Attorney General Alberto R. Gonzales. One, dated January 22, 2002, is entitled "Application of Treaties and Laws to al Qaeda and Taliban Detainees."[26]
The second, dated August 1, 2002, is entitled "Standards of Conduct for Interrogation under 18 U.S.C. §§ 2340–2340A."[27] Both memos employ deliberative
rhetoric in order to justify a policy that would drastically reduce the legal
strictures protecting captured members of the Taliban and al-Qaeda against

---

policies of the Bush administration on terrorism, as symbolized by the fact that the Guantanamo
detention facility continues to operate? What about Obama's drone policy, which raises a whole range
of new and serious moral problems? Does this mean that Obama is also "prophetic" in his reaction to
Islamic militancy? In my judgment, it does not. Politicians may offer vastly different rationales for
engaging in the same actions or policies. Obama's attitudes on these matters seem more indebted to
the realism of Reinhold Niebuhr than to prophetic contestation. Let me emphasize that I do not think
Obama's actions are more justifiable than Bush's because they are not "prophetically" motivated.
There are serious problems with his reasoning on these matters, which amounts to a type of conse-
quentialism that I reject. See, for example, Cathleen Kaveny, "Regret Is Not Enough: Why the
President Should Read Paul Ramsey," *Commonweal,* January 27, 2012, 8.

26. Jay S. Bybee, "Application of Treaties and Laws to al Qaeda and Taliban Detainees," January
22, 2002, in *The Torture Papers: The Road to Abu Ghraib,* ed. Karen J. Greenberg and Joshua L. Dratel
(New York: Cambridge University Press, 2005), 81–117. This memo was based almost entirely on a
memo prepared by Deputy Assistant Attorney General John Yoo; see his "Application of Treaties and
Laws to al Qaeda and Taliban Detainees," January 9, 2002, in Greenberg and Dratel, eds., *The Torture
Papers,* 38–79.

27. Jay S. Bybee, "Standards of Conduct for Interrogation under 18 U.S.C. §§ 2340–2340A," August 1,
2002, in Greenberg and Dratel, eds., *The Torture Papers,* 172–217.

harsh treatment by their American captors.[28] Their overarching goal is to clear away any legal obstacles under international law or American law that would impede President Bush's freedom to control the interrogation of prisoners captured in the war on terror. Consequently, the memos belong to the genre of legal advocacy rather than to that of moral and legal inquiry.

More specifically, the memos make use of the finely grained tools of deliberative rhetoric to advance the objectives of the president of the United States, who stands in the role of Bybee's client. Bybee does not treat the legal sources he analyzes, including the Geneva Conventions, as a source of moral wisdom with which to illuminate a difficult decision; neither does he interpret the letter of the law governing treatment of enemy prisoners according to its animating moral spirit. Nonetheless, it would be wrong to say that the memos are devoid of moral concern. On the contrary, they treat the obligation of the president to protect the citizens of the United States against terrorism not only as morally imperative but also as overriding all other moral concerns. Bybee's analysis, in other words, is not the exercise of moral discernment in the course of practical reasoning; rather, it is the deployment of a powerful set of analytical tools to eliminate what he views as a potential impediment to a morally and politically imperative course of action.

Consider first the January 22 memo, which, by intricately detailed legal analysis, argues that the Geneva Convention protections governing treatment of prisoners of war (POWs) apply neither to the conflict with al-Qaeda nor to the conflict with the Taliban. After arguing that members of al-Qaeda do not meet the qualifications for POWs, the January 22 memo goes on to claim that the president has the constitutional power to suspend the Geneva Conventions as a whole with respect to Afghanistan or, alternatively, to interpret them as excluding POW eligibility for the Taliban. Systematically eliminating all legal protections for the enemy, the January 22 memo proceeds to deny that al-Qaeda or the Taliban qualify for the protections of Common Article 3, which is a provision shared by all four Geneva Conventions and requires "humane treatment" for those placed outside combat by "sickness, wounds, detention, or

---

28. According to one article in the New York Times, the August 1 memo was prepared in order to provide post hoc justification for harsh interrogation procedures used by the CIA on high-level al-Qaeda operatives, in particular Abu Zubaydah, a top aide to Osama bin Laden, after his capture in April 2002. David Johnston and James Risen, "Aides Say Memo Backed Coercion Already in Use," New York Times, June 27, 2004, A1.

any other cause." The effect—and it seems the purpose—of Bybee's analysis is to leave al-Qaeda and Taliban operatives in a legal no-man's land, entirely at the mercy of American forces.

The January 22 memo acknowledges that the president's decision to suspend the Geneva Conventions may not be recognized as valid under international law.[29] One would think that such a prospect would prompt the author to reconsider his reasoning. Instead, and significantly, it triggered an expression of defiance: "customary international law cannot bind the President or the executive branch, in any legally meaningful way, in its conduct of the war in Afghanistan."[30] Why such a reaction? Perhaps because the intricate arguments of the January 22 memo were not meant to provide disinterested legal analysis; instead, they were formulated as an effective means to achieve a desired legal and political end. This explanation becomes more plausible when one considers a memo of White House Counsel Alberto R. Gonzales to President George W. Bush bluntly highlighting the advantages of the January 22 memo's approach. Gonzales notes that it preserves flexibility in fighting this "new kind of war" and "[s]ubstantially reduces the threat of domestic criminal prosecution under the War Crimes Act (18 U.S.C. 2441)."[31]

Whereas the January 22 memo removes general legal protections from American enemies, the August 1 memo[32] gets down to brass tacks, so to speak. It is dedicated to enhancing the administration's ability to obtain information pertaining to future acts of terrorism without incurring a significant threat of domestic criminal prosecution under the Convention Against Torture and Other Cruel, Inhuman and Degrading Treatment or Punishment, as that

29. Bybee, January 22 memo, 102–7.

30. Ibid., 115.

31. Alberto R. Gonzales, "Decision Re Application of the Geneva Convention on Prisoners of War to the Conflict with Al Qaeda and the Taliban," in Greenberg and Dratel, eds., *The Tortune Papers,* 118–21, at 119. President Bush listened to his lawyers; he issued a memorandum stating that the Geneva Conventions do not apply to al-Qaeda and that he had the authority to suspend the conventions as between the United States and Afghanistan, although he declined to do so at that time. Bush also announced that neither the Taliban nor al-Qaeda qualified for protections as prisoners of war or under Common Article 3 of the conventions. George W. Bush, "Humane Treatment of al Qaeda and Taliban Detainees," February 7, 2002, in Greenberg and Dratel, eds., *The Torture Papers,* 134–35.

32. In December 2004, immediately before the Senate Judiciary Committee hearings on the nomination of Alberto R. Gonzales to serve as attorney general of the United States, the Justice Department significantly retreated from the analysis outlined in the August 1 memo. See Neil A. Lewis, "U.S. Spells Out New Definition Curbing Torture," *New York Times,* January 1, 2005, A1.

convention is implemented in federal law.[33] The cumulative effect of the arguments set forth in August 1 memo is to encourage the president to authorize interrogators to obtain such information by any means necessary because a number of factors render it highly unlikely that they will be punished for their acts.

The August 1 memo begins by analyzing the applicable provision in the United States Code, which makes it a crime for any person "outside the United States [to] commit or attempt to commit torture."[34] It elaborates on the elements of the crime, noting in particular that, to convict a defendant, the prosecution must prove that the defendant acted with the specific intent to cause severe physical or mental pain or suffering, and the possible difficulties involved in providing such proof.[35] The memo also attempts to define the prohibited acts of torture as narrowly as possible. It contends, for example, that "[f]or purely mental pain or suffering to amount to torture under Section 2340, it must result in significant psychological harm of significant duration, e.g., lasting for months or even years."[36] The memo next proceeds to erect two further barriers to enforcement of the relevant statutory provision. First, it maintains that, in current circumstances marked by the threat of terrorism, the provision "would represent an unconstitutional infringement of the President's authority to conduct war."[37] Less dramatically, but no less definitely, the memo maintains that the legal defenses of self-defense or necessity might justify interrogators in engaging in techniques that were indisputably barred as torture by the law, given the magnitude of the threat posed to the United States after the attacks on September 11, 2001.[38]

Taken together, the import of Bybee's two memos is that there are few, if any, limits to what American interrogators can do in order to extract information from al-Qaeda and Taliban prisoners. In tone, argument, and structure, the memos suggest that Bybee views his analysis as a broom with which to sweep away the web of international and national law protecting prisoners detained by the United States in the war on terror to facilitate American

33. 18 U.S.C. §§ 2340–2340A.
34. Bybee, August 1 memo, 173.
35. Ibid., 174–75.
36. Ibid., 172. The memo goes on to limit the type of mental suffering that qualifies as torture.
37. Ibid., 173.
38. Ibid.

victory. Two features of his analysis are worthy of comment. First, Bybee's choice of deliberative techniques is governed, in large part, by the end he seeks. His driving question is, "How can the impact of applicable laws against torture on my client's course of action be minimized?" not "How should my client shape his course of action in view of applicable laws against torture, and the moral values they instantiate?" Second, Bybee's approach is designed to create a sphere of action for the president that is comparatively unencumbered by the relevant legal norms and the underlying moral vision those norms embody. It is not designed to *extend* the legal and moral norms embodied in statutory and case law, moving by analogy from a familiar situation to an unfamiliar situation. Bybee's use of deliberative rhetoric, in other words, is *not* the exercise of practical reason in an effort to assess in good faith what ought to be American policy toward prisoners detained as part of the war on terror; rather, it is an effort to eliminate the external barriers that the law imposes on his client's efforts to *win* the war on terror.

The torture memos exemplify how moral and legal deliberation can be so thoroughly distorted that it becomes nothing more than an attempt to rationalize a course of action already chosen for other reasons. In other words, it exemplifies casuistry—in the pejorative sense in which it is unfortunately commonly understood. As Albert Jonsen and Stephen Toulmin observe in their history of casuistry, one definition provided by the *Oxford English Dictionary* proclaims that "[c]asuistry destroys by distinctions and exceptions all morality, and effaces the essential difference between right and wrong."[39] Understanding how and why bad casuistry operates as a distorted form of deliberative discourse makes it easier to see the justification it provides for the exercise of prophetic rhetoric as well as the possibilities of a guilty conscription of casuistry by prophecy.

For those inclined to argue that the torture memos exemplify the pejorative meaning of casuistry, one particularly apt piece of evidence is the manner in which Bybee developed his narrow definition of torture in the August 1 memo.[40] He notes that, as codified in American law, the Convention Against Torture and Other Cruel, Inhuman and Degrading Treatment or Punishment "makes it a criminal offense for any person 'outside the United States [to]

39. Albert R. Jonsen and Stephen Toulmin, *The Abuse of Casuistry: A History of Moral Reasoning* (Berkeley: University of California Press, 1988), 12.

40. Bybee, August 1 memo.

commit or attempt to commit torture.'"[41] He goes on to observe that under Section 2340, torture is defined as an "act committed by a person acting under the color of law specifically intended to inflict severe physical or mental pain or suffering (other than pain or suffering incidental to lawful sanctions) upon another person within his custody or physical control."[42]

But what counts as "severe physical or mental pain or suffering"? To answer this question, Bybee does not turn to other discussions of torture in international law or in the scholarly literature. Instead, he searches the United States Code for other instances of the isolated term *severe pain,* finally finding what he is looking for in "statutes defining an emergency medical condition for the purpose of providing health benefits."[43] Without a hint of incongruity, Bybee contends that, "[a]lthough these statutes address a substantially different subject . . . they are nonetheless helpful for understanding what constitutes severe physical pain." On that basis, he maintains that the infliction of severe pain "must rise to a similarly high level—the level that would ordinarily be associated with a sufficiently serious physical condition or injury such as death, organ failure, or serious impairment of body functions—in order to constitute torture."[44]

But there is incongruity aplenty to be found in Bybee's analysis. The specific statutory provisions pertaining to an "emergency medical condition" cited by Bybee all pertain to the requirements that healthcare providers must meet in order to receive federal funding through the Medicare and Medicaid programs.[45] Taken together, these statutory provisions express Congress's overarching concern to ensure that no one in need of emergency medical treatment will be denied such treatment. This concern not only extends to enrollees in Medicare and Medicaid programs but also to those who are unable to pay for such treatment, even illegal aliens. Taken together, they express the conviction that the moral imperative to alleviate the severe physical suffering of another human being overrides other important national goals and policies. For Bybee to invoke these provisions—without paying attention to their

41. Ibid., 173. The bracketed word was inserted by Bybee.
42. Ibid.
43. Ibid., 176.
44. Ibid.
45. Ibid.

broader statutory context—in order to justify the infliction of severe physical suffering is deeply troubling, both intellectually and morally.

In my view, a close reading of Bybee's analysis reveals serious logical flaws. Consider what is perhaps the most well-known of the statutory provisions that he draws upon in developing his definition of the term *severe pain*, the Emergency Medical Treatment and Active Labor Act (EMTALA).[46] Colloquially known as the anti-dumping law, EMTALA prohibits hospitals that have executed Medicare provider agreements from refusing to serve any patient who presents with an "emergency medical condition" on the grounds that he or she does not have the financial means to pay for the emergency services provided.[47] *Severe pain* is not defined in EMTALA—or in any of the other statutes he cites. It is one of the *defining criteria*, however, of an "emergency medical condition." From a logical perspective, the EMTALA provision followed in the structure of "If there is A (severe pain), then B may also present (the elements of an emergency medical condition)." Bybee's casuistry attempts to extend this analysis by reversal, by making other qualifying elements of the emergency medical condition define the term *severe pain*.[48] But the reversal is logically illegitimate.[49]

More broadly, Bybee seems immured to the particular incongruities involved in evoking the terms of the anti-dumping law in order to justify a narrower reading of the law prohibiting torture. EMTALA explicitly included

46. 42 U.S.C. § 1395dd.

47. EMTALA imposes two requirements upon a hospital's emergency department: (1) it must screen for an emergency medical condition, and (2) it must stabilize any individual with such a condition before transferring him or her to another facility.

48. Under EMTALA, an "emergency medical condition" is "a medical condition manifesting itself by acute symptoms of sufficient severity (including severe pain) such that the absence of immediate medical attention could reasonably be expected to result in—

    (i) placing the health of the individual (or, with respect to a pregnant woman, the health of the woman or her unborn child) in serious jeopardy,

    (ii) serious impairment to bodily functions, or

    (iii) serious dysfunction of any bodily organ or part"

42 U.S.C. § 1395dd(e)(1)(A). The following subsection goes on to define an "emergency medical condition" with respect to women in active labor.

49. Bybee defines *severe pain* for purpose of the anti-torture law as pain requiring that "the victim must experience intense pain or suffering of the kind that is equivalent to the pain that would be associated with serious physical injury so severe that death, organ failure, or permanent damage resulting in a loss of significant bodily function will likely result." Bybee, August 1 memo, 183.

"severe pain" in the list of triggering conditions for an emergency medical condition in order to ensure that no one in severe pain would be denied medical screening and stabilizing medical treatment because of their inability to pay—even if the pain was unaccompanied by any other symptoms.[50] It is incongruous—indeed some might say perversely so—to invoke federal legislation imposing an obligation to *alleviate* physical suffering in order to justify the *infliction* of physical suffering.

Some of the argumentation in the torture memos therefore exemplifies the sort of distorted moral reasoning that tends to give casuistry a bad name. The arguments are faulty, the analysis is specious, the distinctions strained. While apparently deliberating in good faith about what to do in light of applicable law and policies, the authors in fact appear to be concocting a process of reasoning to justify decisions reached on entirely different grounds. It is, of course, this apparent misuse of moral reasoning to further existing desires and rationalize predetermined outcomes that has long drawn the ire of rigorist critiques of casuistry, most famously the *Provincial Letters* of Blaise Pascal (1657).[51]

The crucial feature of corrupt casuistry is that its practitioners rig or distort moral deliberation, sometimes quite dramatically, in order to achieve other purposes. What are those purposes? In some cases, they can include some form of venal personal gain—wealth, material comfort, and physical satisfaction. It is also possible, however, for corrupt casuistry to be deployed for other, less self-centered ends. In fact, corrupt casuistry can be conscripted

---

50. It has been argued that severe pain, by itself, is not an "emergency medical condition." See, for example, Robert A. Bitterman, MD, "Is 'Severe Pain' Considered an Emergency Medical Condition under EMTALA," *ACEP Now*, April 1, 2013, www.acepnow.com/article/severe-pain-considered -emergency-medical-condition-emtala/. It is true that the wording of the statutory provision is unclear and even inadequate. See, for example, Sandra H. Johnson, "The Social, Professional, and Legal Framework for the Problem of Pain Management in Emergency Medicine," *Journal of Law, Medicine & Ethics* 33, no. 4 (Winter 2005): 741–60. As Johnson observes, "EMTALA appears, then, to adopt the traditional, though now dated, perspective of emergency medicine that pain is merely a symptom"(p. 752). Yet the vast majority of hospitals have implemented the Joint Commission on Accreditation of Health Care standards pertinent to pain assessment and management. Moreover, failure to treat pain appropriately amounts to professional negligence. Consequently, Johnson suggests, correctly in my view, that EMTALA may indirectly include the duty to assess and control pain, through its incorporation of professional standards of care. The importance of EMTALA has diminished, but not disappeared, in view of the expansion of health care coverage provided by the Affordable Care Act.

51. Blaise Pascal, *Pensées and the Provincial Letters*, trans. W.F. Trotter and Thomas M'Crie (New York: Modern Library, 1941).

in a project that is essentially prophetic in its sensibilities—as the torture memos show.

A careful reading of the memos reveals that their ultimate form of self-justification is broadly prophetic, not deliberative in nature. Understandably, the sense of urgency about the war on terror pervades the memos. Undergirding the legal analysis in the memos is a vision of conflicting fundamental moral values between America and her enemies that is highly characteristic of prophetic discourse. It is that prophetic vision that propels the memos' use of a distorted form of casuistry to clear the way to employ any means necessary in fighting America's terrorist opponents. Accordingly, the persuasive power in the torture memos does not come from the elaborate legal analysis itself. Instead, it stems from the underlying imperative for national survival against the threat of a merciless enemy.

For example, consider Bybee's justification of nearly limitless presidential power in prosecuting the war on terror in the August 1 memo.[52] He does not tell his readers what would be gained by a decision to authorize a broader range of interrogation techniques; indeed, it is questionable whether techniques verging on torture are even effective means of obtaining information. Instead, he presents his readers with the specter of what might be lost if interrogators do not have all necessary means at their disposal. After recounting the acts and objectives of al-Qaeda, most prominently, the attacks on September 11, 2001, Bybee then proceeds to suggest that engaging in aggressive, and possibly torturous, interrogation techniques may be necessary to preserve the nation itself:

> Interrogation of captured al Qaeda operatives may provide information concerning the nature of al Qaeda plans and the identities of its personnel, which may prove invaluable in preventing further direct attacks on the United States and its citizens. Given the massive destruction and loss of life caused by the September 11 attacks, it is reasonable to believe that information gained from al Qaeda personnel could prevent attacks of a similar (if not greater) magnitude from occurring in the United States.[53]

52. Bybee, August 1 memo, 200–207.
53. Ibid., 201–2.

On this basis, Bybee goes on to argue that "the President enjoys complete discretion in the exercise of his Commander-in-Chief authority and in conducting operations against hostile forces."[54] If interrogators acting pursuant to a presidential directive were to be charged with a violation of Section 2340A's strictures against torture, they might appropriately invoke the defenses of necessity or self-defense—which expands to include defense of country.

The normative substratum of Bybee's legal analysis presents al-Qaeda as an enemy that must be defeated at all costs. It is a substratum characteristic of prophetic indictment, resonating with those sections of the prophetic books commonly referred to as the oracles against the nations.[55] The prophets of Israel and Judah not only condemned their own people for faithlessness and moral ruin, they also chastised the pagan nations who were the enemies of the Jewish people. It is instructive, for example, to consider the oracles against Babylon in the biblical books of Isaiah and Jeremiah.[56] Consider the following passage from Isaiah, which is directed against the king of Babylon:

> All the kings of the nation lie in glory,
>> each in his own tomb;
> but you are cast out, away from your grave,
>> like loathsome carrion,
> clothed with the dead, those pierced by the sword,
>> who go down to the stones of the Pit,
>> like a corpse trampled underfoot.
> You will not be joined with them in burial
>> because you have destroyed your land,
>> you have killed your people.

54. Ibid., 202.

55. See, for example, Isaiah 13–23, Jeremiah 46–51, Ezekiel 25–32, and Amos 1–2. Contemporary biblical scholars take pains to point out how the oracles against the nations were shaped by those editing the canonical texts "to modify the negative attitude of these oracles and to open them up more favorably toward the nations." Carroll Stuhlmueller, "The Major Prophets, Baruch, and Lamentations," in Donald Senior, gen. ed., *The Catholic Study Bible* (New York: Oxford University Press, 1990), RG 293.

56. Jerusalem, the capital of Judah, fell to Nebuchadnezzar II, king of Babylon, in 587 BCE. The Temple and the city were destroyed, and many Jews were exiled to Babylon. Judah lost its status as a sovereign state and became a Babylonian province.

> May the descendants of evildoers,
>> nevermore be named!
> Prepare slaughter for his sons
>> because of the guilt of their father.
> Let them never rise to possess the earth,
>> or cover the face of the world with cities.[57]

On the basis of the "severity of the critique," biblical scholar David L. Peteresen argues that these verses against the king of Babylon were likely inspired by Babylon's total destruction of Judah (under King Nebuchadnezzar) in the sixth century BCE.[58] Over twenty-five centuries later, the words aptly capture the underlying attitude of the torture memos toward Osama bin Laden and al-Qaeda. Bin Laden was a leader of a tightly knit organization bent on destruction of the United States; he was "like loathsome carrion" as a leader. We must be willing to deal harshly with his ideological "sons," lest they "rise to possess the earth."

In light of the prophetic oracle against the nations in the August 1 memo, its strained analysis becomes more intelligible. The president of the United States must have unfettered discretion in using any means necessary to defeat this new "king of Babylon," Osama bin Laden. The memo simply clears away the legal brambles that may hamper "[t]he President's constitutional power to protect the security of the United States and the lives and safety of its people."[59]

The fact that the distorted form of casuistry practiced by the torture memos is actually motivated by a prophetic worldview gives us, I think, insight into one reason why some of torture's prophetic opponents chose not to parse the arguments and expose the false assumptions in the torture memos. If one's interlocutor is not actually engaged in moral and legal deliberation, that is, in the honest effort to determine what is to be done in a particular case, then it makes no sense to offer a deliberative response to them. Effectively countering their arguments requires unmasking and critiquing the prophetic stance that motivates them.

---

57. Isaiah 14:18–21.

58. David L. Petersen, *The Prophetic Literature: An Introduction* (Louisville, KY: Westminster John Knox Press, 2002), 57.

59. Bybee, August 1 memo, 204.

Toward a More Fruitful Relationship

Is there a way to move beyond the apparent impasse between deliberative discourse and prophecy? What would moving around this impasse require? Can we articulate the conditions under which each mode of discourse is appropriate? It seems to me that, in order to answer these questions, we need first to take a step backward and attempt to articulate the fundamental purposes of each mode of discourse.

What is the purpose of deliberative discourse? Fundamentally, it is an aspect of practical reasoning. It is an effort to discern the appropriate course of action in the case at hand by taking account of what has been judged the appropriate course of action in similar cases. Practical reasoning is our ordinary way of proceeding in the face of the countless decisions we must make every day, decisions that have concrete moral implications. We deliberate about the decision facing us by describing the relevant particular facts and general situation, by framing the relevant moral principles and action guides, and by comparing the case at hand to comparable cases faced by others or ourselves on previous occasions.

Because deliberative discourse is an aspect of practical reasoning, those who hope to practice it well must possess the virtues characteristically associated with good practical reasoning. Chief among these, according to Aquinas (and Aristotle), is the virtue of prudence—right reason with respect to things to be done. It is the practice of moral deliberation by one who is bereft of prudence and its associated virtues that gives it a bad name. More specifically, there are two situations in which deliberative discourse tends to go wrong. First, moral deliberation can be employed disingenuously. By "disingenuous" I mean that the one employing deliberative tools only appears to be engaged in a form of practical reasoning. In reality, such a person is not in fact committed to moral discernment in this particular case but is using its trappings to justify a decision that was reached on other grounds. I have argued above that prophets can misuse deliberative reasoning for such a purpose. That, in fact, was the central problem in the torture memos. Prophets are not, however, the only culprits. Any of us can misuse deliberative reasoning when we attempt to rationalize post hoc a decision that we have actually reached previously and purely on other grounds (such as fear or some other untutored passion).

A second situation in which moral deliberation can go terribly wrong is when it is engaged in by someone whose practical reasoning is distorted in a morally significant way. In such cases, unlike in the former class of cases, the practitioner of deliberative discourse is genuinely attempting to employ practical reason in order to consider the moral implications of a particular course of action. The attempt is doomed from the start, however, because some of the assumptions and perceptions that shape and guide the agent's process of practical reasoning are skewed. Unfortunately, skewed assumptions and perceptions do not generally remain localized in their effect; they have a way of infecting the whole of one's moral analysis.

How, specifically, can the process of practical reasoning be morally distorted? Answering this question requires particular attention to the virtues associated with prudence: *euboulia, synesis,* and *gnome.*[60] Agents who do not possess the virtue of *euboulia* are not disposed to take good counsel or, more particularly, to inform themselves about the relevant facts affecting the decision at hand. It is tempting to rely on a familiar, comfortable version of "the way things are" rather than to incorporate the best available information into one's decision-making process. Agents who do not possess the virtue of *synesis* are not disposed to perceive a situation just as it is in reality. In some cases, that can mean completely missing a fundamental component of the moral terrain; for example, failing to see that African Americans are equal members of the human community.[61] In other cases, it can mean appreciating the full

60. Thomas Aquinas, *Summa Theologica,* 5 vols., trans. Fathers of the English Dominican Province (New York: Benzinger Bros., 1948), II-II, q. 51. As Aquinas recognized, prudence and its associated virtues can be eroded significantly by sin. A full examination of how sin (both personal and social) corrodes moral perception is beyond the scope of this book.

61. For a powerful account of a situation in which a morally flawed assumption pervasively infected deliberative reasoning in the legal context, see John T. Noonan, Jr., *The Antelope: The Ordeal of the Recaptured Africans in the Administrations of James Monroe and John Quincy Adams* (Berkeley: University of California Press, 1977), which chronicles the fate of a group of stolen slaves held captive on a ship named *The Antelope.* After the ship was captured off the coast of Florida, an international dispute arose over the fate of the slaves, eventually ending up in the Supreme Court of the United States. In his opinion for the Court, Chief Justice Marshall admitted that slavery and the slave trade were contrary to the law of nature, but he also found that they were prohibited by no positive national or international law—a decision that permitted the slaves to be classified as property. The only question for the courts to determine was the monetary compensation deserved by the various claimants for the loss of such property. It would be wrong to say that Marshall did not recognize the humanity of the slaves—in one sense, he clearly did. Yet he failed to allow that recognition to exert its proper influence in his reasoning process; he failed, in other words, to recognize what it would mean to honor that humanity in deciding the concrete legal dispute before him. In Noonan's terms, one could

ramifications of such a component. For example, for approximately a century, the state of Virginia officially acknowledged the full humanity of African
Americans while failing to realize that their laws against miscegenation were
inconsistent with that acknowledgment.[62] Finally, agents who do not possess
the virtue of *gnome* are not able to identify a truly exceptional situation accurately or to judge correctly what the exceptional nature of the situation does
and does not justify them in doing. For example, being in a state of war with
another country creates an exceptional situation. While that exceptional situation may justify a decision not to return property or other resources that will
be used in the enemy war effort,[63] it does not justify suspending the moral
rule against intentional killing of the innocent.[64]

We cannot do without moral deliberation about how to act in concrete
cases. Moreover, we cannot deny the significant potential for such reasoning
to go awry in the ways that I described above. What can be done to put the
discussion on the right track? One remedy is prophetic indictment, at least in
dire cases. To explain how this can be the case, we need to consider the function of prophetic indictment, especially with respect to practical reason.

One thing we may say for certain: Whatever else prophecy may be, it is
essentially *not* moral deliberation. Turning first to the biblical prophets as a
touchstone for the genre in Western culture, it is clear that the *sole* qualification
for being a prophet is being called by God to prophesy. Philosophical acumen

---

say that the prevailing legal framework created masks (in Latin, *personae*) that obscured the faces of
the persons (also, in Latin, *personae*) whose lives Marshall disposed of as chattel property. See John T.
Noonan, Jr., *Persons and Masks of the Law: Cardozo, Holmes, Jefferson, and Wythe as Makers of the Masks*,
2nd ed. (Berkeley: University of California Press, 2002), chap. 1.

62. *Loving v. Virginia*, 388 U.S. 1 (1967).

63. "Now it happens sometimes that something has to be done which is not covered by the
common rules of actions, for instance in the case of the enemy of one's country, when it would be
wrong to give him back his deposit, or in other similar cases. Hence it is necessary to judge of such
matters according to higher principles than the common laws, according to which σύνεσις [*synesis*]
judges: and corresponding to such higher principles it is necessary to have a higher virtue of judgment, which is called νώμη [*gnome*], and which denotes a certain discrimination in judgment."
Aquinas, *Summa Theologica*, II-II, q. 51, art. 4.

64. "[I]t is in no way lawful to slay the innocent." Ibid., II-II, q. 64, art. 6. But note that Aquinas admits
that under certain circumstances, a judge must pronounce sentence and an executioner must carry out
the sentence against a man whom he knows to be innocent. The judge "does not sin if he pronounce
sentence in accordance with the evidence, for it is not he that puts the innocent man to death, but they
who stated him to be guilty." Ibid., II-II, q. 64, art. 6, rep. ob. 3. Aquinas's qualification is an attempt to
reach a deeper understanding of what it means—and what it does not mean—to "slay the innocent."

and practical wisdom are not job requirements for prophets.[65] Prophets do not in the first instance deliberate about the content of their prophetic utterances; rather, they respond to God's command regarding that content.

What about the audience? The fundamental response that the prophet seeks to evoke in his audience is obedience—he urges them to comply with God's demand. A prophet does not encourage his listeners to pay attention to the dictates of their own practical reason, for it is by following those (mistaken) dictates that they have strayed so far from compliance with divine will. The audience's sole task is to decide whether the person claiming the mantle of a prophet is in fact who he claims to be. Once that decision is made affirmatively, the need for deliberative reasoning is diminished, if not entirely eliminated, with respect to the subject matter of the prophecy. One does not quibble with the word of God; one obeys it.

More specifically, accepting a person as a true prophet entails admitting that he is reliably transmitting a message from God. Consequently, there is no room to negotiate and no reason to introduce additional considerations that could only dilute one's commitment to following the divinely mandated course of action. Compliance, not deliberation and discussion, is the order of the day. By contrast, rejecting a prophet's message inevitably entails rejecting *him*, or at least a crucial part of his avowed identity. Repudiating the self-proclaimed messenger is itself a denial of his claim to be a faithful and accurate assistant of God. In so doing, one implicitly suggests that he is either a liar or deeply self-deceived. The purported prophet will be reluctant to pursue a discussion with interlocutors whom he believes to be attacking his character or mental stability, while the interlocutors will not likely believe it worthwhile to engage in prolonged discussion with someone they believe to be duplicitous or unbalanced.

Of course, not everyone who employs prophetic discourse claims to be a true prophet, in the sense of claiming literally to be delivering a message from God. Nonetheless, it strikes me that those who invoke prophetic rhetoric to address a particular issue create the very same limitations on discourse that

65. For example, the prophet Amos was a breeder of livestock and a tender of mulberry figs. Michael L. Barré, S.S., "Amos," in Raymond E. Brown, S.S., Joseph A. Fitzmayer, S.J., and Roland E. Murphy, O.Carm., eds., *The New Jerome Biblical Commentary*, (Englewood Cliffs, NJ: Prentice Hall, 1990) 209. Jeremiah was a "native of a small village" and "heir of a declassed priesthood"—he was likely viewed as a marginal figure by those in Jerusalem. See Petersen, *The Prophetic Literature*, 98.

were produced by the biblical prophets. This fact should not be surprising. While those availing themselves of prophetic rhetoric may not claim to be delivering a message from God word for word, they frequently do claim to be proclaiming God's unequivocal will about a particular matter facing their society. The dividing line between being a messenger of God on the one hand and standing in the tradition of the messengers of God on the other is not as sharp as one might think.[66]

As I have emphasized throughout this book, few of those who employ prophetic discourse in our own time claim literally to be prophets. In fact, most Christian communities would look upon such a claim with great suspicion. Yet the nature and function of prophetic discourse is much the same, whether it is employed by true prophets or by those who "functionally" stand in their footsteps. This is the case because the fundamental point of the message preserved in the prophetic books of Scripture is not innovative, but strives to reinvigorate the root commitments of the community. The Hebrew prophets called upon their fellow Jews to reaffirm their fundamental values, even as they confronted the challenges of new situations as a people. Many of those who now stand in the rhetorical shoes of the biblical prophets are convinced that those commitments and values are unchangeable. In their own view, they do not need to be the recipient of a direct message from God in order to appropriate prophetic themes and tropes in order to confront the moral cancer afflicting their communities.

If prophecy is decidedly not practical reason, how should we describe its relationship with practical reason? In my view, one way it can be viewed is as a kind of *moral chemotherapy*. It is a brutal but necessary response to aggressive forms of moral malignancy, whose uncontrolled growth threatens to corrupt practical reasoning and ultimately to destroy the very possibility of it. More specifically, as I argued above, the practice of moral deliberation can go wrong in a number of ways. It can be practiced in a disingenuous manner; it

66. Abraham Joshua Heschel reminds us that even the biblical prophets did not mechanically transmit God's word in a manner that eliminated their own personal agency: "The prophet is a person, not a microphone. He is endowed with a mission, with the power of a word not his own that accounts for his greatness—but also with temperament, concern, character, and individuality. As there was no resisting the impact of divine inspiration, so at times there was no resisting the vortex of his own temperament. The word of God reverberated in the voice of man." Abraham J. Heschel, *The Prophets* (New York: HarperCollins, 2001), xxii.

can be practiced with distorted assumptions about the nature of reality, or with skewed perception of the importance of the moral values at stake.

If severe enough, these distorted assumptions and skewed perceptions plague moral reasoning like a cancer, causing it to develop and unfold in contorted ways. The rhetoric of prophetic indictment aims its destructive force at the moral cancer, with the ultimate goal of restoring the possibility of the healthy exercise of practical reasoning. How does it function? By destroying the diseased moral reasoning and promoting healthy regrowth based on a secure connection with fundamental religious and moral truths, which alone can serve as the basis for sound practical reasoning.

Again, it is instructive to turn to the biblical prophets for concrete examples. When they chastise the Jewish people, they do so primarily because of Israel's faithlessness, calling upon their fellows to recover the constitutive elements of their identity, particularly the primacy and exclusiveness of the relationship between Yahweh and Israel. The terms of that relationship are articulated most fully in the covenant given to Moses on Mount Sinai. Although the Hebrew prophets focus a significant amount of attention on individual actions or classes of action that exemplify the faithlessness of the Jews to Yahweh, they characteristically do not view those actions as the locus of the exercise of practical reason. Instead, they see them as the symptoms of a moral and spiritual disease that must be eliminated at the root.

For example, the biblical prophets regularly preached against idolatry as the root of all evils suffered and committed by the Israelites. By committing idolatry, the Israelites did not merely raise the suspicion that their practical reasoning was flawed in a localized or occasional manner. Instead, they conclusively demonstrated that they did not even possess the necessary preconditions for the reliable exercise of practical reason. By committing idolatry, the Israelites made manifest the fact that they had obliterated their consciousness of Yahweh's very identity as the one true God and of their own identity as Yahweh's chosen people.

The Book of Hosea furnishes a good case study. As Abraham Joshua Heschel has noted, during the time of Hosea (the mid-eighth century BCE), the people of the Northern Kingdom of Israel could be found worshipping in the Canaanite cult of Baal, without entirely abandoning their devotion to Yahweh. Hosea depicts Israel's lack of faithfulness to the one true God as a type of adultery. He vividly evokes Yahweh's hurt and anger at this betrayal, as well as Yahweh's enduring desire for reconciliation with His people. The evocative nature of his language is attributable in part to the prophet's own agonized experience of marriage to his beloved but serially unfaithful wife Gomer, whom God commanded him to marry.[67]

Consider, for instance, the passage in Hosea where Yahweh expresses his rage at his people for their betrayal:

> Yet I have been the LORD your God
>   ever since the land of Egypt;
> you know no God but me,
>   and besides me there is no savior.
> It was I who fed you in the wilderness,
>   in the land of drought.
> When I fed them, they were satisfied;
>   they were satisfied, and their heart was proud;
>   therefore they forgot me.
> So I will become like a lion to them,
>   like a leopard I will lurk beside the way.
> I will fall upon them like a bear robbed of her cubs,
>   and will tear open the covering of their heart;
> there I will devour them like a lion,
>   as a wild animal would mangle them.[68]

Understandably, in this context, Hosea evinces no interest in discerning the finer points of what precisely constitutes idolatry. Such a discussion would presume the ability of the participants to engage in an undistorted form of practical reasoning, the very ability that had been destroyed by the Israelites' indifference to the exclusiveness of the claims of the one true God. In another time and place, however, such a deliberative discussion would not be out of order, as St. Paul's nuanced assessment of eating meat sacrificed to idols indicates.[69]

---

67. Hosea 1:2–3.
68. Hosea 13:4–8. See Heschel, *The Prophets*, 55–58.
69. See 1 Corinthians 8:4–9:

> Hence, as to the eating of food offered to idols, we know that "no idol in the world really exists," and that "there is no God but one." Indeed, even though there may be so-called gods in heaven or on earth—as in fact there are many gods and many lords—yet for us there is one

Chemotherapy can be dangerous. It kills healthy cells as well as diseased ones. To improve the overall health of the patient, therefore, it must be used both accurately and sparingly. The same can be said of the moral chemotherapy of prophetic discourse. More specifically, as I argued earlier, the use of prophetic language in a particular context disrupts the normal functioning of a deliberative community. It renders the normal interactions of mutual reason giving impossible because the audience's only avenues of response to a prophetic statement are either to acquiesce to the prophet's demands or to engage in what amounts to an ad hominem attack. Prophets, therefore, need to acknowledge and take responsibility for the troublesome side effects of their moral chemotherapy. For example, an additional problem with the torture memos is that they obscure what is really at stake rhetorically. By cloaking his prophetic impulse under a battery of legal reasoning, Bybee delivered his version of moral chemotherapy disguised as a saline drip.

Close analysis of the rhetoric around both abortion and torture cases reveal that it is a mistake to present prophecy and moral deliberation as forms of discourse that are hermetically sealed from one another. In fact, they frequently relate to one another in complicated and unhealthy ways, each attempting to conscript the other as a means to its own ends. That does not mean, however, that they are doomed to exist in a fruitless relationship with each other. There is a way to frame their relationship more productively, if not always less contentiously.

Moral deliberation—as a form of practical reasoning—is our basic and ordinary moral language. It provides the framework for the countless decisions we make every day, which can have a range of implications for our moral life. Prophetic rhetoric is, by its very nature, an extraordinary form of moral discourse; its purpose is not to replace moral deliberation but to return it to health. I have just suggested that we view the language of prophetic indictment as a type of moral chemotherapy. It takes aim at morally cancerous assumptions or perspectives that threaten to destroy the possibility of

---

God, the Father, from whom are all things and for whom we exist, and one Lord, Jesus Christ, through whom are all things and through whom we exist.

It is not everyone, however, who has this knowledge. Since some have become so accustomed to idols until now, they still think of the food they eat as food offered to an idol; and their conscience, being weak, is defiled. "Food will not bring us close to God." We are no worse off if we do not eat, and no better off if we do. But take care that this liberty of yours does not somehow become a stumbling block to the weak.

reliable practical reasoning within a particular community at a particular time. Like chemotherapy, prophetic rhetoric of indictment is inherently destructive, but in service of an ultimately constructive purpose: The goal of prophetic rhetoric is the reestablishment of a healthy, functioning political context for moral deliberation and decision. Yet the destructive aspects of prophetic discourse on the body politic are not negligible, any more than are the deleterious effects of an intensive course of chemotherapy on the human body. Those considering whether or not to invoke prophetic discourse to make their point in a particular instance do well to consider whether the cure will cause more harm than the disease.

IV

TOWARD AN ETHIC
OF PROPHETIC RHETORIC

COMPASSIONATE AND HUMBLE

TRUTH TELLING

Best Practices

Styles of Prophetic Indictment

If a person is truly and actually a prophet, he or she has been called directly by God and commanded to deliver a particular message to a specific group of people. No other human being will be in a position to critique the fitness of the messenger, the content of the message, or the rhetorical framework deployed in order to deliver that message. God's call and command renders all such critiques beside the point—at least to those who see themselves as authoritative conduits of the divine will.

Most of the time, however, the people who employ prophetic rhetoric do not claim to be prophets. They are simply following in the rhetorical footsteps of the prophets. They are making a choice, on a purely human level, to draw on a well-established tradition of prophetic discourse in order to communicate their moral or political point. In other words, their decision to use the rhetoric of prophetic indictment is a deliberate human action and, as such, is subject to moral evaluation. In this chapter, I attempt to develop a normative framework to guide and assess the choice of speakers to avail themselves of a rhetorical pattern of prophetic indictment in the public square. My purpose here is *not* to justify any kind of legal constraints upon public speech of a political nature. My goal is to formulate criteria that citizens and activists can use in scrutinizing the fruitfulness of their own interventions or in evaluating the interventions of others.

The normative framework I propose takes due account of the fact that, in the United States, the rhetoric of prophetic indictment is historically grounded in Puritan political and religious speech, and so has its most important and illustrious representatives in the Protestant tradition. For example, I will propose that the more recent gold standard of the rhetoric of prophetic indictment is Martin Luther King, Jr., whose civil rights activism was deeply shaped by his identity as a Baptist preacher. Of course, one does not have to be a Protestant minister to deploy the rhetoric of the jeremiad.[1] Nonetheless, attention to the Protestant, Puritan roots of the rhetoric of prophetic indictment can be extremely helpful in developing criteria for its fruitful use in the contemporary context. At the same time, it would be foolish to develop an ethics of prophetic indictment that ignores the substantial developments in the genre over the past two centuries.[2] Cotton Mather's jeremiad is not ours, nor for that matter is our culture that of seventeenth-century Massachusetts.

How, then, to proceed? The first section is an effort to grapple with the legal structure of the jeremiad. I draw upon the discipline of legal ethics to consider when it is appropriate for prosecutors to ask a grand jury to issue an indictment. This question highlights the strong connection between the covenant and the jeremiad that structured much political sermonizing in colonial Massachusetts. It also reminds potential jeremiahs in our own time that prophetic discourse is not rightly construed merely as an emphatic way of making a deliberative point; rather, it stems from a different genre entirely. The jeremiad's roots are in forensic, rather than deliberative, discourse.

Of course, it is impossible to cabin today's jeremiad within the tight constraints observed in the sermons of second-generation Massachusetts Puritans. The jeremiad long ago expanded far beyond those constraints. No longer merely a tool to decry social backsliding, it has become a powerful megaphone demanding social change. This is not to say that no continuity can be

---

1. See, for example, the case studies in David Howard-Pitney, *The African American Jeremiad: Appeals for Justice in America*, rev. ed. (Philadelphia, PA: Temple University Press, 2005); and James Darsey, *The Prophetic Tradition and Radical Rhetoric in America* (New York: New York University Press, 1997).

2. Andrew Murphy argues that the progressive strand in the practice of the jeremiad, which appeals to foundational ideals of liberation and equality, is more able to expand to include a wider range of people. In contrast, he argues that the traditionalist strand, which emphasizes moral decline from past practices, "remains imprisoned in an exclusionary 'Judeo-Christian' paradigm—more specifically, in a white European Judeo-Christian paradigm, one that ignores the ever-increasing diversity *within* American Christianity itself, not to mention American society at large—that makes it difficult to see how non-Christian religions can be both radically unique and wholly American." Andrew R. Murphy, *Prodigal Nation: Moral Decline and Divine Punishment from New England to 9/11* (New York: Oxford University Press, 2009), 168 (original emphasis).

found between the older and newer forms of the jeremiad; even far-reaching calls for social reform often can be configured as radical commitment to our nation's deepest values. An effective ethics of prophetic discourse must grapple, with the broader potential for transformation and disruption associated with the contemporary use of the jeremiad. Given American history subsequent to the Puritans, it must also take into account the relationship between the jeremiad and warfare, particularly the discourse surrounding the Civil War. We saw, for example, how dueling jeremiads accompanied, even if they did not cause, armed conflicts between Americans of sharply different views at the time of the Revolutionary and Civil wars. Despite very real differences, I think that contemporary prophetic rhetoric—which can be characterized as verbal warfare—is in significant respects analogous to actual warfare. I therefore propose in the second section to adapt the just war theory in order to develop substantive criteria for "just prophecy" in the second section of this chapter.

The deepest and most influential roots of the jeremiad are not in Puritan sermons but in their sources—the Jewish and Christian Scriptures. In the third section, I turn to the Bible and biblical scholarship in order to glean rhetorical criteria for the ethical use of prophetic discourse in our society. In the final section, to give some specificity to my proposals, I compare and contrast two examples of modern prophetic discourse: Martin Luther King's "I Have a Dream" speech and Father Frank Pavone's "Open Letter to Michael Schiavo." The task is to learn from both Pavone's rhetorical deficiencies and King's rhetorical achievements.

Procedural Constraints

As R. Michael Cassidy, the author of the leading textbook on prosecutorial ethics, emphasizes, the decision to set in motion the legal apparatus of the state against a particular person or group of persons is not to be made cavalierly: "Through the single stroke of a pen in signing an indictment, the prosecutor literally has the capacity to ruin lives and reputations in a fashion that no subsequent acquittal can remedy."[3] While a prophetic indictment does not have the same tangible repercussions for its targets that an actual criminal

3. R. Michael Cassidy, *Prosecutorial Ethics*, 2nd ed. (St. Paul, MN: Thomson Reuters, 2013), 4.

indictment does, prophetic indictments do charge their targets with violating the basic commitments of our society. Except in extreme cases, they do not ruin lives in the manner of actual indictments, although they can tar reputations. Other analogies can be drawn. Just as abuse of prosecutorial discretion disturbs the common good by undermining the integrity of the justice system, so too does abuse of prophetic discretion distort the political conversation by usurping the rightful sphere for deliberative discourse. Their important differences notwithstanding, it is possible to draw a few lessons for the appropriate use of rhetorical indictments from the norms governing actual legal indictments.

GRAND JURIES

The Fifth Amendment to the U.S. Constitution provides in part: "No person shall be held to answer for a capital, or otherwise infamous crime, unless on a presentment[4] or indictment of a Grand Jury, except in cases arising in the land or naval forces, or in the Militia, when in actual service in time of War or public danger."[5] In the federal system, a grand jury is composed of sixteen to twenty-three individuals who are impaneled under the direction of the jurisdiction's presiding judge.[6] Guided by the prosecutor, the grand jury considers witness testimony and documentary evidence, and decides whether or not sufficient cause exists to issue an indictment.

The case presented to the grand jury is one-sided and controlled entirely by the prosecutor. A grand jury may issue an indictment if, after viewing this one-sided evidence, "a majority of its members finds probable cause to believe that the defendant committed the crime in question." The probable cause bar is low.[7] Nonetheless, the requirement of indictment by grand jury serves a clear legal purpose: screening out prosecutions that are clearly motivated by

---

4. A presentment is a formal written charge returned by a grand jury on its own initiative, not in response to the prosecutor's request for a charge.

5. According to the Supreme Court, this provision applies only to federal crimes, not to state crimes. Consequently, many states now use procedures other than grand juries, such as requiring a prosecutor to have a hearing before a judge, to determine whether the legal standard for issuing an indictment is met. See *Hurtado v. California*, 110 U.S. 516 (1884).

6. The states have different requirements. For a list, see University of Dayton Law School, "Federal Grand Jury: Size of Grand Jury," http://campus.udayton.edu/~grandjur/stategj/sizegj.htm

7. Cassidy, *Prosecutorial Ethics*, 23. Cassidy discusses probable cause along with more stringent standards that have been proposed to govern indictments at 12–15.

malice or are obviously unjustified by the law or the facts. Moreover, the requirement serves an important but more nebulous social function. Because a grand jury is not *required* to issue an indictment, it can ensure that the prosecutor does not stray radically away from the mores of the people in whose name prosecutions are carried out. A prosecutor who attempted to revive a legal prohibition that has long since fallen into desuetude might well find his ambitions checked by the common sense (or better, communal sense) of the men and women who comprise the grand jury.

What bearing does the grand jury requirement in the case of criminal indictments have upon the proper use of prophetic indictments? It can and should have an indirect influence, not a direct relationship. The grand jury symbolizes and instantiates the fact that the indictment is not the act of the prosecutor working as an isolated individual advancing a personal vendetta. To indict a member of the community for a criminal violation is to act on behalf of that community, not as a solitary avenger pursuing her own vision of justice. While there is no grand jury requirement applicable to prophetic indictments, the deeper purposes that requirement serves are equally relevant. Would-be prophets ought to orient their normative claims toward the fundamental commitments of *their* political community, not the commitments of a utopian community existing only in their imaginations and hopes.

This task is admittedly more difficult given the evolution of the jeremiad to include advocacy for social change. But its importance is not diminished: If contemporary jeremiahs cannot connect their calls for reform to deep veins of the community's own values, they will be be perceived as cranks or radical revolutionaries, not prophets. A crucial difference between a prophet and a crank is that the former maintains a deep social commitment and connection that grounds his or her call for reform, while the latter's criticisms are rooted in a far less widely shared vision of the good community. At their most extreme, cranks indict the community not on the basis of their own fundamental values but on the basis of the norms furnished by an idiosyncratic utopian vision. Radical revolutionaries want to remove and replace society's foundations, which they believe to be irreparably cracked.

Not every call for social reform, at every point in the nation's history, is appropriately cast in prophetic terms. Some such calls are so far removed from the broad center of American moral commitments that it is imprudent

and counterproductive to frame them in the language of prophetic indictment. It is understandable why activists would be attracted to a prophetic
strategy; the adamant language quickly focuses attention on the issue of
most concern to them. But that focus dissipates just as quickly. First, many
members of the audience may not agree with the prophet's substantive position. Moreover, whether they agree or not, they may not see it as the kind of
issue appropriate for a prophetic stance. Second, for an activist to take a prophetic stance in this situation derails the deliberative discussion that is necessary at this point in the community's political and moral life.

In my view, animal rights, gun control, and climate change are three
pressing moral issues that are not now ripe for prophetic discourse. The reasons differ from case to case. American law and customs have long treated
animals as having an entirely different status from that of human beings. This
treatment is rooted in a particular understanding of the place of human
beings in the natural order. Before prophetic discourse is likely to be effective in changing our practices on this subject, an entirely different view of
the relationship of human and nonhuman animals has to gain significant
public traction.[8]

The issue of gun control has become urgent in light of the mass shootings that seem to be occurring with increasing frequency in the United
States.[9] At the same time, it is not amenable to prophetic indictment. Unlike
slavery, which from the beginning was a neuralgic moral issue subjected to an
uneasy compromise, the right to bear arms is widely seen as protected by the
Second Amendment to the Constitution.[10] Formulating a more vigorous
policy on gun control will depend on nuanced deliberative interpretations of
our fundamental law, not on prophetic denunciations based on it.[11]

8. See, for example, Cass R. Sunstein and Martha C. Nussbaum, eds., *Animal Rights: Current Debates and New Directions* (New York: Oxford University Press, 2004).

9. See Mark Follman, Gavin Aronsen, and Deanna Pan, "A Guide to Mass Shootings in America," *Mother Jones*, February 27, 2013, updated July 24, 2015, www.motherjones.com/politics/2012/07/mass-shootings-map.

10. For two recent Supreme Court cases affirming constitutional protection of the individual's right to bear arms, see *District of Columbia v. Heller*, 554 U.S. 570 (2008) and *McDonald v. City of Chicago*, 561 U.S. 742 (2010). Both cases were decided with 5 to 4 votes.

11. See, for example, Kristin A. Goss, *Disarmed: The Missing Movement for Gun Control in America* (Princeton, NJ: Princeton University Press, 2006).

At first glance, the escalating challenge of climate change seems made for prophetic indictment; indeed, it portends global catastrophe and chaos that amount to a secular apocalypse.[12] No one could dispute the moral imperative of avoiding such a catastrophe. The difficulty with addressing climate change by means of prophetic discourse is that the dispute, in large part, does not turn on moral disagreement or even indifference. It turns instead on a dispute about the underlying facts: Is global warming actually occurring or not? If it is occurring, is it preventable by human beings or not? These questions are quintessential matters for deliberative discourse and debate, not for prophetic discourse.[13]

TEMPTATIONS TO PROSECUTORIAL ABUSE

In the criminal justice system, the requirement of indictment by grand jury is also designed to deter certain kinds of prosecutorial abuse.[14] Prosecutors have an enormous amount of power and freedom in framing the charges that they bring against a particular party. Given the fact that the government's resources are not infinite, they cannot prosecute every crime that is committed. All prosecutors must exercise discretion in choosing which cases to pursue; their choices are appropriately based on the seriousness of the crime, the likelihood of proving it, and broader concerns about deterrence. Prosecutors can abuse their discretion, however, if their charging decisions are motivated by arbitrariness or vindictiveness, which is defined as pursuing those who attempted to vindicate other important constitutional rights.[15] They can also abuse their discretion if their prosecutorial program is determined primarily by their own political ambitions.

12. See, for example, *An Inconvenient Truth*, written by Al Gore, directed by Davis Guggenheim (Los Angeles, CA: Paramount, 2006), DVD. This film, which chronicles Al Gore's campaign to bring attention to global warming, won two Academy Awards, including the 2007 Academy Award for Best Documentary Feature.

13. See, for example, Andrew Dessler and Edward A. Parson, *The Science and Politics of Global Climate Change: A Guide to the Debate*, 2nd ed. (Cambridge: Cambridge University Press, 2010).

14. See, generally, Peter J. Henning, "Prosecutorial Misconduct in Grand Jury Investigations," *South Carolina Law Review* 51, no. 1 (1999): 1–61; and James F. Holderman and Charles B. Redfern, "Preindictment Prosecutorial Conduct in the Federal System Revisited," *Journal of Criminal Law and Criminology* 96, no. 2 (2005–2006): 527–58.

15. See Cassidy, *Prosecutorial Ethics*, chap. 2, "The Charging Decision." These abuses are difficult to prove, given the presumption of the prosecutor's good faith.

Before a charge is made, however, an investigation is conducted by police and other agents of the government. Unlike the minimal constraints upon prosecutors' actions with regard to obtaining indictments, the power of prosecutors to launch an investigation into any alleged criminal activity is nearly unchecked. Prosecutors have the ability to troll for charges, selecting particular *persons* for investigative scrutiny, rather than going after particular *crimes*, no matter who commits them. Even here, of course, matters are not simple. It is one thing to conduct a broad criminal investigation of a person widely known to be a mob boss; after all, the federal government managed to put Al Capone in prison only for income tax evasion, not for murder. It is another thing entirely, however, to use the government's investigative power to target and harass personal and political enemies.

Finally, prosecutors can abuse discretion in the manner in which they present their case to the grand jury. Many of the procedural protections that are present in the context of an actual criminal trial are absent from the indictment stage of the proceedings. There is no right to cross-examination.[16] Hearsay evidence is admissible in grand jury proceedings.[17] There is nothing to stop the prosecutor from presenting a highly tendentious version of the evidence. In fact, there is a controversy among legal ethicists about whether a prosecutor has a duty to present exculpatory evidence to the grand jury.[18] It is one thing for the prosecutor to convince the grand jury that there is probable cause to believe a crime has been committed, which justifies subjecting the defendant to the difficulties, expense, and distress of a trial. It is another thing entirely for a prosecutor to manipulate the grand jury by knowingly presenting an incomplete or distorted version of the evidence. Michael

16. Ibid., 33.

17. See ibid., 24–26. For example, in a criminal trial, the detective who observed the defendant break the window of the jewelry store would be subpoenaed to testify about what he saw. Defense counsel would then be able to cross-examine the detective. In the grand jury context, by contrast, the sergeant whom the detective told about the incident later that day could testify before the grand jury. No cross-examination would be permitted.

18. Ibid., 31–34. See also R. Michael Cassidy, "Toward a More Independent Grand Jury: Recasting and Enforcing the Prosecutor's Duty to Disclose Exculpatory Evidence," *Georgetown Journal of Legal Ethics* 13, no. 3 (2000): 361–403; and Thaddeus Hoffmeister, "The Grand Jury Legal Advisor: Resurrecting the Grand Jury's Shield," *Journal of Criminal Law and Criminology* 98, no. 4 (2008): 1171–30.

Cassidy rightly argues that the prosecutor has an obligation "to preserve the independence of the grand jury as a deliberative body."[19]

Here again, we can work by analogy to glean some guidelines for the appropriate use of prophetic indictments. As Chapter 7 observed, it can be tempting to use prophetic discourse in order to manipulate one's audience so that one can win an argument that may not be winnable purely on the basis of the reasons adduced. It can also be tempting to use prophetic indictment to magnify one's disagreements with political or personal enemies, casting them into the role of enemies of the nation's fundamental values in order to achieve a strategic advantage. Public intellectuals must resist these temptations in the rhetorical sphere, just as prosecutors must resist analogous temptations in the sphere of criminal justice. Both are abuses of the power of indictment.

It is exceedingly important for prosecutors to exhibit integrity in managing the factual basis of a case in which they seek a grand jury indictment. The same sort of integrity is also important in bringing a rhetorical indictment to the jury of public opinion. Those who deploy prophetic indictments in the public square characteristically charge that a certain social practice violates the basic law of the community. Like prosecutors, they also present the facts that support their charge, often in a very vivid manner. As earlier chapters showed, abolitionists, anti-torture activists, and abortion opponents muster searing descriptions and images as evidence that the targets of their indictment aare violating the nation's fundamental moral commitments.

What are the moral responsibilities of a prophet in presenting the factual basis of his or her case? Just as it is too much to expect a prosecutor to assume the mantle of a defense lawyer before the grand jury, so too we cannot expect that prophets will make the exculpatory case for their opponents in the public square. Nonetheless, we can expect them to refrain from outright lies or hoaxes. Moreover, while rhetorical indictments should have a clear and adamant point of view, prophets ought to refrain from sheer manipulation of their audiences. Examples of tactics that fall into this category include taking one isolated incident and blowing it out of proportion, airbrushing

19. Cassidy, *Prosecutorial Ethics*, 24.

or distorting photographic evidence, and presenting as the truth what are really unsubstantiated rumors about egregious activity on the part of one's opponents.

What, positively, might an appropriate relationship between prophetic indictment and the morally responsible use of evidence look like? Moving away from the North American scene, consider the example of Archbishop Oscar Romero of San Salvador, who was assassinated in 1980 in reaction to his persistent and unstinting critique of the mistreatment of the Salvadoran people by the government and the military.[20]

As Roberto Cuéllar, the executive director of the Interamerican Institute of Human Rights, has detailed, Romero's prophetic indictment was rooted in meticulous concern to establish the facts about the abuses committed by military and government officials.[21] In 1977, the year he was appointed archbishop of San Salvador, Romero began working with a legal aid group, Socorro Juridico, founded by a young group of Jesuit-trained lawyers. Over the next few years, Romero and Socorro Juridico defended the human rights of the poorest Salvadorans (campesinos) who were subject to abuse, torture, and "disappearance" for challenging the program of the government. In his weekly Sunday homilies, Romero did not merely denounce human rights abuses in general terms but he also related those abuses in specific detail. He did so by laying out the findings of the young lawyers from Socorro Juridico who traveled to investigate the veracity of the government's account of particular clashes of violence as well as to interview those whose friends and relatives had "disappeared." Cuéllar writes:

> Many of the events that Oscar Romero revealed in his homilies
> were grave human rights violations directed against the poorest

20. Romero is well on his way to becoming a saint officially recognized by the Roman Catholic Church. Pope Francis declared Romero a martyr in February 2015, clearing the way for his beatification, which took place in March that same year. For more about Romero's life, see, for example, Scott Wright, *Oscar Romero and the Communion of Saints: A Biography* (Maryknoll, NY: Orbis Books, 2009); and James R. Brockman, S.J., *Romero: A Life* (Maryknoll, NY: Orbis Books, 1989). A good place to start with Romero's own writings is Oscar Romero, *Voice of the Voiceless: The Four Pastoral Letters and Other Statements*, trans. Michael J. Walsh (Maryknoll, NY: Orbis Books, 1985).

21. Roberto Cuéllar, "Monseñor Oscar Romero: Human Rights Apostle," Romero Lecture (March 21, 2000), Kellogg Institute, University of Notre Dame, http://kellogg.nd.edu/romero/pdfs/humanrightsapostle.pdf. Many thanks to Craig Iffland, for suggesting that I consider Romero in this chapter and for bringing this important lecture to my attention.

Salvadorans. That an archbishop would publicly relate these deeds, often in great detail, resulted in something unprecedented. His was not a calculated gesture; it was his compassionate and indignant response to the national reality. It was the response of a humanist, a democrat, and a Christian. And, of course, there were very few who dared to make such a public response in the dangerous El Salvador of those years.[22]

Cuéllar goes on to note that Romero's denunciations of human rights abuses brought the attention of the international legal community, as well as a broad array of church groups. The well-grounded and specific nature of his factual allegations lent force to his prophetic indictments. Cuéllar observes:

Romero provided a constitutional framework for the defense of those human rights violated on a daily basis by the Salvadoran power structure. Using this perspective, he repeatedly pointed to the corruption of the law in El Salvador and emphasized the dangers that existed because the laws were not an expression of what they should be under "Just Law," a concept he referred to in many homilies in order to remind governments of what they had forgotten or—as in the case in El Salvador at that time—of what they had never learned: that the legitimate power to make laws, to legislate, belongs only to those who exercise it via the delegation of a sovereign people.[23]

Romero's persuasive power is in part attributable to the way in which he honored the deep legal structure of prophetic language. He did not denounce abuses of human rights in the abstract. He did not bend the truth to make a political point. Instead, he argued that specific instances of egregious behavior on the part of the government violated the community's most fundamental law.

22. Ibid., 6.
23. Ibid., 7.

A Virtuous Prosecutor

In a 1940 speech before federal prosecutors, U.S. Attorney General Robert H. Jackson, observed that "the qualities of a good prosecutor are as elusive and as impossible to define as those which mark a gentleman . . . The citizen's safety lies in the prosecutor who tempers zeal with human kindness, who seeks truth and not victims, who serves the law and not factional purposes, and who approaches his task with humility."[24] Jackson's observations can easily apply to prophets who bring their indictments in the public square. Consider first the idea that a prosecutor would temper zeal with kindness. What might that mean in the public square? Kindness towards political opponents means, at the very least, resisting the temptation to whip up the audience's hostility by proffering misleading statements and analogies. It might require, for instance, that prophets refrain from seizing upon badly worded statements of political enemies as evidence of their real motives. It might also require refusing an easy opportunity to treat a fringe element as a central example of an opponent's goals and methods. So, for example, to treat the murderous Philadelphia abortion doctor Kermit Gosnell as emblematic of the pro-choice movement would be untempered zealotry.[25] To treat homicidal activists like Scott Roeder, who killed an abortion doctor in a church service in Topeka, Kansas, as characteristic of the pro-life movement would equally be to engage in disordered prophetic denunciation.[26]

What use can virtuous prophets make of Jackson's proposal that the prosecutor should "seek truth and not victims," and ought to "serve the law and not factional purposes"? It seems to me that these two concerns are

24. Robert H. Jackson, "The Federal Prosecutor," speech delivered at the Second Annual Conference of United States Attorneys, Washington, DC, April 1, 1940, quoted in Cassidy, *Prosecutorial Ethics*, 1. Jackson went on to become an associate justice of the U.S. Supreme Court.

25. Kermit Gosnell, M.D., ran an abortion clinic in Philadelphia. In 2011, he was charged with eight counts of murder and several lesser offenses related to both his female patients and live-born infants that they delivered after botched abortions. In May 2013, Gosnell was convicted of three murder charges. He was sentenced to life in prison without parole, waiving his right to appeal in exchange for the state's agreement not to seek the death penalty. Jon Hurdle, "Doctor Starts His Life Term in Grisly Abortion Clinic Case," *New York Times*, May 16, 2013, A17.

26. Scott Roeder was convicted of first-degree murder for gunning down George R. Tiller in a church in Kansas. Tiller was one of the few doctors who performed late-term abortions in the United States. See Monica Davey, "Abortion Foe Is Found Guilty of First-Degree Murder in Doctor's Killing," *New York Times*, January 30, 2010, A12.

related in the case of prophetic indictment. Both point to the overriding need for prophets to measure their claims—and themselves—by their best conception of a law that promotes the good of the whole community. Using the rhetoric of prophetic indictment as a weapon to ravage personal, professional, or political opponents is actually to set oneself above the law by using it for private ends. Deploying prophetic indictment to serve the goals of political or social factions is actually far more divisive than the bitter rhetoric that characteristically conveys such indictments. Factionalist prophets pretend to honor a universal and generally applicable law while advancing narrow and particular interests and causes. It is a deeply cynical strategy, a strategy that undermines the very ground to which the prophet purports to appeal: the common aims and values that bind together his or her political or religious community.

Substantive Constraints

The purpose of prophetic indictments is to call attention, in the sharpest possible terms, to fundamental moral flaws in a given society or culture, flaws that threaten to undermine the basic tenets of the moral vision animating that society. Accordingly, the sharp language of prophetic speech is designed to pierce through layers of apathy and motivate the audience to repent, reform, and ameliorate the underlying situation. In ancient Israel, for example, the two basic flaws condemned by the prophets were idolatry and mistreatment of the poor.[27] This behavior, according to the biblical prophets, constituted a fundamental breach of the obligations of the Jews in their covenantal relationship with Yahweh. Prophetic language can be a necessary rhetorical tool to combat entrenched social evil in the community, to shake persons out of indifference, to direct scarce resources of attention and concern toward fundamental social issues rather than toward matters that wrongly seem to be more urgent. If an unjust situation has obtained in a particular society for a long while, it may well have become normalized. The harshness of prophetic language can serve as a necessary wakeup call to those who have become accustomed to a situation of grave immorality. At the same time, the fiery language of prophetic

27. See, for example, Gary A. Anderson, *Charity: The Place of the Poor in the Biblical Tradition* (New Haven, CT: Yale University Press, 2013).

indictment can be dangerous and destructive. As earlier chapters explored in
great detail, these destructive elements are present even in the most justifiable
instances of prophetic discourse, but the harm they cause is magnified when
prophetic indictments are used in situations that actually do not call for such
extreme rhetorical measures. How, then, should persons thinking about
whether they ought to use prophetic rhetoric to advance their moral and political goals structure their deliberation?

In the previous chapter, I offered a vivid metaphor for the interjection of
prophetic rhetoric in the public square, suggesting that it is akin to moral
chemotherapy. In actual chemotherapy, physicians introduce a substance into
the bodies of their patients in order to kill the cancers that threaten to kill
them. That substance is poisonous, however; in deciding whether to go ahead
with the treatment, oncologists need to evaluate whether the treatment will
destroy the patient before it destroys the disease. The chemotherapy metaphor is useful in that it focuses attention on the harm to the body politic that
accompanies all uses of prophetic rhetoric and therefore highlights the need
for responsible participants in the public square to engage in a cost–benefit
analysis before deploying the language of prophetic indictment. At the same
time, the metaphor is limited because it fails to highlight the full range of
moral considerations that prospective prophets need to consider.

A related metaphor may also help generate a more adequate normative
framework to guide deliberations about the use of prophetic rhetoric in the
public square. Many people have talked about chemotherapy as part of the
medical war on cancer, cancer that is itself aiming to destroy the patient's
body while trying his or her soul. Moral chemotherapy—prophetic rhetoric—is, or easily can become, the equivalent of verbal warfare, in large part
because it has come to configure the social and political arena as a culture
war. Drawing on the just war theory, part of the common normative patrimony of Western culture, might help us formulate an appropriate framework to evaluate the use of prophetic rhetoric. More specifically, a "just
prophecy" theory can tell us something about when and why it is appropriate
to deploy a sustained pattern of prophetic indictment in order to galvanize
public response to a perceived social problem. (I am not talking here about
the occasional use of such rhetoric but rather the regular attempt to frame a
particular issue in prophetic terms.)

Some might object that comparing war to prophetic discourse trivializes actual warfare. There are, of course, the enormous differences in lethality between verbal attacks and actual bombs and bullets.[28] But with suitable modifications, just war theory can nevertheless provide a fruitful way to consider the moral implications of using the rhetoric of prophetic indictment in the public square. In fact, moralists have appropriated and modified just war theory to assess the implications of other patterns of action whose potential benefit to society is inevitably accompanied by the threat of significant harm. Most notably, the distinguished moralist James F. Childress has developed a framework for analyzing the morality of civil disobedience that draws heavily upon the categories of just war theory.[29]

We can place civil war, civil disobedience, and civil protest in the form of prophetic indictment on a broad continuum marking a range of responses to entrenched forms of social injustice. In reverse order, they constitute graduated forms of resistance to societal wrongdoing. If prophetic indictment alone does not suffice to correct a problem, prophets may graduate to forms of direct and indirect civil disobedience. If civil disobedience does not ameliorate the situation, social activists will consider resorting to civil war to remedy the wrong. Needless to say, given the devastation it inflicts, the cases where war is reasonably perceived to be an appropriate response to entrenched social evil within a democracy are few; they are not however, nonexistent, as demonstrated in U.S. history by the American Revolution (a civil war) in the eighteenth century and the Civil War in the nineteenth century.[30]

While very different in the nature and degree of destructiveness that they inflict, prophetic indictment, civil disobedience, and armed conflict do share certain structural features that make the just war framework suitable for their

28. Yet I do not wish to deny all connection between religious rhetoric and violence. See John D. Carlson and Jonathan H. Ebel, eds., *From Jeremiad to Jihad: Religion, Violence, & America* (Berkeley: University of California Press, 2012). Furthermore, it is important to investigate the connection between the jeremiad, American exceptionalism, and the American empire. See, for example, Ian Tyrrell, *Reforming the World: The Creation of America's Moral Empire* (Princeton, NJ: Princeton University Press, 2010).

29. James F. Childress, *Civil Disobedience and Political Obligation: A Study in Christian Social Ethics* (New Haven, CT: Yale University Press, 1971).

30. Not everyone believes that the Revolutionary War was morally legitimate. See, for example, John Keown, "America's War for Independence: Just or Unjust?," *Journal of Catholic Social Thought* 6, no. 2 (2009): 277–304.

moral analysis.[31] First, all three activities have human *targets*. War is waged against a certain group of people who are executing a certain set of unjust plans. Their leaders, weapons, and military resources are selected for destruction. Civil disobedience also aims to combat a certain group of people with a problematic set of social goals, selecting its immediate targets for their practical or symbolic connection to those people and goals. So, for example, a group of antiwar activists known as the Catonsville Nine broke into government offices in Catonsville, Maryland, in order to burn draft cards that both symbolized and contributed to the Vietnam War they protested so adamantly. Similarly, prophetic indictments have targets: Speakers excoriate the individuals or classes of people whom they believe to be flouting or seriously undermining the fundamental moral law of the nation.

Second, all three practices seriously disturb the practices and rhythms of ordinary life. The disruption caused by the devastation of war is glaringly obvious. A moment's reflection reveals that both direct civil disobedience (such as a sit-in at a segregated lunch counter) and indirect civil disobedience (such as vandalism of government selective services offices) interrupt the normal courses of activity engaged in by workers, customers, and passersby. The disruption caused by a program of prophetic indictment is somewhat different; it does not take place in the physical world but in the realm of deliberation and discussion. Prophetic excoriation of certain practices impedes the normal flow of deliberative discourse; rather than placing barriers in the paths of activity, it places boulders in the paths of conversation. As we saw in Chapters 6 and 7, precisely because the only response that the issuer of a prophetic indictment will accept is repentance and reform, prophetic rhetoric displaces and discourages more nuanced and wide-ranging discussion. Furthermore, as evinced in the contemporary culture wars, the harshness of prophetic discourse dissuades those of a more tentative rhetorical temperament from taking their places in the public discussion.

Third, the moral evaluation of war, civil disobedience, and prophetic

31. I note, of course, that some religious traditions, including Christianity, have at some points in their history endorsed a "holy war"—a war waged principally to advance or defend what its adherents believe to be the true religion. While contemporary just war theorists reject the legitimacy of holy wars, the line between what counts as a just war and what counts as a holy war has not always been clear because moral and political values are infused with religious sensibilities. See, for example, Ioannis Stouraitis, "'Just War' and 'Holy War' in the Middle Ages: Rethinking Theory through the Byzantine Case-Study," *Jahrbuch der Österreichischen Byzantinistik* 62 (2012): 227–64.

indictment appears to involve a number of factors. These include not merely the considerations invoked by a cost–benefit analysis but also other factors, including a moral evaluation of the overall goal of the endeavor and an Zassessment of the means used to bring it about. Furthermore, the just war framework is capable of directing a nuanced consideration of both individual actions and the larger and more complex endeavor to which they contribute. Just as civil disobedience and waging war are not isolated, one-off activities, neither is the practice of prophetic indictment. Generally speaking, the *ius ad bellum* criteria assess the overall project, while the standards for *ius in bello* assist in evaluating particular actions and strategies. With some appropriate adaptation, they can assist us in formulating criteria for the just use of pro-phetic indictment in the public square—or to put it another way, the just engagement of verbal warfare (*bellum verborum*).[32]

Ius Ad Bellum Verborum

The seven commonly identified *ius ad bellum* factors are used to help evaluate whether a general decision to wage a particular war is justified. Suitably adapted, they can assist in discerning whether a general decision to launch a program of prophetic indictment is justified.

1. *Just Cause.* The first criterion is the most basic. Is the cause for which par-ticipants in the public square are contemplating disrupting the normal flow of practical deliberation truly just? This is a big question, and it is impossible to answer exhaustively here. It is possible to set down some guideposts, how-ever, based on the analysis in previous chapters. Chapters 6 and 7 chronicled several unjust reasons to deploy the rhetoric of prophetic indictment. It is not right, for example, to put on the mantle of a prophet simply in order to win a deliberative argument that until that point had not been going one's way. Such behavior is bullying; it is not prophecy.

It is also inappropriate to use what nineteenth-century English social critic Mathew Arnold called the "rhetoric of fire and strength" in order to

32. The literature on just war theory is voluminous. For a good introduction, see James Turner Johnson, *Morality and Contemporary Warfare* (New Haven, CT: Yale University Press, 1999). My list of the criteria for just war theory is taken from the U.S. Catholic bishops' pastoral letter on war and peace. See National Conference of Catholic Bishops, *The Challenge of Peace: God's Promise and Our Response* (Washington, DC: United States Catholic Conference, 1983).

settle prematurely a hard deliberative question that arises within a stable moral framework.[33] As Chapter 7 argued at length, even people who agree that each and every human being counts as an equally protectable person might disagree about precisely when an individual human being comes into existence. They may debate whether an individual human life begins at fertilization, or about a week later when it is no longer possible for a single fertilized egg to split into identical twins or to combine with another fertilized egg to form a chimera. Similarly, it is not appropriate to use prophetic rhetoric to debate whether a particular economic policy (e.g., minimum wage law) actually helps support a decent standard of living for all persons. People who agree that social justice requires developed countries such as the United States to make a decent standard of living available to everyone may disagree about the best method to achieve that objective.

Why is using prophetic indictment in these sorts of cases unjust? First, it short-circuits important factual debates with moral implications, the very heart of the subject matter covered by public practical deliberation. In the first instance, our assessment of when an individual human life begins (and ends) has generally been dependent upon the best insights of biology. The Aristotelian answer to this question was replaced in the mid-nineteenth century by the discovery of the union of the egg and the sperm in the process of fertilization. We cannot, however, freeze science at that particular point in time any more than we could freeze it in Aristotle's era. Ongoing discoveries of the complexities of the process of conception will rightly have ethical implications that merit good-faith debate and discussion. Similarly, the components of our national economic policy are not sacrosanct; an approach that worked well in the mid-twentieth century may not be as adequate in twenty-first-century globalized capitalism. Debate over these matters is a healthy part of democratic deliberation; it is not a sign of deep moral corruption and therefore is not a fit subject for prophetic indictment.

Second, the rhetoric of prophetic indictment is justified in suspending the ordinary process of deliberation and debate only when it is proceeding on the basis of one or more deeply flawed moral premises. In the two preceding

33. See Matthew Arnold, *Culture and Anarchy,* ed. Samuel Lipman (New Haven, CT: Yale University Press, 1994). Arnold differentiates between the language of Greek culture, essentially discursive reason, which he calls "sweetness and light," and the language of Hebraic culture, essentially prophetic indictment, which he calls "fire and strength."

examples, however, the disputants do not differ over fundamental moral premises; they differ over how to evaluate the factual situation to which those premises apply. One might object, of course, that the proposed distinction is unsound because it could be used to rule out clear cases of the appropriate use of prophetic rhetoric. History is full of cases where one group justified its abhorrent treatment of another group on the basis of the latter's "subhuman" status. Moreover, no assessment of facts is entirely value-neutral.[34]

Because space constraints prevent me from addressing this objection fully, I can only point here to key elements of an adequate response. First, there is a difference between a bad-faith assessment of a factual situation, which is often motivated by self-interest, and an honest response to emerging factual complexity. There is no reason why prophetic indictment is not appropriate in the first case. Second, there is such a thing, in my view, as moral progress— genuinely new insights into moral truths. Such progress is best secured by deliberative discussion rather than by deploying the rhetoric of prophetic indictment. So, for example, in our time, we take it for granted that native populations are fully equal in dignity to those newly settling their shores. The initial recognition of that truth, however, was secured not primarily by fiery jeremiads but rather by detailed moral-factual argumentation; consider, for example, Bartolomé de las Casas's painstaking refutation of Juan Ginés de Sepúlveda's argument that the natives of Central America did not merit full treatment as persons.[35] Third, the criteria for a fit subject for a jeremiad may well differ from era to era.

What, then, *are* the markers of a just cause for deploying the rhetoric of prophetic indictment in the public square? The Puritan roots of that rhetoric

34. For accounts of the treatment of Native Americans and African Americans, see, for example, David E. Stannard, *American Holocaust: The Conquest of the New World* (New York: Oxford University Press, 1992); and James Oliver Horton and Lois E. Horton, *Slavery and the Making of America* (New York: Oxford University Press, 2005).

35. For a summary of the debate, see Lewis Hanke, *All Mankind Is One: A Study of the Disputation between Bartolomé de Las Casas and Juan Ginés de Sepúlveda on the Religious and Intellectual Capacity of the American Indians* (DeKalb: Northern Illinois University Press, 1994). See also my reflections on this issue in M. Cathleen Kaveny, "Imagination, Virtue, and Human Rights: Lessons from Australian and U.S. Law," *Theological Studies* 70, no. 1 (2009): 109–39. David M. Lantigua did his doctoral dissertation on the topic: "Idolatry, War, and the Rights of Infidels: The Christian Legal Theory of Religious Toleration in the New World" (Ph.D. diss., University of Notre Dame, 2012). At the same time, it is important not to whitewash Las Casas. See, for example, Daniel Castro, *Another Face of Empire: Bartolomé de Las Casas, Indigenous Rights, and Ecclesiastical Imperialism* (Durham, NC: Duke University Press, 2007).

give us considerable guidance in identifying them. Prophetic rhetoric is rightly used to condemn what the speaker judges to be violations of the basic agreement on which this society is founded. In the Puritan era, that agreement was defined in terms of the national covenant. In our era, it is defined by basic constitutional values. Consequently, prophetic indictment is appropriately used in the public square to decry clear violations of those values. As I indicated earlier, who counts as an equally protectable member of the community—the human beings to whom constitutional protections apply—is an appropriate issue for prophetic indictment.

Not every constitutional question is fundamental. Moreover, not every question touching on a fundamental value justifies prophetic indictment. There are close questions around how best to promote and protect such values, as well as how to reconcile them with other, equally fundamental values. For example, in *Employment Division v. Smith* (1990)[36] the Supreme Court modified the constitutional test used to decide whether a governmental regulation violated the protections afforded to religious liberty; in so doing it significantly constricted the scope of the right. Although the decision may well have been wrong, it did not appropriately trigger prophetic indictment, for two reasons. First, the Court was not denying that religious liberty was an appropriate constitutional value. Second, it did not prevent that value from being protected in other ways, for example, through the legislative process.[37] Not everyone will, of course, agree on what constitutes a threat to a fundamental value. Still, this is a question prospective prophets ought to ask themselves before proceeding.

Reflecting on the nature of an indictment also suggests that prophetic denunciations are more appropriately used to shore up an existing fundamental moral consensus rather than to make a case for moral evolution. Strictly speaking, as we have seen, legal and quasi-legal indictments do not make any kind of a moral argument; instead, they proclaim the violation of an already existing law. It is possible, of course, to frame or to reframe a case for moral development as if it is actually a matter of ensuring consistency

36. *Employment Division v. Smith*, 494 U.S. 872 (1990).

37. Responding to *Smith*, in 1993 Congress passed the Religious Freedom Restoration Act (RFRA), which attempted to restore the more stringent standard previously in place. In the *City of Boerne v. Flores*, 521 U.S. 507 (1997), the Supreme Court struck down RFRA as unconstitutional as applied to the states. Many states, however, have enacted their own statutes to protect religious liberty.

with fundamental and long-standing values. And indeed, much sound moral development can be understood in this way. But articulating this new understanding is generally a matter for practical deliberation, not prophetic indictment. To put it another way, the language of moral indictment ought not to be the primary language for the development of new moral insights. It may be tempting to use it for these purposes; doing so may even be effective. At the same time, the use of prophetic indictment to produce a new consensus may in fact result only in a Pyrrhic victory. As noted in previous chapters, the language of indictment leaves precious little room for discussion, questioning, and debate about the norms it imposes. While it might intimidate opponents into silence, it will not allow them the opportunity to ask the questions that will bring about their internal assent and commitment to the innovative moral program in question.

A legal indictment takes for granted the legitimacy of the law it invokes and focuses attention on whether or not the defendant actually violated that law. That is a factual question. Accordingly, many powerfully justified rhetorical indictments have a strong factual component. So, for example, in pressing the case for desegregation, civil rights activists could point to decades of American history demonstrating that the "separate but equal" regime approved by *Plessy v. Ferguson* in 1896 was anything but equal.[38] That history undermines any claim that *Plessy* constituted a legitimate scheme to implement the civil rights amendments, clearing the way for prophetic indictment of segregation as inconsistent with the basic values of the Constitution.

The vigilant memory of our history, particularly its most shameful moments, also provides a helpful guide to legitimate invocations of prophetic rhetoric. The collective repentance for and repudiation of some of our nation's actions and policies can justify the use of prophetic indictment when it appears that we are heading down the same path in the present. For example, prophetic indictment would be justified if the United States adopted a mass internment program for a discrete group of U.S. citizens analogous to the internment of Japanese Americans in World War II.[39] Similarly, the

38. *Plessy v. Ferguson*, 163 U.S. 537 (1896). *Plessy* was reversed by *Brown v. Board of Education of Topeka*, 347 U.S. 483 (1954). See also, for example, Douglas A. Blackmon, *Slavery by Another Name: The Re-Enslavement of Black Americans from the Civil War to World War II* (New York: Doubleday, 2008).

39. See *Korematsu v. United States*, 323 U.S. 214 (1944), in which the Supreme Court upheld the constitutionality of such internment programs. In the 1980s, internment was proposed as a strategy

nation's shameful experience with involuntary sterilization[40] could ground the prophetic indictment in the event that a future political leader advocates a new eugenics program.[41]

2. *Competent Authority/Competent Stakeholders.* Just war theory requires the use of military force to be decided upon by those with responsibility for the nation.[42] Even in the case of civil wars, it demands that the decision be made by an organized group with both the ability and the will to establish public order, not by private groups acting on their own initiative. Private acts of violence, even for a just end, are rightly considered vigilantism, not legitimate acts of war. In the United States, the power to wage and conduct war ideally rests in a coordinated relationship between Congress and the president, in a system of checks and balances.[43] So too the decision to use prophetic rhetoric in the public square ought not to be the decision of an isolated individual or pundit. Those who use such rhetoric ought to be part of a network of communal leaders, formal or informal, that holds itself accountable—and the would-be prophet accountable—for contributing to the nation's discussion and discernment of the common good. Rather than a network of competent authority, it might be more accurate to say that the use of prophetic rhetoric necessitates a network of competent stakeholders.

Thanks in part to the work of Max Weber, we tend to think of the great biblical prophets as socially isolated figures speaking to their communities

---

to control the spread of HIV/AIDS. See, for example, Christopher Monckton, "AIDS: A British View," *American Spectator,* January 1987, 29–32, at 30. Monckton later became a leader in the climate change denial movement.

40. See *Buck v. Bell* 274 U.S. 200 (1927), in which the Supreme Court upheld the constitutionality of involuntary sterilization with a majority opinion authored by Oliver Wendell Holmes. Generally, see Paul A. Lombardo, ed., *A Century of Eugenics in America: From the Indiana Experiment to the Human Genome Era* (Bloomington: Indiana University Press, 2011).

41. Patient Protection and Affordable Care Act, Pub. L. No. 111–148, 124 Stat. 119 (2010).

42. Since World War II, American presidents have generally declined to ask Congress for a declaration of war before committing American troops in armed conflicts. See, for example, Marvin Kalb, *The Road to War: Presidential Commitments Honored and Betrayed* (Washington, DC: Brookings Institution Press, 2013).

43. Many American military endeavors have not been wars formally declared by Congress. See, for example, Benjamin R. Beede, *The Small Wars of the United States, 1899–2009: An Annotated Bibliography,* 2nd ed. (New York: Routledge, 2010).

from the margins of their societies.[44] Biblical scholarship informs us, however, that this image actually conveys an incomplete picture of prophecy in the ancient world.[45] In many cases, prophets operated with colleagues, who worked together in order to convey a message.[46] The Book of Isaiah, for example, incorporates large sections from persons working in the tradition—and under the name—of that prophet.[47] The Book of Jeremiah also includes passages from prophets writing in the tradition of Jeremiah over the course of generations. How can it be beneficial to situate deliberation about the choice to engage in prophetic indictment in the context of a broader community?[48] If the community is vigorous and self-reflective, it can provide prospective prophets with the impetus and opportunity to consider whether they are motivated by illegitimate reasons, such as attempting to win a deliberative argument with a seemingly more powerful tool. It can also encourage a type of self-reflection and self-purification so that one's prophetic message

44. See Max Weber, *The Sociology of Religion*, trans. Ephraim Fischoff (Boston, MA: Beacon Press, 1993), 46: "We shall understand 'prophet' to mean a purely individual bearer of charisma, who by virtue of his mission proclaims a religious doctrine or divine commandment."

45. For a general introduction, see John J. Collins, *Introduction to the Hebrew Bible*, 2nd ed. (Minneapolis, MN: Fortress Press, 2014); and Norman K. Gottwald, *The Hebrew Bible: A Socio-Literary Introduction* (Philadelphia, PA: Fortress Press, 1985). Other helpful histories include Francois Castel, *The History of Israel and Judah: In Old Testament Times*, rev. ed., trans. Matthew J. O'Connell (Mahwah, NJ: Paulist Press, 1985); and J. Maxwell Miller and John H. Hayes, *A History of Ancient Israel and Judah*, 2nd ed. (Louisville, KY: Westminster John Knox Press, 2006).

46. For an important work looking at prophecy in its social context, see Robert R. Wilson, *Prophecy and Society in Ancient Israel* (Philadelphia, PA: Fortress Press, 1980). See also the older but still helpful volume, Morton Smith, *Palestinian Parties and Politics That Shaped the Old Testament* (New York: Columbia University Press, 1971). For a more theological approach, see Walter Brueggemann, *A Social Reading of the Old Testament: Prophetic Approaches to Israel's Common Life*, ed. Patrick D. Miller (Minneapolis, MN: Fortress Press, 1994).

47. See Joseph Blenkinsopp, *A History of Prophecy in Israel*, rev. ed. (Louisville, KY: Westminster John Knox Press, 1996), chaps. 12, 19, and 21; and Joseph Blenkinsopp, *Opening the Sealed Book: Interpretations of the Book of Isaiah in Late Antiquity* (Grand Rapids, MI: Eerdmans, 2006). For a learned and clear account of the first chapters of the Bible, see Joseph Blenkinsopp, *The Pentateuch: An Introduction to the First Five Books of the Bible* (New York: Doubleday, 1992).

48. For an account of Old Testament theology that is centered on the prophetic texts, see Walter Brueggemann, *Theology of the Old Testament: Testimony, Dispute, Advocacy* (Minneapolis, MN: Fortress Press, 1997). For other theological accounts, see Gerhard von Rad, *Old Testament Theology*, vol. 2, *The Theology of Israel's Prophetic Traditions*, trans. D. M. G. Stalker (Louisville, KY: Westminster John Knox Press, 2001); Brevard S. Childs, *Biblical Theology of the Old and New Testaments: Theological Reflection on the Christian Bible* (Minneapolis, MN: Fortress Press, 1993); Brevard S. Childs, *Old Testament Theology in a Canonical Context* (Philadelphia, PA: Fortress Press, 1986); and Donald E. Gowan, *Theology of the Prophetic Books: The Death and Resurrection of Israel* (Louisville, KY: Westminster John Knox Press, 1998).

does not stem from hatred of one's target audience but instead springs from sincere desire for reform.

I suggested earlier that a broad continuum exists from actual warfare through civil disobedience to the verbal bellicosity of prophetic indictment. Whereas just war theory provides an overall normative framework of analysis, insights from the just practice of nonviolent civil disobedience can be especially helpful in understanding the benefit of communal self-correction. In organizing and recruiting volunteers for the civil rights movement, Martin Luther King, Jr., did not simply round up people who were rightly incensed at racists and racism and slot them into protests, marches, and sit-ins. Instead, King's community of civil rights activists insisted that they prepare themselves and purify their motives before engaging in civil disobedience. In his "Letter from Birmingham Jail," he writes, "In any nonviolent campaign there are four basic steps: collection of the facts to determine whether injustices exist; negotiation; self-purification; and direct action."[49] Accordingly, in organizing the Birmingham campaign, King treated self-control under difficult circumstances as a prerequisite for participation. "We made it clear that we would not send anyone out to demonstrate who had not convinced himself and us that he could accept and endure violence without retaliating. At the same time, we urged the volunteers to give up any possible weapons that they might have on their persons. Hundreds of people responded to this appeal."[50]

---

49. Martin Luther King, Jr., *The Autobiography of Martin Luther King, Jr.*, ed. Clayborne Carson (New York: Warner Books, 1998), 189.

50. Ibid., 178. The literature on King is voluminous. For studies of the religious aspects of his work on behalf of civil rights, see, for example, David J. Garrow, *Bearing the Cross: Martin Luther King, Jr., and the Southern Christian Leadership Conference* (New York: William Morrow and Company, 1986); Lewis V. Baldwin, *Never to Leave Us Alone: The Prayer Life of Martin Luther King Jr.* (Minneapolis, MN: Fortress Press, 2010); Lewis V. Baldwin, *There Is a Balm in Gilead: The Cultural Roots of Martin Luther King, Jr.* (Minneapolis, MN: Augsburg Fortress, 1991); Peter J. Paris, *Black Religious Leaders: Conflict in Unity; Insights from Martin Luther King, Jr., Malcolm X, Joseph H. Jackson, and Adam Clayton Powell, Jr.* (Louisville, KY: Westminster John Knox Press, 1991); Rufus Burrow, Jr., *God and Human Dignity: The Personalism, Theology, and Ethics of Martin Luther King, Jr.* (Notre Dame, IN: University of Notre Dame Press, 2006); and Hak Joon Lee, *We Will Get to the Promised Land: Martin Luther King, Jr.'s Communal-Political Spirituality* (Cleveland, OH: Pilgrim Press, 2006). For a longer historical perspective, see Lewis V. Baldwin with Rufus Burrow, Jr., Barbara A. Holmes, and Susan Holmes Winfield, *The Legacy of Martin Luther King, Jr.: The Boundaries of Law, Politics, and Religion* (Notre Dame, IN: University of Notre Dame Press, 2002). For a look at the more secular aspects of the civil rights movement, see Clayborne Carson, *In Struggle: SNCC and the Black Awakening of the 1960s*, 2nd ed. (Cambridge, MA: Harvard University Press, 1995).

Engaging in the practice of prophetic indictment is, of course, significantly different from participating in a program of nonviolent civil disobedience. Most important, it does not have the same immediate risk of physical violence. Yet those issuing harsh condemnations do risk fanning the flames of hatred in their own hearts as well as immuring themselves in a bunker of their own self-righteousness. King's communal program of self-scrutiny, self-purification, and self-control can be adopted by those who decide to engage in verbal resistance of injustice.

3. *Comparative Justice.* Just war theory generally does not require absolute justice on the part of those going to war, but it does require clear comparative justice when the dispute is considered as a whole.[51] The same is true in the case of decisions to bring the weapons of prophetic indictment into the public square, although for a somewhat different set of reasons. The stance of someone deploying those rhetorical weapons is that of one who is defending the basic moral framework of the community; in religious terms, it is someone who places him- or herself in the position of a divine prosecutor. To dare to adopt such a stance, even for a good cause, without having relatively clean hands oneself undermines one's prophetic message. More specifically, it invites charges of hypocrisy and bad faith, charges that are all the more likely because of the ad hominem nature of prophetic indictment itself. Furthermore, if the messenger's character is sufficiently sullied, the taint begins to mar the integrity of the message itself. We see this phenomenon in the response to efforts of the Roman Catholic bishops to speak prophetically about what they see as sexual immorality in the United States in the immediate wake of the clergy sex abuse scandal. It is not merely that many people do not believe that the bishops are in a position to cast the first stone; more strongly, they think the morally compromised stance of the Catholic hierarchy is a good reason to be skeptical of their ability to provide sound guidance in this area.[52]

---

51. The comparative justice criterion also limits the use of force, forcing a nation to recognize that its enemy's claim may not be entirely devoid of merit. "Far from legitimizing a crusade mentality, comparative justice is designed to relativize absolute claims and to restrain the use of force even in a 'justified' conflict." National Conference of Catholic Bishops, *The Challenge of Peace*, para. 93.

52. See, for example, Frank Bruni, "Beyond the Bedroom," *New York Times*, March 17, 2013, SR3.

While the *ius ad bellum* criteria are meant to help evaluate general decisions to wage war, not to assess particular strategies, those criteria do have significant implications for the manner in which particular battles are conducted. In the realm of political warfare, the criterion of comparative justice points to a decision to avoid prophetic language in the tu quoque arguments that characterize so many debates in the public square.[53] Abortion is an appropriate topic for prophetic rhetoric—on both sides of the issue. However, it is not appropriate to deploy it in the skirmishes between pro-life and pro-choice activists about whether the literature of pro-life crisis pregnancy centers or Planned Parenthood clinics is the more misleading.

4. *Right Intention.* The just war theory does not require simply a just cause; it also requires a nation to wage war with the intention of advancing that just cause, not as cover for another, less meritorious or upstanding reason. An analogous requirement applies in the use of prophetic rhetoric. Those who intervene in the public square actually ought to use prophetic rhetoric to further the cause to which they testify, not merely as a means of agitating their audience in order to advance another cause indirectly. Political operatives and surrogates of both major parties regularly and inappropriately use prophetic rhetoric on hot button issues for just such purely instrumental purposes.

Doubtless some would object that their ardent support of (say) the Republican Party stems directly from its stance on abortion, while others would claim that their loyalty to (say) the Democrats is attributable to that party's commitment to equal rights for gays and lesbians. Fair enough. At the same time, it is important to recognize that the rhetoric of prophetic indictment has few transitive properties, so to speak. More specifically, as we saw earlier, prophetic indictment works best when it is tightly focused on decrying fundamental moral and social evils. Transitioning from a clear negative indictment to a positive program of reform is far more complicated. Political parties stand for much more than for what they oppose—including their positive plan to eliminate the evils that they identify. Consequently, even those who in good faith use prophetic indictment to prompt citizens to reconsider their approach to particular issues (such as abortion or same-sex marriage or

53. A tu quoque ("you too") argument is an effort to deflect the charges made by one's opponents by accusing them of doing exactly the same thing that they complain about.

torture) should stop well short of transferring that rhetoric to bolster a full-blown political program of positive change by condemning anyone who opposes their preferred program.

So prophetic rhetoric against abortion (or against discrimination on the basis of sexual orientation) may be justifiable. Prophetic rhetoric against the entire Democratic Party (because it supports abortion rights) or the entire Republican Party (because it supports broad religious exemptions for those opposed to same-sex marriage) is a step too far. And it is a *bridge* too far to denounce everyone who *fails to support* the Republican Party (because it is pro-life) or the Democratic Party (because it supports marriage equality).

5. *Last Resort.* Has the prospective prophet tried less extreme and less oppositional forms of interaction in order to convince minds and hearts? These less oppositional forms will likely break fewer communal bonds. Moreover, they will likely provide a better basis for formulating and implementing a solution to the problem. Because communal bonds are stronger, there is a broader base of commitment to draw on in enacting reforms whose success is necessarily dependent on wide communal support, such as the introduction of new legislative programs. Second, remaining within the language—and the framework—of practical deliberation will facilitate moving beyond recognition of social problems to the formulation and evaluation of solutions. The language of prophetic indictment, like war itself, is negative in its immediate focus. It is always necessary to rebuild after a war; it is also necessary to rebuild after a campaign of prophetic denunciation. In both cases, if the requisite reforms can be achieved without passing through the destructive phase, so much the better.

6. *Probability of Success.* This criterion is much harder to translate from the military context to the context of prophetic rhetoric, in part because the human and economic resources that can be devoted to warfare are necessarily finite—or at least more finite than the resources necessary for a war of words. At the same time, we can profitably turn the question around and ask whether it seems likely that prophetic speech in the public square has *a significant probability of failure.* It is possible to imagine a country or a community so torn or divided, on so many grounds, at a particular time or in a particular space that prophetic speech on a neuralgic issue will destroy its spirit entirely.

In the most extreme scenario, it will lead to violence. In those situations, of course, the language of prophetic indictment is counterproductive.

One might object that the biblical prophets do not seem to make the prospect of success, at least in the short term, a criterion of their speech. In fact, in some cases, it appears that the opposite is the case. God decides to harden the hearts of the people in response to the prophetic speech so that they pertinaciously continue in their wrongdoing.[54] But this is a point on which those deliberating about whether to use prophetic discourse in the public square must part company from actual prophets. God may decide to harden people's hearts with respect to the message of those whom He calls directly, but it is not appropriate for those imitating the rhetoric of biblical prophets to take it upon themselves to do the same thing as part of a program of political reform.

7. *Proportionality.* Will the harm caused by a strategy of prophetic intervention on a particular issue be justified by the moral benefits to the community? The criterion of proportionality directs prospective prophets to weigh the possibility that their interventions will result in moral and social improvement against the social erosion that it will likely bring about as well.

Ad hominem nature. A prophetic indictment is modeled on a legal complaint—a charge that certain persons are breaking the fundamental law of the community. It is extremely difficult, if not impossible, to make such a charge without directly attacking the audience whom the prophet is addressing. To put it another way, it is hard not to take a criminal indictment personally. Moreover, like criminal indictments, prophetic indictments do not invite interpreting the target audience's alleged behavior charitably. In essence, both legal and rhetorical indictments centrally claim that the indicted parties have set themselves above or beyond the norms marking the true identity and boundaries of the community.

Loss of nuance. The language of prophetic indictment is black and white. It takes for granted that the behavior it condemns violates the basic law of the community. It does not invite the articulation of subtle moral categories,

---

54. Most famously, God hardens the heart of Pharaoh against the pleadings of Moses and Aaron in the Book of Exodus. See also Isaiah 63:17, in which the prophet asks on behalf of his own people: "Why, O Lord, do you make us stray from your ways and harden our heart, so that we do not fear you?"

nuanced application of moral norms to given factual situations, or broader assessment of the motives and alternatives of those engaging in the problematic behavior. In fact, those employing the language of prophetic indictment tend to view with suspicion those who claim that a more variegated assessment of the indicted behavior is necessary.

Dualistic worldviews. Taken together, the ad hominem nature of prophetic indictments, along with their hostility to nuance, can give rise to a starkly oppositional moral worldview framed as a battle between the righteous and the damned, good and evil, or the culture of life and the culture of death. If they draw on religious themes and norms, those issuing prophetic indictments identify themselves with a transcendentally correct cause—God's cause—and those opposing them with the opponents of God. While nonreligious prophets may not invoke divine approbation for their side, they too tend to infuse their claims with a type of transcendentally valid moral righteousness. Such stances, of course, make it very difficult to justify cooperating with the objects of one's prophetic ire on other issues. One does not make common cause, for example, with people one considers minions of the culture of death (from the abortion debate) or hateful bigots (from the same-sex marriage debate). One can only work to defeat them on the issue at hand and avoid interacting with them in other ways to the extent possible.

A stunted plan of positive reform. Prophetic indictments condemn situations of entrenched injustice without necessarily proposing a way to ameliorate them. Not surprisingly, it can be difficult for those who are united in their opposition to a fundamental social evil to agree on the most appropriate and effective way to combat that evil. It is even more difficult to find consensus on the appropriate social structures to deal with the fallout of abolishing that evil. Moreover, the habits of prophetic thinking serve a cause less well in the positive moments of social reform because they can lead people to treat those who advocate different strategies for reform (which invariably involves some realistic assessment of what can be accomplished) as engaged in acts of betrayal of the movement itself.

Dueling prophets and public cynicism. Important battles typically include prophets on both sides of the issue, as American debates over abortion and same-sex marriage show. Each group of prophets feeds off the other's energy, justifying its own commitment with reference to the dangerous ambitions of its opposition. Yet not all members of a community are as energized and engaged by the opposing sets of moral indictments. In fact, the very ferocity of the combat may encourage the "muddled middle" to steer far away from the battleground in order to avoid becoming collateral damage in the culture war.

Ius In Bello Verborum

In addition to the seven criteria for evaluating a decision to go to war, just war theory also encompasses two additional factors that guide appropriate conduct in warfare—*ius in bello*. These factors may be adapted as well to provide a helpful normative perspective on the use of prophetic indictment in particular situations.

1. *Discrimination between Combatants and Noncombatants.* In just war theory, the requirement of discrimination points to the immunity of noncombatants from direct attack. This requirement also applies to verbal warfare as well. Sustained prophetic indictment targeting "innocents" who are connected to wrongdoers is not morally acceptable. Thus it is out of bounds to direct prophetic excoriations against the children of one's political and moral opponents, either directly, by targeting them by name, or indirectly, by organizing protests against their parents outside their homes and schools.[55]

A more complicated question is, "Who is a legitimate target of direct attack?" In some discussions of just war theory and modern warfare, several moralists took the position that anyone who contributed to or supported the enemy's war effort, in no matter how attenuated a fashion, deserved to be considered a combatant susceptible to legitimate attack. Others responded that mere patriotic support, or the indirect contributions to the war effort that come about through basic activities of everyday living, do not make persons combatants. This response is persuasive.[56] In verbal warfare, it is inappropriate to target prophetic rhetoric against those with only tenuous and indirect contributions to the evil being protested. One might denounce a

---

55. See Kathleen Gilbert, "Abortion Protesters Picket Middle School of Clinic Owner's Daughter," *LifeSiteNews*, September 14, 2011, www.lifesitenews.com/news/abortion-protesters-picket-middle-school-of-clinic-owners-daughter .

56. For a dated but still helpful discussion of these positions, see Paul Ramsey, "The Case for Making 'Just War' Possible," in *The Just War: Force and Political Responsibility* (Lanham, MD: University Press of America, 1983), chap. 7, pp. 148–67.

big-box store for contracting with manufacturers in developing countries that exploit their workers; such denunciation is not appropriately directed against the family trying to buy back-to-school clothes at an affordable price. This injunction does not mean, of course, that protesters may not legitimately attempt to use other means, such as deliberative and educational strategies rather than prophetic denunciation, to convince customers not to shop at such stores.

2. *Proportionality.* This requirement appears in both the *ius in bello* criteria *and the ius ad bellum* criteria. Its purpose in this second list is to ensure proportionality with respect to particular strategies and goals, not merely with respect to the overall objective. It is tempting to try to justify the destruction caused in a particular battle by balancing against the good achieved by the global objective of winning the war. This temptation must be resisted. In most cases, losing the battle will not necessarily mean losing the war, and winning the battle will not necessarily mean winning it. Questions of contingency, fortune, and future decisions made by thousands of other people involved in the war on both sides will have an impact on the significance of a particular battle in the context of an entire war. Consequently, just war theory requires intermediate proportionality calculations to be made with respect to each battle. The same principle applies in verbal warfare. In both cases, it is too easy to justify highly destructive courses of action by reference to an ultimate victory whose nature and timing is highly uncertain.

Ius Post Bellum Verborum

The purpose of any just war, even a verbal war, cannot be to trigger endless conflict but must be to enable a more just and therefore more lasting peace. In recent years, just war theorists have given serious attention to the question, "What constitutes right conduct after hostilities have ended?"[57] Two key issues are compensation from the defeated aggressors to their victims and the prospect of rehabilitation. While acknowledging that it is permissible to ask the aggressors to pay reparations, Brian Orend also cautions that it is

---

57. See, for example, Brian Orend, "Justice after War," *Ethics & International Affairs* 16, no. 1 (Spring 2002): 43–56; Richard P. DiMeglio, "The Evolution of the Just War Tradition: Defining Jus Post Bellum," *Military Law Review* 186 (Winter 2005): 116–63; and Mark J. Allman and Tobias L. Winright, *After the Smoke Clears: The Just War Tradition and Post War Justice* (Maryknoll, NY: Orbis Books, 2010).

important to consider what they can reasonably be expected to contribute without going bankrupt. He maintains that the burden of compensation and reparation should fall mainly on the political and military leaders of the losing nation rather than on the civilian population.[58] Orend also believes that it may be permissible for victors in a just war to insist on some sort of program of moral and political rehabilitation, as the United States did with respect to Germany after World War II.[59]

Needless to say, these *ius post bellum* criteria do not apply directly to a situation involving the verbal warfare of prophetic indictment. Most obviously, culture wars do not have the same clear victories and defeats that mark the conclusion of actual wars. There are no surrenders or peace treaties. Nonetheless, the insights of *ius post bellum* theorists regarding reparations and rehabilitation do suggest additional cautions for the practitioners of prophetic indictment. How does one behave after a socially important moral victory? How does one treat opponents now generally viewed as "on the wrong side of history"?[60]

The *ius post bellum* idea of reparations points to payment: Should the winners make the losers of a culture war "pay" for having held a defeated moral position? This is a very dangerous practice, for two reasons. First, it may prompt ordinary citizens to censor their discussions of other controversial issues out of fear that their positions will be held against them at a later point in time. Such self-censorship is inimical to the practical deliberation that is the lifeblood of a liberal democracy. Second, attempts at total humiliation and marginalization of opposing activists may well be counterproductive. They may well respond by nurturing anger and resentment, biding their time for the next opportunity to revive the culture war.

The *ius post bellum* idea of rehabilitation points to moral reformation. The winners of a culture war necessarily want to inculcate their values in the broader community and to extirpate the values they believe to be erroneous.

---

58. Orend, "Justice after War," 47–49. "Respect for discrimination entails taking a reasonable amount of compensation only from those sources that can afford it *and* that were materially linked to the aggression in a morally culpable way" (original emphasis, p. 48). By "discrimination," Orend means the just war principle that prohibits targeting noncombatants.

59. Ibid., 49–52.

60. Given the speed at which American attitudes toward homosexuality are changing, this question may face activists in favor of same-sex marriage regarding their opponents.

It may be tempting for prophets to attempt to do so by continuing with their forensic mode of rhetoric. They may well think that their prophetic indictment resulted in a conviction; why not proceed with an execution of their enemies in order to make an example of them? Yet they ought to resist this temptation. It is the rhetoric of practical deliberation that better facilitates moral pedagogy, in part because it enables students to express doubts and to ask questions, which can then be addressed and answered. After they win a culture war, the prophets need to make room for the deliberators on their team, just as soldiers make way for experts in reconstructive social policy after they win an actual war.

Rhetorical Constraints

The previous pages of this chapter have focused on the substantive constraints on the use of prophetic indictment, drawing a normative framework from the just war tradition. It is now time to articulate some basic rhetorical criteria for the right use of prophetic indictments in the public square, criteria that would promote the benefits of this form of rhetoric while minimizing the liabilities. Successful criteria for the use of prophetic rhetoric need to be developed from an internal perspective, a perspective sensitive to the inner logic and purpose of prophetic speech, rather than imposed from outside, in an arbitrary fashion.

Consequently, I propose to draw on the books named after the great Hebrew prophets themselves for the development of standards guiding the appropriate use of prophetic indictments. These books reveal that the indictment is not the only form of prophetic speech; in fact, prophetic books contextualize indictments with other forms of speech in ways that maximize the beneficial effects of the indictment while minimizing deleterious consequences. For prophetic indictment to heal rather than to harm a community, would-be prophets need not only reflect on the conditions under which its use is appropriate but also to contextualize their indictment in ways that mitigate its harm to the broader community.

RHETORICAL STANCE

Reflections on the prophetic books, together with the best practices of contemporary prophetic rhetoric, also yields insight into the most helpful *rhetorical stance* to take toward the community that the prospective prophet is addressing. In my view, two factors are crucial. First, prospective prophets ought to avoid framing their remarks to their fellow citizens in terms of what biblical scholars frequently refer to as the oracles against the nations and instead orient them according to the framework modeled in the oracles against Israel and Judah.[61] The oracles against the nations are found in several prophetic books, including Amos, Ezekiel, Isaiah, and Jeremiah. In general terms, the prophet condemns each of the enemies of Israel and Judah, usually its neighbors, by name, for cruelty to the Jews. God uses the enemies of Israel and Judah to chastise His covenant partner, but they invariably exceed their retributive mandate in egregious ways. Consequently, the prophets declare that their national enemies will not only be punished severely for their treachery and butchery, but in some cases will even be wiped off the face of the earth. The language is shockingly, unremittingly harsh. Consider, for example, this oracle against Babylon from the Book of Isaiah, which is written in God's voice:

> See, I am stirring up the Medes against them,
>> who have no regard for silver
>> and do not delight in gold.
> Their bows will slaughter the young men;
>> they will have no mercy on the fruit of the womb;
>> their eyes will not pity children.   ·
> And Babylon, the glory of kingdoms,
>> the splendor and pride of the Chaldeans,
> will be like Sodom and Gomorrah
>> when God overthrew them.
> It will never be inhabited
>> or lived in for all generations;

---

61. For a very helpful orientation, see David L. Petersen, *The Prophetic Literature: An Introduction* (Louisville, KY: Westminster John Knox Press, 2002).

Arabs will not pitch their tents there,
　shepherds will not make their flocks lie down there.
But wild animals will lie down there,
　and its houses will be full of howling creatures;
there ostriches will live,
　and there goat-demons will dance.
Hyenas will cry in its towers,
　and jackals in the pleasant palaces;
its time is close at hand,
　and its days will not be prolonged.[62]

In the eyes of the Hebrew prophets, the nations hostile to Israel are not valuable in and of themselves; they are only instrumentally useful for the supporting role that they play in the divine drama between God and His chosen people. Overstepping their moral boundaries, these nations are condemned to thorough destruction. The prophet speaks against them because God Himself is against them. It is precisely for this reason that the oracles against the nations can be contrasted with the oracles against Israel and Judah, in which God chastises His people, frequently in language every bit as harsh as He uses to chastise the nations. The crucial but important difference, however, is that He repeatedly forgives His people. Deutero-Isaiah describes how God relents after afflicting Judah with the Babylonian captivity, promising them a Messiah (Cyrus of Persia) who will allow them to return to their homeland. In the case of Judah, unlike the case of Babylon, the divine edict of destruction is undone. Consider this passage from Isaiah, in stark contrast to the previous one:

Remember these things, O Jacob,
　and Israel, for you are my servant;
I formed you, you are my servant;
　O Israel, you will not be forgotten by me.
I have swept away your transgressions like a cloud,
　and your sins like mist;
return to me, for I have redeemed you.

---

62. Isaiah 13:17–22. The invective against Babylon is particularly harsh, because it conquered Jerusalem and destroyed the Jewish temple in 586 BCE. The Babylonian empire was itself conquered by the Persians in 539 BCE, which allowed the Jews to return to Jerusalem and rebuild the temple.

> Sing, O heavens, for the LORD has done it;
>   shout, O depths of the earth;
> break forth into singing, O mountains,
>   O forest, and every tree in it!
> For the LORD has redeemed Jacob,
>   and will be glorified in Israel.
>
> Thus says the LORD, your Redeemer,
>   who formed you in the womb:
> I am the LORD, who made all things,
>   who alone stretched out the heavens,
>   who by myself spread out the earth;
> who frustrates the omens of liars,
>   and makes fools of diviners;
> who turns back the wise,
>   and makes their knowledge foolish;
> who confirms the word of his servant,
>   and fulfils the prediction of his messengers;
> who says of Jerusalem, "It shall be inhabited,"
>   and of the cities of Judah, "They shall be rebuilt,
>   and I will raise up their ruins";
> who says to the deep, "Be dry—
>   I will dry up your rivers";
> who says of Cyrus, "He is my shepherd,
>   and he shall carry out all my purpose";
> and who says of Jerusalem, "It shall be rebuilt,"
>   and of the temple, "Your foundation shall be laid."[63]

Those who invoke prophetic rhetoric with the goal of calling attention to a fundamental flaw in their community need to construe their audience as fellow citizens of Israel and Judah, not as citizens of Babylon, Assyria, or Egypt. In other words, prophets need to make it clear that they do not see their audience as implacable enemies and that their prophetic indictments are not designed to demand the utter destruction of those who hear those indictments. Instead, they are meant to prepare the way for repentance, reform,

---

63. Isaiah 44:21–28.

and divine mercy. Prophetic language that is modeled on the oracles against the nations cannot heal a political community. It cannot be interpreted in a constructive way. It carries with it only the threat of annihilation, not the (conditional) promise of a world made new.

Second, precisely because they are addressing their own people, would-be prophets would do well to stand with their audience in their trials and tribulations, despite their sins. They ought not to set themselves, rhetorically speaking, over and against the people whom they castigate in God's name.

As the great rabbi Abraham Joshua Heschel wrote, "Those whom he loved he was called upon to condemn. When the catastrophe came, and the enemy mercilessly killed men, women, and children, the prophet must have discovered that the agony was greater than the heart could feel, that his grief was more than his soul could weep for."[64] Heschel observes of Jeremiah: "Standing before the people he pleaded for God; standing before God he pleaded for his people."[65] To be an instrument of divine wrath toward God's beloved people, toward Jeremiah's own people, was too much for the prophet to endure.[66] He cried out:

> Cursed be the day
> > on which I was born!
> The day when my mother bore me,
> > let it not be blessed!
> Cursed be the man
> > who brought the news to my father, saying,
> "A child is born to you, a son,"
> > making him very glad.
> Let that man be like the cities
> > that the LORD overthrew without pity;
> let him hear a cry in the morning
> > and an alarm at noon,
> because he did not kill me in the womb;
> > so my mother would have been my grave,
> > and her womb forever great.

64. Abraham Joshua Heschel, *The Prophets* (New York: HarperCollins, 2001), 153–54.
65. Ibid., 154–55.
66. Ibid., 156–60.

> Why did I come forth from the womb
> to see toil and sorrow,
> and spend my days in shame?[67]

Third, a prophet must experience and express true sorrow over the sins of the people, even when those sins precipitate their destruction. The Book of Lamentations, traditionally attributed to Jeremiah, poetically memorializes the prophet's sorrow at the destruction of the Jewish people after they failed to heed his warnings to reform. Although it was the Babylonian people who devastated Jerusalem, the ultimate cause of that devastation was their own God, who punished them for their faithlessness to the covenant.[68] The prophet does not rejoice that his fiery prophecies of doom were vindicated. Although he recognizes that the divine sentence was just, he also stands with his people in their sorrow and suffering.

> The LORD is in the right,
> for I have rebelled against his word;
> but hear, all you peoples,
> and behold my suffering;
> my young women and young men
> have gone into captivity.[69]

Fourth, and finally, if a prophet's condemnations of sin and call to repentance are to be heard as constructive chastisements, he or she has to situate them within a horizon of hope.[70] It must be possible somehow to turn from sinful paths, to avert disaster, and to reestablish oneself and one's community within divine favor. Prophecies of wrath and doom are situated within the context of divine faithfulness to God's people. The prophet weeps for his people suffering under a just lash and offers them comfort and consolation.

---

67. Jeremiah 20:14–18; also quoted in the Revised Standard Version in Heschel, *The Prophets*, 159–60.

68. For a theological interpretation, see Walter Brueggemann, *The Theology of the Book of Jeremiah* (Cambridge: Cambridge University Press, 2007). See also Delbert R. Hillers, *Lamentations*, 2nd rev. ed. (New York: Doubleday, 1992); and Adele Berlin, *Lamentations: A Commentary* (Louisville, KY: Westminster John Knox Press, 2002). Contemporary scholarship has called into question the view that Jeremiah authored the Book of Lamentations.

69. Lamentations 1:18.

70. Admittedly, it is difficult to see a horizon of hope in the Book of Lamentations. No one biblical book, however, is meant to be read in isolation.

As Heschel writes of the book of Jeremiah, "The rule of Babylon shall pass, but God's covenant with Israel shall last forever."[71]

Thus far, I have outlined four guidelines gleaned from the biblical prophets for the constructive use of the rhetoric of prophetic indictment in contemporary society. First, in offering prophetic critique to your own people, do not adopt the stance of the oracles against the nations; instead, take as a model the oracles against Judah and Israel. Second, identify yourself with the people who are sinning and about to receive divine chastisement; do not stand over and against them. Third, lament the sins of your people; do not rejoice at their destruction on account of those sins. Fourth, offer hope. These guidelines help ensure that prophetic indictments are heard and understood by their audience as beneficial, although painful, chemotherapy rather than as a poison ultimately destructive of the body politic.

Would-be prophets need to remember that the oracles against the nations are part of the prophetic books, but they are not the whole of them. One might also note that contemporary biblical scholarship has emphasized the way in which the prophetic hope for divine deliverance, for the triumph of God's mercy, contextualizes even the indictments in the oracles against the nations. In the book of Isaiah, for example, we find the passage expressing God's will: "'I will give you as a light to the nations, that my salvation may reach to the end of the earth.'"[72] David Petersen argues that this passage "looks to blessing for all peoples."[73] Petersen also argues that Jeremiah's oracles against the nations are "suffused by a motif of hope," not only for Israel and Judah but also for their enemies.[74] It is a hope rooted not in human endeavors but rather in God's infinite patience and creative mercy.

Chastising One's Own People

These guidelines are particularly important for prophetic rhetoric to be effective in the American context, given the prominent role of the jeremiad in our own history. This is not to say that we cannot question the presuppositions of the American jeremiad—indeed, we *must* question them. To the extent, for example, that our religious and political heritage hardens into the message

71. Heschel, *The Prophets*, 165.
72. Isaiah 49:6.
73. Petersen, *The Prophetic Literature*, 87.
74. Ibid., 128.

that God really cares only about the United States and not about other nations on the earth, it must be strongly resisted.[75] But even in prophetically denouncing that message, American prophets ought not to communicate that God hates America (the opposite message), or that they themselves stand separate and apart from the America whose shortcomings they decry, or that there is no hope of a renewed future for our nation. Even in prophetically rejecting prophetic abuses, one can learn from the Hebrew prophets. The controversy surrounding the preaching of Jeremiah Wright in the 2008 presidential election provides an apt lesson of the dangers involved in failing to appreciate the biblical context of prophetic indictment.

In *The African American Jeremiad: Appeals for Justice in America*, David Howard-Pitney describes how African Americans made the jeremiad their own in order to protest against the radical sins of slavery and racism, which violated God's covenant with America. Building on Sacvan Bercovitch's analysis, Howard-Pitney demonstrates how the jeremiad allowed African Americans to mount a sharp critique of unjust practices while at the same time affirming their love and loyalty to the country. In my own terms, Howard-Pitney's work shows how the prophet can claim the role of a loyal dissenter. Eddie Glaude shows how the biblical stories of the escape of the Jews from slavery in Egypt gave nineteenth-century preachers and thinkers an entry point into the American mythology of emigration and "chosenness," as well as a powerful point of critique.[76] More recently, in *The City on the Hill from Below: The Crisis of Prophetic Black Politics*, Stephen H. Marshall introduces a geographical component to the jeremiad: African American political thinkers such as David Walker, Frederick Douglass, and James Baldwin make important contributions to American political thought precisely because they inhabit a part of the "city on the hill" that makes plain its hidden sins.[77]

75. The literature on American exceptionalism is voluminous. Recent volumes include Richard M. Gamble, *In Search of the City on a Hill: The Making and Unmaking of an American Myth* (London: Continuum, 2012); Jason A. Edwards and David Weiss, eds., *The Rhetoric of American Exceptionalism: Critical Essays* (Jefferson, NC: McFarland & Co., 2011); and Deborah L. Madsen, *American Exceptionalism* (Edinburgh: Edinburgh University Press, 1998). Still enlightening is Ernest Lee Tuveson, *Redeemer Nation: The Idea of America's Millennial Role* (Chicago, IL: University of Chicago Press, 1968).

76. Eddie S. Glaude, Jr., *Exodus!: Religion, Race, and Nation in Early Nineteenth-Century Black America* (Chicago, IL: University of Chicago Press, 2000).

77. Stephen H. Marshall, *The City on the Hill from Below: The Crisis of Prophetic Black Politics* (Philadelphia, PA: Temple University Press, 2011).

The fire and strength of prophetic rhetoric in the African American experience was sharply highlighted in the mainstream press in the context of the 2008 presidential election. Jeremiah Wright is senior pastor emeritus at Trinity United Church of Christ in Chicago, Illinois, the church that Barack Obama attended with his family for many years. In March 2008, ABC News broadcast a story that included excerpts from some of his more blistering sermons.[78] One, entitled "The Day of Jerusalem's Fall," was delivered on September 16, 2001 (the first Sunday after the terrorist attacks on New York City and the Pentagon); the other, entitled "Confusing God and Government," was delivered on April 13, 2003. The story generated intense interest from other media outlets and political commentators. Questions were raised about Wright's patriotism, his relationship with the Obama family, and whether Barack Obama endorsed the ideas expressed by Wright. Obama repeatedly distanced himself from the pastor; finally, on May 31, 2008, the Obamas withdrew their membership in Trinity United Church of Christ, expressing their deep disagreement with the "divisive statements of Reverend Wright."[79]

The initial story, and many of the responses that it provoked, demonstrate that even highly educated people are unfamiliar with the rhetorical conventions of American religion. The lead of the original ABC News story suggests that Wright is literally calling on God to consign the United States to perdition: "Sen. Barack Obama's pastor says blacks should not sing 'God Bless America' but 'God damn America.'"[80] The body of the story reveals that the reporters did a great deal of research: "An ABC News review of dozens of Rev. Wright's sermons, offered for sale by the church, found repeated denunciations of the U.S. based on what he described as his reading of the Gospels and the treatment of black Americans." But no amount of research can make up for the lack of real insight. The story presents Wright as drawing on his own idiosyncratic religious vision and deep feelings of racial resentment

78. Wright is a prolific preacher. See, for example, Jeremiah A. Wright, Jr., *Good News! Sermons of Hope for Today's Families*, ed. Jini Kilgore Ross (Valley Forge, PA: Judson Press, 1995); and Jeremiah A. Wright, Jr., *What Makes You So Strong? Sermons of Joy and Strength from Jeremiah A. Wright Jr.*, ed. Jini Kilgore Ross (Valley Forge, PA: Judson Press, 1993). See also Jeremiah A. Wright, Jr., ed., *From One Brother to Another*, vol. 2, *Voices of African American Men* (Valley Forge, PA: Judson Press, 2003).

79. The best summary of the incident I have found is "Jeremiah Wright Controversy," Wikipedia, en.wikipedia.org/wiki/Jeremiah_Wright_controversy.

80. Brian Ross and Rehab el-Buri, "Obama's Pastor: God Damn America, U.S. to Blame for 9/11," ABC News, March 13, 2008, http://abcnews.go.com/Blotter/DemocraticDebate/story?id=4443788.

in order to deliver incendiary messages to his largely black congregation. Without any background or context, the ABC News story quotes passages from Wright's sermons, including the following passages from his April 13, 2003, sermon:

> "The government gives them the drugs, builds bigger prisons, passes a three-strike law and then wants us to sing 'God Bless America.' No, no, no, God damn America, that's in the Bible for killing innocent people," he said in a 2003 sermon. "God damn America for treating our citizens as less than human. God damn America for as long as she acts like she is God and she is supreme."

Many commentators interpreted Wright as straightforwardly calling on God to punish the United States. For example, *National Review* columnist Mark Steyn interpreted Wright as an America-bashing racist:

> God has blessed America, and blessed the Obamas in America, and even blessed the Reverend Jeremiah Wright, whose bashing of his own country would be far less lucrative anywhere else on the planet. The "racist" here is not Geraldine Ferraro but the Reverend Wright, whose appeals to racial bitterness are supposed to be everything President Obama will transcend. Right now, it sounds more like the same-old same-old.[81]

Scholars of religious studies attempted to quell the firestorm by setting Wright's preaching in a broader context. Georgetown's Michael Eric

---

81. Mark Steyn, "Uncle Jeremiah," *National Review*, March 15, 2008, www.nationalreview.com /article/223934/uncle-jeremiah-mark-steyn. Geraldine Ferraro was a U.S. congresswoman from New York who became the first female vice presidential candidate of a major party, running with Walter Mondale at the top of the Democratic ticket in 1984. As Steyn observes in his column, Ferraro remarked that Obama would not be leading the race for the Democratic nomination if he were a white man. As a result of this remark, Ferraro was sharply criticized in the liberal media and dropped from the Obama campaign. Steyn argues that Ferraro was not racist but was simply noting that Obama's appeal came in part from his status as a "symbol of redemption and renewal."

Dyson,[82] Princeton's Eddie Glaude,[83] and the University of Santa Clara's James Bennett[84] described the rhetorical genre of black preaching and high-lighted its roots in the prophetic books of Scripture, as well as in the story of oppression and liberation in the Book of Exodus. Doubtless the controversy surrounding Wright's fiery words stems in part from a broad cultural unfa-miliarity with important forms of African American preaching. Most people, after all, do not know that Martin Luther King wrote an important paper on the Book of Jeremiah while a student at Crozier Theological Seminary.[85] I would add that the controversy, and even the ABC News story itself, also demonstrates the relative unfamiliarity of Americans with the importance of the jeremiad more generally in the nation's political and religious history.

But the problem was exacerbated by the precise way in which Wright's words were taken out of context in the original news story. For example, the phrase "God damn America" as used by Wright is undeniably shocking. It is meant to be. But it is also meant to call America to repentance and humility before God, not to call for her utter destruction. It is an oracle against Israel, in other words, not an oracle against the nations. In the vast majority of news accounts, however, it was misleadingly presented as closer in sentiment to an oracle against the nations, a fact that understandably would provoke a more intense reaction in those who heard it. Happily, there were exceptions. In his interview with Reverend Wright, who served six years in the Navy, Bill Moyers attempts to bring out the larger, constructive purpose of Wright's critique.[86]

82. "Professor, Author Michael Eric Dyson Compares MLK to Jeremiah Wright," Newsvine, April 4, 2008, http://newsguru.newsvine.com/_news/2008/04/04/1410426-professor-author-michael-eric-dyson-compares-mlk-to-jeremiah-wright.

83. "Eddie Glaude on the Wright Issue," The Chicago Blog, March 31, 2008, http://pressblog.uchicago.edu/2008/03/31/eddie-glaude-on-the-wright-issue.html.

84. James B. Bennett, "Obama's Pastor's Words Ring Uncomfortably True," San Jose Mercury News, March 20, 2008, 15A.

85. Martin Luther King, Jr., "The Significant Contributions of Jeremiah to Religious Thought" (1948), in The Papers of Martin Luther King, Jr., vol. 1, Called to Serve, January 1929–June 1951, ed. Clayborne Carson, Ralph E. Luker, and Penny A. Russell (Berkeley: University of California Press, 1992), 181–95. See also the sermons in Martin Luther King Jr., Strength to Love (Minneapolis, MN: Fortress Press, 2010).

86. "Jeremiah Wright," Bill Moyers Journal, April 25, 2008, an interview with Jeremiah Wright, www.pbs.org/moyers/journal/04252008/profile.html.

Bill Moyers: Yeah. But talk a little bit about that. The prophets
           loved Israel. But they hated the waywardness of Israel. And
           they were calling Israel out of love back to justice, not
           damning—

Reverend Wright: Exactly.

Bill Moyers: Not damning Israel. Right?

Reverend Wright: Right. They were saying that God was—
           in fact, if you look at the damning, condemning, if you
           look at Deuteronomy, it talks about blessings and curses,
           how God doesn't bless everything. God does not bless
           gang-bangers. God does not bless dope dealers. God does
           not bless young thugs that hit old women upside the head
           and snatch their purse. God does not bless that. God does
           not bless the killing of babies. God does not bless the
           killing of enemies. And when you look at blessings and
           curses out of that Hebrew tradition from the book of
           Deuteronomy, that's what the prophets were saying, that
           God is not blessing this. God does not bless it—bless us.
           And when we're calling them, the prophets call them to
           repentance and to come back to God. If my people who are
           called by my name, God says to Solomon, will humble
           themselves and pray, seek my faith and turn from their
           wicked ways. God says that wicked ways, not Jeremiah
           Wright, then will I hear from heaven.

It is undeniable that Wright himself took steps that exacerbated the dispute.[87] Nonetheless, the twin roots of the controversy were the unfamiliarity
of many Americans with the rhetorical form of the jeremiad and the misleading media representation of him as engaged in a critique more akin to the
oracles against the nations (calling for utter destruction) rather than an oracle
against Israel or Judah (threatening destruction with a view to provoking
reform). The outcry against Jeremiah Wright vividly exemplified the fact that

---

87. His performance in subsequent appearances at the National Press Club, for example, added
fuel to the flames. See Amy Sullivan, "Jeremiah Wright Goes to War," *Time*, April 28, 2008, www.time
.com/time/politics/article/0,8599,1735662,00.html.

audiences do not respond well to prophets whom they perceive to be calling for the utter destruction of their country.

A Comparative Assessment

To lend specificity to this chapter's development of normative substantive and rhetorical criteria for the use of prophetic indictments, I will critically examine, in comparative fashion, two speeches made by religious figures in the public square about neuralgic issues of political morality and law. The first is Reverend Martin Luther King's "I Have a Dream" speech, delivered at the Lincoln Memorial on August 28, 1963, to more than 250,000 people at a March on Washington for Jobs and Freedom.[88] Martin Luther King was a Baptist minister; the president of the Southern Christian Leadership Conference; and a key figure in the civil rights movement, which drew on the black churches to mobilize support and inculcate the character traits necessary for the discipline of nonviolent civil resistance. The second is Father Frank Pavone's "Open Letter to Michael Schiavo," written to the widower of Terri Schindler Schiavo, in March 2006, a year after her death and published on the Web.[89] As I described in Chapter 2, in a highly publicized case, Mr. Schiavo authorized the withdrawal of artificial nutrition and hydration (ANH) from his forty-two-year-old wife, who had been in a persistent vegetative state for almost fifteen years. This decision was forcefully opposed by Ms. Schiavo's parents in part on the basis of their Catholic faith. In the fall of 2004, Pavone intervened in the moral and legal controversy on the side of the parents. A

88. King, "I Have a Dream," in *Autobiography,* 223–27. For a fascinating account of the composition of the speech, see Drew D. Hansen, *The Dream: Martin Luther King, Jr. and the Speech that Inspired a Nation* (New York: HarperCollins, 2003). For other analyses of King's preaching, see, for example, Gary S. Selby, *Martin Luther King and the Rhetoric of Freedom: The Exodus Narrative in America's Struggle for Civil Rights* (Waco, TX: Baylor University Press, 2008); Valentino Lassiter, *Martin Luther King in the African American Preaching Tradition* (Cleveland, OH: Pilgrim Press, 2001); Mervyn A. Warren, *King Came Preaching: The Pulpit Power of Dr. Martin Luther King Jr.* (Downers Grove, IL: InterVarsity Press, 2001); Clayborne Carson and Peter Holloran, eds., *A Knock at Midnight: Inspiration from the Great Sermons of Reverend Martin Luther King, Jr.* (New York: Warner Books, 2000); Richard Lischer, *The Preacher King: Martin Luther King, Jr. and the Words That Moved America* (New York: Oxford University Press, 1995); and Keith D. Miller, *Voice of Deliverance: The Language of Martin Luther King, Jr., and Its Sources* (Athens: The University of Georgia Press, 1992). See also David L. Chappell, *A Stone of Hope: Prophetic Religion and the Death of Jim Crow* (Chapel Hill: University of North Carolina Press, 2004).

89. Fr. Frank Pavone, "An Open Letter to Michael Schiavo," Catholic Exchange, March 31, 2006, http://catholicexchange.com/an-open-letter-to-michael-schiavo/.

contemporary culture warrior, he founded a new Roman Catholic religious order called Priests for Life, which is dedicated to combating abortion, euthanasia, and other manifestations of the culture of death as described in Pope John Paul II's encyclical *Evangelium vitae.*[90]

According to the criteria developed in this chapter, King's speech constitutes a model for the proper use of prophetic indictments, whereas Pavone's open letter falls far short of the mark. A reader might well question whether this comparison is fair. King's speech, after all, is an undisputable high point of American political and religious rhetoric; who among us could expect to survive a comparative scrutiny that used it as a touchstone?[91] Yet it is important to consider precisely why King's speech is effective, not merely as a general example of political rhetoric but also more specifically as an example of prophetic rhetoric in the public square. Comparative analysis facilitates this task. In addition, it is a mistake to minimize either the political significance of the Terri Schiavo case in American political life or Pavone's role in stirring the sentiments of religious people across the nation against the withdrawal of Terri Schiavo's feeding tube. Thanks in part to the intervention of religious conservatives, a Republican Congress passed the so-called Terri's Law,[92] which took the extraordinary step of giving de novo jurisdiction over one particular case—her case—to the federal courts despite the fact that family law and medical treatment decisions are quintessentially state-court matters. Terri's Law was an extraordinary manifestation of political power, much of it motivated by religious conviction. Father Pavone helped to galvanize that conviction.

A comparison of King and Pavone needs to begin by identifying something they share: both anchor their prophetic speech in a claimed violation of

90. Pope John Paul II, *Evangelium vitae* [The Gospel of Life], 1995.

91. This is not to say that comparisons of King to other important religious and political figures have never been attempted. See, for example, Willis Jenkins and Jennifer M. McBride, eds., *Bonhoeffer and King: Their Legacies and Import for Christian Social Thought* (Minneapolis, MN: Fortress Press, 2010); Johnny Bernard Hill, *The Theology of Martin Luther King, Jr. and Desmond Mpilo Tutu* (New York: Palgrave Macmillan, 2007); J. Deotis Roberts, *Bonhoeffer & King: Speaking Truth to Power* (Louisville, KY: Westminster John Knox Press, 2005); and William M. Ramsay, *Four Modern Prophets: Walter Rauschenbush, Martin Luther King, Jr., Gustavo Gutiérrez, Rosemary Radford Ruther* (Atlanta, GA: John Knox Press, 1986).

92. An Act for the Relief of the Parents of Theresa Marie Schiavo, Pub. L. 109-3, 119 Stat. 15 and 16 (2005).

law or covenant.[93] As both biblical scholars and careful readers of the biblical texts such as the Puritans have recognized, a fundamental agreement
or covenant binding upon the parties in question provides the basis for prophetic indictment well. Not surprisingly, therefore, when we examine both
King's speech and Pavone's open letter, we find the rudiments of a breach of
contract claim.

First, the opening paragraphs of both documents ground their respective
critiques in a fundamental covenant or compact to which their target audiences can be presumed to have assented. More specifically, Martin Luther
King invokes the Declaration of Independence and the Constitution as constituting a "check," a "promissory note," extending rights to African Americans.[94]
Frank Pavone highlights the marriage covenant that obligated Michael Schiavo
to care for and protect his wife, Terri.[95]

Second, each prophet proceeds to develop the factual basis for the indictment, drawing on vivid imagery to do so. King surveys the plight of black
citizens in America, charging that "[o]ne hundred years later, the Negro is still
languished in the corners of American society and finds himself an exile in his
own land."[96] Pavone describes Terri Schiavo's death: "I watched her face for
hours on end, right up to moments before her last breath. Her death was not
peaceful, nor was it beautiful. If you saw her too, and noticed what her eyes
were doing, you know that to describe her last agony as peaceful is a lie."[97]

Third, each proceeds to draw the legal conclusion on the basis of the law
and the facts. King proclaims: "It is obvious today that America has defaulted
on this promissory note insofar as her citizens of color are concerned. Instead
of honoring this sacred obligation, America has given the Negro people a bad
check, a check which has come back marked 'insufficient funds.'"[98] King is

93. Claus Westermann, *Basic Forms of Prophetic Speech,* trans. Hugh Clayton White (Philadelphia,
PA: Westminster Press, 1967).

94. "In a sense, we've come to our nation's capital to cash a check. When the architects of our
republic wrote the magnificent words of the Constitution and the Declaration of Independence, they
were signing a promissory note to which every American was to fall heir. This note was a promise that
all men, yes, black men as well as white men, would be guaranteed the unalienable rights of 'Life,
Liberty and the pursuit of Happiness.'" King, "I Have a Dream," in *Autobiography,* 224

95. "A year ago this week, I stood by the bedside of the woman you married and promised to love
in good times and bad, in sickness and health." Pavone, "An Open Letter."

96. King, "I Have a Dream," in *Autobiography,* 224.

97. Pavone, "An Open Letter."

98. King, "I Have a Dream," in *Autobiography,* 224.

charging the American polity with a type of fraud. Pavone, in contrast, exco-riates Schiavo for murdering his own wife: "We watched, but you had the power to save her. Her life was in your hands, but you threw it away, with the willing cooperation of attorneys and judges who were as heartless as you were. Some have demanded that I apologize to you for calling you a mur-derer. Not only will I not apologize, I will repeat it again."[99]

A comparison of the two prophetic indictments shows that both men aim to provide a type of moral chemotherapy. Both King and Pavone are using these communications to attack what they perceive as a type of moral cancer invading the body politic—a racist regime in the case of King and the culture of death in the case of Pavone. It is also clear that neither prophet leaves much room for legitimate disagreement with their diagnosis. As I argued above, these features are inherent in the very rhetorical structure of prophetic indictments. Further comparisons, however, reveal illuminating differences in the two sources.

First, look more closely at the basis of the prophetic indictment in the two cases. King was focused on the injustice of a whole pattern of laws that was deeply subversive of the full citizenship of African Americans—the Jim Crow regime that had thwarted the full implementation of the antislavery amendments to the Constitution. Like the biblical prophets, he is using a solid foundation—our basic constitutional values—to call attention to the rotting superstructure.[100]

In contrast, the basis for Pavone's indictment is far more restricted. More specifically, the problem he is targeting is not an entire legal regime but the application of relevant law to a particular case. There is no doubt that Terri Schiavo was recognized as a legal person by all those involved in the dispute. Euthanasia was (and remains) illegal in Florida. Moreover, the state's legal framework regarding guardianship and withdrawal of medical treatment—including artificial nutrition and hydration—was not unsound.[101] Pavone and

99. Pavone, "An Open Letter."

100. See, for example, Richard Wormser, *The Rise and Fall of Jim Crow* (New York: St. Martin's Press, 2003).

101. In essence, every person of sound mind has the right to reject whatever form of medical treatment or procedure they wish to reject, including ANH. This right is grounded not in a right to commit suicide but rather in a right to prevent battery—the unconsented touching of one's body, for any reason whatsoever. Furthermore, the state specifies an elaborate system of surrogate decision

his supporters might have argued that the result in the case exemplifies callousness toward people of compromised physical and mental state. Yet an examination of the case file, which runs over a thousand pages long, demonstrates that this is not the case.[102] The legal dispute between the two sides turned on clashing views about whether Terri Schiavo would have wanted ANH to be discontinued were she able to make the decision for herself. Pavone believed that Mr. Schiavo—and the courts—answered this particular question incorrectly because they did not give enough weight to what (according to Pavone) Catholic teaching requires in this instance.[103] The dispute also turned on conflicting views about who should make the decision because Terri could not decide for herself. Pavone thought that Mr. Schiavo had disqualified himself from this role, in part because he had begun a relationship with another woman while Terri was still alive, and in part because he did not respect the manner in which Catholic teaching should have constrained his decision making.

---

makers for incompetent persons such as Ms. Schiavo; their task is to decide for her according to what they believe she would have decided for herself had she been able to make the decision. The state of Florida has specified a higher burden of proof if a surrogate decision maker wants to withdraw ANH from an incompetent patient; the surrogate must prove that the patient would have desired this result by clear and convincing evidence, not merely by a preponderance of the evidence. The relevant legal framework can be found at Fla. Stat. Ann. § 765.101–.404.

102. Ms. Schiavo's parents attempted more than once to have Mr. Schiavo removed as Terri Schiavo's guardian on the grounds of unfitness; they were unsuccessful in their efforts. For a good history of the early years of the case, see the report submitted by guardian ad litem, Jay Wolfson, "A Report to Governor Jeb Bush and the 6th Judicial Circuit in the Matter of Theresa Marie Schiavo," December 1, 2003, http://abstractappeal.com/schiavo/WolfsonReport.pdf.

103. It appeared that Pope John Paul II declared the provision of ANH to be morally required in cases like Schiavo's. See his "Address to the Participants in the International Congress on 'Life-Sustaining Treatments and Vegetative State: Scientific Advances and Ethical Dilemmas,'" March 20, 2004, http://w2.vatican.va/content/john-paul-ii/en/speeches/2004/march/documents/hf_jp-ii_spe_20040320_congress-fiamc.html. Yet the meaning and relative authority of this intervention, along with the broader question of whether the whole sweep of Catholic teaching requires the continuation of ANH for all PVS patients, has continued to be disputed by Catholic moralists. See, for example, Ronald P. Hamel and James J. Walter, eds., *Artificial Nutrition and Hydration and the Permanently Unconscious Patient: The Catholic Debate* (Washington, DC: Georgetown University Press, 2007); and Christopher Tollefsen, ed., *Artificial Nutrition and Hydration: The New Catholic Debate* (Dordrecht, The Netherlands: Springer, 2008). Furthermore, even if it were the case that Catholic teaching so requires, it is not self-evident that Ms. Schiavo would have followed that teaching, despite her Catholicism. Even Pavone acknowledges that the relevant legal question is what Theresa Schiavo would have wanted, not what the Catholic Church teaches.

The *ius ad bellum verborum* criteria I have proposed in this chapter would distinguish between a systematically unjust legal regime, on the one hand, and a basically sound regime that reaches an unjust result in a particular instance, on the other.[104] It is one thing to protest a widespread pattern or practice of treating some people as second-class citizens; it is another to focus on one problematic case. Disagreement about the application of law to facts is inevitable in hard cases, even among those who are committed to the same moral and legal principles. To use prophetic indictment to call into question the goodwill and integrity of someone who reaches a different conclusion about what the law requires in a particular hard case may be momentarily gratifying to the self-proclaimed prophet, but it is not likely to be successful or effective.

The foregoing observations can be applied both to politically liberal prophets and to politically conservative ones. Prospective prophets must consider whether they are confronting an isolated problem or a pervasive pattern or practice. For example, it would have been inappropriate for a later-day civil rights activist to use prophetic invective if O. J. Simpson had been convicted rather than acquitted of murdering his former wife and her male friend in 1995. Even if such a verdict would have been unjust, it would have been an individual instance of injustice in the context of a functioning legal system. In such an instance, prophetic indictment would have been destructive overkill. Conversely, it would have been appropriate for Pavone to protest prophetically a law that declared all persons in persistent vegetative states to be legally dead, or nonpersons, just as it is rhetorically appropriate, given his convictions, for him to use prophetic language to protest *Roe v. Wade*'s exclusion of fetuses from the category of persons. Given his convictions about the importance of recognizing the equal dignity of all human beings, no matter what their state of disability or dependence, laws restricting personhood in this matter would mark a fundamental deficiency in the American legal system.

At the same time, it is essential to acknowledge that there are complicated cases. In 2014, a white police officer shot and killed Michael Brown, an

---

104. This criterion corresponds to the first of two marks of prophetic indictments identified by James M. Gustafson, *Varieties of Moral Discourse: Prophetic, Narrative, Ethical, and Policy* (Grand Rapids, MI: Calvin College and Seminary, 1988), 8: Prophets "usually, though not always, address what the prophet perceives to be the *root* of religious, moral, or social waywardness, not specific instances in which certain policies are judged to be inadequate or wrong."

eighteen-year-old African American male, despite the fact that he was unarmed. The shooting triggered mass protests and civil unrest. The police officer was not indicted for criminal misconduct by either the state or the federal authorities; it appears that he acted in self-defense. But the report issued after an investigation by the U.S. Department of Justice found the Ferguson police department had exhibited a "pattern or practice of unlawful conduct" in its treatment of its African American citizenry.[105] So even if the actual shooting of Michael Brown was not unjustified when viewed in isolation, it took place in a social context permeated by racism and prejudice. The citizens of Ferguson were reasonable in their skepticism whether an eighteen-year-old *white* male engaging in the same behavior would have received the same treatment. Consequently, it was reasonable for civil rights activists to use this situation to indict the state—and the country—for patterns of racial injustice that remain entrenched a half a century after Martin Luther King.

Second, returning to my comparative study, the ultimate motives and goals of the use of prophetic indictment differ significantly in the two cases. King's motive is obviously hope-filled and oriented toward the future; he holds before his audience the possibility of justice and peace for the nation as a whole. Nowhere is this clearer than in the last line of his speech:

> And when this happens, when we allow freedom ring, when we let it ring from every village and every hamlet, from every state and every city, we will be able to speed up that day when all of God's children, black men and white men, Jews and Gentiles, Protestants and Catholics, will be able to join hands and sing in the words of the old Negro spiritual, "Free at last, free at last. Thank God Almighty, we are free at last."[106]

In contrast, Pavone's motive in issuing this prophetic indictment against Michael Schiavo on the anniversary of Terri Schiavo's death is not entirely clear. There is no orientation toward the future in his open letter; he is entirely focused on the events of the past and his tone is predominantly vindictive:

105. United States Department of Justice, Civil Rights Division, "Investigation of the Ferguson Police Department," March 4, 2015, www.justice.gov/sites/default/files/opa/press-releases/attachments/2015/03/04/ferguson_police_department_report.pdf.

106. King, "I Have a Dream," in *Autobiography*, 227.

"Your decision to have Terri dehydrated to death was a decision to kill her. It doesn't matter if Judge Greer said it was legal. No judge, no court, no power on earth can legitimize what you did."[107]

It is important that those deploying the rhetoric of prophetic indictment do not deprive their intended audience of all hope of a better and more harmonious future. Otherwise, they have no incentive to listen to the prophet, much less to change. Moreover, the purely vindictive use of prophetic rhetoric to revisit a past incident is unjustified in terms of the ancillary and inevitable harms of that form of discourse; it also may correlate with the misuse of this form of discourse as a righteous cover for all-too-human motives of anger and self-aggrandizement.

Third, and finally, there is a striking difference in the stance that each prophet takes toward the intended audience of his prophetic indictment. King sees himself as part of the community to whom he is issuing the indictment; he anguishes not only with the African Americans whose just claims he advocates but also with the American people as a whole, who have been harmed by the sin of racism. Like the prophet Jeremiah, King suffers with his people on account of their iniquities; he takes no joy in delivering a message of indictment. He begs Americans to end our shameful history of segregation and racism in order that we might flourish together; the vision of a united, free, and redeemed America with which he culminates his address includes black and white, Jew and Gentile, northerner and southerner. His call for repentance and reformation on the part of racists simultaneously holds out to them the possibility of forgiveness and the renewal of community. The beginning of the second half of the speech, the point at which the litany of King's dreams actually commences, decisively establishes this redemptive horizon:

> Let us not wallow in the valley of despair. I say to you today, my friends: so even though we face the difficulties of today and tomorrow, I still have a dream. It is a dream deeply rooted in the American dream.

107. Pavone, "An Open Letter."

I have a dream that one day this nation will rise up and live out the true meaning of its creed—we hold these truths to be self-evident that all men are created equal.

I have a dream that one day on the red hills of Georgia the sons of former slaves and the sons of former slave owners will be able to sit down together at the table of brotherhood.

I have a dream that one day even the state of Mississippi, a state sweltering with the heat of injustice, sweltering with the heat of oppression, will be transformed into an oasis of freedom and justice.[108]

Pavone, in contrast, gives no evidence that he sees himself as having any real bond with Michael Schiavo. More specifically, in addressing Mr. Schiavo, he sets up a dichotomy between a sinful "you" and a righteous "us." "Your actions offend us. Not only have you killed Terri and deeply wounded her family, but you have disgraced our nation, betrayed the Gospel of Jesus Christ, and undermined the principles that hold us together as a civilized society."[109] At the end of the open letter, he issues a call for repentance, with a mention of forgiveness, but it is brief and perfunctory. In this call, Pavone proffers no possibility of living in a reconstituted community with Michael Schiavo. The God whom he invokes is a distant scorekeeper; He does not reconstitute a redeemed world. Pavone writes: "You have made your mark on history, but sadly, it is an ugly stain. In the name of millions around the world, I call on you today to embrace a life of repentance, and to ask forgiveness from the Lord, who holds the lives of each of us in His hands."[110] It would be wrong to say, however, that Pavone's approach has no analogue in the prophetic books. In his contempt for Mr. Schiavo, as well as his apparent inability to conceive of sharing a common community with him, Pavone's approach to prophetic rhetoric echoes the oracles against the enemies of Israel and Judah.

In short, King recognized, while Pavone did not, that in addressing fellow members of one's political or religious community, it is best not to model the

---

108. King, "I Have a Dream," in *Autobiography*, 226.
109. Pavone, "An Open Letter."
110. Ibid.

tone of prophetic discourse on the biblical oracles against the nations. In addressing their fellow citizens, the Hebrew prophets did not set themselves over and against them; in an important sense they stood with their people as much as they stood with the God whose words they spoke. Still less should a prophet speaking to his own community depict himself as on the side of a God who has utterly and completely rejected the members of the community. The Hebrew prophets preached divine mercy as well as divine judgment; as Abraham Joshua Heschel writes, they force us to ponder "[w]hat hidden bond exists between the word of wrath and the word of compassion, between 'consuming fire' and 'everlasting love.'"[111]

---

111. Heschel, *The Prophets*, 27.

Prophecy, Irony, and Humility

Lessons from Lincoln and Jonah

In this temple, as in the hearts of the people for whom he saved the Union, the memory of Abraham Lincoln is enshrined forever." These words are carved above the statue of the sixteenth American president in the monument dedicated to his honor on the National Mall in Washington, DC. They communicate in compact form the same sense of noble beauty, steadfast goodness, and enduring truth conveyed by the monument as a whole. Dedicated in 1922, nearly six decades after the Civil War, the Lincoln Memorial is constructed of gleaming white marble in the Greek style evoking the Parthenon.[1] The memorial features thirty-six Doric columns symbolizing the states included in the American Union at the time of Lincoln's murder. Immortalized in marble, Lincoln himself sits serenely in the center of the temple, casting his watchful and benevolent gaze across the reflecting pool and down the length of the Mall to the Capitol, whose quotidian machinations doubtless seem petty from the vantage point of eternity.[2]

The historical events for which Lincoln is remembered are depicted in sanitized mythological form in murals high on the north and south walls of

---

1. The memorial's composition was chosen for symbolic purposes by architect Henry Bacon; the materials included marble from Alabama, Colorado, Georgia, and Tennessee; granite from Massachusetts; and Indiana limestone. "A country torn apart by war can come together, not only to build something beautiful, but also explain the reunification of the states." National Park Service, Lincoln Memorial Construction, www.nps.gov/linc/historyculture/lincoln-memorial-construction.htm.

2. The statue of Lincoln was sculpted by Daniel Chester French. The National Park Service maintains a very helpful website on the Lincoln Memorial at www.nps.gov/linc/index.htm.

the memorial.[3] The murals, however, are not the most essential aspects of the memorial. Ultimately, it is Lincoln's own words that hold the monument and, by extension, the country upright and together. Standing small and humble before the immense statue of Lincoln, supplicants visiting this temple will find the Gettysburg Address (1863) inscribed on the south wall to their left and the Second Inaugural Address (1865) engraved on the north wall to their right.

In my view, these two speeches need to be interpreted in light of each other, as well as in light of the concrete historical circumstances that generated them. Understood in such a fashion, they cast an ironic light on the sentiments evoked by the structure of the Lincoln Memorial itself. While the text of the Gettysburg Address is carved bloodlessly in unblemished marble, it commemorates one of the most grisly and brutal battles of the Civil War. While mythology of ancient Greek philosophers inspired the memorial on which it is inscribed Lincoln's Second Inaugural is haunted by the terrible and righteous God of the Hebrew prophets. The memorial proudly celebrates the recognition of eternal realities as the basis for a sound society, but the man whom it honors had come to recognize a disturbing fundamental truth about our own society: The American Constitution, the covenant upon which this nation was founded, was marred by a fatal flaw that precluded God's blessing and invited God's judgment. It endorsed treating one class of human beings as property.

How could a nation that saw itself as chosen by God for special responsibilities and blessings survive an error of this magnitude? How could a nation that was so certain for so long about the terms and conditions of its own compact with God grapple with the recognition that this compact had to be rewritten in the blood of its citizens? And how can that nation's rhetorical tradition of the jeremiad accommodate the fact that the nation's prophets did not always grasp the divine message reliably, much less convey it accurately?

---

3. The murals were painted by Jules Guerín. At the center of "Emancipation," the mural on the south wall, the Angel of Truth breaks the manacles of slavery that are binding the limbs of a vigorous and beautiful family of Africans in tribal dress. To their left are magnificently displayed the sword of Justice and the scroll of Law. To their right, graceful personifications of the virtues of Faith, Hope, and Charity surround the figure of Immortality. In a corresponding position on the north wall is a mural entitled "Reunion," which centrally features the Angel of Truth reuniting North and South. Cypress trees, a classical symbol of eternity, peacefully adorn both murals. No sign of human pain mars the mythological scenes.

Is there room in the national tradition of prophetic indictment for a lively sense of divine inscrutability that is not reducible to agnosticism or simple moral relativism?

These are the questions to which I now turn. In Chapter 8, I proposed a normative framework to assist people in determining whether and when it is ethically and pragmatically appropriate to deploy prophetic rhetoric in a debate about socially controversial matters. Yet no normative framework is self-executing. Any framework can be used well, used badly, or abused, depending on the character and temperament of the human beings who apply it. No matter how subtle they are, rules will never be enough for the judicious exercise of the rhetoric of prophetic indictment. We must therefore ask what personal characteristics—what virtues, if you will—are necessary to cultivate if the jeremiad is to play a constructive role in our public square in the years to come.

In my view, the American tradition of prophetic indictment cannot survive into our future, which will be more pluralistic and globalized and less conventionally religious, without practitioners who possess both humility and a lively sense of irony. These virtues can help the tradition of the jeremiad negotiate the journey from modernity's confidence in the possibility of reasonable persons converging on a universally applicable and accessible morality to postmodernity's pessimism about that possibility. By creating a rhetorical space between a prophet's view of the situation and God's view, humility can help the prophets make room for the perspective of others— including those whose positions or actions are the target of their indictments. A capacity for irony, in my view, facilitates prophetic humility by enabling prophets to view their own words and actions from other vantage points. It also captures something of the postmodern sense that one's commitments and viewpoints are ineluctably contingent—that matters look different from different vantage points. Moreover, and equally important, both humility and an ironic sensibility can help us make sense of the failures in our past, of the times when we sacrificed our principles for political or economic expediency.

I will argue that the basic shape of a suitably chastened form of prophetic rhetoric can be discerned in Lincoln's Second Inaugural Address, which is arguably a high-water mark of the American rhetorical tradition. Two objections immediately come to mind, however: First, Lincoln's Second Inaugural is undeniably powerful. But what basis do we have for treating it as discourse in the tradition of the Hebrew prophets? Does Lincoln's acknowledgment of the tenuousness of his grasp of the divine will place the address outside the genre? Not all prophetic rhetoric invokes the divine will, of course. Nonetheless, if it does invoke God, can it also exhibit a certain tentativeness about the divine will and still remain prophetic rhetoric? Second, and more broadly, how do we continue the American tradition of prophetic rhetoric in light of Lincoln's example? What method do we have for revising our conception of prophetic rhetoric without distorting it beyond all recognition? What literary technique will allow us to acknowledge the gap between God's perspective and our understanding of that perspective without creating a totally unbridgeable chasm between them? It is one thing to suggest that human beings only grasp the moral order through a glass, darkly. It is another thing entirely to say that human beings can have no true insights whatsoever into the moral order. A tradition of prophetic indictment cannot accommodate a thoroughgoing moral agnosticism or nihilism because it needs to articulate a fundamental commitment to serve as the basis for its indictment.

My goal in this chapter is to make a case for humility as a valuable and authentic virtue in the rhetorical practice of prophetic indictment while also taking seriously the foregoing objections. In the first section, I will situate Lincoln's Second Inaugural in a broader historical and rhetorical context that encompasses the Gettysburg Address. Both speeches are not merely texts carved in marble but are also words of hope delivered in the midst of military destruction on a biblical scale. From the time of the Puritans, of course, those who employed the language of prophetic indictment threatened the destruction of the nation if its inhabitants failed to repent and reform. Yet as the nation grew and prospered, those threats could easily be viewed as empty rhetorical flourishes by speaker and audience alike. Lincoln and his audiences did not have that luxury; his two greatest speeches were delivered in the crucible of the Civil War's almost unconceivable devastation. Within that crucible, he reconfigured the American jeremiad to incorporate a significant strain of modesty about the will of God. I will argue that Lincoln completed this reconstruction in his Second Inaugural Address, which overcomes key conceptual and rhetorical stumbling blocks that are apparent in the Gettysburg Address.

Is there a biblical touchstone for those who want to honor and extend the reconfiguration of the jeremiad discernible in the Second Inaugural Address? In the second section, I will place Lincoln's approach in conversation with the

Book of Jonah, which offers important cautions and correctives to those who believe the prophets in the Hebrew tradition must be unfailingly confident about their insight into God's plans. Many people wrongly think that Jonah is a short, simple children's story about a man who was swallowed by a giant fish and lived to tell about it. That belief is deeply mistaken. The book is in fact an intricately woven account of the complicated relationship of Yahweh and Jonah, his reluctant prophet. The book opens up legitimate possibilities of cultivating humility in the deliverance of prophetic indictments, in large part by seeing the irony in the relationship between God and prophet.

Irony, of course, is a complicated and contested literary device. Some literary traditions and some literary theorists maintain that its acids not only dislodge untenable or overly ambitious conceptions of truth but also undermine the very ideal of moral truth itself. Yet there are other defensible ways to think about irony, which I explore in the final section of the chapter. In my view, irony should be treated as a rhetorical and analytical tool—not as a metaphysical or moral master. Situated and deployed within the broad theological framework that continues to be presupposed by many practitioners of American prophetic discourse, the tool of irony does not necessarily promote corrosive cynicism. Instead, it can help to foster a healthy modesty about our knowledge of God's purposes and plans. By extension, for practitioners of prophetic rhetoric who do not invoke God, it can nurture humility about their grasp of the basic compact binding the society together.

The Gettysburg Address and the Valley of Slaughter

> Therefore, the days are surely coming, says the Lord, when it will no more be called Topheth, or the valley of the son of Hinnom, but the valley of Slaughter: for they will bury in Topheth until there is no more room. The corpses of this people will be food for the birds of the air, and for the animals of the earth; and no one will frighten them away. And I will bring to an end the sound of mirth and gladness, the voice of the bride and bridegroom in the cities of Judah and in the streets of Jerusalem; for the land shall become a waste.[4]

4. Jeremiah 7:32–34.

When Abraham Lincoln set foot on the plains of Gettysburg, Pennsylvania, in November 1863,[5] he was entering a place that had witnessed devastation; evoking the Hebrew prophets' descriptions of scenes of divine retribution visited upon an unfaithful Israel. And yet by this point in the war, the devastation was not unfamiliar. As Drew Gilpin Faust argues in *This Republic of Suffering*, for those who lived through the Civil War, "the texture of the experience, its warp and woof, was the presence of death."[6] Not the *idea* of death, but its actual disturbing, disruptive, and often disgusting *presence*. The casualties of the Civil War were staggering. Approximately 620,000 soldiers died in the hostilities, a number that accounted for roughly as many deaths as occurred in all the other U.S. wars combined until the time of Vietnam.[7] Approximately 8 percent of all American men age thirteen to forty-three died in the war, and an estimated sixty thousand men lost limbs due to the hostilities.[8] Moreover, the mortally wounded were not buried at sea or interred in a foreign land; they died in vast numbers in the farmlands and forests of American soil. The decaying flesh of the dead from one battle inflicted a wound on the land even after the living moved on to fight the next battle in another location.

The Battle of Gettysburg, which took place July 1–3, 1863, produced the largest number of casualties in the entire war. After the Union Army beat the Confederate soldiers back into the South, the people of Gettysburg (population 2,400) were left to clean up the carnage in the sweltering summer heat. In addition to 22,000 wounded soldiers,[9] they were confronted with

5. Two recent comprehensive biographies are James M. McPherson, *Abraham Lincoln* (New York: Oxford University Press, 2009); and David Herbert Donald, *Lincoln* (New York: Simon & Schuster, 1995). Many people consider Carl Sandburg's work to be definitive; he distilled his six-volume biography into one volume: *Abraham Lincoln: The Prairie Years and the War Years* (New York: Harcourt, Brace, 1954).

6. Drew Gilpin Faust, *This Republic of Suffering: Death and the American Civil War* (New York: Vintage Books, 2008), xiii.

7. Ibid., xi.

8. See Maris A. Vinovskis, "Have Social Historians Lost the Civil War? Some Preliminary Demographic Speculations," in Maris A. Vinovskis, ed., *Toward a Social History of the American Civil War: Exploratory Essays* (Cambridge: Cambridge University Press, 1990), 7; and Laurann Figg and Jane Farrell-Beck, "Amputation in the Civil War: Physical and Social Dimensions," *Journal of the History of Medicine and Allied Sciences* 48, no. 4 (1993): 454–75. Recently, however, a demographic historian has proposed a far higher estimate: 752,000 deaths. See J. David Hacker, "A Census-Based Count of the Civil War Dead," *Civil War History* 57, no. 4 (December 2011): 307–348.

9. Faust, *This Republic*, 69.

approximately 8,000 slain men and 5,000 dead horses or mules.[10] To put it another way, the town faced the prospect of burying six million pounds of quickly decomposing flesh.[11] Witnesses testified to a scene of postapocalyptic dystopia. A nurse described the "rise and swell of human bodies," expanding with the gasses of decomposition, in the shallow graves. David Wills, a Gettysburg banker, reported to the Pennsylvania governor: "In many instances arms and legs and sometimes heads protrude and my attention has been directed to several places where the hogs were actually rooting out the bodies and devouring them."[12]

The practical and moral challenges that death on this scale posed for the survivors were considerable. On the one hand, preserving health and preventing disease required mass and anonymous burials; on the other hand, the efficient processing of the dead undermined the sense that each man who died in the war was a unique human being with an immortal destiny.[13] As Faust argues, the idea of military cemeteries developed as a way of negotiating these competing claims, by honoring the sacrifice of those who could not always even be identified.[14] The Battle of Gettysburg provided the occasion for the first such cemetery. In July 1863, the governor of Pennsylvania appointed David Wills his agent in order to construct a suitable burial ground for the Union dead. Wills arranged to purchase sixteen acres near the battlefield and commenced to plan the dedication of the new cemetery.[15] The gravediggers faced a Herculean task. They began their work in late October; when they finished in March 1864, they would have reburied more than three thousand bodies. The work was only one-third completed, however,

---

10. See Garry Wills, *Lincoln at Gettysburg: The Words That Remade America* (New York: Simon & Schuster, 1992), 20. See also Stephen W. Sears, *Gettysburg* (New York: Houghton Mifflin Harcourt, 2003), 511; and Faust, *This Republic*, 81. The statistics vary slightly from source to source.

11. Faust, *This Republic*, 69.

12. Wills, *Lincoln at Gettysburg*, 20, 21.

13. See Faust, *This Republic*, 61–101 (chap. 3: "Burying: 'New Lessons Caring for the Dead'").

14. Ibid., 99–101. For a broader perspective, see Wills, *Lincoln at Gettysburg*, 71. He writes: "The dedication of Gettysburg must, therefore, be seen in its cultural context, as part of the nineteenth century's fascination with death in general and with cemeteries in particular." He argues that cemeteries were seen in romantic terms, as a liminal place between life and death, suitable for the moral education of young persons.

15. The purchase price was $2,475.87. See Jim Murphy, *The Long Road to Gettysburg* (New York: Clarion Books, 1992), 98–99. The land purchased by Wills was augmented by the lands purchased by David McConaughy, a leading citizen of Gettysburg, to constitute the heart of the Gettysburg National Military Park. Sears, *Gettysburg*, 511–12.

by November 14, 1864—a few days before the dedication of the new Soldiers' National Cemetery on November 19.[16] Piles of unburied coffins remained stacked at the train station where Lincoln arrived the night before.[17]

There were two speakers at the dedication: Edward Everett (d. 1865), a highly distinguished public servant and renowned rhetorician in the Greek revival style who taught at Harvard, followed by Abraham Lincoln, the sixteenth president of the United States.[18] Everett spoke for two hours; Lincoln for two minutes.[19] Both speeches abstracted from the macabre devastation precipitated by the battle; their gestures toward eternal nobilities seemed to rescue the dead soldiers from the pain and gritty indignities of their own particular deaths.[20] At the same time, for persons whose minds and imaginations had been shaped by Scripture, as Lincoln's doubtless had been, the scene at Gettysburg evoked the wrath of God.

Why did the soldiers being commemorated die? Lincoln portrays them as defending the Union.[21] He does not, however, defend or even discuss the U.S. Constitution in the Gettysburg Address, despite the fact that it was the solemn pact binding the several states together into one nation. It is not hard to appreciate the reason. Without ever using the word *slavery,* the document provided for and protected the South's "peculiar institution" at several key points. For

16. Frank L. Klement, *The Gettysburg Soldiers' Cemetery and Lincoln's Address: Aspects and Angles* (Shippensburg, PA: White Mane, 1993), 63, 73. Confederate soldiers were not buried in the cemetery but were often left in the fields where they fell.

17. Garry Wills, "The Words That Remade America: The Significance of the Gettysburg Address," *Atlantic,* Civil War issue, February 2012, 89.

18. Everett, who is more or less forgotten today, was the most famous rhetorician of his day. See Richard A. Katula, *The Eloquence of Edward Everett: America's Greatest Orator* (New York: Peter Lang, 2010).

19. National Parks Service, Gettysburg National Cemetery, Gettysburg, Pennsylvania, www.nps .gov/history/nr/travel/national_cemeteries/Pennsylvania/Gettysburg_National_Cemetery.html. Everett was the main speaker; Lincoln was asked merely to deliver "a few appropriate remarks."

20. There is some uncertainty about the actual contents of the Gettysburg Address. There are five known manuscripts in Lincoln's handwriting, which differ slightly from each other and from newspaper accounts of the text. The copy most widely duplicated, and found on the wall of the Lincoln Memorial, was sent to Colonel Alexander Bliss and is the last known copy written by Lincoln and the only one that he signed and dated. For more information, see www.abrahamlincolnonline .org/lincoln/speeches/gettysburg.htm.

21. Abraham Lincoln, "Address Delivered at the Dedication of the Cemetery at Gettysburg," in Roy P. Basler, ed., *The Collected Works of Abraham Lincoln,* 8 vols. (New Brunswick, NJ: Rutgers University Press, 1953), 7:23. I am using the "Bliss Copy" of the address, which is widely considered to be the definitive text.

example, the Constitution's Three-Fifths Compromise[22] counted each slave as three-fifths of a human person for purposes of the apportionment of congressional representatives. Section 9 of Article 1 prevented Congress from prohibiting the importation of slaves before 1808, thus allowing the slave trade to continue unimpeded by law for twenty years after the Constitution's enactment. Finally, the Fugitive Slave Clause required that an escaped slave who fled to another state be returned to his or her owner.[23]

Instead, Lincoln focuses his audience's attention on the Declaration of Independence, beginning with his famous first line: "Four score and seven years ago our fathers brought forth on this continent, a new nation, conceived in Liberty, and dedicated to the proposition that all men are created equal." In his magisterial assessment of the speech, Garry Wills proposes that the decision to focus on the Declaration of Independence was a tactical decision on Lincoln's part; it constituted a way "to sneak around the frontal defenses of prejudice and find a back way into agreement with bigots."[24] At the same time, Wills recognizes that Lincoln's way of framing the issue entailed deeper and more theoretical issues about the nature of the American polity. More specifically, Wills argues that "Lincoln distinguished between the Declaration as the statement of a permanent ideal and the Constitution as an early and provisional embodiment of that ideal, to be tested against it, kept in motion toward it."[25] Indebted to the worldview of New England transcendentalist Theodore Parker, Lincoln believed that the ideas of equality proclaimed in the Declaration of Independence were ultimately the "only ground of legitimate union for the American nation."[26] At the same time, as the nation progressively approached

22. The Three-Fifths Compromise is found at art. 1, sect. 2, clause 3 of the 1787 U.S. Constitution. It reads as follows: "Representatives and direct Taxes shall be apportioned among the several States which may be included within this Union, according to their respective Numbers, which shall be determined by adding to the whole Number of free Persons, including those bound to Service for a Term of Years, and excluding Indians not taxed, three fifths of all other Persons."

23. The text of the so-called Fugitive Slave Clause, art. 4, sect. 2, clause 3 of the U.S. Constitution, reads as follows: "No Person held to Service or Labour in one State, under the Laws thereof, escaping into another, shall, in Consequence of any Law or Regulation therein, be discharged from such Service or Labour, but shall be delivered up on Claim of the Party to whom such Service or Labour may be due." The word *slavery* is never used in te Constitution. The clause was never formally repealed, although it was rendered essentially toothless after the Thirteenth Amendment abolished slavery when it was adopted in 1865.

24. Wills, *Lincoln at Gettysburg*, 99.

25. Ibid., 101.

26. Ibid., 120.

full realization of those ideas, preserving the Union was Lincoln's paramount pragmatic goal.[27] This goal renders intelligible Lincoln's earlier acquiescence of the Fugitive Slave Act and other compromises with the South in the decade preceding the Civil War. Wills writes that Lincoln felt that the compromises "proved that one can remain opposed to slavery while making temporary concessions to the South in order to keep the nation together. The one thing Lincoln would not surrender, as Douglas had done, was the continued identification of slavery as an evil, no matter how necessary."[28]

Wills explains some of Lincoln's most controversial actions in the war as entailed by his deep commitment to the enduring nature of the American Union: Lincoln saw the hostilities as civic unrest or "insurrection" by unruly citizens, not a "war" between separate sovereign nations.[29] He could therefore suspend the right to habeas corpus in the North as well as in the South because insurrection against the federal government was "the same crime no matter where it occurred."[30] He could emancipate the slaves in the South but not in the North because their emancipation was a pragmatic measure designed to enervate the Rebel forces and funnel determined men into the Union army. What Lincoln could not do, and the North could not do, was unilaterally dismantle the institution of slavery. "[The Constitution] was the enactment of the whole (single) people, and could be changed only by the whole people—through the amendment process. As the South could not unilaterally secede, the North could not unilaterally emancipate."[31]

Wills depicts Lincoln's spiritual mind-set at the time of the Gettysburg Address as imbued with a melancholy romanticism indebted to transcendentalism and neoclassicism. He highlights the ideological mélange reflected in the speech. "It is made compact and compelling by its ability to draw on so many sources of verbal energy—on a classical rhetoric befitting the democratic burial of soldiers, on a romantic nature-imagery of birth and rebirth expected at the dedication of rural cemeteries, on biblical vocabulary of a

27. "Lincoln's constitutional view had concrete legal consequences that are hard, almost impossible, to understand if one treats his devotion to the Union as a mystical notion or sentiment. Only in this context can one assess as he did the legal aspect of belligerency and his emancipation measures." Ibid., 132–33.

28. Ibid., 123.

29. See, for example, ibid., 133.

30. Ibid., 134.

31. Ibid., 137 (original emphasis).

chosen nation's consecration and suffering and resurrection, on a 'culture of death' that made mourning serve life."[32]

So Wills situates Lincoln's biblical vision in the midst of a long string of influences on the Gettysburg Address, which he sees as closely modeling Pericles's funeral oration. Other writers, however, have given more prominence to the biblical influences on the speech. Adam Gopnik, for example, has noted that "Lincoln had mastered the sound of the King James Bible so completely that he could recast abstract issues of constitutional law in Biblical terms."[33] Several scholars have pointed out that as his life progressed, Lincoln's spirituality was increasingly influenced by Scripture, particularly his reading of the Old Testament.[34] Moreover, the shape of his beliefs about the nation's destiny and his own role heavily correlated with the key ideas of Puritan covenant theology.[35] As one of his letters attests, by 1859, Lincoln had come to recognize slavery as a grievous sin, which would inevitably bring the judgment of a righteous God upon the nation that supported the practice.[36] By the time of the Gettysburg Address, the terrifying nature of divine judgment had become fully apparent to Lincoln. In fact, the judgment was realized directly in front of him. The devastated remains of young men, many of whom had died in agony, and some of whom had yet to be laid to rest, unmasked Julia Ward Howe's popular

---

32. Ibid., 89.

33. Adam Gopnik, "Angels and Ages: Lincoln's Language and Its Legacy," *New Yorker*, May 28, 2007, 32.

34. See, for example, Ronald C. White, Jr., *Lincoln's Greatest Speech: The Second Inaugural* (New York: Simon & Schuster, 2002), chap. 6, 121–49. White notes (p. 101) that the mere fact that Lincoln repeatedly quoted Scripture in the Second Inaugural Address was an innovation. A biblical quotation appears only once in the eighteen preceding inaugural addresses.

35. "Alfred Kazin suggests that Lincoln's God 'was born of war.' Surely Lincoln's faith deepened during the war. Even before the war, however, Lincoln's speeches clearly reveal that the Victorian skeptic, the infidel from Springfield, was already beginning to see the slavery debate and the division between North and South in religious terms. Although he had never joined his parents' church, he had retained the idea from his youth that a judgmental God ruled the universe, a God who punished sinners for their offenses." James Tackach, *Lincoln's Moral Vision: The Second Inaugural Address* (Jackson: University Press of Mississippi, 2002), 72, citing Alfred Kazin, *God and the American Writer* (New York: Vintage Books, 1997), 139. On Lincoln's Second Inaugural as a jeremiad, see White, *Lincoln's Greatest Speech*, 150–56.

36. Tackach, *Lincoln's Moral Vision*, 67, citing Roy P. Basler, ed., *The Collected Works of Abraham Lincoln*, 2:376. The letter, dated April 6, 1859, was addressed to "Messers. Henry L. Pierce & others Springfield, Ills." Lincoln wrote: "This is a world of compensations; and he who would *be* no slave, must consent to *have* no slave. Those who deny freedom to others, deserve it not for themselves; and, under a just God, can not long retain it."

"Battle Hymn of the Republic," as a farce, as a bouncy trivialization of the unfathomably bitter grapes of divine wrath.[37]

Lincoln's own stance on the horrors of war was anything but a farce. Yet his pragmatic and incremental attitude toward eradicating slavery stood in uneasy tension with his increasingly vivid sense that the nation had reached a terrible turning point in its covenant with a righteous God. The tension can be seen at three key interrelated points in the Gettysburg Address. First, with all due respect to Wills, Lincoln's strategy of gliding over the Constitution in order to prioritize the Declaration of Independence as the most complete and adequate statement of American ideals is significantly incongruous with both the facts and the law. As a lawyer himself, Lincoln must have known so. The Declaration of Independence simply proclaimed the colonies' determination to be free of English domination; it was never intended to set forth the basis of their own positive cooperation in the post-Revolutionary era. That was initially the task of the Articles of Confederation, the drafting of which began in mid-1776. Fully ratified by the initial thirteen colonies in 1781, the Articles soon proved inadequate to the challenges of governing the new nation because the federal powers they conferred were too tepid. The Constitution became the governing document of the United States in 1789. From a legal perspective, then, it was undeniably the Constitution, not the Declaration of Independence, which set forth the terms of the covenant of this new nation whose destiny was so special to God. And that covenant undeniably protected slavery, a fact that creates a second set of tensions for Lincoln's way of framing the situation in the speech: While proclaiming the importance of national unity, key aspects of the Gettysburg Address further entrench the fact of national division.

For example, Lincoln describes the major point of contention animating the hostilities as preserving the nation's unity. He does not acknowledge the ironies involved in using lethal military force to keep people *inside* a political union. Death, after all, constitutes a rather critical type of participation in the life of a political community. Furthermore, Lincoln has not yet found a way to acknowledge the peculiar status of the Southern combatants. Although it persisted in identifying the now-protracted hostilities as an *internal* insurrection, the Gettysburg Address does not fully grasp the nettle of this situation

37. See my analysis of Julia Ward Howe's "Battle Hymn of the Republic" in Chapter 3.

in either its conceptual framing or in its rhetoric. Identifying the conflict as a "civil war," Lincoln's analysis places the accent on the word *war*. With appropriate modifications, his words about the Northern casualties could be applied to American soldiers fighting for any noble cause. His words divide the combatants between *Us* (the North), which happens to be fighting to preserve the Union, and *Them* (the South), which happens to be fighting to destroy the Union through secession. *They* are our enemies. *We* are not to blame for the war; *they* are. Fully grappling with the idea of a *civil* war, however, requires Lincoln to go further: He needs to acknowledge *Them* as fellow Americans— as part of *Us*.

The peculiar setting of the Gettysburg Address doubtless contributed to the ironic divide. The new national cemetery for the American war dead only provided a resting place for *Northern* soldiers. At best, most dead *Southern* soldiers who died in the battle were dumped into mass graves and hastily covered with a thin layer of dirt.[38] Many were left to the fierce mercies of the animals and the elements. Their fate was justified, the North would say, because they wanted to break up the national union. But the South *was* willing to remain in the country on the terms set forth in the Constitution— as the Southerners kept insisting, it was the *North* that wanted to change the terms of the compact that united the states. More important, if the Union was, in fact, unbreakable, did not *every American* soldier who died in the battle at least deserve a decent burial?

In the end, it is impossible to avoid the Constitution. It is impossible to sidestep the fact that the basic and long-settled "rights" protected and endorsed by the founding document of this nation centrally included the institution of slavery, which Lincoln increasingly recognized was odious in the divine sight. For that reason, as we have seen, the fiery abolitionist William Lloyd Garrison had famously called the Constitution "a covenant with death" and

---

38. "Confederates at Gettysburg were buried in trenches containing 150 or more men, often hurled rather than laid to rest. Sometimes the rotting bodies ruptured, compelling burial parties to work elsewhere until the stench had dissipated. Soldiers stomped 'on top of the *dead* straightening out their legs and arms and *tramping* them down so as to make the hole contain as many as possible.'" Faust, *This Republic of Suffering*, 71–72. See also, for example, Gregory A. Coco, *Wasted Valor: The Confederate Dead at Gettysburg* (Gettysburg, PA: Thomas Publications, 1990), 17–42. For another account of the sheer number of casualties, see J. David Petruzzi and Steven Stanley, *The Gettysburg Campaign in Numbers and Losses: Synopses, Orders of Battle, Strengths, Casualties, and Maps, June 9–July 14, 1863* (El Dorado Hills, CA: Savas Beatie, 2013).

"an agreement with hell."[39] How does one convinced of the basic truth of a covenantal relationship between God and the nation come to terms with the fact that the American national covenant has long been marred by a fatal moral flaw?

This question focuses our attention on a third tension in the Gettysburg Address. Given the nature of the occasion, Lincoln cannot avoid acknowledging the costs of the war in human lives. Significantly, however, he configures the lost lives, with biblical resonances, as holy sacrifices. "We are met on a great battle-field of that war. We have come to dedicate a portion of that field, as a final resting place for those who here gave their lives that that nation might live. . . . But, in a larger sense, we can not dedicate—we can not consecrate—we can not hallow—this ground. The brave men, living and dead, who struggled here, have consecrated it, far above our poor power to add or detract."

In the economy of the biblical covenant, however, all sacrifices are not equally acceptable. It is the purity of heart of those performing the ceremony that counts; no amount of sacrifice can compensate for a heart hardened on the path of continued wrongdoing. The question that Lincoln has not fully faced in the Gettysburg Address is whether this nation, for whom these men died, *deserved* to live in God's eyes, given its sins. And if the nation did not deserve to live, then the deaths of these young men could not be configured as a holy and acceptable sacrifice—they must be recognized as a condign although terrible punishment.

At the heart of these tensions visible in the Gettysburg Address stands the relationship between the persistence of the institution of slavery and the preservation of the nation. Scholars have documented an evolution in Lincoln's thought on this matter over the course of the war. Early in the conflict, his main objective was to preserve the unity of the nation; ending slavery was an important but ultimately subsidiary goal: In fact, Lincoln once stated, "Much as I hate slavery, I would consent to the extension of it rather than see the Union dissolved, just as I would consent to any GREAT evil, to avoid a GREATER one."[40] It was not the existence of slavery as a "peculiar institution"

---

39. Paul Finkelman, "Garrison's Constitution: The Covenant with Death and How It Was Made," *Prologue* 32, no. 4 (Winter 2000): 231.

40. Abraham Lincoln, "Speech at Peoria, Illinois," October 16, 1854, in Basler, ed., *The Collected Works of Abraham Lincoln,* 2:247–83, at 270.

in the South that forced Lincoln's hand; he could tolerate slavery provided that it remained geographically contained, in the hope that it would eventually wither and die. Yet the *Dred Scott* decision forced him to rethink his gradualist approach.[41] *Dred Scott* held that the Fifth Amendment to the Constitution invalidated any law that would deprive a slaveholder of his property rights in his slaves, even upon their migration into free territory. Functionally, *Dred Scott* invalidated the Missouri Compromise, which prevented the expansion of slavery into the Northern territories. It meant that slavery would no longer be geographically containable. In his famous "House Divided" speech, Lincoln made the case that the nation would inevitably become either all slave or all free, and that the second option was the only morally acceptable one.[42]

But as the war wore on, Lincoln increasingly came to perceive that the central point of the war was in fact to eradicate slavery throughout the nation.[43] He framed the insight in religious terms. As his faith deepened over the course of his presidency, Lincoln increasingly saw himself as an instrument of the divine will. In a letter to Albert G. Hodes dated April 4, 1864, he clearly indicated his view that the war was a punishment for the nation's sins.[44] At the same time, Lincoln grew increasingly uncertain about the precise shape of God's will. This uncertainty did not mean, however, that he conceived of God as a distant and remote first cause. Lincoln was no deist; the God to whom he prayed remained the God revealed in the Bible, particularly the Old Testament. In fact, during the course of the war, Lincoln proclaimed several days of fasting and prayer, or thanksgiving,[45] a practice that fits well

41. *Dred Scott v. Sandford*, 60 U.S. 393 (1857).

42. Abraham Lincoln, "'A House Divided': Speech at Springfield, Illinois," June 16, 1858, in Basler, ed., *The Collected Works of Abraham Lincoln*, 2:461–69.

43. James Tackach makes this case in compelling fashion in *Lincoln's Moral Vision*.

44. "I claim not to have controlled events, but confess plainly that events have controlled me. Now, at the end of three years struggle the nation's condition is not what either party, or any man devised, or expected. God alone can claim it. Whither it is tending seems plain. If God now wills the removal of a great wrong, and wills also that we of the North as well as you of the South, shall pay fairly for our complicity in that wrong, impartial history will find therein new cause to attest and revere the justice and goodness of God." Abraham Lincoln, "To Albert G. Hodges," April 4, 1864, in Basler, ed., *The Collected Works of Abraham Lincoln*, 7:281–283, at 282.

45. These are available on the website of the American Presidency Project at www.presidency .ucsb.edu/proclamations.php: Abraham Lincoln, Proclamation 85—Proclaiming a Day of National Humiliation, Prayer, and Fasting (August 12, 1861); Proclamation 88—Day of Public Thanksgiving for Victories During the Civil War (April 10, 1862); Proclamation 97—Appointing a Day of National Humiliation, Fasting, and Prayer (March 30, 1863); Proclamation 103—Day of Thanksgiving, Praise,

within the covenantal theology of the Puritans.[46] But the war had doubtless taught him that the God of the Bible was neither tame nor subject to human manipulation.

Lincoln's Second Inaugural Address and Chastened Prophecy

I propose that Lincoln's Second Inaugural Address[47] overcomes the conceptual and rhetorical tensions I have just identified in the Gettysburg Address. Furthermore, I want to suggest that it does so by prioritizing the clear-sighted recognition that slavery itself was the central reason of the war. This recognition in turn provides Lincoln with the hermeneutical and moral key to resolve the questions of national unity, the national covenant, and blame for the war. Whereas the word *slavery* does not appear in the Gettysburg Address, it provides the central focus of the Second Inaugural Address. At the beginning of the third paragraph, the central paragraph of the speech, Lincoln declares: "One eighth of the whole population were colored slaves, not distributed generally over the Union, but localized in the Southern part of it. These slaves constituted a peculiar and powerful interest. All knew that this interest was, somehow, the cause of the war." Unlike the Gettysburg Address, where the events precipitating the threat to the Union are left shrouded in abstraction, Lincoln precisely identifies the cause of the war: "To strengthen, perpetuate, and extend this interest was the object for which the insurgents would rend the Union, even by war; while the government claimed no right to do more than to restrict the territorial enlargement of it." At first blush, this sentence, which encapsulates Lincoln's own gradualist policy, seems to exonerate the North for its role in the war. Read in the context of the speech, however, it is a bill of indictment for complicity in the sin of slavery.

---

and Prayer (July 15, 1863); Proclamation 106—Thanksgiving Day, 1863 (October 3, 1863); Proclamation 114—Appointing a Day of National Humiliation, Fasting, and Prayer (July 7, 1864); Proclamation 118— Thanksgiving Day, 1864 (October 20, 1864).

46. Tackach writes: "Nonetheless, the Puritanical beliefs of Lincoln's parents, which were still strongly evident in American culture in the mid-nineteenth century, took hold in him in important ways during his early adult years and remained with him through middle age." Tackach, *Lincoln's Moral Vision*, 62. In short, the fact that Lincoln did not attend church services does not mean that he was devoid of religious sensibilities.

47. Abraham Lincoln, "Second Inaugural Address," March 4, 1865, in Basler, ed., *The Collected Works of Abraham Lincoln*, 8:332–333.

Lincoln distinguishes, but does not divide, North and South in their guilt for slavery. "It may seem strange that any men should dare to ask a just God's assistance in wringing their bread from the sweat of other men's faces; but let us judge not that we be not judged." Most significantly, he clearly recognizes the culpability of both parties to the war before the divine tribunal.

> If we shall suppose that American Slavery is one of those offences which, in the providence of God, must needs come, but which, having continued through His appointed time, He now wills to remove, and that He gives to both North and South, this terrible war, as the woe due to those by whom the offence came, shall we discern therein any departure from those divine attributes which the believers in a Living God always ascribe to Him?

Why was this "woe due to" the North? Lincoln does not say. But it was clear to everyone at the time how much Northerners had profited economically from the slave trade.[48] In addition the North had profited politically from the Constitution, which, as Lincoln elliptically noted, had legitimated slavery even as it limited it.

Moreover, as the foregoing passage illustrates, Lincoln *neither* distinguishes *nor* divides the North and the South in terms of the price each paid for the war. While the Gettysburg Address configured that price paid by the North as a holy sacrifice, the Second Inaugural Address recognizes the devastation and death suffered by both sides as together constituting a just penalty for the nation's grievous sins. "Yet, if God wills that it [the war] continue, until all the wealth piled by the bond-man's two hundred and fifty years of unrequited toil shall be sunk, and until every drop of blood drawn with the lash, shall be paid by another drawn with the sword, as was said three thousand years ago, so still it must be said 'the judgments of the Lord, are true and righteous altogether.'"

Finally, Lincoln does not differentiate between North and South as he articulates the duty to care for the casualties of the war. He importunes the entire country to act: "With malice toward none; with charity for all . . . let us

48. See, for example, Craig Steven Wilder, *Ebony & Ivy: Race, Slavery, and the Troubled History of America's Universities* (New York: Bloomsbury, 2013).

strive on to finish the work we are in; to bind up the nation's wounds; to care for him who shall have borne the battle, and for his widow, and his orphan— to do all which may achieve and cherish a just, and a lasting peace, among ourselves, and with all nations." In the Gettysburg Address, Lincoln treated Southern soldiers as the unmentionable enemy; in the Second Inaugural Address, he configures them as our fellow sinful Americans.

In the Second Inaugural Address, given just months before the end of his own life, Lincoln finally locates the unity of North and South in sin and penance before a just God. The individual men and women who were afflicted in the war were caught up in a cosmic drama whose import they could grasp only hazily. "Neither party expected for the war, the magnitude, or the duration, which it has already attained. Neither anticipated that the *cause* of the conflict might cease with, or even before, the conflict itself should cease." Lincoln does not pretend that he himself fully understands the ways of his fellow human beings, much less the ways of God. He candidly acknowledges that both sides "read the same Bible." He does not demonize those who read the Bible differently, even as he initially judges their reading itself to be "strange" and ultimately the cause of God's terrible wrath against the nation.

Lincoln is rightly lionized as "the President who saved the Union and ended slavery." I have suggested thus far that the Second Inaugural Address invites us to reframe the label and to see him as having saved the Union *by* ending the sin of slavery, for which the entire nation was held responsible by a righteous God. I would now like to propose that Lincoln's Second Inaugural Address gestures toward a way to revise our understanding of the jeremiad to meet the needs of our current era. In Chapter 8, I formulated some moral and rhetorical criteria for those deliberating about whether to use the rhetoric of prophetic indictment in the public square. But no abstract list of criteria can map the paths forged by true moral and rhetorical genius confronted with a terrible crisis.

Lincoln's Second Inaugural Address exhibits several of the characteristics of good prophetic rhetoric that I identified in Chapter 8. He does not use the oracles against the nations as a model for castigating the South; his chastisements are clearly more analogous to the oracles against Israel. He holds the whole people, North and South, responsible for the nation's sins. Moreover, he stands with his fellow citizens as they suffer, as one with them; he does not separate prophetic discourse from lamentation. He is not calling down divine destruction upon an alien population; he is bracing himself along with his own people for the just lash of divine punishment. Mediating between God and his countrymen, he acknowledges that "[f]ondly do we hope—fervently do we pray—that this mighty scourge of war may speedily pass away" while immediately reminding his audience that the scourge is a condign penalty.

Yet the Second Inaugural Address takes an additional and striking step: It carves out a space for prophetic humility. Lincoln notes that both sides of the war "pray to the same God" and "invoke His aid against the other." Calling the situation "fundamental and astounding," he emphasizes the lack of cor-relation between the prophetic word and the subsequent result. Neither party "expected" or "anticipated" the war's duration. Each "looked for an easier triumph." Lincoln creates distance between the prophets of *both* sides and the divine will: "The prayers of both could not be answered; that of neither has been answered fully. The Almighty has His own purposes." Lincoln does not claim for himself, or cede to anyone else, untrammeled access to the mind of God. His closing exhortation, and his call to action, begins, "With malice toward none; with charity for all; with firmness in the right, as God gives us to see the right. . . ." At the same time, Lincoln is no moral relativist; he is utterly clear in his conviction that slavery is an offense in the sight of God. Humility about divine purposes, in his view, ought not lead to moral indiffer-ence but rather to love of neighbor, and even possibly to love of enemy.

Taken in itself, this stance of prophetic humility toward the divine will may not seem remarkable. Viewed in light of the American rhetorical tradi-tion of the jeremiad, however, it is a tremendously significant development, for two reasons. First, as Chapters 4 and 5 explored, the jeremiad is modeled on a legal indictment for violation of the covenant. The prophet is cast into the role of prosecutor. Characteristically, indictments do not express doubts about what the sovereign's law requires, nor do they manifest any tentative-ness in the charge that the defendant broke the law. Second, the biblical tradi-tion that inspired the American jeremiad places a premium on the prophet's ability to discern a certain pattern of cause and effect. In fact, the very legiti-macy of a biblical prophet depends on his ability to communicate divine will reliably. In the biblical context, a prophet whose threats do not materialize is a false prophet who will himself incur the wrath of God. By saying that the prayers of neither side were answered fully, then, Lincoln was actually implying that the prophets of neither side had fully accounted for the will of

God. The next question that arises is whether this implication puts Lincoln outside the genre of prophetic indictment indebted to the Bible. I believe the answer to this question is no, and will draw on the Book of Jonah to support my position.

Reflections on the Book of Jonah

From a religious perspective, a false prophet is a dangerous man. At best, he is deluded; at worst, he is a charlatan. From a political perspective, a false prophet is a divisive distraction—he seduces people to conform to his own false vision of the nation's flaws and their appropriate remedy. The Scriptures make clear that a *false* prophet is very bad news indeed. But what about a *humble* prophet—a prophet who sees through a glass, darkly, who knows that his grasp of God's purposes and plans is not entirely clear? What about a prophet who ought to be humbler—a prophet who ought to guard against the fact that his own feelings and desires may distort the message he is commanded to deliver?

The Bible does contain the story of one prophet who fits this description: That story is found in the Book of Jonah, one of the shorter books in the Old Testament. Unlike most biblical books named after prophets, the Book of Jonah is not a collection of oracles delivered by (or in the tradition of) the man whose name it bears.[49] Jonah delivers only one very brief oracle in the book; moreover, he delivers that oracle quickly and (most commentators say) reluctantly. The book recounts the story of God's relationship to Jonah, not the story of God's relationship to the Hebrew people mediated by messages delivered by Jonah. In fact, the most striking thing about the book is that the oracle is not meant for the Hebrew people at all; Jonah is asked to deliver it to Nineveh, an antagonist of the Jewish people. Moreover, while the oracle initially seems to be a standard form oracle against the nations, promising devastation to the implacable enemies of Israel, it actually portends something new and different: repentance, reform, and renewed life.

Despite its brevity, the Book of Jonah offers its readers an intricate set of hermeneutical puzzles that admit of no easy or univocal resolution. Its

---

49. For a helpful essay situating Jonah in relationship to the other books in the Hebrew Bible, see Hyun Chul Paul Kim, "Jonah Read Intertextually," *Journal of Biblical Literature* 126, no. 3 (2007): 497–528.

ambiguities are readily apparent in the New Testament. Both Matthew and Luke recount how the scribes and Pharisees asked Jesus for a sign, and he replied that they would receive only the sign of Jonah. While the two Gospel writers are clearly telling the same story, they attribute quite different meanings to that sign. For Matthew, the "sign of Jonah" is the three days that the prophet spent in the belly of the fish before rescue, which presages Jesus's three days in the grave before resurrection.[50] For Luke, the "sign of Jonah" was the prophet's message to the people of Nineveh, which prompted them to repent.[51]

Later efforts proved no more successful than those of the Gospel writers in pinning down the meaning of Jonah. What genre is the Book of Jonah? Is it history or historical fiction? Is it a myth? A legend? A short story?[52] Is it satire, parody, or farce?[53] Is the Book of Jonah a parable or a fable or a type of didactic story?[54] Is Jonah a "comic dupe"[55] or a comic hero?[56] Is the story akin to a "biblical cartoon"?[57] All of these ways of reading the book and its central character have been proposed; while some are more plausible than

50. "Then some of the scribes and Pharisees said to him, 'Teacher, we wish to see a sign from you.' But he answered them, 'An evil and adulterous generation asks for a sign, but no sign will be given to it except the sign of the prophet Jonah. *For just as Jonah was three days and three nights in the belly of the sea monster, so for three days and three nights the Son of Man will be in the heart of the earth.* The people of Nineveh will rise up at the judgment with this generation and condemn it, because they repented at the proclamation of Jonah, and see, something greater than Jonah is here! The queen of the South will rise up at the judgment with this generation and condemn it, because she came from the ends of the earth to listen to the wisdom of Solomon, and see, something greater than Solomon is here.'" Matthew 12:38–42 (emphasis mine).

51. "When the crowds were increasing, he began to say, 'This generation is an evil generation; it asks for a sign, but no sign will be given to it except the sign of Jonah. *For just as Jonah became a sign to the people of Nineveh, so the Son of Man will be to this generation.* The queen of the South will rise at the judgment with the people of this generation and condemn them, because she came from the ends of the earth to listen to the wisdom of Solomon, and see, something greater than Solomon is here! The people of Nineveh will rise up at the judgment with this generation and condemn them, because they repented at the proclamation of Jonah, and see, something greater than Jonah is here!'" Luke 11:29–32 (emphasis mine).

52. Jack M. Sasson, *Jonah: The Anchor Yale Bible* (New Haven, CT: Yale University Press 2010), 327. Sasson ends his marvelous commentary with a section surveying the various interpretations of the book of Jonah; see pp. 323–52.

53. Ibid., 331.

54. Ibid., 335.

55. Ibid., 345.

56. Ibid., 348.

57. Yvonne Sherwood, "Cross-Currents in the Book of Jonah: Some Jewish and Cultural Midrashim on a Traditional Text," *Biblical Interpretation* 6, no. 1 (1998) 49–79, at 49.

others, none have been ruled out decisively. Moreover, these divergent readings feed and are fed by differing ways of interpreting the events that transpire in the story.

The distinguished biblical scholar Joseph Blenkinsopp maintains that the purpose of the book is to mount a radical critique of a certain pat understanding of the role of prophecy. He holds that the Book of Jonah "breaks once and for all the bond of what might be called prophetic causality by its emphasis on the divine freedom."[58] How does it go about accomplishing this objective? In my view, this message is communicated by the ambiguities and uncertainties attendant on both plot and character, which have been highlighted by recent work in critical biblical scholarship.

JONAH, AMBIGUITY, AND UNCERTAINTY

The Book of Jonah[59] begins with a call to prophecy: the Lord told Jonah to "[g]o at once to Nineveh, that great city, and cry out against it; for their wickedness has come up before me."[60] After Jonah's detour through the belly of the fish in an unsuccessful attempt to escape his divinely ordained duty, the Lord reiterates the very same commission.[61] Recognizing that resistance is futile, the reluctant prophet finally delivers a pithy oracle to the Ninevites: "Forty days more, and Nineveh shall be overthrown!"[62] Not only do the Ninevites listen to Jonah, they even respond to his message by performing extravagant acts of contrition, with every living being, from the king to the smallest animal, donning sackcloth and abstaining from food and drink. The Ninevites express some hope that they might ward off the threatened destruction: "Who knows? God

58. Joseph Blenkinsopp, *A History of Prophecy in Israel,* rev. ed. (Louisville, KY: Westminster John Knox Press, 1996), 243.

59. Although extremely short, the book is elaborately and painstakingly constructed. See, for example, Phyllis Trible, *Rhetorical Criticism: Context, Method, and the Book of Jonah* (Minneapolis, MN: Fortress Press, 1994), for a detailed structural analysis. See also Ernst R. Wendland, "Text Analysis and the Genre of Jonah" (part 1), *Journal of the Evangelical Theological Society* 39, no. 2 (June 1996): 191–206; and "Text Analysis and the Genre of Jonah" (part 2), *Journal of the Evangelical Theological Society* 39, no. 3 (September 1996): 373–95.

60. Jonah 1:2.

61. Jonah 3:2.

62. Jonah 3:4. Whereas the Babylonian Talmud reads "forty days," the Septuagint reads "three days." This discrepancy has not escaped Jewish or Christian commentators over the centuries, including St. Jerome, who admitted being puzzled by it. For an account of various ways proposed to reconcile the discrepancy, see, for example, R. W. L. Moberly, "Preaching for a Response? Jonah's Message to the Ninevites Reconsidered," *Vetus Testamentum* 53, no. 2: (2003): 156–68.

may relent and change his mind; he may turn from his fierce anger, so that we do not perish."[63] And lo and behold, God does change His mind; seeing their repentance, He decides to contain His wrath.

Jonah's oracle was categorical, not hypothetical: It did not explicitly call on the Ninevites to repent as a necessary and sufficient condition of warding off disaster.[64] Does it follow, then, that Jonah's oracle was false? No. According to many scripture scholars, the Hebrew word that corresponds to "will be overturned" is ambiguous. On the one hand, it normally means "will be destroyed." On the other hand, it can also mean "will be turned around," as in "they turned their lives around."[65] The narrative is carefully structured to lead us to an event that is unexpected but not impossible given the precise language of the oracle.

This ambiguity in the meaning of the oracle stands at the center of a number of other ambiguities and uncertainties in the Book of Jonah. A second such locus can be found in the two different terms used to refer to the deity: *Yahweh,* or "Lord," is used twenty-two times in the Book of Jonah; *Elohim,* or "God," is used thirteen times; and the combination *Lord God* appears four times. Biblical scholars have gleaned a pattern for usage in the first three and a half chapters: *Yahweh* is generally used to refer to the God of the Hebrews, while *Elohim* is a more general term that is also used to refer to the gods worshiped by other peoples, such as the sailors whose ship Jonah boards in order to avoid his divine commission, and the Ninevites to whom

---

63. Jonah 3:9.

64. In his perceptive engagement with the Book of Jonah, Michael Walzer recognizes that Jonah, like the prophet Amos, is "a critic from the outside." Michael Walzer, *Interpretation and Social Criticism* (Cambridge, MA: Harvard University Press, 1987), 91. Yet Walzer does not focus on the remarkable fact that, unlike most oracles against the nations, Jonah is actually sent by God *to* the Ninevites, evidently to provoke the reform of Nineveh. While Amos criticizes the enemies of Israel for their unethical behavior, he was not a messenger sent by God to them but castigated them (and prophesied their doom) from afar. Amos's approach is far more typical of the oracles against the nations than that of Jonah.

65. See, for example, Trible, *Rhetorical Criticism,* 180: "The verb *hpk* holds the opposite meanings of destruction and deliverance." See also Sasson, *Jonah,* 234–35. Sasson notes that even in the rabbinic era Jewish exegetes were arguing the passage ought to be translated, "Nineveh will be reformed." Sasson also points to an ancient tradition that the word *nehpāket* is purposefully ambiguous. But Uriel Simon's commentary for the Jewish Publication Society judges this assertion of a double meaning to be "dubious." He argues that the Hebrew verb used "connote[s] utter and complete destruction" and "particularly calls to mind the categorical punishment of Sodom and Gomorrah on account of their grave sins." Uriel Simon, *Jonah: The JPS Bible Commentary* (Philadelphia, PA: The Jewish Publication Society, 1999), 29.

he was told to prophesy. This schema does not totally account for the usage at the end of the fourth and final chapter of the book, which encompasses God's conversation with Jonah about the salvation of Nineveh.[66] Jonathan Magonet suggested that the term *Elohim* is used when the narrator is describing a punitive divine action, such as when God appoints a worm to attack the plant that had provided shade to Jonah, and a hot wind to target Jonah himself. In contrast, the term *Yahweh* reappears when the narrator's focus shifts to divine mercy or concern—whether for Jonah or the Ninevites.[67]

Functionally, the mixed usage of the terms broadens the reader's sense of the divine being in two ways. First, by associating Yahweh, the familiar God of the covenant, with the more inscrutable and unpredictable Elohim, the book reminds those who are God's covenant partners that the divine power cannot be manipulated in order to achieve human plans and purposes. Second, by associating Elohim, the name used in Scripture for the deities worshiped by pagan nations, with Yahweh, who is evidently focused on the weal and woe of the Jewish people, the book vividly raises the prospect of divine love and concern for those outside the covenant.

Both lessons, in my view, are essential for Americans who have adapted and continued the Puritan vision of this country as a New Jerusalem, in a new covenant with God, which draws on the grace of Christ to fulfill the model exemplified in God's covenant with the Jewish people. Political historians have documented the effect of American exceptionalism on U.S. foreign policy. Ultimately rooted in the belief that the United States stands in a privileged relationship with God, American exceptionalism has been used to justify policies that callously disregard the rights and needs of other peoples when their interests conflict with our own.[68]

Some critics have suggested that combating the dangers of American exceptionalism will require dismantling the covenantal framework expressed in the tradition of the jeremiad. In my view, however, the covenantal imagination is

---

66. James Limburg, *Jonah* (Louisville, KY: Westminster John Knox Press, 1993), 45–47.

67. Ibid., 46, citing Jonathan Magonet, *Form and Meaning: Studies in Literary Techniques in the Book of Jonah* (Sheffield, UK: Almond Press, 1983), 33–38.

68. For different perspectives on American exceptionalism, see, for example, Deborah L. Madsen, *American Exceptionalism* (Edinburgh: Edinburgh University Press, 1998); Andrew J. Bacevich, *The Limits of Power: The End of American Exceptionalism* (New York: Metropolitan Books, 2008); Godfrey Hodgson, *The Myth of American Exceptionalism* (New Haven, CT: Yale University Press, 2009); and Donald E. Pease, *The New American Exceptionalism* (Minneapolis: University of Minnesota Press, 2009).

too deeply ingrained in American rhetoric to be uprooted from our political and religious discourse. Yet what cannot be removed can be reformed. The Book of Jonah limns a way to nourish and maintain a covenantal framework between God and a particular group of people while ensuring that the terms of the covenant are duly respectful of God's broader concerns as the maker and sustainer of all creation.

At the same time, it is impossible to ignore the substantial currents of uncertainty regarding the genre of the book; its date; and the identity and motivation of its characters, narrator, and author. What do we know about the prophet whose adventures are described in the Book of Jonah? This fundamental question immediately raises a number of uncertainties about the text. In the first verse of the first chapter, he is straightforwardly identified as Jonah son of Amittai, who also appears in 2 Kings as a prophet of the Northern Kingdom, active during the reign of Jeroboam II (about 786–746 BCE).[69] During this time period, Israel was engaged in a program of expansion; in fact, the Jonah of 2 Kings urged the king to act aggressively to recover some of his territories. Here, then we find an irony in the name and character of the prophet. The English translation of his name would roughly be "Dove, son of Truth."[70] As many commentators have pointed out, the Jonah of 2 Kings was a hawk, not a dove;[71] his goal was to convince the king to act aggressively to retake land that Israel had lost in previous battles. Is the prophet in the Book of Jonah a hawk? It is not clear. As I will discuss in more detail below, most commentators believe that he was upset that God failed to destroy Nineveh in conformity with the most obvious meaning of his oracle. He is clearly a *dove*, however, at least in some senses. As scholars in the rabbinic tradition have noted, the dove is a bird that characteristically mews and whines and complains—just as Jonah seems to do about his mission from God. But there is an irony in this label as well. Doves are quintessential birds of sacrifice, offered in the temple in expiation for the sins of God's people. Jonah is sent to a foreign

---

69. Blenkinsopp describes the Jonah of Kings as "an optimistic and nationalist prophet." He thinks it is highly unlikely that the book of Jonah "stood originally after the allusion to the Northern prophet of the same name mentioned in Dtr (2 Kings 14:25). Nor can it be described as a midrash on that text." See Blenkinsopp, *A History of Prophecy*, 240.

70. Phillip Cary, *Jonah* (Grand Rapids, MI: Brazos Press, 2008), 30–31.

71. See, for example, David L. Petersen, *The Prophetic Literature: An Introduction* (Louisville, KY: Westminster John Knox Press, 2002), 193.

land and not to the temple.[72] He would understandably fear that the result of this mission was his own death. Yet it appears that if he is a sacrifice, he is certainly an unwilling one.

Is Jonah rightly called a son of truth? This, too, is unclear. On the one hand, in the first three chapters, he seems reluctant to preach God's message to the Ninevites, and in the fourth chapter he seems to be unhappy with the outcome. On the other hand, when his shipmates are threatened by a storm directed against him, he does not hesitate to acknowledge that he is the source of their problems and to urge them to save themselves by throwing him overboard. The *New Jerome Biblical Commentary* translates Jonah's patronym as "trustworthy," noting that the name "provides the first hint of the irony that pervades the narrative: the prophet forthwith demonstrates his untrustworthiness by blatantly shirking his responsibility as a prophet."[73]

Who were the Ninevites and why was Jonah so reluctant to prophesy to them? A straightforward answer to this question immediately presents itself. Nineveh was the capital of the Assyrian Empire, one of the greatest and most brutal enemies of the Hebrew people. Jonah would have been understandably reluctant to enter into the belly of *that* beast in order to deliver what he would have surely anticipated to be an unwelcome prophetic oracle. Upon closer inspection, however, that explanation proves to be less than satisfying, at least if we hold to the claim that the book was composed at the time of Jonah ben Amittai. At the time the Jonah of 2 Kings was advising Jeroboam II, Nineveh was not yet the capital of Assyria. In fact, many scholars believe that it was more like a provincial capital. Nineveh did not become the grand city that the Book of Jonah seems to contemplate until about 700 BCE, when Sennacherib engaged in a vast program of expansion. By that time, the Northern Kingdom of Israel had already disappeared from the scene.[74] Amos, Hosea, and Micah,

---

72. The word *dove* has several uses in the Hebrew Scriptures; see, for example, Sasson, *Jonah*, 69. He notes, for example, the word appears "in listings for sacrificial offerings, as a term of endearment, and as an inspiration for similes and metaphors." For an exploration of Jonah's message in connection with the story of Noah, see Sheila Tuller Keiter, "Noah and the Dove: The Integral Connection between Noah and Jonah," *Jewish Bible Quarterly* 40, no. 4 (2012): 261–65.

73. Anthony R. Ceresko, O.S.F.S., "Jonah," in *The New Jerome Biblical Commentary*, ed. Raymond E. Brown, S.S., Joseph A. Fitzmeyer, S.J., and Roland E. Murphy, O.Carm. (Englewood Cliffs, NJ: Prentice Hall, 1990), 582.

74. More specifically, the Northern Kingdom began to be constricted in the mid-eighth century, when Tiglath-Pileser III reorganized and consolidated the Assyrian Empire. He offered subject states the choice between complete annihilation or existence under repressive terms of vassalage. When the

the writing prophets of the Northern Kingdom, attributed Assyria's success to Israel's faithlessness, while Isaiah and Nahum, prophets of the Southern Kingdom, described the scourge and ultimate survival of the people of Judah as due to their repentance and God's mercy.

Taking note of the foregoing anomalies, many biblical scholars date the Book of Jonah not to the early eighth century BCE and the events described in 2 Kings but rather to the fourth century BCE and the experience of the Judeans after they returned from the Babylonian exile.[75] As Jack Sasson notes, "To the prophets of Israel, even to those who lived after Assyria's fall, the name Nineveh was enough to prompt memory of a bitter and long-lasting yoke."[76] They propose to interpret the book as a prophetic fable, written with the intent of counteracting the "the separatist and exclusivist tendencies" of the post-exile prophets such as Ezra and Nehemiah.[77] Privileging the Jews returning from exile, these prophets cast suspicion upon those who had stayed behind, portraying them as faithless and contaminated by intermarriage with pagans.[78] In this account, Nineveh is not meant to signal so much a

---

Northern Kingdom began to balk at those terms, it was extinguished. In 722 BCE, Sargon II conquered Samaria and deported nearly thirty thousand Israelites to Mesopotamia and Media. The Southern Kingdom of Judah barely survived Sennacherib's invasion in 701. Yet its fortunes took a sudden turn for the better. Sennacherib left Palestine, never to return, after a plague devastated his army before he could conquer Jerusalem. See Jay Lemanski, "Jonah's Nineveh," *Concordia Journal* 18, no. 1 (January 1992): 40–49. For a comprehensive history, see John Boardman, I. E. S. Edwards, E. Sollenberger, and N. G. L. Hammond, eds., *The Cambridge Ancient History,* vol. 3:2, *The Assyrian and Babylonian Empires and Other States of the Near East, from the Eighth to the Sixth Centuries BC,* 2nd ed. (Cambridge: Cambridge University Press, 1991). For a fascinating exploration of the phrase "king of Nineveh," which initially appears to be an anachronism, see Paul Ferguson, "Who Was the 'King of Nineveh' in Jonah 3:6?," *Tyndale Bulletin* 47, no. 2 (1996): 301–314.

75. A helpful overview of the issues involved in dating the book of Jonah can be found in Sasson, *Jonah,* 20–28. He writes: "It must be evident that instead of helping us to pinpoint a definite date for Jonah, the survey leaves us with contestable clues about placing Jonah on either side of that great divide in Israel's history: the Exile-Restoration period (586–438)" (p. 26). His own tentative conclusion is that "a final editing or composing of Jonah took place during the exilic, but more likely during the postexilic, period" (p. 27).

76. Ibid., 70. Sasson goes on to note that the few other references to Nineveh in the Hebrew Bible are unflattering.

77. Ceresko, "Jonah," 581.

78. Blenkinsopp cautions: "But we must also be careful in aligning Jonah with a universalist perspective. Universalism is a slippery term; the salvation offered to gentiles in exilic prophetic writing (e.g., Isa. 45:22; 49:6; 52:10) implies an acknowledgment of the lordship of Israel's God (e.g., Isa 45:23; 51:5) and is sometimes couched in the form of an offer they can't refuse." Blenkinsopp, *A History of Prophecy,* 243. Blenkinsopp also contests the argument made by other biblical scholars that the book of Jonah is written against Ezra and Nehemiah; instead, he sees it as directed against the author of the

particular city at a particular point in time but rather to evoke an idea of a cosmopolitan, corrupt, and ruthless metropolis.[79] In fact, Thomas Bolin has suggested that this stereotypical use of the city can be traced to Hellenistic views of Nineveh as "an opulent but lawless and licentious city."[80] Bolin proposes (somewhat controversially) that "[t]he author and original readers, living in a culture informed by traditions which do not fail to mention Nineveh as a city that no longer exists, would at the end of Jonah not see a loving God who is free to forgive whom he wills, but rather a God who may forgive at will and revoke that forgiveness as well."[81]

JONAH'S RELUCTANCE

Why was Jonah so reluctant to deliver the oracle to the Ninevites? Commentators are divided in ways that both reflect and deepen some of the ambiguities and uncertainties that I just described. An interpretation common, if not dominant, in the history of Christian biblical interpretation is that the Hebrew Jonah did not want to be an agent of salvation for a Gentile population.[82] In this view, Jonah's reluctance to deliver the message of Yahweh to a foreign people is contrasted with the pious and upright response to God's interventions in their lives shown by the Ninevites and even by the pagan sailors before

Isaian apocalypse, which threatens doom to an unnamed city of incompetent people: "This is a people without discernment; / therefore he who made them will not have compassion on them, / he that formed them will show them no favor" (Isa.27:11). Ibid., 243–44.

79. For an exploration of the idea that the city of Nineveh is a character in the story reflecting urban morality, see Mary Mills, "Urban Morality and the Great City in the Book of Jonah," *Political Theology* 11, no. 3 (2010): 453–65. See also Edwin M. Good's *Irony in the Old Testament,* 2nd ed. (Sheffield: The Almond Press, 1981), 48: "In the author's mind, Nineveh is not a quantity but a quality, not a mere metropolis but an immorality. He takes the symbol of the ancient world's most impressive evil, magnifies and intensifies it by mass and sends his timorous prophet into the middle of it."

80. Thomas M. Bolin, "'Should I Not Also Pity Nineveh?' Divine Freedom in the Book of Jonah," *Journal for the Study of the Old Testament* no. 67 (1995): 109–120, at 117. Bolin buttresses his argument with the (not undisputed) scholarly consensus that Jonah was written in the late Persian or early Hellenistic period.

81. Ibid., 109–10.

82. For a contemporary example of this reading, see Cary, *Jonah,* 43: "Of course Jonah has no intention of preaching good news to the Gentiles when he goes to Joppa, heading for Tarshish. But neither did Peter when he went to Joppa, nor Saul when he came from Tarsus." It should be noted that Cary takes great pains to forestall any anti-Semitic sentiments that might follow from this interpretation. See page 174: "Can Jews rejoice that the LORD repents of the evil he threatened to do to Nineveh, to Babylon, to Rome? Can Christians rejoice that the Jews remain forever his chosen people, his dove, his fair one, the very apple of his eye?" For another Christian theologian who also strongly rejects any anti-Jewish reading of the book, see, R. Kendall Soulen, "The Sign of Jonah," *Theology Today* 65, no. 3 (2008): 331–43.

them. The Book of Jonah, then, becomes a case study demonstrating the attractiveness of universalism over against particularism.

Yet this reading of the text has its complications. In her fascinating book on various "mainstream" and "backwater" interpretations of Jonah,[83] Yvonne Sherwood makes the case that tensions between Jewish and Christian communities had affected the way the book was read as early as the first century CE. More specifically, she observes that Babylonian Jews studying the Book of Jonah emphasized themes of God's universal care and concern.[84] In contrast, Jews living in ancient Palestine, immersed as they were in tensions and polemics with the newly emerging Christian community, downplayed these themes in order not to play into the hands of their antagonists. "It may well be the supreme irony of Christian and Jewish interpretation of the book of Jonah that, for several centuries, a pro-Ninevite, universalist Jewish reading was eliminated because *Jews feared the power of Christian supersessionist logic, that would gobble up such readings into vindication of the Church.*"[85] In his extremely helpful introduction to his commentary on Jonah, Uriel Simon explores the debate about universalism versus particularism in the Book of Jonah, which he traces to a particular midrash: *Mekhilta of Rabbi Ishmael.* Simon points out that this midrash is not focused on universalism per se but instead on the relative moral standing of the Jews before God. The midrash depicts Jonah as reluctant to deliver the message to the Ninevites because the quick repentance of the Gentiles will only highlight the recalcitrance of the Israelites before the commands of God.[86]

---

83. Yvonne Sherwood, *A Biblical Text and Its Afterlives: The Survival of Jonah in Western Culture* (Cambridge: Cambridge University Press, 2000). Sherwood provides a trenchant analysis of the way in which anti-Semitism has infected Christian readings of the Book of Jonah; see pages 21–32, 48–87.

84. Ibid., 106–108. Tova Forti situates Jonah's universalism in the context of the wisdom tradition in the Hebrew Bible in "Of Ships and Seas, and Fish and Beasts: Viewing the Concept of Universal Providence in the Book of Jonah through the Prism of Psalms," *Journal for the Study of the Old Testament* 35, no. 3 (2011): 359–74. The ways of reading Jonah have long been multifarious; in a very interesting essay, Louis H. Feldman argues that Josephus's presentation of the biblical book is the result of a complicated political strategy taking into accounts the needs of his Jewish community and the sensitivities of his Roman patrons. See his "Josephus' Interpretations of Jonah," *AJS Review* 17, no. 1 (Spring 1992): 1–29.

85. Sherwood, *A Biblical Text,* 107–8 (original emphasis).

86. Simon, *Jonah,* viii–x. Simon cites *Mekhilta of Rabbi Ishamel,* Masekhta de-Pisha, sec. 1, ed. Horovitz-Rabin, 3–4. For a translation of this classic midrash, see Jacob Z. Lauterbach and David Stern, *Mekhilta de-Rabbi Ishmael,* rev. ed., JPS Classic Reissues (Philadelphia, PA: Jewish Publication Society, 2010).

Sherwood, like other commentators, also notes an alternative, although no more complimentary, understanding of Jonah's motivation that is found in some rabbinic sources. Foreseeing that God meant to save the Ninevites, Jonah did not want to deliver an oracle that would turn out to be wrong. In the biblical framework, a true prophet was a reliable prophet; his oracles unfailingly materialized.[87] On this interpretation, Jonah was reluctant to deliver a true oracle from the one true God because doing so would ironically leave him open to the serious charge of being a false prophet.[88]

The foregoing rabbinic reading of Jonah's motivations does not do much to rehabilitate his character. There is another rabbinic reading, however, that paints him in a much more favorable light. Jonah, like the other great Hebrew prophets, mediates between his God and his people. The factor that distinguishes Jonah is the task with which he is charged, not the attitude that he brings to it. Hosea and Jeremiah wept as they delivered oracles of God's wrath to the Jews, alternatively pleading with their people to repent in order to avoid certain destruction and begging God to relinquish his fierce anger. These prophets were never asked to do what Jonah was asked to do: to act to save the instrument of God's wrath against his own people.[89] On this view, Jonah is not a petulant malingerer; he is a tragic hero. Jonah foresees that his oracle to the Ninevites will cause them to repent and that their repentance will avert divine wrath. He also recognizes, however, that their moral transformation is fleeting. The Ninevites will soon revert to their barbarous ways, to the enduring detriment of the Jews.[90] Jonah, in this view, is caught between his God and his people. If he fails to deliver the oracle, he betrays the one; if he delivers it, he signs the death warrant of the other. Jonah flees and

87. Deuteronomy 18:21–22; Sherwood, A Biblical Text, 120.

88. Sherwood, A Biblical Text, 120: "Many Jewish interpreters find it hard not to empathise with a character who does not want to enter a plot where the words may turn on him, trip him up, and (mis)represent him as a liar." See also Simon, Jonah, x–xii, for a list of rabbinic sources defending this view. Simon is not enamored of this reading, citing "the absence of an adequate basis in the text" and "literary implausibility." Simon, Jonah, xi.

89. For an exploration of biblical and rabbinic sources proposing this interpretation, see Raphael Shuchat, "Jonah the Rebellious Prophet: A Look at the Man behind the Prophecy based on Biblical and Rabbinic Sources," Jewish Bible Quarterly 37, no. 1 (2009): 45–52. For a more contemporary defense of this position, see Chesung Justin Ryu, "Silence as Resistance: A Postcolonial Reading of the Silence of Jonah in Jonah 4.1–11," Journal for the Study of the Old Testament 34, no. 2 (2009): 195–218.

90. Uriel Simon notes: "Hardly any Jewish Bible scholar still adheres to this exegetical line, but it remains attractive to most Christian scholars." Simon, Jonah, ix.

repeatedly expresses the wish to die because death is the only way out of a morally unsustainable position.

A second, more positive (and arguably more modern) view of Jonah, ably defended by Jack Sasson, sees the book as a snapshot of the passionate and tempestuous relationship between a prophet and his God.[91] There is certainly a plethora of evidence for this reading. The book recounts two tumultuous events in the relationship between God and Jonah: the episode at sea and the episode in and around Nineveh. The text allots to Jonah and God the very same amount of dialogue; each character in the narrative is allowed to get his word in, so to speak. Sasson suggests that Jonah's initial decision to run away from his mission was motivated by hurt and anger at the way God was treating him. More specifically, God had commanded Jonah to deliver an oracle to the Ninevites—a foreign people—without sharing the broader plan with him.[92] He feels used and duped. Highlighting the psalm praising God for saving his life that Jonah sings while in the belly of the fish, Sasson proposes that the prophet's new attitude toward his mission reflects a renewed sense of God's personal concern for him. Similarly, Jonah is happy when God makes the qiqayon plant grow not because he needs it for shade (he has already built himself a hut to shelter himself against the elements) but because the tree signals God's tender regard for him. When a worm causes the tree to wither, Jonah is devastated because he thinks that God has withdrawn his care.

Both these positive readings of Jonah's mindset present him as motivated by particularist concerns: either the fate of his people or his own fate. Other rabbinic readings, which have been echoed in contemporary readings of the book, maintain that the prophet is defending the importance of justice against too profligate mercy, even on God's part.[93] This is the view, for example, that is

91. "When we took our leave of Jonah, he believed that he had come to a satisfying resolution of his disagreement with God. For him, the reason for God's mercy to the Ninevites was certainly shrouded in mystery; but when unexpectedly and miraculously God raised a qîqāyôn to shade his head, Jonah decided that, after all, God cared deeply about him; he therefore became 'absolutely delighted over the qiqayon plant.'" Sasson, Jonah, 316.

92. "But when a prophet carries a message of doom, especially to a great city such as Nineveh, and God revokes it without giving his prophet a role to play in the reversal, how could that prophet trust in his own calling? How will Jonah know that he remains God's prophet?" Ibid., 297.

93. See, for example, Hayyim Angel, "'I Am a Hebrew!' Jonah's Conflict with God's Mercy Toward Even the Most Worthy of Pagans," Jewish Bible Quarterly 34, no. 1 (2006): 3–11; and Shimon Bakon, "Jonah: The Conscientious Objector," Jewish Bible Quarterly 37, no. 2 (2009): 95–102. Noting the two possible meanings of the Hebrew word Ivri, Angel writes: "Jonah was indeed . . . [an] Ivri—a

advanced in the *New Jerome Biblical Commentary*, which remarks, "Why did Jonah flee? . . . Jonah could not bear the possibility that God's mercy might be extended to this wicked and hateful people, the Ninevites."[94]

Other commentators, particularly in recent years, have turned their critical attention to the character of God, whose actions toward Jonah they believe to be arbitrary and even cruel. They accordingly propose that Jonah's psalm in chapter two should be interpreted ironically.[95] The verb tenses suggest that Jonah is improbably giving profuse thanks to God for God's gracious kindness even while he is still firmly encased in fish flesh. Jonah sings the divine praises for rescuing him without the slightest acknowledgment that it was God who caused his suffering in the first place. Moreover, as an act of thanksgiving, he promises to offer sacrifice in the temple upon his release from his watery tomb—an act that is to be performed in Jerusalem. Yet it is to Nineveh, not to the temple, that he is forced to go by divine commission. In some modern interpretations, viewing God's acts toward Jonah in less than completely benign terms opens up greater suspicion about God's motives in saving Nineveh. Sherwood points out that when God asks Jonah whether or not He should be "concerned" about Nineveh, the Hebrew word corresponding to "concerned" has strong connotations of utility. Those connotations are strengthened by the text's analogy of the city of Nineveh to the *qiqayon* plant whose demise Jonah mourned. Presumably, on this reading, Jonah was not upset at the loss of the plant for its own sake but because of the additional shelter it provided to him. The analogy suggests that God rightly preserves Nineveh in order to protect its future usefulness to Him.[96] As biblical history attests, this usefulness does not turn out well for either Israel or Nineveh itself. After deploying the Assyrians as a rod to destroy Israel and devastate Judah, God appoints the Babylonians to attack the Assyrians in turn. The reprieve for both Israelites and Ninevites alike is temporary.

This is a far darker reading of the Book of Jonah, a reading in which God's purposes, more or less unfathomable, do not always bode well from

---

prophetic hero of true faith contrasting himself with pagans, and an *avaryan*—a sinner against God." Angel, "I am a Hebrew!," 6.

94. Ceresko, "Jonah," 582.

95. See, for example, Serge Frolov, "Returning the Ticket: God and His Prophet in the Book of Jonah," *Journal for the Study of the Old Testament* 24, no. 86 (1999): 85–105. See also Carolyn J. Sharp, *Irony and Meaning in the Hebrew Bible* (Bloomington: Indiana University Press, 2009), 178–79.

96. Sherwood, *A Biblical Text*, 127–28.

the perspective of those with whom He interacts. It resonates with the profound sense of divine inscrutability that Lincoln communicates in his Second Inaugural Address. Both remind us that there is no way to map God's designs securely, comfortably, and reliably onto human plans. Pleas for divine mercy may be heard and may hold for a time, but they do not always and ultimately trump the unfolding of divine justice.

At the same time, while the darker reading of the book needs to be addressed, it cannot entirely supplant other, more mainstream readings. The last passage in the book ends with a question from God to his recalcitrant prophet:

> But God said to Jonah, "Is it right for you to be angry about the bush?" And he said, "Yes, angry enough to die." Then the LORD said, "You are concerned about the bush, for which you did not labor and which you did not grow; it came into being in a night and perished in a night. And should I not be concerned about Nineveh, that great city, in which there are more than a hundred and twenty thousand persons who do not know their right hand from their left, and also many animals?"[97]

It is difficult to read this divine statement as entirely instrumentalizing the Ninevites. As many commentators have pointed out, God's intervention is structured as an "a fortiori" argument very common in post-exile Jewish writing.[98] God is not mocking Jonah's concern for the plant; instead, He is using it to build a hermeneutical bridge that will allow Jonah to understand the divine perspective on Nineveh. God acknowledges Nineveh as a "great city" but not because of its military might. Instead, it is great because it is teeming with life. Most significantly, God does not present Nineveh here as an undifferentiated mass, as an entity hostile to His chosen people, but as a community of living, breathing beings—human persons *and* animals. The Ninevites are not depicted as a well-oiled fighting machine but rather as a collection of hapless agents who lack any basic orientation in space and time.

97. Jonah 4:9–11. Sasson does not translate the description of Jonah's state as "angry." Instead, he translates it as "utterly dejected," in keeping with his view that Jonah is depressed about his relationship with God. See Sasson, *Jonah*, 300.

98. See, for example, Limburg, *Jonah*, 97.

God is not only familiar with the Ninevites, He appears to have a rather deep affection for them despite their ineptitude. After all, God invites Jonah to see his own fiercely (and perhaps irrationally) protective feelings toward the plant as analogous to God's sentiments toward Nineveh.

Ironizing Prophecy

This picture of God as treating another people as precious and valuable in their own right is a key development in the Jewish thought. Even a cursory glance at the prophetic and historical writings, for example, shows that Israel's neighbors and enemies are generally portrayed as significant primarily for their role as instruments in working out the covenantal relationship between Israel and Judah and God. There is scant acknowledgment that God may indeed have a relationship with these other nations that the Jews know nothing about, or that He may have plans and purposes for them that are uniquely their own rather than ancillary to His plans for the Hebrew people.

More radically, however, this picture, situated in the entire context of the Book of Jonah, highlights the prospect that God's people—and God's prophets—do not have a complete grasp of divine plans, purposes, and relationships more generally. Jonah delivered God's message to the Ninevites only after being pursued almost to the death in order to so; he did not understand the message, which he likely delivered halfheartedly and in cursory fashion. He grumbled and crumpled at the result of his oracle. If this is the case with Jonah, whom the narrative identifies as a true prophet, how much more is this likely to be the case when readers find themselves dealing with those who style themselves rhetorically as God's messengers? Even in the case of the best of them, are not the motives of all prophets mixed? Are not their capacities to grasp the divine plans highly limited? Is there any reason for confidence that they are delivering the message of God in a straightforward, reliable, way—even if they are delivering it in the very words that God communicated to them?

More broadly, the Book of Jonah encourages the audience to take with a grain of salt any prophet's claim that he has privileged access to the mind of God. It does so, in my view, by inviting us to read prophetic indictments ironically. Numerous biblical scholars have noted and scrutinized, to greater or lesser degrees, the presence of irony in the Book of Johah. Joseph Blenkinsopp, for example, writes that "it achieves a level of sophistication in its use of ironic contrast, deliberate exaggeration and distortion."[99] Some of those ironic contrasts have been explored in the preceding paragraphs of this chapter. It is crucial to note, however, that not all commentators identify the key ironies in the same way. Defining irony as "criticism, implicit or explicit, which perceives in things as they are an incongruity,"[100] Edwin Good claims that the Book of Jonah "portrays the prophet in order to ridicule him."[101] By vomiting him up on the shore, the great fish eroded Jonah's dignity and made him feel "silly."[102] Carolyn Sharp offers a more subtle account of the ironies involved, which she sees as targeting God's character as well as that of Jonah. She focuses our attention on the puzzling psalm Jonah delivers from the belly of the sea beast in Chapter 2, which she contends is a key to the book's irony.[103] Sharp observes that the psalm speaks the truth "in a way that is rendered absurd under the circumstances."[104] Most strikingly, while still marinating in misery, Jonah profusely thanks God for a deliverance that he has not yet experienced and has no reason to expect. As Sharp further notes, "figures of speech and images that ordinarily would be employed in metaphorical senses in Israel's psalmody are here used in ways that are hyperbolically literalistic in Jonah's actual briny circumstances."[105] Sharp contends that the mounting incongruities press us toward an ironic interpretation of the psalm and of the book itself, remarking that "the psalm is gradually revealed as a calculated attempt on the part of the unregenerate prophet to manipulate God while

99. Blenkinsopp, A History of Prophecy, 241.

100. Good, Irony in the Old Testament, 30.

101. Ibid., 41.

102. Ibid., 47.

103. I called to the LORD out of my distress, / and he answered me; / out of the belly of Sheol I cried, / and you / heard my voice. / You cast me into the deep, / into the heart of the seas, / and the flood surrounded me; / all your waves and your billows / passed over me. / Then I said, "I am driven away / from your sight; / how shall I look again / upon your holy temple?" / The waters closed in over me; / the deep surrounded me; / weeds were wrapped around my head / at the roots of the mountains. / I went down to the land / whose bars closed upon me forever; / yet you brought up my life from the Pit, / O LORD my God. / As my life was ebbing away, / I remembered the LORD; / and my prayer came to you / into your holy temple. / Those who worship vain idols / forsake their true loyalty. / But I with the voice of thanksgiving / will sacrifice to you; / what I have vowed I will pay. / Deliverance belongs to the LORD! (Jonah 2:2–9).

104. Sharp, Irony and Meaning, 178.

105. Ibid.

remaining unaccountable himself."[106] But God does not escape the author's critical gaze either. Because the psalm's profuse expressions of gratitude sharply contrast with the way God has actually treated Jonah thus far, Sharp argues that it ironizes the common tendency of the Hebrew psalmists to attribute the virtue of mercifulness to God.[107]

The Book of Jonah is firmly ensconced as a prophetic book in both the Jewish and the Christian canons. It is also a book replete with irony, the target of which arguably includes the practice of prophetic indictment itself.[108] Precisely because it is in the canon, it can be read as legitimating and facilitating an ironic, self-critical spirit about the practice of delivering messages from God about the state of the covenant. In my view, then, it can also help us think more critically about the practice of prophetic indictment in the American public square. It can help us, in other words, ironize the American jeremiad, the roots of which can be found in the prophetic books of the Hebrew Bible and Old Testament. Moreover, the example of the Book of Jonah can help us avoid the charge that any attempt to ironize prophetic indictment is to introduce a discordant and destructive note into this venerable form of religious and political rhetoric.

Before looking more closely at what these claims might mean, it is worth highlighting the difficulty of the rhetorical task that is involved. As I have argued, the jeremiad's prophetic indictments are rhetorically modeled on legal indictments. And no communicative discourse is *less* deliberately ironic on the part of the communicator than is a legal indictment. It is meant to be a particular charge against a particular person (or group of people) for having committed a particular act. Indictments are not designed to be ambiguous and still less are they meant to have a hidden meaning. Quite the contrary, they are meant to inform defendants (and their attorneys) of the specific nature of their alleged violation of communal norms to enable them to

---

106. Ibid., 179.

107. Ibid., 185–86.

108. The *New Jerome Biblical Commentary* observes: "In Jonah, one of the last representations of a prophetic figure, we find not someone of heroic stature but a caricature of a prophet. There is certainly irony in this, and even satire, which may reflect something of the disillusionment with and disappearance of prophecy that marked this period. But it also reflects a profound humility. The author turns the audience's gaze away from the prophetic messengers themselves to the One whose messengers they were, the One who is able to achieve his ends sometimes even in spite of envoys like Jonah." Ceresko, "Jonah," 580.

respond to the charges in a judicial proceeding. The fundamental rhetorical question that arises, therefore, is: How can irony operate in the vicinity of a type of speech modeled on a legal indictment without entirely distorting that speech?

Is an Ironic Jeremiad a Contradiction in Terms?

To answer this question, we need to delve more deeply into the nature and functions of irony as a rhetorical tool. It is not a simple tool to grasp or to wield. It has been subject to significantly different definitions over the centuries, and its literary and philosophical uses have been varied and at points contradictory. Before addressing the particular question of irony and the jeremiad, therefore, I need to provide some general context and to clarify the way in which I myself will be using the term *irony*.

In its earliest usages, the Greek noun *eirōneia* is generally understood in a pejorative way, to mean "deception" or "dissembling." The *eirōn* is a liar, self-serving in his own deceptive presentation of himself.[109] Not long after Aristophanes (d. 386 BCE), however, irony began to refer to a dissimulation that was *designed* by the author to be recognized by the discerning reader. The great Roman orator Quintilian (d. 100 CE) defined irony as a figure of speech in which "the contrary of what is said is to be understood."[110] The key classical figure in understanding irony, of course is Socrates; Socratic irony is generally defined as feigning ignorance in order to pursue a line of questioning that reveals the ignorance of others.[111] At the same time, there is significant debate both about the nature of Socratic irony and the purpose with which Socrates deployed it, which is complicated by the fact that Socrates does not present his own views but rather appears as a figure in the works of others—Aristophanes, Xenophon, and Plato.[112]

---

109. Gregory Vlastos, *Socrates: Ironist and Moral Philosopher* (Ithaca, NY: Cornell University Press, 1991), 24. Vlastos's account of Socratic irony is extraordinarily influential but not without its critics.

110. Quintilian, *Institutes of Oratory*, bk. 9, chap. 2, v. 44.

111. See Melissa Lane, "The Evolution of *Eirōneia* in Classical Greek Texts: Why Socratic *Eirōneia* Is Not Socratic Irony," in *Oxford Studies in Ancient Philosophy*, vol. 31, ed. David Sedley (Oxford: Oxford University Press, 2006), 49–83; Paul Muench, "Socratic Irony, Plato's *Apology*, and Kierkegaard's *On the Concept of Irony*," in *Kierkegaard Studies Yearbook 2009: Kierkegaard's Concept of Irony*, ed. Niels Jørgen Cappelørn, Hermann Deuser, and K. Brian Söderquist (Berlin: Walter de Gruyter, 2009), 71–125.

112. One key question is whether Socrates deployed irony primarily in a negative way, simply to expose weaknesses in the thought patterns of his interlocutors, or whether he was also interested in the positive project of constructing a more sound view of human life and interaction. This question,

For many centuries, irony referred generally to a figure of speech, like allegory. Over time, however, especially in the context of nineteenth-century Romanticism, irony became a way to describe a full-blown strategy of approaching one's own existence. In the postmodern era, the concept of irony underwent further expansion and metamorphosis, to the point where it threatened to undermine itself. More specifically, deconstruction raised the possibility that everything, without exception, is ironic—but if everything is ironic, it is at least possible that nothing is.[113]

Needless to say, thinking carefully about the role of irony in the political context requires some line drawing. In fact, the postmodern philosopher Richard Rorty maintains that irony is a tool for private self-creation that is not appropriate for public life. He argues that "liberal political discourse would do well to remain as untheoretical and simpleminded as it looks."[114] The irony is that for someone who so passionately decries foundationalism and essentialism, Rorty has a very constricted, almost Rawlsian, view of liberal political discourse. If discourse in the public square could (let alone should) really be constrained along Rawlsian lines, there would be no need for irony. But it cannot be so constrained, as I argued in Chapter 2. We need to ask, therefore: what *kind* of irony will be helpful?

In his perceptive book on the topic, Wayne Booth develops a taxonomy of irony that will help us answer this question. His central and basic example is indebted to classical views of irony and has four characteristics: It is intended, covert, stable, and finite.[115] A reader happens upon a word or phrase that seems incongruous, decides that a literal reading of that word or phrase cannot be right, attempts to try out other meanings, makes an assessment of the beliefs of the author in question, and chooses a new reading that makes better sense of the passage. So one character in a Jane Austen novel may describe another character as "sober" and "sensible," when it is clear from the

---

in turn, raises two other issues. First, how consistent is the identity of Socrates as portrayed in the earlier and middle Platonic dialogues? Second, does Plato portray Socrates more accurately in his earlier dialogues while using him as a character to advance his own position in his later writings? This is Vlastos's position.

113. I am drawing here from Claire Colebrook's history in *Irony: The New Critical Idiom* (London: Routledge, 2004), 1–8.

114. Richard Rorty, *Contingency, Irony, and Solidarity* (Cambridge: Cambridge University Press, 1989), 121.

115. Wayne C. Booth, *A Rhetoric of Irony* (Chicago, IL: University of Chicago Press, 1974), 5–6.

context that Austen herself *intends* to convey, *covertly*, that the character is far more accurately described as "profligate" and "silly." The ironic meaning is *stable* in that it seems highly unlikely that Austen is inviting further ironization of "profligate" and "silly." The irony is *finite* in that it is situated within a broader landscape of sentences and descriptions that are not meant to be taken ironically. Booth sees this sort of irony in geographical terms; he suggests that the author is inviting the wise and discerning reader to leave a particular location (the literal meaning) and climb with the author to a higher vantage point with a better view on the situation at hand, a vantage point occupied by the decoded ironic meaning.[116]

At the same time, Booth cautions us to remember that reading irony is not akin to operating a secret decoder ring. Irony creates meaning but not necessarily a highly particularized meaning. It is crucial to recognize that an ironic meaning cannot be "fully paraphrased" in a nonironic proposition.[117] Moreover, in more complicated cases, there is room for some range of defensible reconstructions in meaning. Each reader will fill out the landscape of that higher vantage point that he or she occupies with the author somewhat differently. For Booth, unlike for Rorty, the practice of (some sorts of) irony can be socially and politically constructive because the range of permissible reconstructed meanings can be useful for building community. Taking as his example the passage from Mark's Gospel where the soldiers cry, "Hail, King of the Jews," Booth argues that the scene was meant by the author to be interpreted ironically. It offers an "account of the man-God who, though *really* King of the Jews, was reduced to this miserable mockery."[118] Yet Booth notes that anyone who has any basis for empathizing with Jesus's plight will morally resist the soldiers' actions, not merely those who actually believe Jesus to be the Messiah. By inviting the scene to be interpreted ironically, therefore, the Gospel writers created a larger, more sympathetic community than they would have had they made a more straightforward, nonironic claim, such as "Roman soldiers shamefully put to death the Messiah while mocking his

---

116. "The movement is always toward an obscured point that is intended as wiser, wittier, more compassionate, subtler, truer, more moral, or at least less obviously vulnerable to further irony. Since there is always a sense in which part of the new view is a look back upon the old inferior dwelling, the moving van is perhaps better described as traveling upward to a nicer part of town." Ibid., 36.

117. Ibid., 39.

118. Ibid., 28–29.

identity." More people can find reason to object to Jesus's treatment at the hands of the Romans than will agree with the Gospel writers about his actually identity as the Messiah.[119]

Booth, in short, highlights the generative possibilities of irony by pointing to the range of legitimate reconstructed meanings that an ironic portrayal can trigger in a range of readers with different views. We can go a step further and say that it is possible even for a single reader (or community of readers) to acknowledge the potential validity of a range of reconstructed meanings after irony does its work. These meanings can exist alongside each other, sometimes challenging each other, sometimes providing a different setting in which the other can be viewed. We can see how this process might occur by borrowing from Booth's real estate metaphor. Booth says that the new and better real estate of the reconstructed meaning on the heights yields perspective on the initial, straightforward meaning that languishes in the valley below. We can press his point further and say that the view from any piece of property on the heights is affected by the houses that surround it. As real estate agents regularly insist, after all, their mantra is "location, location, location."

When we read the Book of Jonah, therefore, we do not need to commit firmly to one of the many reconstructed meanings offered to us by critics over the centuries, some of which I alluded to above. We do not need to say that God is scamming Jonah (by cruelly maneuvering Jonah into delivering the oracle) or that Jonah is scamming God (by trying to manipulate God with a psalm of praise). Allowing both ironic possibilities to influence each other, we can interpret them in light of each other, just as the houses on the heights take some of their character from their neighbors, not merely from the dwellings they look down upon in the valley. The author of the Book of Jonah, in short, can be reasonably understood as inviting the ironic construction of a *city* on a hill, not merely a single-family home with a view of the valley.

IRONY AS A MORAL VIRTUE

The philosopher and psychoanalyst Jonathan Lear allows us to take Booth's insight one step further. He proposes not merely the possibility of multiple ironic meanings coexisting with each other but the far more radical possibility of ironic meanings coexisting with a dominant, nonironic meaning. Drawing on thinkers as diverse as Søren Kierkegaard and neo-Freudian analyst Hans

119. Ibid., 29.

Loewald, Lear argues that the aim of psychoanalysis should be construed in part as a way of helping a patient develop his or her own capacity for irony. This capacity, in Lear's view, can provide a balm for patients whose unconscious thoughts and desires disrupt and destroy their dominant, conscious lives. Rather than suppressing unconscious life, or allowing unconscious drives to derail reflective plans and purposes entirely, a person with the capacity to reflect ironically on his or her own actions, words, thoughts, and feelings can nurture a set of relationships between the conscious and unconscious that is more productive than otherwise possible. Lear maintains that psychotherapy teaches how irony allows "a gentle connection that runs through meaning" to mediate between the unconscious and one's conscious self.[120] Irony allows us to recognize, acknowledge, and name the ghosts from our past—and then to lay them down respectfully without attempting to destroy them or to deny their existence.[121]

In his most recent book on the topic, Lear makes it clear that the development of irony is not a neutral, therapeutically useful strategy; it also has a strong ethical component to it. The sense of incongruity or "uncanniness" that is brought about by the disruptions of the unconscious upon the pretensions of conscious life turn out to be, for Lear, just one type of several possible vehicles for irony. More broadly, an ironic sensibility helps us perceive the gap between the ideals of a social role that we pretend to occupy on the one hand and the grubby little reality that we actually live on the other. Here, he draws on Kierkegaard's question, "In all of Christendom, is there a Christian?" as precisely the sort of ironic query that exposes this sort of gap.[122] "When irony hits its mark," writes Lear, "the person who is its target has an uncanny experience that the demands of an ideal, value, or identity to which he takes himself to be already committed dramatically transcend the received social understandings."[123]

Lear argues that the development of a capacity for irony is a human excellence in which one acquires the capacity to "deploy irony in the right sort of way at the right time in the living of one's life."[124] We ought not, he emphasizes, approach *everything* ironically—he does not mean to deny the claims of

120. Jonathan Lear, *Therapeutic Action: An Ernest Plea for Irony* (New York: Other Press, 2003), 211.
121. Ibid.
122. Jonathan Lear, *A Case for Irony* (Cambridge, MA: Harvard University Press, 2011), 12.
123. Ibid., 25.
124. Ibid., 30.

nonironic categories upon us. Moreover, a capacity for irony is not meant to dissolve all truth but instead to disclose the unpleasant truth that our ways of understanding are flawed. Developing a capacity for ironic excellence "would be a manifestation of a practical understanding of one aspect of the finiteness of human life: that the concepts with which we understand ourselves and live our lives have a certain vulnerability built into them."[125]

It seems to me that Lear's understanding of irony provides us with a fruitful way to approach the rhetoric of prophetic indictment, as exemplified in Lincoln's Second Inaugural Address. We can think about a capacity for ironic excellence as a virtue appropriate for public life, not merely for private life. A capacity for ironic excellence, understood as Lear understands it, would not need to destroy the idea of prophetic indictment or the more basic idea of a nation in covenant with God. It would, however, point to the fact that our idea of what it means to be in covenant with God is very likely not identical to God's idea. We can see Lincoln's reflection that both sides in the Civil War read the same Scriptures and prayed to the same God as an instantiation of ironic excellence. So too is the last line in the Book of Jonah, which gives the reader a mysterious window into God's strange relationship with the Ninevites.

It is evident that, with Lear's analysis, we have moved far beyond Booth's central case of covert, stable, local irony.[126] Lear is deeply indebted to the idea of irony as a way of life, an idea that was developed by Romantic writers and others in the nineteenth century.[127] A key purpose of that form of irony was to produce a particular type of social destabilization. As Kierkegaard notes, the power of irony is personally liberating; it breaks the chains of an ossified worldview that is too constrictive, certain, and smothering, thereby promoting "negative independence."[128] Irony in this form tends to be unstable

---

125. Ibid., 31.

126. "For our present purposes, it is important only to recognize the absolute split between works designed to be reconstructible on firm norms shared by authors and readers, and those other 'ironic' works that provide no platform for reconstruction. In the one kind, all or most of the ironies are resolved into relatively secure moral or philosophical perceptions or truths; in the other, all truths are dissolved in an ironic mist." Booth, *A Rhetoric of Irony*, 151. For a more sympathetic account of postmodern irony, see Colebrook, *Irony*, chap. 5, 95–110.

127. See Colebrook, *Irony*, chap. 3 ("Romantic Irony").

128. Kierkegaard insightfully contrasts irony and doubt: "In doubt, the subject continually wants to enter into the object, and his unhappiness is that the object continually eludes him. In irony, the subject continually wants to get outside the object, and he achieves this by realizing at every moment that the object has no reality." Søren Kierkegaard, *The Concept of Irony with Continual Reference to*

and pervasive; it provides a powerful way of smashing through any and every constraint. Kierkegaard, in fact, refers to it as "infinite absolute negativity" in *The Concept of Irony*.[129] He toys with the idea that "[b]oredom is the only continuity the ironist has."[130]

The Concept of Irony was Kierkegaard's doctoral dissertation; its central focus was on Socrates's view of irony. The later Kierkegaard, however, regretted his earlier self's flirtation with restless nihilism.[131] And even in his dissertation, there were passages that signaled some limits, saying that "[i]rony as the negative is the way; it is not the truth but the way."[132] Irony is a tool to demolish rigidity, not a full-blown plan of life. Someone who does not know irony, says Kierkegaard, "does not know the refreshment and strengthening that come with undressing when the air gets too hot and heavy and diving into the sea of irony, not in order to stay there, of course, but in order to come out healthy, happy, and buoyant and to dress again."[133] Lear, too, emphasizes the nature of irony as a practical virtue; the goal is to scrutinize and revise one's commitments, not wallow in an endless series of ironies that forestall commitment.[134]

Lincoln's Second Inaugural Address does not make the mistake of taking a fatal detour through unstable irony. He ends with an action plan, not a dissolution of agency in the solvent of ironic detachment. While the tide had turned in their favor, Union soldiers must continue to fight to win the war. Corporal works of mercy must be performed—thousands of soldiers must be buried or nursed to health, and countless widows and orphans must be protected and succored. Despite our humble grasp of God plans, we (like Jonah) have no choice but to do the right "as God gives us to see the right." Ironizing the jeremiad leads to humility before God and a certain type of empathy with one's opponents. It does not need to generate moral relativism or lead to political paralysis.

Socrates, together with Notes of Schelling's Berlin Lectures, ed. and trans. Howard V. Hong and Edna H. Hong (Princeton, NJ: Princeton University Press, 1989), 257.

129. Ibid., 259. Kierkegaard is clearly influenced by Hegel here.

130. Ibid., 285.

131. Lear, *A Case for Irony,* 33.

132. Kierkegaard, *The Concept of Irony,* 327.

133. Ibid.

134. "[D]eveloping a capacity for ironic disruption may be a manifestation of seriousness about one's practical identity. It is not merely a disruption of one's practical identity; it is a form of loyalty to it." Lear, *A Case for Irony,* 22.

THE LIMITS OF IRONY

The purpose of this final chapter has been to explore how the tradition of the jeremiad can be developed in a way that nurtures the virtue of humility in the face of God and God's plans, and charity in the face of one's political opponents. I have tried to illustrate how the tradition of biblically based prophetic indictment possesses significant internal resources to aid this development: the Book of Jonah in the biblical tradition, and Abraham Lincoln's Second Inaugural Address in the tradition of American political rhetoric.

More broadly, I have explored how irony can be a tremendously useful tool for dismantling ossified or overconfident frameworks of prophetic indictment. As Kierkegaard reminds us, however, it is a *tool*—not an end in itself. Irony does not set its own limits. Those limits must come from elsewhere. Booth emphasizes that, in literature, the reader determines the limits of irony by paying attention to the world created by the text. Only *Pride and Prejudice,* he says, can tell us where irony begins and ends in *Pride and Prejudice.* The same reminder can be applied analogously with respect to the political-religious world created by the jeremiad. In the end, irony must stop when it threatens to undermine key normative commitments that provide the linchpins of the moral and political world it is hoping to refresh.

On the moral level, I maintain irony must stop when confronted with human degradation and death. Lincoln can, for example, appropriately ironize the fact that both sides in the Civil War read the same Bible and pray to the same God—he cannot (and does not) treat the deaths of 600,000 young men in the same fashion. The tears of their parents will not allow it. On a theological level, I think irony must stop before a bedrock commitment about the nature of God. As the foregoing pages of this chapter have shown, it is possible to read the Book of Jonah abstractly in many different ways, which raises deep and troublesome questions about the divine nature. That book, however, is part of two sacred texts—the Hebrew Bible and the Christian Bible, which are read and interpreted not in the abstract but within the context of worshiping communities. Kierkegaard is quite correct that irony allows us to escape the mustiness and heat of ossified traditions by conceptually undressing in order to bathe in an intoxicating and troubling sea of conceptual possibilities. Scriptural insights about who God is give us some clues about what raiment we should don once refreshed by our ironic baths.

Abraham Joshua Heschel, in my view the most profound thinker of the twentieth century on the Hebrew prophets, devotes only two out of more than six hundred pages in his book to the story Jonah.[135] Not surprisingly, he goes to the heart of the matter. The story of Jonah is the story of God's power to change his mind—for the good. "This is the mysterious paradox of Hebrew faith: The All-wise and Almighty may change a word that He proclaims. Man has the power to modify His design. . . . The anger of the Lord is instrumental, hypothetical, conditional, and subject to His will."[136] Heschel reads Jonah as a prophet who has staked too much on the reliability of the divine word.

> God's answer to Jonah, stressing the supremacy of compassion, upsets the possibility of looking for a rational coherence of God's ways with the world. History would be more intelligible if God's word were the last word, final and unambiguous like a dogma or an unconditional decree. It would be easier if God's anger became effective automatically: once wickedness had reached its full measure, punishment would destroy it. Yet, beyond justice and anger lies the mystery of compassion.[137]

Lincoln's Second Inaugural Address, like the Book of Jonah, deals with the mysterious relationship of justice and mercy. The jeremiad, like all indictments, prophetic or otherwise, places the emphasis on justice. Yet maybe justice, to be sustainable or even finally intelligible, needs to be situated in the context of God's mercy. Without denying for a minute the terrible injustices that practitioners of the American jeremiad have decried over the past centuries, we must not forget that this tradition has its origins in a view of God

135. Abraham Joshua Heschel, *The Prophets* (New York: Harper Collins, 2001), 367–68. Thomas Bolin also argues that the book of Jonah advances a more radical conception of divine freedom, entertaining a somewhat darker view of divine purposes than does Heschel. See Bolin, "Should I Not Also Pity Nineveh?" and his monograph *Freedom Beyond Forgiveness: The Book of Jonah Re-Examined*, JSOTSup 236 (Sheffield, UK: Sheffield Academic Press, 1997).

136. Heschel, *The Prophets*, 367. See also Yossi Feintuch, "Jonah: A Transitional Prophet," *Jewish Bible Quarterly* 27, no. 3 (1999): 199–201, arguing that Jonah is a key figure in the developing awareness in the prophetic tradition of God's power to turn back and repent of his wrath. For a Christian articulation of the same position, see John H. Walton, "The Object Lesson of Jonah 4:5–7 and the Purpose of the Book of Jonah," *Bulletin for Biblical Research* 2 (1992): 47–57.

137. Heschel, *The Prophets*, 368.

whose compassion tempers justice, sometimes unaccountably. In the Jewish tradition, the Book of Jonah is read in its entirety on the feast of Yom Kippur—the Day of Atonement. In the Roman Catholic tradition, before the Second Vatican Council, it was read on Holy Saturday—the day that Jesus is believed to have descended into hell before resurrection on Easter Sunday.

If the American tradition of prophetic indictment will be able to contribute the repentance, reform, and renewal of our Union, even in our increasingly pluralistic society, it will have to make room for compassion, even for our moral opponents. Here too, the story of Jonah is helpful. As I noted earlier, the book ends with God's question to Jonah: "And should I not be concerned about Nineveh, that great city, in which there are more than a hundred and twenty thousand persons who do not know their right hand from their left, and also many animals?"[138] What was Jonah's answer? The narrator does not say. Yet a medieval Jewish sermon fascinatingly speculates: "At that very moment [Jonah] fell flat on his face, saying 'Direct your world according to the attribute of mercy, as is written, 'Mercy and forgiveness belong to the Lord our God.'"[139]

138. Jonah 4:11.

139. Sasson, *Jonah*, 320. The quotation is from *Midrash Yona*, taken from A. Jellinek, *Bet ha-Midrasch Sammlung: Kleiner Midraschim und vermischter Abhandlungen aus der ältern jüdischen Literatur*, part 1, 2nd ed. (Jerusalem: Bamberger & Wahrman, 1938), 102.

Conclusion

The American public square is not a seminar room. The conversations it hosts are not well-ordered; indeed, they are often cacophonous. The participants talk past and over each other. In examining issues of grave moral and political import, they proffer comments that are fueled not only by reason but also by passionate moral and religious commitment. In short, the discourse of the American public square includes prophetic condemnations of great moral and social evils, as well as nuanced considerations of competing values and policy goals. To borrow from the late Mathew Arnold, Americans not only address fundamental matters of law and policy in the irenic and balanced tones of "sweetness and light."[1] They also draw regularly on the more combative language of "fire and strength" to condemn violations of the moral law in unequivocal terms.

To understand the function of religious arguments in the public square of a pluralistic society, it is not enough to focus on deliberation and discursive argumentation, as Alasdair MacIntyre and John Rawls both do, although in very different ways. To grapple with dissension fueled by religious commitment, it is not sufficient to call for civility and respect, as Stephen Carter does. Understanding the role of religious discourse in the American context requires coming to terms with the nature, function, and limits of prophetic indictment. At once both religious and political, prophetic rhetoric is an enduring aspect of American public life.

---

1. Matthew Arnold, *Culture and Anarchy,* ed. Samuel Lipman (New Haven, CT: Yale University Press, 1994).

Modeled on the blistering condemnations of the Hebrew prophets, who chastised their people for violating fundamental aspects of their communal covenant with God, the jeremiad became a staple of political life in the New England colonies. The Puritans saw themselves as the New Israel, as a divinely chosen and covenantal nation. Their belief in Christ, they thought, enabled them to live out those commitments more fully than had the people of Judah and Israel; consequently, they believed their colony in the New World would be rich in blessings, both spiritual and temporal. Ironically, however, the jeremiad proved to be more resilient and popular than the Puritan theocracy that generated it. In particular, the jeremiad made the transition from colony to province, from province to nation, from nation to superpower, and (now) from superpower to superconsumer in a globalized economy. Along the way, these transitions augmented the contentiousness of the jeremiad by loosening its tight connection to a covenant whose terms were the subject of significant agreement.

I have argued that the rhetoric of prophetic indictment is akin to moral chemotherapy. It is powerful medicine that appropriately targets moral cancers threatening the very existence of the body politic. As stinging words of condemnation from abolitionists such as William Lloyd Garrison well illustrate, the American jeremiad is not polite or nice. Nonetheless, at its best, it can be profoundly civil in that it calls on one's fellows to repent of their violations of fundamental terms of the political covenant. If it is not used carefully, however, the jeremiad can inflict considerable harm on the national body it hopes to save. Just like actual chemotherapy, great care in dosage and targeting has to be exercised by those using the medicine of prophetic indictment lest the cure kill the patient.

Unless speakers actually believe themselves to be true messengers of God, they *make a choice* to frame a particular intervention in the public square in terms of the adamant claims of prophetic indictment rather than in the more nuanced and qualified terms of practical deliberation. Drawing on a number of interdisciplinary sources, I have attempted to articulate the moral, pragmatic, and rhetorical considerations that should guide that choice. These considerations are not only reflected in the prophetic books of the Bible but also in the words Martin Luther King, Jr., who is the exemplar of prophetic best practices in recent times. Two overarching criteria govern my specific recommendations. First, the rhetoric of prophetic indictment is meant to be radical—that is, to target fundamental violations of the nation's basic social compact. It should not be used to target less serious violations of our common life. Second, the rhetorical style of the indictment is best modeled on what biblical scholars call the oracles against Israel and Judah rather than the oracles against the nations. In the former, the Hebrew prophets stand with the people they condemn, as their own people, weeping for their sins and praying for their repentance. In the latter, the prophets condemn the sins of the enemies of their people, calling down God's judgment without a word of mercy. Only the former, in my view, can be a constructive form of political speech between and among citizens and other participants in our pluralistic liberal democracy.

Finally, I suggest that the judicious use of prophetic indictment is a matter not only of content and style but also of character and virtue. In the contemporary political context, increasing in both pluralism and polarization, the virtue of humility will become an increasingly important quality to cultivate for those who want to deploy prophetic rhetoric successfully. The type of humility I have in mind is multifaceted and includes intellectual humility with respect to one's general knowledge of God's plan or purposes; moral humility with regard to one's own comparative righteousness in the eyes of God; and social humility regarding the status of other peoples, including one's enemies, in God's affections. Admittedly, the articulation of these sensibilities may seem inconsistent with the practice of prophetic indictment in both the Hebrew Bible and in the history of the American jeremiad. I argue, however, that illuminating precedents can be found in the Book of Jonah and in Abraham Lincoln's Second Inaugural Address. Both texts can teach us how to integrate humility into the practice of prophetic indictment without sacrificing a strong commitment to moral realism.

The Book of Jonah, in my view, creates rhetorical and moral space for a humble (and humbled) prophet in large part through the pervasive use of irony and humor. It destabilizes the platform on which the prophet stands and invites the audience to escape from under the prophetic indictment in order to move to higher ground and cast a critical eye on the prophet's own motives and commitments. This phenomenon raises, I think, the next important question to consider in developing a more complete picture of religious and moral discourse in the public square: How do different forms of rhetoric react to and even correct each other?

Here is my own hypothesis, which will require another book to develop and demonstrate. What I have called the language of practical deliberation is the ordinary discourse of public morality, social policy, and law. Participants in public discussions reason from fundamental premises to conclusions and offer nuanced assessments of actions, policies, and consequences. They often immerse themselves in the detailed language of case law, regulations, and white papers. What happens, however, when practical deliberation goes off the rails—when it tacitly or explicitly betrays the fundamental commitments that serve as its only sound basis?

Here, I think, the outraged rhetoric of prophetic indictment plays its rightful role—its powerful and bitter medicine is meant to wake deliberators from their moral coma and revive their commitment to the true foundational principles of the community. *Prophecy without Contempt: Religious Discourse in the Public Square* has shown how prophetic rhetoric can operate as an important corrective to practical deliberation that has become corrupted because it has lost its connection to fundamental commitments. I have not addressed in sufficient detail, however, the next logical question: What controls out-of-control prophetic rhetoric, of the sort we are all too familiar with in the heat of battles in the culture war?

This is not an easy issue to address. Engaging in practical deliberation with opponents committed to prophetic denunciation of your position is not likely to be effective because they believe that your deliberation is proceeding on the basis of seriously faulty premises. The only response they will accept is repentance and reform. It is tempting to return fire, to denounce those who denounce you. While such a rejoinder may be emotionally satisfying, it will only pour oil on the rhetorical flames. As I observed in Chapters 6 and 7, prophets committed to one side of a contentious social issue generally have a grudging respect for their activist opponents because they too see the issue of paramount importance. Moreover, prophetic activists are likely to be energized by their true opponents, leading to an escalation in rhetoric.

What to do, then, if it is futile to reason with irresponsible jeremiahs and unwise to engage them in a game of dueling prophetic indictments? As my discussion of the Book of Jonah indicated, it is possible to deploy the rhetoric of irony as well as that of satire, irony's first cousin. Poking fun at self-proclaimed prophets delegitimizes their assertions of their own moral insight and deflates the status of the issues they propose as fundamental. It is no accident, I believe, that the brilliant satires of *The Daily Show with Jon Stewart* and *The Colbert Report* emerged as influential progressive commentators just as American conservatives adopted an increasingly insistent vocabulary of prophetic indictment. Mockery, however, does not solve social problems. When satire gets too distracting and work is pressing, someone in authority, someone with moral gravitas, will likely say, "Knock it off. It's time to get back to work." Then the hard work of practical deliberation in a pluralistic society begins again. Then the cycle of moral and rhetorical correction begins a new round.

Acknowledgments

The idea for *Prophecy without Contempt: Religious Discourse in the Public Square* did not come to mind in one clearly defined moment of insight. Instead, like Topsy, it grew of its own accord, slowly taking shape over the past decade. More specifically, writing this book required me to spend a great deal of time honing the questions I was asking about the nature and function of prophetic rhetoric in the public square long before I could even begin to contemplate articulating the answers.

Puzzling about both the questions and the answers required me to extend my research in directions that were significantly new to me. I would like to thank Robin Darling Young for her sage advice in many conversations over the years on how to grapple with the prophetic aspects of the Hebrew Bible and the Christian tradition. Gerhard Böwering and Margaret Farley gave me the encouragement necessary to tackle such a big project. Understanding the place of prophetic indictment in American history required additional guides; I extend my appreciation to John McGreevy and Mark Noll for helping me to set my course early in my explorations. Grasping the nature and function of different kinds of rhetoric has been a crucial task for this project. I am much indebted to John O'Malley, particularly his *Four Cultures of the West,* for helping me see the overall rhetorical pattern in which my reflections could be situated.

I have given talks on prophetic discourse on many occasions and in many contexts in the past decade. I would like to thank all those who have had the patience to listen and converse with me. I am uniquely indebted, however, to Villanova University Law School for inviting me to deliver 28th Annual Donald A. Giannella Memorial Lecture, which allowed me to work out some of my initial thoughts on the relationship between prophetic and deliberative discourse.

Chapters 6 and 7 incorporate and expand upon significant portions of my article "Prophecy and Casuistry: Abortion, Torture, and Moral Discourse," 51 *Vill. L. Rev.* 499

(2006). Chapter 8 conjoins relevant sections from two previous publications: "Democracy and Prophecy," in James Boyd White and Jefferson Powell, eds., *Law and Democracy in the Empire of Force* (Ann Arbor: University of Michigan Press, 2009) 33–57, copyright © 2009 University of Michigan; and "Prophetic Discourse in the Public Square," *2008 Santa Clara Lecture,* the Ignatian Center for Jesuit Education, copyright © 2009 Santa Clara University.

As *Prophecy without Contempt* was assuming its final shape, I had the privilege of serving as a visiting professor at Princeton University and Yale University, which gave me the opportunity to talk about the book with new discussion partners. I am grateful to Princeton's Religion Department for inviting me to present a chapter at a departmental colloquium. In particular, I would like to thank Gustavo Maya for serving as a perceptive respondent, and Jeffrey Stout for his insightful questions at the session. I greatly enjoyed my conversations not only with the faculty members but also with many graduate students, especially my teaching assistants, who included not only Gustavo Maya but also Davey Henreckson and Alda Balthrop-Lewis, who was kind enough to read the manuscript with an eye that was in equal parts critical and charitable.

Yale's Department of Religious Studies also offered me the opportunity to participate in an extremely helpful and vigorous departmental colloquium, for which I am very grateful. I am particularly appreciative of the perceptive suggestions made by Yale doctoral students who read the entire manuscript during my time in New Haven: Ryan Darr, Andrew Forsyth, and Graedon Zorzi.

Other friends and colleagues have been extraordinarily kind in offering comments on various aspects of this project, including Kent Greenawalt, Alasdair MacIntyre, Michael Perry, Jefferson Powell, James Boyd White, and John Witte. I am particularly indebted to Robin Lovin, Mark Noll, John Robinson, and William Werpehowski for reading through the entire manuscript. They offered many astute observations on the argument's consistency and flow as well as its substance.

I was fortunate to begin this project while a faculty member at the University of Notre Dame, where I taught for over fifteen years. Lu Ann Nate, my staff assistant, helped me with the initial formatting of the manuscript and with every other aspect of my teaching and scholarship. The Notre Dame Law School research librarians exhibited extraordinary patience and ingenuity in responding to my requests to find arcane documents and sources. I would like to extend special thanks to my research assistants from Notre Dame who worked on the book over the years: Brian Bushman, Robert Koneck, and Craig Iffland. They not only checked the citations, they also offered valuable comments on both style and substance.

It is a great delight to be able to complete this book as a faculty member at Boston College. I am grateful to all my new colleagues in both the Theology Department and the Law School for a very warm welcome. In particular, thanks to members of the Theology Department's Ethics Colloquium for discussing an early draft of the last chapter and especially to James Keenan for his generosity as a respondent. Special thanks go to Conor Kelly for his helping me put the manuscript into final form, as well as to John Carter and Rohan Oberai for their patient assistance with last minute corrections.

Lindsay Waters and Amanda Peery of Harvard University Press offered their guidance, support, and patience in bringing this project to fruition. The two anonymous reviewers offered very useful suggestions for further improvement.

Finally, I would like to express my deep gratitude to my friends and family for so graciously bearing with me and my obsession with the topics covered in this book for so many years. I am in their debt, in so many ways, and for so many things.

Index

Abolitionist jeremiads, 225; Bible and, 226–228; anti-abolitionists and, 227–230; legal indictment and, 229; jury nullification and, 229–230

Abolitionists, 228, 385–386; consistency of, 75; political emergency of, 75–76; public reason of, 75–76, 76n78; King and, 75–77, 76n78, 80–83, 81n88; proviso and, 76–77; expressivist discourse of, 80–82; reasonableness of, 80–82, 81n88; expressivist freedom of, 81; tone of, 82; quotes of, 82–83; roots of, 82–83; language of, 83–84, 112; Phillips as, 112, 116–117, 117n98, 226–227; Howe as, 115–116, 116n97

Abortion debates, 7–8, 259; rhetorical style in, 242–243; due account in, 261; strategy in, 261; tensions from, 261–262, 286. *See also* 2004 presidential election

Abortion description, 265–266, 265n63, 266nn64,65

Abortion, 261n48, 272n80, 330, 330n25; torture related to, 7–8, 242–243, 259–262, 264, 275–277, 286; arguments on, 16–17, 58–59, 290–291, 336; as murder, 17, 86–87; frustration about, 17–18, 17n7; Roman Catholic Church and, 31, 31n65, 262–265,

263n55; Obama and, 38–41, 39n99, 41n101, 88; public reason on, 58–59, 59n33, 61, 64; by Tiller, 85–86, 330n26; civility constraints about, 85–89; casuistry in, 264–265; moral manuals in, 265. *See also* 2004 presidential election

Abraham, 138

Abu Ghraib Prison, 278, 287; torture debates and, 260, 260n46, 276, 276n84; torture deliberative responses about, 281–285, 281n97, 284n105

Academics, 3–4

Accountability, 44–45, 44n107

Adam and Eve, 138

Adams, John, 224

Adams, John Quincy, 3

Adams, William, 159, 159n86

Ad hominem attacks, 79, 101; moral reasoning and, 37–38, 38n90; covenant evolution and, 209–210; in mixed-form discourse, 256–257

Ad hominem nature of argumets, 346

Adoption, 55, 100

The African American Jeremiad: Appeals for Justice in America (Howard-Pitney), 358

African Americans, 309–310, 358–363, 360n81, 362n87; Ferguson shooting and,

African Americans (continued)
   368–369. See also King, Martin Luther, Jr.;
   Slavery
After Virtue (MacIntyre), 15–16
The Age of Reason (Paine), 224
Agreements, 170, 212–213; covenants as, 167,
   169, 208–209, 234. See also Consensus;
   Disagreement
Aliens, illegal, 250, 250n30
Ambiguity, 392–398, 393nn50,51, 394n62,
   395n65
American Center for Law and Justice, 67
American Civil Liberties Union, 67
American Constitution. See Constitution
American exceptionalism, 231–234, 396–397
American jeremiads, 118–119, 320n2, 374,
   420–421; assumptions about, 125–126,
   357–358; African Americans and, 358–363,
   360n81, 362n87; in rhetorical constraints,
   358–363, 360n81, 362n87; irony in,
   375, 377
American Puritanism, 128n5, 129–130,
   129n7, 131n11; covenant of, 127–128;
   toleration and, 131–134, 131n14, 195;
   dominion of, 133, 159, 188; autonomy of,
   133–134. See also Covenantal framework
American values: Roman Catholic Church
   and, 262–263, 263n59, 263nn55,56,57; in
   torture prophetic challenges, 280–281,
   280n95, 281n96
Amos (prophet), 311n65, 395n64
Anderson, Ryan T., 60n36
Andros, Edmund, 133, 159
Angel, Hayyim, 403n93
Anglican Church, 29–30, 30n56, 40; Hooker
   and, 140–141, 140n29, 249–250
ANH. See Artificial nutrition and hydration
Animal rights, 324
Animal testing analogy, 256–257
Anti-abolitionists, 227–230
Anti-Catholicism, 223
Antinomians, 137, 148, 151n58
Anti-Semitism, 107, 107n72, 400n82, 401n83

Apostacy, 161
Aquinas, Thomas (saint), 33, 77, 249–251, 258,
   258n42; virtues of, 309–311, 310nn63, 64
Arbitrariness, 19–20, 19n15
Arguments, 45, 126; on abortions, 16–17,
   58–59, 290–291, 336; for moral shrillness,
   36–37; same-sex marriage and, 59–61,
   60n36
Aristotelian schema, 249, 336
Aristotelian-Thomistic schema, 249–252
Aristotle, 20–21, 78, 80n87, 258, 258n42
Arminians, 137, 148
Arnold, Matthew, 112, 243n6, 335–336,
   336n33, 419
Arrogance, 9–10
Artificial nutrition and hydration (ANH),
   72, 73n4, 366–367, 366n101, 367n103
Artillery sermons, 219, 219n93
Assumpsit, 167
Audience, 62–63, 208–209, 211–213
August 1 memo, 299, 299n32; justification
   in, 300; torture definition in, 300–302,
   300n36, 302n41; Book of Isaiah and,
   306–307, 306nn55,56
Authenticity, 311–312, 368, 368n104
Authority, 203–204, 204n63; moral shrillness
   and, 30, 30n60, 37; Roman Catholic
   Church on, 30–31, 31n62. See also
   Competent authority
Autonomy, 133–134. See also Congregational
   autonomy

Babylon, 306–307, 306n56, 352–353, 353n62
Bacon, Henry, 373, 373n1
Bailyn, Bernard, 221n100
Baptists, Southern, 113–114
Barr, James, 259, 259n43
Barton, John, 244n10
"Battle Hymn of the Republic" (Howe),
   42n102, 116
Battle of Gettysburg, 378–380, 379n10,
   379nn14,15; Southern soldiers in, 380n16,
   385, 385n38

Beliefs, 163; of Catholics, 31, 31n62, 31nn64,65; of Puritans, 149–150

Benedict XVI (pope), 270–271, 270n74, 271n77

Bennett, James, 360–361

Bercovitch, Sacvan, 126, 177–178, 182–183, 182n1

Berrigan, Daniel, 41–42, 42n102

Bible, 10, 208, 222, 222n103; values related to, 67, 67n56; covenant lawsuits in, 135n21, 170, 170n127; Old Testament, 143; in covenant evolution, 213; abolitionist jeremiads and, 226–228; slavery and, 226–230; Second Inaugural Address and, 383n34. *See also* New Testament; *specific books*

Biblical prophets. *See* Prophets

Bin Laden, Osama, 307

Biology, 291–292, 291n8, 292n11

Blenkinsopp, Joseph, 394, 397n69, 399n78, 406–407

Bliss, Alexander, 380nn20,21

Bolin, Thomas, 400, 400n80, 417n135

Booth, Wayne, 410–412, 411n116

Bradley, Gerard, 59–60

Brenzel, J. B., 21n22

A Brief History of the Warr with the Indians in New England (I. Mather), 150, 150n56

A Brief Recognition of New-England's Errand into the Wilderness (Danforth), 157

Brown, John, 79

Brown, Michael, 368–369

Brownback, Sam, 68

Buck v. Bell, 340n40

Bulkeley, Peter, 145, 146n45

Burke, Raymond, 39n99, 266n64, 290

Bush, George W., 57, 68–69, 234; abortion and, 260, 260n45, 267, 270–271; torture debates and, 270–271; war on terrorism and, 295n25, 296–297, 296n24; Geneva Conventions and, 299n31

Bush, Jeb, 67, 69, 69n66

Bybee, Jay S., 276n84, 282–284, 284n105. *See also* Torture memos

Calef, Robert, 192

Callahan, Sidney, 271

Calvin, John, 136

Cardinal Newman Society, 39

Carter, Jimmy, 39n99

Carter, Stephen, 5, 91–92, 125, 239, 419; on civility's American Protestant *agape,* 109–113, 109n76. *See also* Civility

Cassel, Elaine, 70

Cassidy, Michael, 321, 322n7, 326–327

Casualties, 389–390

Casuistry, 264–265, 390; in torture memos, 301–305, 303n49, 307

Catholic Bishops, 100, 267, 267n69, 288; National Conference of, 263n59, 280, 280n93

Catholics, 217–218, 223; beliefs of, 31, 31n62, 31nn64,65; homosexuality and, 31, 31n64; moral shrillness of, 31–32, 31nn61,62, 31nn64–65; civility of, 38. *See also* Roman Catholic Church

Catonsville Nine, 41–42

Center for Reproductive Rights, 272n79

Chaput, Charles J., 71

Charles I (king), 129, 131, 131n11, 203–205

Charles II (king), 132–133, 132n15, 217n89

Childbirth, 303n48

Childress, James, 333

Chosenness, 196, 231–232

Christianity, 34n77, 104, 109, 109n76; of civility, 94–95, 95n34; Book of Jonah and, 400–402, 400n82, 401n83, 402n90

The Churches Quarrel Espoused . . . (Wise), 206–207

Church of England, 29n52, 30n56, 117, 118n101

The City on the Hill from Below: The Crisis of Prophetic Black Politics (Marshall), 358

Civic friendship, 50

Civic peace, 84; reciprocity in, 52, 54–55, 54n27; divisiveness from, 52–53, 52n25, 53n26; public reason in, 54–58, 54n27; reasons in, 55–56; language in, 55–57

Civil, 120

Civil complaints, 170–171

Civil disagreement, 97–98, 97n48

Civil discourse, 95–96

Civil disobedience, 333–334, 333n30,
342–343

Civility, 38; manners of, 92–94; self-restraint
in, 93; generosity for, 93–94; requirements of, 93–94; sacrifice for, 93–96; of
civil rights activists, 94; hospitality in, 94;
Christianity of, 94–95, 95n34; God in,
95–96; language of, 95–96, 99–100;
demonization and, 96; civil disagreement in, 97–98, 97n48; respect in, 97–98,
100–101; exclusion and, 98; emotional
framing and, 99; conclusory labels in,
99–100; about torture debates, 99–100;
compartmentalization and, 99–102;
messengers in, 100–101; mistakes and,
101; of Roman Catholic Church, 106–107.
See also Uncivil Protestants

Civility constraints, 89n17; about abortions, 85–89; in new media, 88–89; truth
or, 89; surface of, 90–91; protests
against, 91; respect in, 91; analyses on,
91–92, 91n23

Civility: Manners, Morals, and the Etiquette of
Democracy (S. Carter), 91–92

Civility's American Protestant agape:
Christian love in, 109, 109n76; integralism and, 109–110; community in,
110–111; disagreement in, 111; norms in,
111; abolitionists in, 111–112; culture wars
in, 113; sloth in, 113

Civil listening, 97–98

Civil religion, 102n57, 117; Protestant
denominationalism as, 102–108

Civil rights, 203–206, 204n63, 206n69

Civil rights activists, 94

Civil war, 333, 333n30

Civil War, 385; deaths in, 378–380, 378n8,
379n10, 379nn14–15, 380n16. See also Battle
of Gettysburg; Gettysburg Address

Classic texts, 10–11

Climate change, 325, 325n12

CNN poll, 240n1

Combatants, 348–350, 350n58

Common law, 251, 251n32

Common sense, 185, 207–209, 207n72

Common Sense: Address to the Inhabitants of
America (Paine): natural rights in,
221–222; political language of, 221–222,
221n100; Scripture in, 222, 222n103;
Puritan jeremiad compared to, 222–223;
personal insults in, 222–224; anti-
Catholicism in, 223; morality in, 223;
John Adams against, 224

Communal guilt, 179

Communism, 82

Communities, 110–111; moral disagreement
remedy in, 24–25; in 2004 presidential
election, 241–242, 241n5; of prophets,
341–342

Comparative assessment, 363–372. See also
King-Pavone comparison

Comparative justice, 343–344, 343n51, 344n53

Compartmentalization, 99–102, 108

Competent authority, 294, 294n16;
decisions from, 340–342, 340n42,43; just
war theory and, 340–343, 340nn42,43,
341n44, 343n51, 344n53; nonviolent civil
disobedience and, 342–343

The Concept of Irony (Kierkegaard), 414n128,
415, 415n129

Conclusory labels, 99–100

Condemn (word), ix–x

Condemnation, x, 344–345

Confederacy, 380n16, 385, 385n38

Confession, 192n28, 193

Confession of Faith, 164–165, 164n110

Confidence, 139

Congregational autonomy, 207n74;
Proposals against, 206; common sense in,
207, 207n72; democracy of, 207–208;
papacy and, 207–208, 207n76. See also
Covenant evolution

Congregational model, 139–140, 139n27

Conscription, 255, 286–287

Consensus, 339–340, 339n38; about Puritan
jeremiads, 179–180, 183–184
Consequentialism, 23, 23n29, 252–253,
296n25
Conservative Judaism, 105
Conservativism, 82–83
Consistency, 75
Constitution, 46–48, 106, 322, 322nn4,5; just
cause and, 338–340, 338n37; Gettysburg
Address and, 380–382, 381nn22,23, 382n27,
384–386
Constitutional principles, 73–74, 73n75
Contemn (word), ix–x
Contemporary jeremiad, 320–321, 320n2
Contemporary national covenant:
divisions within, 232; penalties and, 232,
234; unity and, 232; inversion in, 232–233;
breaches in, 232–234; obligations in, 233;
exceptionalism in, 233–234; political
parties in, 233–234; prosperity in, 233–234;
agreement and, 234; prophetic
indictment in, 234–235
Contempt, x
Contraception, 100, 262; sterilization as,
339–340, 340n40
Contracts, 167–170, 169n124, 172
Controversy, 73–75, 210
Convincing, 62
Corrective affliction, 177–178
Cotton, John, 130, 158, 158n82
Courts, 67–69. See also Massachusetts
General Court; Supreme Court
Covenantal framework, 134–135, 135n21;
God and, 136–139, 136n23; series in,
137–138; Jesus Christ in, 138; pragmatism
of, 138–139; confidence from, 139;
ubiquity of, 139; congregational model
of, 139–140, 139n27; membership for,
140, 140n28; political covenant from,
140–143
Covenantal obligations, 233; content in,
197–199; England in, 198; materialism in,
198, 198n43; political reform in, 198; in
covenant bond, 198–199; piety in,

198–199; social improvement in, 199,
199n49; hope in, 200
Covenantal theology, 193–194
Covenant bond, 186, 199; God in, 187–195;
covenant partners' identity in, 195–198;
jeremiad rhetoric in, 200–202
Covenant breach, 175, 232–234; agreements
in, 169–170; jeremiad related to, 169–172,
185–186, 230–231
Covenant evolution, 202n58, 206n69;
federal theology and, 202–203; secularization in, 203–206, 204n63; congregational autonomy in, 206–208, 207n72,
207n74, 207n76; natural rights in, 207n76,
208–210; common sense in, 208–209;
self-evidence of, 209; ad hominem
attack and, 209–210; Revolutionary
jeremiads and, 210–211, 213–214;
interpretation in, 212–213; Scripture in,
213; halfway covenant in, 220, 220n98
Covenant lawsuits, 135n21, 170–172, 170n127
Covenant partners' identity, 197n41;
accommodation in, 195; deism and, 195;
religious pluralism in, 195–197; in
covenant bond, 195–198; chosenness in,
196; New England in, 196–198; uncertainty in, 197–198, 231
Covenant renewal sermons, 159, 160n88
Covenants, 6, 147n48, 185, 406; of American
Puritanism, 127–128; Puritan jeremiads
and, 135–136, 180; of works, 137–138,
146n45; of grace, 138, 140–141, 143, 146n45;
Judaism and, 141–142, 254–255; national,
147–148, 186; in fast day sermons, 153–155;
use of term, 165–166; legal use of, 166; as
agreements, 167, 169, 208–209, 234;
assumpsit and, 167; contracts compared
to, 167–170, 169n124, 172; in King-Pavone
comparison, 365, 365nn94,95. See also
Contemporary national covenant;
Political covenant
Criminal indictments, 171; structure of,
172–173, 173n135, 173n138; terms of,
173–174, 174n140

Cromwell, Oliver, 118n101, 131, 131n11

Cuddihy, John Murray, 102–108, 104n62. *See also* Civility's American Protestant *agape;* Civil religion

Cuéllar, Roberto, 328–329

Cultures, 112n87, 243n6, 253–255, 253n34

Culture wars, 60, 60n37, 113; over public reason limited descriptive reach, 65–73, 66n51

Cumings, Henry, 217

Cushing, Jacob, 215–216, 216n84, 216n87

Cynicism, 347–348

Dalrymple, John, 223

Danforth, Samuel, 157

D'Arcy, John, 39

Darsey, James, 82–83, 247, 320

The Day of Doom (Wigglesworth), 152n62

days of humiliation, 150–151, 151n58

Deaths, 291, 291n7, 385–386; by murder, 17, 86–87, 249–250, 250n29; by executions, 192, 192n24, 192n28; in Civil War, 378–380, 378n8, 379n10, 379nn14–15, 380n16

Debt, 166–167

Decisions, 250–251, 268–269, 386–387; from competent authority, 340–342, 340nn42,43

Declaration of Independence, 381–382, 384

Declassification, 276, 276n84

Deism, 188, 188n6, 195

Delay, Tom, 68

Deliberative discourse: disingenuousness in, 308; practical reason for, 308; distortion in, 309–310; prophetic indictment and, 311–316, 314n69. *See also* Moral deliberation; Torture, deliberative responses to; Virtues

Deliberative discourse, prophetic misuse of: divine command theories in, 294, 294n15; just war debate compared to, 294–296, 294n16, 295nn18,19, 296nn22,23; torture memos and, 296–297, 296n24

Deliberative moral discourse, 5–6

Deliberative rhetoric, 4

Deliberators, 252, 274–275; in 2004 presidential election, 268–273, 270nn73,74, 271n77, 272nn79,80; cooperation of, 269–270, 270n73, 270n74; facts-and-circumstances test of, 269–270, 270n73; proportionality for, 269–273, 270nn73,74, 271n77, 272nn79,80; character for, 270–271, 270n73; moral issue of, 271–272, 271n77, 272nn79,80; issue range of, 272–273

Democracy, 207–208

Democracy and Tradition (Stout, J.), 63–64

Demonization, 96

Denison, Daniel, 198n43

Despair, 19, 19n12

Detinue, 166–167

Differences: about public reason, 48–50; in King-Pavone comparison, 366–367, 366n101, 367nn102,103

Differentiation, 103–104

Dignitatis humanae, [The Declaration on Religious Freedom] (Vatican II), 33, 36

Disagreement, 3, 15–16, 51–52; within religions, 241–242, 241n5; over just cause in warfare, 336, 336n33. *See also* Moral disagreement

Discipline, 162

Disclosure, 62

A Discourse Concerning Unlimited Submission and Non-Resistance to Higher Powers (Mayhew), 203–205

Discourse style, 242–243

Discretion, 325–326, 325n15

Disingenuousness, 308

Disrespect, 55–58, 84

Divine command theories, 294, 294n15

Divine mind discernment, 194–195, 194nn35,36, 195n37

Divisions, 232; in 2004 presidential election, 240–242

Divisiveness: from civic peace, 52–53, 52n25, 53n26; in jeremiad evolution, 183–185, 184n4

Dobson, James, 68
Dominion, 133, 159, 188
Doubts, 187–188, 414n128
Douglas, Stephen, 266n68
Douthat, Ross, 32
Doves, 397–398, 398n72
Dred Scott decision, 387
Dreher, Rod, 87
Dudley, Joseph, 133
Due account, 261
Dummer, Jeremiah, 203
Dylan, Bob, 244, 244n10
Dyson, Michael Eric, 360–361

Earthquake, 149–150, 149n53
Ecclesiastical tyranny, 204
Economic Justice for All, 288
Edwards, Jonathan, 200–201, 201n53
Effectiveness, 296, 296n23
Election day sermons, 156, 156nn74,75,
    157n79, 205–206, 206n69; Israel in,
    157–158; conclusion of, 158; of J. Cotton,
    158, 158n82; conflict over, 158–159, 158n83;
    criminal indictments in, 172
Elizabethan Puritanism, 128–129, 128n5
Elizabeth I (queen), 129
Elohim (God), 395–396
Emergency medical treatment, 250,
    250n30
Emergency Medical Treatment and Active
    Labor Act (EMTALA), 303n47, 304;
    emergency medical condition in, 303,
    303nn48,49, 304n50
Emotional framing, 99
Emotivism: appeal of, 18–19; moral
    disagreement and, 18–20, 18n10, 19n12,
    19n14; moral reasoning and, 19, 19n12,
    19n14; arbitrariness and, 19–20, 19n15
Employment Division v. Smith, 338, 338n37
EMTALA. *See* Emergency Medical
    Treatment and Active Labor Act
England, 133; Reformation in, 128–129,
    132n17, 145; Protectorate of, 131–132,
    131n11; Restoration in, 132, 132n15,

187–188; in covenantal obligations, 198;
    in Revolutionary jeremiads, 217–218
Enlightenment, 15–16, 188; moral
    disagreement and, 21–22, 21nn21,22,
    22n25
Episcopal Church, 29, 40
*An Essay for the Recording of Illustrious
    Providences* (I. Mather), 189
Ethics, 8–10
Euboulia, 309–310, 310n63
Eugenics, 339–340, 340n40
Evangelical Protestants, 119, 148n51; torture
    debates and, 28–29; Judaism and,
    104–105, 104n62; Roman Catholic
    Church and, 105–108, 107n72
Evangelicals for Human Rights, 28, 28n48
Evangelium vitae [The Gospel of Life], 69
Evans, John H., 31n65
Everett, Edward, 380, 380nn18,19
Evolutionary naturalism, 21n22
Exceptionalism, 231–234, 396–397
Exclusion, 98
Executions, 192, 192n24, 192n28
Exodus, Book of, 346n54
Expressivist discourse, 80–82
Expressivist freedom, 81

Facts: in 2004 presidential election, 241; in
    just cause, 336–337, 339–340, 339n39; in
    King-Pavone comparison, 365–367,
    366n101, 367nn102,103
Facts-and-circumstances test, 269–270,
    270n73
Fairness, 47–48
Faithlessness, 147, 313–314
Faith traditions, 27–28, 164–165, 164n110
False prophets, 392
Family Research Council, 68, 89
Fast day sermons, 151n58, 152n62; form of,
    151–152, 151n59; sins in, 151–155; God in,
    152–155; covenant in, 153–155; repentance
    in, 154–155, 199; sufferings in, 154–155;
    love in, 155
Faust, Drew Gilpin, 378

Federal theology, 137–139, 138n25, 143, 202–203

Feeney, Leonard, 107–108, 107n72

Feldman, Louis H., 401n84

Ferguson shooting, 368–369

Ferraro, Geraldine, 360, 360n81

Finances, 201, 201nn56,57

Finnis, John, 59–60, 60n36

First Amendment, 46–48

First principles, 37

Fisher, Anthony, 269

Fletcher, John, 213

Foner, Eric, 221

Forensic rhetoric, 4

Forti, Tova, 401n84

Foster, Stephen, 128

France, 217–218, 217n89

Francis (pope), 32, 263n56

Franklin, Benjamin, 201n57

Franklin, James, 201n57

French and Indian War, 217n89, 218–219, 218n90

Frist, Bill, 68, 68n59

Frustration, 17–18, 17n7, 23

Fugitive Slave Clause, 380–382, 381n23, 382n27

GAFCON. See Global Anglican Future Conference

Garrison, William Lloyd, 79–80, 83, 112, 117n98, 385–386

Gaudium et spes, [Pastoral Constitution on the Church in the Modern World] (Vatican II), 33

Generosity, 93–94

Geneva Conventions, 284, 298–299, 299n31

George, Francis, 39

George, Robert P., 59–60, 60n36

German Lutherans, 104–105

Gettysburg Address (Lincoln), 374, 377; Second Inaugural Address compared with, 376; Battle of Gettysburg and, 378–380, 379n10, 379nn14,15; delivery of, 380, 380nn19,20; Constitution and,

380–382, 381nn22,23, 382n27, 384–386; Union and, 380–382, 382n27, 384–385, 387; Declaration of Independence and, 381–382, 384; ideology of, 382–384; stance of, 384–385; death in, 385–386

Gildrie, Richard, 199

Glaude, Eddie, 358–359, 360–361

Global Anglican Future Conference (GAFCON), 29–30

Glorious Revolution, 133, 188, 205

Gnome, 309–310, 310n63

God, 141, 346, 346n54; in civility, 95–96; predestination and, 136–137, 136n23; covenantal framework and, 136–139, 136n23; federal theology on, 137–139, 138n25, 143; secondary causes from, 139–140, 149; New England and, 146–147, 149–150; chance and, 149–150, 149n53; through humans, 150, 150n56; in fast day sermons, 152–155; Yahweh as, 170–172, 254, 313–314, 395–396; in covenant bond, 187–195; prophetic indictments and, 311–312, 314n69; of Lincoln, 383–384, 383nn35,36, 387–388, 387n44, 387n45, 388n46; in Book of Jonah, 395–397, 403–408, 403nn91,92,93, 405n97, 417–418. See also Divine mind discernment

God's Controversy with New-England: Written in the time of the great drought Anno 1662 (Wigglesworth), 152–156, 152n62

God's Eye on the Contrite (W. Adams), 159, 159n86

God's waning interest in New England, 191; doubts in, 187–188; military strategy or, 189–190; judgment and, 190; witchcraft and, 193–195, 193n32, 194nn35,36, 195n37

Gonzales, Alberto R., 299, 299n31; torture debates and, 276, 276nn84–85, 278–279, 278n88; responses to, 278–279

Good, Edwin, 407

Good judgment (synesis), 309–310, 310n63

Goodwin, John, 191

Gosnell, Kermit, 330, 330n25

Government, 140–147, 140n29

Grace, 138, 140–141, 143, 146n45

Grand juries: procedural constraints and, 322–323, 322nn4,5,6,7; prosecutorial abuse and, 325–327, 326n17

Great Awakening, 199, 199n50, 201n53

Greek language, x, 259n43, 309, 336n33, 409

Greenawalt, Kent, 52n25

Greer, George, 68–69

Griffith, David, 277n86

Grisez, Germain, 292n11

Gun control, 324, 324n10

Gustafson, James, 246–247, 277, 368n104

Halfway covenant, 220, 220n98

Hebrew language, 244–245, 244n7, 336n33

Hebrew prophets. See Prophets

Hegemony, 50–51

Heimbach, Daniel R., 28

Henotheism, 104–105

Hentoff, Nat, 66

Herberg, Will, 105

Heresy, 44–45

Heschel, Abraham Joshua, 314; on prophets, 245–246, 312n66, 372; on Book of Jeremiah, 355, 357; on Book of Jonah, 417, 417nn135,136

History, 5–6, 21, 21n22; prediction related to, 142–143

Holy Communion, 267n69

Holy Trinity, 138

Holy war, 334, 334n31

Homeland Security Department, 250, 250n30

Homosexuality, 31, 31n64, 55; Anglican Church and, 29–30, 30n56, 40; mainline Protestantism and, 29–30, 29n53, 30n56; same-sex marriage, 59–61, 60nn36,37, 61n38, 263, 263n56, 350n60

Hooker, Richard, 140–141, 140n29, 249–250

Hope, 155, 369–370; from Puritan jeremiads, 178, 182n1; in covenantal obligations, 200; in rhetorical stance, 356–357, 356n70

Hosea, Book of: covenant lawsuits in, 171–172; torture debates and, 277n86; on faithlessness, 313–314

Hospitality, 94

Howard-Pitney, David, 320, 358

Howe, Julia Ward, 42n102, 115–116, 116n97, 383–384

Hubbard, William, 157–158, 157n79, 198n43

Human embryonic stem-cell research, 290; biology and, 291–292, 291n8, 292n11; individuated life in, 291–292, 291nn7,8, 292n10; rhetoric over, 292–293, 292n11, 293n12, 293n14

Human rights, 28, 28n48, 34–35, 328–329

Humans, 150, 150n56

Hume, David, 21, 21n23, 26n44

Humility, 9–10, 97, 375; days of humiliation, 150–151, 151n58; witchcraft related to, 194n37, 195; Second Inaugural Address and, 376, 391; Book of Jonah and, 377, 392–393, 421

Hussein, Saddam, 270, 278, 278n87

Hutchinson, Anne, 146n45

Idealism, 56

"The Idea of Public Reason" (Rawls), 58–59

"The Idea of Public Reason Revisited" (Rawls), 59

Identification, 355–356

Identity, 132, 195–198; of Jonah, 397–398, 397n69, 398n72. See also Covenant partners' identity; Moral identity

"I Have a Dream" (King), 369–371

Illusion, 19, 19n14

Immigrants, 104, 119, 250, 250n30

Income, 272n80

An Inconvenient Truth, 325n12

Indictments, 321, 322n4; jeremiads as, 4, 175–176; legal, 44, 179–180, 229; definition of, 172–173, 173n135; Supreme Court on, 322, 322n5. See also Criminal indictments; MacIntyre's moral indictment; Moral indictment; Prophetic indictments

Indifferentism, 107–108

Individual rights, 73, 73n74

Infidelity, 147

In God's Shadow: Politics in the Hebrew Bible
  (Walzer), 253–254, 253n34

Institutional structure, 32

Institutions, 25–26, 25n40

Instrumentality, 296

Insults, personal, 222–224

Integralism, 104–110, 119

Intemperance, 162, 164

Intention, 344–345

Internment, 339–340, 339n39

Interpretation, 212–213

Interventions, 240–241

Investigation, 325–326

Iraq, 240n1, 270–271

Irony, 375, 377, 422–423; Book of Jonah and,
  397–398, 407–408, 407n103, 408n108, 412;
  use of term, 409–412, 409n109, 409n112,
  411n116; psychotherapy related to,
  412–414, 414n126; as moral virtue, 412–415,
  414n126, 414n128, 415n129, 415n134; Second
  Inaugural Address and, 414, 415–417;
  limits of, 416–418, 417nn135,136

Isaiah, Book of, 280, 288–289, 341; August 1
  memo and, 306–307, 306nn55,56;
  rhetorical stance of, 352–354, 353n62

Islamic extremists, 1, 307; Al-Qaeda,
  298–299, 298n28, 299n31, 305–306;
  Taliban, 298–299, 299n31

"Is Polite Society Polite?" (Howe), 115

Israel, 143–144, 306n56; in election day
  sermons, 157–158; in Revolutionary
  jeremiads, 210–211, 214–216, 216n84;
  oracles against, 214, 216n87, 352–355, 357

Israel's political culture, 253–255, 253n34

Ius ad bellum verborum (just decision to go
  to war), 335–348, 368

Ius in bello verborum (just conduct in
  waging verbal war), 348–349

Ius post bellum verborum (just conduct after
  waging verbal war), 349–351, 350n58,
  350n60

Jackson, Robert H., 330

James I (king), 129

January 22 memo, 297–299, 297n26, 299n31

Jeremiad ethic, 8–9. *See also* King, Martin
  Luther, Jr.

Jeremiad evolution, 180–181, 182n1;
  revolutions and, 182–183; abolitionists
  and, 183; divisiveness in, 183–185, 184n4;
  common sense in, 185; covenant in, 185

Jeremiad rhetoric, 3–4; in covenant bond,
  200–202; finances and, 201, 201nn56,57

Jeremiads, 2–5, 83, 176; covenant and, 6,
  180; arrogance and, 9–10; public reason
  and, 64–65; language of, 82, 210, 331–332;
  form of, 126–127; national covenant and,
  147–148; covenant breach related to,
  169–172, 185–186, 230–231; contemporary,
  320–321, 320n2. *See also* American
  jeremiads; Puritan jeremiads; Puritan
  sermons

Jeremiah (prophet), 355–356, 356n68. *See
  also* Jeremiah, Book of

Jeremiah, Book of, 2, 172, 341; oracle
  against nations in, 214–215, 215n81;
  rhetorical stance in, 355–356, 356n68

Jesuits, 31–32, 106–107

Jesus Christ, 143, 195, 393, 393nn50,51,
  411–412; in covenantal framework, 138;
  just war debate and, 296, 296n23

Jews, 203, 306n56; Puritans compared to,
  143–144, 147, 196–197, 212. *See also* Israel

Joachim of Fiore, 244n10

John Paul II (pope), 73n74, 262–263, 266,
  367n103; *Evangelium vitae* of, 69

Johnson, Sandra H., 304n50

Jonah (prophet), 398n74, 399–402, 400n82,
  402n88; sign of, 393, 393nn50,51; identity
  of, 397–398, 397n69, 398n72; psalm of,
  407–408, 407n103. *See also* Jonah, Book
  of

Jonah, Book of, 10, 376, 394n59; humility
  and, 377, 392–393, 421; ambiguity in,
  392–398, 393nn50,51, 394n62, 395n65;
  oracle against nations in, 393, 394–396,

395n64, 402; meaning of, 393–394, 393n52, 399–400, 399n78, 400n79; God in, 395–397, 403–408, 403nn91,92,93, 405n97, 417–418; American exceptionalism and, 396–397; irony and, 397–398, 407–408, 407n103, 408n108, 412; Nineveh in, 398–406, 400n79; time of, 398n74, 399–400, 399n75, 400n80; universalism and, 400–401, 401n84; Christianity and, 400–402, 400n82, 401n83, 402n90

Jonsen, Albert, 301

Josephus, 401n84

Judah, 352–355, 357

Judaism, 107n72, 135; evangelical Protestants and, 104–105, 104n62; covenant and, 141–142, 254–255; *Mekhilta of Rabbi Ishmael*, 401. *See also* Israel; Jews

Judgments, 100, 190, 200, 254; synesis as, 309–310, 310n63

Jury nullification, 229–230

Just cause, 335, 340n40; disagreement over, 336, 336n33; facts in, 336–337, 339–340, 339n39; moral premises in, 336–337, 337n35; Constitution and, 338–340, 338n37; moral consensus in, 339–340, 339n38

Just conduct after verbal warfare: (*Ius post bellum verborum*), 350–351

Just conduct in waging verbal war *(Ius in bello verborum)*, 348–349

Just decision to go to verbal war *(Ius ad bellum verborum)*, 335–348, 368

Justice, 26n44; as fairness, 47–48. *See also* Comparative justice

Just law, 77–78

Just war debate, 294, 294n16, 295n19; pacifism in, 294n18, 295–296, 296nn22,23; Jesus Christ and, 296, 296n23

Just war theory, 332, 333n28, 335n32; civil war and, 333, 333n30; disruption in, 334; holy war and, 334, 334n31; targets in, 334, 334n31, 348–349; goal in, 335; just cause in, 335–340, 336n33, 337n35, 338n37, 339nn38,39, 340n40; competent authority and, 340–343, 340nn42,43, 341n44, 343n51,

344n53; comparative justice in, 343–344, 343n51, 344n53; condemnation in, 344–345; right intention in, 344–345; last resort in, 345; probability of success in, 345–346; proportionality in, 346–349; combatants and noncombatants in, 348–350, 350n58; reparations in, 349–350; victory in, 349–350, 350n60; rehabilitation in, 350–351

Kahane, Meir, 113

Kant, Immanuel, 21, 21n23, 252

Kelley, James R., 272, 272n80

Kennedy, George A., 80n87

Kerry, John, 260, 266–268, 266n68, 267n69

Kestenbaum, Sara, 94

Kierkegaard, Søren, 21, 21n23; on irony, 414–415, 414n128, 415n129

Kindness, 330

King, Martin Luther, Jr., 4, 9, 34, 34n78, 79, 363; abolitionists and, 76n78, 80–83, 81n88; "Letter from a Birmingham City Jail" by, 77, 342; natural law of, 77–78; prophetic rhetoric of, 78, 80; self-control of, 342–343; "I Have a Dream" by, 369–371

King-Pavone comparison, 363, 364n91; covenant in, 365, 365nn94,95; law in, 365–366; similarities in, 365–366, 365nn94,95; facts in, 365–367, 366n101, 367nn102,103; moral chemotherapy in, 366; differences in, 366–367, 366n101, 367nn102,103; prophetic indictment and, 368, 368n104; motives in, 369–370; oracles against nations in, 370–371; stance in, 370–371

King Philip's War, 150, 150n56, 159, 187

Korematsu v. United States, 339n39

Labor, 303n48

Lack of discipline, 162

Lambeth Conference 2008, 29

Lamentations, Book of, 356, 356n68, 356n70

Langerak, Edward, 97–98, 97n48

Language, 243n6, 419; Latin, ix–x; Greek, x, 259n43, 309, 336n33, 409; in civic peace, 55–57; of jeremiads, 82, 210, 331–332; of abolitionists, 83–84, 112; of civility, 95–96, 99–100; of Revolutionary jeremiads, 210; political, 221–222, 221n100; prophetic, 244, 244n10, 331–332; Hebrew, 244–245, 244n7, 336n33

Larkin, Edward, 221

Las Casas, Bartolomé de, 337, 337n35

Last Judgment, 200

Last resort, 345

Latin, ix–x

Laud, William, 129

Lauinger, Anthony J., 40–41, 41n101

Laws, 174, 251, 251n32, 365–366; virtues related to, 43–44. See also Covenant lawsuits; Natural law; Terri's law

Leach, David, 86

Lear, Jonathan, 412–415, 415n134

Lederman, Marty, 283

Legal advocacy, 297–298, 298n28

Legal indictment, 44, 179–180, 229

Legal realm, 296

"Letter from a Birmingham City Jail" (King), 77, 342

Letter to the Galatians (Saint Paul), 38n90

Liberalism, 48, 73–74; moral shrillness and, 33–35, 33n75, 34n76, 35n80,81; same-sex marriage and, 61, 61n38

Liguori, Alphonsus (saint), 269

Lincoln, Abraham, x, 9; slavery and, 380–390, 382n27, 383n36; God of, 383–384, 383nn35,36, 387–388, 387n44, 387n45, 388n46. See also Gettysburg Address; Second Inaugural Address

Lincoln Memorial, 11, 373–374, 373nn1,2, 374n3

Literacy, 167

Lobbying, 67–68

Locke, John, 140–141, 140n29, 199

Lopez, Kathryn Jean, 87–88

Love, 109, 109n76, 155

Loyalists, 213–214, 219–221

Luke (gospel), 393, 393n51

Mac Donald, Heather, 282–284, 284n105

MacIntyre, Alasdair, 4–5, 32, 125, 239; moral reasoning of, 15–16; tradition theory of, 24, 24n35; Rawls compared to, 46–47, 52. See also Moral disagreement

MacIntyre's moral indictment, 45n109; moral deliberation in, 42–43, 43n103; virtue theory in, 43–44; law in, 43–44; legal indictment in, 44; accountability in, 44–45, 44n107; moral argument and, 45; normative traditions and, 45

Madison, James, 1

Magnalia Christi Americana (C. Mather), 196–197, 197n41, 212

Mainline Protestantism, 29–30, 29n53, 30n56

Manager, 20

Manipulation, 19–20, 19n15, 56

Manners, 92–94

Mark (gospel), 411

Marshall, Stephen H., 358

Martinez, Mel, 68, 68n59

Martino, Renato, 71

Massachusetts Bay Colony, 2, 82, 130–133, 141–142. See also New England; Puritans

Massachusetts Body of Liberties, 174

Massachusetts General Court, 131n14, 133, 143, 151n58; on provoking sins, 160, 160n89, 164–165, 164n110

Materialism, 185, 198, 198n43

Mather, Cotton, 2–3, 149–150, 156n75; against witchcraft, 191–193, 191n20, 192n26, 192nn28,29; covenant partners' identity and, 196–198, 197n41; covenantal obligations and, 199–200; covenant evolution and, 212

Mather, Increase, 133, 150, 150n56, 156n75, 160n89; covenant renewal sermons and, 159, 160n88; God's waning interest and, 187, 189; witchcraft and, 192, 192n29

Mather, Richard, 156nn74–75

Matthew (gospel), 393, 393n50

Mayhew, Jonathan, 189–191, 203–206, 204n63, 206n69

McInerny, Ralph, 39, 39n98

Media, 88–89

Medical-moral questions, 72, 72n72. *See also* Human embryonic stem-cell research; King-Pavone comparison

Mekhilta of Rabbi Ishmael, 401

Mellen, John, 217n89

Membership, 140, 140n28

Metacomet, 150, 150n56

Micah, Book of, 170–171, 288

Migration, 130

Military strategy, 189–190

Miller, Perry, 126, 129n7, 136, 151–152, 193; on New England, 142–143; on covenant, 165–166; on Puritan jeremiad, 178–179

Miscegenation, 310

Mixed-form discourse, 259–260; conscription in, 255; effects of, 255–257; ad hominem attack in, 256–257; without moral deliberation, 256–257. *See also* Abortion

Modernism, 33

Monarchy, 253–255

Moral admonition, 288–289

Moral argument, 45, 126

Moral chemotherapy, 315–316, 332, 366, 420

Moral concern, 298

Moral consensus, 339–340, 339n38

Moral deliberation, 42–43, 43n103, 243, 315–316; description of, 248–249; motives in, 249–250, 250n29; Aristotelian-Thomistic schema in, 249–252; immigrants and, 250, 250n30; exceptions in, 250–251; in common law, 251, 251n32; complexity of, 251, 284–285; virtue theory in, 251–252; consequentialism in, 252–253; in terminology's limits, 252–253; mixed-form discourse without, 256–257

Moral deliberation–prophetic indictment clash, 285; in priorities, 257–258; in moral analysis, 258; in rationale, 258; in character, 258–259, 258n42; in society, 259; in time, 259, 259n43

Moral disagreement: abortion in, 16–17; frustration in, 17–18, 17n7, 23; paradox of,

18; emotivism and, 18–20, 18n10, 19n12, 19n14; despair about, 19, 19n12; illusion in, 19, 19n14; manipulation and, 19–20, 19n15; moral tradition in, 20–21, 21n21; history in, 21, 21n22; Enlightenment and, 21–22, 21nn21,22, 22n25; moral theory on, 21–22, 22nn25,26; consequentialism in, 23, 23n29; protest and, 23; utilitarianism and, 23, 23nn29,30

Moral disagreement remedy, 27; norms in, 23–24; tradition theory in, 24, 24n35; in communities, 24–25; three-dimensional context of, 25–26, 25n37, 25n40, 26n44, 26nn41,42

Moral discourse, 5–6, 126

Moral identity, 279n91, 281n96; of responses, 279–281, 280n95

Moral indictment, 126; against Obama, 40–41, 41n101; moral reasoning and, 40–42, 42n102; by Berrigan, 41–42, 42n102; of torture prophetic challenges, 277–279, 277n86, 285; excoriation of, 289. *See also* MacIntyre's moral indictment

Morality, 223

Moral life, 26, 26n44

Moral manuals, 265

Moral premises, 337, 337n35

Moral reasoning, 15–16, 19, 19n12, 19n14; ad hominem attacks and, 37–38, 38n90; University of Notre Dame and, 38–41, 39nn98,99, 41n101; moral indictment and, 40–42, 42n102

Morals, 327–328

Moral shrillness, 29n53, 30n56; faith traditions and, 27–28; traditions and, 27–28, 32–33, 33n70; evangelical Protestants and, 28–29; authority and, 30, 30n60, 37; of Catholics, 31–32, 31nn61,62, 31nn64,65; institutional structure and, 32; utilitarianism and, 32; limitations about, 32–33; modernism and, 33; politics and, 33–34, 33n75, 34n76; liberalism and, 33–35, 33n75, 34n76,

Moral shrillness *(continued)*
35n80,81; natural law and, 35–36;
arguments for, 36–37; ad hominem
attacks in, 37; first principles and, 37
Moral theory, 21–22, 22nn25,26; in
three-dimensional context, 26,
26nn41,42
Moral tradition, 20–21, 21n21
Moral values, 239–240, 240n1
Moral virtue, 25; irony as, 412–415, 414n126,
414n128, 415n129, 415n134
Moses, 143, 346n54
Motivation, 403–404, 403nn91,92
Motives, 249–250, 250n29, 369–370
Moyers, Bill, 361–362
Murder, 249–250, 250n29; abortion as, 17,
86–87
Murphy, Andrew R., 182n1, 247, 247n25,
320n2
Murray, John Courtney, 106–107, 262
Muster sermons, 219, 219n93

National Association of Evangelicals, 28
National Catholic Prayer Breakfast, 39n99
National Conference of Catholic Bishops,
263n59, 280, 280n93
National covenant, 145–148, 186. *See also*
Contemporary national covenant
National Right to Life, 40–41, 41n101, 67
Native Americans, 150, 150n56, 159, 187, 219
Natural law, 35–36, 77–78
Natural rights, 207n76, 208–210, 221–222
Neuhaus, Richard John, 281n97
New England, 119, 142, 150n56, 196–198;
Israel related to, 143–144; national
covenant for, 145–146; God and, 146–147,
149–150; earthquake in, 149–150, 149n53
New England Puritan jeremiads. *See*
Puritan jeremiads
New Jerome Biblical Commentary, 398,
403–404, 408n108
New Testament, 143; civil rights from,
203–204, 204n63; Luke in, 393, 393n51;
Matthew in, 393, 393n50; Mark in, 411

Niebuhr, Reinhold, 104–105, 296n25
9/11, 260, 359
Nineveh, 399n76; in Book of Jonah,
398–406, 400n79
Noll, Mark, 117, 199, 199n50, 201n53, 228
Noncombatants, 348–350, 350n58
Nonviolent civil disobedience, 342–343
No Offense: Civil Religion and Protestant Taste
(Cuddihy), 102
Noonan, John T., Jr., 35–36, 88
Normative decision, 250
Normative discussion, 10–11
Normative traditions, 45
Norms, 23–24, 74, 111
Norton, John, 132, 132n17
Nostradamus, 244
Noyes, Nicholas, 142
Nuance, 346–347
Nuclear deterrence, 263–264, 263n59

Oakes, Urian, 143–145
Obama, Barack, 86, 86n4, 90, 234; abortion
and, 38–41, 39n99, 41n101, 88; moral
indictment against, 40–41, 41n101; war
on terrorism and, 296n25; Wright and,
359–363, 360n81, 362n87
Obergefell v. Hodges, 263n56
Objections, 375–376
Objective, 346–348
Obligations, 169–170, 233. *See also*
Covenantal obligations
Olbermann, Keith, 89n17
Old Testament, 143
O'Malley, John, 243n6
"Open Letter to Michael Schiavo"
(Pavone), 363–364
Operation Rescue, 85–87
Oracles against Israel and Judah, 214,
216n87, 352–355, 357
Oracles against nations, 306, 306n55,
370–371; in Book of Jeremiah, 214–215,
215n81; in Revolutionary jeremiads,
214–220, 215n82, 216n84, 219n93, 220n98;
on French and Indian War, 217n89,

218–219, 218n90; in rhetorical stance, 352–353, 353n62, 357; in Book of Jonah, 393, 394–396, 395n64, 402

The Ordeal of Civility: Freud, Marx, Levi-Strauss, and the Jewish Struggle with Modernity (Cuddihy), 104n62

Ordination, 29n52

O'Reilly, Bill, 86–87, 89n17

Orend, Brian, 350–351, 350n58

Ortiz, Dianna, 279n91

Oxford English Dictionary, ix–x, 301

Pacifism, 295n18, 295–296, 295nn22,23

Pain, severe, 302–304, 303n49, 304n50

Paine, Thomas, 220–221, 221n100. See also *Common Sense: Address to the Inhabitants of America*

Palm Sunday Compromise, 68, 68n59

Pamphlets, 221, 221n100

Papacy, 207–208, 207n76; of Francis, 32, 263n56; of John Paul II, 69, 73n74, 262–263, 266, 367n103; of Paul VI, 262; of Benedict XVI, 270–271, 270n74, 271n77

Papists, 217–218

Parallelism, 252

Parker, Kathleen, 88

Parker, Theodore, 381–382

Parsons, Talcott, 103

Passions, 162

Patriots, 1

Paul (saint), 38n90, 176, 290, 314, 314n69, 400n82

Pauline Christianity, 104

Paul VI (pope), 262

Pavilschek, Keith, 28

Pavone, Frank, 363–364. See also King-Pavone comparison

Peace, 263–264, 263n57, 263n59. See also Civic peace

Penalties, 230–232, 234, 389–390

Pentagon, 282

Perkins, Tony, 89

Perry, Michael, 59–60

Persecution, 224

Peter (saint), 38n90, 400n82

Petersen, David L., 307, 357

Pew Forum. See *U.S. Religious Landscape Survey*

Pew Research Center, 281n96

Phillips, Wendell, 112, 116–117, 117n98, 226–227

"Philosophy of the Abolition Movement" (Phillips), 226–227

Photographs, 293; in torture prophetic challenges, 277–278, 277n86, 285

Piety, 198–199

Planned Parenthood v. Casey, 262n54

Plato, 258, 258n42

Plessy v. Ferguson, 339, 339n39

Pluralism, 97, 97n48, 102–103, 195–197

Political authority, 203–204, 204n63

Political covenant: from covenantal framework, 140–144; for government, 140–147, 140n29

Political culture, 253–255, 253n34

Political emergency, 75–76

Political failure, 187–188

Political language, 221–222, 221n100

Political liberalism, 48, 73–74

Political Liberalism (Rawls), 47–48

Political parties, 233–234, 344–345

Political power, 190–191

Political reform, 198

Politics, 4, 129–130; moral shrillness and, 33–34, 33n75, 34n76; civility constraints in, 88–89, 91nn22,23

Poor persons, 199, 199n49, 272n80

Post Revolutionary jeremiads, 225–230

POWs. *See* Prisoners of war

Practical deliberation, 5, 421–422; prophetic indictment-practical deliberation relationship, 286–287, 308–316

Practical reason, 308; prophetic indictment and, 313–316

Pragmatism, 138–139

Preachers, 201n56, 202

Prediction, 142–143, 244

Press, Eyal, 86–87

Pride, 161

Prisoners of war (POWs), 298–299, 299n31

Probability of success, 345–346, 346n54

Probable cause, 322, 322n7

Procedural constraints: in prophetic indictment styles, 321–325, 322nn4,5,6,7; social reform and, 323–325, 324n10

Profanity, 161

Progressive jeremiads, 247–248, 247n25

Pro-life activists, 84–88, 86n4; public reason's limited descriptive reach and, 65–67, 69, 72. See also Human embryonic stem-cell research

Pro-life argument, 290–291, 336

Pro-life prophets, 273–274

Prophecy, 142–143, 147n48, 265, 275

Prophetic discourse, 289; definition of, 244, 246; in terminology's limits, 252–253; over human embryonic stem-cell research, 290–291; on gun control, 324; on climate change, 325, 325n12. See also Mixed-form discourse

Prophetic discourse, deliberative misuse of: moral admonition in, 288–289; tentativeness in, 289–290. See also Human embryonic stem-cell research

Prophetic indictment–practical deliberation relationship, 286–287, 308–316. See also Prophetic discourse, deliberative misuse of; Torture memos

Prophetic indictments, 52, 243, 244n10, 323; uncivil Protestants and, 119–121; of Puritan jeremiads, 134–135, 135n21; in contemporary national covenant, 234–235; definition of, 245–246; characteristics of, 246, 420–421; of progressive jeremiads, 247–248, 247n25; of traditionalist jeremiads, 247–248, 247n25; moral deliberation-prophetic indictment clash, 257–259, 258n42, 259n43, 285; as moral chemotherapy, 287–288; authenticity of, 311–312, 368, 368n104; God and, 311–312, 314n69; deliberative discourse and,

311–316, 314n69; practical reason and, 313–316; targets of, 321–322; prosecutorial abuse and, 327–328; King-Pavone comparison and, 368, 368n104; Second Inaugural Address and, 391–392

Prophetic indictment styles, 319–320, 422–423; procedural constraints and, 321–325, 322nn4,5,6,7, 324n10; prosecutorial abuse and, 325–329, 325n15, 326n17, 328n20; prosecutorial virtue and, 330–331, 330nn25,26; substantive constraints and, 331–351, 333n28, 333n30, 334n31, 335n32, 336n33, 337n35, 338n37, 339n39, 339nn38,39, 340n40, 340nn42,43, 341n44, 343n51, 344n53, 350n58, 350n60; rhetorical constraints and, 351–363, 353n62, 356n68, 356n70, 358n75, 360n81, 362n87; comparative assessment of, 363–372

Prophetic language, 244, 244n10, 331–332

Prophetic rhetoric, 8, 80n87, 120, 319; of King, 78, 80; of Garrison, 79–80, 83; as moral chemotherapy, 315–316, 332, 420; in Second Inaugural Address, 390–391. See also Jeremiads; Just war theory

The Prophetic Tradition and Radical Rhetoric in America (Darsey), 82–83

Prophetic witness, 71–74, 72n72

Prophets, ix, 2, 244n10, 313–314; definitions of, 244–245, 244n7; Heschel on, 245–246, 312n66, 372; in terminology's limits, 252; monarchy and, 253–255; pro-life, 273–274; choice of, 275–277; community of, 341–342; false, 392

Proportionality, 294, 294n16; for deliberators, 269–273, 270nn73,74, 271n77, 272nn79,80; nuance and, 346–347; objective and, 346–348; in just war theory, 346–349; reform and, 347; worldviews and, 347; cynicism and, 347–348; of strategies, 349

Proposals, 206

Prosecutorial abuse: discretion and, 325–326, 325n15; investigation and,

325–326; grand juries and, 325–327, 326n17; in prophetic indictment styles, 325–329, 325n15, 326n17, 328n20; protections from, 326–327, 326n17; morals and, 327–328; prophetic indictment and, 327–328; human rights and, 328–329

Prosecutorial virtue, 330, 330nn25,26

Prosperity, 233–234

Protections, 326–327, 326n17

Protectorate, 131–132, 131n11

Protestant-Catholic-Jew (Herberg), 105

Protestant denominationalism, 102; crisscross in, 103; differentiation in, 103–104; immigrants and, 104; ordeal of, 104; henotheism and, 104–105; against integralism, 104–108

Protestants, 1, 319–320, 320n2. *See also* Civility's American Protestant *agape;* Evangelical Protestants; Mainline Protestantism; Puritans; Uncivil Protestants

Protests, 23, 91; Vietnam War, 41–42, 42n102

Proviso, 51, 57–58; abolitionists and, 76–77

Provoking sins: Massachusetts General Court on, 160, 160n89, 164–165, 164n110; Reforming Synod on, 160–164, 160n89, 165n113; Apostasy, 161; pride, 161; profanity, 161; Sabbath-breaking, 161; intemperance, 162, 164; lack of discipline, 162; passions, 162; worldliness, 162; unbelief, 163; Confession of Faith about, 164–165, 164n110

Prudential judgments, 254

Psalm, 407–408, 407n103

Psychotherapy, 412–414, 414n126

Public discourse limitations, 4–5

Public reason: justice as fairness in, 47–48; requirements of, 47–48; political liberalism in, 48; of reasonable citizens, 48–49, 63–64; differences about, 48–50; content of, 49–50, 50n13; civic friendship

in, 50; reciprocity in, 50, 52, 54–55, 54n27; hegemony in, 50–51; proviso in, 51; disagreement in, 51–52; limitations in, 51–52, 58–59, 59n33; prophetic indictment and, 52; in civic peace, 54–58, 54n27; on abortion, 58–59, 59n33, 61, 64; same-sex marriage and, 59–61, 60nn36,37, 61n38; alternative to, 61–62; consistency in, 61–62; convincing in, 62; disclosure in, 62; audiences of, 62–63; respect and, 63; jeremiads and, 64–65; rhetorical style and, 64–65; of abolitionists, 75–76, 76n78

Public reason, limited descriptive reach of: pro-life activists and, 65–67, 69, 72; culture wars over, 65–73, 66n51; Terri's Law and, 67, 67n54; courts on, 67–69; lobbying in, 68; Palm Sunday Compromise in, 68, 68n59; reasons related to, 70–71; prophetic witness or, 71–74, 72n72; medical-moral questions and, 72, 72n72; process and, 72, 74; respect and, 72; individual rights and, 73, 73n74; constitutional principles and, 73–74, 73n75; political liberalism and, 73–74; national controversy over, 73–75; rhetorical style and, 74

Public reason, limited normative grasp, 74. *See also* Abolilitionists; Civility constraints

Puritan jeremiads, 118, 180n150, 222–223, 420; immigrants and, 119; form of, 134; prophetic indictment of, 134–135, 135n21; covenant and, 135–136, 180; Puritan sermons or, 148–149, 148n49; uniqueness of, 148–149; fast day sermons as, 150–156, 151nn58,59, 152n62, 199; election day sermons as, 156–159, 156nn74,75, 157n79, 158n82; revival and covenant renewal sermons as, 159, 160n88; framework of, 175; purpose of, 176; popularity of, 176–179; as corrective affliction, 177–178; reassurance of, 177–178; hope from, 178, 182n1; stimulant of, 178; expiation of,

Puritan jeremiads *(continued)*
179; acknowledgment in, 179–180;
consensus about, 179–180, 183–184; as
legal indictment, 179–180; breach
reversal in, 230–231

Puritans, 2, 82; in uncivil Protestants,
117–119, 118n101; integralism and, 119;
New England Unitarians and, 119; social
unity of, 127; label of, 128–129; Jews
compared to, 143–144, 147, 196–197, 212;
beliefs of, 149–150; literacy of, 167; social
class of, 167–168

Puritan sermons: changes of, 148, 148n51;
structure of, 148, 148n49; Puritan
jeremiad or, 148–149, 148n49; artillery
sermons, 219, 219n93

Al-Qaeda, 298–299, 298n28, 299n31,
305–306. *See also* Torture memos

Quintilian, 409

Racism, 368–369

Radicalism, 247

Ramsey, Paul, 291n7, 292, 292n11

Ramus, Peter, 202, 202n58

Randolph, Edward, 133

Rationalists, 148n51

Ratzinger, Joseph, 270–271, 270n74, 271n77

Rawls, John, 5, 83, 90, 125, 239; MacIntyre
compared to, 46–47, 52. *See also* Public
reason

Reasonable citizens, 48–49, 63–64

Reasonableness, 80–82, 81n88

Reasonable pluralism, 97, 97n48

Reasons, 55–56, 78, 336n33. *See also* Public
reason

Reciprocity, 50, 52, 54–55, 54n27

Redemption, 192n28, 193

Reform, 198, 323–325, 324n10, 347

Reformation, 128–129, 132n17, 145

Reforming Synod, 160–164, 160n89, 165n113

Rehabilitation, 350–351

Religions, 112n87; survey on, 31, 31nn61,62,
31nn64,65; civil, 102–108, 102n57, 117;

Great Awakening of, 199, 199n50, 201n53;
disagreements within, 241–242, 241n5

Religious Freedom Restoration Act
(RFRA), 338n37

Religious pluralism, 195–197

Religious texts, 10–11

Religious traditionalists, 81

Religious worldviews, 52–53, 52n25, 53n26

Reparations, 349–350

Repentance, 154–155, 199

Resources, 10–11

Respect, 72, 79, 83, 274; public reason and,
63; in civility constraints, 91; in civility,
97–98, 100–101. *See also* Civic peace

Responses, 279n91; to Gonzales, 278–279;
moral identity of, 279–281, 280n95. *See
also* Torture, deliberative responses to

Revelation, 78, 217–218, 218n90

Revelation, Book of, 217–218, 218n90

Revival and covenant renewal sermons,
159, 160n88

Revivalists, 148n51

Revolutionary jeremiads, 225–230; controversy of, 210; language of, 210; covenant
evolution and, 210–211, 213–214; Israel in,
210–211, 214–216, 216n84; audience of, 211;
orientation of, 211; Loyalists and, 213–214,
219–220; oracles against nations in,
214–220, 215n82, 216n84, 219n93, 220n98; by
Cushing, 215–216, 216n84, 216n87; England
in, 217–218

Revolutionary War, 213–214, 219–220

Revolutions, 182–183; Glorious, 133, 188,
205; political authority in, 203–204,
204n63

RFRA. *See* Religious Freedom Restoration
Act

Rhetoric, 80n87, 421–422

Rhetorical analysis, 254–255; time and, 6–7;
participants in, 7; abortion in, 7–8;
torture in, 7–8; tensions in, 8; prophetic
rhetoric related to, 80

Rhetorical constraints, 351, 356n68, 358n75;
rhetorical stance in, 352–358, 353n62,

356n70; American jeremiads in, 358–363, 360n81, 362n87

Rhetorical stance: oracles against nations in, 352–353, 353n62, 357; of Book of Isaiah, 352–354, 353n62; oracles against Israel and Judah in, 352–355, 357; in Book of Jeremiah, 355–356, 356n68; identification in, 355–356; hope in, 356–357, 356n70

Rhetorical studies, 3–4, 10–11

Rhetorical style, 64–65, 74; in abortion and torture debates, 242–243

Ricard, John, 280

Rich Aesthetes, 20

Right intention, 344–345

Robertson, Pat, 71

Robinson, Gene, 29n53

Roeder, Scott, 30n26, 86–87, 330

Roe v. Wade, 60, 262n54; in 2004 presidential election, 72n79, 260, 260n45, 267–268, 271–272, 271n77

Roman Catholic Church, 328n20; on authority, 30–31, 31n62; abortion and, 31, 31n65, 262–265, 263n55; Second Vatican Council of, 33, 262–263, 263n55; contraception and, 100, 262; evangelical Protestants and, 105–108, 107n72; civility of, 106–107; indifferentism in, 107–108; Feeney and, 107–108, 107n72; American values and, 262–263, 263n59, 263nn55,56,57; war and peace and, 263–264, 263n57, 263n59; Holy Communion in, 267n69; Vatican newspaper, 280, 280n95; sexual immorality and, 343. *See also* Papacy

Romero, Oscar, 328–329, 328n20

Rorty, Richard, 410–411

Rules of Civility: The 110 Precepts That Guided Our First President in War and Peace (Washington), 91n23

Rutten, Tim, 88

Sabbath-breaking, 161

Sacrifice, 93–96

Salem witchcraft trials. *See* Witchcraft

Same-sex marriage, 263, 350n60; arguments and, 59–61, 60n36; public reason and, 59–61, 60nn36,37, 61n38; culture wars and, 60, 60n37; Supreme Court on, 60, 60nn36,37, 263, 263n56; liberalism and, 61, 61n38

Samuel (prophet), 197n41, 244

Sandburg, Carl, 378n5

San Salvador, 328–329

Santorum, Rick, 68, 68n59

Sasson, Jack, 393n52, 395n65, 398n72, 405n97; on Nineveh, 399–400, 399n76; on time, 399–400, 399n75; on motivation, 403–404, 403nn91,92

Satire, 201n57, 206, 408n108, 422–423

Schaffer, Frank, 87

Schiavo, Michael, 64, 67–68, 69n66, 363–364. *See also* King-Pavone comparison

Schiavo, Theresa Marie Schindler, 65–70, 366–367. *See also* King-Pavone comparison; Public reason

Schindlers, 66–67, 69, 73n74

Science, 17, 58–59, 336

Scripture. *See* Bible

Sebelius, Kathleen, 86, 86n4

Second Inaugural Address (Lincoln), x, 9, 114, 114n93, 374; objections to, 375–376; humility and, 376, 391; Bible and, 383n34; slavery in, 388–390; penalty in, 389–390; Union in, 389–390; prophetic rhetoric in, 390–391; prophetic indictment and, 391–392; irony and, 414–417. *See also* Jonah, Book of

Second Vatican Council, 33, 262–263, 263n55

Secularization, 203–206, 204n63

Self-control, 342–343

Self-criticism, 9–10

Self-defense, 250–251

Self-evidence, 209

Self-restraint, 93

Sensenbrenner, James, 70, 70n68

Sermons. *See* Puritan sermons

Severe pain, 302–304, 303n49, 304n50

Sexual immorality, 343

Shannon, Rachelle, 85

Sharp, Carolyn, 407–408, 407n103

Shepard, Thomas, 172

Sherwood, Yvonne, 401–402, 401n83, 402n88

Silence, 281

Simon, Uriel, 401, 401n86, 403n91

Simpson, A. W. B., 166n118, 167

Sins, 151–155. *See also* Provoking sins

Slavery, 75, 78–79; Bible and, 226–230; Fugitive Slave Clause, 380–382, 381n23, 382n27; Lincoln and, 380–390, 382n27, 383n36; *Dred Scott* decision and, 387; in Second Inaugural Address, 388–390. *See also* Abolitionists

Smolinski, Reiner, 152n62

Social class, 114–117, 117n98, 167–168

Social conditioning, 102, 102n57

Social critic, 244n10

Social improvement, 199, 199n49

Social reform, 323–325, 324n10

Social roles, 25, 25n37

Social unity, 127

Society, 25n37, 259

Socrates, 409, 409n112

Sorrow, 356

Southern Baptists, 113–114

Southern soldiers, 380n16, 385, 385n38

Spectral evidence, 192, 192n29

Stakeholders. *See* Competent authority

Stance: in King-Pavone comparison, 370–371; of Gettysburg Address, 384–385. *See also* Rhetorical stance

Stephens, Alexander, 227

Sterilization, involuntary, 339–340, 340n40

Steyn, Mark, 360, 360n81

Stoddard, Solomon, 202

Stoughton, William, 147

Stout, Harry, 134, 146n45, 148–149

Stout, Jeffrey, 63–64, 71, 78; on abolitionists, 80–84, 81n88

Strategies, 189–190; in abortion and torture debates, 261; of torture memos, 301; proportionality of, 349

Stringfellow, Thornton, 227

Substance, 55, 126–127

Substantive constraints, 331. *See also* Just war theory

Sufferings, 154–155

Summa Theologica (Thomas Aquinas), 249

Supreme Court, 69, 262, 262n54; on same-sex marriage, 60, 60nn36,37, 263, 263n56; on indictments, 322, 322n5; *Employment Division v. Smith*, 338, 338n37; *Korematsu v. United States*, 339n39; *Buck v. Bell*, 340n40

Survey, 31, 31nn61,62, 31nn64,65

Symbolism, 114, 224

Synesis (good judgment), 309–310, 310n63

Taliban, 298–299, 299n31. *See also* Torture memos

Targets, 321–322; in just war theory, 334, 334n31, 348–349

Tentativeness, 289–290

Terminology's limits: parallelism in, 252; prophet in, 252; moral deliberation in, 252–253; prophetic discourse in, 252–253; prudential judgments in, 254; rhetorical analysis in, 254–255

Terri Schiavo Life & Hope Network, 69n66

Terri's Law, 67, 67n54, 364

The Terror of the Lord (C. Mather), 149–150

Terry, Randall, 66, 87–88

Thavis, John, 280n95

Theological pluralism, 102–103

Theology, 193–194; federal, 137–139, 138n25, 143, 202–203

A Theory of Justice (Rawls), 47–48

Therapists, 20. *See also* Psychotherapy

This Republic of Suffering (Faust), 378

Three-dimensional context: social roles in, 25, 25n37; institutions in, 25–26, 25n40; moral life in, 26, 26n44; moral theory in,

26, 26nn41,42; practices in, 26, 26n41; virtues in, 26, 26n42, 26n44

Three-Fifths Compromise, 380–381, 381n22

Tiller, George, 85–88, 330n26

Time, 6–7, 259, 259n43; in 2004 presidential election, 267–268; of just cause, 337–338; of Book of Jonah, 398n74, 399–400, 399n75, 400n80

Toleration, 131–134, 131n14, 196

Tone, 82

Torture, 279n91; abortion related to, 7–8, 242–243, 259–262, 264, 275–277, 286

Torture, debates on, 264, 281, 281n96; abortion debates and, 7–8, 242–243, 259, 261–262; evangelical Protestants and, 28–29; liberalism and, 35, 35n81; civility about, 99–100; Abu Ghraib Prison and, 260, 260n46, 276, 276n84; George W. Bush and, 270–271; Gonzales and, 276, 276nn84–85, 278–279, 278n88; Book of Hosea and, 277n86

Torture, definition of, 300–302, 300n36, 302n41

Torture, deliberative responses to: silence in, 281; anomalies in, 281–282; about Abu Ghraib Prison, 281–285, 281n97, 284n105; distinctions in, 282–283; Weigel in, 282; MacDonald in, 282–284, 284n105

Torture, prophetic challenges to: photographs in, 277–278, 277n86, 285; moral indictment of, 277–279, 277n86, 285; utopia and, 279, 279n91; moral identity in, 279–281, 279n91, 280n95, 281n96; American values in, 280–281, 280n95, 281n96

Torture memos: declassification of, 276, 276n84; Abu Ghraib Prison and, 278, 282, 287; responses to, 278–281, 279n91, 280n95; deliberative discourse prophetic misuse and, 296–297, 296n24; legal advocacy of, 297–298, 298n28; January 22 memo in, 297–299, 297n26, 299n31; moral concern of, 298; August 1 memo in,

299–302, 299n32, 300n36, 302n41, 306–307, 306nn55,56; strategy of, 301; casuistry in, 301–305, 303n49, 307; incongruity of, 302–303; severe pain and, 302–304, 303n49, 304n50; EMTALA and, 303–304, 303nn47,48,49, 304n50; worldview and, 305–308, 306nn55,56; bin Laden and, 307

Toulmin, Stephen, 301

Traditionalist jeremiads, 247–248, 247n25

Traditionalists, religious, 81

Traditional societies, 25n37

Traditional Values Coalition, 67, 67n56

Traditions, 45; moral shrillness and, 27–28, 32–33, 33n70

Tradition theory, 24, 24n35

Trinity United Church of Christ (Chicago, Illinois), 359

Truth, 89, 325n12

2004 presidential election, 6–7, 265n62; *Roe v. Wade* and, 72n79, 260, 260n45, 267–268, 271–272, 271n77; moral values and, 239–240, 240n1; interventions in, 240–241; divisions in, 240–242; facts in, 241; overlap in, 241; community in, 241–242, 241n5; discourse style in, 242–243; abortion description in, 265–266, 265n63, 266nn64,65; time in, 267–268; deliberators in, 268–273, 270nn73,74, 271n77, 272nn79,80

Tyranny, 204–205

Unbelief, 163

Uncivil Protestants: Southern Baptists as, 113–114; social class of, 114–117, 117n98; Puritans in, 117–119, 118n101; prophetic indictment and, 119–121

Union: Gettysburg Address and, 380–382, 382n27, 384–385, 387; in Second Inaugural Address, 389–390

Unitarianism, 117, 119, 148n51

Unity, 127, 232

University of Notre Dame, 38–41, 39nn98,99, 41n101

UN Universal Declaration on Human Rights, 34–35
Upham, Charles, 192
U.S. Constitution. *See* Constitution
U.S. Religious Landscape Survey, 31, 31nn61,62, 31nn64,65
Utilitarianism, 293, 293n14; moral disagreement and, 23, 23nn29,30; moral shrillness and, 32
Utopia, 247; torture prophetic challenges and, 279, 279n91

Values, 100, 239–240, 240n1, 250; Bible related to, 67, 67n56. *See also* American values
Vatican II. *See also* Second Vatican Council
Vatican newspaper, 280, 280n95
Victory, 349–350, 350n60
Vietnam War Protest, 41–42, 42n102
Virtues, 26, 26n42, 26n44, 375; laws related to, 43–44; of Thomas Aquinas, 309–311, 310nn63,64. *See also* Moral virtue; Prosecutorial virtue
Virtue theory, 43–44, 251–252

Wadsworth, Benjamin, 198–199
Walker, George, 169
Walzer, Michael, 147n48, 244n10; Israel's political culture and, 253–255, 253n34
War and peace, 263–264, 263n57, 263n59
War Crimes Act, 299, 299n31
War on terrorism: George W. Bush and, 296–297, 296n24, 296n25; Obama and, 296n25
Warren, Rick, 90
Wars, 333, 333n30; culture, 60, 60n37, 65–73, 66n51, 113; King Philip's, 150, 150n56, 159, 187; Revolutionary, 213–214, 219–220; POWs, 298–299, 299n31. *See also* Civil War; French and Indian War; Just war debate
Washington, George, 91n23, 219–220

WASP. *See* White Anglo-Saxon Protestant
Weber, Max, 340–341, 341n44
Webster v. Reproductive Health Services, 262n54
Weigel, George, 282
Weir, David, 139
Weithman, Paul, 59–60, 60n36
Westermann, Claus, 134–135, 135n21
When War Is Unjust: Being Honest in Just War Thinking (Yoder), 295–296, 295nn18,19
Whitaker, Nathaniel, 219–220
White Anglo-Saxon Protestant (WASP), 114
Whose Justice? Which Rationality? (MacIntyre), 24, 24n35, 32
Wigglesworth, Michael, 152–156, 152n62, 201n56
Wilberforce, William, 92–93
William of Orange, 133, 198
Williams, Rowan, 29–30
Williamson, Kevin, 89
Wills, David, 379, 379n15
Wills, Garry, 381–383
Wilson, Joe, 88–89
Winthrop, John, 2, 129–130, 142, 145–146
Wise, John, 201n57, 206–207
Witchcraft: C. Mather against, 191–193, 191n20, 192n26, 192nn28,29; executions for, 192, 192n24, 192n28; spectral evidence and, 192, 192n29; confession of, 192n28, 193; covenantal theology and, 193–194; God's waning interest and, 193–195, 193n32, 194nn35,36, 195n37; divine mind discernment and, 194–195, 194nn35,36, 195n37; humility related to, 194n37, 195
Women, 279n91; ordination of, 29n52; in labor, 303n48
Women's Christian Temperance Union, 34n77
Women's suffrage, 34n77
Works, covenant of, 138, 146n45

Worldliness, 162

Worldviews, 51; religious, 52–53, 52n25, 53n26; torture memos and, 305–308, 306nn55,56; proportionality and, 347

Wright, Jeremiah, 359–363, 360n81, 362n87

Yahweh (God), 170–172, 254, 313–314, 395–396

Yoder, John Howard, 295–296, 295nn18,19, 296nn22,23

Yoo, John, 276n84, 287, 297n26

Zaret, David, 168–169, 169n124